Factionalism

Factionalism is widely understood to be one of the distinguishing characteristics of Chinese politics. The Chinese Communist Party has a long history of purges and infighting among its elite members and, after 1949, of seemingly irrational and frequently vicious struggles for succession to leadership. Almost all of the successors to Mao and Deng, with the exception of China's President Jiang Zemin – including Liu Shaoqi, Lin Biao, Hua Guofeng, Hu Yaobang, and Zhao Ziyang – were purged. What is not as well understood is how this divisive feature could coexist with another linchpin of post-1949 political power and legitimacy: Party unity. Nor do scholars agree upon the exact relationship between factional politics and policy outcomes. In this book Jing Huang examines the role of factionalism in leadership relations and policy making. His detailed knowledge of intra-Party politics offers scholars and students a new understanding of long-disputed struggles behind the walls of leadership in Zhongnanhai.

Huang traces the development of factional politics from its roots in the various "mountaintops," or power bases, headed by guerrilla leaders during the communist revolution, and describes the enduring impact of the personal bonds formed between Mao and his supporters at the Yan'an Round Table. He explains how factionalism led to Mao's unleashing of the Cultural Revolution, and how Deng Xiaoping manipulated factionalism to orchestrate his rise to power.

The nature of Chinese Communist Party politics, Huang argues – including highly personalized relationships between political contenders and their supporters, a barely institutionalized political process, and uncertain rules of decision making – has allowed factionalism to prevail. Huang's analysis concludes that it is not power struggles that give rise to factional activities, as the predominant theories on leadership relations and decision making presume; it is factionalism that turns power into an overriding goal in CCP politics. Thus, factional activities were a key source of inconsistency in Party policy; policy outcomes switched constantly between "Left-adventurism" and "Right-conservatism" under Mao's leadership and between those favoring "emancipation of the mind" and "socialist spiritual civilization" in the Deng era. Huang asserts, however, that, paradoxically, factionalism is not necessarily unstable and chaotic. In the long run, it may play a positive role in political development.

Jing Huang is Associate Professor of Political Science at Utah State University and Research Associate at the John King Fairbank Center for East Asian Research at Harvard University.

Cambridge Modern China Series
Edited by William Kirby, *Harvard University*

Other Books in the Series

Warren I. Cohen and Li Zhao, eds., *Hong Kong under Chinese Rule: The Economic and Political Implications of Reversion*

Tamara Jacka, *Women's Work in Rural China: Change and Continuity in an Era of Reform*

Shiping Zheng, *Party vs. State in Post-1949 China: The Institutional Dilemma*

Wenfang Tang and William L. Parish, *Chinese Urban Life under Reform: The Changing Social Contract*

Michael Dutton, *Streetlife China*

Edward S. Steinfeld, *Forging Reform in China: The Fate of State-Owned Industry*

Factionalism in Chinese Communist Politics

JING HUANG

Utah State University

CAMBRIDGE
UNIVERSITY PRESS

CAMBRIDGE UNIVERSITY PRESS
Cambridge, New York, Melbourne, Madrid, Cape Town, Singapore, São Paulo

Cambridge University Press
The Edinburgh Building, Cambridge CB2 2RU, UK

Published in the United States of America by Cambridge University Press, New York

www.cambridge.org
Information on this title: www.cambridge.org/9780521622844

© Jing Huang 2000

This publication is in copyright. Subject to statutory exception
and to the provisions of relevant collective licensing agreements,
no reproduction of any part may take place without
the written permission of Cambridge University Press.

First published 2000
This digitally printed first paperback version 2006

A catalogue record for this publication is available from the British Library

Library of Congress Cataloguing in Publication data

Huang, Jing.
Factionalism in Chinese Communist politics / Jing Huang.
p. cm. – (Cambridge modern China series)
Includes bibliographical references and index.
ISBN 0-521-62284-0
1. Chung-kuo kung ch'an tang – History. 2. Political purges – China. 3. China – Politics and government – 1949– I. Title. II. Series.

JQ1519.A5H8725   2000
324.251'075'09 – dc21
99-29408
CIP

ISBN-13 978-0-521-62284-4 hardback
ISBN-10 0-521-62284-0 hardback

ISBN-13 978-0-521-03258-2 paperback
ISBN-10 0-521-03258-X paperback

For Xiuping

Contents

List of Figures and Tables	*page* xi
Preface	xiii
List of Abbreviations	xvii

	Introduction	1
	Factionalism in Leadership Relations and Decision Making	1
	Western Analysis of Factionalism in Leadership Relations and Decision Making	3
	Conditions for the Development of Factionalism in CCP Politics	6
	Mountaintops and Leadership Relations with Mao in Command	8
	The Two-Front Arrangement, Elite Conflicts, and Policy Inconsistency	12
	"Bringing Up Successors" and the Vicious Cycle of Succession Struggles	18
	Continuity and Changes: Factionalism in the Deng Period	20
1	Factionalism, the Puzzle of Chinese Communist Politics	26
	Conflict Models and Their Explanations of Factionalism	26
	Factionalism, a Puzzle of CCP Politics	42
2	Factionalism and the Political System in China	55
	Conditions for the Development of Factionalism	55
	Factional Activities and the Shaping of Leadership Relations	74
3	The Establishment of the Yan'an Round Table	107
	Mao Zedong Strives to Achieve the Party Leadership	107

Contents

	The Yan'an Rectification and the Establishment of the Yan'an Round Table	119
	Mountaintops under Mao's Command	141
4	The Transition of the Yan'an Round Table	159
	Policy Differences: Prelude to the Gao-Liu Power Struggle	160
	The Gao-Rao Affair: An Inevitable Clash	173
	The Structural Change of the Yan'an Round Table	197
5	Crises in Leadership Relations with the Two-Front Arrangement	211
	The Rise of the Party Bureaucrats	213
	Mao versus the Party State	238
	Conclusion: The Overall Crisis of the Yan'an Round Table	256
	Appendix 5.1: The Game between Mao and Liu in Early 1962	260
	Appendix 5.2: The Game with the Deng Factor in Early 1962	264
6	The Collapse of the Yan'an Round Table and the Unleashing of Factionalism	267
	The Destruction of the Party System	268
	Lin Biao's Rise and Fall: Disconnection of the Military from the Yan'an Round Table	287
	Deng Xiaoping's Return and Fall: The Collapse of the Yan'an Round Table	325
7	Deng Xiaoping's Dominance: Factionalism Prevails over the Party Spirit	350
	The Establishment of Deng Xiaoping's Dominance	350
	Factionalism over the Party Spirit	365
	Deng's Struggle to Maintain His Dominance	387
8	Conclusion	411
	Factionalism and Political Outcomes in China	411
	The Impact of Factionalism on Chinese Politics	417
	Selected Bibliography	429
	Index	441

Figures and Tables

FIGURES

I.1	The Structure of the Yan'an Round Table	page	9
I.2	The Two-Front Arrangement, 1954–1966		13
2.1	The Process of *Zhengdun* (Rectification) Campaign		84
2.2	Prisoners' Dilemma between the Leader and His Successor		89
2.3	The New Player in a Succession Struggle: Working Model		94
2.4	Extensive Form of the Game: Players Move Simultaneously		101
2.5	Extensive Form of the Game: Deng Moves First		103
3.1	Reorganization of CCP Forces under Mao's Command, August 1937		109
3.2	A Tentative Yan'an Round Table after the Sixth Plenum, November 1938		118
3.3	The Yan'an Rectification under Mao's Command		123
3.4	The Yan'an Round Table under Mao's Command		137
4.1	Civilian Leaders and Their Policy Areas (*kou*) in 1953		182
4.2	The Transition of the Yan'an Round Table at the Eighth Party Congress, 1956		208
5.A1	Normal Form of the Game between Mao and Liu		262
5.A2	Extensive Form of the Game between Mao and Liu		262
5.A3	The Game between Mao and Liu with the Deng Factor		266
6.1	The Ties between PLA Leaders and Their Mountaintops		288
6.2	A Transformed Yan'an Round Table after the Ninth Party Congress		315
7.1	Leadership Relations under Deng Xiaoping's Dominance, 1982		384

Figures and Tables

| 8.1 | Factionalism and Power Struggle in CCP Politics | 413 |
| 8.2 | Factionalism and Policy Outcomes in CCP Politics | 415 |

TABLES

2.1	Elite Conflicts and *Zhengdun* (Rectification) Campaigns since 1949	83
2.2	Preference Orders of Leader and Successor in a Prisoners' Dilemma	92
2.3	Hardliners' Preference Order on the Outcomes of a Succession Struggle	99
2.4	Strategies, Outcomes, and Payoffs of a Succession Struggle in Deng's Period	100
3.1	Major Mountaintops under Mao's Command (1949–1952)	152
4.1	An Ziwen's List of CCP Politburo Members	178
4.2	Positions of the Military Leaders after the Gao-Rao Affair	205
5.1	Changes in Production Targets for 1967	214
5.2	High-Ranking Officers Implicated in Peng's Case	229
5.A1	Outcome, Strategy, and Payoffs in the Mao-Liu Game	261
5.A2	Outcome, Strategy, and Payoffs with the Deng Factor	265
6.1	Liu's Whereabouts and the Happenings in Beijing, March 26–April 19	279
6.2	Factional Conflicts in the PLA RMCs (1967–1968)	297
6.3	The Leadership Formed at the Tenth Party Congress (August 24–28, 1973)	327
6.4	Deng Xiaoping's Return and the Decline of Zhou Enlai's Power (1971–1973)	336
6.5	Deng's Progress and Mao's Criticism of the Gang of Four (1974–1976)	340
7.1	Personnel Arrangements at the Politburo Meeting (December 25, 1978)	364
7.2	Power Struggles between Deng and the Hardliners (1978–1987)	408

Preface

My interests in Chinese politics started in 1973–5 when I was receiving "reeducation" in a remote mountain village in Yunnan Province. In addition to heavy manual labor in the field, all the readings available to me there were the four-volume *Selected Works of Mao Zedong*, and the *Yunnan Daily* and *People's Daily*, which always arrived a week late. A tennager hungry for everything, material and spiritual, I virtually devoured every word in these publications. What fostered my interests in CCP politics, however, were the many questions I had in reading Mao's works and the gap between the newspaper propaganda and reality. I soon indulged myself in frequent correspondences with my friends in which we exchanged our ideas, knowledge, and opinions drawn from questions in Mao's works and the constantly changing situation during those turbulent years. Although such exchanges would continue for years, I actually tried to suppress my interests in CCP politics after I entered college, where I majored in English literature and later earned an M.A. degree in history. An essential reason was that the study of CCP politics was seen as a dangerous activity in China, for any steps outside the official line could result in a purge. Yet I could not really give up my interests in Chinese politics because my life experiences in the CCP political system made my desire for the answers insuppressible.

I was fortunate to sit in Roderick MacFarqhuar's class at Harvard University in 1987. His exhaustive analyses and his insights of political affairs in China have benefited my study tremendously, and his constant encouragement and unwavering support have always been a great source of inspiration. As my mentor, he read each chapter of my manuscript with such care that even a punctuation error would not escape his attention, and his advice and comments were perceptive and to the point. Working with MacFraquhar has been the most exciting and satisfactory

Preface

experience in my academic life. My gratitude to him is beyond expression.

My heartfelt thanks also go to Timothy Colten, whose expertise in Soviet politics has broadened the prospective of my study; to Jean Oi, whose sharp and apropos comments and critique have forced me to clarify my ideas more accurately with rigid analyses; and to Kenneth Shepsle, from whom I have learned not just game theory per se but what it can reveal so eloquently – that is, depending on the players' preferences, the rules and procedures determine the final outcomes. Thus, a political crisis is caused essentially by the failure of the process rather than by conflicting interests or policy disputes. Factional politics is prone to crisis not necessarily because of constant factional struggles, but because personal ties, or *guanxi*, often override the adopted rules and procedures in political interactions.

This book would not have been completed but for the generous support and help from numerous people and organizations. A Harvard-Yenching scholarship in 1986–8 permitted me to study at Harvard in the first place. Fellowships from the Mellon Foundation enabled me to concentrate on my research and writing in 1991–3. The late Professor Hu Hua in China gave me good advice on source materials. The more than two dozen people whom I interviewed in China – some of them are prominent Party historians – not only provided me with firsthand information and access to source materials but also shared their insights with me. Nancy Hearst at the John King Fairbank Center for East Asian Studies at Harvard University has offered the most crucial help in locating and sorting out source materials. She also edited the drafts of my first two chapters with painstaking care. In various stages of my work on this book, I have benefited from discussions with Ellis Joffe, Hao Yufan, and Wu Guoguang; from the thoughtful suggestions of Edward Steinfeld, who read the drafts of Chapters 4 and 5 with great care; and from the constructive comments and critiques of Andrew Nathan, who read the first draft of the manuscript in late 1994. I also wish to express my sincere thanks to the anonymous manuscript reviewers from whose relentless critiques and perceptive comments I have profited in revisions of the manuscript.

I am also indebted to a greater circle of friends, scholars, and colleagues from whose works and wisdom I have drawn in this study and to whom I can only express my gratitude by their acknowledgment in

Preface

my footnotes and bibliography. Any errors that remain are, of course, all mine. I am also grateful to those whose help was indispensable in bringing this book into print. Mary Child at Cambridge University Press has played an essential role in converting the manuscript into a publishable book. Brian MacDonald has been a truly devoted production editor, who made a painstaking effort to ready the manuscript for publication; working with him has not only been a pleasant experience but also a learning process. Anne Holmes has made an excellent index, which I believe has enhanced the general quality of this book.

My ultimate thanks, however, go to my wife, who sacrificed her own chances for an advanced degree so that I could fully concentrate on my work. With a full-time job as a librarian assistant, two young children, and a husband who usually showed up at midnight, she somehow managed to help me out, working as my research assistant, librarian, typist, and file keeper. This book is dedicated to her.

Abbreviations

AJPS	American Journal of Political Science
APSR	American Political Science Review
AS	Asian Survey
BR	Beijing Review
Cankao	Zhonggong dangshi jiaoxue cankao ziliao (The CCP History Teaching Reference Materials), compiled by Guofang daxue dangshi dangjian zhenggong jiaoyanshi (Teaching and Research Office of the Party's History, Construction, and Political Work, National Defense University), 27 vols., 1986
CB	Current Background
CC	Central Committee of the CCP
CCB	Central China Bureau
CCP	Chinese Communist Party
CFEG	Central Financial and Economic Group
CFEC	Central Financial and Economic Commission
CLG	Chinese Law and Government, a journal of translations, Armonk, NY: M. E. Sharp, 1968–
CLOPCG	The Collection of Laws and Orders of the People's Central Government, Beijing: Law Press
CMC	Central Military Commission
CO	(military) commander
CPB	Central Plain Bureau
CPSU	Communist Party of the Soviet Union
CQ	China Quarterly
CR	Cultural Revolution
CRG	Cultural Revolutionary Group
CYLC	Communist Youth League of China

Abbreviations

ECB	East China Bureau
FCP	Four Cardinal Principles
FYP	Five-Year Plan
GLF	Great Leap Forward
ICC	investment in capital construction
Jueyi	The CCP Central Committee, *Guanyu jianguo yilai dang de ruogan lishi wenti de jueyi* (The Resolution on Several Questions of Our Party's History since the Establishment of the PRC), Beijing: Sixth Plenum of the Eleventh Central Committee, June 27, 1981
KMT	Kuomintang (National Party)
MZT	Mao Zedong Thought
NB	North Bureau
NCFEC	North China Financial and Economic Commission
NEB	Northeastern Bureau
NPC	National People's Congress
NWB	Northwestern Bureau
PB	Party bureaucrats
PC	National Party Congress of the CCP
PC	*Problems of Communism*
PD	*People's Daily*
PLA	People's Liberation Army
PRC	People's Republic of China
PSC	Politburo Standing Committee
RMC	Regional Military Command (*da junqu*)
RWZ	Hu Hua, ed., *Zhonggong lishi renwu zhuan* (Biographies of Personalities in CCP History), Taiyuan: Shanxi People's Press, 1978–
SEC	State Economic Commission
SPC	State Planning Commission
SWCY	Chen Yun, *Selected Works of Chen Yun*, 2 vols., Beijing: Foreign Languages Press, 1984
SWDXP	Deng Xiaoping, *Selected Works of Deng Xiaoping, 1975–1982*, 2 vols., Beijing: Foreign Languages Press, 1984
SWLSQ	Liu Shaoqi, *Selected Works of Liu Shaoqi*, 3 vols., Beijing: Foreign Languages Press, 1984
SWMZD	Mao Zedong, *Selected Works of Mao Zedong*, 5 vols., Beijing: Foreign Languages Press, 1981

Abbreviations

SWZEL	Zhou Enlai, *Selected Works of Zhou Enlai*, 2 vols., Beijing: Foreign Languages Press, 1989
Wansui	*Mao Zedong sixiang wansui* (Long Live Mao Zedong Thought), 3 vols., n.p., 1967, 1969
Wengao	*Jianguo yilai Mao Zedong wengao* (Manuscripts of Mao Zedong since the Establishment of the PRC), compiled by Department for Research on Party Literature, CCP Central Committee, 13 vols., Beijing: CC Document Press, 1987–98
Xuanbian	*Shierda yilai zhongyao wenxian xuanbian* (Selection of the Important Documents since the Twelfth Party Congress), compiled by Department for Research on Party Literature, CCP Central Committee, 2 vols., Beijing: People's Press, 1989
Xuandu	*Shiyijie sanzhong quanhui yilai zhongyao wenxian xuandu* (Selected Readings of the Important Documents since the Third Plenum of the Eleventh Party Congress), compiled by Department for Research on Party Literature, CCP Central Committee, 2 vols., Beijing: People's Press, 1987
Xulie	*Zhongguo renmin jiefangjun fazhan xulie 1927–1949* (The Development of the PLA Organizational System), Beijing: PLA Press, 1985
Yanjiu 1	*Dangshi yanjiu* (The Study of the Party History)
Yanjiu 2	*Zhonggong dangshi yanjiu* (The Study of the CCP History)
YB	Yangtze Bureau
YR	Yan'an Rectification
Zhuanji	*Xuexi "lishi jueyi" zhuanji* (Monograph on the Study of "The Resolution on Several Questions of Our Party's History"), compiled by the Association of the CCP History, 3 vols., Beijing: Press of the Central Party School of the CCP, 1982
Ziliao	*"Wenhua da geming" yanjiu ziliao* (Research Materials of "the Cultural Revolution"), compiled by Guofang daxue dangshi dangjian zhenggong jiaoyanshi (Teaching and Research Office of the Party's History, Construction, and Political Work, National Defense University), 3 vols., 1988

Introduction

FACTIONALISM IN LEADERSHIP RELATIONS AND DECISION MAKING

Factionalism, a politics in which informal groups, formed on personal ties, compete for dominance within their parent organization, is a well-observed phenomenon in Chinese politics. In addition to frequent references to factional activities in the literature, a few studies focus on this topic specifically: Andrew Nathan explores factionalism in Chinese Communist Party (CCP) politics in terms of clientalism;[1] William Whitson attributes factional tendencies in the military to the CCP's Field Army system during the war;[2] Lucian Pye elucidates factionalism from the perspective of Chinese political culture;[3] and Frederick Teiwes depicts the 1954 Gao-Rao Affair as essentially an outcome of factional struggles among the elite members.[4]

The study of factionalism in CCP politics, however, remains strikingly deficient. There are few thorough and systematic examinations of how factionalism has developed in CCP politics. Theoretically, it is hard to imagine how factions, which tend to divide the Party, can exist in the CCP, not necessarily because the CCP leadership has always vowed to

---

1 Andrew Nathan, "A factionalism model for CCP Politics," *CQ*, 53 (January 1973), pp. 34–66.
2 William Whitson, *The Chinese High Command: A History of Communist Military Politics, 1927–71*, London: Macmillan, 1973.
3 Lucian Pye, *The Dynamics of Chinese Politics*, Cambridge, MA: Oelgeschlager, Gunn & Hain, 1981.
4 Frederick Teiwes, *Politics at Mao's Court: Gao Gang and Party Factionalism in the Early 1950s*, New York: M. E. Sharp, 1990.

eliminate factional activities in the Party, but because the CCP is a Leninist party, the unity of which is vital for its rule. More pragmatically, if factionalism forms the essential dynamics in the policy process, how can we distinguish a genuine policy dispute from the unprincipled factional conflicts? Or, as some may suggest, if the two entangle, to what extent can factional activities affect a policy outcome, or vice versa? Furthermore, how can factionalism affect the overall political development in China? In short, factionalism remains a puzzle of, rather than an answer to, Chinese politics. As Kenneth Lieberthal and Michael Oksenberg point out: "Few questions [about factionalism] have so engrossed outside observers of Chinese politics as these, yet on few issues is there as little certainty."[5]

Factionalism in China has drawn so much attention yet still remains a puzzle because it involves two major issues that have remained the most problematic in our study of CCP politics: leadership relations and leadership decision making. *Leadership relations* have been infamously unpredictable, marked by frequent purges ever since the CCP was established in 1921 and by a particularly vicious cycle of succession struggles after 1949. Except for Jiang Zemin, who was handpicked by Deng Xiaoping after the May 1989 crisis, all the successors – Liu Shaoqi, Lin Biao, Hua Guofeng, Hu Yaobang, and Zhao Ziyang – were purged. Moreover, all were toppled by their patrons, Mao Zedong and Deng Xiaoping, with the exception of Hua, who was ousted by Deng after Mao's death. *Leadership decision making* in China has also puzzled us, not necessarily because of its secrecy, but because of its inconsistency. Policy outcomes switched constantly between "Left-adventurism" and "Right-conservatism" in Mao's period, or between "emancipation of mind" and "socialist spiritual civilization" in Deng's. As a well-known metaphor in China says, "the Party's policy is like the moon – the one on the first night of the month is different from the one on the fifteenth."

This book is designed to explain leadership relations and decision making from the perspective of factionalism. The aim is to show to what extent factionalism affects changes in leadership relations and policy outcomes.

---

5 Kenneth Lieberthal and Michael Oksenberg, *Policy Making in China: Leaders, Structure, and Processes*, Princeton: Princeton University Press, 1988, p. 58.

Introduction

WESTERN ANALYSIS OF FACTIONALISM IN LEADERSHIP RELATIONS AND DECISION MAKING

Chapter 1 examines the evolution of Western analysis of leadership relations and decision making in China. The explanations can be generalized by three predominant models: the policy-choice model, the structure model, and the power-struggle model. All three highlight factional activities, yet their explanations vary greatly.

The policy-choice analysts argue that leadership relations are determined by the leaders' *choices* in policy making. Different diagnoses by these leaders of an existing problem lead to different policy choices. Factional activities, if there are any, emerge in policy confrontations in which those with shared views team up in order to make their choice prevail. Harry Harding notes that "the leaders of post-Mao China fall into two groups. More conservative leaders are cautious and skeptical about dramatic departures from the planned economy, state-owned industry, and centralized political system that were the legacy of the Soviet model. Radical reformers, in contrast, entertain bolder and riskier measures that would launch China in the direction of a market economy, new forms of public ownership, and a more pluralistic political order."[6]

Drawing on the theory of bureaucratic politics, the structure analysts argue that leadership relations reflect the leaders' positions in the *structure* of policy making, and their *institutional interests* determine their policy choices. Factional activities are essentially underlain by interest conflicts among the agencies involved in the policy process. Policy making appears inconsistent because, given "the segmented and stratified system of authority," bureaucratic interactions, interwoven with factional activities, often lead to "unintended outcomes" in the policy process.[7] Thus, the structure analysts see similar career paths as a major criterion for factional alignments. Lieberthal and Oksenberg point out that all the prominent members of the "petroleum faction" rose to power from the oil industry.[8]

The power-struggle analysts maintain that leadership relations are

---

6 Harry Harding, *China's Second Revolution*, Washington, DC: Brookings Institution, 1987, pp. 2–3.
7 Lieberthal and Oksenberg, *Policy Making in China*, esp. p. 137.
8 Ibid., pp. 42–51, 60–1.

determined by the *distribution of power* among the elite members, and leadership decision making essentially reflects the vision of those who have prevailed in the power struggle.[9] Factionalism has its roots in endless power struggles. As Lucian Pye explains, "the prime basis for factions among cadres is the search for career security and the protection of power.... The strength of Chinese factions is the personal relationships of individuals who, operating in a hierarchical context, create linkage networks that extend upward in support of particular leaders who are, in turn, looking for followers to ensure their power."[10]

Explanations involving the three models, however, are based on a problematic assumption that factionalism is a dependent variable that results from policy disputes, conflicts of institutional interests, or power struggles. A close examination shows that the CCP leaders with shared policy preferences did not always get along. Liu Shaoqi supported Mao most of the time in policy making,[11] but his desperate effort to keep up with Mao did not prevent a merciless purge by Mao. Although Lin Biao's "attitude was truly one of 'Do whatever the Chairman says,'" his relationship with Mao ended up in an ultimate "tragedy."[12] Indeed, the CCP leaders with shared policy preferences often had different factional alignments: both the Gang of Four and Lin Biao supported the Cultural Revolution (CR), yet the fierce power struggle between them was an underlying factor in Lin's eventual fall (see Chapter 4); Chen Yun and Peng Zhen were both known for their conservative attitudes in the Deng period, yet Chen played a crucial role in blocking Peng from entering the Politburo Standing Committee (PSC); and both Hu Yaobang and Zhao Ziyang were reform-minded leaders, yet Zhao kept an indifferent attitude to the toppling of Hu (see Chapter 7).

Conflicts of institutional interest can constitute an essential dynamic in the policy process, yet it would be difficult to explain the final policy outcomes if "there is no way precisely to measure the real authority of any particular group of officials." Moreover, how can we define institutional interests if it is not the institutional arrangements but personal ties, or

---

9 Roderick MacFarquhar, *The Origins of the Cultural Revolution*, 3 vols., New York: Columbia University Press, 1974, 1983, 1997.
10 Pye, *The Dynamics*, pp. 7–8.
11 MacFarquhar, *The Origins*, 1:2–3.
12 Frederick Teiwes and Warren Sun, *The Tragedy of Lin Biao: Riding the Tiger during the Cultural Revolution*, London: C. Hurst, 1961, p. 161.

Introduction

guanxi, that not only "bind different agencies together" but also "constitute the single most important ingredient which integrates the system and enables it to function"?[13] Nonetheless, the structure model reveals a significant reality in CCP politics: the offices are distributed as spoils among those who dominate. A leader strives to advance the interests of his office essentially because it has been knitted into his *guanxi* networks, and its well-being has a substantial impact on the strength of his faction. Thus, a leader's power is determined not so much by his official position as by the support he can generate through his *guanxi* networks. Deng and Chen Yun, for example, remained the most influential figures until they died in 1997 and 1995, although they held no official positions after 1989.

The power-struggle model has perhaps provided the most compelling explanation of factionalism in CCP politics. However, its analysis invites more profound questions. If a leader's power comes from his factional networks instead of his institution or the support to his policy choices, how can he develop and control these networks in the CCP political system, a totalistic system in which the Party's unity is a necessary prerequisite? How can he adjust the interests of his faction to those of the institution over which he presides in policy making?

In a fundamental departure from previous scholarship, I argue that factionalism is an independent variable in the shaping of leadership relations and in leadership decision making in CCP politics. Specifically, a leader's power is based on the strength of his factional networks; his relationships with his peers are shaped not so much by their pros and cons to his policy choices as by the consequences of their interactions with his power in a hierarchical context; and decisions are made according to the vision of those who have prevailed in the power struggles rather than through the due process in which everyone is entitled to present his preferences. The axis of my analysis – the relationship between factionalism and power – appears consistent with the power-struggle model. But the fundamental difference must be stated precisely: power struggles do not give rise to factional activities; rather, it is factionalism that turns power into an overriding goal in CCP politics, in which authorities are highly personalized, institutionalization of the political process is deficient, and the procedures and rules for decision making are uncertain.

---

13 Lieberthal and Oksenberg, *Policy Making in China*, pp. 137–8, 156.

Factionalism in Chinese Communist Politics

CONDITIONS FOR THE DEVELOPMENT OF FACTIONALISM IN CCP POLITICS

An inevitable question arises from the assumption that factionalism is an *independent variable* in the shaping of leadership relations and decision making: how could factionalism develop and prevail in CCP politics despite the CCP leadership's repeated denouncement of, and vows to eliminate, factionalism in political affairs? Chapter 2 addresses this question from the perspective of the CCP system, a system in which (1) power is entrusted to individual leaders in a hierarchical context, (2) the Party monopolizes all the legal channels for the expression of diverse interests, (3) a formal process for decision making has never really been adopted, and (4) the military frequently intervenes in political affairs. Factionalism is innate to CCP politics because these four features provide the development of factionalism with necessary and sufficient conditions.

The CCP carried out its revolution with Mao's strategy of "setting up base areas in the countryside and encircling cities from the rural areas." Thus, the CCP forces were developed separately by various leaders in their base areas, which were isolated from each other. In a perilous situation during the war, these leaders were allowed a large degree of independence in decision making, and they entrusted power to their subordinates according to the strength of their forces and, more importantly, the degree of their loyalty. This pattern of personal entrustment of power fostered close personal ties, or *guanxi*, between a leader and his followers, and the former needs the latter's support as badly as the latter needs the former's protection in political affairs.[14] These *guanxi* created "old-boy networks" and prepared the roots for factional development.

However, it is the *single-party rule* that turns the universally existing old-boy networks into political factions. In China, the CCP monopolizes all the legal channels for the expression of political and socioeconomic interests. But these interests are rarely harmonious, because situations across China vary greatly. Thus, as Mao said, "intra-party struggles are inevitable because different social interests will eventually find expressions within the Party."[15] When differences emerge, however, the CCP

---

14 See Pye, *The Dynamic*, pp. 6-8.   15 *SWMZD*, 4:124.

Introduction

leaders are not allowed to make them public, because the Party's appearance of unity is vital for its rule; that is why whenever differences in the CCP leadership broke out, a purge would follow, and the victims were always accused of "scheming to split the Party." Thus, the involved leaders have to seek support through informal channels – old-boy networks – to solve their differences. My examination shows that in CCP politics *guanxi* networks function as (1) exclusive channels of communications among political associates, (2) outlets for their particular interests, and (3) the command system of their forces – functions that are normally assumed by the political organizations in a pluralistic political system. Repeated abuse of personal ties in a system of single-party dictatorship turns the universally existing old-boy networks into political factions.

A solution to the conflict between the single-party rule and diverse socioeconomic interests is to institutionalize the policy-making process, namely, to establish a formal process through institutional arrangements in which formal rules, compliant procedures, and standard operating practices are abiding in policy making. While keeping the system essentially intact, formal institutional arrangements can provide plural channels for the expression of diverse interests in the policy process; compliant procedures can override personal ties, or *guanxi*, in decision making; and standard operating practices can make it difficult to abuse one's power in political affairs. All this strengthens the authority of institutions rather than individual leaders.[16]

But institutionalization of the political process has not been achieved in China. Power has always concentrated in the hands of individual leaders. In retrospect, an important reason, which has largely been overlooked in the literature, why Mao and Deng maintained their command was their exclusive privilege to violate any established rules and procedures in decision making whenever they felt their dominance was being threatened. As a result, all the formal arrangements in decision making

---

16 After Stalin's death, for example, factional phenomena – frequent purges based on personal implications and the abuse of personal ties in political affairs – faded away in Soviet politics as the political process was institutionalized. For institutionalization of the policy process in the ex-Soviet Union and its impact, see Jerry Hough, *Soviet Union and Social Science Theory*, Cambridge, MA: Harvard University Press, 1977, pp. 23–31; and Robert Daniels, "Soviet politics since Khrushchev," in John W. Strong, ed., *The Soviet Union under Brezhnev and Kosyqin*, New York: Van Nostrand-Reinhold, 1971, pp. 22–3.

became a facade, beneath which *guanxi* to the powerful leaders became indispensable to achieving the desired policy goals. The dependence on *guanxi* networks in political affairs has promoted factional activities.

The other major consequence of the lack of a formal process is, as rational-choice theory predicts, that the policy process is bound to collapse when the policy makers' preferences are intransitive – that is, when there are differences in kind among them.[17] A policy crisis emerges in such a situation. To solve this crisis and to ensure the operation of the system, the dominant leader, namely Mao or Deng, had to resort to military intervention to enforce his choice, which happened repeatedly in CCP history. Given that most of the CCP factions originated from the armed forces during the war, repeated military intervention has not only consolidated the dominant leaders' power but also strengthened their factional alignments. As a result, the military has become the most important power base in CCP politics. Without military support, a Party leader could not be dominant in policy making, no matter how influential he appeared. Leaders like Liu Shaoqi in Mao's period and Chen Yun in Deng's were typical examples.

MOUNTAINTOPS AND LEADERSHIP RELATIONS WITH MAO IN COMMAND

Factionalism played an essential role in the establishment of Mao's command. Mao pointed out that "China's revolution was made by many mountaintops."[18] Mountaintops, or *shantou*, refers to the CCP base areas, which were usually developed in the mountainous areas ideal for guerrilla warfare during the revolution. Since these base areas were isolated from each other and the CCP forces in these areas had to fight independently, strong personal bonds were forged between the leaders and their forces, and among the cadres and officers from the same mountaintop. These personal bonds formed the foundation of the CCP factions. Thus, "mountaintop" has become a synonym for political faction, and "mountaintop mentality" (*shantou zhuyi*) refers to factionalism in the CCP jargon.

---

17 See Thomas Schwartz, *The Logic of Collective Choice*, New York: Columbia University Press, 1986, pp. 12–17.
18 *Wansui*, 2:479.

Introduction

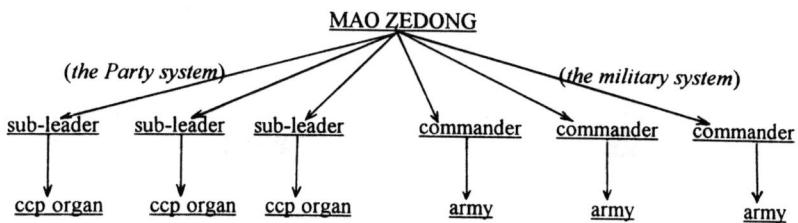

Figure I.1. The structure of the Yan'an Round Table (solid arrow = direction of control based on personal loyalty)

Chapter 3 examines how all the mountaintops came under the leadership of the Yan'an Round Table[19] – the first-generation leadership with Mao in command[20] – after Mao and his followers prevailed in the struggles against the mountaintops led by Zhang Guotao in the military and by Wang Ming in the Party. More significant was the establishment of Mao Zedong Thought as the CCP's "guiding principle" during the Yan'an period in 1937–45. This not only marked the CCP's ideological independence from Moscow, but it also made Mao's command unchallengeable, for any challenges to his command would eventually undermine the Party's ideological legitimacy.

But the structure of the Yan'an Round Table was faction-ridden. As shown by Figure I.1 (a simplified version of Figure 3.4), it was Mao's authority based on personal loyalties, rather than institutional arrangements, that secured the stability of leadership relations. Mao's command was supported by the mountaintops in both the Party and military systems, which are virtually independent of each other in the CCP polit-

---

19 The term is coined by Roderick MacFarquhar. It refers to the first generation of CCP leaders "whose comradeship had been forged by the Long March, Japanese aggression, and civil war." (MacFarquhar, *The Origins*, 1:1.)

20 The Mao-in-command model was formalized by Michael Oksenberg, "Policy making under Mao," in John M. H. Lindbeck, ed., *China: Management of a Revolutionary Society*, Seattle: University of Washington Press, 1971, pp. 79–115. For Mao's path to power, see Jin Chongji, ed., *Mao Zedong zhuan, 1983–1949* (A Biography of Mao Zedong, 1983–1949), Beijing: Central Document Press, 1996; and Frederick Teiwes and Warren Sun, "From a Leninist to a charismatic party: The CCP's changing leadership, 1937–1945," in Tony Saich and Hans van de Ven, eds., *New Perspectives on the Chinese Communist Revolution*, New York: M. E. Sharp, 1995, pp. 339–87. Teiwes and Sun's analysis overlaps with Chapter 3 in this book. Yet my analysis differs from theirs in perspectives, source materials, and their explanations and evaluations of various events and figures involved in the establishment of Mao's command.

ical system, and Mao was the *only* one who had control of both systems. While the generals' loyalties enabled Mao to secure his hegemonic position in the Party, the principle that "the Party commands the gun" provided Mao with political legitimacy to command the military.

The Yan'an Round Table provided the CCP with a strong and cohesive leadership in its revolution, which was carried out by various mountaintops. It not only embodied the comradeship among the mountaintop leaders and their loyalty to Mao, but also created a structural shackle on the factionalism embedded in CCP politics. Leadership relations were structured in such a way that a subleader who attempted to expand his power base would have to engage in a zero-sum struggle with the other leaders, and his expansion could also face Mao's suppression because it posed a potential threat to his command. To be precise, by entrusting the supreme authority to Mao on the one hand and creating a system of checks and balances among Mao's comrades on the other hand, the Yan'an Round Table secured the stability of faction-ridden leadership relations. The status quo could be maintained as long as Mao wanted to, because no one but Mao – *the* leader who had full control of both the Party and military and whose Mao Zedong Thought provided this leadership with ideological legitimacy – could exert an external force to break the leadership stability.

But the problems in faction-ridden leadership relations were exposed soon after 1949. Rapid expansion of the CCP forces after the collapse of Kuomintang (KMT) brought about a situation in which China was virtually divided up by various CCP mountaintops, and their leaders became the "kings" in the areas controlled by their forces.[21] Meanwhile, Liu Shaoqi's mountaintop grew so powerful that Liu's men began to manipulate the policy process at the Center. In an effort to prevent "independent kingdoms" and to undermine Liu's forces, Mao moved all the mountaintop leaders to Beijing. The effort of centralization led to an overall redistribution of power among the CCP leaders. This broke the stability of the Yan'an Round Table.

Chapter 4 focuses on the first major elite conflict after 1949 – the Gao-Rao Affair in 1954 – in order to demonstrate the significant transition of the Yan'an Round Table after 1949. The Gao-Rao Affair was not an aber-

---

21 Mao called these regional leaders *ge lu zhuhou* (dukes and princes from their territories).

Introduction

ration resulting from Gao's "misunderstanding" and "miscalculation" of Mao and the other leaders' intention, as suggested by the conventional explanations.[22] My examination suggests:

1. The affair resulted from an inevitable clash between the two major mountaintops in the Party led by Gao and Liu during the process of centralization.
2. It was Mao who spurred Gao to take on Liu in order to undermine Liu's mountaintop. But the ongoing redistribution of power made the entire episode more explosive, hence more difficult for Mao to maneuver as he had expected.
3. Mao eventually abandoned Gao because Gao's brazen intervention in personnel affairs, especially his reckless lobbying among the military leaders, formed a direct threat to Mao's command.

Indeed, Mao's "betrayal" of Gao further reveals a crucial feature in Mao's command, namely, that Mao was the only one in the CCP leadership who was allowed to have control of both the Party and the military systems. As my study shows repeatedly, Mao would not permit anyone to expand his influence in a system to which he did not belong. Like Gao's fall, a major factor in the purges of Peng Dehuai in 1959 and Lin Biao in 1971, the "containment" of Zhou Enlai in 1973–5, and Deng Xiaoping's second fall in 1976, was that they all tended to develop, or had already developed, substantial influence in the system they were not supposed to lead.

More significantly, the Gao-Rao Affair exposed two *structural flaws* in the Yan'an Round Table. First, while each individual leader was responsible to Mao in a hierarchical context, there were few institutional arrangements for the relationships among the subleaders in the policy process. All manner of control – information, directives, recommendations, reports, complaints – had to flow directly to and from Mao. It is not difficult to see why this was important for Mao's command: while it ensured Mao's direct control over each subleader, it also minimized the possibility of coalition formations among the subleaders, for such coalitions could threaten Mao's command. This feature, however, also created a dilemma for Mao, especially after 1949: although Mao had to keep all manner of control flowing directly to him in order to secure his

---

22 See *Zhongguo gongchandang lishi* (History of the CCP), compiled by the Party History Research Office of the CC Party School, Beijing: People's Press, 1990, 3:190–7; and Teiwes, *Politics at Mao's Court*, p. 38.

command, it was too much of a task for him to follow every policy issue closely. As a result, those who had access to Mao could either try to manipulate the policy process, as Liu did in 1951–3, or use Mao's name for their own gains, as Gao did in his lobbying activities in 1954.

Moreover, as the CCP leaders became the new rulers of China, what they faced daily was no longer a common enemy but various problems, diverse interests, and hence different policy goals. But deficient institutional arrangements prevented them from examining a problem from various perspectives, presenting their points of view adequately, and coordinating different policy goals effectively. All this resulted in unexpected conflicts and instability in the policy process. Dramatic examples include the discord between Mao and Liu on the policy toward the "national bourgeoisie" in 1950, inconsistent policies on land reform in the early 1950s, and the controversy caused by Bo Yibo's tax reform in 1953, which triggered the Gao-Rao Affair.

The second structural flaw is that the supreme leader's eventual departure could immediately destabilize leadership relations by leaving a huge power vacuum at the top, which would in turn break the status quo and provoke fierce power struggles. As a matter of fact, jockeying for a better position could happen long before the supreme leader's expected departure. Gao's attack on Liu, for example, was essentially motivated by his ambition to replace Liu as the one next in the line.

The CCP leaders' effort to overcome these two structural flaws has had a fundamental impact on leadership relations and decision making in both the Mao and Deng periods.

THE TWO-FRONT ARRANGEMENT, ELITE
CONFLICTS, AND POLICY INCONSISTENCY

The solution to the first structural flaw is the so-called *two-front arrangement* in policy making (Figure I.2). Chapter 5 examines how this arrangement, which was formalized at the 1956 Eighth Party Congress (PC), brought about tremendous changes in leadership relations and decision making. The key points yielded by my analysis are:

1 Incompatibility between Mao's command, which was based on personal loyalties, and the effort by the Party leadership to formalize the policy process, which led to the reshaping of leadership relations according to

Introduction

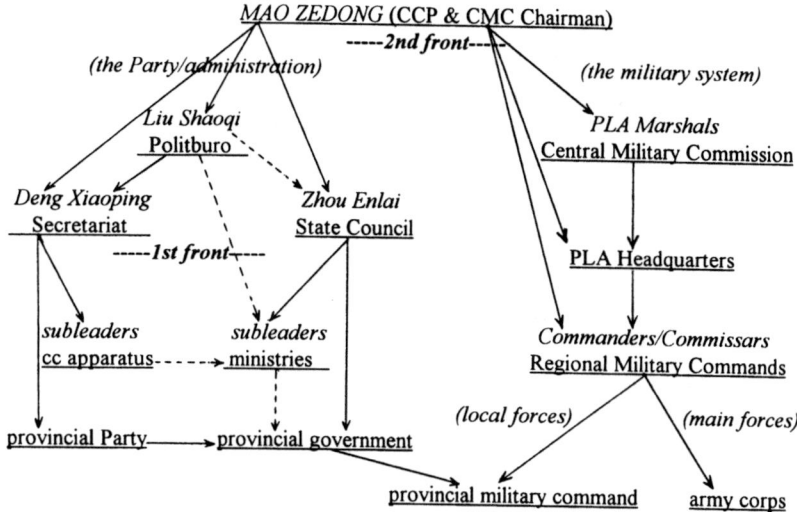

Figure I.2. Two-front arrangement, 1954–1966 (solid arrow = direct control; dashed arrow = indirect control)

various interests in the policy process, formed the essential source of elite conflicts.
2 Policy inconsistency was essentially caused by Mao's repeated violations of the established institutional arrangements in policy making.
3 Mao launched an onslaught to the Party establishment – the Cultural Revolution – not necessarily because of his deep-seated "antibureaucraticism"[23] or his personal dismay at Liu Shaoqi and his colleagues, but because the Party establishment embodied a formal process that empowered the Party bureaucrats while constraining Mao's personal authority in policy making.

The most distinctive change in the structure of leadership relations, as we compare Figure I.2 to Figure I.1, is that the civilian leaders were divided into two fronts in the policy process: while Mao stayed with the second front to "decide on the issues of principle," the other leaders managed daily policy affairs at the first front – hence it is called the two-front arrangement. Noticeably, the first front leaders were assigned to various institutions with specific functions in policy making. Liu, for

---

23 See Maurice Meisner, *Mao's China and After: A History of the People's Republic*, rev. ed., New York: Free Press, 1986, p. 445.

13

example, ran the Politburo, which oversees the entire policy process; Zhou took charge of the State Council, which was the administrative center; and Deng headed the CCP Secretariat, which handled daily affairs and served as the information hub. These institutional arrangements substantially improved coordination and communication among the leaders and, more importantly, created a *formal process* for policy making. All this was crucial for the stability and consistency of the policy process.

The two-front arrangement was also designed to solve Mao's dilemma in policy making without undermining his command. Staying with the second front, Mao could have shaken off the burden of daily affairs while still maintaining his command because of his direct control over the first-front leaders, among whom a system of checks and balances was embodied in the institutional arrangements of policy making. Mao's direct control of the military would have provided his command with extra security. (There was no two-front arrangement in the military system. Mao still maintained his direct control of the military.) But it was not to be.

As an essential step toward institutionalization of the policy-making process, the two-front arrangement brought about fundamental changes in leadership relations and decision making. When a problem emerged in the policy process, the first-front leaders' assessment and diagnosis were not always in accord with Mao's vision. While Mao could envision the problem from the perspective of "revolutionary principles," the first-front leaders had to devise a solution to the problem that would satisfy their policy goals. Although the first-front leaders tried to maintain their loyalty to Mao, their responsibility for the designed policy goals bound their best interests to the objective policy outcomes. As a result, when differences in policy making emerged between Mao and the first-front leaders, the latter had to stick together in order to achieve their policy goals, and the established institutional arrangements enabled them to manipulate the policy process without defying Mao directly. Thus, unexpectedly to Mao, the two-front arrangement undermined, rather than secured, his command, for it not only created common interests among the first-front leaders, but it also embodied due procedures for policy making that exerted constraints on Mao's power.

Thus, contrary to the conventional view that Mao's absolute power is

Introduction

a key factor leading to the CR,[24] my analysis shows that the two-front arrangement in policy making had constrained Mao's authority to such an extent that Mao felt he was losing control at the Center.[25] As Mao admitted to Edgar Snow in 1970, he had to allow his personality cult to be created on the eve of the CR to make up for his declining power and to "stimulate the masses to destroy the anti-Mao Party bureaucracy."[26]

To demonstrate how the two-front arrangement checked Mao's power and how his violation of this arrangement destabilized the policy process and eventually leadership relations, my examination focuses on two periods during which we witnessed the most dramatic policy changes before the CR: the late 1950s, when the policy waltzed from the first leap forward to "resolute retreat" and then to the Great Leap Forward (GLF); and the early 1960s, when the pragmatic approach in economic policies formed a sharp contrast to the increasingly radical policies in the political sphere. The obvious policy inconsistencies in these two periods were essentially caused by Mao's repeated violations of the two-front arrangement in order to prevent his command from eroding. Although Mao was able to enforce his vision to the first-front leaders, he was unable to convert his ideas into concrete policies without going through the established process controlled by the Party bureaucrats. Increasingly frustrated and suspicious, Mao had to seek support from outside the Party and launched an all-out assault on the entire Party establishment. The result was the CR. In this sense, the massive purge of the Party elite did not necessarily mean that Mao betrayed, or felt he was being betrayed by, his former comrades. Rather, they had to go because Mao wanted to destroy the Party institutions over which they presided. Thus, although there is adequate evidence that purging Liu Shaoqi and his

---

24 See, among others, *Jueyi*, pp. 314–18; Jin Chunming, *"Wenhua da geming" shigao* (A Draft of History of the "Cultural Revolution"), Chengdu: Sichuan People's Press, 1995, pp. 132–4; Hong Yung Lee, *The Politics of the Chinese Cultural Revolution*, Berkeley: University of California Press, 1978; and Harry Harding, "The Chinese state in crisis, 1966–69," in Roderick MacFarquhar, ed., *The Politics of China: 1949–1989*, Cambridge: Cambridge University Press, 1993, p. 235.
25 See *Wansui*, 2:641, 658, 674.
26 See Edgar Snow, *The Long Revolution*, New York: Random House, 1972, p. 169. Mao also made the same point in his July 1966 "Mao's Letter to Ch'iang Ching," *Issues & Studies*, 9, no. 4 (January 1973), p. 95.

men, including Peng Zhen, was Mao's personal desire, leaders like Deng Xiaoping and Luo Ruiqing were essentially the victims of the falling Party institutions.

The CR caused substantial damage to the legitimacy of the CCP's rule.[27] Although few would disagree that "the ultimate responsibility for the CR rests squarely with" Mao,[28] questions still remain on how the CR could eventually wipe out virtually the entire Yan'an Round Table – not just the Party elite but also the military leaders whose support enabled Mao to launch the CR in the first place. Thus, the CR also caused devastating damage to Mao himself, for the Yan'an Round Table was the very foundation of his command. Whatever his purpose might be, how could Mao eventually destroy the foundation of his own leadership?[29]

Chapter 6 addresses this question from the perspective of factionalism during the CR. I argue that the collapse of the party system removed the organizational shackles on factionalism embedded in CCP politics. The consequent outbreak of factional struggles brought about a fundamental dilemma for Mao: he needed support from the strongest faction to maintain his command, yet he could not let this faction become dominant in political affairs. Mao's effort to solve this dilemma led to a vicious cycle of power struggles. First, Mao had to give his blessing to the prominent faction(s) in exchange for its support; but as this faction became dominant under his patronage, Mao had to shift his weight to the weaker faction(s) in order to prevent the dominant faction from becoming too strong.[30] In his constant change of positions in the factional struggles, Mao used the policy issues as means to manipulate the political situation. All this caused continuous instability in leadership relations and repeated inconsistency in policy making.

My examination focuses on three major issues in leadership relations and decision making in this period: the role of the military in the launching of the CR, the Mao-Lin (Biao) conflict, and Deng Xiaoping's come-

27 Roderick MacFarquhar, "End of the Revolution," *New York Review of Books*, July 20, 1989, pp. 8–10.
28 Harding, "The Chinese state in crisis," pp. 232–6.
29 Mao seemed to foresee that the CR could eventually hurt him, as he said in "Mao's Letter to Ch'iang Ching," p. 96, "I am now prepared to be broken to pieces."
30 This finding provides an explanation for Nathan's central assumption in his "A factionalism model," p. 66: "no faction will be able to achieve overwhelmingly superior power."

Introduction

back and its impact. The findings in my examination depart from the conventional explanations. First, despite the crucial role of the Maoist radicals like Jiang Qing and Zhang Chunqiao, it was the support from *all* the military leaders, not just Lin Biao, that enabled Mao to launch the CR. Second, Mao's dependence on the military forced him to take sides in factional struggles among the military mountaintops, which broke out immediately after the collapse of the Party. With Mao's patronage, Lin's mountaintop expanded rapidly at the others' expense. This eventually led to a "prisoners' dilemma" between Mao and Lin (see the discussion in next section). Lastly, Lin's fall enabled Zhou Enlai to gain control of both the Party and military systems, not necessarily because of his crucial role in the Lin Biao Incident, but because he was the only one left in the leadership who had access to the factional networks in both systems. This formed an unprecedented threat to Mao's command – for the first time a CCP leader other than Mao was able to control both the Party and the military. Thus, Mao had to bring back Deng Xiaoping to contain Zhou, for Deng was *the* one who could have Mao's trust and, more important, had widespread *guanxi* networks in both systems.

But Deng faced an unsolvable dilemma in his mission: he had to bring back the "old boys" in order to consolidate his position and to restore stability, yet by doing so he would virtually "reverse the verdict of the CR." Deng's choice put him in a deadly clash with the Maoists and eventually with Mao himself. His second fall was inevitable, and it marked the final collapse of the Yan'an Round Table.

In retrospect, the Yan'an Round Table was bound to collapse because its faction-ridden structure could not be adapted to the formalization of the political process after 1949. The formalization, which was necessary for leadership stability and policy consistency, demanded the reshaping of leadership relations according to different positions of the leaders in the policy-making structure rather than their personal relationships. Ultimately, Mao only had two choices: either to adapt his command to the formal process, which would exert constraints on his personal authority as it did on the other leaders', or to do away with this process so as to maintain his absolute command. Consciously or not, Mao tried the former first, but eventually he chose the second. What Mao failed to realize is that it was not his former comrades who betrayed him, but rather it was the formal process, on which the Party bureaucracy was established, that undermined his power. Mao's onslaught on the Party bureaucracy removed the organizational shackles on factionalism embedded in the CCP political system, and the massive purge set off a chain of factional strife for power. Eventually, as these factional struggles brought down the entire Yan'an Round Table, Mao's command became virtually baseless. That is why Mao became increasingly Machiavellian and his personality cult reached its climax in his final days, for this was the only way to make up for the eroding base of his command, which appeared so absolute yet in fact became so fragile that it could not tolerate even the slightest differences in policy making.

"BRINGING UP SUCCESSORS" AND THE VICIOUS CYCLE OF SUCCESSION STRUGGLES

A puzzle in CCP politics is the vicious cycle of succession struggles, which is examined in this book from the perspective of the faction-ridden structure of leadership relations. As I discussed earlier, the other *structural flaw* of the Yan'an Round Table was its vulnerability to sudden collapse with the departure of the supreme leader. The CCP leadership tried to solve this problem by "bringing up a successor" while the supreme leader was still in power. Since the successor would assume the leadership at the moment of the supreme leader's departure, chaos caused by his death could be prevented.

However, given the faction-ridden leadership structure, whose stability essentially depended on a balanced distribution of power among the subleaders on the one hand and the supreme leader's absolute command on the other, "bringing up a successor" was a move that would undermine this stability. To make sure that the successor would not be challenged by the other mountaintop leaders, the supreme leader would have to entrust more power to his successor, who in turn would take the opportunity to expand his forces so as to secure his position. Sooner or later, the successor's expansion would break the balance of power among the leaders and hence jeopardize the status quo. The successor could become so powerful that even the supreme leader would feel threatened. At this point, the leader had two choices: to continue his patronage of the successor, or to contain the successor in order to secure his own command. Meanwhile, the successor could either stop his expansion or continue it in order to consolidate his power. This scenario can be modeled precisely by a prisoners' dilemma in which both the leader and

Introduction

successor would suffer because both of their positions were jeopardized (see Chapter 2).

But the leader and his successor were not prisoners who "must choose without the opportunity for explicitly coordinating their actions."[31] Why couldn't they solve the problem through communications? It seems unimaginable indeed that there were no communications between the leader and his successor when the problems began to emerge. Yet the evidence shows that this was exactly what happened during a succession struggle. Liu Shaoqi "had no clue" about Mao's intention, "nor did he understand (why there should be) the CR at all" before he was purged.[32] Lin Biao did not even know Mao's whereabouts during the Mao-Lin conflict.[33] Hu Yaobang was dying to "have a heart-to-heart talk (with Deng)" after he sensed that Deng was unhappy with him.[34] Zhao Ziyang tried desperately to have "a sincere exchange of opinions" with Deng at the eve of his toppling, but he was not even informed of Deng's whereabouts.[35]

This is not surprising, for what the prisoners' dilemma captures is essentially *a crisis of trust* between the two players. What triggered a succession struggle, as my examination shows, was not necessarily the lack of communication, but the erosion of trust between the leader and his successor when the former felt threatened by the latter's growing power. Whereas the leader was suspicious that the successor would not stop his expansion, the successor could not believe that the leader would continue the patronage despite his continuous expansion. Given that their relationship is originally established on mutual loyalty and trust – a nec-

---

31 Peter Ordeshook, *Game Theory and Political Theory: An Introduction*, Cambridge: Cambridge University Press, 1986, p. 99.
32 Liao Gailong, ed., *1949–1989: Xin zhongguo biannian shi* (1949–1989: A Chronology of the New China), Beijing: People's Press, July 1989, pp. 272, 279.
33 See Wang Dongxing, "*Mao Zhuxi zai fensui Lin Biao fan geming jituan de rizi li*" (Chairman Mao in the days of smashing Lin Biao's counterrevolutionary coup plot), in Ke Yan, ed., *Mao Zedong de lichenn – yige weiren he ta de huihuang shidai* (Mao Zedong's Career – a Great Man and His Splendid Era), 2 vols., Beijing: PLA Art Press, 1996, 2:359–67.
34 Li Rui, who was close to Hu Yaobang, told me that he had a "long conversation" with Hu a few days before his death. He said that "Hu strongly felt that he was wronged," and that "Hu really wanted have a heart-to-heart talk (with Deng). But he was never given a chance."
35 A former aide to Zhao Ziyang said that Zhao tried desperately to contact Deng after the students launched the hunger strike on May 13, 1989, but in vain.

essary condition for one to be chosen as the successor is that he has to be seen by the leader as the most trustworthy – the loss of trust means the end of this relationship. The lack of trust would prevent the two from seeking a "rational" compromise. As a result, a succession struggle evolves into a duel in which, given the intolerant nature of a totalistic political system, neither of them can feel secure unless his opponent is politically eliminated.

The prisoners' dilemma provides a rational explanation of the seemingly irrational and tragic relationship between the leader, Mao or Deng, and his successors, Liu Shaoqi and Lin Biao or Hu Yaobang and Zhao Ziyang, in both the Mao and Deng periods. It also reveals why the effort of "bringing up a successor" brought about a vicious cycle of succession struggles: a successor's rise to power would lead to a deadly struggle with his patron. But a succession struggle was essentially structure-induced, by a faction-ridden structure of leadership relations that required a leader to bring up a successor, and that also predetermined the coming of a prisoners' dilemma between the leader and his successor.

CONTINUITY AND CHANGES: FACTIONALISM IN THE DENG PERIOD

Ruthless factional struggles during the CR turned CCP politics into a series of treacheries, plots, and purges. The sense of comradeship among the CCP members was lost, their faith in ideology eroded, and the coherence of the Party was damaged. As a result, although the Party system has been restored, the organizational shackle it can place on factionalism has become far less effective. Factional activities have become rampant in political affairs in the post-Mao period.

Chapter 7 examines how Deng Xiaoping prevailed in the fierce factional struggles after Mao's death and to what extent factionalism affected political outcomes in the Deng period. My examination shows that Deng's path to power is in fact similar to Mao's: both leaders rose to power through factional struggles, and they prevailed essentially because of their exclusive control of the mountaintops in both the Party and military systems. Thus, it is no surprise that the structure of leadership relations established in the Deng period resembled that of the Yan'an Round Table, for it was only with this structure that Deng could secure his dominance and stabilize faction-ridden leadership relations. Given the same

Introduction

structure, all the essential problems in leadership relations and decision making in the Mao period reappeared in the Deng period.

First of all, Deng faced the same dilemma Mao did in policy making, so he adopted the same solution – the two-front arrangement (see Figure 7.1) – in order to solve this dilemma. He then became increasingly alienated from this arrangement and resorted to his personal authority – the antithesis of the formal process he had created – in his effort to maintain his dominance.[36] This led to the same problem Mao had: the deterioration of his relationships with the first-front leaders, namely Hu Yaobang and Zhao Ziyang. Not surprisingly, like Mao, Deng eventually toppled these two successors he had brought up himself, which in turn undermined his own power base.

The similarity between Mao and Deng has more significant implications. It provides a strong case that, despite the remarkable differences between Mao and Deng in vision, personality, experience, and knowledge and, more ironically, despite Deng's evident unwillingness to follow in Mao's footsteps, Deng's behavior astonishingly resembled Mao's because their choices in decision making were subject to similar constraints of the faction-ridden structure of leadership relations. More important, both Mao and Deng had to put up with factionalism – no matter how earnest they appeared in their efforts to eliminate it from political affairs – because it is innate within the CCP political system. Thus, the political systems do make a difference, and political outcomes are eventually system-induced.

Unlike Mao, however, Deng was never able to provide his leadership with its own ideological legitimacy. Although Deng repudiated Mao's "gross mistakes" in order to legitimate his own comeback and, more importantly, his reform policy, which departs radically from the Mao legacy, he could not afford to denounce Mao because the legitimacy of the CCP's rule was essentially based on Mao Zedong Thought. Thus, Deng's reform had to be "incomplete."[37] Yet the essential cause of Deng's "partial reform" was not just his effort to balance the two often

---

36 Stuart Schram, "China after the 13th congress," *CQ*, 114 (June 1988), pp. 177–97, points out that Deng had to adopt some institutional arrangements to formalize the reform, yet when these arrangements began to exert constraints on his power, he resorted to his personal authority in policy making.

37 Lowell Dittmer, "China in 1989: The crisis of incomplete reform," *AS*, 30, no. 1 (January 1990), pp. 25–41, first raised the concept of "incomplete reform" in the Western analysis.

self-contradictory goals, economic growth and stability,[38] but ultimately it was his inability to overcome a fundamental dilemma he created for himself. That is, he had to depend on the Four Cardinal Principles – adherence to the socialist road, the people's democratic dictatorship, the CCP leadership, and Marxism–Leninism–Mao Zedong Thought – in order to provide his leadership with ideological legitimacy, yet meanwhile, he had no choice but to push for a radical reform policy centered on a market economy in order to save the CCP's rule. The problem was, the more success his reform policy had, the more it undermined the Four Cardinal Principles, which provided ideological legitimacy not only for Deng's leadership but ultimately for the entire CCP's political system. Deng's ultimate dilemma had a profound impact on factional politics in the post-Mao period:

1 Deng's weakness in ideology made him vulnerable in this area. As a result, factional struggles tended to concentrate in the ideological sphere, for control of the ideological high ground was crucial for one to justify his policy choices as well as his attack on his opponents in the factional struggles for power.
2 Without its own ideological legitimacy, Deng's leadership was maintained largely through his constant compromise making with his opponents. Thus, although conflicts were more frequent due to rampant factional activities, the struggles were confined to a smaller scale, the purges were less brutal, and damages to leadership stability and policy making were less serious.
3 Policy inconsistency and changes in leadership relations were caused not so much by Deng's victory or defeat as by his compromises with his opponents in the endless factional struggles for power.
4 Unable to obtain absolute command in the Party, Deng had to depend more on the military support in policy making. The increase of the military's role in politics further undermined the "Party spirit" (*dangxing*) but promoted "factional mentality" (*paixing*).

All these changes in the Deng period resulted in relatively more stable leadership relations as compared with those in the Mao period, and policy making was also more consistent despite frequent factional strug-

---

38 For the discussion of "partial reform" and its causes, see David Zweig, "Dilemmas of partial reform," in Bruce Reynolds, ed., *Chinese Economic Policy*, New York: Paragon House, 1989, pp. 13–38; Richard Baum, ed., *Reform and Reaction in Post-Mao China: The Road to Tiananmen*, New York: Routledge, Chapman and Hall, 1991, pp. 1–17; and Susan Shirk, *The Political Logic of Economic Reform*, Berkeley: University of California Press, 1993.

Introduction

gles. For example, the May 1989 crisis did appear horrifying, especially with the whole world watching. But it was not so much a tide-turning event as a hiccup in the reform process. Although Zhao Ziyang was victimized as part of the compromise between Deng and the hardliners, the policy outcomes have remained relatively consistent, and leadership relations have been stable ever since.

Thus, as I conclude in Chapter 8, my examination does not fully confirm the conventional wisdom that factionalism hinders China's political development because it undermines political stability. Rather, my study demonstrates that stability becomes most vulnerable after a political faction has achieved hegemony in policy making. It is true that factional politics could be unstable and potentially chaotic, but the establishment of a dominant leader does not guarantee political stability, nor will the formal political process adopted under a dominant leader bring about the desired policy consistency.[39]

An essential point in my argument throughout this book is that the dominant leader's authority, which is based on personal loyalty forged during the factional struggles for power, is incompatible with the formal process adopted under his leadership for the stability of the system. First, his authority based on loyalty has to be absolute, yet a formal process exerts indiscriminating constraints on all individual leaders in decision making. Second, a formal process will reshape leadership relations according to each leader's position in the structure of policy making, rather than the personal loyalty upon which the dominant leader's authority has been established. All this formed the essential source of instability in leadership relations and inconsistency in leadership decision making.

Indeed, when the dominant leader faces a credible challenge, or feels that he is challenged, he is reluctant to make any compromises even though this challenge may reflect a legitimate policy dispute. As a result, a policy dispute, which could be solved through the adopted formal process, always evolves into a ruthless showdown of power in which the weak are purged, but the fundamental problem – the incompatibility

---

[39] Tang Tsou, *The Cultural Revolution and Post-Mao Reform: A Historical Perspective*, Chicago: University of Chicago Press, 1986, pp. 105–10, suggests that factional politics is temporary, unstable, and chaotic. A dominant leader will emerge through factional struggles, and then adopt a formal process in order "to enhance the capability of the political system"; this is the normal and stable state of affairs in CCP politics.

between the dominant leader's authority and the formal process – remains unsolved. This was the case in the early 1950s when Liu Shaoqi's mountaintop had achieved dominance in the policy process at the Center, in those turbulent years during the CR when one mountaintop after another obtained dominance in policy making with Mao's patronage, in 1976–7 when the "whatever faction" was confident that it had full control of the situation, and in 1984–9 when Deng's forces had achieved nearly complete dominance in policy making. However, we observed the most stable political situation and policy consistency in the mid 1960s when Mao's authority was to a certain extent balanced by the Party bureaucrats who managed the policy process at the first front; and in the Deng period, it is surprising but significant that the political stability was maintained with steady economic growth after the 1989 crisis.

It is the lack of hegemony that makes compromise possible. Factional politics may appear unstable and potentially chaotic. But, as this book demonstrates, instability is not caused by factional pluralism per se but by the uncompromising nature of dictatorship. In other words, it is the dominant faction's intolerance of any differences in policy making on the one hand and the other factions' uncontrollable effort to promote their interests on the other hand that form the essential source of instability and policy inconsistency. But in a situation where no single faction is able to dominate the political process, such as what has happened since the 1989 crisis, mountaintop leaders have to seek compromises constantly instead of plotting political purges in political struggles. In this sense, the slow but steady improvement of the political situation in China since 1989 is not because the reform-minded leaders have again gained the upper hand. On the contrary, it is the inability of any single faction to dominate the policy process that has compelled the elite members to be gentler and more tolerant in solving their differences.

As an essential source of the intra-Party strife, what factionalism has steadily undermined is the CCP's coherence. This tendency has been increasingly obvious in the past two decades. As the rapid but uneven development has greatly diversified the Chinese society, differences in policy making become a daily reality as various factions find themselves representing different socioeconomic interests. But the fear of instability on the one hand, and the increasingly balanced distribution of power among various mountaintops on the other hand, force the CCP leaders to seek compromise rather than "a life-and-death struggle" as they used

Introduction

to do. As a result, the uncompromising nature of the single-party dictatorship has been gradually but irrevocably changed. More importantly, in their constant effort to seek as much support as possible in order to make the best deal, various mountaintops can actually represent a greater range of socioeconomic interests and therefore enlarge the scope of political participation. All this suggests that factionalism in the long run may actually promote the progress toward a more open and pluralistic system.

1

Factionalism, the Puzzle of Chinese Communist Politics

CONFLICT MODELS AND THEIR EXPLANATIONS OF FACTIONALISM

From Unity to Conflict

Factional politics is a politics of conflict. Before the Cultural Revolution (CR) unfolded in 1966, factionalism was barely noticed in the study of Chinese politics because the field was predominated by *unity* analyses. These analyses see Chinese politics as a united entity, integrated by ideology and organizations, maintained by discipline and a strong leadership, and safeguarded by the People's Liberation Army (PLA) commanded by the Party.

A *totalitarian* model was applied in the 1950s and the early 1960s. As Oksenberg points out, this model stresses the Soviet-like qualities of the CCP regime: "the adherence of its leaders to Marxism-Leninism, the totalitarian grip of the top political leaders upon the entire society and culture, and the centrally planned economy in which resources were allocated through political command."[1] Ironically, this description corresponds to the CCP's nostalgic view, which sees the initial years of the PRC as "a period not only when the Party's policies were usually correct, but also when leadership relations were marked by a high degree of unity and democracy."[2]

---

1 Michael Oksenberg, "Politics takes command: An essay on the study of post-1949 China," in Roderick MacFarquhar and John K. Fairbank, eds., *Cambridge History of China*, Cambridge: Cambridge University Press, 1987, 14:579. The preeminent works on this model include Richard Walker, *China under Communism: The First Five Years*, London: Allen and Unwin, 1956; John Lewis, *Leadership in Communist China*, Ithaca: Cornell University Press, 1963; and Doak A. Barnett, *Communist China and Asia*, New York: Harper and Brothers, 1960.
2 Frederick Teiwes, *Politics at Mao's Court: Gao Gang and Party Factionalism in the Early 1950s*, New York: M. E. Sharpe, 1990, p. 3.

The Puzzle of Chinese Communist Politics

Indeed, this was a period of startling accomplishment for the CCP: a Stalinist system was established, the confrontation with the hostile forces led by the United States in the Korean War boosted national confidence, the economy recovered and was molded into the Soviet central-planning model with an astonishing speed. All this transformed a family-oriented traditional China into a state-centered socialist nation in which, as MacFarquhar observed, "the Party state swiftly came to dominate all sections of society."[3]

This achievement was unmistakably reflected in the literature. Franz Schurmann advanced an *ideology* model, depicting the PRC polity as the realization of Lenin's dream of the unity of theory and action – the combination of ideology and discipline produced effective organizations and brought a new life to a fragmented old nation.[4] A variant of this model resulted from the debate on the originality of "Maoism."[5] It stresses the importance of Maoism in the maintenance of ideological consensus and effective organizations, which are crucial for activating and regulating the massive political participation.[6] Like the totalitarian model, these studies were based on the unity-centered analysis, although they were more objective and therefore had a higher scholarly value.

A few China watchers, however, tried to see through the unity facade of Chinese politics. Lucian Pye argued from a unique cultural perspective that traditional patron-client relations still played a crucial role in CCP politics. His study reveals a dilemma of the CCP system: the deep-seated fear of insecurity drives those working in the system into an endless search for support and protection by knitting patron-client ties

---

3 Roderick MacFarquhar, "Epilogue," in MacFarquhar and Fairbank, *Cambridge History of China*, 14:539; and *The Origins of the Cultural Revolution*, 1: *Contradictions among the People, 1956–1957*, New York: Columbia University Press, 1974, pp. 15–25.
4 Franz Schurmann, *Ideology and Organization in Communist China*, Berkeley: University of California Press, 1966.
5 See Benjamin Schwartz, *Chinese Communism and the Rise of Mao*, Cambridge, MA: Harvard University Press, 1961; and "The legend of the 'legend of Maoism,'" *CQ*, 2 (April 1960), pp. 35–42; Karl Wittfogel, "The legend of 'Maoism,'" *CQ*, 1 (January 1960), pp. 72–86, and 2 (April 1960), pp. 16–30; and Arthur Cohen, "How original is 'Maoism?'" *PC*, 10, no. 6 (November 1961), pp. 31–42.
6 Stuart Schram, *Mao Tse-tung: A Political Biography*, New York: Simon and Schuster, 1966; Benjaming Schwartz, "Modernization and Maoist vision," in Roderick MacFarquhar, ed., *China under Mao*, Cambridge, MA: MIT Press, 1966, pp. 3–19. The influence of this approach can still be seen in Maurice Meisner's *Mao's China and After: A History of People's Republic*, New York: Free Press, 1988.

in a hierarchical context, yet the frustration and anger caused by the eventual inability of such a relationship to provide for the desired security makes the seemingly stable structure vulnerable to collapse.[7] Roderick MacFarquhar highlighted policy disputes among the leaders behind the pretense of unity. The departure is not necessarily his elaboration on Mao's dominance in politics, but his analysis on how Mao manipulated the policy-making process despite differences among the CCP leaders.[8] The conflict-centered analysis, however, was drowned out by the grand chorus of "unity."

This chorus was soon overwhelmed by the CR. The political storm initiated by Mao blew away the entire Party establishment, let alone the facade of its unity. Yet all this was done under Mao's command, except that the CR further exposed the totalitarian feature of the regime. As Oksenberg notices, "the politicization of all aspects of the society, culture, and economy reached its apogee..., the deification of the leader climaxed in a cult of personality rarely attained before in history, and terror became a way of life."[9]

A Mao-in-command model emerged. It holds that Mao's command was so absolute that any departure from his line in policy making would be intolerable. Thus, all elite conflicts ended up with the purge of those who were at odds with Mao.[10] The Mao-in-command model, which predominated in the field from the late 1960s through the 1970s, reflected a profound shift of scholarly perspective in the study of CCP politics: from unity to conflict, and from stability to change. Indeed, the CR revealed the reality of CCP politics: the commitment to ideology could not hold the leaders to the same line, the cohesiveness of organization could not prevent internal strife, and discipline was undermined by increasing corruption. All this validated the conflict-centered analyses: although power

---

7 Lucian Pye, *The Spirit of Chinese Politics*, Cambridge, MA: MIT Press, 1967.
8 Roderick MacFarquhar, "Mao Tse-tung and the Chinese communists' rectification movement," *World Today*, August 1957, pp. 330–41; and "Communist China's intra-Party dispute," *Pacific Affairs*, 31, no. 4 (December 1958), pp. 323–35.
9 Oksenberg, "Politics takes command," p. 583.
10 See Philip Bridgham's series, "Mao's Cultural Revolution: 1: Origin and development," *CQ*, 29 (January 1967), pp. 1–35; "2: The struggle to seize power," *CQ*, 34 (April 1968), pp. 6–37; and "3: The struggle to consolidate power," *CQ*, 41 (January 1970), pp. 1–25. For a more sophisticated version of the Mao-in-command analysis, see Michael Oksenberg, "Policy making under Mao," in John M. Lindbeck, ed., *China: Management of a Revolutionary Society*, Seattle: University of Washington Press, 1971, pp. 79–115.

The Puzzle of Chinese Communist Politics

is centralized in a totalistic system, CCP politics is still conflict-ridden – policies emerge from disputes, and stability is maintained through endless struggles.

Yet the conflict-centered analyses invited a more fundamental debate: what is the dynamics of the conflicts in CCP politics? In other words, what are the causes of the conflicts among the leaders despite their strong commitment to the communist ideology and the virtually unchallengeable authority of the supreme leader, first Mao and later Deng Xiaoping?

Two books published in 1974 have perhaps exerted the most influence in the field. One is Doak Barnett's *Uncertain Passage*,[11] the other is Roderick MacFarquhar's *The Origins of the Cultural Revolution, 1: Contradictions among the People*.

Drawing on rational-choice theory, which assumes that a policy maker's rationale is determined by his assessment of means and ends, and costs and gains in light of his interest preferences,[12] Barnett argues that a conflict originates from the leaders' different views of the national interests, which in turn leads to differences in their evaluations of the problems and calculations of means and ends. All this results in different priorities in their policy choices. But not all the priorities can be met, given limited resources. A conflict results. Thus, to understand CCP politics "requires identification of the problems that the Chinese leadership faces, assessment of alternative ways these problems may be handled, and analysis of the possible effects of external events on the policies the Chinese pursue both at home and abroad."[13]

MacFarquhar's book provides a nearly exhaustive analysis of CCP politics at the eve of the Great Leap Forward. His inference is that a conflict among the leaders, either triggered by a policy dispute or provoked by personality clashes, will eventually be solved in a power struggle, for power is not only necessary for a leader to make his vision prevail, but it also provides him with security in the jungle of CCP

---

11 Doak Barnett, *Uncertain Passage*, Washington, DC: Brookings Institution, 1974.
12 Anthony Downs's *An Economic Theory of Democracy*, New York: Harper and Row, 1957, is the pioneering volume that applies the rational-choice theory in political science. Graham Alison has perhaps provided the most implicit discussion of the application of this theory to policy making in his *Essence of Decision: Explaining the Cuban Missile Crisis*, Boston: Little, Brown, 1971.
13 Barnett, *Uncertain Passage*, p. xi.

politics. The Mao-Liu (Shaoqi) conflict provides a strong case for MacFarquhar's approach:

> A careful examination of the evidence suggests that neither Mao nor Liu was consistent; that Mao and Liu were not always opponents; that many men who survived the cultural revolution, notably Premier Chou En-lai, had opposed Mao on crucial issues when Liu had stood by the Chairman; that some of Liu's supposed supporters, notably Teng Hsiao-p'ing, the Party's General Secretary, had been more often on Mao's side than Liu's. . . . But as always in the affairs of men there were also bitter feuds over power and status.[14]

These two books represent two different approaches that have had a profound impact on the study of CCP politics. Barnett's approach is employed mostly in the studies that examine how a specific policy is produced in response to the perceived problem(s).[15] Although these studies often incorporate some aspects of the power-struggle approach, they see power essentially as means for the desired policy goals. Thus, an elite conflict is essentially over policy choices rather than over power itself. Harry Harding formalized this approach into a policy-choice model. He argues that an elite conflict is essentially a policy confrontation between the leaders with different policy preferences. Thus, in order to explain a policy the Chinese leaders have adopted, we have to understand their diagnoses of the problems they have encountered and the debate they have conducted.[16] Harding explains the policy outcomes in the post-Mao period as a result of the ongoing struggles between the conservative leaders who were "cautious and skeptical about dramatic departures from the planned

---

14 MacFarquhar, *The Origins*, 1:2–3.
15 See Michael Oksenberg, "The Chinese policy process and the public health issue: An arena approach," *Studies in Comparative Communism*, 7, no. 4 (Winter 1974), pp. 375–408; and "Economic policy making in China: Summer 1981," *CQ*, 90 (June 1982), pp. 165–94; David Lampton, *Health, Conflict, and the Chinese Political System*, Ann Arbor: University of Michigan Center for Chinese Studies, 1974; Richard Suttmerier, *Research and Revolution: Scientific Policy and Societal Change in China*, Lexington, MA: Lexington Books, 1974; Benedict Stavis, *The Politics of Agricultural Mechanization in China*, Ithaca: Cornell University Press, 1978; David Zweig, *Agrarian Radicalism in China, 1968–78: The Search for a Social Base*, Cambridge, MA: Harvard University Press, 1989; and Dorothy Solinger, *Chinese Business under Socialism*, Berkeley: University of California Press, 1984.
16 Harry Harding, *Organizing China*, Stanford: Stanford University Press, 1981, p. 1.

economy, state-owned industry, and centralized political system" and the reformers who entertained "bolder and riskier measures that would launch China in the direction of a market economy, new forms of public ownership, and a more pluralistic political order."[17]

MacFarquhar's approach has been elaborated as the *power-struggle* model. Although the scholars who have adopted this model differ on how a conflict could occur, they echo one another that such a conflict, whether it was about policy choices or personality clashes, would eventually evolve into a power struggle in which the losers would be victimized.[18] On the causes of the CR, for example, some emphasize the disputes in the 1950s and/or the disastrous GLF in 1958–61,[19] others focus on Mao's growing anger with the resistance from Liu and the other leaders to Mao's policy of mass movement at the eve of the CR.[20] But all agree that the Mao-Liu conflict was essentially a power struggle rather than "a two-line struggle." Thus, the ultimate rationale in CCP politics is drawn from the calculations on how to prevail in ruthless power struggles. The revival of the GLF after the 1959 Lushan Conference, for example, was not because the policy was right or it was based on a consensus, but because, as MacFarquhar argues, Mao "did not want to acknowledge that Peng Dehuai had been right." Meanwhile, the other leaders like Liu Shaoqi and Lin Biao chose to support Mao because of their own ambitions for power or, like Zhou Enlai and Chen Yun, were silenced by the deterrence of Peng Dehuai's fate.[21]

Lieberthal and Oksenberg departed from the above two models and advanced a *structure* model. Drawing upon the theory of bureaucratic politics, they explain a conflict and its policy consequence from the perspective of the structure of policy making. They argue that, like the

---

17 Harry Harding, *China's Second Revolution*, Washington, DC: Brookings Institution, 1987, pp. 2–3.
18 See, among others, Parris H. Chang, *Power and Policy in China*, 2nd ed., University Park: Pennsylvania State University Press, 1978; and Teiwes, *Politics at Mao's Court*.
19 See Byung-joon Ahn, *Chinese Politics and the Cultural Revolution*, Seattle: University of Washington Press, 1976; Hong Yung Lee, *The Politics of the Chinese Cultural Revolution*, Berkeley, University of California Press, 1978.
20 See Lowell Dittmer, *Liu Shao-ch'i and the Chinese Cultural Revolution: The Politics of Mass Criticism*, Berkeley: University of California Press, 1974; and "The Chinese Cultural Revolution revisited: The role of the nemesis," *Journal of Contemporary China*, 5, no. 13 (1996), pp. 255–68.
21 See Roderick MacFarquhar, *The Origins of the Cultural Revolution, 2: The Great Leap Forward, 1958–1960*, New York: Columbia University Press, 1983, pp. 333–5.

leaders in other countries, the Chinese "leaders might propound views of the bureaucracy over which they preside, and that elite contention over policy and/or power might be a manifestation of bureaucratic conflict."[22] Thus, a conflict in CCP politics, caused by either a policy dispute or power struggles, is rooted essentially in the institutional structure of policy making whereby interests of the involved institutions clash; the leaders act as representatives of the institutions over which they preside; and their behavior and policy choices are subject to the constraints imposed by this structure. Such a conflict, however, can become very complicated because of the segmented and stratified system of authority in China. As a result, its outcomes are difficult to predict, and, more often than not, unintended outcomes result, which cause policy inconsistency and destabilize leadership relations.[23]

Thus, the three predominant models vary greatly in the explanations of conflicts in CCP politics, although all three highlight the decisive role of the supreme leader, Mao or Deng, in political affairs. The differences among the three models are seen not only in their identification of the causes of conflicts – that is, policy disputes, power struggles, or conflicts of institutional interests – but also in the ways the leaders interact in a conflict. The policy-choice model focuses on the achievement of consensus in the solution of a policy dispute. Its analyses of the *process* through which the consensus was achieved often reveal the constraints this process exerted on the supreme leader, Mao or Deng, despite his dominance in policy making, for a consensus usually resulted from a compromise of various policy preferences presented by the involved leaders, including the supreme leader himself.[24]

---

22 Kenneth Lieberthal and Michael Oksenberg, *Policy Making in China: Leaders, Structure, and Processes*, Princeton: Princeton University Press, 1988, p. 17.
23 Ibid., p. 137.
24 There are several cases in this point. On Mao's "retreat" from the first leap forward due to pressures from his colleagues (see Chapter 5); on radical policy changes in the early 1960s despite Mao's resistance (see Kenneth Lieberthal, "The Great Leap Forward," in Roderick MacFarquhar, ed., *The Politics of China: 1949–1989*, Cambridge: Cambridge University Press, 1993, pp. 117–22; and Chapter 5); on Deng's repeated compromises with the conservative leaders, which in a large part resulted in "partial reform" (see Chapter 7; David Zweig, "Dilemmas of partial reform," in Bruce Reynolds, ed., *Chinese Economic Policy*, New York: Paragon House, 1989, pp. 13–38; Richard Baum, ed., *Reform and Reaction in Post-Mao China: The Road to Tiananmen*, New York: Routledge, Chapman and Hall, 1991, pp. 1–17; and Susan Shirk, *The Political Logic of Economic Reform*, Berkeley: University of California Press, 1993).

The Puzzle of Chinese Communist Politics

The power-struggle analysis focuses on leadership relations in a conflict, and how the changes in these relations affect the final outcomes. Given that a conflict, provoked by either a policy dispute or personality clashes, will eventually be solved in a power struggle, the power-struggle analysts tend to treat the policy issues as means, rather than ends, in a conflict, for what matters in the end is not who has the right idea but who prevails in the power struggle. Thus, a policy choice prevails not necessarily because it is right but essentially because it is the preference of those who dominate in politics. Cases in point are numerous: the revival of the GLF after the 1959 Lushan Conference,[25] the criticism of ultra-rightism after Lin Biao's fall in 1971,[26] the halt of "emancipation of mind" with the "four cardinal principles" in 1979 (see Chapter 7), and the crackdown on the student movement in 1989.[27] The power-struggle analysis is most supportive to the grand model of Mao-in-command or, later, Deng-in-command.

The structure analysts see conflict as routine in bureaucratic politics. Its solution does not necessarily result from a rational debate because it is difficult to distinguish right from wrong, given different perspectives from which the involved leaders are competing for their institutional interests; nor is it necessarily determined by those who appear more powerful because the bureaucratic structure exerts indiscriminating constraints on everyone involved in the process. Those who prevail may not be the most powerful or righteous leaders, but they happened to be in the most advantageous position in the structure of policy making. The more complicated the bureaucratic structure is, the harder it is for the leaders to control the interactions among the involved agencies, and hence more difficult to predict the final outcomes.[28]

Thus, while the power-struggle approach reinforces the Mao-in-command model, the analyses of the policy-choice and structure models actually depart from this grand model. The most significant contribution of the two models is perhaps their discovery that, like his colleagues, the supreme leader is also subject to the constraints of the adopted process

---

25 MacFarquhar, *The Origins*, 2:233–51.
26 Roderick MacFarquhar, "The succession to Mao and the end of Maoism," in MacFarquhar, *The Politics of China: 1949–1989*, pp. 281–7.
27 Richard Baum, "The road to Tiananmen: Chinese politics in the 1980s," in MacFarquhar, *The Politics of China: 1949–1989*, pp. 441–50.
28 Lieberthal and Oksenberg, *Policy Making in China*, pp. 136–7.

or the structure of policy making. But the ultimate question remains unanswered: how could the supreme leader maintain his dominance in policy making, even though his "gross mistake" had repeatedly brought disasters to the Party? Or, if his authority is subject to the constraints of the adopted process or the structure of policy making, why did he always have the last say during the periods of crisis? In short, what really constitutes the power bases for the supreme leader? Moreover, how could he keep his power bases strong and loyal to him in a forever-changing political situation? The factionalism analysis is to provide an answer to these questions.

Factionalism Analyses and Their Unanswered Questions

Factionalism in CCP politics began to draw attention as the analyses shifted to the conflict models. The issue of factionalism was first raised in the study of the military,[29] partly due to the obvious factional tendencies in the PLA, but largely because of the crucial role of the military in CCP politics. William Whitson's examination of military politics in China revealed that factionalism in the armed forces was rooted in the CCP's Field Army system during the revolution. He argued that the commanders of each field army had developed strong personal authority over their forces, and the officers from the same field army had also cultivated close personal relations among them. Factionalism was developed upon such old-boy networks. Whitson held that the stability of the system depended largely on a balanced distribution of power among the military leaders.[30]

Among many factionalism analyses,[31] the most influential is perhaps

---

29 See David A. Charles, "The dismissal of Marshal P'eng Teh-huai," *CQ*, 8 (October 1961), pp. 63–76; Ralph L. Powell, "The party, the government and the gun," *AS*, 10, no. 6 (June 1970), pp. 441–71; and William Parrish, "Factions in Chinese military politics," *CQ*, 56 (October 1973), pp. 667–9.

30 William Whitson, "The field army in Chinese communist military politics," *CQ*, 37 (January 1969), pp. 1–30; see also his *The Chinese High Command*, New York: Praeger, 1978.

31 See Liao Kuang-sheng, "Linkage politics in China: Internal mobilization and articulated external hostility in the Cultural Revolution," *World Politics*, 28, no. 4 (July 1976), pp. 590–610; Tang Tsou, "Prolegomenon to the study of informal groups in CCP politics," in his *The Cultural Revolution and Post-Mao Reform: A Historical Perspective*, Chicago: University of Chicago Press, 1986, pp. 102–21; Edward E. Rice, "The second rise and fall of Teng Hsiao-p'ing," *CQ*, 67 (September 1976), pp. 494–500; Jurgen Domes,

The Puzzle of Chinese Communist Politics

Andrew Nathan's factionalism model of CCP politics.[32] His thesis is that the CCP politics is structured essentially as one of "complex faction": a faction is built on the patron-client relationships between the leaders and their followers, and a leader's power is based on the strength of his faction. Nathan argues that factionalism has played such a crucial role that it was the cause of all the major intrastruggles in CCP history. Yet he holds that factionalism only exists at the central level; authorities at the provincial level and below are well institutionalized and faction-free.[33]

Two questions arise from the above factionalism analyses. How does factionalism affect the political outcomes in China? What are the causes for factionalism, whether it is originated in the military or not, to have become such an essential dynamics in CCP politics?

Nathan's analysis implies that factionalism undermines political stability because "no faction will be able to achieve overwhelmingly superior power," and "one faction may for the moment enjoy somewhat greater power than rival factions, but this power will not be so great that the victorious faction is capable of expunging its rival and assuring permanent dominance."[34] Thus, Nathan sees the CR as "an episode in which the long-standing factional system attempted to defend its existence against an attack based on outside social forces" mobilized by Mao, whose goal was to bring "an end to factionalism and its associated policy oscillations, and an institutionalization of the Party as an instrument of Maoist will, capable of outliving Mao himself."[35]

Generalizing on the pre-1949 factional struggles in CCP history, Tang Tsou suggests that factionalism reflects a political crisis in which the CCP leadership has either collapsed or been seriously challenged. But a hegemonic faction under a strong leader will eventually emerge through factional struggles; and as soon as the new leader gains the dominance, he will adopt a formal process in order to "enhance the capability of the

---

"The Gang of Four and Hua Kuao-feng: Analysis of political events in 1975–76," *CQ*, 71 (September 1977), pp. 473–97; Kenneth Lieberthal, "The internal political scene," *PC*, 24, no. 3 (May–June, 1975), pp. 1–10, and his "The politics of modernization in the PRC," *PC*, 27, no. 3 (May–June 1978), pp. 1–18; Michael Oksenberg, "The exit pattern from Chinese politics and its implications," *CQ*, 67 (September 1976), pp. 501–18.

32 Andrew Nathan, "A factionalism model of CCP politics," *CQ*, 53 (January 1973), pp. 34–66.

33 Ibid., pp. 37–42. 34 Ibid., p. 66. 35 Ibid., pp. 54–5.

political system." Thus, Tsou sees factional politics as a form of transition toward hegemony, and it is therefore temporary, unstable, and potentially chaotic, whereas hegemonic politics is the normal and stable state of CCP politics.[36] A great insight in Tsou's analysis is that a formal process can effectively check factionalism and the informal politics caused by it. Yet his analysis provides little explanation of how factionalism could develop in CCP politics in the first place and, more importantly, why the supreme leader, despite his hegemonic position, cannot eliminate the rival factions, which will rise to challenge his dominance whenever there is a chance.

But it is the first question on the causes of factionalism in CCP politics that has sparked more discussions in the literature. Not surprisingly, various explanations fall in line with the three predominant models. The policy-choice analysts see factional activities as a result of policy confrontations in which the leaders with shared views team up in order to make their choices prevail. Thus, factional activities are policy-oriented and tend to appear only after the consensus breaks down.[37] Viewing factionalism as an on-and-off phenomenon, some policy-choice analysts prefer "group" to "faction," and a group is formed vis-à-vis its members' policy preferences.[38]

The assumption that factionalism emerges after the collapse of consensus falls in line with Tsou's position that factional politics reflects a leadership crisis. More significantly, the policy-choice analysis demonstrates that the *formal process* in policy making can effectively suppress factional activities – again, this supports Tsou's proposition that the predominant leader adopts formal politics to secure stability. Indeed, personal ties, on which factional linkages are cultivated, become important only when an external force, usually exerted by the supreme leader,

36 Tsou, "Prolegomenon to the study of informal groups," pp. 107–10.
37 Jurgen Domes, *The Government and Politics of the PRC*, Boulder, CO: Westview Press, 1985, pp. 80–4. For a more substantial analysis, see Frederick Teiwes, *Leadership, Legitimacy, and Conflict in China,* New York: M. E. Sharpe, 1984. On the Gao-Rao Affair in 1954, however, Teiwes initially believed that it was an unprincipled factional strife with little involvement of policy issues. But in a later modification, he acknowledges that there were significant policy issues involved as Gao Gang "did use the debates surrounding the new general line to attack the policies of others" – namely, Liu Shaoqi and his followers. Teiwes, "The establishment and consolidation of the new regime," in MacFarquhar, *The Politics of China: 1949–1989*, p. 47.
38 For example, the word "faction" is carefully avoided by Harding in his *China's Second Revolution* and by Solinger in her *Chinese Business under Socialism*.

The Puzzle of Chinese Communist Politics

breaks the formal process of political affairs.[39] In this sense, what triggers factional activities is not necessarily the collapse of consensus but the breakdown of the adopted political process.

The shared-view assumption on factional orientation, however, invites questions as we apply it to the reality of CCP politics. The grand consensus on reform, for example, was achieved after the "whatever faction" led by Hua Guofeng was ousted in 1978, but this did not stop fierce factional activities among the CCP leaders.[40] Although certain policy priorities have been the trademark of particular factions, what underlie these priorities are factional interests. Factional activities not only turn policy outcomes into vehicles for their particular interests, but also cause policy inconsistency because, as my analysis in the following chapters will show, each faction would try to skew the adopted policy to its own advantage. Had factions been merely "clusters of leaders" with shared views, Peng Dehuai might have had a quite different fate, given that he enjoyed substantial support at the 1959 Lushan Conference;[41] the combined effort of Liu Shaoqi, Zhou Enlai, Deng Xiaoping, and other powerful leaders might have prevented the CR;[42] Chen Yun could have formed a coalition with Peng Zhen to halt Deng's reform rather than spoiling Peng's effort

---

39 See Teiwes, *Leadership, Legitimacy, and Conflict in China*, and *Politics at Mao's Court*. For example, Teiwes argues that although Gao's uncontrollable ambition was the essential motive for his attack on Liu, it was Mao's intervention on Bo Yibo's tax reform that triggered the entire Gao-Rao Affair.

40 Some may argue that there has never been a consensus on the reform among the CCP elite members. But as Richard Baum, "The road to Tiananmen: Chinese politics in the 1980s," in MacFarquhar, *The Politics of China: 1949–1989*, p. 340, argues: "Although members of the reform coalition forged by Deng Xiaoping could agree among themselves, in principle, on the need for economic reform and opening up to the outside world, they differed over just how far and how fast to move toward revamping the basic ideology and institutions of Chinese socialism." The consensus, however, was not just on economic reform. The decision to depart from the Mao legacy itself stood out as a radical political policy. Indeed, there had to be a reform, both in the economic and political spheres, in order to save the system – this was the consensus upon which Deng Xiaoping, Chen Yun, and other senior leaders like Li Xiannian and Luo Ruiqing could form an alliance in the late 1970s to topple the "whatever faction" led by Hua Guofeng, who, on the contrary, insisted on adhering to whatever policies Mao had made. The differences among Deng and his allies were on *how to reform* and *what to be reformed*. Also cf. Harding, *China's Second Revolution*, p. 63.

41 See MacFarquhar, *The Origins*, 2:187–251.

42 Cf. Yen Jiaqi, "*Wenhua da geming*" *shinian shi 1966–1976* (Ten-Year History of the "Cultural Revolution," 1966–1976), Tianjin: Tianjin People's Press, 1986, pp. 92–100, 126–49, 238–50.

to enter the PSC; and Zhao Ziyang could have defended Hu Yaobang, rather than being indifferent, when Hu was toppled in early 1987 (see Chapter 7).

The problems in its explanation of factionalism reveal a basic flaw in the policy-choice model. Viewing conflicts in CCP politics as policy confrontations, this model assumes that the policy-making process in CCP politics is a cooperative game of complete information,[43] where a dispute is about how to utilize the resources for an objective goal, rather than a struggle for the control of these resources, and the division between the leaders is clear vis-à-vis their policy choices, which reflect their evaluation of an existing problem. Thus, this model tends to predict a consensus when a majority is formed in a policy dispute.

But cases like this are few in CCP politics, where interactions among the leaders resemble a noncooperative game because of the uncertainty of rules and procedures. More often than not, the line-up between the CCP leaders was obscure, and so were their preferences, when a conflict emerged in an environment where the political process was barely institutionalized. As Lieberthal and Oksenberg point out,

> [Policy-choice analysts] have generally not explored the constraints upon China's top leaders which may preclude their attaining the rationality which the scholars assume. Thus, the policy analysts tend not to probe decisional constraints upon the leaders due to the limited information available to them, the ambiguities and ambivalence in the minds of the leaders concerning their hierarchy of value preferences, and the time pressures they confront in comprehensively evaluating their alternatives.[44]

Indeed, the policy-choice model can be very powerful because it is

---

43 See Peter C. Ordeshook, *Game Theory and Political Theory: An Introduction*, Cambridge: Cambridge University Press, 1986, pp. 162–5, 302–4. A "cooperative game" is defined as a process "in which communication not only is possible, but also stands as a central feature of human interaction." The game becomes "cooperative" because communication among the players leads to the formation of coalitions, which represents, briefly, "an agreement among two or more persons to coordinate their actions (choices or strategies)." "Complete information" refers to the situation in which the players have an exact knowledge of each other's preference orders.
44 Lieberthal and Oksenberg, *Policy Making in China*, p. 13.

The Puzzle of Chinese Communist Politics

based on rational-choice theory, which has rigid requirements on the context of the game, definition of the variables and players, their relationships, and the procedures of their interplays. Yet, as I will elaborate in Chapter 2, the CCP leaders interact with each other in an environment in which (1) a formal process is barely existent in decision making, (2) access to the resources and information are seized by the leaders who seek to monopolize these assets, and (3) the rules and procedures are manipulated by the dominant leaders. All this undermines the strength of the policy-choice model. Thus, policy outcomes in CCP politics often appeared irrational from the perspective of rational-choice theory. We were "surprised" repeatedly by political events in China, not necessarily because we had failed to envision all the possible outcomes, but because more often than not it was the most "irrational" choice we could imagine that prevailed, instead of the "rational" ones we believed were more credible outcomes. The factor that is often overlooked by the policy-choice analysis is that Mao, and later Deng, enjoyed exclusive privileges in political affairs: not only did he control the information flow – all the information had to go through him – in decision making, but he could also violate any established rules and procedures if necessary. All this makes it difficult to analyze the outcomes in CCP politics in a "rational" fashion because the very basis for the rational-choice theory – the formal process, compliant procedures, and standard operating practice in decision making – is uncertain in CCP politics.

The structure approach attributes factionalism to "the flaws of the structure" of policy making.[45] It argues that conflicting "institutional interests" motivate factionalism in the policy process. Thus, similar career paths are seen as the key criterion for factional alignments, and the institutions as bases for factional activities. A case in point is the "petroleum faction" in the 1970s and early 1980s, which was formed by a group of leaders rising from the oil industry.[46]

No doubt the different interests of the involved agencies can constitute the underlying dynamics of policy making. But in Chinese politics "there is no way precisely to measure the real authority of any particular group of officials [who propound the views of the bureaucracy over

---

45 See Teiwes, *Politics at Mao's Court*, pp. 3–5.
46 Lieberthal and Oksenberg, *Policy Making in China*, pp. 42–51, 60–1.

which they preside]"[47] because instead of institutional arrangements, it is *guanxi*, or personal ties, that "bind different agencies together" and "constitute the single most important ingredient which integrates the system and enables it to function."[48] All this makes it difficult to determine and weigh the interests of the agencies involved in a given policy process, and to analyze the final outcomes from the structural perspective.

Thus, the structure explanation of factionalism suffers from its uncertainty over the relationship between "institutional interests" and factional interests, and from difficulties in distinguishing factional activities from interactions among the involved institutions in the policy process. All this has caused inconsistency in the explanation of factional development, the role of factions, and the rise and fall of leaders in the structural analysis of factionalism.[49] As a result, the structure model seems to be handicapped by the very reality it has disclosed, namely, that more often than not political offices in China are distributed as spoils among those who have achieved dominance. A leader strikes to promote the interests of his office because it has been intertwined with his *guanxi* network – the office's well-being is therefore closely related to the strength of his network. The "institutional arrangements" become a facade, beneath which interactions among the involved *guanxi* networks form the essential dynamics in the policy process. Thus, as Lieberthal and Oksenberg have observed, "what on paper appears to be a unified, hier-

---

47 Ibid., pp. 137–8. The latter half of the sentence is: "it is possible to make informed estimates based on the formal structure of authority and the more subtle, informal considerations." Yet, how possible can it be if "the formal structure of authority" is a facade of the stratified system, and the major parts of the "informal consideration" turn out to be a cadre's rank and stature and his links with others? (Ibid., pp. 136–7, 145–51, 155–7.)
48 Ibid., pp. 155–6.
49 See ibid., pp. 42–51, 59–61, 252–5, 264–7. On the one hand, the analysis highlights the existence and the important role of factions: it sees a cluster of leaders rising from Daqing oil field as the "petroleum faction" because of their common career background, close personal ties, and shared policy preferences. On the other hand, it argues that such a faction was just a "group" of leaders who "were viewed as a faction more in the eyes of their non-members than of their members" because of their shared policy preferences rather than other factors such as the pursuit of power. Moreover, while *guanxi* and the control of crucial resources account for the rapid rise of the "petroleum faction" in the late 1960s, it remains unclear why this faction ceased to be a political force after the reform started, although its priorities like rapid growth and the use of foreign capital have been adopted as major reform policies.

archical chain of command turns out in reality to be divided, segmented, and stratified."⁵⁰ Indeed, the influence of an institution depends largely on its leader's position in the structure of leadership relations rather than the structure of policy making. The priorities of a leader in policy making are determined not so much by his institutional interests as by his calculation of the policy consequences on his relationships with the other leaders, especially the dominant one(s).

The power model provides the most consistent explanation of factionalism in CCP politics. Its strength rests on its revelation that power is an overriding goal in the CCP political system where institutionalization is barely existent. As Nathan argues, a leader's power is based essentially on the strength of his faction, which is built on his *guanxi* networks. Thus, a leader's rationale in policy making is not necessarily drawn from the extent to which the designated policy can promote the collective interests but on his calculations of the consequences of his choice on his status in the power distribution. As Lucian Pye points out, "those who are actively engaged in [factional politics] in China do not have the luxury of deciding their stand on new issues on the basis of an objective weighing of all the pros and cons."⁵¹

On the basis of his "fundamental hypothesis" that in Chinese politics "power considerations are generally decisive because power is seen as the least ambiguous and most predictive of all factors in social life,"⁵² Pye argues:

> The prime basis for factions among cadres is the search for career security and the protection of power.... Thus, the strength of Chinese factions is the personal relationships of individuals who, operating in a hierarchical context, create linkage networks that extend upward in support of particular leaders who are, in turn, looking for followers to ensure their power.⁵³

According to the *security* explanation, a leader who is riding high should have a large number of followers who follow him not because his policy is right but because he can provide reliable protection. Yet this explana-

---

50 Ibid., p. 137.
51 Lucian Pye, *The Dynamics of Chinese Politics*, Cambridge, MA: Oelgeschlager, Gunn & Hain, 1981, p. 7.
52 Ibid., p. 127.   53 Ibid., pp. 7–8.

tion can hardly account for some outcomes – for example, the unpopularity of the Gang of Four, even when they were riding high during the CR;[54] the break between Deng Liqun and Hu Yaobang, who had been comrades-in-arms in the 1978 debate over practice as the sole criterion of truth in the early 1980s (see Chapter 7); and the split between Zhao Ziyang and Deng Xiaoping in the 1989 crisis.

The explanations of factionalism offered by the three major models have captured certain aspects of factionalism in CCP politics, yet some crucial problems remain unanswered. The essential reason is that all the factionalism analyses share a fundamental assumption, namely, that factionalism is a dependent variable in the political conflicts in the CCP system, resulting from policy disputes, a clash of institutional interests, or power struggles. Thus, factionalism is generally seen as a temporary and unstable state of affairs in CCP politics. Although few would disagree that factionalism has an undeniable impact on policy outcomes, it draws our attention only during the periods of crisis. As a result, although we recognize the existence of factionalism, we cannot see its roots; and although we are intrigued by its effect on leadership relations and decision making, we have little understanding of how a faction has been developed. As Lieberthal and Oksenberg point out, "few questions have so engrossed outside observers of Chinese politics as these [about factionalism], yet on few issues is there as little certainty."[55]

FACTIONALISM, A PUZZLE OF CCP POLITICS

Problems for the Study of Factionalism in CCP Politics

Factionalism is characterized by two symbiotic phenomena: informal groups linked by personal ties compete for dominance within their parent organization, and informal personal influences prevail over the formal due process in decision making. Thus, factional activities are usually seen in a system of single-party rule in which various interest groups have to operate within the ruling party's organizational frame in order to participate in the political process, or in a system of dictat-

---

54 Pye (ibid., pp. 119–20) sees this problem himself. But he attributes it to the Gang of Four's radical policies, which were in reality against the interests of their potential followers. Yet this argument is obviously inconsistent with his central hypothesis.
55 Lieberthal and Oksenberg, *Policy Making in China*, p. 58.

The Puzzle of Chinese Communist Politics

orship in which the authority of "strongmen" can override any due processes in policy making – hence personal ties and influences become crucial for political participation. Factionalism, however, is rarely seen in a democratic system where political participation is practiced through multiparty competitions and, more important, the political process is fully institutionalized:

1. Power stays ultimately with the institutions rather than in the hands of individual leaders.
2. A system of checks and balances of power is established and maintained by institutional arrangements, which embody the formal processes, compliant procedures, and standard operating practices that are abiding in policy making.
3. All manner of political control and participation – directives, reports, complaints, policy initiatives, lobby activities, elections, voting – are channeled through these institutional arrangements.

A multiparty system deactivates factionalism because it legalizes peaceful competitions for political offices by various interest groups; and institutionalization suppresses factionalism because it effectively checks the abuse of personal power and connections that promotes factional activities in political affairs.

Indeed, factionalism usually prevails in a nondemocratic system where the political offices are monopolized by the ruling party and institutionalization of the political process is insufficient. In such a system, power often goes with individual leaders, and their authority can override the due process in policy making. As a result, institutional arrangements, if there are any, become a facade, beneath which personal connections form the essential source of power. All this leads to the abuse of personal power and connections, which in turn promotes factional activities and turns the old-boy networks into factions in political affairs.

Thus, factionalism in the CCP political system is not unexpected because it is a system of single-party rule where, as I will elaborate in Chapter 2, the political process has never been fully institutionalized. But differences and difficulties in explaining factionalism in CCP politics reveal our extremely inadequate knowledge about this important issue. The first and foremost question is, What is a CCP faction? Few would disagree with Lucian Pye that CCP factions "lie between the extremes of the intimately knit cliques and the diffuse mass parties that are common in the politics of other countries."[56] But this reveals the problem rather than solving it. The prevailing *guanxi* networks in CCP politics and their substantial influence over policy outcomes are too complicated and too subtle to be depicted as "personal groups" with shared interests. Nor can they fit into the quasi-political organizations as Nathan implies,[57] for there are no principles, rules, and disciplines in the operation of a CCP faction and, more importantly, any such quasi organizations would be intolerable in the CCP's totalistic political system.

The lack of a consistent definition for a CCP faction has caused great confusion. While some scholars treat factionalism as activities of "informal groups," or "forces, categories, and the like" with shifting alignments and opinions,[58] others describe factions as political forces either linked by similar career experiences,[59] or bound by shared policy preferences.[60] But the alignments of some factions like the Gang of Four and the "whateverists" were very stable, and their opinions rarely shifted. As I show in the following chapters, similar experiences did not prevent fierce strife between the CCP leaders like Liu Shaoqi, Gao Gang, Deng Xiaoping, Chen Yun, and Peng Zhen, and we have also observed the struggles between Lin Biao and the Gang of Four, and the obvious division between Hu Yaobang and Zhao Ziyang, although they did have shared policy preferences.

These problems indicate a striking deficiency in the study of factionalism in CCP politics, because few have ever examined how and under what conditions factionalism has developed in CCP politics. We know little about how the factional networks are extended in the CCP system, how the members of a faction are related to each other, and how various factions interact in political affairs. As a result, we do not really understand the internal dynamics for a faction to develop and operate, nor do we know much about the relationships between a faction and its leaders, and among various factional networks. While factional activities at the elite level have been extensively observed, it is unclear whether

56 Pye, *The Dynamics of Chinese Politics*, p. 6.
57 Nathan, "A factionalism model," pp. 37–42.
58 Tsou, "Prolegomenon to the study of the informal groups in CCP politics," pp. 107–10, and Peter R. Moody Jr., *Chinese Politics after Mao: Development and Liberalization 1976 to 1983*, New York: Praeger, 1983, p. 9.
59 Pye, *The Dynamics of Chinese Politics*, pp. 22–7.
60 See Michael Oksenberg and Steven Goldstein, "The Chinese political spectrum," *PC*, 23, no. 2 (March 1974), pp. 1–13.

The Puzzle of Chinese Communist Politics

and how the factional linkages can extend from the elite members to local cadres.[61]

The lack of knowledge about relations between factions as well as within the factional networks has resulted in neglect of changes in the political situation to which factional alignments and their strength and relations are highly responsive. This has in turn caused great difficulties in estimating the power and influence of leaders and their relationships in political affairs. Observers were "surprised" repeatedly by events like the Gao-Rao Affair in 1954, the massive purge of the Party elite in 1966–8, Lin Biao's fall in 1971, Deng Xiaoping's comeback in 1973 followed by his purge in 1976, Hu Yaobang's "resignation" in early 1987 and his comeback at the Thirteenth Party Congress, and the May 1989 crisis and its aftermath.

Another problem for the study of factionalism is the uncertainty over the relationship between factionalism and policy outcomes. While tremendous factional activities in the policy process have been observed, little has been done about their impact on the policy outcomes. The study of factionalism in CCP politics must involve the policy process in order to disclose to what extent factional activities can affect the policy outcomes and by what means a faction seeks to manipulate the policy process to its advantage. Otherwise, policy making in China will, to a large extent, remain a puzzle because two important questions remain unanswered in the perspective of factionalism. Why and how is a faction involved in the policy process? And to what extent can a faction influence a policy outcome and, in return, benefit or suffer from its implementation?

Last but not least, we know little about the relationship between factionalism and the working of the CCP system. We are uncertain whether factionalism in CCP politics is inevitable because of the way the system operates, or is just a by-product of the political behavior determined by elements like political culture, policy confrontations, and constraints of the policy-making structure. Nor are we sure how factionalism has

---

[61] For example, Nathan, "A factionalism model," pp. 52–62, believes that factionalism exists only among the central elite members, and local authorities are faction-free. Goodman, "Provincial party first secretaries in national politics: A categoric or a political group?" in David Goodman, ed., *Groups and Politics in the People's Republic of China*, New York: M. E. Sharp, 1984, pp. 68–82, highlights the important roles of the intermediate and high-intermediate cadres in policy making. But his examination is unclear about how they are related to the central elite members.

impacted the system itself. Does factionalism undermine the system so as to contribute to its final collapse from within, or does it reinforce it and lock it into an endless cycle of power struggles, or will it eventually evolve the system into a kind of political pluralism?

Indeed, the gap between the explanations of factionalism in the literature and factional activities we have observed reveals some important unanswered questions in the study of CCP politics. Moreover, the inconsistency and confusion in our knowledge about factionalism have greatly hindered our efforts to build a theoretical approach upon which rigorous analyses of Chinese politics can be advanced.

Guanxi and Patron-Client Relationships

An empirical but crucial problem in the study of factionalism in CCP politics is the definition of *guanxi*, a term that is frequently used in the description of factional behavior in China. Few would disagree that *guanxi* is vital to the development of factionalism. Yet there is hardly any consensus on its exact implications in terms of Chinese politics. A few interpret *guanxi* as comprising old boy networks,[62] but the tendency is to trace an analogy between *guanxi* and patron-client relations.[63]

Conditions for the development of patron-client relations are ripe in Chinese society,[64] a society where all the accesses to socioeconomic goods are largely monopolized by the Party given the nature of a socialist state. Thus, it is not surprising that clientalism has been a popular topic in the study of contemporary China since Pye first highlighted the issue in 1967.[65] In his study of the unique *danwei* (unit) system in the PRC, Andrew Walder reveals that patron-client relations often exist between workers and their leader(s). Such relations have developed in *danwei* because the *danwei* leaders function not only as business managers, but

62 See Whitson, "The field army in Chinese communist military politics."
63 Nathan, "A factionalism model"; and Pye, *The Dynamics of Chinese Politics*, pp. 139–40.
64 For a general discussion on necessary and sufficient conditions for the development of patron-client relations, see Christopher Clapham, "Clientalism and the state," in Christopher Clapham, ed., *Private Patronage and Public Power: Political Clientalism in the Modern State*, New York: St. Martin's Press, 1982, pp. 7–9.
65 See Pye, *The Spirit of Chinese Politics*. Pye's argument on this issue is further elaborated by Richard Solomon in *Mao's Revolution and Chinese Political Culture*, Berkeley: University of California Press, 1971.

also as distributors of socioeconomic benefits. Walder concludes that such patron-client relations have reinforced the political loyalty toward the regime.[66]

Lynn White has also observed the wide existence of patron-client relations in China. He argues that the CCP's administrative policy has resulted in an individual's dependence on his patron(s) – usually a CCP cadre. But such a relationship can backfire once the tight control is relaxed, or even breaks down, because of elite strife. The frustration and anger caused by the patrons' inability to provide the desired benefits and protection can lead to massive violence. The Cultural Revolution serves as a typical case for White's study.[67]

Jean Oi has conducted a study specifically on patron-client relations in Chinese rural politics. She argues that a type of interest-maximizing patron-client tie between the peasants and the local cadres has played a crucial role in social and economic activities in the rural areas. The dependence of the peasants on the cadres who control the access to socioeconomic benefits is the key to the development of this relationship.[68]

These studies show that patron-client relations in Chinese society are by their nature not different from those widely seen in the other developing countries. The patron-client relationship is generally defined as:

1 "A relationship of exchange between unequals."
2 A persistent and regular relationship developed upon the exchange of well-understood benefits and rights.
3 A relationship based on a personal or private morality of obligations between individuals.
4 A relationship that is not exclusive, because the same individual can be "simultaneously a client in relation to those above him in hierarchy, and a patron in relation to those below."

---

66 Andrew Walder, *Communist Neo-Traditionalism: Work and Authority in Chinese Industry*, Berkeley: University of California Press, 1986.
67 Lynn White, *Policies of Chaos: The Organizational Causes of Violence in China's Cultural Revolution*, Princeton: Princeton University Press, 1989, esp. pp. 15–7, 226–7, 263–5, 318–19, sees the other two consequences of the the CCP's "institutionalized" administrative policy as equally important. They are the polarization of social divisions between the good and the bad, and the legitimation of violence in massive campaigns.
68 Jean C. Oi, *State and Peasant in Contemporary China*, Berkeley: University of California Press, 1989, esp. chaps. 7, 9.

5 An interest-oriented relationship that "is by its nature competitive" – it can be abrogated by either member when it is no longer profitable to him.[69]

Undoubtedly, there are similarities between political *guanxi* and patron-client relations. *Guanxi* in its broad sense also refers to a type of personal tie through which the participants can gain something they otherwise can hardly obtain. Yet, there are substantial differences between the two kinds of relationship. From the perspective of factionalism, *guanxi* in CCP politics is characterized by personal ties that are cultivated in the Party's organizational framework. Since *guanxi* tends to promote "small cliques" in the Party, its existence undermines the Party's coherence and unity, which are vital for the CCP's rule. So the CCP leadership always denounces *guanxi* and tries to eliminate it from the Party's political life. Yet the cultivation of *guanxi* between a leader and his followers and among the cadres is inevitable given the nature of the CCP political system (see Chapter 2 for details). As a result, unlike a patron-client tie, which can exist openly between the two participants as long as it can bring benefits to both of them, *guanxi* has to be underground and the participants always tend to deny its existence, especially when they are under attack. Ironically, this situation further strengthens political *guanxi* because its failure could bring about a disaster for its participants.

Second, patron-client relations are by nature economic relations. Exchanges between the participants are objective and can be measured in both quantity and quality. Yet, *guanxi* in CCP politics is based on personal loyalty forged through years of mutually endured tests and hardships. What the participants exchange are essentially loyalty and trust, which in turn bring about common interests, that is, political security, in their careers. These are the exchanges that can hardly be measured in quantity. In fact, the extent to which one is obliged to his *guanxi* is regarded as a yardstick of his trustworthiness in the Chinese political culture, in which loyalty is the core of the primary ethics. Indeed, loyalty is the key element in all four cornerstones of Chinese traditional values:

69 Clapham, "Clientalism and the state," pp. 4–7; James Scott, "Political clientalism: A bibliographic essay," in Steffan W. Schmidt, Laura Guasti, Carl H. Lande, and James C. Scott, ed., *Friends, Fellows, and Factions: A Reader in Political Clientalism*, Berkeley: University of California Press, 1977, pp. 483–505; and Nathan, "A factionalism model," p. 37.

The Puzzle of Chinese Communist Politics

zhong (loyalty to superior), *xiao* (filial piety), *ren* (benevolence to the inferior), and *yi* (loyalty to friends). A public figure in China must be absolutely loyal to his superior (*zhong*); and he must dutifully take care of the people he governs (*ren*). As a private man, he must be unconditionally obliged to his parents (*xiao*); and he must be wholeheartedly devoted to his friends (*yi*). Otherwise, he is not trustworthy. It is doubly ironic but significant that political loyalty is always emphasized by the CCP leadership, yet the CCP propaganda has never stopped attacking the "old political traditions" that are centered on *zhong*, *xiao*, *ren*, and *yi*.

Third, since *guanxi* is based on loyalty and trust, its participants, unlike those in patron-client relations, are essentially *equal partners*, although it may be developed between a superior and his inferior in a hierarchical context. Thus, political *guanxi* is more coercive and abiding than patron-client relations. The mutually obliged loyalty in *guanxi* creates a situation in which, as Pye observes, "there is much greater acknowledgment that the inferior can victimize the superior, and there is also much greater use of stratagems in creating feelings of responsibility and obligation on the one hand and indebtness on the other."[70]

What must be emphasized, however, is that *guanxi* is not exactly a factional linkage yet, for *guanxi* is based on loyalty and trust, whereas the formation and maintenance of factional linkages need common interests in political affairs. In the development of a faction, *guanxi* networks provide a handy base on which factional linkages are cultivated, given the CCP political system (see Chapter 2).

Factionalism or Bandwagon and Balance-of-Power Politics

Avery Goldstein has applied bandwagon and balance-of-power theory in his explanation of CCP politics.[71] His work deserves special attention here because he specifically challenges the factionalism analyses, although he acknowledges that his analysis, especially the argument on balance-of-power politics, has "several parallels" with the factionalism approach.[72] "Bandwagon" and "balance of power" are originally two

---

70 Pye, *The Dynamics of Chinese Politics*, p. 142.
71 Avery Goldstein, *From Bandwagon to Balance-of-Power Politics: Structural Constraints and Politics in China, 1949–1978*, Stanford: Stanford University Press, 1991.
72 Ibid., p. 12.

behavior patterns captured by Kenneth Waltz's structural theory of international politics.[73] Waltz argues that the rationale for all actors in international politics is the same – to pursue power while containing others – because international politics is anarchically structured. Thus, the stability depends on a balance of distribution of capabilities among these actors, and any changes in the established balance constitute a potential source of war. When such a change occurs, the actors will respond by forming or dissolving coalitions to restore the balance. Balance-of-power politics results in an endless cycle of balancing and counterbalancing.[74]

However, Waltz points out that when an actor (or a group of actors) breaks a balance of power and emerges as a probable winner, "nearly all [actors] jump on the bandwagon rather than continuing to build coalitions intended to prevent anyone from winning the prize of power. Bandwagoning, not balancing, becomes the characteristic behavior."[75]

Applying bandwagon and balance-of-power theory to CCP politics, Goldstein tries to examine CCP politics from the perspective of structure that constrains the actors' behavior. He states his thesis as follows:

> [T]he China case is introduced to demonstrate the usefulness of ... balance-of-power theory and bandwagon theory. These theories identify how context, or more precisely political structure, shapes behavior and outcomes in characteristic ways.... Hierarchic arenas of the particular sort seen in China between 1949 and 1966 give rise to political patterns explained by bandwagon theory. Anarchic realms like that seen in China between 1966 and 1978 – the period of the Cultural Revolution – are characterized by political patterns best explained by balance-of-power theory.[76]

73 See Kenneth Waltz, *Theory of International Politics*, Reading, MA: Addison-Wesley, 1979; also Robert Keohane, ed., *Neo-Realism and Its Critics*, New York: Columbia University Press, 1986, esp. chaps. 1, 3–7, 11.
74 See Kenneth Waltz, *Man, the State and War*, New York: Columbia University Press, 1959, esp. chaps. 4, 6, 7; also Hans Morgenthau, *Politics among Nations*, 4th ed., New York: Knopf, 1967.
75 Waltz, *Theory of International Politics*, p. 126.
76 Goldstein, *From Bandwagon*, p. 3.

The Puzzle of Chinese Communist Politics

For Goldstein, the unity maintained among leaders under Mao's command before the CR, even during the periods of crisis, was determined by the hierarchical structure of bandwagon politics whereby Mao was perceived as the established victor who "was inextricably bound up with the legitimacy of the regime."[77] Therefore, it was a rational choice for all the leaders to bandwagon with Mao. As the CR unfolded in 1966, however, bandwagon behavior disappeared as the political structure became anarchic, resulting from the collapse of the organization. Thus, although the attitude of actors could remain unchanged, balance-of-power behavior prevailed as Chinese politics became "essentially the politics of survival in an anarchic self-help realm."[78] All the actors, including Mao himself, were engaged in balance-of-power politics. As a result, fierce power struggles and ruthless purges became routine in political affairs.

Yet, as Goldstein acknowledges, neither bandwagon nor balance-of-power politics can explain political outcomes in the post-Mao period because, as he implies, Chinese politics has evolved into a different structure.[79] If this is the case, his structure theory would not be of much use because it fails to account for the changes in Chinese politics.

For the Mao period, however, Goldstein's approach is also flawed, for Waltz's structure theory of international politics does not fit Chinese politics, which was never in a state of anarchy, even during the CR. Thus, explaining it with a "bandwagon" perspective is highly questionable. Although Mao was in command, it is misleading to assert that the leaders bandwagoned with Mao in decision making. Otherwise, how can we explain frequent conflicts, in which Mao himself was usually involved? As a matter of fact, Mao was not always a Machiavellian; more often than not he used his position astutely to manipulate the other leaders in political affairs. A typical case is the 1954 Gao-Rao Affair. Liu Shaoqi barely prevailed not because the other leaders "bandwagoned" with him, as Goldstein argues,[80] but because Mao abandoned Gao as he had become a liability to Mao and, more importantly, Gao's reckless lobbying activities had jeopardized Mao's own position (see Chapter 4).

77 Ibid., p. 10.   78 Ibid., pp. 5–6.   79 Ibid., p. 255.   80 See ibid., pp. 83–6.

There were also cases in which Mao was actually forced to accept opinions against his well-documented ideas, as manifested in the 1956 antiadventurism,[81] in the 1957 rectification,[82] and during the economic recovery of 1962–4.[83] In fact, more often than not the CCP leaders did not bandwagon with Mao. Rather, as Teiwes noticed, they "could on the whole collectively and openly thrash out problems" at Mao's doorstep during the pre-CR period.[84] When they sided with Mao, they were either sharing his vision, as Liu, Deng, and the like (except Zhou Enlai and Chen Yun) did in the launching of the GLF;[85] or were driven by their own ambitions for power, as Liu and Lin Biao were at the 1959 Lushan Conference and at the 7,000-Cadre Conference in early 1962 (see Chapter 5).[86]

The balance-of-power explanation for political outcomes during the CR is also misleading, for the collapse of the Party establishment during the CR did not turn Chinese politics into anarchy. Even during the most turbulent years of 1967–8, the hierarchical structure of CCP politics continued because of the very hierarchical nature of the way the Red Guards and the masses were mobilized. The leaders around Mao never lost their grasp of the situation, although the chaos was obviously beyond their expectations. Power struggles during the CR were not caused by continuous forming and dissolving coalitions among the leaders; rather, these struggles reflected fierce competitions among the beneficiaries of the CR to fill the power vacuum caused by massive purges. Factional linkages in a hierarchical context became vital in such a situation not only because

81 See Chapter 5. See also MacFarquhar, *The Origins*, 1:57–9, 86–91.
82 Goldstein, *From Bandwagon*, pp. 94, 288n59, argues that the decision to halt the rectification and launch an antirightist campaign was made because Mao changed his mind. However, the fact is that Mao's "cues" were not positively responded to, let alone "zealously" followed by his colleagues; and Mao had to, whether forced or not, reverse the policy in the direction in which Liu Shaoqi, Peng Zhen, and Deng Xiaoping had persisted.
83 See Huang Zeng, "*Liu Shaoqi yu liuushi niandai chu de guomin jingji tiaozheng*" (Liu Shaoqi and the readjustment of the national economy in the early 1960s), *Yanjiu 1*, 1986, 1:1–7. See also Chapter 5.
84 Teiwes, *Leadership, Legitimacy, and Conflict in China*, p. 64. My analysis on the reasons that the CCP leaders could do this to Mao differs fundamentally from Teiwes's (see Chapter 5).
85 MacFarquhar, *The Origins*, 2:51–116.
86 Goldstein, *From Bandwagon*, pp. 10, 87–90, argues that the leaders bandwagoned with Mao in order to secure the political health of the regime. He did not mention the 7,000 Cadre Conference in his analysis.

The Puzzle of Chinese Communist Politics

the formal political process had collapsed,[87] but also because it was through these linkages that Mao was able to manipulate political struggles and maintain his command (see Chapter 6). Indeed, it was these factional linkages that enabled the leaders to keep their followers under control in such a chaotic situation, provided factional associates with channels for information flow in the conspiratorial political affairs,[88] and constituted the command system of one's forces in fierce power struggles (see Chapter 2).

If there was a balance-of-power game during the CR, it existed only among subleaders, and it was manipulated by Mao in order to secure his own supreme authority – it was balance-of-power politics among Mao's followers under Mao's command. By using his power and his image as "a sure winner" astutely, Mao was able to maintain his command through to the end. Ironically, "bandwagon" seems a more exact description for actors' behavior during the CR, though it is somewhat superficial.

But Goldstein's analysis does highlight the problem that has for years perplexed scholars of CCP politics: why and how could the CR occur? Goldstein argues that the CR resulted precisely from bandwagon politics in which the virtually unconditional obedience of the leaders to Mao led to disastrous events like the GLF and the suppression of expertise in various political campaigns. All this caused a sharp decline of the regime's authority, which accounted for the outburst of the CR.[89] Yet the CR was not initiated from the bottom up but was launched by Mao from above. This brings about a key problem that Goldstein's analysis has failed to address. That is, why was it so hard for Mao, despite his image as a "sure winner," to pursue goals that appeared inconsistent with those of his colleagues? Thus, Mao had no choice but to resort to the forces outside the CCP organization to settle "differences in kind" between him and his colleagues.[90] It would be superficial to assert that the Party

---

87 Tsou, "Prolegomenon to the study of the informal groups in CCP politics," pp. 101–6, raises the issue first, namely, that the collapse of the "formal process" can activate factional politics.
88 Goldstein, *From Bandwagon*, pp. 162–5, also notices the importance of personal ties in political affairs during the CR. But he sees this as a criterion of a state of anarchy.
89 Ibid., pp. 138–44.
90 Ibid., pp. 148–53, stresses that the differences between Mao and the leaders purged in the CR "were, at most, differences in degree rather than kind." He claims that these

leaders who were purged in the initial years of the CR intentionally lined up against Mao, or that they all belonged to the same faction. What is true is that they were pursuing their interests and thus became obstacles to Mao in pursuing his goals. Then, what were their interests? How could they resist Mao the Commander? And where did they draw power in their resistance? Last but not least, what made Mao, and later Deng, such an absolute winner in political conflicts, regardless of whether the other leaders bandwagoned with him or engaged in balance-of-power politics? All these questions are unanswered in Goldstein's analysis, but they will be addressed in this book from the perspective of factionalism.

<blockquote>
leaders were still trying to bandwagon with Mao even after the CR was launched. But they were unable to keep pace with Mao during the rapid devolution of the situation. Thus, Mao's initiatives in 1966 to prevent the occurrence of revisionism brought about an unintended outcome: the CR.
</blockquote>

2

Factionalism and the Political System in China

The fundamental departure of this study from the literature on factionalism in CCP politics is that factionalism is an *independent variable* in the shaping of leadership relations and leadership decision making. This chapter shows why and how factionalism is *embedded* in the CCP political system, a system that has provided the necessary and sufficient conditions for the development of factionalism in political affairs. The analysis then focuses on how factionalism has reinforced itself through cadre promotion and changes in leadership relations.

CONDITIONS FOR THE DEVELOPMENT OF FACTIONALISM

Proposition 1: Power is entrusted to individuals instead of institutions in a hierarchic context. This pattern of personal entrustment of power provides a sufficient condition for the development of factionalism, for it fosters *guanxi* between a leader and his appointees on which factional linkages can be developed as common political interests emerge in repeated exploitations of their *guanxi* in political affairs.

Personal Entrustment of Power

The pattern of power distribution in CCP politics is rooted in the process of its revolution. The perilous situation after the bloody setback in 1927 forced the CCP to embark on an arduous route for power, a route best summed up by Mao as "setting up the armed independent regimes in the countryside and encircling the cities from the rural areas."[1] With this

---

1 Hao Mengbi and Duan Haoran, *Zhongguo gongchandang liushi nian* (The Sixty Years of the CCP), Beijing: PLA Press, 1984, 1:94 (hereafter *Liushi nian*).

strategy, the CCP cadres were sent to the remote and usually mountainous regions where the authority of the incumbent government could barely reach. Their task was to "educate the masses" of poor peasants with communist ideology, "mobilize" them with the promise of a better life, "organize" them into the armed struggle for power, and "arm" them with whatever weapons were available. As a result, an armed force was developed and began to build up its "armed independent regime," or base area. It was not unusual that only after a troop and its base area had been developed was this force formally integrated into the CCP forces and its leaders given official positions in the Party's commanding system. This tactic of "spreading seeds, taking root, blossoming, and bearing fruit" (*buozhong, shenggen, kaihua, jieguo*) was very successful indeed. Yet it also brought about two consequences that would exert a significant impact on CCP politics in the years to come.

First, all the CCP forces were controlled by the individual leaders who had developed them. Given that the base areas were isolated from each other and the armed forces there had to fight on their own during the revolution, these leaders were not only military commanders but also administrators in the areas controlled by their troops. Their positions in the CCP leadership were essentially determined by the strength of their forces and the degree of their loyalty to the supreme leader; and these leaders distributed power in their base areas in the same fashion. Thus, from the very beginning, power was not located with the institutions but was entrusted to individuals in a hierarchic context. An office was set up not necessarily because it was needed, but to fit the power and position of an established leader. When this leader fell, it would either be dissolved or rewarded as spoils to someone who had *guanxi* to the prevailing leader(s). Thus, the role and influence of an office were determined not so much by its designated functions as by the power its leader possessed.[2]

---

2 Cases like this were numerous, especially during the revolution. For example, the CC Secretariat was first established as the Party's supreme organ by the Moscow-trained students at the Fourth Plenum of the Sixth PC. But it became virtually nonexistent after Mao began to dominate at the Zunyi Conference. The Secretariat resumed its functions after Mao subdued the returned students and retained his full command of the CCP during the Yan'an Rectification (see Chapter 3). The other example is the fate of the CCP Front Commission (*qianwei*) led by Mao. The commission was set up to "lead the armed struggle" in the Jinggangshan area. But after the Fourth Red Army was devel-

The Political System in China

Second, the administration of a base area was militarized. The entire administrative system was set up, safeguarded, and hence controlled by the military. As a result, the pattern of personal entrustment of power was extended from the military to the administrative system from day one. So it is not surprising that most of the CCP factions have strong military connections.

This situation changed little after the regime was established in 1949. Almost all the newly established local administrations were controlled by the officers who had just "liberated" these areas, partly due to the shortage of cadres in the hasty construction of the regime, but largely for the convenience of arrangement and control (see Chapter 4). Moreover, this practice was soon routinized as a system of *zhuanye*, or transferring a discharged officer to a civilian position equivalent to his military rank. The PLA has since become "a big cadre school" for the regime. Thus, *guanxi* forged in the military was smoothly extended to all the levels of administration. More importantly, the *zhuanye* system also paved the way for military involvement in political affairs in the years to come.

The hasty construction of the regime was in fact a process of dividing up China among the mountaintop leaders according to the strength of their forces and the territory they occupied. These leaders were the de facto kings in their regions. Because the CCP leadership undoubtedly realized the danger of these potential "independent kingdoms," as soon as the situation was stabilized in the summer of 1952 all the regional administrations were downgraded;[3] their powerful leaders – Gao Gang

---

oped in this area in the late 1920s, another Party organ, the CCP Fourth Red Army Commission (*junwei*), was set up under the leadership of Chen Yi and Zhu De. A power struggle soon occurred between the two parallel organs. Lin Biao, then a regiment commander, was "the only one who wrote to Mao and unambiguously asked Mao not to leave the Fourth Red Army." Although the Fourth Red Army Commission was dissolved in June 1929, Mao resigned with the excuse of poor health; the real reason was that he did not have the majority support. But Lin's firm support impressed Mao so much that he rewarded Lin with over four decades of trust and patronage. See Wei Li, *1965 qian de Lin Biao* (Lin Biao Prior to 1965), Lhasa: Tebet People's Press, 1996, pp. 58–66.

3 The centralization started with the dissolution of the Northeast People's Government in August 1952. On November 11, 1952, Beijing issued an order to downgrade all four civil and military commissions in Northwest, South, Southwest, and East China into the administrative councils. See *CLOPCG*, pp. 38–9. But North China was an exception: the People's Government of North China, which was controlled by Liu Shaoqi's

Factionalism in Chinese Communist Politics

from the Northeast, Rao Shushi and Chen Yi from the East, Lin Biao and Deng Zihui from the South, Deng Xiaoping and He Long from the Southwest, and Peng Dehuai and Xi Zhongxun from the Northwest – were all "promoted" to the Center.[4] This radical centralization broke the stability of leadership relations. The Gao-Rao Affair resulted from the redistribution of power among the newly promoted regional leaders and the central elites (see Chapter 4).

The Gao-Rao Affair alarmed the CCP leaders in two respects. It exposed the danger of letting power be concentrated in the hands of individual leaders; and it indicated the need to institutionalize (or formalize) the policy-making process so as to stabilize policy outcomes as well as leadership relations. The effort of institutionalization brought about substantial changes in leadership relations. In his report to the Second Plenum of the Eighth Central Committee (November 10–15, 1956), Liu Shaoqi emphasized the need to put *all* the leaders under the Party's supervision, to promote "democracy" within the Party, and to "exert certain checks on the power of the state leaders."[5] A result was that Mao had to subordinate his priority of "faster" development to the majority headed by Zhou Enlai and Chen Yun, who preferred "con-

---

mountaintop, was upgraded into the PRC Central Government in July 1949. This arrangement greatly boosted the influence of Liu's mountaintop (see Chapters 3 and 4).

4 Cf. Frederick Teiwes, *Politics at Mao's Court: Rectification and the Decline of Party Norms, 1950–1965*, New York: M. E. Sharpe, 1979, table 1, pp. 22–4. But Teiwes's second column, "Important Historical Ties to Key Leaders," is confusing and inadequate. It actually contains two kinds of relations: the superior-inferior relationship and co-worker relationship. Obviously, *guanxi* can be cultivated on both relationships. But co-working experience could also lead to rivalry, from which competing factional networks could be developed. For example, Liu Shaoqi and Chen Yi are linked in the table. But there was tension between the two, not only because Chen, as the commander of the New Fourth Army, had gone through a humiliating *zhengshen* (political examination) conducted by Liu when the latter was the commissar of the New Fourth Army (1940–1), but also because Liu was the patron of Chen's bitter rival, Rao Shushi, who leveled a ferocious attack on Chen in 1942–3 (see Chapter 4).

5 Liu Shaoqi, "*Yao fangzhi lingdao renyuan teshu hua*" (Privileges of the leaders must be prevented), in *Liu Shaoqi lun Dang de jian she* (Liu Shaoqi on the Construction of the Party), compiled by the CCP Department for Research on Party Literature, Beijing: CCP Central Document Press, 1991, pp. 644–5. Also cf. Liao Gailong, ed., *1949–1989: Xin zhongguo biannian shi* (1949–1989: A Chronology of the New China), Beijing: People's Press, 1989, p. 114.

The Political System in China

tinuous consolidation" at the Third Plenum (September 20–October 9, 1957).[6] Although their moderate approach was reversed in 1958, caused in large part by Mao's violation of the adopted policy-making process, the GLF was not just the result of Mao's "personal crusade" as Avery Goldstein argues.[7] But it was caused essentially by the "collective impatience of Comrade Mao Zedong and many central and local leaders for a quick success"[8] (see Chapter 5).

However, when Peng Dehuai's criticism of the GLF at the 1959 Lushan Conference posed a test of whether the institutionalized authority could overcome personally entrusted power, the latter prevailed: Mao won the battle he should have lost. When Mao drew a line between Peng and himself, he was sure that he would win. But the question concerning leadership relations in this conflict is what had turned Mao into such a godlike figure that "however serious his policy error and violations of official norms in 1959, [his] colleagues could not separate him from the Party or the nation."[9] The undeniable collective responsibility shared by the majority of leaders on the GLF was surely a major factor.[10] A more profound reason, however, lies both in the unchallengeable power that was *personally* entrusted to Mao and in the ideological dependence of the Party on Mao Zedong Thought (see Chapter 3). The power entrusted to Mao was so absolute that the system could hardly operate without his leadership during the period of crisis, and the ideological legitimacy of the CCP's cause was essentially based on Mao Zedong Thought, adopted as "the Party's guiding principle." It is true that Peng's criticism was about issues, but his attack was a challenge to Mao's unchallengeable position. Thus, the line Mao drew at Lushan was not just between himself and Peng, but between the Party and

---

6 Parris H. Chang, *Power and Policy in China*, 2nd ed., University Park: Pennsylvania State University Press, 1978, esp. pp. 38–55.
7 See Avery Goldstein, *From Bandwagon to Balance-of-Power Politics: Structural Constraints and Politics in China, 1949–1978*, Stanford: Stanford University Press, 1991, pp. 104–6.
8 See *Jueyi*, p. 18.
9 Frederick Teiwes, *Leadership, Legitimacy, and Conflict in China*, New York: M. E. Sharpe, 1984, p. 67.
10 See *Jueyi*, p. 17; *SWDXP*, esp. pp. 280–2; and *Zhuanji*, 1:142. See also Roderick MacFarquhar, *The Origins of the Cultural Revolution, 2: The Great Leap Forward, 1958–1960*, New York: Columbia University Press, 1983, chaps. 2–6, 9.

anyone who dared to challenge his leadership. *Mao was the Party.* His absolute authority was not, and could not be, based on institutional arrangements, but it was based on personal loyalties that had been forged during the revolution. Lamentably, this is exactly where *Mao de beiju* (Mao's tragedy, the term used in *Jueyi*) was: the power entrusted to him was so overwhelming that Mao was entrapped in the situation where he, as a public figure, had to take it as his personal mission to keep the critically flawed system working in order to keep his dream alive, but as a private man, he had to be a cunning Machiavellian in order to maintain the absolute authority necessary for his mission to be unchallengeable.

From this perspective we see an astonishing parallel between Mao and Deng Xiaoping, despite Deng's obvious unwillingness to follow in Mao's footsteps and tremendous differences between the two in terms of personality, experiences, education, and vision. But the resemblance is inevitable because it is *system-created*. It is not surprising that Deng's earnest effort of institutionalization, or "legalization" (*fazhi hua*) in Deng's term, after 1980 was fruitless but nevertheless stirred up power struggles, for the first and foremost obstacle to institutionalization was his own personally entrusted power.[11] It was beyond Deng's ability and willingness to change this flawed pattern of power distribution, not necessarily because he did not have the absolute power Mao had, but because like Mao, he could not have carried out his reform without the power entrusted to him personally. It is in this sense that Pye's description of the CCP leadership as a "deserving elite"[12] becomes comprehensible.

Moreover, the pattern of personal entrustment of power has created a Mao-type tyranny at every corner the Party authority can reach. This tyranny's power is personally entrusted to him by his superior, and he therefore has absolute authority in the area where he

---

11 Stuart R. Schram, "China after the 13th congress," *CQ*, 114 (June 1988), pp. 177–97, keenly observed Deng's self-contradictory behavior on institutionalization of the political process. Deng had to adopt a set of institutional arrangements to formalize the reform, yet as these arrangements began to constrain his power, he violated them but resorted to his personal power in order to maintain his dominance in policy making.

12 Lucian Pye, *The Dynamics of Chinese Politics*, Cambridge, MA: Oelgeschlager, Gunn & Hain, 1981, pp. 193–4.

The Political System in China

is in charge. A more profound consequence is that *guanxi* networks have been cultivated throughout the entire CCP system, for personal entrustment of power turns the relationship between a superior and his followers into one of mutual dependence in a hierarchic context. A leader can take credit or be blamed for his followers' achievements or mistakes; and his fall would virtually bring an end to his followers' political careers. Thus, when a conflict emerges, a leader needs his followers' support as badly as the latter need his protection. This mutual dependence turns *guanxi* networks into factional linkages.

However, political relationships similar to *guanxi* are not a unique phenomenon in China. Old-boy networks that universally exist in all politics resemble much of the *guanxi* networks. Thus, the pattern of personal entrustment of power, which is essential to the formation of *guanxi* networks, is not a necessary but a sufficient condition for the development of factionalism. It is the system of single-party dictatorship that turns *guanxi* networks into political factions.

> *Proposition 2*: The system of single-party dictatorship provides a necessary condition for the development of factionalism. It turns political *guanxi*, or personal ties based on comradeship and trust, into factional linkages. Under the Party's dictatorship, *guanxi* networks provide the political associates with an outlet for their particular interests, exclusive channels of communication, and the commanding system of their forces. As *guanxi* networks assume the functions that are normally performed by a political organization in a pluralistic system, they are transformed into a faction.

The CCP's Dictatorship

The feature of a Soviet-type single-Party dictatorship is well discussed in the literature.[13] Yet, the CCP's control is more penetrating,[14] and it is

---

13 Cf. Carl J. Friedrich and Zbigniew K. Brzezinski, *Totalitarian Dictatorship and Autocracy*, New York: Praeger, 1961; and Irving Howe, ed., *1984 Revisited: Totalitarianism in Our Century*, New York: Harper & Row, 1983, pp. 103–48, 209–67.
14 See Yan Huai "Understanding the political system of contemporary China," *Papers from the Center for Modern China*, 10 (August 1991).

effectively reinforced by two unique systems: the *hukou* (household registration)[15] and the *danwei* (unit) systems.[16]

The system of single-party dictatorship, however, created a fundamental dilemma for the CCP leaders. The effectiveness of organization, the monopoly of resources, and the control of all the sources of information, including education, media, and the press, made it virtually impossible for any independent political organizations to emerge in China. As a result, the Party has been the sole provider of legal channels to aggregate a multiplicity of socioeconomic interests into coherent policy-making agendas. But these interests are rarely harmonious, given enormous differences in the level of development, ethnic traditions, and natural conditions across China. Ironically, the CCP's efforts to promote development often made these interests even more divergent.[17] As a result, intra-Party struggles are inevitable because, as Mao recognized, the conflicting socioeconomic interests "will inevitably find expressions in our Party."[18] Yet the Party's cohesiveness, the self-conscious commitment to the Party's cause, and the rigid disciplines that are prerequisites for the CCP's rule have exerted such strict constraints on the CCP leaders that they could not reveal any differences among themselves in an open and honest manner. Nor could they make any individual effort to seek support within or outside the Party through the legal channels. Thus, they had to resort to *informal* channels in search of support. As Pye observes, "leadership (in CCP politics)

---

15 See Tiejun Cheng, "The Household Registration (Hukou) System in China," Ph.D. diss. Binghamton: State University of New York, 1992. *Hukou* grows out of the traditional *bao-jia* system, which can be traced up to the Qin Dynasty (221–207 B.C.). Each *jia* consisted of ten households, and each *bao* had ten *jia*. The essential aim of the *bao-jia* system was to secure tax collections and to control the mobility of the population in an agrarian society. The *bao-jia* system was also an effective instrument to strengthen rule. If a member committed a crime, the whole *jia*, sometimes even the whole *bao*, would be punished unless it assisted the authority promptly to detain this person. But *hukou* is more effective than *bao-jia* because it is directly related to one's employment, housing, schooling for the children, and supply of daily necessities.
16 See Andrew Walder, *Communist Neo-Traditionalism: Work and Authority in Chinese Industry*, Berkeley: University of California Press, 1986.
17 Cf. J. M. Montias, "Economic conditions and political instability in communist countries," *Studies in Comparative Communism*, 13, no. 4 (Winter 1980), pp. 283–99, for relations between economic development and political stability in the communist world. 18 *SWMZD*, 4:124.

does not operate through legally defined channels but as a deserving elite."[19]

In retrospect, a major characteristic of CCP politics is that when a conflict emerged, the leaders would usually exchange their ideas and opinions via informal channels in a secret manner before they made their attitude and stand (*biaotai zhandui*) clear in public. As I examine in the following chapters, all the elite conflicts since 1949 were initiated through informal channels. (This does not mean that the pre-1949 period was an exception!) When a conflict eventually found its expression through the legal channels, the point of no return had already been reached because any compromises would have damaged the Party's appearance of unity and cohesiveness, which is vital for its rule.

The same dilemma also haunts every leading cadre. He is virtually the only legitimate representative of the area or unit he governs. Thus, he is responsible for advancing the interests of the people under his governance, and his own well-being usually depends on whether he can succeed in doing so. Yet these interests are often at odds with those from the other areas or units, and they are not always consistent with the perceived goals of the Party. It is difficult, and painful indeed, for a local leader to "harmonize the interests of the state, the collective, and the individuals under the guidance of the Party's line" while competing with his peers for priority. Not surprisingly, special *guanxi* with the superiors becomes highly desirable in this situation, not only for extra protection when things go sour but also to exert a certain influence on the higher authority in the policy process.

True, in any politics those who have close ties with their superiors have a greater leverage in policy making. Yet, in CCP politics, where diverse interests have to be expressed through informal channels and different opinions are suppressed in order to maintain the Party's unity, *guanxi* networks have to function as:

1 The outlet for the particular interests and demands of leaders and their followers.
2 The exclusive channels of communication among the political associates.
3 The commanding system of a leader's forces in political affairs.

19 Pye, *The Dynamics of Chinese Politics*, pp. 193–4.

In a pluralistic system, all these functions are performed by legitimate political organizations. Thus, like those of a political organization, the effectiveness and strength of *guanxi* networks in CCP politics depend on the extent to which they can penetrate the system. A CCP leader's power is essentially based on his *guanxi* networks. The more penetrating and effective his networks are, the more support, hence more power, he can generate in political affairs.[20]

Yet no *guanxi* networks have ever been able to evolve into even a tentative organization despite their significant role and function in CCP politics. This is revealing indeed: the Party's appearance of unity and cohesiveness is so vital that the sacrifice of any interests of its members can be justified if the Party's "unity" is at stake. That is why whenever a large number of devoted CCP members were purged, usually immediately after the fall of a (group of) top leader(s), like Li Lisan, Wang Ming, Peng Dehuai, Liu Shaoqi, Lin Biao, Deng Xiaoping, and Zhao Ziyang, the Party's unity is raised to dizzying new heights, and those who were victimized were always accused of "scheming to split the Party." The massive purge of the Party cadres for their alleged anti-Party crimes during the CR was the most dramatic example.

Repeated exploitations of *guanxi* networks in political affairs have not only made them tighter and more effective, but also transformed the nature of this relationship. As *guanxi* networks, forged originally by comradeship and friendship, have been transformed into the relationships based on common political interests, factional linkages come into being.

> *Proposition 3*: The lack of institutionalization provides the other necessary condition for the development of factionalism. Uncertainty of the rules and procedures in policy making leads to a cellular and fragmented structure of the policy process, hinders

20 Goldstein, *From Bandwagon*, pp. 163–4, 177–8, 310n64, argues that personal ties in CCP politics became significant only after "the collapse of organization" in the CR and, therefore, was a major indicator of anarchically structured politics. This is misleading, given that when the organization functioned normally, personal ties were no less significant, if not more so, in cases like the 1954 Gao-Rao Affair (see Chapter 3), and virtually in all the major events after the Tenth PC (August 24–28, 1973) as well. Moreover, attributing the significance of personal ties to "the collapse of organization" misses the crux of the issue – that it is the CCP's dictatorship and its intolerant nature that have made personal ties so important in CCP politics. The collapse of organization only made *guanxi* networks more visible in political affairs.

The Political System in China

communication and coordination among the policy makers, and provokes panic and chaos when a crisis emerges. All this results in dependency on the leaders' authority, charisma, and skills in the political process, especially during a period of crisis. Factional activities are therefore promoted because *guanxi* networks with powerful leaders become indispensable in the operation of the system.

The Lack of Institutionalization

The handicap of the single-party dictatorship in responding to diverse interests can be remedied considerably by institutionalizing the political process without changing the essence of the system. Scholars of Soviet politics have long noticed the dilemma of the single-party dictatorship versus diverse interests. Robert Daniels describes it in this fashion:

> In any complex modern bureaucratic organization, it is impossible to function purely from the top down: all manner of influence – information, advice, recommendations, problems, complaints – must flow upwards. . . . The problems of managing a complex economy and technology have made it abundantly clear to the Soviet leadership that they must allow this reverse stream of influence to flow freely, and their main concern is that *the flow be kept within the organizational structure of the Communist Party.*[21]

The post-Stalin Soviet leadership, however, made a remarkable effort to institutionalize the political process. As a result, both the frequency and the brutality of purges were remarkably reduced, and massive purges based on personal implications were rarely seen in the post-Stalin period. Moreover, power began to relocate with the institutions, especially those "vertical administrative units" that had control of important resources, and local governments gained more autonomy.[22] More significantly, the

---

21 Robert Daniels, "Soviet politics since Khrushchev," in John W. Strong, ed., *The Soviet Union under Brezhnev and Kosyqin*, New York: Van Nostrand-Reinhold, 1971, pp. 22–3. Emphasis added.
22 See J. F. Hough, *Soviet Union and Social Science Theory*, Cambridge, MA: Harvard University Press, 1977, esp. pp. 23–31.

role of personal ties became less prominent and even faded away in political affairs compared with circumstances in the Stalin period.[23]

The essence of institutionalization is to establish a *formal process* based on institutional arrangements that embody formal rules, compliant procedures, and standard operational practices for governance. With the ultimate authority staying with the institutions, institutional arrangements not only improve communication and coordination among the policy makers, but also help secure the stability and consistency of the policy process.[24] Although it is a persuasive argument that "institutional pluralism" fostered a monstrous bureaucracy that "ossified" the entire Soviet system,[25] few could dispute that policy making in the Soviet Union

---

23 Timothy J. Colton, "Moscow's party organization," *PC*, 37 (January 1988), esp. pp. 40–1, 40n70, demonstrates that personal ties had been a noticeable factor in one's promotion in the Soviet Party organizations during the 1930s. His examination shows that Khrushchev, Malenkov, and Bulganin were the fastest rising stars in the 1930s, largely due to their previous association with the then Moscow Party boss Kaganovich, "the best comrade-in-arms" of Stalin at the time. But such a phenomenon was rarely seen in the post-Stalin period. As Barbara B. Green, *The Dynamics of Russian Politics: A Short History*, Westport, CT: Praeger, 1994, pp. 69–70, noticed, the new generation of Soviet leaders rose to power as technocrats, and the growth of institutional pluralism enabled them to solve conflicts through bargaining and compromises.

24 This is perhaps the most important contribution of game theory to our understanding of the political process. This contribution is manifested in two aspects. First, once a formal process is established, it is the *rules* and *procedures* that determine the final outcomes in policy making. See Peter Ordeshook, *Game Theory and Political Theory: An Introduction*, Cambridge: Cambridge University Press, 1986, p. 257. Thus, it is not surprising that the focus of the neo-institutional analysis has shifted from the *functions* of institutions, that is, state, government, and bureaucracy (see, among others, Peter B. Evans, Dietrich Rueschemeyer, and Theda Skocpol, ed., *Bring the State Back In*, Cambridge: Cambridge University Press, 1985), to the *structure* of institutional arrangements, that is, "the formal rules, compliant procedures, and standard operating practices that structure the relationship between individuals in various units of the polity" (Peter Hall, *Governing the Economy: The Politics of State Intervention in Britain and France*, New York: Oxford University Press, 1986, p. 19). Second, the stability of policy making is *structure-induced*. Although a policy maker can change his preferences or shift his alignment in the policy-making process, his choice is eventually subject to the structural constraints – his power and obligations are defined by his position in the *institutional arrangements*. These constraints check the "spatial coalition formations" (or the so-called logrolling) among the legislators when their preferences are "intransitive" and hence prevent a policy dispute from evolving into a crisis. Stability is therefore induced. See, among others, Kenneth A. Shepsle and Barry Weingast, "Structure-induced equilibrium and legislative choice," *Public Choice*, 37 (1981), pp. 503–19.

25 But this "ossification" argument appears misleading. What really "ossified" the ex-Soviet Union was a bureaucracy based on a centrally planned economy, which put the

The Political System in China

became more stable – which means predictable – in the post-Stalin period, especially after the ousting of Krushchev in 1964.

Indeed, while keeping the system and the organizational structure of the Party essentially intact, institutionalization relocates power from individuals to institutions, creates the abiding rules and procedures in policy making so as to improve the stability and consistency of the policy process, and provides plural legal channels through institutions for the expression of diverse socioeconomic interests so as to reduce the anxiety and tension caused by the dilemma of the single-party dictatorship versus diverse interests. All this may be the reason for Tang Tsou's claim that "a formal process" can "enhance the capability of the [CCP] political system."[26] As we observed in the post-Stalin Soviet Union, institutional arrangements improved communication and coordination among the policy makers; the due procedures checked the abuse of personal ties in political affairs; and the interaction of institutional interests overrode personal interests in policy making. Ironically, all this enabled the Soviet state to play the essential role in policy making at the expense of the party organization.[27]

Yet the institutionalization has been strikingly deficient in CCP politics, though the effort was made at least twice during the Mao and Deng periods. The first effort was seen at the 1956 Eighth Party Congress (PC). The major concern of this congress was the transformation of the CCP from a revolutionary organization to a ruling party.[28] The necessity of institutionalization was stressed; collective leadership was enforced; the two-front arrangement was formalized (see Chapter 4); Mao's role was cautiously downplayed; and Mao Zedong Thought was dropped from the Party Constitution.[29]

---

entire economy in the hands of the bureaucrats. It would be a real surprise had such a bureaucracy not been rotten and eventually ossified. But we can also view this from a positive perspective because the "ossified bureaucracy" hastened the demise of the Soviet communist regime.

26 Tang Tsou, *The Cultural Revolution and Post-Mao Reform: A Historical Perspective*, Chicago: University of Chicago Press, 1986, p. 108.
27 Cf. Colton, "Moscow's party organization," pp. 46–52, 56–9.
28 Cf. *Jueyi*, Article 15.
29 See MacFarquhar, *The Origins of the Cultural Revolution,* 1: *Contradictions among the People, 1956–1957*, New York: Columbia University Press, 1974, chap. 8, esp. pp. 99–109. Xu Qingqing and Wang Diming at the CCP Central Archives, "*Mao Zedong lingdao le bada wenjian de qicao gongzuo*" (Mao Zedong led the work of the drafting of the Eighth PC documents), pp. 64–6, argue that Liu Shaoqi had little to do with down-

Factionalism in Chinese Communist Politics

Nevertheless, as I explain in detail in Chapter 4, the drive for institutionalization in 1956 was not so much a self-conscious effort as an instinctive response to the 1954 Gao-Rao Affair, and even more to the fear of instability caused by the "unprincipled" but brutal succession struggles in Soviet politics.[30] Thus, the emphasis on collective leadership stemmed from the collective desire for an "institutional guarantee" (*zhidu shang de baozheng*) for a smooth power transition in succession, and Mao's low profile at the congress was actually a precaution to prevent a CCP

playing Mao's role and dropping Mao Zedong Thought from the Party's Constitution, given the personnel arrangements in the drafting group of the Party Constitution and the official record that the group was working under Mao's supervision instead of Liu's. Yet the new information they reveal has actually made MacFarquhar's questions more significant: (1) Who made the decision or, more precisely, who tacitly consented to downplaying Mao's role and dropping Mao Zedong Thought? (2) Why, how, and when was the decision made? It may be true that the drafting group was officially under Mao's supervision. But this list, which is revealed for the first time, including An Ziwen, Liu Lantao, Song Renqiong, Li Xuefeng, Hu Qiaomu, Ma Mingfang, Yang Shangkun, Deng Xiaoping, and Tan Zhenlin, shows the remarkable influence of Liu: An, Liu, Li, Hu, and Yang were all from Liu's mountaintop. To put this group under Mao's *nominal* supervision does not mean that Mao is in actual charge of the drafting; rather, it indicates that the issue was so sensitive that nobody, except for Mao himself, was able to take official responsibility for its consequences.

Second, Xu and Wang emphasize that *"none* of the CC leaders ever suggested adding the part about Mao Zedong Thought in the Party Constitution of the Seventh PC to [the new one of the Eighth PC] during its five drafts" (p. 66). This statement throws more doubt rather than light on the issue: how could Mao's comrades be so insensitive about the dropping of Mao Zedong Thought, which they had proudly written into the Party Constitution at the Seventh PC? Unfortunately, Xu and Wang did not offer any explanations.

Third, Xu and Wang claim that no one had questioned the dropping of Mao Zedong Thought during the entire drafting process, because "there was a *generally accepted attitude of understanding within the Party (leadership)* for the dropping of Mao Zedong Thought from the Party Constitution" (p. 66). How was this attitude created and "generally accepted"?

Fourth, Xu and Wang claim that the documents of the Eighth PC, especially the "Resolution on the Political Report," were not done in a rush as MacFarquhar observed, but through careful discussions. But only a few lines later they acknowledge that Mao had to read the drafts of the "Resolution" during the nights of September 24 and 26 in order to send out his opinion "before the night was over"; and by the time Mao read over the final draft, it was already 2:00 A.M. on September 26, the very day the document was to be approved by the Eighth PC.

30 Bo Yibo, *Ruogan zhongda juece yu shijian de huigu* (Review of Several Important Decisions and Events), Beijing: CCP Party School Press, 1991, 1:472 (hereafter *Huigu*), recalls that after the CPSU's Twentieth Congress, Mao warned repeatedly that the CCP should "take [the events in] the Soviet Union as a mirror [*yisu weijian*]."

The Political System in China

version of the post-Stalin drama.[31] The lack of an essential understanding of and determination on institutionalization among the CCP leaders sowed the seeds for the eventual failure of the effort they made at the Eighth PC. The institutionalization was confined to economic policy making, but barely existent in the political areas like ideology and propaganda, massive political campaigns, personnel arrangements, and the military commanding system. Moreover, the relationship between the Party and its leaders, particularly Mao, was never ascertained. It was in these areas that Mao initiated struggles leading to the CR, which not only "eventually denied the correct line of the Eighth PC," but also destroyed the entire Party establishment (see Chapter 5).[32]

The second effort was initiated by Deng Xiaoping after he prevailed in the struggle with the "whatever faction" in 1978.[33] In his speech at the Enlarged Politburo Meeting in August 1980, Deng emphasized the importance of reforming "the institutions of the Party and state leadership" in order to "prevent the power from overconcentrating in the hands of individuals."[34] This speech was republished on July 1, 1987, as reform leaders resumed the offensive in the struggle against the conservatives after Hu Yaobang's resignation in January 1987. Wan Li, a close associate of Deng, published an article on the first page of *People's Daily*, arguing that institutionalization of the policy process is "the key to the political reform."[35]

Although the CCP leaders were earnest in their effort of institutionalization this time – they surely should have learned the lesson well – their effort only led to fierce factional struggles for power essentially because none of the elite members was willing to compromise his power in the absence of an absolute authority like Mao. Thus, the CCP leaders failed to reach any consensus on the scope, the pace, and the methods of institutionalization, while each of them attempted to capitalize on the opportunity that the ongoing redistribution of power had provided (see Chapter 7).

31 Cf. MacFarquhar, *The Origins*, 1:43–8, 105–9.
32 Cf. *Jueyi*, Articles 17, 21, 23.
33 See Harry Harding, *China's Second Revolution*, Washington, DC: Brookings Institution, 1987, esp. pp. 202–36.
34 See *SWDXP*, pp. 302–25. *Zhidu* in Chinese can mean "system" and/or "institutions," depending on the context. In *SWDXP*, as in all the writings by the CCP leaders, *zhidu* is translated indiscriminately as *system*. But *zhidu* in this speech refers to the *institutions* of leadership, rather than the CCP *system*.   35 *PD*, July 1, 1987.

The failure of institutionalization has exerted a far-reaching effect on the political process in China. First, the administrative buildup was problem-oriented. The government agencies were set up largely in response to the emerging problems. There were few thought-through designs on how best to utilize the available resources to achieve the desired policy goals. As a result, whenever a policy process was triggered by an emerging problem, the tasks of the relevant offices would be respecified to see if any new ones needed to be set up to improve effectiveness, or any existing ones be abolished to increase efficiency. Whether a new agency was established or an existing one abolished, the process itself created an opportunity for the involved leaders to grasp more resources, hence more power in the policy process.

Nevertheless, the administration has kept growing as more and more offices were set up or expanded to cope with the newly emerged problems, and such a growth was unplanned and hence poorly coordinated. A paradox has resulted: a centralized system together with the cellular structure of the policy-making process, characteristics that have been captured in the literature.[36] On the one hand, even a small issue tends to rise to the top level for a decision because the agency in charge is not empowered to coordinate the relevant offices to execute the decision it has made. On the other hand, difficulties in coordinating the cellularly structured government agencies have made the intervention by powerful leaders crucial for the working of the system. Thus, an elite member's leadership is evaluated by his ability to broker power in political affairs and to arbitrate endless conflicts between his subordinates in the policy process. Not surprisingly, given the noninstitutionalized environment, those who have penetrating and widespread *guanxi* networks would be in an advantageous position in such a situation.

Second, communication and coordination become difficult in the noninstitutionalized political process because there are few legally defined channels to secure the exchange of ideas, opinions, and information. As we have observed repeatedly in the past decades, the stratified structure of the policy process has often skewed or even blocked the information needed by the policy makers. When differences occur in the

---

36 Cf. Kenneth Lieberthal and Michael Oksenberg, *Policy Making in China: Leaders, Structure, and Processes*, Princeton: Princeton University Press, 1988, pp. 135–7.

The Political System in China

policy process, a leader may be reluctant to release the information he has obtained because, as game theory teaches us, there is little chance for a sincere actor to prevail in a game that is played with incomplete information.[37] Again, *guanxi* networks become necessary for the policy makers to exchange information and formulate the preferences among the associates in the policy process.

Third, as I will further elaborate, the lack of institutionalization makes the policy process vulnerable to crisis whenever the status quo breaks down. Although majority rule is emphasized as a principle in all the CCP constitutions, any outcomes, as McKelvey has proved, are possible in a given policy space under majority rule.[38] Institutional arrangements are necessary not only to prevent the policy process from collapsing but also to secure the stability of the outcomes.[39] The deficiency in institutional arrangements in CCP politics has resulted in dependency on powerful leaders in decision making, because policy outcomes rest on these leaders' ability to manipulate the interactions in the policy-making process.

Last, it would be foolish for anyone to abide by the adopted rules and procedures in the policy process because these rules and procedures could be easily overridden by the intervention of a higher authority who is coordinating the parallel subordinates. Given the inevitable conflicts in the cellularly structured policy process, the uncertainty about the rules and procedures further aggravates the dependency on a personalized authority for the daily operation of the system.

As a result, *guanxi* thrives in politics. People cultivate and exploit *guanxi* because of the obvious benefits it can bring to them – the subordinate gets advantage and protection, and the superior enjoys support and loyalty. More significantly, more often than not *guanxi* is the only practical way to obtain the necessary information and get things done promptly. As a result, the *guanxi* networks have become an important

---

37 See Ordeshook, *Game Theory and Political Theory*, chap. 6, esp. pp. 291–8.
38 See Richard D. McKelvey, "Intransitivities in multidimensional voting models and some implications for agenda control," *Journal of Economic Theory*, 16 (1976), pp. 472–82. See also Robin Farquharson, *Theory of Voting*, New Haven, CT: Yale University Press, 1969.
39 See Kenneth Shepsle and Barry Weingast, "Structure-induced equilibrium and legislative choice," pp. 503–19. See also Gordon Tullock, "Why so much stability," *Public Choice*, 37 (1981), pp. 189–202, for an alternate argument.

political resource whereby one can draw the power necessary to muscle through the administrative morass and to prevail in disputes. The abuse of *guanxi* networks eventually transforms them from personal ties forged through comradeship or friendship into factional linkages based on common interests.

> *Proposition 4*: The lack of institutionalization makes the policy process vulnerable to crisis when there are differences in kind among the policy makers. When such a situation emerges, the dominant leader has to resort to military support to solve the crisis. Repeated military involvement provides another sufficient condition for the development of factionalism because it consolidates the pattern of personal entrustment of power and, therefore, reinforces factional alignments.

Military Involvement

Military intervention in policy making is not unexpected, given that the regime was established through the armed struggle for power. Although the Party's principle is that "the Party commands the gun,"[40] such a principle was a facade during the Mao and Deng periods, concealing Mao's and Deng's personal authority, which kept the military under control (see Chapters 3 and 7). Thus, more often than not the military was involved in politics not necessarily because the CCP system was in danger, but because the supreme leader's position was challenged, either in a policy dispute or in a power struggle.

This is not surprising given the pattern of personal entrustment of power through which the generals' loyalty toward the supreme leader was cultivated. What must be highlighted here, however, is that the unique system of *zhuanye* has enabled the military leaders to extend their factional networks into the civilian system. As a result, military involvement is not just a phenomenon at the central level but has happened systematically, becoming an integral part of the CCP political machinery.

Moreover, the lack of insitutionalization makes military intervention a necessary and the most effective instrument for the dominant leaders

---

40 *SWMZD*, 2:224.

The Political System in China

to solve a policy crisis. As I have already discussed, a major consequence of deficient institutional arrangements in policy making is that the policy process is bound to collapse when there are differences in kind among the policy makers.[41] A formal process of policy making is necessary because the rules and due procedures embodied in this process "can induce stability even if social preferences are intransitive, whereas the outcome that prevails depends on the particular procedure used."[42]

But in CCP politics where the rules and procedures of policy making are rarely abiding – they could be easily overridden by the authority of the supreme leader – a policy crisis tended to emerge whenever there were differences in kind among the leaders. To solve this crisis, the supreme leader had to resort to military intervention to enforce his policy choice so as to ensure the operation of the system. What Mao and Deng did in the launching of the CR and in the 1989 crisis, for example, represents the extremes of military intervention on behalf of the supreme leader in order to solve the policy crisis.

Military intervention reinforces the pattern of personal entrustment of power. While it can certainly help strengthen the supreme leader's authority, a more significant impact is that military intervention breaks the status quo in leadership relations, and hence creates new opportunities for those who have prevailed to expand their *guanxi* networks in the redistribution of power. In retrospect, every time the military was involved in political affairs, an adjustment in the distribution of power would follow; and the process of redistribution of power was not immune to yet a new round of military intervention given the military connections in leadership relations. The larger an adjustment, the stronger and more violent the military intervention.

Repeated military intervention has promoted and consolidated factional alignments in CCP politics because it reinforces *guanxi* networks formed through personal entrustment of power. That is why a CCP leader could not dominate without military support, no matter how influential he appeared in the policy process. Leaders like Liu Shaoqi in the Mao period and Chen Yun in the Deng period were typical examples.

---

41 See Thomas Schwartz, *The Logic of Collective Choice*, New York: Columbia University Press, 1986, pp. 12–17.
42 Ordeshook, *Game Theory and Political Theory*, p. 257.

FACTIONAL ACTIVITIES AND THE SHAPING OF LEADERSHIP RELATIONS

The factional activities we have observed among the CCP leaders stem from the faction-ridden nature of leadership relations, rather than from interactions among them in the policy-making process. The following is a depiction of how factionalism has affected leadership relations and how leaders maintain control in the political process.

Proposition 5: *Guanxi* is the most crucial factor in the cadre promotion or demotion system. The most effective way to cultivate and/or expand factional linkages is to promote cadres through *guanxi* networks. Thus, changes in personnel arrangements usually result from an adjustment in the distribution of power among various factions, rather than any adjustments in policy making.

Guanxi *and the Formation of Factional Networks*

An incumbent in China is appointed by his superior(s) instead of winning his office through an open competition. There are few rules and regulations for cadre promotion.[43] Although talent and virtue (which means loyalty to the Party) are always stressed, and a "cadre examination system" was introduced in the mid 1980s,[44] what really counts in a cadre appointment is the appointee's *guanxi* to his superior; ability and virtue are of secondary importance.

This practice paved the way for the cultivation of factional linkages.

---

43 The Party authority in the rural areas virtually collapsed after the People's Commune was abolished. Nowadays a grass-roots cadre is often elected rather than appointed. While this is one of the most significant changes the reform has brought to the political system, most of the leading cadres at the township level and all the leaders at the county level and above are still appointed by the higher authority.

44 A cadre must go through the process of "self-recommendation or nomination by the superior, mass appraisal, and assessment of higher authorities" before he can be promoted. But the key point is the "assessment of higher authorities"; and it is uncertain whether this system is seriously carried out. But even this half-minded effort was aborted after the May 1989 crisis. Political *biaoxian* (performance) has been reemphasized as the top priority in cadre promotion.

The Political System in China

When a position is open, leaders at the equal authority level often have different candidates for it, because they see the appointment as a chance to expand their influence. Thus, the appointment becomes a zero-sum game in which one's gain means the other's loss. If the involved leaders are equally powerful, the appointment will involve a complicated bargaining process among them. Not surprisingly, the final outcome often appears as a "package": when a candidate is confirmed, the new appointments or transfers of other incumbents are also made as a compromise with the leaders who have failed to put their candidates on the position. Such cases have been repeatedly observed in the post-Mao period during which an absolute authority like Mao was absent in CCP politics.

More important is the consequence of the appointment. The promotion has shown to all the existence of *guanxi* between the newly promoted incumbent and the superior who made the appointment – they are now in the same boat. So the inferior will do what he can to support the superior; meanwhile, the latter has to do his best to protect his appointee, for his failure will at least prove this leader's poor judgment, or even destroy the power base he has entrusted to his appointee because his rival will take the advantage by filling the vacancy with someone whose loyalty is not toward him. As a result, the former *guanxi* between the leader and his appointees is transformed into factional linkages that embody their common interests and well-being.

The coerciveness of this relationship on both the leader and his followers is perhaps best demonstrated by the 1971 Lin Biao Affair, the 1987 Hu Yaobang resignation, and Zhao Ziyang's fall in the May 1989 crisis. As I elaborate later, the biggest losers in these cases were not necessarily the inferiors, Lin, Hu, or Zhao, who were victimized or even killed, but their patrons, namely Mao and Deng, whose positions were undermined to the extent that they were never able to restore their former dominance. Mao never recovered his former status, mentally or physically, after Lin's death. The fact that Mao was increasingly isolated from the other leaders, both in the left and the right wings, and appeared more and more Machiavellian indicated that the charm of his leadership was no longer irresistible and that he was less and less confident of his ability to control. In Deng's case, his momentum was brought to a halt when Hu was toppled, and reversed altogether after Zhao's fall.[45]

Factional linkages in CCP politics can in fact be traced from a top leader down to the grass-root levels of authority. These linkages are quite different from the patron-client ties I discuss in Chapter 1, although both types of relationship do share some basic elements. A factional linkage has the following characteristics:

1 A factional linkage is secured by the common political interests.
2 Its crux is the exchange of political obligations that concern the well-being of both participants in a hierarchic context.
3 It is equally coercive to both participants. Abrogation by either of them can bring about damage or even disaster to both participants.
4 Each participant holds a position of authority at a given level. But direct relations usually exist only between the superior and his immediate inferiors.
5 A factional linkage is not inclusive. Although a leader can develop such linkages with the other followers so as to maximize his support, it will be disastrous for a follower to seek multiple linkages with more than one leader. This would give a leader enough reason to suspect his loyalty and hence to withdraw his protection.
6 It can be extended: both ends can be linked to the next higher or lower level of authority in the same fashion.

It has long been observed that an ordinary officer or cadre in China is rarely transferred out of the army or system where he began his career.[46] This phenomenon can be explained from the factionalism perspective: an officer or a cadre has been knit into factional networks after working in his army or system for years. The officer or cadre who is moved out of his army or system will be uncomfortable in a new environment where he is alien to the factional networks there. More signifi-

---

45 Some pundits worried that "Deng has no sense yet of the damage he has done" in the May 1989 crisis (Robert Jacobson, "China after-shocks," *Chronicle of Higher Education*, Washington DC, July 19, 1989, p. A30). This is unnecessary, for Deng was well aware what the damage was. What we have to figure out is why Deng's decision that seemed incredibly irrational turned out to be the *only* rational choice for Deng at the time.
46 See William Whitson, *The Chinese High Command*, New York: Praeger, 1978. Though the distinction between the field armies has faded away since the beginning of professionalization in the early 1980s, an officer is rarely moved out of his army or, if his rank is high, his regional military command. For the cadres, see Doak Barnett, *Cadres, Bureaucracy, and Political Power in China*, New York: Columbia University Press, 1967.

The Political System in China

cantly, such a move will break the factional chain in his previous system because it cuts off the factional linkage that has been established through years of cultivation. The higher his rank, the bigger the shock. But to move along in the same system is more manageable.

Proposition 6: A leader's power is essentially based on the strength of his factional networks. The leaders who have the most access to factional networks dominate.

Factionalism and Leadership Relations

Factional networks are a result of years of cultivation. Given that the regime was established after twenty-one years of armed struggle for power, most of the veteran CCP leaders had strong factional connections with the military. Liu Shaoqi and Gao Gang, however, deserve special attention, not just because of their more prominent civilian backgrounds, but because of their similar paths to power. Both were excellent organizers whose support of Mao was indispensable for him to expand his command from the military to the whole Party at the expense of the Moscow-trained Wang Ming faction (see Chapter 3). Liu's remarkable success in restoring and expanding the CCP organization in North China in the late 1930s laid the ground for the rapid development of the communist forces in this area during the Anti-Japanese War.[47] Gao Gang played a crucial role in the establishment of Mao's command during the Yan'an period: as head of the CCP Northwest Bureau and a native of northern Shaanxi, Gao provided the necessary support to Mao in his struggle against the Wang Ming faction. True, Mao's trust and patronage were necessary for their dramatic rise to power – in a few years Liu became Mao's second in command and Gao entered the Politburo despite his junior status (see Chapter 3). Yet a more significant factor in their rise was the substantial strength they had developed in the CCP organizations, which, not surprisingly, made them the brightest stars in CCP politics immediately after 1949.

Kang Sheng's assignment in February 1949 provided a contrary example. Although Kang was a senior leader with Mao's trust, he had few reliable ties with either the CCP organizations or the military. Thus, he was assigned to a humble position – the secretary of the CCP

---

47 See Hao and Duan, *Liushi nian*, pp. 187–94, 201–2, 217–21.

Shandong Subbureau under the leadership of Rao Shushi, secretary of the East China Bureau who was junior to Kang. Such a position suggested a radical decline of Kang's power in political affairs.[48]

The strength of factional networks is best shown in the changes in leadership relations, especially during the periods of transition. As I explain in Chapter 6, those who rose to power after the massive purges in 1966–7 were not only the Maoists such as Chen Boda, Kang Sheng, Jiang Qing, and Zhang Chunqiao, but also the regional leaders like Li Desheng, Chen Xilian, Ji Dengkui, Hua Guofeng, and Wei Guoqing, who, as local military leaders, had the power and ability to rebuild the local authorities and factional networks after the old ones collapsed. These new leaders, however, never retained the power the senior leaders like Liu Shaoqi, Deng Xiaoping, and Peng Zhen had possessed because they could not in a short period of time build up the factional networks penetrating the entire system. Their eminence was caused either by their close relations with Mao, in the case of the Maoists, or, in the case of the regional leaders, by their newly developed local power bases. As a result, although Mao repeatedly expressed his dismay about his cult, his deification was necessary because of the sharply skewed distribution of power on the one hand and the lack of personal acquaintance between Mao and the newly promoted leaders on the other. The unprecedented emphasis on loyalty to Mao reflected the extraordinarily unbalanced distribution of power.

Ironically, Lin Biao, the only surviving senior leader who had strong factional networks, suffered from this situation. When Lin established his control of the PLA central command after the 1968 Yang (Chengwu)-Yu (Lijin)-Fu (Congbi) Affair,[49] the newly developed local factions were

---

48 Zhong Kang, *Kang Sheng pingzhuan* (A Critical Biography of Kang Sheng), Beijing: Red Flag Press, 1982, pp. 106–11. Kang and Rao joined the CCP at about the same time. But Kang entered the Politburo at the Fifth Plenum of the Sixth PC (January 1934) and played an important role in the 1941–3 Yan'an Rectification, when Mao's command was established. Kang's unhappiness about this position was illustrated by the fact that he feigned illness until Rao fell in 1954.
49 Yang was acting chief of staff, Yu, air force commissar, and Fu, commander of the Beijing Garrison. All three were toppled on March 22, 1968, for "scheming a coup" (see Chapter 6). They were replaced by Lin's followers Huang Yongsheng, Wu Faxian (concurrently CO of the air force), and Wen Yucheng. At that time, Li Zuopeng and Qiu Huizuo, also Lin's men, had already been the navy commissar and director of the General Logistic Department. Thus, the PLA Headquarters was under the control of Lin's faction.

too strong to be subdued.[50] This gave Mao the decisive edge for the forthcoming Mao-Lin strife. After the Beijing Regional Command, where Lin's faction had substantial influence, was reorganized following the North China Conference (December 22, 1970–January 25, 1971),[51] Vice-Commander Lin appeared helpless and could only rely on his twenty-six-year-old son Lin Liguo, who, together with a handful of his sworn followers, schemed to assassinate Mao. When the plot was aborted, Lin was doomed.

Lin Biao's fall exacerbated the incoherence of leadership relations. Soon, it was clear that the Control Committee (CC) leadership had difficulty controlling the situation.[52] True, the intensifying conflict between Zhou Enlai and the Gang of Four was an obvious factor, but a more profound reason was that none of the elite members had total control of the factional networks. As I examine in Chapter 6, Deng's comeback in 1974 was surprising but logical: he was the only one who had both Mao's trust and, more importantly, access to the factional networks in both the army and civilian systems due to his long military career and rich administrative experience. With Mao's support, the first thing Deng did after his return was to shuffle the commanders of the eight major regional commands in order to cut off these regional bigwigs with their faction networks. This not only enabled the CCP leadership to quickly restore its control but also paved the way for Deng to tame local factional networks during his nationwide rectification in 1975. The rapid expansion of Deng's force not only led to a new prisoners' dilemma between Mao and

---

50 All commanders and commissars of the eleven major RMCs joined the CC. Jurgen Domes, *The Government and Politics of the PRC: A Time of Transition*, Boulder, CO: Westview Press, 1985, pp. 56–7, observed that the percentage of the officers increased from 31% in the Eighth CC to over 50% in the Ninth, and more significantly, the percentage of *regional* military leaders increased from 2.2% in the Eighth CC to 26.6% in the Ninth.

51 The meeting was convened at Mao's request to "criticize Chen Boda." But Zhou Enlai, who presided over the meeting, caught the attendees by surprise by announcing in his summary speech on the last day (January 24, 1971) that the CCP leadership, namely Mao, had decided to reorganize the Beijing Regional Command. This threw Lin and his people into panic. See Jin Daying, "*9.13 shijian shimuo ji*" (The whole story of the September 13 Incident), *Shidai de baogao* (Reports of an Era), 4 (December 1980).

52 The situation quickly deteriorated in 1973. In 1974 the growth of the GNP dropped to 1.4% – the lowest since 1962. See Fang Weizhong, *Zhonghua renmin gongheguo jingji dashi ji, 1949–1980* (The Economic Chronology of the PRC, 1949–1980), Beijing: Chinese Social Science Academy Press, 1984, pp. 538–9 (hereafter *Jingji dashi ji*).

Deng, but also tended to "reverse the verdict of the CR" (see Chapter 6). Deng fell again in early 1976, and Hua Guofeng, the new player Mao brought in the game, was the winner.

Factionalism became increasingly prominent in the shaping of leadership relations after Mao's death in 1976. On the one hand, no one has ever obtained the absolute command Mao had. Although Deng maintained his dominance in policy making due to his exclusive access to the factional networks in both the Party and military systems, his inability to provide his reform policy with ideological justification made him vulnerable to criticism, especially in the ideological field (see Chapter 7). Thus, Deng tended to seek compromises, rather than to engage in a "life-and-death struggle" as Mao used to, with his opponents in a conflict. This resulted in more and increasingly overt factional activities in political affairs, for frequent deal makings constantly exposed the involved factions' strength and alignments. Meanwhile, Deng became increasingly dependent on military support in an effort to carry out his reform policy. The increasing role of the military in policy making further consolidated factional alignments.

On the other hand, few central elite members, either the veterans who had survived the CR or the new rising stars, had factional networks as penetrating and widespread as those of the pre-CR elite members, partly due to the massive damage to the old mountaintops, but in large part due to the lack of *guanxi* among the new-generation leaders, especially between the Party elite who rose as technocrats and the new generals who were promoted as professional soldiers. As a result, a tendency that emerged in the later years of the Mao period has been further consolidated in CCP politics. That is, the leaders who have access to regional factional networks have been increasingly influential in policy making, whereas the power and influence of those whose power bases rest in "systems" (*xitong*) have steadily declined.[53] The increasing power of the

---

53 Those who enjoyed strong support from the regional factional networks include leaders like Peng Zhen (Beijing), Zhao Ziyang (South China, Sichuan), Wan Li (Anhuai, Shandong), Li Ruihuan (Tianjin), Zhu Rongji (Shanghai), Ye Xuanping (Guandong), Jiang Chunyun (Shandong), and even Jiang Zemin himself, who has been labeled as the head of the Shanghai faction. The leaders whose support comes mainly from the systems include Qiao Shi (interior), Hu Yaobang (the CYLC), Bo Yibo (finance and planning), Li Peng (hydraulic power), Li Lanqing (education and culture), and Yao Yilin (commerce and finance).

regional authorities can be attributed to very complicated causes,[54] but a significant consequence is that policy making is no longer dominated by a few central predominant factions. It is true that substantial involvement of regional factional networks in CCP politics embodies a potential threat to stability, but it also broadens political participation and, more important, it gradually but steadily undermines the uncompromising nature of the single-party dictatorship. From this perspective, the increasing role of factionalism in CCP politics may promote, rather than hinder, China's overall development toward a pluralistic system (see Conclusion).

> *Proposition 7*: Any significant changes in leadership relations will followed by a *zhengdun* (rectification) in the entire system in order to eliminate the fallen leaders' factional networks and, more important, to consolidate and expand the ones of those who have prevailed in the struggle. The larger a change is, the bigger and more penetrating a *zhengdun* campaign.

Factionalism and the Zhengdun Campaigns

The CCP leaders have developed and benefited from the factional networks. Yet factionalism has posed a serious problem for them, especially when a crisis provokes radical changes in leadership relations, because

---

54 Some attribute the rise of regional power to "decentralization" during the reform. They argue that such a trend hinders China's development because it undermines political stability, weakens the "overall capability" of the Chinese state, and ultimately encourages fragmentation. So, as they suggest, "decentralization" must be halted and the central authority must be strengthened. This "decentralization" argument is misleading. The power of a government is defined in two dimensions. First, the scope of its governance, in which decentralization should occur because it means that a central government confines its governance to a smaller scope and lets the local authorities take care of more policy areas; and, second, the effectiveness of its authority, which has little to do with decentralization. The "decentralization" argument confuses the two dimensions. What the CCP leadership suffers from nowadays is not so much "decentralization" as the decrease in its authority. As a matter of fact, the "scope" of China's central government still remains extraordinarily large, and it can still intervene in many areas if it wants to. The essential source of the rise of regionalism is the increasing regional gap, which is caused mainly by the policy-induced uneven development across China in the past twenty years. See Jing Huang, "*Buduan kuoda de diqu chaju jiqi dui woguo zhengzhi anding de yingxiang*" (The increase in regional differences and its impact on political stability in our country), *Gaige* (Reform), no. 5 (August 1996), pp. 34–8.

political factions are very sensitive to changes that can directly affect members' political well-being. Any rise or fall of a leader can set off a series of domino responses among the factional networks which extend throughout the system. Unless checked effectively, these responses can lead to a chaotic situation that will jeopardize political stability. Moreover, the toppling of a leader does not necessarily mean that his influence is eliminated. As long as his factional networks remain intact, he can still have substantial influence in political affairs. This is a potential threat to stability as well as the existing leadership. The extent to which the dominant leaders can destroy the factional networks of the toppled leader(s) will to a large degree determine whether he can make a later comeback.

A solution to this problem is to consolidate the dominant factional networks at the costs of the defeated ones. For this purpose, a top-down campaign in the entire system will be launched whenever there is a dramatic change in leadership relations. Such a campaign is called *zhengdun*, or rectification. Its tasks include: *rectification*, in order to achieve the political consensus; *reorganization*, in order to eliminate the fallen leader's factional networks; and *consolidation*, in order to stabilize the situation under the dominant leader. The bigger the changes in leadership relations, the larger a *zhengdun* campaign. In retrospect, whenever there was a purge among the CCP leaders, a top-down *zhengdun* would be launched (Table 2.1).

The process of *zhengdun* is illustrated in Figure 2.1. Its focus is on the leadership at each level of authority. By "integrating the criticism [of the fallen leader] with the local reality [*lianxi bendi shiji*]," *zhengdun* is aimed at eliminating the fallen leader's "pernicious influence organizationally as well as ideologically." As Deng Xiaoping points out, a *zhengdun* campaign is to wipe out "factionalism" and build up "a tough and able leading body" that will keep in step with the CC leadership at each level of authority,[55] needless to say that those who are accused of "factionalism" are the members of the defeated factions. So the struggles against them "will have the support of the CC and the provincial Party committees."[56]

However, a *zhengdun* campaign may fail to achieve its goals if the

---

55 See "On the general principle of our work," *PD*, October 7, 1975.
56 *SWDXP*, pp. 18–19.

The Political System in China

Table 2.1. *Elite Conflicts and* Zhengdun *(Rectification) Campaigns since 1949*

Changes in Leadership	Name of *Zhengdun*/Year	Focus Areas
Gao-Rao Affair	*Zhengdun*, 1954	East/Northeast China
Peng Dehuai's fall	Antirightist deviation, 1959–61	Army/Party organization
Purge of the Party leaders	Exposing and criticizing the capitalist roaders, 1966–8	Entire system
Chen Boda's fall	Criticizing Chen and rectification, 1970–1	Ideology and propaganda
Lin Biao Incident	Criticizing Lin and rectification, 1970–1	Entire system, especially in the army
Deng Xiaoping's comeback	*Zhengdun*, 1975	Entire system
Zhou's death and Deng's second fall	Counterattacking the right-deviationist restoration, 1976	Entire system
The fall of the Gang of Four	Exposing and criticizing the Gang of Four, 1976–8	Entire system
Toppling of Hua Guofeng	Exposing and criticizing the "three-category people," 1979–85	Entire system, especially in administration
Toppling of Hu Yaobang	Antispiritual pollution, 1986–7	Party and administration
Zhao Ziyang's fall	Rectifying the Party, 1989–91	Entire system

factional networks of the toppled leader are so strong that their resistance turns the campaign into a facade (*zou guo chang*). This can also happen when more than one leader shares the dominance at the Center. An example of the first case is the campaign of Counterattacking the Right-Deviationist Restoration in 1976, aimed at eliminating Deng Xiaoping's influence. This *zhengdun* went essentially nowhere, although the propaganda controlled by the Gang of Four made it appear mammoth to the public. The essential reason was that few among the central leaders, including Hua Guofeng, and particularly the Gang of

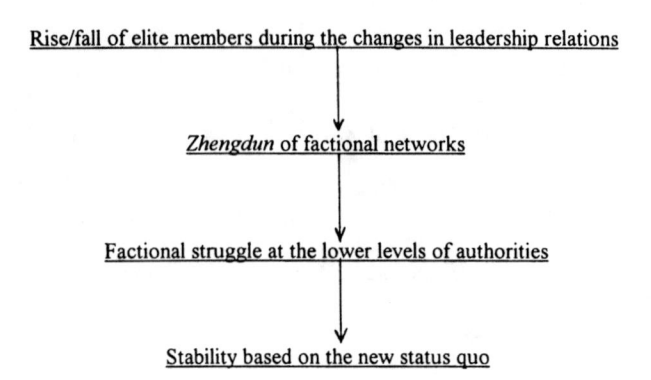

```
Rise/fall of elite members during the changes in leadership relations
                            |
                            v
            Zhengdun of factional networks
                            |
                            v
       Factional struggle at the lower levels of authorities
                            |
                            v
             Stability based on the new status quo
```

Figure 2.1. The process of a *zhengdun* (rectification) campaign

Four, had any access to the factional networks in various systems and localities. The failure of this *zhengdun* guaranteed Deng Xiaoping's quick comeback in late 1977 and, more important, the establishment of his dominance in 1978–9.

An example of the second case is the 1979–85 *zhengdun*, which was launched after Hua's "whatever" faction was cornered by the Deng-Chen (Yun) coalition. The first half of this *zhengdun* was effective. By the time of the Eleventh PC in September 1982, the "three-category people" (*san zhong ren*) had either been driven out of the administration and military or demoted to insignificant positions.[57] Thus, the Maoists and the beneficiaries of the CR were deprived of their power bases. Thereafter, however, this *zhengdun* slowed down because every elite member tried to take advantage of the campaign to expand his own forces in the absence of a hegemonic faction. As the campaign became an endless power struggle among the existing mountaintops, the second half of this *zhengdun*, which was the longest in the CCP history, was barely carried to the provincial level.[58] It failed to achieve the desired

---

57 "The three-category people" refers to (1) the followers of the Gang of Four, (2) the rebels who rose to power during the CR, and (3) those who beat the other people, smashed the state's property, and looted the others' belongings during the CR. The ultimate task of this *zhengdun* was to eliminate those who had risen to power during the CR from the Party and the administration.

58 Hu Yaobang, "*Zai quanguo dangdaihui kaimushi shang de jianghua*" (Opening speech at the CCP National Conference), *Xuandu*, 2:915, announced that the *zhengdun* "would

cooperation between the reformers and the conservatives who had been allies in the struggle against the "whatever" faction, nor did it increase the central authority as had been expected. On the contrary, the collective authority of the central leaders decreased to its lowest ebb while the local factional networks consolidated themselves under the patronage of their bosses who were struggling for dominance.

A significant phenomenon during *zhengdun* is the massive transfer of leading cadres. For example, in the two *zhengdun* that covered the period from the 1982 Twelfth PC to the early 1990s, personnel assignments at the provincial level were thoroughly rearranged – the transsystem rearrangements of the subleaders were done three times in this period.[59] The large-scale reorganizations at the subordinate levels of authority demonstrated how promptly the factional networks responded to the changes in leadership relations.

The transfer of subordinate leaders during a *zhengdun* serves as a double-edged sword in factional politics. For the fallen leaders' factional networks, a massive transfer of subleaders cuts off the links between these leaders and their supporters, so it undermines the former's position while making it easier to reorganize the latter. Meanwhile, leaders from the dominant factions are sent to the places where those of the defeated factions either have been purged or have moved away. Thus, if a transfer of a subordinate leader is to undermine his faction, he is moved alone, so that he will immediately become powerless in the new environment where he is alien to the factional networks there, though he may be given the same or even a higher position. Examples are numerous, such as the reshuffling of commanders of the regional commands in 1974, the "promotion" of Xu Shiyou to the National People's Congress (NPC) as a vice-chairman in the early 1980s, Mao Zhiyong's transfer from Hunan to Jiangxi as the first Party secretary in 1984, and the "promotion" of Ye Xuanping to the CC leadership in 1990.

But if a transfer of a subordinate leader is to strengthen a dominant faction, he will usually bring a group of his supporters to his new place and assign them to crucial positions, so that they can quickly and effectively take over the local factional networks. We saw that cadres from

be brought to a temporary end" as all the leading bodies from the central level down to the provincial level in the administration and to the divisional level in the military had been reorganized.

59 Yan, "*Zhongguo dalu zhengzhi tizhi qianlun*," p. 18.

the Communist Youth League of China (CYLC), where Hu Yaobang had been the first secretary, and from Guangdong and Sichuan, where Zhao Ziyang had been the first Party secretary, appeared simultaneously in Beijing when Hu and Zhao were promoted to the top leadership in the late 1970s. The second generation of "returned students" also have occupied quite a few important offices in Beijing after Li Peng entered the Politburo on September 24, 1985. Noticeably, virtually all the prominent leaders have worked in more than two systems or regions, ensuring strong support from widespread factional networks.

The preceding discussion has touched upon an important problem in relations between the subordinate and central leaders in CCP politics. Normally, the former are well under the latter's control, not only because of the norms and disciplines, but also because of the factional linkages between the subleaders and the central elites. A subleader who is active in the policy process is usually associated with a dominant leader at the Center. During the Mao period, Ke Qingshi of Shanghai, Wang Renzhong of Hubei, and Xu Shiyou of the Nanjing Regional Command were among Mao's favorites; Peng Zhen of Beijing and An Ziwen of the CC Organization Department were Liu Shaoqi's confidants; and Huang Yongsheng of Guangzhou Regional Command and Tan Furen of Kunming Regional Command were Lin Biao's sworn followers. During the Deng period, Qin Jiwei of Beijing Regional Command, Wan Li of Anhui, Xu Jiatun of Jiangsu, and Song Ping of Gansu had direct access to Deng; Hu Jintao of Guizhou and Zhu Houze of the Propaganda Department were close to Hu Yaobang; and Yang Rudai of Sichuan and Liang Xiang of Hainan were Zhao Ziyang's associates. Not surprisingly, most of these eminent subleaders were later promoted to Beijing to strengthen their patrons' positions.

During periods of political transition, however, the subleaders, especially those who have obtained regional or even national influence – such as Gao Gang in the early 1950s, Tao Zhu in 1965–6, Chen Zaidao in 1967, Xu Shiyou in the late 1970s, Mao Zhiyong in the early 1980s, Ye Xuanping in the late 1980s, and Xie Hua in the mid 1990s – can constitute threats to the central authority. The potential danger lies not so much in the strong local support they enjoy as in the lack of factional links between these powerful local leaders and the central elites. In other words, the Center's control of these "independent kingdoms" becomes less effective, even though the institutionally defined commanding system appears intact.

The Political System in China

It is true that the uneven development across China and the centralized political system together make central-local tensions inevitable. In the perspective of factionalism, such tensions could emerge after a massive purge destroyed the linkages between the central and local leaders, such as in the initial years of the CR; or when the central elites were so preoccupied with the struggle for dominance that the ambitious local bigwigs seized the chance to foster their own forces, such as was the case during the post-Mao period.

Yet the treatment of eminent subleaders during the Mao period was different from that during the Deng period due to the changes in structures of power distribution. Under Mao's command, it was easier for an eminent subleader to find a way to the top level because the more actors in the central arena, the greater Mao's leverage in his manipulation of competitions among his followers. When Mao foresaw a struggle between himself and his colleague(s), he would tour the country to rally the local leaders while cutting off his perceived opponents. Mao was eager to promote an eminent local leader to the Center because the fewer the players at Mao's court, the more he felt threatened. Thus, we saw a "charismatic Mao" when his colleagues competed for his favor, but a Machiavellian Mao who brought new players into the game when certain strong leaders – Liu Shaoqi in the mid 1960s, Lin Biao after the Ninth PC, Zhou Enlai after Lin's fall, and Deng Xiaoping in late 1975 – had overwhelmed their rivals at the Center.

In contrast, Deng was reluctant to let those self-made local bigwigs step into the already crowded decision-making circle, for that would make the situation less manageable, given his barely maintained dominance. Thus, Deng either kicked the local leaders upstairs (as he did with Xu Shiyou, Li Desheng, and Ye Xuanping) or cut them off by transferring them to new places (moving An Pingsheng from Guangxi to Yunnan in 1978 and Mao Zhiyong from Hunan to Jiangxi in 1984).[60] The rise of Deng's men – Wan Li, Hu Yaobang, Zhao Ziyang, Qin Jiwei, Hu Qili, Tian Jiyun, Jiang Zemin, and Zhang Zhen – resulted not so much from his single-handed promotion as from hard bargaining with his rivals. That is why we also witnessed the simultaneous rise of

60 Li Ruihuan is an interesting exception. Li is the only leader who was favored by both Deng and Chen Yun, though he is hardly seen as a loyal follower of either; and he could not get along with the reform leaders like Hu and Zhao, or the hardliners like Li Peng and Deng Liqun.

those who were obviously not Deng's favorites, for example, Yao Yilin, Deng Liqun, Li Peng, Hu Qiaomu, Chen Muhua, Wang Hanbin, and Li Ximing.

Proposition 8: The supreme leader entrusts more power to his most loyal and capable follower in order to secure his control and to prevent instability at the time of his departure. Yet, the latter's rapid expansion will eventually jeopardize the dominant leader's position. Thus, a prisoners' dilemma occurs between them. To break it, the leader must bring new players into the struggle to subdue the increasingly powerful successor, such as in the Mao period, or to strike a deal with his opponents to topple the alienated successor, such as in the Deng period.

Prisoners' Dilemma and Succession Struggles

Deng's second fall at the eve of Mao's death fully exposed the succession problem resulting from the system's dependence on personalized authority due to factional politics. The supreme leader must entrust more power to his successor, who was chosen among his most loyal supporters, not only as a precaution to prevent instability at the time of his departure but also to keep a firm grasp on the factional networks. Inevitably, this follower will take advantage of the leader's patronage and expand his own forces as fast as he can in order to secure his successor's position. Eventually, this successor will be so powerful that even the supreme leader himself feels threatened (see Introduction).

At this point, the leader, **L**, has two strategies: **L1**, to continue patronage to his successor in order to show his trust, and **L2**, to contain his successor's power in order to secure his control. The successor, **S**, also has two strategies: **S1**, to stop his expansion in order to show his loyalty, and **S2**, to continue his expansion in order to consolidate his position. Depending on their strategies S(**L**, **S**) in their interactions, there are four possible outcomes, **O**, with different payoffs for the leader and his successor, **u(L, S)**:[61]

---

61 All the "payoffs" are based on their cardinal, instead of ordinal, values. They reflect the *intensity* of the players' preferences, rather than the objective utilities attached to each outcome.

The Political System in China

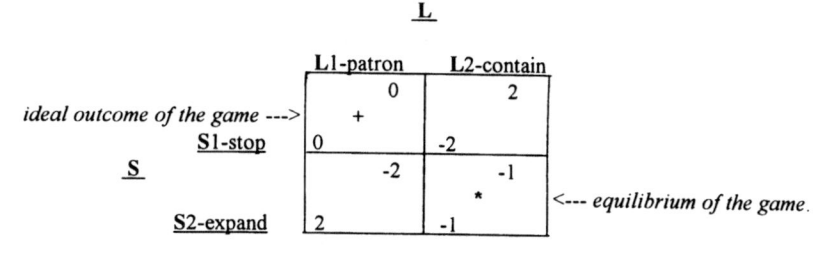

```
                          L
                  L1-patron    L2-contain
                       0           2
ideal outcome of game →  +
          S1-stop   0          -2
   S                   -2          -1
                                    *      ←--- equilibrium of the game
          S2-expand  2          -1
```

Figure 2.2. Prisoners' dilemma between the leader and his successor

O1: s(L1, S1), u(0, 0). The leader continues his patronage, and the successor halts his expansion. The status quo remains.
O2: s(L1, S2), u(−2, 2). The leader continues his patronage, and the successor keeps expanding. As the successor gains more power at the leader's cost, he may take over the command.
O3: s(L2, S1), u(2, −2). The leader contains his successor who halts his expansion. As the successor's power declines, he may lose his position as the successor.
O4: s(L2, S2), u(−1, −1). The leader contains his successor who keeps expanding. A conflict results, which undermines both of their positions.

This scenario can be modeled precisely by the prisoners' dilemma (Figure 2.2). The normal form of the game shows that **O1**: S(L1, S1), u(0, 0), is an ideal solution of the dilemma – both the leader and successor have their positions secured as the former continues his patronage, while the latter stops his expansion. But an ideal choice is not necessarily rational given the uncertainty involved in this game. As we can see from the game model, the dominant strategy for the leader is **L2** (to contain the successor) because

$$u.L2(2,-1) > u.L1(0,-2),$$

while the dominant strategy for the successor is **S2** (to continue his expansion) because

$$u.S2(2,-1) > u.S1(0,-2).$$

This means that if the leader chooses **L1**, the successor will take the advantage by choosing **S2**, resulting in **O2**: S(L1, S2), u(−2, 2), that is, the successor gains at the leader's cost. Or, if the successor chooses **S1**, the leaders will take the advantage by choosing **L2**, resulting in **O3**: S(**L2, S1**), **u**(2, –2), that is, the leader gains at his successor's cost.

As a result, **O4**: S(**L2, S2**), **u**(–1, –1), prevails. Both the leader and successor suffer because their positions are jeopardized in the looming leader-successor conflict.

But prisoners' dilemma is a noncooperative game in which the prisoners "must choose without the opportunity for explicitly coordinating their actions."[62] The leader and his successor are not prisoners. Why can't they prevent prisoners' dilemma through communications? It seems unimaginable indeed that the leader and his successor do not communicate with each other as the problem emerges. Yet this was exactly what happened during the succession struggles in CCP politics. Liu Shaoqi was unable to have any substantial contacts with Mao before he was purged. He "had no clue" about Mao's intention, "nor did he understand the CR at all."[63] Lin Biao did not even know Mao's whereabouts during the Mao-Lin conflict.[64] Hu Yaobang was dying to "have a heart-to-heart talk with Deng" after he sensed Deng's unhappiness with him,[65] but the writing for him had already been on the wall when he was summoned to Deng's residence on the last day of 1986. Zhao Ziyang tried desperately to "have a conversation" with Deng on the eve of his fall, but he was not even informed of Deng's whereabouts.[66]

Why? Let us assume that the leader and his successor intend to solve their problem through communication. After exchanges of their concerns, they make a compromise: the leader will continue his patronage,

---

62 Ordeshook, *Game Theory and Political Theory*, p. 99.
63 Liao Gailong, ed., *1949–1989: Xin zhongguo biannian shi* (1949–1989: A Chronology of the New China), Beijing: People's Press, pp. 272, 279.
64 See Wang Dongxing, "*Mao Zhuxi zai fensui Lin Biao fan geming jituan de rizi li*" (Chairman Mao in the days of smashing Lin Biao's counterrevolutionary coup plot), in Ke Yan, ed., *Mao Zedong de lichenn – yige weiren he ta de huihuang shidai* (Mao Zedong's Career – a Great Man and His Splendid Era), Beijing: PLA Art Press, 1996, 2:359–67.
65 A former deputy director of the CCP organizational department, who was very close to Hu Yaobang, told me that he had a "long conversation" with Hu three days before his death. He said "Yaobang strongly felt that he was wronged, . . . and he always believed that he could have convinced Deng had he been given a chance to have a heart-to-heart talk [with Deng]."
66 A former aid to Zhao Ziyang said that after the students launched the hunger strike on May 13, 1989, Zhao tried desperately to arrange a meeting with Deng. A well-placed source told me that Zhao also tried to get to Deng through Deng's children. But all his effort was in vain.

The Political System in China

and the successor will halt his expansion. Thus, it is expected that the status quo will remain, that is, **O1**: S(L1, S1), **u**(0, 0).

But how can the leader, or the successor, be sure that the other side will keep his promise? It must be pointed out that the prisoners' dilemma is a game of *complete information*, which means that both players know the game tree, the payoffs, and the node at which they have to make their choices. So the final outcome, **O4**: S(L2, S2), **u**(−1, −1), is *not unexpected*. **L2** is a rational choice for the leader because it could yield his most preferred outcome, **O3**: S(L2, S1), **u**(2, −2); and **S2** is a rational choice for the successor because it could yield his, **O2**: S(L1, S2), **u**(−2, 2). But both of them are aware that **O4** can prevail because each of them makes his choice with the anticipation that the other side will do the same, that both the leader and his successor share the same rationale: they choose (**L2**, **S2**) not to maximize their interests, but to prevent the other from maximizing his interests at one's own cost. They anticipate the outcome, **O4**, which ranks third in their preference orders, not because they give up the status quo, **O1**, which ranks second in their preference orders, but because they want to prevent the worst outcome – **O2** for the leader and **O3** for the successor – from befalling them (Table 2.2).

Thus, it is not communication, but the extent to which the leader and his successor can *trust* each other that determines whether they can achieve **O1**: S(L1, S1), **u**(0, 0). Then, how much trust between them is enough that when one chooses **L1**, or **S1**, the other will not choose **S2**, or **L2**, for the best payoff at the former's expense? To answer this question, we have:

$$t(0) \geq (1-t)(2),$$

where:

- t = trust that is needed between the leader and successor to maintain status quo;
- 0 = the payoff for the leader and successor when *both* of them choose **L1** and **S1**; and
- 2 = the payoff for the leader with S(L2, S1), or for the successor with S(L1, S2).

Solving the above inequality, we have: $t \geq 1$, which means that unless there is an *absolute* trust – no less than 100 percent – between them, it would be irrational for the leader to choose **L1**, or for the successor to choose **S1**!

Factionalism in Chinese Communist Politics

Table 2.2. *Preference Orders of Leader and Successor in a Prisoners' Dilemma*

Leader		Successor	
Outcome	Payoff	Outcome	Payoff
O3: S(L2, S1)	2	O2: S(L1, S2)	2
O1: S(L1, S1)	0	O1: S(L1, S1)	0
O4: S(L2, S2)	−1	O4: S(L2, S2)	−1
O2: S(L1, S2)	−2	O3: S(L2, S1)	−2

Thus, what the model of the prisoners' dilemma captures is essentially a *crisis of trust* between the leader and his successor. Given that the successor is selected from those who are the most loyal and trustworthy to the leader, the loss of trust between the leader and his successor means the end of their relationship. As I have discussed before, although a succession struggle was usually triggered by a policy dispute, the lack of trust prevented them from seeking a "rational" compromise. As a result, the struggle always evolved into a duel in which, given the intolerant nature of a totalistic political system, neither of them can feel secure unless his opponent is politically eliminated.

But why did the leader, Mao or Deng, always prevail in succession struggles no matter how powerful his successor appeared? While detailed examinations of each succession struggle will be made in various chapters, here I incorporate the game theory models to provide an explanation to the seemingly irrational behavior of the leader and his successor in a succession struggle. The aim is to show that it is the faction-ridden structure of leadership relations that enabled the leader to prevail in this struggle.

Mao's Solution to a Succession Struggle: Bringing in a New Player

During the Mao period, once a succession struggle emerged, a *new player* would become actively involved and play a crucial role in the struggle against the successor. Lin Biao's support of Mao was indispensable in the toppling of Liu Shaoqi in 1966, and so was Zhou Enlai's in Lin Biao's fall in 1971.

The Political System in China

But how could this new player get involved and, more importantly, side resolutely with Mao? The available evidence shows that the new player supports Mao not necessarily because of the policy differences, as the policy-choice analysis implies.[67] Lin's involvement in the struggle against Liu was in a large part motivated by his ambition or, as Teiwes argues, because of his attitude of "do whatever the Chairman says."[68] In Lin's case, a close examination reveals that Zhou and Lin got along quite well prior to the Mao-Lin clash. It was Zhou who confirmed the formula that Lin was Mao's "closest comrade-in-arms" and was "our vice-commander." In return, Lin "cared greatly for the Premier's health" and "instructed specifically" that medical personnel and equipment "must accompany the Premier wherever he goes."[69] As a matter of fact, when the Mao-Lin conflict surfaced over the issue of state chairmanship in August 1970, Zhou's attitude was ambiguous. Instead, it was Lin's former allies, the Maoist radicals, who took on Lin on Mao's behalf (see Chapter 6).[70]

From the perspective of factional politics, the new player had the same primary goal as the leader and his successor in the game, namely, *power*. So the question is, How could he gain more power by participating and siding with Mao in a succession struggle? Moreover, how could Mao benefit from his participation? To answer these questions, I first construct a working model to illustrate the effect of his participation on the final outcomes of a succession struggle.

For the convenience of analysis, we first assume that the new player, **P**, is an *indifferent player* in the working model – that is, although his choices have an essential effect on the outcomes of the game, he is *indifferent to the payoffs*. It must be emphasized, however, that his participation does not change the nature of the succession struggle: it is a power struggle in which the leader, **L**, and successor, **S**, have to either *fight* or *give in* because, as we have discussed already, the possibility of compro-

---

[67] Cf. Harry Harding, "The Chinese state in crisis," in Roderick MacFarquhar and John Fairbank, eds., *Cambridge History of China*, Cambridge: Cambridge University Press, 1991, 15:116–18.

[68] Frederick Teiwes and Warren Sun, *The Tragedy of Lin Biao: Riding the Tiger during the Cultural Revolution,* London: C. Hurst, 1996, p. 161.

[69] Chen Hua, *Zhou Enlai he ta de mishu men* (Zhou Enlai and His Secretaries), Beijing: China Media and Television Press, 1992, p. 526.

[70] Roderick MacFarquhar, "The succession to Mao and the end of Maoism," in MacFarquhar and Fairbank, *Cambridge History of China*, 15:317–20.

Factionalism in Chinese Communist Politics

Extensive Form of the Game

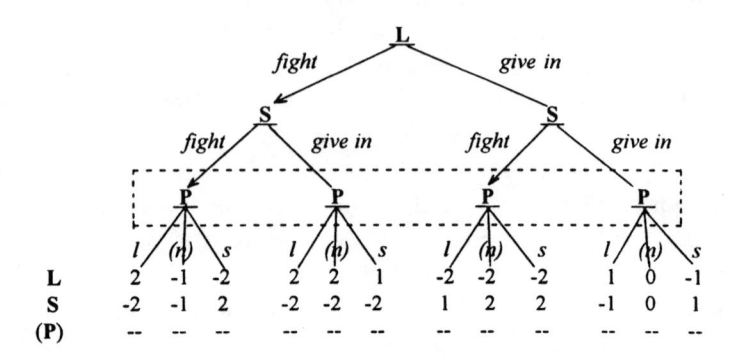

	fight			give in			fight			give in		
	l	(*n*)	*s*	*l*	(*n*)	*s*	*l*	(*n*)	*s*	*l*	(*n*)	*s*
L	2	-1	-2	2	2	1	-2	-2	-2	1	0	-1
S	-2	-1	2	-2	-2	-2	1	2	2	-1	0	1
(P)	--	--	--	--	--	--	--	--	--	--	--	--

Normal Form of the Game

		L fight		**L** give in	
		S fight	**S** give in	**S** fight	**S** give in
P	*l*	-2 / 2 / --	-2 / 2 / --	1 / -2 / --	-1 / 1 / --
	s	2 / -2 / --	-2 / 1 / --	2 / -2 / --	1 / -1 / --
	(*n*)	-1 / -1 / --	-2 / 2 / --	2 / -2 / --	0 / 0 / --

Figure 2.3. The new player in a succession struggle: Working model (solid arrow = dominant strategy)

mise has been eliminated as soon as prisoners' dilemma emerges between them. But the new player has three choices in the game: *l*, to side with the leader; *s*, to side with the successor; and *n*, to remain neutral between the leader and successor (Figure 2.3).

As shown by the game tree, **P**'s participation creates an *information asymmetry* in the game: while he knows the choices of the leader and successor – either *fight* or *give in* – they are not sure about his. (The dotted line around **P**'s decision nodes shows that the information set of **P** is unknown to the leader and his successor.) Thus, the new player has

The Political System in China

an exclusive advantage in this game of *incomplete information*, although he is the least powerful among the three.

However, if the new player chooses *n* – to remain neutral in the struggle – his participation has no effect at all: all the possible outcomes of the game duplicate those of prisoners' dilemma. This implies that in practice he shall be replaced by another subleader who will take sides. Only when he takes sides – either *l* or *s* – does his participation exert a *decisive* effect on the game: the succession struggle is no longer a duel with indeterminate outcomes, but a game of winner-take-all in which one has no chance under the combined attack of two. (If the leader, or successor, chooses *give-in*, the value of the new player's choice of *l*, or *s*, is 1.)

This working model reveals the most important aspect of a succession struggle: it is the new player's choice, rather than "Mao's supreme power" as the conventional explanation implies, that determines the final outcome of a succession struggle. In other words, whether Mao or the successor could prevail in this struggle depended on his *ability to form a coalition* with the new player. It is in this aspect that Mao had a decisive advantage: he had direct access to each of the subleaders in the leadership structure (see Figure 1.2). This exclusive position enabled him not only to bring in a new player, but also to manipulate his behavior in the game. As a result, the information asymmetry became the sole disadvantage of the successor, while Mao and the new player formed a "winning coalition."[71]

By contrast, the power of the successor, either Liu or Lin, was subject to the constraints of leadership structure: he had little control of the system other than his own, and except with his own followers, his communication and coordination with his peers are barely existent due to the deficiency in institutional arrangements. Such structural constraints are deadly to the successor in a succession struggle because they prevent him from forming a coalition with the other leaders. The successor's inability to form coalitions with the other elite members in a succession struggle prevented "Euclidean coalition formations," or endless coalition formations among the elite members, which would lead to an overall crisis.

No wonder that the new player Mao brought in a succession struggle always came from a system other than the successor's – Lin Biao was a

---

71 See Ordeshook, *Game Theory and Political Theory*, p. 314.

Factionalism in Chinese Communist Politics

preeminent military leader in the struggle against Liu Shaoqi, a Party leader, in 1966, and Zhou Enlai, the administrative leader in the struggle against Lin in 1971. By supporting Mao in the struggle, not only was the new player rewarded with more power, but he also gained access to *both* the Party and the military systems – a noticeable exception Mao had to tolerate *only* during a succession struggle. Lin jumped from the sixth to the second in the rank of Politburo and was actively involved in civilian affairs in the CR; and Zhou, who held no military positions at all, was entrusted to maneuver the entire military in the struggle against Lin (see Chapter 6). During the most critical four days of the Lin Biao Incident, September 13–16, 1971, Zhou's authority was such that he could and did move all the Politburo members, including Mao himself, to the People's Hall, where they could not leave without Zhou's permission.[72]

Deng's Solution to a Succession Struggle: Joining in the Opposition

Deng took a different strategy in the succession struggles. Instead of bringing in a new player, Deng in fact struck deals with his opponents, usually the conservatives, in the toppling of his successors: Hu Yaobang in 1987, and Zhao Ziyang in 1989. However, this does not mean that Deng gave up his policy choices, nor does it indicate that Deng had abandoned his followers. On the contrary, as soon as the successor was toppled, Deng would regroup his forces and resume his reform policy despite strong resistance from his former allies, the hardliners.

Deng's solution to a succession struggle seemed self-destructive, for it strengthened the hardliners at his own cost. Hu's fall in 1987 resulted in the hardliners' takeover of the State Council: Li Peng became the premier. The purge of Zhao in 1989 enabled the conservative forces to roll back the achievement of reform to the extent that Deng was unable to resume the reform momentum until 1992. All this resulted in a decline of Deng's power – he became less capable of doing what he wanted than he was in the mid-1980s when his dominance peaked.

However, beneath Deng's seemingly irrational behavior was a substantial change in the leadership structure (see Chapter 7). Unlike Mao, who stayed with the second front all by himself while maintaining

[72] Chen, *Zhou Enlai he ta de mishu men*, pp. 448–9.

The Political System in China

direct control over each subleader, Deng had to share the second front with the other senior leaders who also had access to the first-front leaders, although Deng was the only one who had access to both the Party and army systems (see Figure 7.1). This change, which reflected differences in the distribution of power in the Deng period, put Deng in a more challenging situation than the one Mao had faced in a succession struggle.

Mao had defeated all his rivals during the revolution and established his command over all the factions (see Chapter 3). Thus, the challenge Mao faced in a succession struggle was from the successor's mountaintop, which was just *one* of all the mountaintops under his command. When Mao got a new player involved in the game, he was virtually setting the new player's mountaintop against the successor's. But Deng was never able to subdue the opposition formed by the hardliners. It was his exclusive access to both the Party and military systems that enabled him to form the strongest coalition and establish his dominance in the faction-ridden political process (see Chapter 7). Thus, Deng always chose his successor from within his own forces: both Hu and Zhao were long-time Deng followers. When a succession struggle emerged, however, the challenge Deng faced was from *within his own mountaintop*. That put Deng in a dilemma about whether to bring a new player into the game. Deng would prefer to bring in one of his followers to whom he had exclusive access, so that he could secure a winning coalition against the successor. But this could aggravate the rift among his forces and allow the hardliners to take more advantage. Deng was reluctant to get Zhao Ziyang and Wan Li involved in the toppling of Hu Yaobang, and, as a result, both Zhao and Wan maintained a low profile.[73]

---

[73] Ruan Ming, *Deng Xiaoping diguo* (The Deng Xiaoping Empire), Taipei: Shipao Press, 1992, pp. 188–9, claims that Zhao played "an important role" in the toppling of Hu. But a source who was very close to Hu and had a "long conversation" with Hu a few days before his death does not think so. In my presence, he questioned Ruan one afternoon in June 1993: "Where is your evidence [that Zhao played a role in the toppling of Hu]?" Ruan admitted: "I was told that Zhao wrote a letter to Deng, complaining that Hu had intervened into his work. I may exaggerate a little bit . . ." Cutting off Ruan, this source pointed out: "It is totally groundless! How could you know Zhau wrote a letter to Deng? Have you seen it? You can imagine according to your opinion, but when you put it in writing, you've got to have evidence." Ruan promised that he would "earnestly revise this part according to the evidence." See also Wu Guoguang, *Zhao Ziyang yu zhongguo zhengzhi gaige* (Political Reform under Zhao Ziyang), Hong Kong: Pacific Century Institute, 1997, pp. 242–3.

But should Deng bring someone from outside of his forces into a succession struggle, he could not eliminate the possibility that this new player would make a deal with the other senior leaders who had access to him. Moreover, without exclusive access to the new player, Deng could not fully overcome the information asymmetry in the game (see Figure 2.2). As a result, Deng and his successor would be in equally disadvantageous positions: neither of them would know the new player's strategy for sure. With the existence of a formidable opposition in the leadership, it became even more risky for Deng to bring in someone over whom he did not have exclusive control.

The existence of an opposition force, however, also provided Deng with a chance to prevail in a succession struggle, though he had to pay a price. With Deng staying with the second front, his successor, who was entrusted with daily affairs at the first front, was in constant battle with the hardliners in the policy process (see Chapter 7). Thus, it seems natural that the hardliners would be allies available to Deng when a succession struggle emerged. But this interpretation is superficial. Ultimately, what the hardliners wanted was to *upset the dominance of Deng's reform forces*. They chose to side with Deng in a succession struggle not because they had been fighting with Deng's successor, but because it could weaken Deng's reform forces. So it is not surprising that Deng and the hardliners would break up as soon as the successor was toppled. Indeed, there seems no reason why the hardliners could not side with the successor if such a coalition could enable them to upset Deng's dominance.

The following game model reveals the rationale of Deng and the hardliners in forming a coalition against the successor. When a prisoners' dilemma triggered a succession struggle, the hardliners had three strategies to choose from: d, to support Deng against the successor; n, to remain neutral between Deng and his successor; and s, to support the successor against Deng.

As an opposition, the hardliners' most preferred outcome of a succession struggle is that Deng's dominance be upset, and the last thing they want to see is the consolidation of Deng's forces (Table 2.3). Given the choices of Deng and his successor – f (fight) or g (give in) – and their preference orders in a succession struggle (see Table 2.2), interactions among **D**, **S**, and the hardliners, **H**, can result in different outcomes, depending on the strategies, S(**D**, **S**, **H**), they choose in the game. Con-

The Political System in China

Table 2.3. *The Hardliners' Preference Order on the Outcomes of a Succession Struggle*

Outcome	Payoff
Deng's dominance is upset in the succession struggle.	3
Deng's forces are substantially undermined because of the fall of Deng's successor.	2
Deng's forces suffer from a continuous succession struggle with uncertain outcomes.	1
The status quo remains because of a compromise between Deng and his successor.	0
The reform forces are consolidated under Deng's leadership, because his successor gives in, or vice versa. The hardliners would be partially compensated if they took the right side – they support the winner, either Deng or the successor who prevails.	–1
The reform forces are consolidated under Deng's leadership, because his successor gave in, or vice versa, while the hardliners maintain a neutral position.	–2
The reform forces are consolidated under the leadership of Deng because his successor gave in, or vice versa. The hardliners suffer most because they took the wrong side – they supported the successor, or Deng, who gave in.	–3

sequently, they will have different payoffs, **u(D, S, H)**, with various outcomes (Table 2.4).

We assume that the three players, **D, S**, and **H**, move simultaneously in the game because of the *imperfect information*. The game tree shows that Deng has a dominant strategy (Figure 2.4), to fight, because

$$\mathbf{u.D}f(2,2,-1,2,-2,2) \geq \mathbf{u.D}g(-2,0,-2,0,-2,0).$$

The successor also has a dominant strategy, to fight, because

$$\mathbf{u.S}f(-2,2,-1,2,2,2) \geq \mathbf{u.S}g(-2,0,-2,0,-2,0).$$

The hardliners do not have a dominant strategy in the game because no matter which strategy they take, the set of payoffs for each outcome is essentially indifferent (*I*) to them:

Table 2.4. *Strategies, Outcomes, and Payoffs of a Succession Struggle in Deng's Period*

S(D, S, H)	Outcomes	u(D, S, H)
f, f, d	The hardliners support Deng to topple his successor. Although Deng prevails, his forces are undermined because of the successor's fall.	2, –2, 2
f, f, n	Deng's forces suffer from the continuous conflict between Deng and his successor. This benefits the hardliners who remain neutral in the struggle.	–1, –1, 1
f, f, s	The hardliners and the successor join forces to upset Deng's dominance.	–2, 2, 3
f, g, d	Deng consolidates his forces because his successor gives in. The hardliners are partially compensated because they support Deng.	2, –2, –1
f, g, n	Deng consolidates his forces because his successor gives in. The hardliners suffer because they remain neutral in the struggle.	2, –2, –2
f, g, s	Deng consolidates his forces because his successor gives in. The hardliners suffer most because they support the successor.	2, –2, –3
g, f, d	Deng gives in, which enables the successor to take over the reform forces. The hardliners suffer most because they support Deng.	–2, 2, –3
g, f, n	The hardliners remain neutral while Deng gives in, which enables the successor to take over the leadership of the reform forces.	–2, 2, –2
g, f, s	Deng gives in, which enables the successor to take over the reform forces. The hardliners are compensated because they support the successor.	–2, 2, –1
g, g, d	Deng and his successor make a compromise, even though the hardliners support Deng. The status quo remains.	0, 0, 0
g, g, n	The hardliners remain neutral while Deng and his successor reach a compromise. The status quo remains.	0, 0, 0
g, g, s	Deng and his successor make a compromise, even though the hardliners support the successor. The status quo remains.	0, 0, 0

The Political System in China

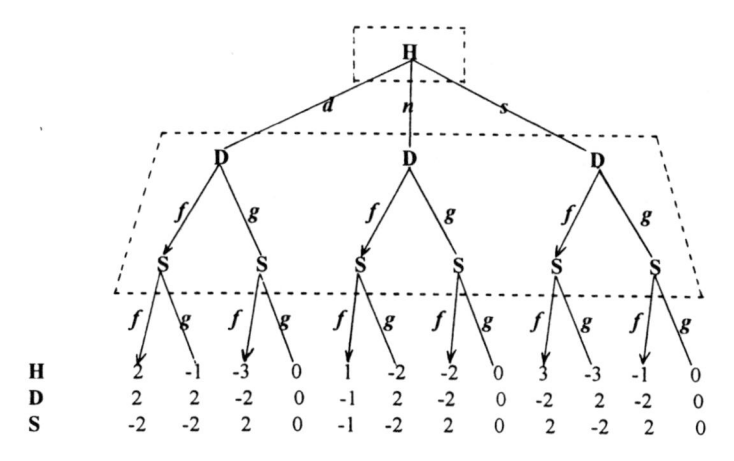

H	2	-1	-3	0	1	-2	-2	0	3	-3	-1	0
D	2	2	-2	0	-1	2	-2	0	-2	2	-2	0
S	-2	-2	2	0	-1	-2	2	0	2	-2	2	0

Figure 2.4. Extensive form of the game: Players move simultaneously (solid arrow = dominant strategy)

$$\mathbf{u.H}d(2,-1,-3,0) \ / \ \mathbf{u.H}n(1,-2,-2,0) \ / \ \mathbf{u.H}s(3,-3,-1,0).$$

However, had the hardliners known that "to fight" is the dominant strategy for both Deng and his successor, their best response strategy would have been s, to support the successor, because if both Deng and his successor choose f,

$$\mathbf{u.H}s(3) > \mathbf{u.H}d(2) > \mathbf{u.H}n(1).$$

In other words, had the hardliners been sure that there was no possibility of compromise between Deng and his successor, they would have sided with the successor to upset Deng's dominance. This confirms the earlier assumption that it was Deng, rather than his successor, who was the hardliners' ultimate target in political struggles.

But this is a game of *incomplete information*. Although the hardliners could see the emerging conflict between Deng and his successor, as *outsiders* they could not be sure what strategy Deng and his successor would choose in this struggle *within* Deng's forces. The dotted line around the decision nodes of Deng and his successor in Figure 2.4 shows the information sets unknown to the hardliners. Without the assurance that Deng and his successor would choose to fight, the hardliners could not afford to gamble by betting on the successor. Should the successor give in, the

Factionalism in Chinese Communist Politics

hardliners' support to him would virtually help Deng to consolidate his dominance, the last thing the hardliners wanted to see.

Deng and his successor were unsure how their common opponents, the hardliners, would respond to a looming succession struggle, either. The dotted line around the hardliners' decision nodes in Figure 2.4 shows the information set unknown to Deng and his successor. However, Deng and his successor were much less affected than the hardliners by the incomplete information in their choice making, because both of them had a dominant strategy. This created a de facto *information asymmetry* unfavorable to the hardliners.

Moreover, this is a game of *imperfect information* in which the choice of the player who moves first has a substantial effect on the choices of the players who move after him. This feature is especially vital for Deng because it would be disastrous for Deng had the hardliners figured out the situation and made the first move to support the successor, or had the successor moved first and made it clear that to fight (f) was his *dominant strategy*. If so, whatever strategy Deng would choose, he would be the loser – should the hardliners choose to support the successor (s), given that the successor's dominant strategy is f, we have:

$$u.Df(-2) = u.Dg(-2).$$

So Deng had to move first and make a deal with the hardliners while preventing his successor from doing the same. Again, the leadership structure provided Deng with an exclusive advantage, while it laid constraints on his successor. Sharing the second front with the other veteran leaders, Deng was able to communicate with them, including Chen Yun, who led the conservative forces. But the successor, who managed daily affairs at the first front on Deng's behalf, had limited access to the other veteran leaders except Deng (see Figure 7.1). As a result, while the successor's strategy was unknown to the hardliners, Deng moved first and initiated a deal with them at the second front.

Moreover, by moving first, Deng was able to manipulate the hardliners' choice making in the game. As the game tree shows (Figure 2.5), the hardliners faced a dilemma after Deng made it clear that his dominant strategy was f. Obviously, s would be the hardliners' best response strategy if, and only if, the successor would also choose f because

$$u.Hs(3) > u.Hd(2) > u.Hn(1).$$

The Political System in China

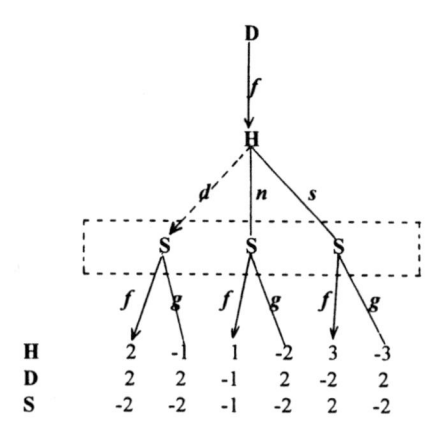

```
            D
            |f
            ↓
            H
         d´ |n  s
      ┌─────────────────┐
      | S    S    S     |
      └─────────────────┘
       f/\g  f/\g  f/\g

H      2  -1   1  -2   3  -3
D      2   2  -1   2  -2   2
S     -2  -2  -1  -2   2  -2
```

Figure 2.5. Extensive form of the game: Deng moves first (solid arrow = dominant strategy; dashed arrow = best response strategy)

This strategy, s, however, could bring about the worst outcome for the hardliners should the successor choose g because

$$u.Hs(-3) < u.Hn(-2) < u.Hd(-1).$$

From the above inequality, we can also see that d, to support Deng, would be the hardliners' best response strategy should the successor choose g.

But the hardliners were uncertain of the successor's choice of strategies because they had no access to him – the dotted line around the successor's decision nodes in Figure 2.5 shows the information set is unknown to them. Given the uncertainty of the game, the hardliners' rational choice was to support Deng, not necessarily because it could bring about their second-best payoff, $u.Hd$ (2), if the successor would choose f, but because *it eliminates the possibility of the worst outcomes* – $u.Hs$ (−3) and $u.Hn$ (−2) – no matter what strategy the successor would choose. In other words, in reality the hardliners opted to *minimize* the risk rather than maximize the gains, that is, they chose gains over uncertainty in a game in which they suffered from information asymmetry.

This was exactly what happened during the succession struggles in the Deng period. In the cases of both Hu and Zhao, Deng moved first and struck a deal with the other veteran leaders at the second front. But neither Hu nor Zhao was allowed any chance to explain himself in front of the veteran leaders *before* he was toppled. In both cases, while the successor was still fighting hard against the hardliners at the first front, the decision to dump him was made among the veteran leaders behind the scenes. However, as the game model shows, the hardliners agreed to cooperate with Deng because it enabled them to lock in a positive payoff, namely, that the successor's fall would undermine Deng's reform forces, though the gains were not as much as they would like. But they would break the coalition with Deng and resume their opposition to Deng's reform as soon as the successor was toppled.

It must be noted, however, that Deng's treatment of his toppled successors, Hu and Zhao, was lenient compared with Mao's. Mao eliminated the toppled successors and, moreover, would immediately launch a massive *zhengdun* in order to destroy the fallen successor's mountaintop. By contrast, Deng not only protected his former successors after they were toppled, but he also stopped any attempts by the hardliners to launch *a massive* campaign in the *entire* system so as to prevent them from taking further advantage through a massive purge of his former successors' followers, who were, after all, still the members of Deng's own forces.

The succession struggles in CCP politics were induced by the faction-ridden structure of leadership relations. The seemingly irrational outcomes in these struggles resulted from rational choices made by the CCP leaders under the constraints of this structure. Different solutions to the succession struggles between the Mao and Deng periods, however, did not change this structure but reinforced it somewhat because the independent variable in the shaping of leadership relations, namely factionalism, remains unchanged. Thus, as soon as a successor is purged, the need for a new one emerges. But this need is more urgent than before, not only because the leader is older, but also because the successor's fall has created a power vacuum that has to be filled immediately in order to prevent further leadership instability. As a result, the same game would start all over again: the new successor's rise sows the seeds for his inevitable fall. Liu Shaoqi's rapid rise after the 1954 Gao-Rao Affair made him the sure target of Mao in the 1960s; the height of Lin Biao's power at the Ninth Party Congress in 1969 marked the beginning of his fall; the enormous authority Zhou Enlai gained in the struggle against Lin Biao caused Mao's suspicion and containment – Zhou's death in

The Political System in China

January 1976 saved his political life, but victimized his ally Deng Xiaoping, who fell again immediately after Zhou's death. In the Deng period, the rapid rise of Hu Yaobang in the mid-1980s incurred Deng's suspicion and eventual withdrawal of patronage; and Zhao Ziyang's glory at the Thirteenth Party Congress in 1987 was soon overshadowed by his fall in May 1989.

It is a double irony that the faction-ridden leadership structure induces different outcomes in the process of leader-successor relations. It makes "bringing up a successor" necessary in order to prevent instability on the leader's death. But the successor's rise leads to a prisoners' dilemma that jeopardizes the leadership stability. After a succession struggle emerges, the constraints of the leadership structure prevent the successor from making deals with the other elite members, and therefore eliminate the possibility of "Euclidian, or spatial, coalition formations," which could lead to an overall crisis of leadership relations. As a result, the leader can topple his successor swiftly without destabilizing the entire leadership stability. In this perspective, the findings of this study are surprisingly consistent with the inference that the stability of policy outcomes in a democratic system is essentially *structure-induced*.[74]

In the long run, however, the vicious cycle of succession struggles has contributed to the gradual decay of the faction-ridden leadership structure. The leader's effort to "bring up a successor" always backfired. It actually intensified the potential instability on his death. Every succession struggle emerged when a successor had become too powerful to be trusted by the leader. As a result, the successor who survived the leader has always been weaker than his predecessors simply because he did not have time to make himself powerful enough under the leader's patronage. No wonder that Hua Guofeng was soon ousted by Deng after Mao's death. Similarly, there had been widespread skepticism of Jiang Zemin's ability to survive the power struggles in the post-Deng period. But Jiang seems to have consolidated his authority, partly due to the absence of a senior leader like Deng who had access to both the Party and military systems after the ousting of Yang Shangkun in early 1993, but largely because of the overwhelming priority shared by all the CCP elites in the post-Deng period – political stability.

---

[74] See Shepsle and Weingast, "Structure-induced equilibrium and the legislative choice," pp. 503–19.

Factionalism in Chinese Communist Politics

The parallel between Hua and Jiang, however, exposes an essential factor in succession struggles: the leader's ability to control the military. This factor has become more important because, without the absolute power Mao had enjoyed, Deng was increasingly dependent on the military to maintain his dominance. As a result, not only did the military become more involved in the political process, but the potential instability on Deng's death also increased. Unlike their predecessors whose authority over the military was based on personal loyalties forged during the revolution, the third-generation leaders like Jiang Zemin have no military careers. Their relations with the generals are shaped by the interests that emerged in political affairs. Loyalty sustains, and so does the personal authority based on it; but interests change, and so does the commitment that goes with them. It is in this sense that we see why the potential instability on Deng's death drew so much concern. What was at stake was not necessarily whether Deng's last successor, Jiang Zemin, could survive the power struggles in the post-Deng period, but whether the new leader could keep the military under control. The development after Deng's death, however, suggests that Jiang has retained the authority over the military through institutionalization of the Party's command of the gun, rather than reinforcing his personal power. Yet institutionalization has not only brought the state into military operations that used to be an exclusive domain of the Party, but it has also changed the two-system structure of leadership relations. Although the military still remains an independent system in this structure, its subordination to the Party was now secured not so much by the supreme leader's authority as by institutional arrangements.[75]

---

75 See Jing Huang, "Transition of civil-military relations in China: First-cut analysis of interviews with the PLA officers," paper presented at the Conference of China in Transition, Utah State University, September 10–12, 1998.

3

The Establishment of the Yan'an Round Table

MAO ZEDONG STRIVES TO ACHIEVE THE PARTY LEADERSHIP

Mao's Command over the CCP Forces

Mao pointed out that "the Chinese revolution was made by many mountaintops."[1] These mountaintops, however, were barely a unified force when the Long Marchers settled down in northern Shaanxi in 1937. They had been isolated from each other since their establishment, and, moreover, a political hierarchy among their leaders was yet to be established. What kept them together were their shared ideological faith and strong enemies. Those who assumed the CCP leadership before Mao Zedong – Chen Duxiu, Qu Qiubai, Li Lisan, and Wang Ming – were the *messengers* who knew how best to explain the ideology, rather than the *organizers* who had developed these mountaintops. Thus, whenever the CCP suffered a setback, a new messenger would emerge to reexplain the ideology, and then take over the leadership. The dramatic rise of the Wang Ming faction, formed by the Moscow-trained Chinese students, at the Fourth Plenum of the Sixth Party Congress (PC) in January 1931[2] demonstrated the CCP's incoherence as an organization and adolescence as a communist party.

Furthermore, each time the leadership changed hands, a top-down purge would follow. A typical example was the large-scale purge after the Wang Ming faction seized the Central Committee (CC)

---

1 *Wansui*, 2:479. See the Introduction for the definition of mountaintop.
2 See Jin Chonji, ed., *Zhou Enlai zhuan* (Biography of Zhou Enlai), Beijing: People's Press, 1988, pp. 225–34; Zhou Guoquan, Guo Dehong, and Li Mingsan, *Wang Ming pingzhuan* (A Critical Biography of Wang Ming), Hefei: Anhui People's Press, 1989, pp. 120–57; Gai Jun and Yu Jinan, "*Chen Shaoyu shi zenyang shangtai de*" (How Chen Shaoyu [i.e., Wang Ming] rose to power), *Yanjiu 1*, no. 2, 1981.

leadership.³ An essential reason was that personal loyalties had been cultivated between the fallen leaders and their followers during the development of their mountaintops – it was personal loyalties, rather than the ideological faith, that had kept a mountaintop in line with its leader. Thus, the new leadership could hardly obtain effective control of various mountaintops without a penetrating reorganization in order to purge those who were loyal to the fallen leaders and promote the ones who pledged to be loyal to the new leaders.

Mao's rise at the Zunyi Politburo Conference in January 1935 marked the beginning of a transfer of power from the messengers to organizers, although this transfer would not be completed till a thorough reorganization of the CCP forces in northern Shaanxi, where the major mountaintops gathered together after the Long March. At the enlarged Luochuan Politburo Conference, held August 22–25, 1937, Mao was elected chairman of the new Central Military Commission (CMC), with Zhu De and Zhou Enlai as its vice-chairmen. Its members were Peng Dehuai, Ren Bishi, Lin Biao, He Long, Liu Bocheng, Zhang Guotao, Xu Xiangqian, and Ye Jianying.⁴ After the conference, the Red Army and its guerrilla forces in South China were reorganized into the Eighth Route Army and the New Fourth Army. The leaders rising from Mao's Jinggang Mountaintop formed an overwhelming majority in the reorganized commanding system (Figure 3.1).

Among the reorganized forces, Mao was most concerned with the 129th Division because it grew out of the remnants of the Fourth Front Red Army controlled by Mao's most formidable rival, Zhang Guotao. But it was difficult, and risky indeed, for Mao to send in his men to take over this division immediately. It was difficult because, although the main forces of the Fourth Front Army were lost in the 1936–7 Western Expedition,⁵ its remnants were still over 7,000 men strong; it was risky

---

3 Zhou, Guo, and Li, *Wang Ming pingzhuan*, pp. 158–201; see also Li Renbao, "*Zhongyang geming genjudi shiqi de yichang yanzhong douzheng*" (A serious struggle during the period of Central Revolutionary Base Area), *Yanjiu* 2, no. 3, 1985.

4 Hao Mengbi and Duan Haoran, *Zhongguo gongchandang liushi nian* (The Sixty Years of the CCP), Beijing: PLA Press, 1984, 1:211 (hereafter *Liushi nian*). See also *Zhongguo gongchan dang lishi* (The CCP History), compiled by *zhonggong zhongyang dangshi yanjou shi* (CCP Party History Research Center), Beijing: People's Press, 1991, 1:471–4.

5 In October 1936, the main forces of the Fourth Front Army formed the Western Route Army (WRA), commanded by Commissar Chen Changhao and Commander Xu

The Establishment of the Yan'an Round Table

Mao Zedong/CMC Chairman
Zhu De[a]/general CO   Ren Bishi/general commissar

	8th Route Army Peng Dehuai[a]/front CO Ye Jianying[a]/chief of staff	**New 4th Army** Ye Ting/CO Xiang Ying/vice-CO
(Red Army) **1st-Front Army** Mao Zedong/Zhu De Peng Dehuai (Liu Bocheng) Ye Jianying Lin Biao Nie Rongzhen Luo Ronghuan Xiao Jinguang	─> **115th Division** Lin Biao[a]/CO Nie Rongzhen[a]/vice-CO Luo Ronghuan[a]/commissar **Yanan Garrison** Xiao Jinguang[a]/CO	**1st Detachment** Chen Yi[a]/CO Fu Qiutao[a]/vice-CO **2nd Detachment** Zhang Dingcheng[a]/CO Su Yu[a]/vice-CO
2nd-Front Army ─> Ren Bishi/He Long Guan Xiangying	**120th Division** He Long/CO Guan Xiangying/commissar	**3rd Detachment** Zhang Yunyi/CO Tan Zhenlin[a]/vice-CO
4th-Front Army ─> Zhang Guotao Xu Xiangqian Liu Bocheng (August 1935)	**129th Division** Liu Bocheng[a]/CO Xu Xiangqian/vice-CO Deng Xiaoping[a]/commissar (January 1938)	**4th Detachment** Gao Jingting/CO

[a] Leaders from Mao's Grant Jinggang Mountaintop.
CO = commander.

Figure 3.1. Reorganization of CCP forces under Mao's command, August 1937

Xiangqian. The WRA marched westward into the Gansu-Ningxia area, controlled by warlord Ma Bufang, in an effort to open up a new base area. After three months of bloody fighting, the WRA was eliminated. Li Ruqing, *Bixue huangsha* (Red Blood and Yellow Sand), *Kunlun*, no. 2, Beijing: PLA Literature Press, 1988, provides a detailed account of this heroic but tragic operation. Li quotes numerous original documents, most of them being telegrams between the WRA and the CCP headquarters in northern Shaanxi. These documents raise some important yet unanswered questions: Why were the CCP leaders so reluctant to send reinforcement to their desperate comrades? Why did Zhang Guotao bet so much on this operation that he could hardly allow his army to withdraw, even though he knew it had been trapped in a hopeless situation? Why did Chen Changhao, Zhang's right-hand man, force the WRA back into the deadly trap they had barely escaped from? But one thing is clear: after nearly 25,000 Red Army soldiers lost their lives, Zhang Guotao lost his advantage in the power struggle with Mao. Mei Jian, ed., *Yan'an mishi* (The Untold Stories of Yan'an), Beijing: Red Flag Press, because, at the time when the exhausted Red Army was still surrounded by the KMT forces, a hostile take over of Zhang's forces could have provoked fierce struggle and endangered the entire CCP force.[6]

Liu Bocheng, a prestigious general who had worked with Mao since the late 1920s, assumed the command of the 129th Division. As chief of staff of the Fourth Front Army,[7] Liu had been virtually in charge of the Fourth Front Army after its main forces left for the Gan-Ning area in late 1936. Thus, it was natural for Liu to assume the command of the new division. Xu Xiangqian, the former commander of the Fourth Front Army, could only be grateful to be named its vice-commander, for he had just lost all his troops in the Western Expedition (see note 5).[8] As a compromise, Zhang Hao (a.k.a. Lin Yuying, Lin Biao's uncle) was named the division's political director.[9] As a senior member of the CCP Mission to the Comintern, Zhang Hao had been an arbitrator between Mao and Zhang Guotao.[10]

The pressure from the KMT forces, however, was soon relieved because of the anti-Japanese united front and the panicky withdrawal of the KMT forces in front of the Japanese forces. Thus, Zhang Hao was

1996, 1:7–62, reveals that only after the WRA's defeat did Mao decide to "settle accounts" (*qingsuan*) with Zhang. The failure of the Western Expedition still remains one of the most controversial events in the CCP history.

6 The criticism of Zhang exerted such pressure on those from Zhang's forces that Xu Shiyou and a group of high-ranking officers from the Fourth Front Red Army plotted to desert Yan'an and go back to the South to "make a revolution of their own." The plot was aborted, and Xu and his men were arrested. But instead of "punishing them for their counterrevolutionary crime," Mao personally visited each of the arrested officers and showed his respect to them, especially Xu. Xu was moved and pledged his loyalty to Mao. See Mei, *Yan'an mishi*, 1:47–50.

7 Liu assumed this position in August 1935 as part of the deal between Mao and Zhang at the Shawo Conference, August 5–6, 1935. See Benjamin Yang, *From Revolution to Politics: Chinese Communists on the Long March*, Boulder, CO: Westview Press, 1990, pp. 151–4.

8 I raised the question about Xu Xiangqian's appointment in my interview with a former officer of the Fourth Front Red Army in the summer of 1995. He said: "We were lucky not to be purged. [A lot of] officers had been executed [in 1933–5] just because they had lost a battle, but we had lost all our troops [in the Western Expedition]. We were grateful to Chairman Mao [because] he protected us."

9 After the reorganization "commissar" was replaced by "political director," the title used by the KMT forces. But "commissar" was restored two months later in the CCP forces at Peng Dehuai's suggestion.

10 See Mei, *Yan'an mishi*, 1:36–9; see also Ban Ying and Zuo Xiaohui, "*Heimao baimao – ping Han Shan Bi 'Deng Xiaoping zhuan'*" (Black cat or white cat – a critique to Han Shanbi's *A Biography of Deng Xiaoping*), *Tansuo* (Quest), no. 2 (1992), pp. 62–3.

The Establishment of the Yan'an Round Table

"promoted" to chair the CCP's National Trade Union. Deng Xiaoping, a Mao protégé who was then the deputy director of the Political Department of the Eighth Route Army, succeeded Zhang as the division's commissar in mid-January 1938.[11] Deng had been a member of Mao's clique since he was purged as a follower of Mao's "Right-opportunist line" in 1933. He rose rapidly after Mao returned to the CC leadership at the Zunyi Conference.[12] This appointment was one of the three decisive promotions in Deng's career (see Chapter 4) – Deng became Mao's chief watchdog over one-third of the CCP's main forces and, more importantly, this position enabled Deng to develop his own mountaintop in the years to come. Deng's appointment marked Mao's full attainment of the command over the CCP forces. Mao's dominance in the Party, however, was yet to be achieved.

Yan'an versus the CCP Yangtze Bureau

On November 29, 1937, Wang Ming, head of the CCP Mission to the Comintern, landed at Yan'an, together with Kang Sheng, vice-head of the mission, and Chen Yun.[13] They were met by all CCP elite members at Yan'an. Mao made a humble welcome speech: "Welcome you, gods [*shenxian*] descending from the Kunlun Mountain! . . . What a tremendously happy event that you have come back to Yan'an. [Since you return by airplane,] it is indeed 'happiness befalling from heaven'!"[14] Mao

---

11 Deng's appointment was made on January 5. See Xu Baoqi, "*Deng Xiaoping ren 129shi zhengwei shijian kao*" (On the time of Deng Xiaoping's appointment of the commissar of the 129th Division of the Eighth Route Army), *Dangshi Yanjiu zhiliao* (Research Materials of the Party History), 1980, 1:9–14; and Maomao, *Wuode fuqin Deng Xiaoping* (My Father Deng Xiaoping), Hong Kong: Joint Publishing, 1993, p. 263.

12 Li Weihan, *Huiyi yu yanjiu* (Memory and Study), Beijing: CCP Historical Materials Press, 1986, 1:36–8; also Maomao, *Wuode fuqin Deng Xiaoping*, pp. 273–9.

13 When Wang left Shanghai for Moscow on October 18, 1931, he named Bo Gu, Zhang Wentian, Kang Sheng, Chen Yun, Lu Futan, and Li Zhusheng as members of the newly created Provisional Politburo. Bo, Zhang, and Lu formed the Standing Committee. See Zhou, Guo, and Li, *Wang Ming pingzhuan*, pp. 223–4. Kang Sheng left Shanghai for Moscow in July 1933. Chen Yun went to the Comintern in May 1935 to report on the Zunyi Conference. See Xiang Qing, *Gongchan guoji yu zhongguo gemin guanxi lunwenji* (Collection of Papers on the Relationship between the Comintern and China's Revolution), Shanghai: Shanghai People's Press, 1985, pp. 186, 385–6.

14 Quoted from Liu Junmin, "*Shilun Wang Ming youqing jihuizhuyi luxian de xingcheng*" (On the development of Wang Ming's Right-opportunist line), *Journal of Qiqihar Teacher's College*, no. 1, 1982. See also Mei, *Yan'an mishi*, 1:230–1.

Factionalism in Chinese Communist Politics

reminded people specifically that "when [you] enjoy the good situation, never forget its cause [*yinshui siyuan*]" because, as Mao emphasized, the CCP-KMT anti-Japanese united front was initiated by "our Party's leader Comrade Wang Ming" in the "August 1 Declaration."[15]

However, the tension between Mao and Wang soon surfaced at the Politburo Conference (December 9–14). Except for Deng Fa and Wang Jiaxiang, who were in Moscow, all the Politburo members – Zhang Wentian, Mao, Wang Ming, Zhou Enlai, Bo Gu, Ren Bishi, Xiang Ying, Zhang Guotao, Peng Dehuai, Kang Sheng, Chen Yun, Kai Feng, Liu Shaoqi, and Lin Boqu – attended the conference. Mao insisted on the CCP's political and military independence in the united front with the KMT.[16] But Wang advocated that the CCP should commit itself to the united front and even merge, if necessary, its forces into the KMT's, so that China could fight the Japanese under "unified command, unified discipline, unified equipment, unified supply, and unified operational plan."[17] Wang's proposal was consistent with the policy of "a universal antifascist front," adopted by the Comintern. To Mao, however, giving up the independence of the CCP's armed forces meant surrendering his power base.

Among the attendees, Xiang Ying and Zhang Guotao supported Wang.[18] Except for Liu Shaoqi, who "sided with Mao firmly," the attitude of the other attendees, including Peng Dehuai and Zhou Enlai, leaned

---

15 The "August 1 Declaration," issued by the CCP Mission to the Comintern on August 1, 1935, was drafted by Wang Ming. See Xiang Qing, "*Bayi xuanyan xingcheng de lishi guocheng*" (The historical process of the writing of *August 1 Declaration*), *Dangshi ziliao chongkan* (Collections of the Party's Historical Materials), no. 3, 1983.

16 This was the policy Mao advocated at the Luochuan Conference in August 1937. Although there was a dispute over this policy between Mao and the other leaders, notably Zhou Enlai and Zhang Guotao, at the time, Zhang Guotao, *Wuode huiyi* (My Memoirs), Hong Kong: Mingpao Monthly Press, 1973, 3:1296, dramatized these differences for obvious personal reasons. Kuo Warren (Hualun), *Zhonggong shilun* (Analytical History of the CCP), Taipei: Institute of International Relations, 1970, 3:231–3, seems to have exaggerated these differences in order to discredit Mao's vision. See also Yang, *From Revolution to Politics*, pp. 244–8.

17 Liu, "*Shilun Wang Ming youqing jihuizhuyi luxian de xingcheng*," pp. 230–1.

18 Notably, both Xiang and Zhang were mountaintop leaders. Wang's proposal was attractive to Xiang because his New Fourth Army was sandwiched between the Japanese and KMT forces. So it was difficult, and dangerous indeed, for his forces to maintain independence. Zhang sided with Wang largely because of his bitter relationship with Mao.

The Establishment of the Yan'an Round Table

toward Wang.[19] Yet Wang failed to prevail at the conference, largely because Zhang Wentian, then "the person in general charge of final decision making," refused to take sides.[20] A compromise resulted: although Wang failed to achieve a resolution based on his proposal, Mao had to let Wang lead the CCP delegation to the KMT headquarters in Wuhan, and later to accept Wang's self-appointment as the secretary of the CCP Yangtze Bureau (YB), which was newly created to supervise the CCP organizations and the New Fourth Army in central-south China on behalf of the CC.[21]

This compromise revealed the limit of Mao's power. More threatening to Mao's position, however, was its consequences. On December 25, 1937, two days after the first joint meeting of the YB and the CCP delegation,[22] the YB issued "The CC's Declaration on the Current Situation" without even consulting Yan'an.[23] Moreover, on February 8,

19 See Mei, *Yan'an mishi*, 1:245.
20 Zhang Wentian was often mistaken for the CCP's *zong shuji* (general secretary) after the Zunyi Conference. Even Deng Xiaoping made the same mistake in his speech at Zhang's Memorial Meeting. In fact, Zhang was chosen at the Zunyi Conference as *zong fuzi zuihou jueding* (person in general charge of final decision making). The title "general secretary" ceased to be used after Xiang Zhongfa's betrayal in 1931 until Hu Yaobang assumed the CCP leadership in 1982. See *Zunyi huiyi shiliao ji* (Collection of the Historical Materials of the Zunyi Conference), compiled by the Office of Collecting the Materials of Party History, Beijing, 1983, p. 29; and Han Taihua, "*Zhonggong zhongyang zuigao lingdaoren zhiwu chengwei de yanbian*" (Evolution of the title for the supreme CCP leader), *Yanjiu 2*, 1990, 6:87–8.
21 The CCP delegation consisted of Wang Ming, Zhou Enlai, Bo Gu, Ye Jianying, and Dong Biwu. The YB was originally formed by Zhou, Xiang Ying, Bo, Ye Ting, and Lin Boqu, with Zhou as its leader. Wang was not even on the list. His mission was to meet Chiang Kai-shek. See Jin, *Zhou Enlai zhuan*, p. 392. But Wang remained in Wuhan and took over the YB. See Yang Xiaoyi and Tong Xiumei,"*Kangzhan shiqi dang zai Wuhan huodong dashiji*" (Chronology of the Party's activities at Wuhan during the initial years of the Resistance War), *Wuhan dangshi tongxun* (Wuhan Bulletin of the Party History), no. 5, 1985. See also Mei, *Yan'an mishi*, 1:246–7.
22 Wang chaired this conference where the YB and CCP delegations merged into one. Wang appointed himself the YB secretary and Zhou Enlai, vice-secretary. Wang also took charge of the YB's Newspaper Committee. Yan'an never approved, or disapproved, the foregoing decisions. See Liao Xinwen, "*Kangri zhangzheng chuqi changjiang zhongyangju de zuzhi biandong qingkuang – jiantan Wang Ming shi zenyang dangshan shuji de*" (The organizational changes of the YB during the initial years of the anti-Japanese War – and on how Wang Ming became (its) secretary), *Wenxian yu yanjiu* (Documents and Studies), no. 1, 1987; also Jin, *Zhou Enlai zhuan*, pp. 393–4.
23 *Zhonggong zhongyang wenjian xuanji* (A Selected Collection of Documents of the CCP Central Committee), compiled by the CCP Central Archives, Beijing: CC Party School Press, 1991, vol. 11 (1936–8), pp. 410–13.

1938, Wang published "Mr. Mao Zedong's Conversation with *New China* Reporter Qi Guang" in *Xinhua Daily*, the CCP's mouthpiece in the KMT areas. But Wang composed this article himself without Mao's consent.[24]

Mao's dismay was obvious at the Politburo conference in early March, where the dispute between Mao and Wang on the policy toward the KMT-CCP united front was again the dominant topic. Again, the conference failed to achieve a consensus, although Wang seemed to have the support of the majority.[25] Given Wang's previous performance at the YB, Mao demanded: "Wang Ming cannot go back to Wuhan in today's situation!" But both sides had to settle with a compromise again: Wang was let go on the agreement that he would "stay there [i.e., the YB] for only one month"[26] – Wang would not come back until the Sixth Plenum in September. More annoying to Mao was that as soon as he arrived in Wuhan, Wang published his "Summary of the March Politburo Conference" on April 23. In this article, Wang not only posed himself as the top CCP leader but also brought his differences with Mao into public.[27]

The Mao-Wang conflict was essentially a power struggle. Whereas Mao dominated at Yan'an because of his predominance in the Eighth Route Army, Wang's eminence was based on his connection to the Comintern and his theoretical prowess. But it was the support from Xiang Ying, the head of the New Fourth Army, and the control of the YB that enabled Wang to develop a power center outside Yan'an. With such a strong mountaintop, Wang even attempted to make Yan'an follow his baton. On March 21, 1938, Wang drafted "The CC's Suggestions to the KMT Provisional National Congress (PNC)" and submitted it to the KMT without Yan'an's authorization. This "CC's suggestion" was obviously at odds with the CC at Yan'an, which sent its own "The CC's Telegram to PNC" to Wuhan on March 25. However, Wang withheld this genuine CC "Telegram" and instructed Yan'an on April 2: "You must not

---

24 Zhou, Guo, and Li, *Wang Ming pingzhuan*, pp. 321–2.
25 See Mei, *Yan'an mishi*, 1:252–5. But there is little evidence to support Mei's claim that Wang was authorized to draft a summary for the conference.
26 See Liao, "Kangri zhanzheng chuqi changjiang zhongyang ju de zuzhi biandong qingkuang," p. 56.
27 See *Wang Ming yanlun xuanji* (Selected Speeches and Articles of Wang Ming), *Neibu* ed., Beijing: People's Press, pp. 578–89.

The Establishment of the Yan'an Round Table

publish the second 'suggestions' [i.e., Yan'an's March 25 telegram] written by you anywhere and in any form. Otherwise, a tremendous harmful political effect will occur in and outside the Party."[28] In July, the CC sent Mao's *On Protracted War* to the YB, expecting it to be published in *Xinhua Daily*. Wang turned it down with the excuse that it was too long.[29] The real reason was that Mao's vision of a protracted war against Japan was at odds with Wang's idea of a quick victory by the joint forces of the CCP and KMT.

Indeed, Wang, who had a close relationship with the Comintern, was extraordinarily influential in the CCP, which was still subject itself to instructions of the Comintern. Although most Politburo members like Zhu, Zhou, Zhang (Wentian), Chen, and Peng saw Mao's strategy of maintaining independence in the KMT-CCP united front as practically correct, they could not justify this strategy with the Comintern's policy of "a universal antifascist front." So they maintained an ambiguous attitude, and sometimes even leaned toward Wang. Only Liu Shaoqi supported Mao firmly. Wang was so confident that when Lin Boqu urged him to consult Yan'an before making important decisions, Wang sneered: "Not necessary. There are more Politburo members outside Yan'an!"[30] Wang was right: among fourteen Politburo members (Zhang Guotao defected in April), only six of them – Mao, Zhang (Wentian), Kang, Chen, Kai Feng, and Liu – were at Yan'an. Wang (Jiaxiang) and Ren were in Moscow; Wang, Zhou, Bo, Xiang, and Lin (Boqu) were in Wuhan; and Peng was in Shanxi. Wang's influence was such that Mao "sometimes found himself so isolated that his words could hardly be heard beyond the cave where he dwelled."[31]

The Sixth Plenum of the Sixth CC

But the situation was developing in a direction favorable to Mao. Wuhan was lost in late June 1938. The collapse of the KMT forces not only confirmed Mao's prediction of a protracted war but also but also crushed Wang's dream of a quick victory. Moreover, Wuhan's fall made nonsense of Wang's slogan "all through the united front" because the CCP

---

28 *Zhonggong zhongyang wenjian xuanji*, 11:481–8. The PNC opened on March 29, 1938.
29 Zhou, Guo, and Li, *Wang Ming pingzhuan*, p. 342.
30 *Lin Boqu zhuan* (Biography of Lin Boqu), Beijing: Red Flag Press, 1987, p. 224.
31 Li, *Huiyi yu yanjiu*, 1:442–3.

and KMT forces were now geographically separated by the Japanese army.

Unbeknownst to Wang, the decisive blow against him had already been delivered by the Comintern. Wang Jiaxiang returned from Moscow in July 1938. He brought instructions from Dimitrov, general secretary of the Executive Committee of the Comintern: "The Comintern thinks that the CCP's political line is correct.... [Differences] in the leadership should be settled under Mao Zedong's leadership.... [You] must recognize that Comrade Mao Zedong is the leader emerged from the concrete struggle of the Chinese revolution.... Please tell Comrade Wang Ming, do not compete [with Mao] any more."[32] This instruction was passed to the CCP leaders at Yan'an on September 14 at a Politburo conference, whereupon it was decided to hold the Sixth Plenum immediately.[33] But Wang Ming, who was not informed of Dimitrov's instruction, insisted that if a plenum had to be held, it should be convened in Wuhan. He even asked Wang Jiaxiang to go to Wuhan and report to him in person on the Comintern's instruction. Mao would not compromise this time. He instructed Wang Jiaxiang to respond immediately: "Please come to Yan'an in time to attend the Sixth Plenum and to listen to the Comintern's important instruction. You must obey the CC's decision. Otherwise, you have to be responsible for all the consequences."[34]

Wang Ming caved in. The Sixth Plenum was convened at Yan'an from September 29 to November 6, 1938. This was an enlarged plenum: among the fifty-five attendees, only seventeen were CC members,[35] the other thirty-eight were newly emerged mountaintop leaders from North and Northwest China. Not surprisingly, all of them were Mao supporters.[36] The self-educated Chinese communists, or the mountaintop organizers,

---

32 Xu Zehao, "*Wang Jiaxiang dui liujie liuzhong quanhui de gongxian*" (Wang Jiaxiang's contribution to the Sixth Plenum of the Sixth PC), *Wenxian yu Yanjiu* (Documents and Studies), no. 4, 1986, pp. 11–15.
33 The decision was a surprise to leaders outside Yan'an, for it was decided at the December 1937 Politburo conference to convene the Seventh PC instead of another plenum.
34 Zhu Zhongli (Mme Wang Jiaxiang), *Liming yu wanxia* (Dawn and Sunset), Beijing: PLA Press, 1986, pp. 287–8.
35 The seventeen CC members were Mao, Zhu, Zhou, Wang, Zhang, Xiang, Bo, Kang, Wang (Jiaxiang), Peng, Liu, Chen (the preceding twelve were Politburo members), Guan Xiangying, Zhang Hao, Yang Shangkun, Li Fuchun, and Li Weihan.
36 See Hao and Duan, *Liushi nian*, 1:238. Among the thirty-eight non-CC member attendees, Peng Zhen, Gao Gang, Luo Ronghuan, Nie Rongzhen, Deng Xiaoping, He Long, and Luo Ruiqing were the most eminent ones.

The Establishment of the Yan'an Round Table

prevailed over the Moscow-trained students. The plenum adopted *The Political Resolution* based on Mao's report. It criticized "the Right-opportunists" who tended to "sacrifice our Party's political and organizational independence, and ... turn the proletariat and its party into the bourgeoisie's tail."[37] Although the use of the Bolshevik jargon was less sophisticated than that which would have flowed from the pens of the Moscow-trained students, the message was unambiguous. Thus, as Mao recalled, "the dispute with Wang Ming started in 1937 and ended in August 1938."[38]

But Mao's leadership would have been unstable but for a thorough reorganization. The YB was dissolved with the excuse of Wuhan's fall. While Wang was detained at Yan'an, the former YB members were assigned to two newly created CCP bureaus: the Central Plain Bureau (CPB) led by Liu Shaoqi, and the Southern Bureau led by Zhou Enlai.[39] Thus, Wang was deprived of his major power base. Moreover, this reorganization also contained Zhou and Xiang. The Southern Bureau led by Zhou no longer supervised any armed forces. Its mission was to deal with the KMT government and to supervise the CCP organizations in South China ruled by the KMT. The CCP Southeastern Subbureau led by Xiang was upgraded to the Southeastern Bureau, but his power actually decreased because of the cutoff between Xiang and Wang and, moreover, the division of the New Fourth Army (about thirty thousand men in 1939). The Third Detachment in southern Anhui was still under Xiang's control, even though it was the strongest (about nine thousand men); the CPB led by Liu controlled the Fourth and Fifth Detachments in northeastern Anhui;[40] and Chen Yi commanded the First and Second Detachments in northern Jiangsu.[41] In November 1940 the North and South Headquarters of the New Fourth Army merged into the new Central Plain General Headquarters, with Chen as its commander, and

---

37 *Zhonggong zhongyang wenjian xuanji*, 11:757.
38 *Wansui*, 2:164–5. There is a one-month difference between August and September in Mao's account, presumably because Mao confused the lunar calendar with the solar calendar.
39 The CPB was formally set up on November 9, 1938, to supervise "the Party's work in Henan, Hubei, Anhui, and Jiangsu north of the Yangtze River." *Zhonggong zhongyang wenjian xuanji*, 11:783.
40 See *Liu Shaoqi zai wandong* (Liu Shaoqi in East Anhui), Hefei: Anhui People's Press, 1985, pp. 27–8; and *Xulie*, pp. 164–5.
41 *Xulie*, pp. 165–6.

Factionalism in Chinese Communist Politics

MAO ZEDONG
(Party)   (Military)

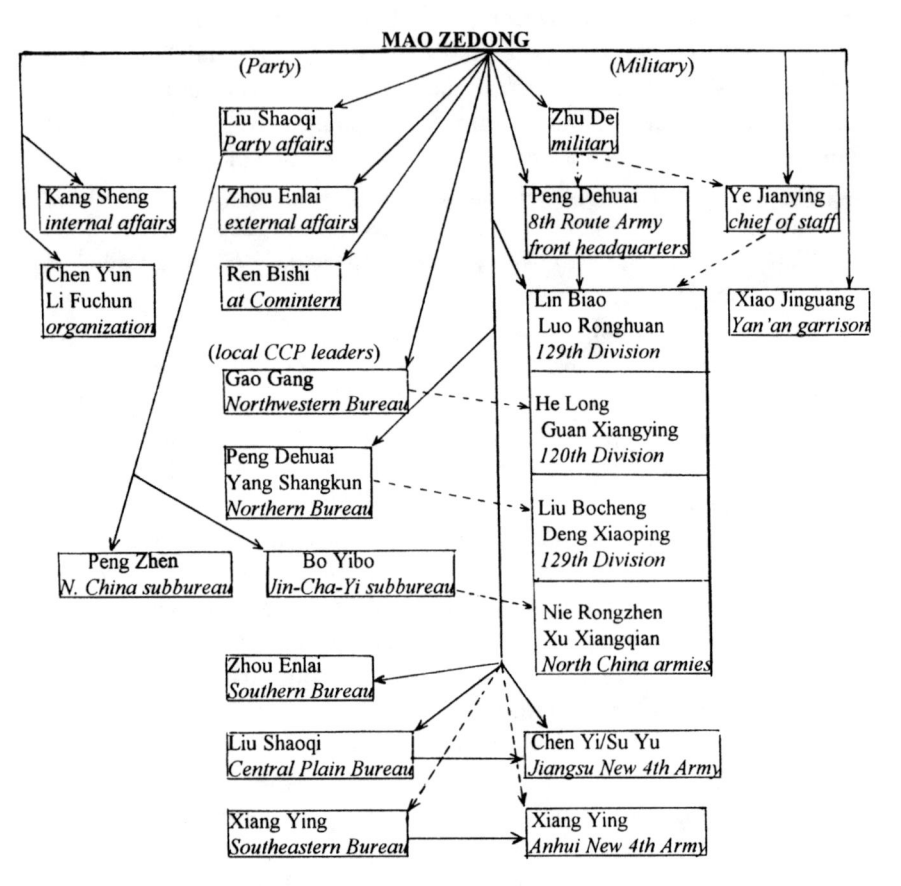

```
Kang Sheng                Liu Shaoqi              Zhu De
internal affairs          Party affairs           military

Chen Yun                  Zhou Enlai              Peng Dehuai          Ye Jianying
Li Fuchun                 external affairs        8th Route Army       chief of staff
organization                                      front headquarters

                          Ren Bishi               Lin Biao             Xiao Jinguang
                          at Comintern            Luo Ronghuan         Yan'an garrison
                          (local CCP leaders)     129th Division

                          Gao Gang
                          Northwestern Bureau     He Long
                                                  Guan Xiangying
                          Peng Dehuai             120th Division
                          Yang Shangkun
                          Northern Bureau         Liu Bocheng
                                                  Deng Xiaoping
Peng Zhen                 Bo Yibo                 129th Division
N. China subbureau        Jin-Cha-Yi subbureau
                                                  Nie Rongzhen
                                                  Xu Xiangqian
                                                  North China armies
                          Zhou Enlai
                          Southern Bureau

                          Liu Shaoqi              Chen Yi/Su Yu
                          Central Plain Bureau    Jiangsu New 4th Army

                          Xiang Ying              Xiang Ying
                          Southeastern Bureau     Anhui New 4th Army
```

Figure 3.2. A tentative Yan'an Round Table after the Sixth Plenum, November 1938 (solid arrow = direct control; dashed arrow = indirect/loose control)

Liu commissar.[42] Thus, the bulk of the New Fourth Army was under the command of Liu and Chen.

By now, the Yan'an Round Table under Mao's command was in shape. Figure 3.2 demonstrates each individual leader's duty and his relationship with Mao; and it also shows that Mao's authority began to expand into the Party organizations with the support of Liu Shaoqi and Gao Gang. Yet there was a striking weakness in this tentative Yan'an Round Table – the lack of ideological control. Mao's command was still vulner-

---
42 Ibid., p. 167.

The Establishment of the Yan'an Round Table

able because ideological legitimacy was a prerequisite for him to assume the top leadership of the CCP, a party that was glued together by ideology. The Wang Ming faction, which had dominated the Party leadership because of its theoretical training and unconditional obedience to the Comintern, still occupied most of the ideological front. Mao had to take over this front in order to establish the ideological legitimacy for his command. The essential aim of the Yan'an Rectification (YR) of 1941–4 was to discredit the Wang Ming faction – it would be accused of dogmatism and be held responsible for the CCP's disastrous setback in the early 1930s – and to establish Mao's "correct line," on which Mao Zedong Thought would be developed.

THE YAN'AN RECTIFICATION AND THE ESTABLISHMENT OF THE YAN'AN ROUND TABLE

The Yan'an Rectification

Wang Ming's setback at the Sixth Plenum was largely due to the Comintern's recognition of Mao's leadership; and the attack on him was justified essentially by "the Party's concrete experience," rather than on ideological grounds. Even Peng Dehuai, the front commander of the Eighth Route Army, was "confused" by the ongoing Mao-Wang struggle. Although Peng's bitterness toward the Moscow-trained students was well known, his "clear objection to the Wang Ming line" at the Sixth Plenum was because this line "did not work in practice."[43] Peng's confusion revealed a dilemma he and the other leaders faced in the Mao-Wang conflict: they supported Mao's strategy of independence, but they could hardly justify this position with the Comintern's united-front policy. Indeed, at a time when Marxism-Leninism was the *sole* source of ideological legitimacy for the CCP's cause and the Moscow-trained students were regarded as the ones who had mastered the communist ideology, Mao's dominance in the Party was vulnerable unless he took over the ideological high ground from the Wang Ming faction.[44]

---

43 See Peng Dehuai, *Peng Dehuai zishu* (Autobiography of Peng Dehuai), Beijing: People's Press, 1981, pp. 224–9.
44 Wang still remained a secretary at the CC Secretariat (analogous to today's PSC) and a Politburo member. He was in charge of the CCP publications, including the CC's official newspaper *New China*. Cf. Deng Liqun, "*Xuexi 'guanyu jianguo yilai dangde*

Mao certainly realized the problem. He initiated "a study campaign" at the Sixth Plenum. The aim, as Mao emphasized repeatedly, was to "have a real grasp of the essence of Marxism" instead of simply "babbling Marxist-Leninist phraseology" – the innuendo was targeted at the returned students.[45] Meanwhile, Mao made a remarkable effort to build up his own doctrine, which would "explain Marxism-Leninism with the practice of China's revolution." Mao's effort resulted in volumes 2 and 3 of the four-volume *Selected Works of Mao Zedong*, both written during the 1937–43 period.

The study campaign led to "a great increase in the whole Party's understanding of Marxism."[46] As a result, the "messengers" were no longer needed. Moreover, they had to be criticized, because they brought dogmatism, factionalism, and stereotyped jargon into the Party. The YR "was aimed at eliminating these abominable styles of work," the style that had undermined the Party and hindered the Chinese revolution.[47]

By now the Wang Ming faction had become virtually helpless: the only substantial support Wang had in the CCP forces disappeared with Xiang's death in the 1941 Wannan Incident,[48] and the Comintern was too preoccupied with "The Great Patriotic War" to attend to the CCP's internal affairs. Mao seized the opportunity and convened an enlarged Politburo conference from September 10 to October 22, 1941.[49] "This was

ruogan lishi wenti de jueyi' de wenti he huida" (Questions and answers for the study of *The Resolution on Several Questions of Our Party's History since the Establishment of the PRC*), *Zhuanji*, 2:131.

45 See *SWMZD*, 2:208–10.
46 See "*Guanyu ruogan lishi wenti de jueyi*" (Resolution of several historical problems), adopted at the Seventh Plenum of the Sixth PC, April 20, 1945.
47 See *SWMZD*, 3:35–50.
48 In January 5–15, 1941, the KMT forces attacked the New Fourth Army led by Xiang Ying in southern Anhui. Xiang was killed. On January 20 the CC appointed Chen Yi the acting commander and Liu Shaoqi the commissar of the New Fourth Army. Meanwhile, the CC dispatched "the Decision on Xiang and Yuan (Guoping)'s Mistakes" within the Party. (Yuan, who was also killed in the event, was the political director of the New Fourth Army.) The two were criticized as "Right-opportunists." See *Liuda yilai – dangnei mimi wenjian* (Since the Sixth PC – the secret party documents), Beijing: People's Press, 1980, 1:237–8.
49 See Hu Qiaomu, *Hu Qiaomu huiyi Mao Zedong* (Hu Qiaomu's Memory of Mao Zedong), Beijing: People's Press, 1994, p. 193. The formal attendees of the conference were Mao, Ren, Wang, Wang (Jiaxiang), Zhu, Zhang, Kang, Chen, Kai, Bo, and Deng Fa. Li Fuchun, Yang Shangkun, Li Weihan, Chen Boda, Gao Gang, Lin Boqu, Ye Jianying, Wang Ruofei, and Peng Zhen were also present at the conference.

The Establishment of the Yan'an Round Table

a rectification conference," which marked the beginning of the YR.[50] In his opening speech, Mao attacked Wang Ming and his like, accusing them of carrying a line of "Left-opportunism, subjectivism, and factionalism," the line that had caused devastating damage to the Party during its dominance in 1934–36.[51] Following Mao's lead, not only did Zhu De and Lin Boqu attack Wang Ming and his like,[52] but Kang Sheng and Chen Yun also turned on their former boss.[53] Zhang Wentian made a self-criticism and then surrendered his position as "the person in general charge of final decision making" at the CC Secretariat.[54] After "the examination of the problems in the Party's history,"[55] the conference reached the following conclusion: "From the Fourth Plenum of the Sixth PC to the Zunyi Conference, the error of the CC leadership is the *error of line*.... Its ideological roots are subjectivism and formalism."[56] Crestfallen and isolated, Wang refused to attend the conference with the excuse of "illness" on October 12, and after that he virtually ceased to work.[57]

On February 1, 1942, Mao issued the report "Rectify the Party's Style of Work" at the Central Party School. A week later he delivered the other report "Oppose Stereotyped Party Writing" at the Yan'an Cadre Conference.[58] The CC Propaganda Department, which was now led by Ren Bishi and Kang Sheng, issued a resolution on April 3, emphasizing that Mao's two reports "expounded the task and principles for this rectification campaign" and therefore had to be studied by every CCP member.

50 Hao and Duan, *Liushi nian*, 1:278.
51 See Hu, *Hu Qiaomu huiyi Mao Zedong*, pp. 193–5.
52 See *Zhu De nianpu* (A Chronicle of Zhu De's Life), compiled by the CC Documentary Study Office, Beijing: People's Press, 1986, p. 242; and *Lin Boqu zhuan*, p. 270.
53 Zhong Kan, *Kang Sheng pingzhuan* (A Critical Biography of Kang Sheng), Beijing: Red Flag Press, 1982, p. 79. The tension between Wang and Chen, then director of the CC Organization Department, surfaced on personnel arrangements in February 1941. Chen prevailed with Mao's support. Cf. *SWCY*, pp. 157–8.
54 See Wu Liangping, "Huiyi Wentian" (Memory of Wentian), in *Huiyi Zhang Wentian* (The Memory of Zhang Wentian), Changsha: Hunan People's Press, 1985, p. 51; and Hu, *Hu Qiaomu huiyi Mao Zedong*, p. 195.
55 Xiao Chaoran and Sha Jiansun, *Zhongguo geming shigao* (History of the Chinese Revolution), Beijing: Beijing University Press, 1984, p. 326.
56 Quoted from *Zhonggong yanjiu* (Study of the CCP), 17, no. 2 (1973), Taipei, pp. 74–5 (emphasis added).
57 See Hu, *Hu Qiaomu huiyi Mao Zedong*, pp. 199–202; Mei, *Yan'an mishi*, 1:285–95; and Zhou, Guo, and Li, *Wang Ming pingzhuan*, p. 393.
58 For the two reports, see *SWMZD*, 3:53–68.

Factionalism in Chinese Communist Politics

On the same day, the General Study Commission was set up as the headquarters of the YR, with Mao as its director, and Kang, vice-director.[59] The YR was officially launched with a series of measures to secure Mao's absolute control of the campaign:

1. On February 28 the Central Party School, where the high-ranking cadres were trained, was put under the direct control of the CC Secretariat. Mao personally supervised its political studies; Ren was in charge of its organizational affairs; and Peng Zhen took care of its daily affairs.[60]
2. In April various study commissions were set up in all the systems (*xitong*) in northern Shaanxi to strengthen the CC's control of the headquarters area. These commissions were led by Kang, Li Fuchun, Ke Qingshi, Wang Shoudao, Chen Boda, and Cao Yiou (Kang's wife) in the CC apparatus; Wang Jiaxiang and Chen Yun in the CMC apparatus; and Kai Feng and Li Weihan in the propaganda and culture spheres.
3. Ren and Gao were in charge of the Study Commission of the local Party, administrative, and military systems. There were three subcommissions, which were led by Chen Zhengren in local Party and mass organizations; Lin Boqu and Xie Juezai in administrative systems; and Xiao Jinguang and Wang Zhen in the garrison forces.[61]
4. The CC General Office was set up to handle the information flow, with Li Fuchun as its head. The other two key members, Chen Boda and Hu Qiaomu, also served as Mao's personal secretaries.[62]
5. On May 13, 1942, the Shaanxi-Shuiyuan Military Region, led by He Long, and the Yan'an Garrison, led by Xiao Jinguang, were merged into the newly created Shaan-Gan-Ning-Sui Joint Command. The aim was to put all the CCP forces in the Northwest under direct control of the CMC. He Long was named its commander, Guan Xiangying, commissar, Xu Xiangqian and Xiao Jinguang, vice-commanders, and Gao Gang, vice-commissar (who soon became the acting commissar due to Guan's poor health).[63]
6. In order to control propaganda, Kang Sheng, Chen Boda, Wang Ruofei, and Deng Liqun formed the editorial board of *Xuexi* (Study), the offi-

---

59 See Hao and Duan, *Liushi nian*, p. 278.
60 Tang Peiji, "*Jianguo yiqian ershiba nian lishi de huigu*" (A review of twenty-eight years of history before the establishment of the PRC), *Zhuanji*, 1:81.
61 See *Jiefang ribao* (Liberation Daily), April 19, 1942.
62 Li was also the acting director of the CC Organization Department; Chen came from the CC Propaganda Department; and Hu was recommended by his patron, Liu Shaoqi, from the CYCL Propaganda Department.
63 *Xulie*, p. 135; and Wang Jianying, *Zhongguo gongchandang zuzhi shiliao huibian* (Collection of Materials of the CCP's Organizational History), Beijing: Red Flag Press, 1983, pp. 412–13.

The Establishment of the Yan'an Round Table

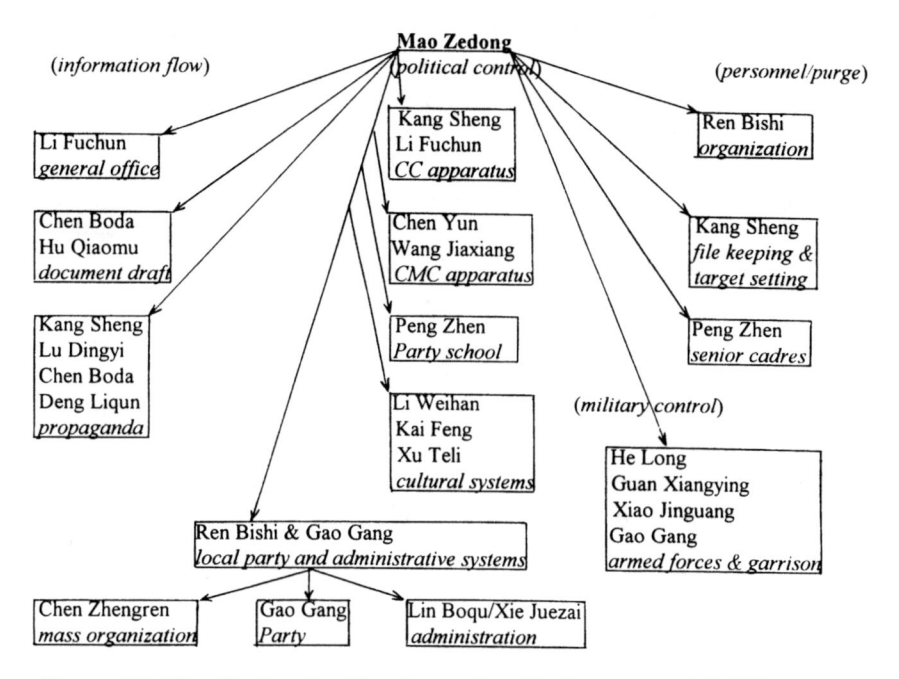

Figure 3.3. The Yan'an Rectification under Mao's command (solid arrow = direct control; dashed arrow = indirect control)

cial magazine of the General Study Commission, in June. Lu Dingyi was appointed chief editor of the CC's newspaper *Jiefang ribao* (Liberation Daily) in September.[64]

Indeed, the YR was thoroughly prepared and organized under Mao's command in order to wipe out the influence of the Wang Ming faction and, more importantly, to provide Mao's command with ideological legitimacy (Figure 3.3).

Compared with the command structure in Figure 3.2, a distinctive change was that Mao had overcome his weakness, the lack of ideological control. His command now extended to the entire ideological area. Two men rose into prominence in this change: Kang Sheng and Li

---

64 Wang, *Zhongguo gongchangdang zuzhi shiliao*, p. 380. *New China*, controlled by Wang, and *Today's News*, led by Zhang Wentian, were merged into *Liberation Daily* on May 16, 1941. Bo Gu was appointed its director, but the real boss was Chief Editor Yang Cong, a member of Mao's study group. Yang died in September 1941, and he was succeeded by Lu Dingyi, Liu's associate, and Ai Siqi, Mao's philosophy tutor.

Factionalism in Chinese Communist Politics

Fuchun. Kang was in charge of interior affairs, propaganda, file keeping, and setting up targets during the YR. As the purge went to the extreme in 1942, Kang attracted much negative attention.[65]

Li had been a member of Mao's clique since December 1931, when he was appointed the secretary of the Jiangxi Provincial Party Committee under direct leadership of Mao, who was then the chairman of the Central Soviet Area.[66] At the Zunyi Conference, Li, the acting director of the First Front Army's Political Department, "severely criticized Wang Ming and firmly supported Comrade Mao Zedong's leadership."[67] In July 1937 Li succeeded Deng Xiaoping as the CC's secretary general, and he was concurrently the deputy director of the CC Organizational Department. As the YR reached the "crucial moment" in early 1942, Mao put Li in charge of the newly created General Office to control the information flow. Although Li kept a low profile in the YR, Mao would not have given Li such an important job had Li not won Mao's trust. As a senior CCP cadre described: "Kang Sheng was a crazy dog during the YR, but Li Fuchun passed the information to and from Mao in decision making."[68]

The two-year campaign "purified the Party both in organization and in spirit," and massive purges made it clear to everyone who the real boss was. The conclusion of the YR was made at the enlarged Seventh Plenum of the Sixth PC, which lasted from May 21, 1943, to April 20, 1944 – the longest plenum in the CCP history. The agenda of the plenum was to "discuss the problems in the Party history, especially those that occurred between early 1931 and the end of 1934," during which time the Wang Ming faction controlled the CC leadership. The plenum adopted *The Resolution on Several Historical Problems*, drafted by Hu Qiaomu under Mao's supervision.[69] It denounced the Wang Ming faction

65 See Zhong, *Kang Sheng pingzhuan*, pp. 82–95.
66 Li's wife, Cai Chang, was a sister of Mao's best friend, Cai Hesen, who was executed by the KMT in 1927. Cai was among a few who had a substantial influence on Mao. See "*Cai Hesen Zhuan*" (A Biography of Cai Hesen), *RWZ* (1978), 2:6–12.
67 "*Li Fuchun zhuan*" (A Biography of Li Fuchun), *RWZ* (1990), 44:32.
68 Source A. In this study I interviewed quite a few well-informed sources, among whom four were very helpful because of their personal involvement in the events examined in this book. I will identify them as Sources A, B, C, and D, according to the sequence in which they are cited.
69 According to Mei, *Yan'an mishi*, 2:491–3, the first draft of the Resolution was done by Ren Bishi in May 1944; Hu Qiaomu then made a thorough revision – the second draft; and Zhang Wentian made the third draft based on Hu's. After that, Mao revised the

The Establishment of the Yan'an Round Table

and its "Left-opportunist line ..."; highly evaluated Mao Zedong's brilliant contribution to the Chinese revolution; and expounded the great immediate and historical significance of the establishment of Mao Zedong's leadership."[70]

The Beginning of the Chairman Mao Era and the Rise of Gao Gang and Liu Shaoqi

It would have been difficult for Mao to establish his dominance in the Party without the support of the Party elite members, especially Liu Shaoqi, Gao Gang, Ren Bishi, and Kang Sheng. However, they played different roles and had different relations with Mao in the establishment of Mao's command. They therefore obtained different positions in the emerging Yan'an Round Table.

Ren supported Mao in the Mao-Zhang struggle during the Long March,[71] and he played a crucial role in winning the Comintern's support for Mao.[72] After Ren returned to Yan'an in March 1940, Mao entrusted to him not only daily affairs at the CC Secretariat but also organizational affairs. Ren also participated in the drafting of *The Resolution on Several Historical Problems*. But as a CCP leader who had his own mountaintop – the armed forces led by He Long – and had close ties with the CCP organizations in the Northwest, Ren was not so much Mao's follower as his trustworthy ally.[73]

Kang was a calculating and keen player of elite politics. Although he had been close to Wang Ming, he quickly won Mao's trust and favor after the Sixth Plenum[74] due to his keenness at reading Mao's mind, his theoretical training, his ability to stir up emotions, and, above all, his

---

draft seven times with Hu Qiaomu's assistance before it was approved at the plenum on April 20, 1945. Hu, *Hu Qiaomu huiyi Mao Zedong*, p. 66, implies that Chen Yun also played a substantial role in the drafting. This must be treated with caution because it is not so much a historical fact as Hu's effort to flatter Chen.

70 Hao and Duan, *Liushi nian*, 1:280.
71 Tang, "*Jianguo yiqian ershiba nian lishi de huigu*," 1:68–9; see also Yang, *From Revolution to Politics*, pp. 129–61, 204–6, 210–18.
72 Xiang, *Gongchan guoji yu zhongguo geming*, pp. 218–19, 390–2; and Yu Jundao, *Zhongguo geming zhong de gongchan guoji renwu* (People from the Comintern in China's Revolution), Chengdu: Sichuan People's Press, 1986, pp. 74–7. Ren left Yan'an for the Comintern as the CCP's new chief representative on March 16, 1938.
73 Cf. Yang, *From Revolution to Politics*, pp. 199–200.
74 See Zhong, *Kang Sheng pingzhuan*, pp. 38–73, 82–95.

willingness to do unpleasant tasks for Mao. Kang's eminence, however, was based partly on his control of the CCP Social Department in charge of internal affairs, but largely on Mao's favor rather than his own power base, as Kang did not have his own mountaintop. This determined his absolute obedience to Mao, who in turn found himself a reliable file keeper.

Although Gao was junior to the other three,[75] he rose quickly under Mao's patronage after the Long Marchers arrived in northern Shaanxi in October 1935. In return, Gao made a crucial contribution to the establishment of Mao's command. Purges by the pre-1935 CC leadership and shared enmity against the Moscow-trained students formed the natural basis for the closeness between Mao and Gao.[76] A more objective reason, however, was that Mao and his followers were all southerners who felt alien to the local tradition and culture. A native elite like Gao was needed to secure popular support in the headquarters area in the ongoing Mao-Wang struggle.[77] As Mao admitted: "I came to northern Shaanxi five or six years ago, yet I cannot match with comrades like Gao Gang in my knowledge of conditions here and in my relations with people of this region."[78]

Indeed, the "northwestern faction" formed by the local cadres, also known as the "donkey faction,"[79] played a crucial role in discrediting the Wang Ming faction during the YR. Their strong desire to reverse the 1935 verdict against them and their shared bitterness toward the Moscow-trained students made them the most zealous participants of the YR.[80]

75 Gao, who joined the CCP in 1926, was a leader of the northern Shaanxi base area in the early 1930s, where Liu Zhidan was the military commander, Gao was in charge of the Party, and Xi Zhongxun led the government. See *"Liu Zhidan zhuan"* (A Biography of Liu Zhidan), *RWZ* (1981), 3:206–8.
76 When the Long Marchers arrived in northern Shaanxi, a massive purge had been under way there. All the local leaders, including Liu, Gao, and Xi, were arrested by the representatives of the pre-1935 CC leadership. They were accused of "Right-opportunism" and carrying "a rich peasant line." Mao ordered a stop to the purge as soon as he learned of it. See Li, *Huiyi yu yanjiu*, 1:269–72; also *"Liu Zhidan zhuan,"* pp. 208–10.
77 Cf. Hu, *Hu Qiaomu huiyi Mao Zedong*, p. 138.
78 Quoted from Conrad Brandt, Benjamin Schwartz, and John K. Fairbank, *A Documentary History of Chinese Communism*, New York: Atheneum, 1967, p. 387.
79 Most members of this faction were donkey riders, because their ranks were not high enough to ride horses, a privilege for cadres above the county and regiment levels. Donkey was also the major livestock in the region.
80 The tension between the local cadres and the representatives of the pre-1935 CC leadership had never ceased since the 1935 purge. Although the latter were criticized in

The Establishment of the Yan'an Round Table

Notably, Gao's leadership over the "donkey faction" was formalized when the YR was launched. On May 13, 1941, the CCP Northwestern Working Commission, led by Zhang Wentian, and the CCP Shaan-Gan-Ning Border Region Bureau, led by Ren Bishi, merged into the CCP Northwestern Bureau (NWB). Gao, who was then not even a CC member, became the secretary of the NWB, although it had been expected that Zhang or Ren – both sitting Politburo members – would assume this position.[81]

Gao soon proved his worthiness. Soon after his appointment, Gao led an investigation team down to the NWB's grass-root units to "unify the thinking" for the YR; and he did it again in early 1942 after the YR was officially launched. After 3,689 cadres of the NWB had participated in rectification studies,[82] the NWB convened the Northwestern High-Ranking Cadre Conference (NWHCC) on October 19, 1942. The aim was to "resolve three particularly big problems of the Shaan(xi)-Gan(su) Party: its history, its leadership, and its tasks."[83] Not surprisingly, the target was the pre-1935 CCP leadership.

Ren presided over the NWHCC; but it was Gao who had prepared and organized this significant gathering. Discussions at the NWHCC soon focused on the 1935 purge of the local cadres; and the pre-1935 CC leadership was under fire. "Under Mao Zedong's guidance," the criticism escalated into an overall attack on the Left-deviationists, namely the Moscow-trained students.[84] This NWHCC, originally scheduled to end on November 8, 1942, lasted till January 14, 1943; and it became the largest gathering of the CCP organization before 1949. Not only did all 266 cadres at the county and regiment levels and above in the region attend the conference, but all the members of the Central High-Ranking Cadre

---

November 1935, they remained in their positions. Some of them were even promoted, because the Wang Ming faction was still influential at the time. Moreover, as Li, *Huiyi yu yanjiu*, 1:373, admitted: "The local cadres [who had been purged] were still labeled as Right-opportunists. So their work assignments, especially for those high-ranking cadres, were generally unfair." After Liu Zhidan was killed in a battle in April 1936, Gao and Xi were seen as the leaders of these local cadres. Cf. "*Liu Zhidan zhuan*," pp. 272–3.

81 Li, *Huiyi yu yanjiu*, 2:452.
82 Zhu Chengjia, *Zhonggong dangshi yanjiu lunwen ji* (Collection of Papers on the Study of the CCP History), Shanghai: Shanghai People's Press, 1988, 2:42.
83 Tang, "*Jianguo yiqian ershiba nian lishi de huigu*," p. 81.
84 Xu Xiangqian, *Lishi de huigu* (History in Retrospect), 2 vols., Beijing: PLA Press, 1987, 2:693–5.

Study Group and the advanced students at the CC Party School were also present throughout its eighty-eight days of heated discussion.

The significance of the NWHCC is that it generated a momentum at the CCP headquarters area to denounce Wang Ming and his like as "the Left-opportunists," while Mao's leadership was justified by his "line of proceeding from practice and seeking truth from facts."[85] After the NWHCC, Mao was confident enough to convene a Politburo conference in March 16–20, 1943. The aim was to discuss "the issues of the Party leadership and its organizational structure." A new CC Secretariat – analogous to today's PSC – was formed by Mao, Liu, and Ren. Mao assumed the chairmanships of the Secretariat, the Politburo, and the CMC; he was also the secretary of the CC Propaganda Commission, and the president of the CC Party School.[86] The Chairman Mao era had begun.

Gao was rewarded handsomely. He was praised as "the leader of the revolution in Northwest ... and the representative of the correct line of Mao Zedong."[87] Although he was a local leader who had never been a CC member, Gao was helicoptered into the Politburo and ranked eighth among the thirteen members at the First Plenum of the Seventh CC in June 1945.[88] A rising star, Gao not only was the youngest but also had direct access to Mao among the Politburo members.

Unlike Gao, Liu was a senior CCP leader. He entered the Politburo as an expert on the workers' movement during the Wang Ming period.[89] Liu's substantial rise started in March 1936 when he was sent to Tianjin

---

85 See Kuo, *Zhonggong shilun*, 2:396.
86 Hao and Duan, *Liushi nian*, 1:279.
87 See "*Yan Hongyan zhuan*" (A Biography of Yan Hongyan), *RWZ* (1984), 26:97. Some local cadres led by Yan, who would become the Party secretary of Yunan Province after 1949, had different opinions on Gao at the NWHCC. But Kang ironed them out.
88 The Politburo members were Mao, Liu, Zhu, Zhou, Ren, Chen, Kang, Gao, Peng Zhen, Dong Biwu, Lin, Zhang, and Peng Dehuai.
89 Liu went to Moscow in late 1920, where he joined the CCP in 1921. After he returned to China in 1922, Liu was engaged in the workers' movement. He was appointed the secretary of the CC Workers' Movement Committee in early 1928. He was soon moved from this position because of his criticism of the then CC leaders, Qu Qiubai and Li Weihan, for their "Left-adventurism." Cf. *Zhonggong zhongyang wenjian xuanji*, 11:812. After that, Liu headed the CCP Hebei Provincial Committee till January 1930, and then the CCP Manchuria Committee till August 1930, when he was sent to Moscow, where he stayed till the fall of 1931 as the CCP's chief representative at the Workers' International. See Xiang, *Gongchan guoji he zhongguo geming guanxi lunwenji*, pp. 266–7. Liu entered the Politburo as an alternate member at both the Fourth and Fifth Plenums of the Sixth CC. See Hao and Duan, *Liushi nian*, 1:162, 171.

The Establishment of the Yan'an Round Table

to rebuild the CCP Northern Bureau (NB).[90] In this mission Liu demonstrated his prowess as a political organizer. Under his leadership, the CCP organization expanded rapidly in North China, particularly in Shanxi and Hebei provinces, which the CCP leadership had foreseen as "the key areas" for strategic development.[91] With the assistance of his trio of followers, Peng Zhen, Rao Shushi, and Bo Yibo – all three had been working in North China since the late 1920s[92] – Liu soon expanded the NB into the largest bureau in the CCP. The NB was actually seen as the "front office" of Yan'an after it was moved from Beiping to Shanxi in August 1937. Liu also made a remarkable effort to develop the CCP's administrative systems in the vast rural areas where the KMT rule had collapsed, but the Japanese forces were too stretched to exercise effective control.[93] All this paved the way for the rapid expansion of the CCP forces in North China in the late 1930s.[94] Meanwhile, Liu also built up a strong mountaintop for himself in the CCP organizations.

90 Zhang Wentian chose Liu for this mission at the Wayaobao Politburo Conference in December 1935, because Liu, the former secretary of the CCP Hebei Provincial Committee, had reliable connections with the CCP activists in North China. See Zhao Shu, "*Zhang Wentian yu Wayaobao huiyi*" (Zhang Wentian and the Wayaobao Conference), *Yanjiu 2*, 1990, 5:23–30. Liu was sent to Tianjin before – in August 1933 when the Red Army reached its peak – but that mission turned out to be fruitless.
91 Hao and Duan, *Liushi nian*, 1:190.
92 Peng, the Party boss in Beiping, had been close to Liu since the late 1920s. He moved to Shanxi with the NB in August 1937. In January 1938 Peng was named secretary of the CCP Jin-Cha-Yi Committee, which later grew into the Northern Subbureau. Rao Shushi, a.k.a. Xiao Yao, was one of Liu's major assistants in the workers' movement in Hebei and Manchuria in the late 1920s. After Liu returned to the NB, Rao worked under Liu's direct leadership. He was later sent to the CCP Southeast Bureau as its vice-secretary after the Sixth Plenum, obviously to contain its secretary, Xiang Ying. Bo Yibo was sent to his hometown in Shanxi after he was released from the KMT's jail in Beiping in 1936. In 1941 Bo succeeded Peng, who was promoted to vice-president of the Central Party School.
93 See Bo Yibo, "*Liu Shaoqi tongzhi de yige lishi gongji*" (A historical contribution of Comrade Liu Shaoqi), *Shanxi geming huiyi lu* (Reminiscence of Revolution in Shanxi), compiled by Shanxi Social Science Academy, Taiyuan: Shanxi People's Press, 1983, pp. 33–7.
94 The entire Eighth Route Army entered Shanxi after the August 1937 reorganization. The 115th Division expanded eastward, and developed the Jin-Cha-Yi base area, led by Nie Rongzhen, and the Shandong base area, led by Luo Ronghuan. (Lin Biao was injured by friendly fire in 1938 and was sent to Moscow for treatment until 1942.) The 120th Division expanded northward and developed the Jin-Shui (yuan) base area. The 129th Division expanded southeastward and developed the Jin-Yi-Lu-Yu base area. See Hao and Duan, *Liushi nian*, 1:217–26.

Factionalism in Chinese Communist Politics

It was during this mission that Liu began his ferocious attack on the Moscow-trained students. In a long letter to Zhang Wentian on March 4, 1937, Liu relentlessly criticized the pre-1935 CC leadership for its constant "mistakes of Left adventurism and factionalism." Liu lashed out: "The [pre-1935] CC did not have any major achievements in the white areas.... Their mistakes have exerted the most influential and far-reaching (damaging) effect in the Party, and their damage to our Party was also the greatest."[95] Liu's harsh criticism dismayed Zhang and Zhou Enlai, who had been in charge of the work in the white areas, to the extent that he was summoned back to Yan'an, criticized, and demoted to a humble secretary at the Organizational Department.[96]

But this episode laid the foundation for the Mao-Liu honeymoon. Although Liu was in fact "isolated" due to the demotion and criticism, Liu's attack on the Moscow-trained students, according to his wife, Wang Guangmei, won him many supporters, "among whom the most crucial and strongest one was Mao Zedong."[97] This was not surprising, for Mao's policy of independence justified Liu's effort to expand the CCP organizations, and his own mountaintop as well, in the CCP-KMT united front, while Liu's support boosted Mao's strength in the Party. Indeed, Wang Ming's policy that "everything (must be decided) through the united front" was the last thing Liu wanted; had the CCP's activities gone through the united front led by the KMT, Liu's expansion would have been extremely difficult, because it undermined the KMT's influence in North China. Thus, "Liu Shaoqi sided with Mao firmly"[98] in the Mao-Wang struggle at the two Politburo conferences in December 1937 and in March 1938. Given that Wang's stance was justified by the Comintern policy, and that Xiang Ying sided with Wang while the other Politburo members were either indifferent, or even leaned toward Wang, Mao could have lost to Wang had Liu not firmly supported him. It is not surprising that Liu became Mao's right-hand man immediately after the

95 *Zhonggong zhongyang wenjian xuanji*, 11:801–17.
96 According to Sources A and C, Zhang and Zhou would have expelled Liu from the Politburo but for Mao's rejection. However, they still managed to demote Liu in May 1937. Yang Shangkun, the youngest among the Moscow-trained students, replaced Liu as the NB secretary. But Liu maintained solid control of the NB through his trio: Peng, Rao, and Bo.
97 Wang Guangmei, "*Yujun tongzhou, fengyu wuhui*" (No regret for being your company for life), *Xinhua wenzhai* (New China Digest), no. 240 (December 1998), p. 127.
98 See "*Liu Shaoqi zhuan*" (A Biography of Liu Shaoqi), *RWZ* (1991), 49:46.

The Establishment of the Yan'an Round Table

March 1938 conference; and Liu's name was signed right below Mao's in all eleven published internal CC directives dispatched from Yan'an during the period when he stayed with Mao at Yan'an – from March 1938 to the end of the Sixth Plenum.[99]

Not surprisingly, Liu played a leading role in criticizing Wang Ming at the Sixth Plenum. He lashed out at Wang: "If 'everything through the united front' means everything through Chiang Kai-shek..., it was nothing but one-sided obedience."[100] Liu launched a more ferocious attack on Wang and his like after the plenum. In his "How to Be a Good Communist," Liu totally discredited the Moscow-trained students. He lashed out:

> These people knew absolutely nothing about Marxism-Leninism and could only babble Marxist-Leninist phraseology, and yet they regarded themselves as "China's Marx" or "China's Lenin," posed as such in the Party, and had the impudence to require that our Party members should revere them as Marx and Lenin are revered, support them as "the leaders," and accord them loyalty and devotion. They went so far as to appoint themselves "the leaders" without being chosen, climbed into positions of authority, issued orders to the Party like patriarchs, tried to lecture our Party, abused everything in the Party, wilfully attacked and punished our Party members and pushed them around. Those people... were just careerists in the Party, termites in the communist movement.[101]

---

99 See *Zhonggong zhongyang wenjianji*, 11:475–552. Mao kept Liu by his side after the March 1938 conference, even though Zhang and Zhou agreed to let Liu go back to NB. See "*Zhongyang guanyu beifangju lingdao fengong de jueding*" (The CC's decision on the work assignments of the NB leaders), March 24, 1937, ibid., p. 477. This decision ordered that all the subleaders of the NB "must report *directly* to Comrade Hu Fu [i.e., Liu] in addition to Comrade Yang Shangkun," who was then the NB secretary (emphasis added).

100 Wang Shoudao, "*Jianding de zhanzai zhengque luxian yibian*" (Firmly stand on the side of the correct line), *Mianhuai Liu Shaoqi* (Cherish the Memory of Liu Shaoqi), Beijing: People's Press, 1983, p. 20. Mao, *SWMZD*, 2:527, also quoted Liu's words.

101 *SWLSQ*, 1:115–16. Ironically, the Red Guards during the CR saw these words as "solid evidence of Liu's vicious attack on" Mao. But Liu's ferocious attacks on others, including Zhou, during the YR provided perhaps a key reason why, among the senior cadres, the sympathy toward his tragedy in the CR was so weak, compared with that toward other CR victims like Chen Yi, He Long, and even Lin Biao. Liu's men, notably Peng and Bo, were cautious in talking about Liu's activities during the YR.

Factionalism in Chinese Communist Politics

This article delighted Mao so much that he asked Liu to make a formal report on it to the Yan'an Marx-Lenin Academy, an institute where the high-ranking CCP cadres were gathered for theoretical training. Thus, Liu was called back to Yan'an from the newly created CPB in Anhui in March 1939, two months after he had arrived there.[102] Liu remained at Yan'an till September, although the New Fourth Army assigned to his CPB was undergoing its "most difficult time" during this period.[103]

Liu soon expanded his power base. After the 1941 Wannan Incident (see note 48), Liu's CPB absorbed the badly damaged Southeastern Bureau, and was renamed the Central China Bureau (CCB) in May. Liu was appointed its secretary, and Liu's protégé, Rao Shushi, vice-secretary. By now, Liu emerged as the most powerful Party leader under Mao's command: he controlled two of the four CCP bureaus at the time, the NB and the CCB (the other two, the NWB and the Southern Bureau [SB], were led by Gao and Zhou).

On July 2, 1941, Liu delivered another timely report, "On Inner-Party Struggle," at the CCB Party School. Liu argued that, as "a reflection of the class struggle outside the Party," the inner-Party struggle "is absolutely indispensable in preserving the Party's purity and independence, in guaranteeing the conformity of its actions with the line that represents the highest interests of the proletariat."[104] Meanwhile, Liu denounced the Wang Ming faction as "the Chinese Bolsheviks" who picked on others "just to show how well they had been 'Bolshevist' [so as] to enhance their prestige."[105]

This report was exactly what Mao needed on the eve of the YR. Mao had it published in the *Liberation Daily*, the CC's mouthpiece, on October 9, 1942. Mao personally wrote the "Editor's Comment," demanding that "every comrade must read" Liu's report, because it "solves an important problem on the inner-Party struggles."

102 Liu, the new CPB secretary, left Yan'an for Anhui on November 23, 1938. He arrived at the CPB in early January 1939. He left Anhui for Yan'an in mid-March and delivered the report "How to Be a Good Communist" at the Yan'an Marx-Lenin Academy on July 8. See "*Liu Shaoqi zhuan*," pp. 49–50.
103 Ibid., pp. 57–61.
104 *SWLSQ*, 1:181–2. It is interesting to notice that there is an obvious parallel between Liu's justification for "inner-Party struggles" and the "class-struggle theory" Mao put forward at the Tenth Plenum of the Eighth CC in 1962, the theory that latter justified Mao's launching of the CR (see Chapter 5).
105 Ibid., p. 207.

The Establishment of the Yan'an Round Table

At this time, Liu was on his way to Yan'an to help Mao "rectify the thinking of the high-ranking cadres." As soon as he arrived at Yan'an,[106] Liu made a high-profile speech at the ongoing NWHCC. In this speech Liu attacked Wang Ming by name for the first time, accusing Wang and his like of "a tremendous *crime against the Party*."[107] This was a bombshell indeed, for "a crime against the Party" was the accusation used only against those who had betrayed the Party, such as Zhang Guotao, but the term "error" was the one used in the criticism against those who still remained in the Party, such as Li Lisan, Qu Qiubai, and even Chen Duxiu. Liu's attack on Wang sent a clear message to all the Party because, according to Source C, "a crime against the Party" was an accusation that could lead to execution at that time.

Liu's crucial role in the struggle against the Wang Ming faction and his devotion to Mao's leadership paid off. He entered the newly created three-man Secretariat at the Politburo conference in March 1943. He also became the CMC vice-chairman despite his lack of military experience. His other positions included secretary of the Organizational Commission and director of the Central Research Bureau, created during the YR to provide theoretical justifications for the policies adopted by the CCP leadership. Liu was also "in charge of the Party's overall work in central China."[108] Thus, Liu "actually rose to the No. 2 position in the Party (leadership)."[109]

It must be noted, however, that there was an interesting and, indeed, significant exchange of benefits between Mao and Liu *after* the March 1943 Politburo conference. In all the *original editions* of Liu's publications prior to this conference, Mao's name was not even mentioned, let alone any tribute to his great leadership.[110] But in "Eliminate

---

106 Liu left the CCB on March 5, 1942. But he would not have arrived at Yan'an until December 30 because Mao wanted him to "inspect the rectification campaigns in the base areas in Henan, Shandong, Hebei, and Shanxi." See *"Liu Shaoqi zhuan,"* p. 50.
107 Ibid., p. 55 (emphasis added). In this account, Liu's speech at the NWHCC was mistakenly dated in "late October." Liu was still in Shandong at that time. Liu's speech had to be made between December 30, 1942, the day Liu arrived at Yan'an, and January 14, 1943, the day the NWHCC ended.
108 Hao and Duan, *Liushi nian*, 1:279.
109 Hu, *Hu Qiaomu huiyi Mao Zedong*, p. 275.
110 I noticed this phenomenon when I was a graduate student of history at Fudan University in Shanghai in the early 1980s. I have since then been careful in comparing the pre-1943 editions of Liu's works with the ones after 1943. Amazingly, all the admiring words to Mao were added in the revised editions *after* March 1943.

Menshevist Ideology within the Party," Liu's first publication after the March 1943 conference,[111] Liu zealously admired Mao, claiming that all previous policy disputes between Mao and the other leaders were "the line struggles." Liu concluded:

> [O]ur Party, the proletariat and the revolutionary people of our country have finally found their own *leader* in Comrade Mao Zedong.... Our Party members and, above all, our cadres must ... put every field of work and every department under the guidance of Comrade Mao Zedong....
>
> Throughout our [Party's] history, two lines and two traditions have existed. One is the *line* and tradition of Bolshevism, the other, the line and tradition of Menshevism. The exponent of the former is Comrade Mao Zedong, and that of the latter, the various cliques of opportunists in the Party....
>
> All cadres and all Party members should carefully study and grasp Comrade Mao Zedong's theory, ... [they must] arm themselves with the *thought of Mao Zedong*.[112]

Thus, Liu raised a complete line of concepts: Mao the *leader*, his *line*, and his *thought*. It was along this line that Mao Zedong Thought (MZT) was established and was virtually equaled to Marxism-Leninism as the CCP's guiding principle at the 1945 Seventh Party Congress.[113] This was indeed the most important contribution Liu made to the establishment of Mao's command.

Although there is little documentary evidence of any deals between Mao and Liu around the March 1943 Politburo conference, the objective

---

111 The article was published on July 6, 1943, in *Liberation Daily* to celebrate the CCP's twenty-second anniversary.

112 *SWLSQ*, 1:294, 296, 300–1 (emphasis added).

113 Liu's words in Chinese read: *Mao Zedong de sixiang*. It is still unclear who initiated the term MZT, and when. *Huiyi Wang Jiaxiang* (Memory of Wang Jiaxiang), compiled by the Editing Group of *Selected Works of Wang Jiaxiang*, Beijing: People's Press, 1985, p. 3, says that Wang Jiaxiang first used the term MZT in his "The road of the CCP and China's national liberation," in July 1943. In my readings, however, Chen Yi first raised the notion of MZT in his "*Weida de ershiyi nian*" (Great twenty-one years), published in *Liberation Daily* on July 1, 1942. Chen said: "Comrade Mao Zedong has established his correct *line of thought* [*sixiang tixi*]." But it was Liu Shaoqi who formalized the term MZT and made "an excellent explanation" of MZT at the Seventh PC in 1945. See Hu, *Hu Qiaomu huiyi Mao Zedong*, p. 380.

The Establishment of the Yan'an Round Table

exchange of benefits between the two is undeniable: Mao was recognized as "the great leader of the CCP" due to Liu's zealous preaching. In return, Mao also praised Liu as "the leading figure of the correct (line)" in the white areas and noted that "Comrade Liu Shaoqi's view is the truth because it has been proved so by ... the direct fact."[114] Mao rarely gave such a praise to the other CCP leaders. Liu achieved the number two position in the CCP leadership and was recognized as Mao's successor.

However, Mao's gain was much more significant. His command was no longer justified merely by his correct strategy as it was in his rise at the Zunyi Conference. Rather, his leadership had since been established on the ideological legitimacy thereafter provided by his own MZT. The other far-reaching implication of the establishment of MZT was that it marked the beginning of the CCP's political independence from Moscow. The CCP would no longer depend on Marxism-Leninism for its ideological legitimacy, and hence it would no longer want to be seen as a little brother of Moscow. It has since become the largest communist party under the guidance of MZT, which was "the product of integrating the fundamental tenets of Marxism-Leninism with the practice of the Chinese revolution."[115]

The Faction-Ridden Structure of the Yan'an Round Table

When the Seventh Party Congress was held in April 1945, Mao had already achieved the status of, in MacFarquhar's words, "both the Lenin and Stalin of the Chinese revolution."[116] Not only had Mao subdued all the mountaintops and established his command in *both* the Party and the military, but MZT also became the source of ideological legitimacy for the CCP's cause. Thus Mao was now an unchallengeable figure in the CCP, because any challenges to Mao would eventually undermine the legitimacy of the Party.

The Yan'an Round Table, with Mao in command, was formalized at the Seventh PC. Not surprisingly, it was based on the support from

114 Quoted from ibid., p. 274.
115 The CCP Constitution, adopted at the Seventh PC.
116 Roderick MacFarquhar, *The Origins of the Cultural Revolution*, 1: *Contradictions among the People, 1956–1957*, New York: Columbia University Press, 1974, p. 10.

various mountaintops.[117] The Yan'an Round Table had four main structural characteristics (Figure 3.4):

1 The structure of the Yan'an Round Table consisted of two systems: the Party and the military. Mao's command was based on the support from both systems. Although the principle is "the Party commands the gun" – all the Politburo members were Party leaders, except Zhu and Peng – it was the gun that enabled Mao to maintain his leadership in the Party: the generals formed the majority at the Yan'an Round Table.

Thus, Mao's command was secured, because he was the *only* one who had full control of *both* the Party and the military. The Party provided Mao with the organizational framework as well as ideological legitimacy to command the military. However, as the *only* leader who sat at the point where the Party and the military systems met, Mao could always seek military support when a conflict emerged in the CCP leadership. As a result, the military became an integral part of the CCP leadership structure, and it also served as the most crucial power base in CCP politics. Without its support, a CCP leader could not dominate the policy process, no matter how influential he appeared: Liu Shaoqi in Mao's period and Chen Yun in Deng's were typical examples. Thus, this structure laid the foundation for military interventions in policy making – a distinctive feature of Chinese politics in the years to come.

2 The Party and military systems were virtually independent of each other. There were barely any formal institutional arrangements for the relationship between the two systems, except that both were under Mao's command. The cross-posting practice – the local Party leaders were appointed commissars in the garrison forces and the generals took leading positions in the local CCP organizations – was adopted for convenience rather than as a thought-through policy. As a result, personal connections played an essential role in Party-military relations.

The cross-posting practice integrated the administration into the commanding system during the revolution. Since the armed struggle for

---

117 Mao Zedong, "*Di qijie zhongyang weiyuanhui de xuan ju fangzhen*" (The principles for the election of the Seventh CC), in *Dang de wenxian* (The Party's Historical Documents), by the CCP Department for Research on Party Literature, 1995, 2:3, 6, discussed specifically the issue of mountaintops in the CC election. Mao concluded that the new CC should include representatives of all mountaintops. The outcome of the election shows that mountaintops were a major factor in the formation of the Seventh CC. Also see Hu, *Hu Qiaomu huiyi Mao Zedong*, p. 381.

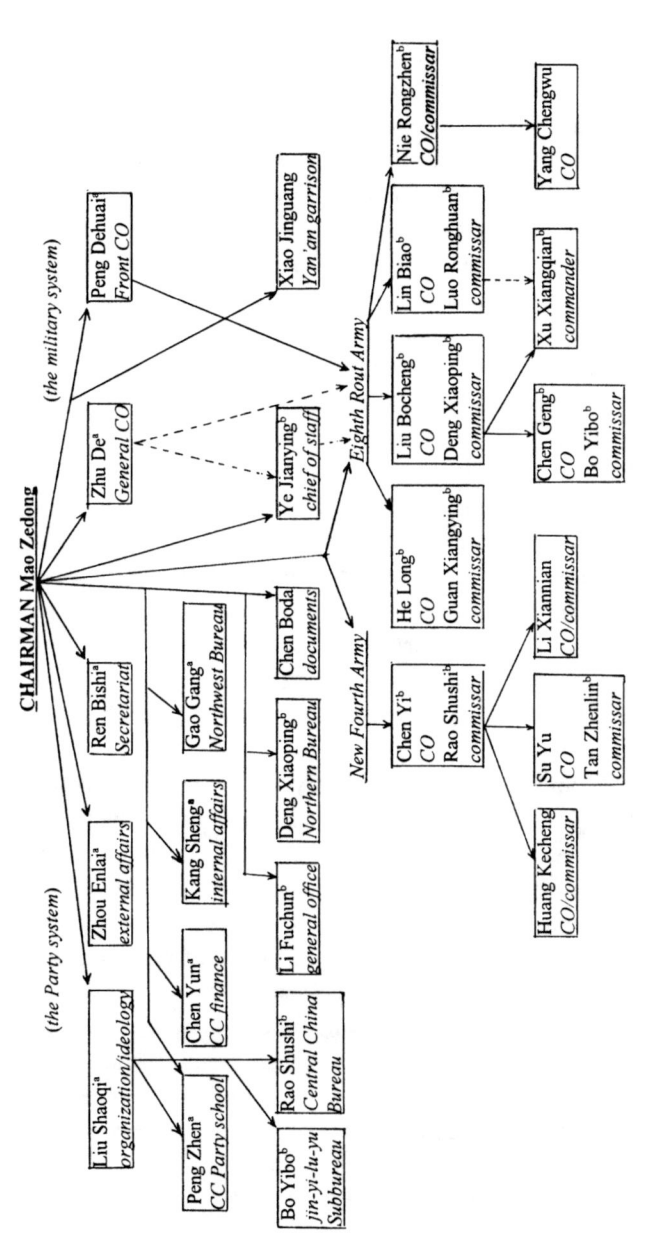

Figure 3.4. The Yan'an Round Table under Mao's command (solid arrow = direct control; dashed arrow = indirect control)

[a] Politburo members.
[b] CC members; the rest are alternate CC members.
CO = commander.

power was the top priority, the commanders were usually in overall charge in their base areas, but the commissars' duty was mainly to maintain the local administrations, except for Liu, who was the commissar of the New Fourth Army in 1941–3, and Deng, the commissar of the 129th Division, who served as Mao's watchdog. This practice, however, was never formalized as an institutional arrangement before it was abolished in 1983. The definition of the duties and power of a commander or a commissar were often subjective rather than clear-cut. Although a commissar was routinely appointed as the head of the local CCP organization after 1949, his role in military affairs was usually overshadowed by the commander, although in those cases where he was more favored by Mao, and later Deng, he could take over the commanding system. It was not unusual that a general was concurrently both the commander and commissar. The lack of formal arrangements in the Party-military relationship and the confusion of duties and power of the commanders and commissars formed a sharp contrast to civil-military relations in the ex–Soviet Union, where the commanding system was incorporated into the Party's formal government structure. As the formal representatives of the CPSU in the armed forces, the commissars usually had more say and even veto power over the commanders in decision making.[118]

The military's independence from the Party's government structure was crucial for Mao to maintain his command. Had the commanding system been incorporated into a formal government structure, Mao's command over the military would have been subject to the formal rules, compliant procedures, and standard operating practices that would have been applied to military operations. Moreover, without the exclusive control of the military, it would have been difficult for Mao to override the other leaders' decisions in policy making, especially when Mao was among the minority in a policy dispute. It is revealing that Mao rarely allowed his followers, either from the Party or the military, to expand their influence into the system they did not belong to, especially when a conflict emerged in the leadership. A crucial factor in the purges of Gao Gang in 1954, Peng Dehuai in 1959, Lin Biao in 1970, the containment of Zhou Enlai in 1973–5, and Deng Xiaoping's second fall in 1976 was

---

118 See Timothy Colton, *Commissars, Commanders, and Civilian Authority: The Structure of Soviet Military Politics*, Cambridge, MA: Harvard University Press, 1979.

The Establishment of the Yan'an Round Table

that they were developing, or had already developed, substantial power bases in the *other* system.

> 3 Most members of the Yan'an Round Table had their own mountaintops. Their relations with the supreme leader Mao and among themselves were structured in a typical fashion of "complex faction."[119]

Mao's command was based on personal loyalties from the members of the Yan'an Round Table. These members controlled their own mountaintops in the same fashion. Those who appeared to be without a power base in the Yan'an Round Table, however, played special roles in the political process: Zhu was Mao's necessary, though not always significant, military partner; Zhou served as Mao's housekeeper internally and personal envoy externally; Kang was Mao's file keeper (but only when he was needed); and Chen Boda was Mao's secretary. As Mao's de facto staff members, they would all come and go with him, except Chen, who fell in 1970 after he jumped onto Lin Biao's boat.

Two leaders deserve special attention: Chen Yun and Ye Jianying. Both appeared without any power bases. But Chen would gradually develop his coterie in the financial system, especially after the financial centralization in 1951–2. As the CCP's "chief accountant," Chen would be extraordinarily influential whenever there was an economic crisis or a major change in economic policy. As for Ye, the position of chief of staff enabled him to gain access to various military mountaintops, although he had rarely controlled any. Ye's special role as a liaison between Mao and various military mountaintops not only enabled him to survive the Cultural Revolution, but also put him in a key position in the arrest of the Gang of Four on October 6, 1976. Ye's eminence, however, faded away after the real mountaintop bosses like Deng returned to power in the late 1970s (see Chapter 7).

> 4 Institutional arrangements for communications and coordination among the subleaders were strikingly deficient. All manner of control – orders, directives, complaints, reports, and the like – flowed directly to and from Mao.

This feature was crucial for Mao to keep his command. It resulted in a unique process of policy making. When a policy issue emerged, any policy

---

119 See Andrew Nathan, "A factionalism model for CCP politics," *CQ*, 53 (January 1973), p. 41.

initiatives had to be submitted to Mao first, who would then authorize the circulation of these initiatives among the elite members for their opinions. Only after the circulation was completed and all the members' comments went back to Mao would a meeting be held to discuss this policy issue. As a result, Mao knew everyone's preference even before the policy was formally discussed.

Furthermore, when a policy dispute emerged, this process helped Mao minimize the possibility of coalition formations among the elite members, because it prevented them from exchanging ideas with one another before the formal discussion – anyone who violated this procedure would be accused of "irresponsible liberalism" or even "sabotaging the Party's unity." As a result, while the procedure prevented the elite members from seeking alliance through exchanging the information about their interests, Mao's direct access to each leader enabled him to make deals with them while cutting off his opponent(s). This exclusive advantage enabled Mao to manipulate leadership relations in a conflict.

However, it must be noticed that the leaders who had developed horizontal connections in the system would *all* be extraordinarily active in CCP politics after 1949. They were Liu Shaoqi, who had built up a big mountaintop in the CCP organizations through Peng Zhen, Rao Shushi, and Bo Yibo; Gao Gang, whose control of the NWB, and later Northeast China, enabled him to develop a widespread factional network; and Deng Xiaoping, Rao Shushi, Peng Zhen, and Bo Yibo, who had held dual positions in the Party and the military during the revolution, even though all four were cut off from the military after 1949.

The Yan'an Round Table had indeed provided the strongest leadership for the Chinese revolution. Its structure also fit perfectly in the system of the CCP's dictatorship. It embodied not only the comradeship among the first-generation CCP leaders and their loyalties to Mao, but also the source of ideological legitimacy for their cause, namely, MZT. All this enabled the Yan'an Round Table members, who were geographically isolated from and structurally independent of each other, to "unite as one" under Mao's command during their armed struggle for power.

More important, the Yan'an Round Table created the structural shackles on factionalism embedded in leadership relations. In this structure, anyone who attempted to expand his power base without Mao's

The Establishment of the Yan'an Round Table

patronage would not only engage in a zero-sum game with his peers because his expansion would undermine their power bases, but he would also face Mao's possible suppression because the increase in his power would pose a potential threat to Mao's command. Mao was the only one who could break the status quo, because in this structure any changes in the distribution of power would be suppressed unless they were initiated by Mao himself. Thus, Mao's absolute authority was guaranteed not only because his vision embodied in MZT was accepted as "the Party's guiding principle," but also because his position in the leadership structure – he was the only one who had control of both the Party and military systems and he maintained exclusive access to each mountaintop – enabled him to manipulate the other leaders in political affairs.

MOUNTAINTOPS UNDER MAO'S COMMAND

Reorganization in 1945

After the establishment of the Yan'an Round Table at the Seventh PC, an overall reorganization of the CCP forces took place as the triumphant leaders seized the opportunity to expand and consolidate their forces. Japan's surrender and the mounting pressure from the KMT forces further justified this reorganization.

Foreseeing that a confrontation with the KMT was inevitable, the CC leadership decided to strengthen the base areas in North China and build up forces in Manchuria, but to withdraw the forces from Central China into Shandong and the Jiangsu-Anhui-Henan areas.[120] Beginning in late August 1945, the CCP leadership made the following major organizational adjustments:

1 The Party organizations in the Northwest remained unchanged. All the CCP forces were under the command of He Long.[121]

---

[120] See Xiao and Sha, *Zhongguo geming shigao*, pp. 319–20; Hao and Duan, *Liushi nian*, 1:318–21.
[121] There were two groups in the CCP forces in the Northwest: the Yan'an Garrison, which grew out of Peng Dehuai's Third Red Army Corp of the First Front Red Army and the local red army, and He Long's army, which grew out of the Second Front Red Army. On March 17, 1947, two days before the KMT forces seized Yan'an, the CMC decided to let Peng Dehuai command the main forces in the Northwest, which later grew into the First Field Army. He Long commanded the forces in the Jin-Shui area, which would be dispatched to the Southwest in 1949. This reorganization took away

Factionalism in Chinese Communist Politics

2 The CCP Northern Bureau was divided into the Jin (Shanxi)-Ji (Hebei)-Lu (Shandong)-Yu (Henan) Bureau led by Secretary Deng Xiaoping and Vice-Secretary Bo Yibo, and the Jin-Cha (har)-Ji Bureau led by Secretary Nie Rongzhen and Vice-Secretaries Liu Lantao[122] and Luo Ruiqing.
3 Liu Bocheng and Deng Xiaoping commanded the Jin-Ji-Lu-Yu Field Army, which later grew into the Second Field Army. Nie Rongzhen led the CCP forces in the Jin-Cha-Ji area, which later grew into the Central Military Corp.
4 The forces in Shandong, led by Luo Ronghuan, and the forces in northern Jiangsu, led by Huang Kecheng – both forces grew out of Mao's First Front Red Army – were dispatched to Manchuria.[123]
5 The New Fourth Army led by Chen Yi and Rao Shushi in northern Jiangsu took over the Shandong base area left by the forces that had been dispatched to Manchuria. The New Fourth Army that remained in northern Jiangsu and Anhui was commanded by Su Yu and Tan Zhenlin.

The reorganization in Northwest and North China went smoothly, for it actually redefined the boundaries of the established mountaintops. So the commanding systems were unified and the Party leaders were put in place. By contrast, the arrangements in Manchuria and East-Central China – the CCP's two strategic front areas – were far from complete. The Party leaders were not selected yet, nor were the commanding systems unified. Given the faction-ridden leadership relations, in the areas where either no base areas had been developed (in Manchuria)

---

a bulk of the forces from He, a major military leader who did not rise from Mao's Jinggang mountaintop. But He resented Peng, and the relationship between the two had been tense since then.

122 Liu Lantao had been a close associate of Liu Shaoqi since the late 1920s. He was one of the sixty-one CCP cadres who made a collective confession to the KMT authority in 1936 under the CC's directive. After that, he was promoted quickly in the CCP Northern Bureau.

123 On August 10, 1945, Mao sent a cable to Stalin, informing him that the CCP's forces would "go all out to cooperate with the [Soviet] Red Army" in Manchuria. The next day, Yan'an sent an urgent cable to the CCP forces in Shandong (about 50,000 men led by Luo Ronghuan), northern Jiangsu (30,000 men led by Huang Kecheng), Hebei (9,000 men led by Wan Yi and Li Yunchang), and the Jin-Shui area (6,000 men led by Lu Zhengcao), ordering them "to enter the Northeast immediately at any cost." With the help of the Soviet army, the CCP had gathered 100,000 troops and over 20,000 cadres in Manchuria by the end of August. *Zhongguo renmin jiefangjun zhanshi jianbian* (A Concise History of the PLA), compiled by the Editing Group of the PLA's Concise History in the Chinese Military Academy, Beijing: PLA Press, 1989, pp. 474–5.

The Establishment of the Yan'an Round Table

or the boundaries between the existing mountaintops were uncertain (in East-Central China), the reorganization provoked differences among the mountaintop leaders, because it provided them with an opportunity to expand their forces. Although the conflicts caused by these differences were soon overwhelmed by the confrontation with the KMT forces, they had substantial implications for the development of various mountaintops and therefore to CCP politics in the years to come.

Differences among the Leaders

Not surprisingly, Liu Shaoqi, acting chairman of the CCP during Mao's absence – Mao was in Chongqing from August 28 to October 11, 1945, to negotiate with Chiang Kai-shek – seized the opportunity to expand his mountaintop. He convened a CC conference on September 14, whereby Peng Zhen, Chen Yun, Cheng Zihua, Wu Xiuquan, and Lin Feng (Liu's secretary) formed the CCP Northeastern Bureau (NEB). Its task was to provide "the overall leadership on behalf of the CC" in Manchuria. Liu's associate Peng Zhen, who ranked ninth in the Politburo, was appointed the bureau's secretary,[124] but Chen Yun, who was ranked sixth in the Politburo and was more senior than Peng,[125] was just a member. Meanwhile, the CCP East China Bureau (ECB) was also set up on the basis of the former Central China Bureau. Again, Liu's associate Rao Shushi was appointed its secretary, while Chen Yi and Tan Zhenlin, both of whom were more senior than Rao, served as a vice-secretary and a member.

These arrangements were telegraphed to Mao in Chongqing on September 17. Mao responded two days later. Although Mao did not object to Liu's arrangements, he instructed the CC to appoint Lin Biao the commander, and Xiao Jinguang, vice-commander, of the CCP forces in Manchuria (these forces later grew into the Fourth Field Army). On the same day, Lin and Xiao, who had just arrived in Henan from Yan'an, received "a most-urgent telegram" from Mao, ordering them to "turn

---

124 *Liu Shaoqi zhuan*, p. 59.
125 Before Mao left for Chongqing on August 28, Chen Yun was still ranked above Peng Zhen when the two were added to the Secretariat, equivalent to today's PSC, as the alternate members. See *Zhongguo gongchan dang lishi* (The CCP History), compiled by the CCP Party History Research Center, 1:674.

around" and go to Manchuria immediately.[126] Moreover, Mao also "suggested" sending Gao Gang, Zhang Wentian, Luo Ronghuan, and Li Fuchun to Manchuria; all were Mao's men except Zhang, who held a grudge against Liu. Soon, the CCP regional commissions were set up in northern, western, and eastern Manchuria, and were led respectively by Gao, Li, and Xiao Hua.[127] Thus, only southern Manchuria was under control of Peng Zhen, the newly appointed NEB secretary.

But a dispute soon occurred over whether KMT's forces should be confronted in southern Manchuria. Peng favored a more frontal strategy because, as he argued, should the KMT seize southern Manchuria, the connection between the CCP's base areas in Manchuria and North China would be cut off; furthermore, an economically advanced southern Manchuria would strengthen the KMT regime. But Lin, Gao, and Chen held that the CCP should build up its forces in the countryside but avoid frontal confrontation with the stronger KMT forces.[128]

It is not surprising that Peng advocated a more frontal strategy, because southern Manchuria was his bailiwick, and its connection to North China was crucial for Peng to build up his forces in the Northeast. Yet Lin was reluctant to confront the KMT forces that outgunned and outnumbered his army. Lin's strategy to develop the CCP forces in northern Manchuria was supported by Gao and Chen, who were building up their constituencies there. Although Mao initially favored a frontal confrontation with the KMT forces in order to gain advantages at the negotiating table, he soon chose to back Lin, not necessarily because Mao favored his strategy, but because Mao never wanted his most trusted force, Lin's army, to be thrown into the conflict before the KMT forces were sapped by the other CCP forces.[129] Mao sent a telegram to the NEB

126 Xiao Jinguang, *Xiao Jinguang huiyi lu* (Xiao Jinguang's Memoir), Beijing: PLA Press, 1987, p. 326. Lin and Xiao left Yan'an for Shandong on August 24, three days before Mao went to Chongqing. The original plan was to let them command the CCP forces there.
127 Xiao Hua rose from Mao's Jinggang Mountaintop. He was the political director of the First Front Red Army during the Long March and was assigned to the same post in Lin Biao's army during the war.
128 See Lin's telegram to the CC on November 21, Peng's telegram to Lin, Gao, and Chen, and Gao and Chen's response to Peng on December 5, 1945, in Zhang Zhenglong, *Xuebai xuehong* (Red Blood on White Snow), Beijing: PLA Press, 1991, pp. 11–12, 116, 192n18.
129 Mao's plan for the CCP forces in the civil war was that the forces led by Liu Bocheng and Deng Xiaoping in north China march to Central China; Chen Yi and Su Yu's army

The Establishment of the Yan'an Round Table

on December 28, 1946: "our Party's present task in the Northeast is to build up base areas, stable military and political base areas in eastern, northern, and western Manchuria."[130]

Southern Manchuria was not on the list. Yet, the dispute continued. The wishful thinking of the CCP leadership that it could gain a better position at the negotiating table by winning a big battle in Manchuria led to the bloody Siping Battle from April 18 to May 18, 1946.[131] Even after the CCP forces withdrew from the battle due to heavy losses,[132] Peng still insisted at the NEB conference on May 19 that the CCP forces should hold fast to Changchun in order to keep at least part of southern Manchuria under the CCP's control. Lin, Gao, and Chen insisted that they withdraw all the CCP forces to northern Manchuria.[133] Not surprisingly, Liu at Yan'an supported Peng. Although he had to change his position later, his support for Lin – if there was any – was reluctant.[134]

---

in East China would head toward Jiangna (the lower reaches of the Yangtze River); He Long's forces in northern Shaanxi would attack the KMT areas in the Northwest; and the forces led by Nie Rongzhen and Xu Xiangqian would remain in North China. *After* the KMT forces are torn apart by these operations, Lin's army would dash from Manchuria down to Central South China. Thus, Lin's army would suffer the least but gain the most. See Nie Rongzhen, *Nie Rongzhen huiyi lu* (Nie Rongzhen's Memoirs), Beijing: PLA Press, 1984, 3:674. Also see Ban Ying and Zuo Xiaowei, "Heimao baimao – ping Han 'Deng Xiaoping zhuan'" (Black cat or white cat – a critique to Han Shanbi's *A Biography of Deng Xiaoping*), *Tansuo*, no. 3 (1992), p. 70. The plan was carried out almost exactly as Mao planned except: (1) the forces in the Northwest were split into two (see note 121), and (2) the Third Field Army's attack on Jiangnan was delayed for about a year, because at the Nanzhuang Secretariat Meeting in May 1948 Mao accepted Su Yu's suggestion of destroying the main forces of the KMT in north of the Yangtze River before crossing the Yangtze River. Also cf. Jin, *Zhou Enlai zhuan*, p. 721.

130 *SWMZD*, 4:81.
131 See Han Xianchu, "*Siping baoweizhan*" (The battle of defending Siping), *Dangshi yanjiu ziliao* (Research Materials of CCP History) (1986), 1:1–5, 2:1–6.
132 Zhang, *Xuebai xuehong*, pp. 129–37, 154–63, describes in detail the Siping Battle and the difference between Lin/Goa/Chen/Huang Kecheng and Peng, who was backed up by the CC leadership on the strategy in Manchuria.
133 See "*Luo Ronghuan zhuan*" (A Biography of Luo Ronghuan), *RWZ* (1987), 32:63.
134 A report by the Special Investigation Group for Liu's Case on October 18, 1968, says: "As the Liberation War broke out, Liu Shaoqi supported Peng Zhen's erroneous line in the Northeast behind Mao's back." In his self-criticism on October 23, 1966, Liu admitted: "At the beginning of 1946, I made an error on the principle in the Northeast. My support to Comrade Lin Biao at that time was insufficient." See *A Special Collection of Materials on Liu Shaoqi*, compiled by the Institute for the Study of Chinese Communist Problems, Taibei, 1970, p. 623. A reliable source said that although

Factionalism in Chinese Communist Politics

Lin eventually prevailed partly because of Mao's support, but largely because of the KMT's increasing military pressure.

Thus, Peng's base in southern Manchuria vanished as the KMT forces marched forward. The NEB was reorganized on June 16, 1946. Lin, "Mao's best pupil," who was concurrently the commander and commissar of the CCP forces in Manchuria, replaced Peng as the NEB secretary. Peng became one of the four vice-commissars and vice-secretaries: Luo Ronghuan, Gao, Chen, and Peng. But Luo was Lin's first vice-commissar (he was promoted to commissar in August 1948); Gao was the de facto Party boss (he took over the NEB in August 1948); and Chen was in charge of economy. So Peng was virtually jobless. Seeing that Peng was getting nowhere in Manchuria, Liu, then the secretary of CC's Working Committee,[135] summoned Peng back to his side in the summer of 1947.[136]

Unlike the struggle in Manchuria in which Peng lost out, a compromise was made on the leadership arrangements in East-Central China: Rao Shushi remained the ECB secretary,[137] but Chen Yi was appointed commander, and Su Yu, vice-commander and vice-commissar, of the CCP forces in East China, which would grow into the Third Field Army. Competition and the old scores between Chen and Rao[138] prevented Liu's further expansion in this area.

Thus, although Liu tried to take advantage of the reorganization to expand his mountaintop, it was Mao who consolidated his command. All the forces originating from Mao's Jinggan Mountaintop were strength-

there are "forced confessions" in Liu's self-criticism, the foregoing words were true because it "can be proved by the documentary record [*youan kecha*]."
135 After the KMT forces seized Yan'an on February 19, 1947, the CC leadership was split into two: Mao, Zhou, and Ren remained in northern Shanxi; Liu, Zhu, and Dong went to Hebei and formed the CC Working Committee to handle daily affairs. Hao and Duan, *Liushi nian*, 1:331.
136 Peng left Manchuria before the summer of 1947 to attend the Land Conference convened by Liu in July–September 1947. Peng remained with Liu after the meeting.
137 After Mao returned to Yan'an on October 11, 1945, Rao was dispatched to Manchuria as the CCP's representative in the Military Mediating Group. He resumed the post of ECB secretary after the Civil War broke out.
138 In 1943 Rao, whom Liu handpicked to succeed him as CCB secretary and commissar of the New Fourth Army, leveled an attack on Chen, the army's commander and the bureau's vice-secretary. Chen was criticized as "a grand anti-Mao general" (*fan Mao dajiangjun*). See Deng Xiaoping, Chen Yi, and Tan Zhenlin, "Report on the Discussion Meetings on the Rao Shushi Question," in Frederick Teiwes, *Politics at Mao's Court: Goo Gang and Party Factionalism in the Early 1950s*, New York: M. E. Sharp, 1990, pp. 247–8.

The Establishment of the Yan'an Round Table

ened and deployed in the strategically important areas: Lin's army controlled Manchuria; Nie Rongzheng's troops guarded the Jin-Cha-Ji base area, or "the front door" of Yan'an; and Peng Dehuai commanded the forces in northern Shaanxi. By contrast, the forces growing out of the mountaintops other than Mao's were either divided, as those from He Long's Second Front Red Army and those under the command of Xu Xiangqian, or deployed to the forefront of the Civil War, as those from the Fourth Front Red Army led by Liu Bocheng and Deng Xiaoping, and those from the New Fourth Army led by Chen Yi, Rao Shushi, and Su Yu.

The 1945 discord, however, revealed the vulnerability of the faction-ridden Yan'an Round Table. That is, whenever a power vacuum appeared, leadership relations would be disturbed because every mountaintop leader would try to grasp the chance to expand his forces. This discord soured the relationships between Liu's mountaintop and the trio in Manchuria – Lin, Gao, and Chen – for the trio virtually drove Liu's right-hand man, Peng Zhen, out of Manchuria.[139] Gao perhaps gained most in this episode. The role he played in Manchuria not only further indicated that he was Mao's favored Party man but also enabled him to develop a power base that was strong enough to challenge Liu later. More significantly, this episode showed that Mao began to contain Liu's power even when their honeymoon had barely ended. Thus, it was not surprising that Mao would spur Gao to take on Liu later (see Chapter 4). Mao's choice in this episode was rational because, given the faction-ridden structure of the Yan'an Round Table, any member who became excessively powerful could form a potential threat to Mao's command. From this perspective, it is not an aberration that Mao would later take similar precautions against Lin Biao as early as 1967 and against Zhou Enlai after Lin's fall (see Chapter 6).

Mountaintops under Mao's Command

The 1945 discord was solved even before it fully surfaced, partly because of the pressure from the KMT forces, but largely because the triumphant war against the KMT provided enough space for the CCP's dramatic expansion in 1946–9. Yet, the victory that came unexpectedly fast also

---

139 In our discussion of why Chen blocked Peng from entering the PSC in the post-Mao period, a former political secretary of Chen told me that the tension between the two started in 1945–7, when both were vice-secretaries of the NEB.

brought about a new challenge:[140] the administrative construction could barely keep up with the military victory. For example, a report from the CCP South China Subbureau to the CC in September 1950 demanded at least the addition of 1,000 leading cadres and 6,000 ordinary ones for the newly established administration in Guangdong and Guangxi provinces, although over 30,000 CCP cadres had already been there.[141]

To solve this shortage, the CCP resorted to the militarization of administration, the model that had been successful in its base areas.[142] Thus, the PLA officers took up the leading posts in the newly established administration in the places they had seized.[143] Millions of the PLA officers were assigned to civilian posts,[144] and this practice was soon routinized into a system called *zhuanye* (transferring the officers to civilian posts).[145] As a result, most local administrative posts were filled by the officers from the armies that had seized the area. Although numerous cadres were transported from the base areas to the new areas,[146] these

---

140 Mao and his comrades had planned to defeat the KMT in fifteen years, then shortened it to five at the September 1948 Politburo Conference. See Jin, *Zhou Enlai zhuan*, p. 728.
141 Zhao Wei, *Zhao Ziyang zhuan* (A Biography of Zhao Ziyang), Beijing: China News Press, 1989, pp. 58, 63.
142 "The Resolution of the Second Plenum of the Seventh CC," *Cankao*, 19:1–5, ordered that the "field armies in the new areas should all be transferred into work teams ... [and] should be a big cadre school" for the construction of administration.
143 After the PRC was established, the CC "decided that the commanders of each field army would concurrently be the chairmen of the Military and Administrative Committee (MAC)," and the commissars would be secretaries of the CCP bureaus in the regions they occupied. But East China was an exception: Rao took up the posts of both MAC chairman and the ECB secretary. (See Deng, Chen, and Tan, "Report on the Discussion Meetings on the Rao Shushi Question," p. 248.) Meanwhile, the CC also recommended the practice in Guangdong to the other newly liberated areas, that is, the armed forces took over the administration in the areas they occupied – specifically, each army had to assign 500–700 officers to the civilian posts. See *Wengao*, 2:187–8.
144 According to Nie Rongzhen, *Nie Rongzhen huiyi lu*, 3:721, over 1.4 million PLA men left the army for civilian posts in 1949–50.
145 There are two kinds of arrangement for a PLA man who leaves the army, depending on his status. A discharged soldier usually returns to the place where he came from (*fuyuan*), but an officer is usually transferred to a civilian post equivalent to his rank (*zhuanye*).
146 "The Resolution of the Second Plenum of the Seventh CC (March 13, 1949)," *Cankao*, 19:1–5, ordered the CCP organizations in the base areas to send 53,000 cadres to the new areas.

The Establishment of the Yan'an Round Table

cadres were usually grouped in their local places and followed the army that had been stationed there. For example, among the 8,050 cadres who went to Guangdong and Guangxi after they were seized by Lin's Fourth Field Army, 7,750 came from Manchuria and Central China, controlled by Lin's army.[147]

A unique phenomenon resulted: the northeastern accent was popular among the cadres in South China seized by Lin's Fourth Field Army; the accent of Shandong and northern Jiangsu, former base areas of Chen Yi and Rao Shushi's Third Field Army, dominated in the offices in East China; the Shanxi accent was the hallmark of a cadre in the Southwest, seized by Deng Xiaoping's Second Field Army coming from Shanxi's Taihang Mountain; and the northern Shaanxi accent could surely identify a cadre in the Northwest, occupied by Peng Dehuai's First Field Army. Not surprisingly, these new rulers felt alien in the local environment. Yet this further strengthened their comradeship and self-conscious identity. As a result, *guanxi* thrived in political life at all levels of authority.

While the PLA officers played the dominant role in the administration of the newly liberated areas, the Party leaders took over the base areas after the armies pulled out to the new areas. Gao Gang became "the king of the Northeast" as he assumed all the top positions in Manchuria: Party secretary, government chairman, director of economic affairs, and military commander and commissar; Xi Zhongxun was a predominant figure in the Northwest, especially after Peng was sent to command the Chinese forces in Korea in October 1950; and Rao Shushi dominated in Shandong and northern Jiangsu. But the expansion of Liu Shaoqi's mountaintop was more significant.

In February 1947 Liu led the CCP central apparatus to Hebei due to the mounting pressure of the KMT forces and handled daily affairs on behalf of the CC, while Mao remained in northern Shaanxi. Mao would not come to Hebei until May 26, 1948.[148] When Liu arrived

---

147 See Zhao, *Zhao Ziyang zhuan*, p. 58.
148 Bo Yibo, *Ruogan zhongda juece gu shijan de huigu* (Review of Several Important Decisions and Events), Beijing: CCP Party School Press, 1991, 1:3 (hereafter *Huigu*), 1:3, says that Mao came to Hebei on March 23, 1948. But Mao did not arrive in Xibaipo until May 26. Mao stayed at Chennazhuang, where the headquarters of the Jin-Cha-Ji base areas was located, to prepare for a secret visit to Moscow. The trip was postponed because of the unexpectedly fast development of the situation. See Jin, *Zhou Enlai zhuan*, pp. 717–18.

in the North China base areas, three mountaintops were predominant there: Liu's own, which was rooted in the North China Party organizations; the forces led by Liu Bocheng and Deng Xiaoping; and the forces led by Nie Rongzhen. After Liu and Deng's army left for Central China in the summer of 1947, Liu attempted to unify the commanding system of all the CCP forces in North China. But his effort met with strong resistance from Nie Rongzhen and the remaining forces of Liu (Bocheng) and Deng, which were then led by Xu Xiangqian. Thus, Liu made little progress until Mao endorsed his suggestion to merge the CCP Jin-Yi-Lu-Yu Bureau, led by Bo Yibo, and the Jin-Cha-ji Bureau, led by Nie, into a new North China Bureau (NCB). The establishment of the NCB on May 9, 1948, marked that Liu's mountaintop finally achieved its dominance in North China, although as a compromise, all the armed forces in North China were reorganized into the Central Military Corps commanded by Nie.[149] Liu was the NCB's first secretary, but daily affairs were handled by Second Secretary Bo Yibo.

Moreover, the PRC Central government virtually grew out of the CCP North China government.[150] Thus, Liu's associates occupied all the key areas at the Center: Peng Zhen was the boss of Beijing, Bo controlled the financial system, An Ziwen managed personnel affairs, Lu Dingyi was in charge of propaganda, Liu Lantao led the Party and administration in North China, Liao Luyan took charge of agricultural affairs, and Yang Xianzhen was predominant in the theoretical sphere. The CCP headquarters virtually became "the party of Liu Shaoqi, Peng Zhen and their associates."[151]

Thus, under the pressure caused by the collapse of the KMT, the CCP leadership divided China virtually among various mountaintops in the rush of regime construction. Although this solved the problems like urgent cadre shortages and, more importantly, brought about political stability by concentrating all the political, administrative, and military powers in the hands of a few mountaintop leaders, there were hardly any

149 See "*Liu Shaoqi zhuan,*" pp. 72–3; Bo, *Huigu,* 1:1–3. But Mao also gained in this deal because he eventually deprived Xu Xiangqian of the commandership of his forces. Xu was virtually demoted as Nie's vice-commander, although Mao allowed him to concurrently command the Eighteenth Army Corps.
150 Bo, *Huigu,* 1:3–4.   151 MacFarquhar, *The Origins,* 1:144.

The Establishment of the Yan'an Round Table

well-thought-out plans for state construction, nor were there any pre-designed institutional arrangements for the policy process. The structure of power distribution remained unchanged and was transplanted intact into the administrative systems during the hasty conversion of a military organization into a penetrative regime. As a result, the administrative system was not institutionally structured, though it appeared to be so on paper; its operation still relied on personal loyalties forged during the war between the leaders and their followers; and the mountaintops were therefore integrated into the system from the beginning. In general, the factional networks in the former base areas were controlled by the Party elite; but in the areas south of the Yellow River, military leaders were more influential.

At the Center, however, Liu's predominance in the policy process was obvious, although Zhou continued to be Mao's top steward. Chen Yun would gain considerable influence in the financial system, Peng Dehuai would become a powerful defense minister after the Korean War broke out, Nie and Luo Ruiqing controlled security, and Luo Ronghuan led the PLA General Political Department (Table 3.1).

Financial Unification and Chen Yun's Rise

The faction-ridden structure of the Yan'an Round Table began to handicap the policy process even before the PRC was established. Since each mountaintop was independent of each other during the war, the Yan'an Round Table did not embody a financial mechanism. This became an obstacle for the leadership to maintain effective control as the CCP gained the upper hand in the war. In order to overcome this problem, the North China Financial and Economic Committee (NCFEC) was created after the September 1948 Politburo Conference.[152] Dong Biwu was its director, but the real boss was Vice-Director Bo Yibo. Its tasks were first to unify the financial system of North, Northwest, and East China, and then to centralize finance and revenue of all the areas under the CCP's control.[153]

However, little progress was made due to strong resistance from Northeast, East, and South-Central China, the most advanced regions,

---

152 See Jin, *Zhou Enlai zhuan*, 1:723–4.   153 See Bo, *Huigu*, 1:68.

Factionalism in Chinese Communist Politics

Table 3.1. *Major Mountaintops under Mao's Command (1949–52)*

Names	Main Positions	Areas Controlled
Liu Shaoqi[a]	Vice-chairman, NCB first secretary	The policy process at the Center
Peng Zhen[a]	Beijing party secretary	Capital
Bo Yibo[b]	NCB second secretary, Central FEC vice-director, and finance minister	Finance, tax revenue, and budget
Lu Dingyi[b]	Director, CC propaganda department	Propaganda and cultural affairs
Lin Feng[b]	Vice-chairman, Northeast government	Liu's watchdog in Northeast
Liu Lantao[c]	NBC vice-secretary, minister of North China affairs	Party and administration in North China
An Ziwen	Acting director, CC organization dept.	High-ranking cadre personnel
Liao Luyan	Deputy director, CC rural work dept.	Agriculture and rural affairs
Yang Xianzhen	Vice-president, central Party school	Party school and theoretical area
Peng Dehuai[a]	Defense minister, NWB first secretary, Northwest CMC chairman, and Northwest military commander	PLA headquarters and the armed forces in Northwest
Xiao Jinguang[b]	PLA navy commander	PLA navy
Huang Kecheng[c]	PLA deputy chief of staff, Tianjin party secretary, and Hunan party secretary	PLA headquarters Tianjin (3–12/1949) Hunan (1950–2)
Xu Guangda	PLA armored force commander	PLA armored forces
Gao Gang[a]	NEB secretary, Northeast government chairman, Northeast military CO and commissar, Northeast FEC director	Northeast China

152

The Establishment of the Yan'an Round Table

Table 3.1. (cont.)

Names	Main Positions	Areas Controlled
Ye Jizhuang[b]	Northeast military vice-commissar	
Sun Xiushan	Northeast government vice-chairman	Foreign trade
Zhang Mingyuan	Northeast FEC vice-director	
Mao Hong	Director, NEB organization dept.	
Chen Yun[a]	Central FEC director	Finance and banking
Yao Yilin	Deputy commerce director	Commerce and foreign trade
Lin Biao[b]	CSB secretary, Central-South CMC chairman, Central-South military CO	Military in Central-South China
Liu Yalou	PLA air force commander	PLA air force
Huang Yongsheng	Guangzhou garrison commander	Military in Southeast China
Tao Zhu	SCSB secretary	Southeast China Party & administration
Nie Rongzhen[b]	PLA acting chief of staff and Beijing-Tianjin garrison commander	PLA headquarters and military in North China
Luo Ruiqing[c]	Public security minister and head of the central bodyguard	Security and police
Yang Chengwu	Beijing-Tianjin garrison vice-commander	Military in North China
Chen Yi[b]	ECB second secretary, Shanghai mayor, and East China military commander	Military in East China and Shanghai
Su Yu[c]	East China military vice-commander, Zhejiang party secretary	Military in East China Zhejiang

Table 3.1. (cont.)

Names	Main Positions	Areas Controlled
Tan Zhenlin[b]	Shandong military commander	Military in Shandong
Zhang Yunyi[b]	Guangxi Party secretary	Guangxi
Luo Ronghuan[b]	PLA political department director	Party organizations in the armed forces
Tan Zheng[c]	PLA political dept. deputy-director	
He Long[b]	SWB second secretary, Southwest CMC chairman, and Southwest military CO	Military in Southwest and Southwest administration
Li Jingquan	Southwest CMC vice-chairman and Southwest military vice-commissar	Southwest Party and Sichuan administration
Zhou Shidi	PLA air defense commander	PLA air defense forces
He Bingyan	Southwest military vice-commander	Southwest military
Liao Hansheng	PLA first military corp commissar, Qinghai Party secretary	Military in Northwest, Qinghai Party and administration
Deng Xiaoping[b]	SWB first secretary, and Southwest military commissar	Southwest Party and administration
Chen Geng[c]	Southwest military vice-commander	Military in Southwest China
Hu Yaobang	Northern Sichuan Party secretary and northern Sichuan military commissar	northern Sichuan Party and administration
Song Renqong	Yunnan military commissar	Yunnan Party and administration
Rao Shushi[b]	ECB first secretary, East China CMC chairman, and East China military commissar	East China Party and administration

The Establishment of the Yan'an Round Table

Table 3.1. (cont.)

Names	Main Positions	Areas Controlled
Xiang Ming	Shandong Subbureau secretary	Shandong
Xi Zhongxun[c]	NWB secretary, Northwest CMC chairman, and Northwest military commissar	Northwest Party and administration
Jia Tuofu	Central FEC vice-director	Light industry
Xu Xiangqian[b]	PLA deputy chief of staff and Beijing-Tianjin garrison vice-commander	North China military
Li Xiannian[b]	Hubei Party secretary	Hubei
Wang Shusheng	Hubei military commander	Military in Hubei

Notes: CMC = Civil and Military Commission; CSB = CCP Central-South Bureau; ECB = CCP East China Bureau; FEC = Financial and Economic Commission; NCB = CCP North China Bureau; NEB = CCP Northeast Bureau; NWB = CCP Northwest Bureau; SCSB = CCP South China Subbureau; SWB = the CCP Southwest Bureau.
[a] Politburo members.
[b] CC members.
[c] Alternate CC members.

on which the CC leadership counted as the major revenue sources.[154] The Center summoned the leaders of these regions: Lin, Gao, Luo Ronghuan, Rao, Chen Yi, and Liu Bocheng, to a Financial and Economic Forum on January 1, 1949. But all that the participants had in common were complaints about the fragmented financial system.[155] With Liu's support, Bo attempted to upgrade the NCFEC into a central authority, managing the entire revenues for the emerging PRC. But the other leaders, especially

---

154 The revenues, calculated by the amount of grain collection, of the six regions in 1949 are: Northeast China, 8,600 million kilograms; East China, 3,350; North China, 1,400; Central-South China, 1,100; Northwest China, 400; and Southwest China, 100. *Cankao*, 19:31–2.
155 See Bo, *Huigu*, 1:69.

Gao and Rao, demanded more involvement in management.[156] The forum was actually fruitless, because every mountaintop leader wanted to gain in this zero-sum game.

Interestingly, Mao maintained an indifferent attitude in this dispute, which could be seen by people like Gao as an encouragement for their resistance to Liu's effort to expand his control to the financial system. Thus, the issue was brought to the Second Plenum, where a compromise was achieved. On May 31, 1949, the Central Financial and Economic Committee (CFEC) was created to "lead the state's financial and economic work."[157] But Chen Yun was summoned from Manchuria to head the new CFEC. Chen's seniority and experience in finance made him an ideal candidate for the job.[158] More importantly, Chen was acceptable to all mountaintop leaders, because he was then a low-profile leader, without a mountaintop.[159] Bo was appointed the CFEC vice-director.

Although the CFEC was empowered to control the expenditures, it still relied on the local authorities to collect tax revenues. Every mountaintop tried to keep the revenue collected in its bailiwick while competing with others for the Center's money.[160] A huge deficit, 46.4 percent of total expenditure, appeared at the end of 1949.[161] The revenue collected in February 1950 only made up 60 percent of what had been expected.[162] The situation forced the CCP leadership to strengthen the financial centralization, particularly the tax revenues.[163] The Government Administration Council (GAC, the predecessor of the State Council) issued "The Resolution on Unifying the Nation's Financial and Eco-

---

156 This was the first time Gao and Rao stood on the same side. According to a reliable source, Liu was very upset. He blamed Gao for "demanding independence from the Party." But Gao implied that Zhou, Bo, and Yang Lisan, then director of the PLA Logistic Department, were the ones who should be blamed.
157 See Bo, *Huigu*, 1:69.
158 Chen's career in financial management started in 1942, after Ren Bishi replaced him as director of the Organization Department. He was assigned to supervise financial affairs of the base areas in the Northwest. Chen was director of the Northeastern Financial and Economic Committee in 1946–9.
159 Source B, a former confidant of Gao Gang, said that Liu wanted Dong Biwu to take up the post, so Bo could continue to be the real financial boss. But Mao turned to Zhou for his opinion, and Zhou wisely suggested Chen.
160 Cf. Fang Weizhong, ed., *Zhonghua renmin gongheguo jingji dashi ji, 1949–1980* (The Economic Chronology of the PRC, 1949–1980), Beijing: Chinese Social Science Academy Press, 1984, p. 12 (hereafter *Jingji dashi ji*).
161 Ibid., p. 9.   162 Bo, *Huigu*, 1:82.   163 Cf. ibid., p. 83.

The Establishment of the Yan'an Round Table

nomic Work" on March 3, stipulating that the finance, revenue, and monetary systems had to be centralized, and the size and expenditure of the localities had to be regulated. The CFEC was authorized to set up the subordinate offices in all the systems and localities to ensure its control over the finances and tax revenues. On the same day, the CC leadership dispatched a circular, instructing all the Party authorities to "take all the necessary measures to guarantee the absolute implementation of the [GAC] resolution."[164]

The financial centralization boosted Chen's power. The CFEC even overshadowed its superior office, the GAC, in the policy process.[165] Chen's gain was that, as the CCP's financial boss, he was able to develop a strong power base in the financial system of the CCP regime. Compared with his colleagues, Chen seemed to have been exceptionally lucky since 1949. Although he suffered a few criticisms and Red Guard attacks, he was never really purged. The reason was not just that, as Teiwes argues, Chen always managed to fade "into the background whenever the Chairman was on a different wavelength, only to reemerge when Mao was more willing to listen,"[166] but it lies in the fact that, from the perspective of factionalism, his control of the financial system was virtually irreplaceable, despite all the political storms after 1949.

Financial unification was the prelude to the overall centralization that would be started soon after the consolidation of the regime. A Stalin-type system could not tolerate powerful local authorities, and the Yan'an Round Table would not have survived had the mountaintops evolved into "independent kingdoms." However, the tendency of "independent kingdoms" just reflected the vital flaws in the structure of the Yan'an Round Table. After the CCP seized the state power, the stability of the faction-ridden leadership relations became vulnerable because of the

---

164 This Resolution was based on Chen's report, "Resolution on unifying financial and economic works," to the first National Financial and Economic Conference in February 1950. Cf. Fang, *Jingji dashi ji*, pp. 13–14; and Liao Gailong, *1949–1989: Xin zhongguo biannian shi* (1949–1989: A Chronology of the New China), Beijing: People's Press, July 1989, pp. 15–16. For the full text of the two documents, see *Cankao*, 19:107–10.

165 Bo, *Huigu*, 1:72, 110, says that the CFEC directly reported to the Center on Financial and Economic Affairs. Teiwes, *Politics at Mao's Court*, p. 27, also notices the confusing relationship between the GAC and the CFEC.

166 Teiwes, *Politics at Mao's Court*, p. 32; also see David M. Bachman, *Chen Yun and the Chinese Political System*, China Research Monograph, no. 29, Berkeley: University of California, 1985, pp. 146–8.

two inevitable developments in subsequent CCP politics. First was the disappearance of a common enemy to the CCP leaders. Despite their shared ideological faith, diverse interests emerged in the policy process that would force them to pursue different policy goals, and they would evaluate an emerging problem from different perspectives. As a result, differences would replace harmony as the routine in policy making. However, deficiency in institutional arrangements and Mao's absolute command would make it difficult for them to communicate and coordinate their actions in a honest manner. Thus, the eventual solution would still depend on the political skills and personal authority of the supreme leader, namely Mao. As Mao's authority became increasingly absolute, however, it became more difficult to conduct any structural changes in the Yan'an Round Table, which in turn further increased the system's dependency on Mao's personal authority. As a result, the political process entered into a vicious cycle.

Second, the effort to stabilize policy outcomes would lead to an effort to formalize the policy-making process, resulting in the adoption of various formal arrangements and procedures in order to secure communications and coordination in policy making. But these arrangements would reshape leadership relations in the light of various interests that emerged in the policy process. This would in turn undermine Mao's command, which was based essentially on personal loyalties. Thus, the process of institutionalization was incompatible with Mao's command, and it weakened his ability to manipulate leadership relations. As I explain in detail in the following chapters, Mao's effort (and later Deng's) to maintain his command would not only hinder the process of institutionalization, but also constantly destabilize leadership relations and leadership decision making.

The Yan'an Round Table was bound to collapse, because its structure was ill-suited to the political process of a modern state, and it could not be adapted to new relationships between the leaders who had transmuted themselves from revolutionaries into administrators by the time their revolution ended successfully in 1949. Lamentably, the desperate, and often unconscious, efforts of Mao and his colleagues to save the integrity of their glorious Yan'an Round Table made the eventual outcome even more tragic for all of them, including Mao himself, and for the cause to which they had devoted themselves.

4

The Transition of the Yan'an Round Table

The centralization started in August 1952: the Northeastern People's Government was downgraded into an administrative council, and the Civil and Military Commissions in the other five regions followed three months later.[1] All the regional leaders were moved to Beijing in 1952–3: Gao Gang from the Northeast; Peng Dehuai and Xi Zhongxun from the Northwest; Rao Shushi from the East; Lin Biao, Deng Zihui, and Ye Jianying from the Central-South; and Deng Xiaoping and He Long from the Southwest. This resulted in an overall redistribution of power, which in turn provoked a fierce power struggle among the Yan'an Round Table members: the Gao-Rao Affair.

Although opinions vary on this event,[2] the CCP official account[3] and the Western analysis appear consistent in their explanations – that a power-hungry Gao Gang "misinterpreted" Mao's intention and "miscalculated" the situation, and that Gao and Rao were purged because their activities jeopardized the Party's unity.[4] Although Teiwes highlighted factionalism in his analysis, its implications are mostly seen in Gao's "search of allies."[5] But my examination of this event suggests:

---

1 See *CLOPCG*, pp. 38–9.
2 See Frederick Teiwes, *Politics at Mao's Court: Gao Gang and Party Factionalism in the Early 1950s*, New York: M. E. Sharp, 1990, pp. 5, 277–8nn5–9.
3 See Bo Yibo, *Ruogan zhongda juece yu shijian de huigu* (Review of Several Important Decisions and Events), Beijing: CCP Party School Press, 1991, 1:309–10 (hereafter *Huigu*). Bo's opinion and description could be biased because of his involvement in this affair, although he tries to be objective in his account. Also see Chen Shihui, "Questions concerning opposition to the anti-party conspiratorial activities of Gao and Rao," and Deng Xiaoping, "Report on the Gao Gang, Rao Shushi anti-Party alliance," in Teiwes, *Politics at Mao's Court*, pp. 258–60.
4 See Teiwes, *Politics at Mao's Court*, pp. 37–9, 112.
5 Ibid.

Factionalism in Chinese Communist Politics

1. A power struggle emerged during the centralization that involved a redistribution of power in the Party system. Given the faction-ridden structure of leadership relations, this struggle evolved into a clash between the two major mountaintops, led by Liu Shaoqi and Gao Gang respectively, in the Party.
2. It was Mao who spurred Gao to take on Liu in an effort to contain Liu's mountaintop that had become dominant at the Center. This led to an overall crisis in leadership relations because there were few institutional arrangements at the Yan'an Round Table to secure communications and coordination in decision making (see Chapter 3). Thus, while Mao had to maintain an ambiguous attitude before he could see each leader's stand, the other leaders were also reluctant to show their attitude before they could see where Mao stood. All this made the final outcome more explosive.
3. Mao eventually abandoned Gao because Gao's aggressive lobbying among the elite members, especially those in the military, posed a threat to Mao's command. Had Gao successfully rallied the military leaders to upset Liu, he would have achieved the position Mao enjoyed exclusively, receiving support from both the Party and military systems.
4. The Gao-Rao Affair resulted in a *structural* change in leadership relations: the two-front arrangement in the policy-making process.

POLICY DIFFERENCES: PRELUDE TO THE GAO-LIU
POWER STRUGGLE

The Tension between Liu Shaoqi and Gao Gang

The tension between Liu and Gao started even before the CCP took over the state power. The CCP Northeast Bureau (NEB) led by Gao was the first CCP bureau that had experience in running the metropolises like Shenyang. Thus, the CC leadership dispatched the NEB's report on the takeover of Shenyang to the other CCP bureaus on December 14, 1948.[6] Meanwhile, it instructed the NEB to send cadres with experience in urban administration down south to help take over the big cities,[7] which had been seized by Lin's Fourth Field Army. For example, Tianjin was taken over in January 1949 by cadres and officers led by Huang Kecheng, a vice-commander of the Fourth Field Army.

6 This report was drafted by Chen Yun, then the NEB's vice-secretary in charge of urban administration. See Liao Gailong, *1949–1989: Xin zhongguo biannian shi* (1949–1989: A Chronology of the New China), Beijing: People's Press, July 1989, p. 9.
7 Bo, *Huigu*, 1:8–9.

The Transition of the Yan'an Round Table

But frictions soon surfaced between the cadres from Gao's Northeast party and those from Liu's North China party.[8] The cadres from the Northeast insisted on the NEB's takeover policy, which was summarized by Chen Yun as "take over all units" from the top down first, and then "place each [unit] under the administration of the appropriate division."[9] But this policy backfired in Tianjin, where the economy was primarily light industry and commerce. By April 1949, over 70 percent of private businesses in Tianjin were shut down because their owners were afraid that their properties would be "taken over." A high rate of unemployment and the shortage of daily necessities caused economic chaos, which jeopardized stability.[10]

Liu Shaoqi went to Tianjin on April 10.[11] During his one-month inspection there, Liu gave a series of talks with the thesis that the interests of China's capitalists had to be protected and their business activities encouraged. Given that thousands of workers were on the street, Liu argued: "Capitalist exploitation is not evil, but has rendered great service" to the society because "it helps to improve people's lives and promote social progress." Thus, "the more capitalist exploitation, the better."[12]

Liu's Tianjin talks were a departure from the policy orientation

---

8 A former secretary of Chen Yun said that cadres from the Northeast often complained to Huang Kecheng, then the Party secretary of Tianjin, about the local cadres' "localism" and discrimination against the cadres from the other areas. The local cadres, however, complained that the cadres from the Northeast were cocky and rude. Even Huang Kecheng felt that the local cadres had "their own system" (*zicheng xitong*) and were "reluctant to cooperate with the cadres from the Northeast" (see also note 14).
9 See *SWCY*, 1926–49, p. 260.
10 Bo, *Huigu*, 1:50–1. However, as a mountaintop leader from North China, Bo's account could be biased against the cadres from the Northeast.
11 Teiwes, *Politics at Mao's Court*, p. 42, asserts that Mao dispatched Liu to Tianjin. This is inconsistent with Mao and Zhou's accounts (see note 18). Bo, *Huigu*, 1:51, recalled: "One day in the first ten days of April, [Liu] came to the North China Bureau [NCB].... He said that he was going to Tianjin to inspect work.... He also said that his activities in Tianjin would be reported to the NCB by Tianjin Party Committee, but some important issues should be reported to the CC and Chairman Mao by me [i.e., Bo]. The directives from the CC and Chairman Mao should also be passed to him by me." However, Bo does not explain why Liu would not keep direct contact with the CC but through the NCB, although the NCB was also located in Beijing; nor does he mention whether, and what, he reported to Mao on Liu's activities.
12 Ibid., 1:51–3; see also *A Special Collection of Materials on Liu Shaoqi*, compiled by the Institute for the Study of Chinese Communist Problems, Taibei, 1970, pp. 449–51 (hereafter *Materials on Liu Shaoqi*).

adopted at the Second Plenum of the Seventh CC: "to *use, restrict,* and *transform*" China's capitalists.[13] His talks justified the local cadres' criticism of "the cadres from the Northeast" but puzzled the latter.[14] In order to drive his points home, Liu turned down "The Outline of Economic Composition and Principles of Economic Construction in the Northeast" submitted by the NEB.[15] He drafted a telegram to the NEB on May 30, "criticizing the NEB for its Left-deviationist error on the issue" of the national bourgeoisie. The next day, Liu cleverly dispatched Mao's approval of an NCB report on national bourgeoisie to *all* the CCP bureaus and the headquarters of field armies in the name of the CC,[16] implying this was the Party's general policy.

The NCB, led by Bo Yibo, immediately instructed all its subordinate offices to "widely propagate every issue Comrade Shaoqi explained in his Tianjin talks."[17] But Gao's NEB was not enthusiastic about Liu's Tianjin talks; and Gao resented the May 31 telegram drafted by Liu. A former confidant of Gao recalled that Gao ordered that the information not be distributed to the NEB's subordinate offices, arguing that "the situation in the Northeast was exceptional." Moreover, Gao made a special file of Liu's talks that he obtained through informal channels and submitted it to Mao, asking if it represented the CC's "*new* spirit (*xin jingshen*)." Gao called it "new" to remind Mao that it was at odds with the policy adopted at the Second Plenum.

It is unlikely that Liu's Tianjin talks were "fully in accord with Mao's

---

13 See *Cankao,* 19:1–5.
14 For example, Huang Kecheng, then the Tianjin Party secretary, was puzzled by Liu's talks. He asked Mao to let him return to his army with the excuse that he was "not adapted to urban work." The real reason, according to the same source, was that he could not get along with Tianjin's Mayor Huang Jing (Jiang Qing's former husband), who was Bo's confidant. Liu's talks made it more difficult for Huang to remain in the driver's seat. So Mao sent him to his hometown, Hunan, as the Party secretary in September 1949.
15 This "Outline" was actually drafted by Zhang Wentian, a vice-secretary of NEB in charge of economic affairs in Manchuria after Chen Yun left. See *Cankao,* 19:70.
16 Bo, *Huigu,* 1:57, claims that Mao authorized the dispatch of Liu's telegram to all CCP bureaus. But according to the CC documents available today, what Mao actually agreed upon was the report from the NCB to which Liu's telegram is attached. The report did suggest that members of the national bourgeoisie "are our friends," and that the Party should adopt a moderate policy toward them. Mao's comment reads: "I think your currently adopted policy of adjusting the industry and commerce and improving the relationship between the public and private sectors is correct." *Wengao,* 1:380.
17 Bo, *Huigu,* 1:53–4.

The Transition of the Yan'an Round Table

policy directive" at the time.[18] On the contrary, Mao was upset when he saw the *full text* of Liu's Tianjin talks from the "files" Gao submitted.[19] He summoned Bo and Yang Shangkun, head of the CC General Office, in mid-June. He pointed out that Liu's words on capitalist exploitation were "improper" (*butuo*) and "inconsistent" (*buyizhi*) with the Party's policy.[20] Mao emphasized on June 30: "[The national bourgeoisie] can only play its proper role under the leadership of the proletariat. The national bourgeoisie is *a class that will be eliminated* gradually during socialist revolution. . . . The people have the state power in their hands;

---

18 See Teiwes, *Politics at Mao's Court*, pp. 42, 72–3, 290n113. Teiwes's argument is essentially based on two articles: Zhang Kai, "*'Tianjin jianghua' shimuo*" (The whole story of the "Tianjin Talks"), *Yanjiu 1*, 1980, 2:17–28, and Ye Wuxi and Shao Yunduan, "*Chong ping 'Tianjin jianghua'*" (A reappraisal of "Tianjin Address"), *Lishi yanjiu* (Historical Research), Beijing: Chinese Social Science Academy Press, no. 2 (1980), pp. 47–58. The two articles, however, were actually written to justify the reversal of Liu's case. Zhang Kai's article claim that Mao not only knew Liu's Tianjin talks but also expressed his delight when Liu's wife, Wang Guangmei, reported them to him. Mao said, "We sent him [i.e., Liu] to Tianjin. The aim is to let him work on the capitalists" (p. 25). Noticeably, though, neither article mentions Mao's critical attitude toward and unhappiness about Liu's Tianjin talks later. Teiwes asserts that Mao changed his attitude in late 1952 and became critical of Liu's talks. But Mao, *Wansui*, 2:655, said at a Politburo meeting on October 22, 1966, "[Liu] went in for the independent kingdom, and did not consult me on many things. For example, . . . the Tianjin talks." Zhou Enlai, *Materials on Liu Shaoqi*, p. 552, confirmed Mao's account on August 9, 1967: "Liu Shaoqi went to Tianjin and gave talks to the capitalists in early May without asking Chairman Mao for his instructions. . . . Someone may ask why you [the CC leadership] did not pay any attention to him at that time. When such a leading comrade [i.e., Liu] goes out to give talks, isn't it improper to send people to follow him everywhere he goes?"

The key question is to what extent Mao knew about Liu's Tianjin talks – the full text or just basic ideas – *before* he allegedly authorized the dispatch of Liu's telegram on May 31, 1949. Bo Yibo, who is perhaps best qualified to answer this question, carefully avoids this question in his account. Bo, *Huigu*, 1:54, only mentions in a pair of brackets that "(Mao had agreed)" that the NCB "required [its subordinate offices] to propagate the issues Comrade Shaoqi expounded in his Tianjin talks." But Bo fails to tell us *when* and on *what issues* Mao agreed to propagate. The evidence available today indicates that Mao first learned about Liu's Tianjin talks from the report of Liu's wife, Wang Guangmei, but just some major points instead of the full text, and Bo later submitted a cleaned-up version to Mao. For even Bo has to admit that Mao was very upset after he saw *the full text* of Liu's Tianjin talks, which were part of the "files" Gao submitted to Mao in mid-June.

19 Interviews with Sources B and D. The last time I talked to D, a former secretary of Mao, on the Gao-Rao Affair was in July 1993.

20 Bo, *Huigu*, 1:55, admits that Mao was upset by Liu's words on "capitalist exploitation" when he "reported to Mao on Liu's Tianjin talks." But again, Bo fails to tell who initiated this conversation and when.

they are not afraid of the national bourgeoisie's rebellion."[21] This, according to Zhou Enlai, was "Chairman Mao immediate response" to Liu's Tianjin talks, of which Mao "was informed *later*."[22]

But it is unclear if there were any direct exchanges between Mao and Liu on this issue. Understandably, the issue was downplayed because assuaging the bourgeoisie's fear was vital to the stability after the PLA seized Shanghai on May 27, especially when the CCP was trying to lure "democratic personages" into its new government.[23] Thus, Liu's talks were reported in the *People's Daily* on July 4, two months after Liu's Tianjin trip. The report, however, did not mention Liu's words on the policy toward the capitalists at all. But it downgraded Liu's Tianjin talks as the ones dealing with the local labor-capital disputes, rather than being concerned with the Party's policy. It praised the fact that Liu's talks clarified the position of the government "on labor-capital relations, . . . relieved the capitalists' fear . . . (and) let both the labor and capitalists understand the principle of mutual benefit." Thus, Liu's talks did not need to be transmitted within the Party. Even Deng Xiaoping "did not see the original record of the Tianjin talks," but only "heard of it."[24] Ironically, Gao was later accused of "launching an attack on the Party" by "making and spreading a 'file' of Comrade Liu Shaoqi's Tianjin talks."[25]

Yet Liu soon attacked Gao again. On January 4, 1950, Gao published his speech at the Forum on Rural Work in the Northeast, held in December 1949. He advocated that the Party should immediately organize "the overwhelming majority of the peasants [to] evolve from the individual to collective farming."[26] On the same day, the NEB sent a report to the CC Organization Department, inquiring about the policy toward Party members who hired laborers for private farming.

Liu had different ideas. On January 23 he instructed An Ziwen, a Liu confidant who was deputy director of the Organization Department:

21 *SWMZD*, 4:12 (emphasis added).
22 *Materials on Liu Shaoqi*, p. 552 (emphasis added).
23 Cf. Xiao Chaoran and Sha Jiansun, eds., *Zhongguo geming shigao* (History of the Chinese Revolution), Beijing: Beijing University Press, 1984, p. 440; and Li Weihan, *Huiyi yu yanjiu* (Memory and Study), Beijing: CCP History Materials Press, 1986, 2:683–4.
24 *SWDXP*, 1938–65, p. 193. 25 Bo, *Huigu*, 1:57.
26 See the *Northeast Daily*, January 4, 1950.

The Transition of the Yan'an Round Table

> The present mutual-aid teams in the Northeast are based on the bankrupt and poor individual economy.... Can the mutual-aid teams develop into future collective farms? I do not think it is possible.... The new democratic phase cannot be confused with the socialist phase. "What if a Party member becomes a rich peasant?" This question is asked too early.... Now it is a society of *private* ownership.... It is dogmatic to hold that a Party member cannot go in for exploitation.

On the same day, An's office conveyed Liu's idea to the NEB in a formal letter: "Based on the individual economy in today's countryside, the development of rural capitalism to a certain degree is inevitable.... It is too early to ask what if a Party member becomes a rich peasant, and it is an erroneous [question]."[27]

A few weeks later, Gao personally submitted the minutes of the Liu-An conversation to Mao.[28] Mao's "resentment of Liu's talks could be seen clearly from his facial expression [*xingyu yanse*]."[29] But again, Mao had to hold his temper because he had to focus on the "major contradiction" at that time, namely, the land reform in the newly liberated areas.

The tension between Liu and Gao stemmed from their different interests in policy making. North China had been strategically the CCP's most important area, and it had been the model for the other base areas to follow.[30] Yet its role as a model was fading as the focus of policy making

---

27 See Bo, *Huigu*, 1:197–8 (emphasis added). Because both documents were dated on January 23, Bo deliberately pointed out that Liu talked to An in the *evening*, implying that Liu talked to An *after* the letter from An's office was sent to the NEB. But in this letter it is stated that it is written "in the light of a CC leader's directive." Those who were then recognized as the CC leaders were Mao, Liu, Zhu, and Zhou. It could not be Mao because it turned out later that he was mad about this letter; neither Zhu nor Zhou would handle such an issue because Party affairs were none of their business. So it has to be Liu. The reason why An and Bo tried to twist this fact is that they want people to believe that An's office wrote to the NEB on its own. Liu merely endorsed it afterward. Thus, it looks like Liu and An just followed the standard procedures on this matter instead of engaging in factional activities.
28 The exact date of Gao's meeting with Mao in Beijing is unknown. But it has to be between February 17, the date Mao returned from the Soviet Union, and February 25, the last day of the National Financial and Economic Conference (February 13–25, 1950), which Gao attended.
29 Bo, *Huigu*, 1:198.
30 Bo Yibo, "*Liu Shaoqi tongzhi de yige lishi gongji*" (A historical contribution of Comrade Liu Shaoqi), in *Shanxi geming huiyi lu* (Reminiscence of Revolution in Shanxi),

165

shifted to socialist transformation after 1949. It was unrealistic indeed to bring North China into the planned economy, given the region's unevenly developed agriculture – the poor mountainous west and more advanced but densely populated east – and an urban economy based on fragmented light industry and commerce. Such conditions led Liu to advocate a "new democratic phase" lasting fifteen to twenty years prior to socialist transformation. The kernel of his argument was that since socialism could be built only upon an advanced economy, the CCP should first focus on economic development after its victory in 1949. So the CCP would have to tolerate, or even encourage, a certain degree of capitalism, which could help to speed up economic development.[31] Liu's Tianjin talks and his instruction to An reflected his vision.

Liu's vision, however, was challenged by the development in the Northeast, then the most advanced area in China. Over 50 percent of heavy industry was located there;[32] and most enterprises there were large ones previously owned by the KMT regime or by big businessmen. This not only justified the NEB's radical takeover policy, but also made it less difficult to bring the region into the planned economy. On the other hand, although the land reform had increased the living standards of 64 percent of the rural population in the Northeast, economic gaps among the peasants soon emerged. Thus, "be organized to develop production" was not only a policy for the NEB to promote the collective economy but also a necessary measure to prevent "class polarization" in the rural areas.[33]

Ironically, Gao's policy preferences based on the situation in the Northeast could have best justified Liu's argument that socialist transition could take place only upon a developed economy. But why could not Liu see this? Why did he pick on Gao repeatedly for his "Left-

compiled by the Shanxi Social Science Academy Taiyuan: Shanxi People's Press, 1983, pp. 35–7.
31 Liu first advanced this "new democracy" theory in his report, "On the problem in the construction of new democracy," at a Politburo conference in September 1948. But a more systematic exposition of the new democratic system is his "CCP's historical tasks in the future," a lecture at the Marx-Lenin Institute on July 5, 1951.
32 *Cankao*, 19:23–6.
33 See the *Northeast Daily*, January 4, 1950. Bo, *Huigu*, 1:202, recalls that Zhang Wentian, the NEB's vice-secretary, wrote to Mao on May 17, 22, 23, 1950. He held that cooperation was a way to prevent "class polarization" and to promote production in the rural areas. But Liu argued that any form of co-ops would "hinder the development of the rural economy." Mao sided with Zhang in this dispute.

The Transition of the Yan'an Round Table

deviationist errors"? An objective explanation is that Liu felt threatened by Gao's success. If Gao could succeed in turning the Northeast into a model for socialist transition, his influence in policy making would increase. Given the faction-ridden structure of the Yan'an Round Table, this would undermine Liu's mountaintop, which was predominant at the Center. Thus, although Gao's policy was rational, judging from the conditions in the Northeast, Liu still attacked it as too radical from the perspective of the conditions of the other areas.

It must be noticed, however, that the Liu-Gao disagreement was in fact unseen in the policy-making process. The tension between them appeared only *after* Gao adopted and implemented the policy in the area under his authority. This is not surprising because deficient institutional arrangements prevented the leaders from communicating with each other in policy making. Yet, given faction-ridden leadership relations, the success of a leader's policy in his area formed a threat to the other leaders' positions. Thus, a conflict emerged after this leader's policy was carried out successfully, and, due to the uncertainty of rules and procedures in conflict solution, this conflict would soon evolve into a power struggle (see Chapter 2).

Gao Gains Momentum in the Mao-Liu Discord

The lack of institutional arrangements was also shown in that Liu and Gao rarely confronted each other but exchanged their objections via Mao. But Gao gained momentum soon after differences between Mao and Liu on socialist transition emerged in July 1951.

Although both Mao and Liu agreed that China would experience a new democratic period after 1949, there was a fundamental difference between them. Seeing this period as "an inevitable phase," Liu wanted to "*establish* a new-democratic system" in which private ownership had to be sustained, because it had "a positive role in increasing social productivity."[34] But Mao regarded "new democracy" as a *transition* period, during which the CCP would promote "socialist factors" while "using, restricting, and transforming" the private sector to pave the way for overall socialist construction.

---

34 Bo, *Huigu*, 1:60.

An example of this difference is Mao's correction of Liu's revision of a document on October 26, 1949:[35]

> on page 29 (you write), "do not adopt measures that will *prematurely* restrict the private capitalist economy." [My] correction is: "do not *prematurely* adopt measures that will restrict the private capitalist economy *that at present is still beneficial to the national economy and the people's livelihood.*" Since our economic policy as a whole is to restrict private capital, only private capital that is beneficial to the national economy and the people's livelihood does not belong to the category of restriction. "Be beneficial to the national economy and the people's livelihood," *this is itself an enormous restriction.*[36]

Thus, Mao changed the entire meaning of the sentence by not only adding new words, but also reordering the words.

Yet, this difference was concealed by the external factor (i.e., the Korean War), and internal pressures in 1949–51, when Mao's major concerns were stabilizing the economy and promoting land reform. Mao realized that cooperation from the bourgeoisie was vital for economic recovery. He said in his opening speech at the Third Plenum of the Seventh CC, held June–September 1950: "The national bourgeoisie will eventually cease to exist. But at this stage we should rally them around us and not push them away. . . . It is in the interests of the working class to unite with them. We need to adopt these *tactics now*."[37] Mao also suggested protecting the rich peasants in the land reform "for the time being" in order to "isolate the landlords" and, more importantly, "to set the minds of the national bourgeoisie at rest," because they were "closely tied up with the land problem."[38] But Liu insisted that protecting the rich peasants was "of course not a temporary policy, but a long-term policy" for the entire new-democratic phase.[39]

---

35 This document is "The Outline of the Economic Composition and Principles of Economic Construction in the Northeast" (see note 15).
36 Quoted from Bo, *Huigu*, 1:23 (emphasis added). The Chinese original of Liu's words reads: "*jue buke caiqu guozao de xianzhi siren ziben zhuyi jingji de banfa.*" Mao's correction reads: "*jue buke guozao de caiqu xianzhi xianshi hai youyi yu guoji minsheng de siren ziben zhuyi jingji de banfa.*"
37 *SWMZD*, 5:35 (emphasis added).
38 Ibid., pp. 24–5.   39 See Bo, *Huigu*, 1:120–31.

The Transition of the Yan'an Round Table

The differences between Mao and Liu surfaced in 1951 when the land reform was completed in most areas except in the Southwest and Northwest;[40] the economy had been "decisively improved";[41] and the peace negotiations in Korea started on July 10.[42] In fact, Mao reminded the Party as early as February at an enlarged Politburo conference: "We have twenty-four months left" to complete the plan adopted at the Second Plenum: "three years for preparation and ten years for the construction of a *planned economy.*" Mao urged the cadres that they "should be clear in their minds about relying on the working class."[43] But Mao's warning was neglected or, more precisely, ignored by Liu and his men. On May 7 Liu changed Mao's formulation into "three years for preparation and ten years for the construction" – Mao's words "a planned economy" were omitted. Moreover, Liu stressed that *only after* "ten years for construction" would socialist transition "be considered."[44] A confrontation between Mao and Liu occurred in July.

The Shanxi Party Committee submitted a report to the NCB on April 17, suggesting to strengthen the agricultural mutual aids and co-ops by "expanding collective accumulation" and "distributing according to one's work" instead of according to the quantity of his property used in the production. The aim was to "shake, cripple, and eventually deny" private ownership in order to promote collectivization.[45] This was consistent with Gao's preference: "pushing for socialist transition immediately after the land reform without allowing for a new-democratic phase."[46] Liu was upset, especially since this report was from his

---

40 Cf. Fang Weizhong, ed., *Zhonghua renmin gongheguo jingji dashi ji, 1949–1980* (The Economic Chronology of the PRC, 1949–1980), Beijing: Chinese Social Science Academy Press, 1984, p. 60 (hereafter *Jingji dashi ji*).
41 By the end of 1950, the industrial production increased 36.4%, and the agricultural output, 17.8%, though there was a deficit of 290 million yuan. The economy was improved "decisively" in 1951 – the revenue increased 104%. For the first time there was a surplus of 1.6 billion yuan in the budget. Ibid., pp. 37–8, 60–1.
42 See Liao, *Xin zhongguo biannian shi*, pp. 36–7.
43 *SWMZD*, 5:45 (emphasis added).
44 Liu's speech on May 7, 1951, at the CCP National Conference for the Propaganda Work was not published, presumably because it was obviously at odds with the Party's principle. His published summary report on May 23 at the conference was heavily edited. But even in the edited version, we can still see that Liu advocated to "encourage the development of the economies of the bourgeoisie, petty bourgeoisie, and [rich] peasant class." *SWLSQ*, 2:83.
45 See *Materials on Liu Shaoqi*, pp. 245–6.   46 Bo, *Huigu*, 1:197.

turf.[47] Not only did he instruct the NCB to turn down this report on May 4, but he also "criticized the Shanxi Party Committee on several occasions."[48] Liu authorized the circulation of this report among the CCP bureaus on July 3 with this comment: "the suggestion that [we] should shake, cripple, and eventually deny the basis of private [ownership], that [we] should upgrade the agricultural mutual-aid teams into agricultural production co-ops . . . is an *erroneous, dangerous, and utopian notion of agrarian socialism*. This report by the Shanxi Provincial Committee is an example that displays such a notion."[49] Two days later, Liu made a systematic criticism of "agrarian socialism" in his lecture at the Marx-Lenin Institute. Bo also published an article in the *People's Daily*, ridiculing the attempt to leap from the mutual aids to collectivization as "a sheer fantasy" of agrarian socialism.

Mao was annoyed, not necessarily by Liu's attack on "agrarian socialism,"[50] but because Liu again, without Mao's authorization, expressed his opinion publicly in the name of the CC on the issue concerning "the Party's principle." Mao felt that his "great power was taken away (*daquan pangluo*)."[51] Mao summoned Liu, Bo, and Liu Lantao, deputy secretary of the NCB, after the NCB submitted its report on this case on July 25. Mao told them flatly that he was against them and sided "with the minority who hold the truth." Liu and his men caved in. The NCB withdrew its report; and Liu recalled his lecture at the Marx-Lenin Institute.[52] On December 15, the CC issued a *Resolution* on agricultural

---

47 In fact, Liu expressed his resentment in early 1951, when he learned the stand of the Shanxi Party Committee. But he withheld his criticism, wishing that the Shanxi Party authority would cave in under the pressure of their superior body, the NCB led by Bo. See ibid., p. 186.
48 Ibid., pp. 187–9.
49 Quoted from ibid., pp. 188–9 (emphasis added).
50 Teiwes, *Politics at Mao's Court*, p. 42, asserts that "there were notable similarities with the Tianjin talks issues" in this case, because the disagreement was caused essentially by the shift of Mao's focus toward socialist transition. He claims that Mao was annoyed by Liu's attack on "agrarian socialism," the term Mao himself "used in 1948 to attack leftist excesses." But Mao used the term then to criticize the "absolute egalitarianism" in the land reform, caused by the "leftist" policy adopted at the Land Conference Liu chaired in July–September 1947. Liu picked up the term in 1951, as Bo admitted, to ridicule the effort to achieve "agricultural collectivization through gradually shaking, crippling, and eventually denying private ownership in the mutual-aid teams." But this was exactly what Mao intended to do.
51 See *Wansui*, 2:655.
52 See Bo, *Huigu*, 1:191. Again, Bo fails to tell the exact date of the meeting.

The Transition of the Yan'an Round Table

mutual aids and co-ops, affirming that "to be organized" was the direction for agriculture.[53] Mao announced that the implementation of this policy was a "major task" of the Party.[54]

This was just the beginning of Mao's rebuff of Liu's new-democracy theory. The wrongdoings of the capitalists, exposed during the Five Anti Campaign,[55] convinced Mao that "the long-term coexistence between the socialist and capitalist economies was impossible."[56] The rapid expansion of the public sector and the fully recovered economy[57] further strengthened Mao's confidence in pushing for socialist transition.

On June 6, 1952, Mao declared that the national bourgeoisie "should no longer be defined as an intermediate class."[58] At a CC Secretariat meeting on September 24, Mao initiated a "general line" for the transition period: "to accomplish the country's industrialization and socialist transformation of agriculture, handicrafts and capitalist industry, and commerce in ten to fifteen years."[59] After consulting with Stalin in October,[60] this general line was formally adopted at the enlarged Politburo conference on June 15, 1953. At the same conference, Mao denounced Liu's idea of a new democratic system: "'Firmly establish the new-democratic social order.' That is a harmful formulation.... (It) goes against the realities of our struggle and hinders the progress of the socialist cause.... 'Sustain private property'... is not right, either."[61]

Gao benefited greatly from the Mao-Liu discord. In fact, the success of the planned economy in the Northeast was a major factor impelling

---

53 Liao, *Xin zhongguo biannian shi*, pp. 37–8. This document was drafted by Chen Boda.
54 See *SWMZD*, 5:71.
55 This campaign was launched on January 26, 1952, after the Three Anti Campaign, started in December 1951 against corruption, waste, and bureaucracy among CCP officials, revealed "a large amount of five evils among capitalists": tax evasion, bribery, theft of state property, cheating on government contracts, and stealing of economic information. See Bo, *Huigu*, 2:138–83; and Liao, *Xin zhongguo biannian shi*, pp. 42–3.
56 Chen Wei, "*Jiben wancheng shihui zhuyi gaizao de qinian*" (Seven years of basic completion of socialist transformation), *Zhuanji*, 1:99, 103.
57 See Xue Mugiao, *Zhongguo shehui zhuyi jingji wenti yanjiu* (The Study of the Problem in China's Socialist Economy), Beijing: Social Science Academy Press, 1981, pp. 31–2.
58 *SWMZD*, 5:77; see also Li Weihan, *Huiyi yu yanjiu*, 2:729.
59 *SWMZD*, 5:93.
60 Cf. Bo, *Huigu*, 1:212–30; Liao, *Xin zhongguo biannian shi*, pp. 56–7.
61 *SWMZD*, 5:93–4; see also *Wengao*, 4:251. Liu raised the slogan "firmly establish the new-democratic social order" at the First National Conference on Organizational Work in March–April 1951.

Mao to push for socialist transition. As early as June 1950 Mao cited the Northeast as a model: "Construction of the planned economy has begun in the Northeast. Why can the Northeast do so well? It is because there are three conditions: the land reform has been completed; industry and commerce is on the right track; and the government expenditure has been retrenched, so that much money is used for the economic investment."[62]

After Mao confronted Liu in July 1951, Gao submitted a timely report on the mutual aids and co-ops on October 14.[63] Gao suggested that the Party should focus on mutual aids and co-ops in order to lead the peasants in the right direction. Mao was so delighted that he dispatched Gao's report to the Party on July 17, affirming that "the principle (raised by Gao) is correct."[64]

Mao was also pleased by Gao's initiation of the Three Anti and Five Anti campaigns.[65] On December 13, Mao urged the other CCP bureaus to follow the NEB's example and launch a nationwide campaign.[66] All this enabled Gao to ride high even before he was appointed chairman of the State Planning Commission (SPC) on November 15, 1952.[67] Not only was the Northeast seen as a model for the rapid Soviet-style development,[68] but Gao's correct policy and achievements also increased Mao's trust in him.

However, Gao seemed reluctant to take up this new post.[69] Allegedly, he complained to Mao that it might be "difficult for me to do the job" because he and Liu had "some different opinions [*butong de kanfa*] on several issues." Mao, who knew what Gao meant, explained to Gao that

---

62 Quoted from Bo, *Huigu*, 1:99.
63 According to Source B, Gao submitted this report partly because an article, published in Gao's name in the *People's Daily* on October 1, "distorted his view." Teiwes, *Politics at Mao's Court*, p. 36, cites this article as evidence of Gao's "rightist leaning" because it warned "that agricultural co-operativization should not push ahead rapidly in the absence of mechanization." But Gao claimed that these words were "smuggled in" by Liu's men at the *People's Daily*, and he later used it as evidence of "Liu's conspiratorial activities."
64 See *Wengao*, 2:476–8.
65 The Three Anti Campaign was launched in the Northeast in September; and the Five Anti Campaign, in late October. Gao submitted a report on the two campaigns to Mao on November 1, 1952. Ibid., 2:513–14.
66 See *Cankao*, 19:386–7.   67 *CLOPCG*, pp. 38–9.
68 Teiwes, *Politics at Mao's Court*, p. 35.
69 See ibid., p. 25.

The Transition of the Yan'an Round Table

the SPC was a crucial policy-making organ in the upcoming construction of the planned economy. He also promised Gao that "[I] shall back you up (*gei ni chengyao*)." Mao also expressed his displeasure with "the Right-opportunist tendency in the Party."[70] Mao then suggested to Gao: "Why don't you have a chat with Shaoqi?"[71]

It is unclear whether Gao went to Liu for a chat – Bo Yibo implies that Gao "turned a deaf ear to Mao's suggestion."[72] But soon, Bo's "terrible mistake" in the change of the tax system and An Ziwen's inept manipulation of the production of a new Politburo provided Gao with god-sent opportunity to orchestrate a siege of Liu's mountaintop.

THE GAO-RAO AFFAIR: AN INEVITABLE CLASH

Liu's Mountaintop under Siege

The CCP "basically inherited the old [tax system]" after 1949 with a special tax relief to the state-owned enterprises.[73] However, as the public sector in the economy expanded quickly, the tax revenue stagnated as the production by private enterprises decreased sharply, especially after the Five Anti Campaign. Thus, the CFEC convened the Financial and Economic Conference in September, 1952. This conference decided to "adjust the tax system."[74] Bo Yibo, a CFEC vice-director and concurrently finance minister, was in charge of the drafting of a new tax law. There were two major changes in the new tax law, published on December 31, 1952:

1 "Equality between the public and private enterprises" in order to "secure the tax revenue."

---

70 Basically, this is what Gao told the other leaders during the Gao-Rao Affair. Although the exact date is unknown, this conversation is confirmed by Sources A, B, and D. But D believed that Gao exaggerated Mao's support to him. This conversation should occur around a Politburo conference held sometime in mid-December 1952 to discuss the 1953 plan and the first five-year plan. See Fang, *Jingji dashi ji*, p. 85. Teiwes, *Politics at Mao's Court*, pp. 5, 37–9, also learned from an "authoritative oral source" that "Mao and Gao had three private conversations sometime after Gao's arrival in the capital."
71 Source A. This source speculates that Mao's words that Gao should "have a chat with Liu" were passed to Liu via his staff members.
72 Cf. Bo, *Huigu*, 1:312.
73 Cf. Fang, *Jingji dashi ji*, pp. 5, 10.
74 Cf. Bo, *Huigu*, 1:232.

2 Levying taxes directly on manufactures instead of the wholesale enterprises. The aim was to "stop up the loopholes" by "simplifying the tax payment links"[75]

The public sector was doubly hurt. Not only did it loose all the tax privileges, but it was virtually taxed twice, on factory turnovers and wholesale enterprises, because the two were strictly separated in the state-owned enterprises in order to prevent corruption. Yet a private owner could combine the factory turnover and wholesale categories into one by wholesaling his own products, so that he was taxed only once. Thus, the new system not only benefited the private sector at the cost of the public one, but it also stirred up a disturbance in the market because people expected that factories would increase prices to make up for the taxes they paid.[76]

Strong objections came from all over the country, for the new tax system, implemented "without notifying the local Party and government leaders,"[77] deprived the localities of a major source of revenue. Because the local governments had little control over tax revenues after the 1950 financial centralization, a chunk of their income came from the profits of the local public industry. Such profits dropped sharply, because all public industry had to pay taxes now.[78]

Mao was annoyed, not just because the new tax system undermined the public sector in the economy, but because it was made and implemented without his approval. On January 15, 1953, Mao sent a "note" to the four leaders who were involved in tax reform: Zhou Enlai, Chen Yun, Deng Xiaoping, and Bo: "The issue of the new tax law had not been discussed at the Center, nor had various (CCP) bureaus, subbureaus, and provincial committees been notified. It was published in a rush without preparation. This seems to have stirred up disturbance all over the country, not just in Shanghai and Beijing. How should it be dealt with? Please let me know after you consider and discuss it. *I came to know this*

---

75 Ibid., p. 233.
76 Cf. Fang, *Jingji dashi ji*, p. 88.
77 See Bo, *Huigu*, 1:234–6. Even the Beijing government, a stronghold of Liu's mountaintop, joined in the protest.
78 For example, the enterprises under the Heavy Industry Ministry had to pay nearly 50 million yuan of tax, all from the profit; and the state enterprises in the Northeast lost over 20 million yuan of profit in 1953. See Fang, *Jingji dashi ji*, p. 88.

The Transition of the Yan'an Round Table

matter after I saw it in a newspaper. I still cannot fully understand [the new tax law] after I read it [from the newspaper]."[79]

The four reacted differently. Zhou "wrote to Mao in the same night, reporting on the measures to resolve [the problem]."[80] Although Zhou *routinely* chaired the 164th GAC session on December 26, which approved the new tax law,[81] the issue was then submitted to Liu Shaoqi, who handled daily affairs at the Center, and to the CC General Office headed by Yang Shangkun. Yet, according to a source who had worked in Zhou's office in the 1950s and 1960s, Zhou "only blamed himself" and "did not mention the other people."

Chen pleaded illness.[82] Although the new tax law was issued by the CFEC led by Chen, he was not responsible for it, and he had actually voiced his disagreement indirectly before the new tax law was issued. Interestingly, Deng, who had been a vice-premier since July 1952 to assist Zhou in administrative affairs, also pleaded illness. Thus, Deng joined Chen, Lin Biao, and Kang Sheng in what was then called "the club of patients" by the elite members.[83] Deng remained inactive until Mao activated him in August 1953.

Bo was held responsible, as was fitting. Bo had been very active in the policy process, partly because of Liu's patronage, and partly because the CFEC grew out of the NCFEC (see Chapter 3).[84] True, the CFEC approved the levying of taxes on the public sector, but "equality of treatment" was Bo's own idea. Altering the tax payment link from wholesale enterprises to factory turnovers also resulted from Bo's "gentleman's agreement with" the capitalists.[85] Although some leaders "had expressed

---

79 *Wengao*, 4:27 (emphasis added).
80 Ibid., p. 234.   81 See *PD*, January 1, 1953.
82 When Mao sent out his "note," Chen had already left for his hometown, Hangzhou, where he usually spent the winter.
83 Deng was last seen in Beijing on February 11, when he spoke at a central government conference. He appeared in Sichuan on February 28, celebrating the establishment of the Southwest Administrative Council, of which Deng was a vice-chairman. He remained there for most of the time till August. Kang pleaded illness in early 1949 (see Chapter 2). Nie Rongzhen, *Nie Rongzhen huiyi lu* (Nie Rongzhen's Memoirs), Beijing: PLA Press, 1984, 3:733–6, said that Lin Biao pleaded illness in September 1950 after he declined the appointment as the commander of the Chinese army in Korea.
84 Cf. Bo, *Huigu*, 1:70–1.
85 *SWMZD*, 5:107; also see Bo, *Huigu*, 1:236–7.

their objections clearly" to the new tax law,[86] Bo "did not pay serious attention."[87] Yao Yilin also opposed the new tax system, despite his junior status at the time. This should reflect Chen Yun's displeasure, given the close relationship between the two.

The Finance, Commerce, and Grain Ministries submitted a joint report on the problems caused by the new tax system on February 10. This report intensified Mao's anger. He lashed out at a Politburo meeting where Bo was ordered to report on the new tax law: "The slogan 'equality between private and public enterprises' violated the resolution of the Second Plenum of the Seventh CC. [Bo] failed to report to the Center on changing the tax law, but [he] consulted with the capitalists, seeing them as more important than the Center. This new tax law is applauded by the capitalists. It is an error of "Right-opportunism."[88]

Two points must be noticed in Mao's words. First, it was "the resolution of the Second Plenum," instead of that of the Third Plenum, that was violated. This indicated that what really counted in Mao's mind was the Second Plenum, which emphasized "the major contradiction between the working class and the bourgeoisie," rather than the Third Plenum, which decided to "unite the national bourgeoisie" for economic recovery.

Second, Bo "failed to report to the Center," namely Mao. This made Mao determined to reconstruct the policy-making process, especially the CC Secretariat,[89] in order to improve the situation about which Mao complained: "Practically nothing comes to my ear in Beijing."[90]

Mao told Gao of his intention to reorganize the Politburo and the CC apparatus in a conversation in late February. Although there is still controversy over exactly what Mao said to Gao,[91] this conversation indicated that Mao began to shift his trust to Gao, for it was Liu, not Gao, who

86 The Ministry of Commerce, the Ministry of Light Industry, and the Federation of Supply and Marketing Co-operatives were opposed to the new system. See ibid., p. 107. The three ministries were then led by Zeng Shan, Jia Tuofu, and Zhang Wentian. Two sources, A and C, confirmed that Ye Jizhuang and Deputy Commerce Minister Yao Yilin also opposed the new tax system. Thus, except for Li Fuchun, who was in Moscow at that time, most leaders at the CFEC were at odds with Bo on this issue.
87 Bo, *Huigu*, 1:236.
88 *SWMZD*, 5:103–5, 107. Cf. Bo, *Huigu*, 1:235.
89 Ibid., p. 312; also Liao, *Xin zhongguo biannian shi*, p. 59.
90 *SWMZD*, 5:104.
91 Both Sources A and C confirmed that Gao later claimed that Mao initiated the idea in February 1953 that Gao should run the Politburo; Liu, the NPC; and Zhou, the government.

The Transition of the Yan'an Round Table

had been in charge of organizational affairs since March 1943 (see Chapter 3). Thus, it is not surprising that Liu appeared anxious after he learned of Mao's intention. He went to consult Gao on whether to adopt the Soviet system of Council of Ministers, but Gao gave him a cold shoulder. Instead, "Gao Gang passed the content of Chairman Mao's conversation with him to An Ziwen," deputy director of the Organization Department who was a Liu confidant.[92]

Whatever Gao's motives were in passing Mao's words to An,[93] two inferences seem reasonable. First, Gao had not yet formed an alliance with Rao Shushi, who had just been appointed director of the Organization Department. Gao went to An, instead of his boss Rao, presumably because Gao saw Rao as less reliable and more difficult to deal with, given Rao's long-term affiliation with Liu and his senior status. Second, and more significantly, Liu's mountaintop was dominant in the policy process because it was hard to initiate a policy without Liu's intervention. But An made two inept moves that triggered the Gao-Rao affair: he drew up a list of the prospective Politburo members; and he went to "consult" Gao on this list.

Not surprisingly, An's list reflected the interests of Liu's mountaintop in the changes in leadership relations after 1949 (Table 4.1). In his list the Politburo would consist of the five members of the CC Secretariat (equivalent to today's PSC): Mao, Liu, Zhou, Zhu, and Chen, and the heads of the six CCP bureaus.[94] But Kang Sheng, Dong Biwu, Lin Boqu, and Zhang Wentian, who were all the sitting Politburo members, would be demoted to alternate members – this was not surprising because they were all leaders without a mountaintop. Li Fuchun's and Xi Zhongxun's rises were not unexpected. Li had Mao's trust and played a crucial role in the policy process (see Chapter 3); Xi headed the NWB

---

92 Bo, *Huigu*, 1:313.
93 Teiwes, *Politics at Mao's Court*, p. 97, learned from a "best-informed source" that the Organizational Department submitted a report to the 1955 CCP National Conference, accusing Gao of "an ulterior motive" in passing Mao's words to An – to ensnare An and Liu Shaoqi. Yet, except for Source A, who vaguely said that "this is not impossible" (*zhe bushi meiyou keneng*), none of the sources I asked, including those who had direct access to the archives, knew about it. But Mao stressed repeatedly that Gao's crime was to "split the Party"; the rest were all "minor matters." Had Mao allowed the people to dig into the "minor matters," Mao himself would have been in trouble.
94 Gao claimed that Lin Biao, Xi Zhongxun, and even Zhu De were not on An's original list. They were added because of Gao's "strong objection." An denied Gao's allegation, and Bo, *Huigu*, 1:313, also comes to An's defense.

Table 4.1. An Ziwen's List of CCP Politburo Members

Rank 1953/1945	Affiliation[a]	Main Post	Association[b]
Politburo members			
1/1 Mao Zedong	P/A/G	CCP chairman, CC secretary	
2/3 Liu Shaoqi	P/G	CC secretary, NCB first secretary	
3/4 Zhou Enlai	G	CC secretary, prime minister	
4/2 Zhu De	A	CC secretary	
5/6 Chen Yun	G	CC secretary, CFEC director	
6/8 Gao Gang	P/G	NEB secretary, SPC chairman	
7/– Lin Biao	A	SCB secretary, CMC vice-chairman	M
8/13 Peng Dehuai	A	NWB secretary, CMC vice-chairman	(M)
9/– Deng Xiaoping	P/G/A	SWB secretary, vice-premier	M
10/– Rao Shushi	P/G	ECB secretary, organizational department director	L
11/– Bo Yibo	P/G	NCB 2nd secretary, CFEC vice-director, finance minister	L
12/– Deng Zihui	G	SCB 2nd secretary, SPC vice-chair, rural work dept. director	M
Alternate Politburo members			
13/10 Dong Biwu	G	Chief procurator of the PRC	
14/11 Lin Boqu	G	Politburo member	
15/9 Peng Zhen	P	Beijing Party secretary	L
16/12 Zhang Wentian	P/G	Deputy minister of Foreign Affairs	
17/7 Kang Sheng	P	Shandong subbureau secretary	(M)
18/– Li Fuchun	G	CFEC vice-director	M
19/– Xi Zhongxun	P/G	NWB second secretary	G
20/– Liu Lantao	P/G	NCB third secretary	L

[a] A = army; G = government; P = Party.
[b] G = Gao; L = Liu; M = Mao; (L) = leaning to Liu; and (M) = leaning to Mao.

The Transition of the Yan'an Round Table

and had been commissar of the First Field Army. What appeared astonishing in An's list were: (1) Liu Lantao, the bottom man among the alternate CC members of the Seventh CC, jumped into the Politburo – an obvious faction-oriented promotion; and (2) Peng Zhen's rank declined sharply.[95]

An's arrangement would strengthen Liu's position. As Rao Shushi, Bo Yibo, and Liu Lantao joined in, Liu's men in the Politburo increased from one (i.e., Peng Zhen) to four, outnumbering even Mao's people there: Lin Biao, Deng Xiaoping, and Li Fuchun. Given the key positions occupied by Liu's people, the balance leaned favorably to Liu.

To draw up such a list was inept, especially on the eve of an overall redistribution of power. Not only was Mao angered by this list, which he saw as "illicit,"[96] but he was also alerted by the extent to which Liu's men could manipulate political affairs, for An was not even an alternate CC member. Stranger still was that An consulted Gao on this list. This is really unintelligible, not only because the Liu-Gao tension was an open secret, but also because Gao had never been officially assigned to handle organizational affairs, which had been Liu's business since 1943. An might have been much better off had he followed the normal procedure: to submit the list to Liu.

But Liu, who was dying to know how Mao would respond to this list, would not dare to discuss these arrangements with Mao, not just because he had lost track of Mao's mind on this issue, but because there were few legally defined institutional arrangements to secure communications among the leaders in decision making. Thus, they had to depend on informal channels to exchange their intentions. When such channels were closed during a crisis, they were all in the dark. The strong could force their way out, but the weak had to feel their way out; in this situation – after Mao discussed with Gao, instead of Liu, the leadership reorganization – Liu had to allow, or even encourage, An to draw up a list and to consult Gao in order to sound Gao, and eventually Mao, out.[97] Risky

---

[95] This indicates that Peng had not recovered from the 1946 setback and, moreover, the existence of a competition between Peng and Bo/An/Liu (Lantao) in Liu Shaoqi's mountaintop. This might be why Peng was unusually inactive during the Gao-Rao Affair.

[96] *SWMZD*, p. 161.

[97] Gao said, "An Ziwen showed me the list in order to sound me out." Bo, *Huigu*, 1:313, denied Gao's charge. But he failed to offer any explanation for An's ineptness.

and silly though it appeared, this was Liu's best bet indeed, given the anxiety and pressure Liu felt at that time.

Liu got what he wanted, although it was not what he would like to see. As Mao made it known to all about his anger with An's list, Gao cashed in, using this list to stir up resentment among the elite members, especially those in the military, who had long harbored sour feelings toward Liu's mountaintop.[98] It is intriguing to notice that, although Mao would later condemn Gao and Rao for "spreading rumors" on this list,[99] he kept his attitude on this issue unclear for a good nine months (March–November) during which rumors, speculations, and resentment toward Liu and his men were rife among the elite members.

A significant by-product of An's list was that it blew Rao Shushi out of Liu's camp. Both the CCP official account[100] and the Western analysis emphasized that Rao "quickly joined forces with" Gao because he was "undoubtedly influenced by both Gao's increasing prominence and signs of Mao's dissatisfaction with Liu."[101] But Rao's alienation from Liu's mountaintop was not unexpected, given Rao's hunger for power and, more importantly, the faction-ridden nature of leadership relations. The way power is distributed in CCP politics creates a constant possibility of a prisoners' dilemma between a leader and his strongest follower: as the latter expanded rapidly at the former's patronage, a conflict would emerge between the two (see Chapter 2). Rao's betrayal of Liu is just another example of such a development.

Thus, although Liu "had held [Rao] in high regard"[102] and "promoted him to the key positions,"[103] mutual suspicion gradually developed after Rao built up his own mountaintop in East China. The friction between the two started as early as February 1948, when Rao resisted Liu's attempt to put Shandong, which had been Rao's turf, under the control of the newly created NCB.[104] Rao's resistence, which aborted Liu's

---

98 Cf. Teiwes, *Politics at Mao's Court*, p. 98.
99 *SWMZD*, pp. 161–2; also Bo, *Huigu*, 1:318.
100 Deng Xiaoping, Chen Yi, and Tan Zhenlin, "Report on Rao Shushi," in Teiwes, *Politics at Mao's Court*, p. 246; Bo, *Huigu*, 1:318; and Chen Shihui, "Questions concerning opposition to the anti-Party conspiratorial activities of Gao Gang and Rao Shushi," in Teiwes, *Politics at Mao's Court*, p. 161.
101 Teiwes, *Politics at Mao's Court*, p. 45.
102 Bo, *Huigu*, 1:316.
103 Deng, "Xuexi 'jueyi' de wenti he huida," *Zuanji*, 1:85.
104 Bo, *Huigu*, 1:2.

The Transition of the Yan'an Round Table

attempt, was not surprising, for Rao's ECB would have been much smaller had Shandong, the second most populous province and a major CCP base area, been taken away. Rao was also opposed to financial unification under Bo Yibo's NCFEC in early 1949 (see Chapter 3). In February 1952, when Bo was dispatched to oversee the Five Anti Campaign in Shanghai,[105] the CC sent a cable to Rao, asking him to come to Beijing to treat his eye illness. Rao was so suspicious that "one night about 3 A.M." he went to Mao, *instead of his long-term patron Liu* who was in charge of personnel affairs, to make sure that he still had Mao's trust.[106] In fact, Xiang Ming, a Rao confidant who was the acting secretary of the CCP Shandong Subbureau, was the first one who wrote to Mao on January 9, 1953, to complain about the new tax law.[107] Evidently, Rao had long felt alienated by Liu's North China faction, and this feeling turned into anger when he knew that his deputy director An Ziwen had made a list of Politburo membership behind his back.[108] Thus, joining forces with Gao was a sweet revenge as well as a rational bid for power. Indeed, it was not that Gao and Rao started the affair; rather, it was the affair that brought the two together.

The Gao-Rao Affair, an Inevitable Clash

The GAC's General Party Group was dissolved on March 10, 1953, so that all the ministries were placed directly under the CC leadership.[109] This marked the beginning of the redistribution of power among the Party leaders, which was completed on May 15 (Figure 4.1).

This "leadership adjustment" was not so much a structural change as a reshuffling of leaders to the newly designated policy areas (*kou*), with each area covering a few related systems (*xitong*). There were hardly any institutional arrangements to define the relationships among these

---

105 Ibid., pp. 173–4.
106 Deng, Chen, and Tan, "Report on Rao Shushi," p. 249.
107 Ibid., p. 234.
108 This was obviously not the first time An bypassed Rao and went directly to Liu. An's secretary Han Jingcao (Chen Yeping and Han Jingcao, *An Ziwen zhuanlue* [A Brief Biography of An Ziwen], Taiyuan: Shanxi People's Press, 1985, pp. 99–100) recalled that at a meeting of the Organizational Department, Rao "pointed rudely at [An], demanding to know why [An] had not reported certain problems to him but instead to Liu."
109 Cf. Liao, *Xin zhongguo biannian shi*, p. 59.

Factionalism in Chinese Communist Politics

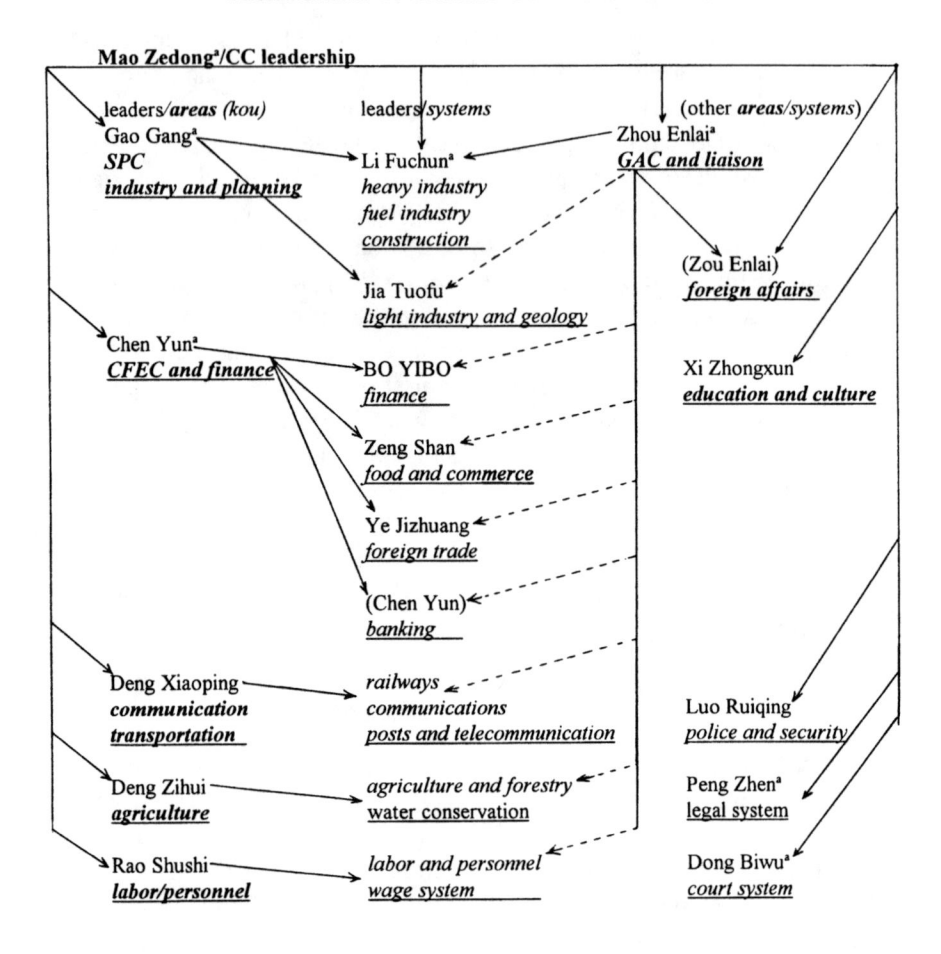

Mao Zedong[a]/CC leadership

```
leaders/areas (kou)        leaders/systems              (other areas/systems)
Gao Gang[a]                                             Zhou Enlai[a]
SPC                        Li Fuchun[a]                 GAC and liaison
industry and planning      heavy industry
                           fuel industry
                           construction
                                                        (Zou Enlai)
                           Jia Tuofu                    foreign affairs
                           light industry and geology
Chen Yun[a]                                             Xi Zhongxun
CFEC and finance           BO YIBO                      education and culture
                           finance
                           Zeng Shan
                           food and commerce
                           Ye Jizhuang
                           foreign trade
                           (Chen Yun)
                           banking
Deng Xiaoping              railways
communication              communications               Luo Ruiqing
transportation             posts and telecommunication  police and security
Deng Zihui                 agriculture and forestry     Peng Zhen[a]
agriculture                water conservation           legal system
Rao Shushi                 labor and personnel          Dong Biwu[a]
labor/personnel            wage system                  court system
```

[a] Politburo members.

Figure 4.1. Civilian leaders and their policy areas (*kou*) in 1953 (solid arrow = direct control; dashed arrow = indirect control)

leaders. The five major policy areas "were relatively independent of each other,"[110] and the leaders in charge of them reported directly to the Center – that is, Mao.

The reshuffling revealed some crucial changes in leadership relations. First of all, Liu was an odd man out. He was not in charge of any spe-

110 Bo, *Huigu*, 1:72.

The Transition of the Yan'an Round Table

cific *kou*, nor would any leaders report to him in the policy process. The decline of Liu's power was further indicated when, with the exception of Bo, all the other five CCP bureau secretaries – Gao, Rao, the two Dengs, and Xi – were assigned to a *kou*. Moreover, except Peng Zhen, who was in charge of the "law" system, all the other important members of Liu's mountaintop – Lu Dingyi, An, and the like – were senior staff members in the policy process.

By contrast, Zhou Enlai maintained his crucial position in policy making, despite the speculation that the dissolution of the General Party Group at the GAC was to cripple Zhou's wings.[111] As "the liaison among various [policy] areas and systems,"[112] Zhou's office was the information hub in the policy process, and Zhou was the one who reported to Mao on daily affairs.[113] Indeed, Zhou's unique position as housekeeper in CCP politics was irreplaceable, essentially because he did not, and never intended to, have his own mountaintop despite his seniority, extraordinary interpersonal ability, and administrative talent. Thus, Zhou was not only acceptable to all mountaintops but also trusted by Mao because he was not a threat.

Notably, Mao picked on Liu and Yang Shangkun immediately after this leadership adjustment for their "breach of discipline in issuing documents in the name of the CC without authorization." Mao emphasized on May 19: "From now on, *only after* I read them can the documents and telegrams issued in the name of the CC be sent out. Otherwise, they are invalid. Please take note."[114] This was obviously the strategy of "killing

---

111 A Party historian who specializes in Zhou is convinced that the dissolution of the GAC's General Party Group (GPG) in March 1953 was to contain Zhou's power. He argues that the GPG, which was set up to supervise the GAC on behalf of the Politburo, further empowers the GAC, the administrative center, because it enables the GAC to prove its own actions. Thus, the Politburo becomes a figurehead. The dissolution of the GPG contained Zhou's power because all the ministries came directly under the CC leadership. Bo, *Huigu*, 1:310, also implies that the dissolution of the GPG contained Zhou's power.

112 *Zhonghua renmin gongheguo jingji guanli dashi ji*, (Chronology of the PRC Economic Management), compiled by the "Contemporary China's Economic Management" Editorial Board, Beijing: China's Economic Press, 1986, p. 41 (hereafter *Jingji guanli dashi ji*).

113 A Party historian who specializes in Zhou's career as well as several other sources confirmed that it was always Zhou who reported to Mao on regular basis. None of the other leaders, including Liu Shaoqi, Lin Biao, and Deng Xiaoping, had ever achieved such a unique position.

114 *SWMZD*, 5:92; cf. also *Wengao*, 4:229–31. It is unclear how many documents Liu and

the rooster to scare the monkey," namely to punish Liu and Yang to show everyone that Mao was the boss.

The arrangement – each leader took charge of one *kou* under Mao's command – reflected the faction-ridden structure of the Yan'an Round Table. It was caused not so much by the CCP leaders' "inexperience" in administration as by their addiction to the pattern of power entrustment formed during the revolution (see Chapter 2). Yet, unlike the revolution during which an army could, and did, fight on its own in an area, problems in each policy area were interwoven. Performance in one area – say, industry – depended on the other areas like transportation, finance, marketing, and communication. Moreover, the cost each area had to bear was often inconsistent with the benefit it would receive. Thus, institutional arrangements are necessary in a complex organization in order to secure stable and consistent policy outcomes.[115] But this was absent in leadership relations after the redistribution of power in 1953. The lack of institutionalization determined the dependency on the personalized authority in policy making. When this authority was unable to arbitrate an emerging conflict, policy outcomes were difficult, and so was the maintenance of stability (see Chapter 2).

This was what Gao faced in 1953. Gao emerged as the most preeminent leader under Mao's command after the centralization: his SPC "was called 'the economic cabinet' and was independent of the GAC."[116] Besides the entire industrial sector, Gao also took over a crucial area from Chen Yun: the economic planning, including the first five-year plan.[117] As a huge deficit in the 1953 budget surfaced in

Yang had dispatched without Mao's authorization. But the most serious ones include Liu's instruction to An in January 1950, the Shanxi Party Committee's report with Liu's comment in July 1951, and the new tax law in December 1952.
115 See Peter Ordeshook, *Game Theory and Political Theory: Introduction*, Cambridge: Cambridge University Press, 1986, pp. 53–6; also Kenneth Shepsle and Barry Weingast, "Structure-induced equilibrium and legislative choice," *Public Choice*, 37 (1981), pp. 503–19.
116 Bo, *Huigu*, 1:71.
117 The drafting of the five-year plan started in early 1952 under the leadership of Zhou Enlai, Chen Yun, Bo Yibo, Li Fuchun, and Nie Rongzhen. But the first draft was rejected by the Soviet experts in August 1952 after Zhou, Chen, and Li went to Moscow with first draft. Li then remained in Moscow until next May to consult the Soviets on details. See *"Li Fuchun zhuan"* (A Biography of Li Fuchun), *RWZ* (1990), 44:52–3; and Bo, *Huigu*, 1:286–7. Gao's SPC began to revise the first five-year plan in early 1953. An overall redrafting started on June 9, 1953, after Gao and Li came back from Moscow (Gao went there in May 1953). See Fang, *Jingji dashi ji*, pp. 98–9.

The Transition of the Yan'an Round Table

March,[118] the drafting of the annual plan was also moved from the CFEC to the SPC.[119] Thus, it was well known among the elite members that when "five horses (i.e., Gao, the two Dengs, Rao, and Xi) enter Beijing, one (i.e., Gao) runs ahead of the others."[120]

As a leading horse, Gao had to make the others go his way in order to fulfill the mission entrusted to him. Yet Gao had little access to the financial and organizational systems – both were the domain of Liu's mountaintop. As a senior cadre who was involved in the Gao-Rao Affair says: "Gao was ambitious and bullish indeed. But as the SPC chairman, how could he fulfill his work if he could not get the *money* and *people* he wanted? Some people made things hard for him on purpose [*youyi he ta biejin*]. So he was forced to fight [*bishang Liangshan*]."[121]

Thus, Gao's attack focused on Bo and An, Liu's right-hand men who were in charge of the financial and organizational systems. The battle unfolded at the National Conference on Financial and Economic Work (NCFEW), held from June 14 to August 12, and the National Conference on Organization Work (NCOW), held from September 21 to October 27, 1953.[122]

The official account condemns Gao-Rao's strategy at the two conferences as "criticizing Bo to shoot at Liu, denouncing An to attack Liu" (*pi Bo she Liu, tao An fa Liu*). Specifically, Gao and Rao accused Bo and An of the words Liu had said and the things Liu had done.[123] But Mao did exactly the same in his criticism of Bo at the NCFEW: "Bo Yibo said that the road from individual farming to collectivization through mutual aid and cooperation 'is sheer fantasy, because the present mutual-aid teams, based on the individual economy, cannot develop gradually into collective farms, still less can such a road lead to the collectivization of agricul-

---

118 There was a huge deficit in the 1953 budget made by Bo on February 12, 1953 (see *Cankao*, 20:31–40). But Bo covered it up by counting 3 billion yuan of credit funds left over from 1952 as the 1953 revenue. A financial crisis emerged soon after the budget was published. Fang, *Jingji dashi ji*, p. 92.
119 See ibid., pp. 96–7.　　120 See Bo, *Huigu*, 1:309.　　121 Source C.
122 Deng, "Report on the Gao Gang, Shao Shushi anti-Party alliance," p. 254.
123 Bo, *Huigu*, 1:242, 318; see also Chen, "Questions concerning opposition to the anti-Party conspiratorial activities," p. 163. However, in his 1955 "Report on the Gao-Rao Anti-Party Alliance," pp. 254–76, Deng rarely mentioned this "major conspiratorial activity of Gao and Rao," presumably because Bo had not recovered from his tax-reform setback yet.

ture as a whole.' This runs counter to the Party's resolution."[124] The words Mao quoted as Bo's were actually from Liu in his instructions to An in January 1950. Indeed, "criticizing Bo to shoot at Liu" was less a conspiracy than a reflection that Bo closely followed Liu in policy making. Bo himself admitted that Mao's criticism to him "in fact also embodied Chairman Mao's criticism of the view of Comrade [Liu] Shaoqi."[125]

Gao and Rao's other major "conspiratorial activity" was that they spread a "file" of all Liu's words that were at odds with Mao's since 1945. Their aim was to show that the "Right-opportunist mistakes" made by Liu and his men were *systematic* and had *ideological* roots. Ironically, this was the method Liu used in his attack on Wang Ming (see Chapter 3). Gao and Rao also accused Liu of forming his own "circle" at the Center.[126] All this was evidently in accord with Mao's intention. As Mao ordered Bo on July 12, "You should examine yourself at a deeper level, explaining [your] problem in terms of *ideology*, policy, *organization*, and working-style."[127]

In his self-criticism on July 13, however, Bo attributed his mistakes to his breach of discipline, his carelessness, and his misjudgment of the situation, but he insisted that his mistakes had no roots in ideology and organization, which implied that he did not make any errors of line, nor was he involved in any factional activities. This was unacceptable. So Bo had to make another self-criticism on August 1 at Zhou Enlai's order. But it was essentially the same as the first. As Zhou pointed out in his summary speech at the NCFEW, Bo "again failed to expose the roots of his mistakes,"[128] Thereafter, Bo "decided not to utter a word in order to *prevent the problem from expanding to the core of the CC leadership*," which means that Bo would rather sacrifice himself in order to protect his patron Liu Shaoqi.[129] After that, Liu's associates "adopted the struggle method of 'silence is better than sound at this time' [*cishi wusheng sheng yousheng*] and resolutely refused to talk."[130]

Meanwhile, Mao's attitude was undergoing a subtle but significant

---

124 *SWMZD*, 5:106..   125 Bo, *Huigu*, 1:194.
126 Chen, "Questions concerning opposition to the anti-Party conspiratorial activities," pp. 163–4; Bo, *Huigu*, 1:242, 312.
127 Quoted from Bo, *Huigu*, 1:240 (emphasis added).
128 See *Cankao*, 20:139.   129 Bo, *Huigu*, 1:240, 243.
130 Chen and Han, *An Ziwen zhuanlue*, p. 102.

The Transition of the Yan'an Round Table

change. In the evening of August 1, Zhou reported to Mao that the conference was deadlocked because Bo refused to talk in front of fierce attacks. Mao suggested to Zhou: "Why don't you send for reinforcement [*banbing*]! Invite Comrades Chen Yun and Deng Xiaoping back [to Beijing], let them take part in the conference."[131]

Chen returned from Beidaihe on August 3. He "clearly expressed his objection of [Gao's] formulation [*tifa*] of a two-line struggle" in his speech to the leading group of the NCFEC on August 6.[132] Deng also made a similar speech at the NCFEW in early August.[133] After their speeches "changed the atmosphere of the conferences," Mao cut out all the words of "the error of line" from Zhou's summary report on the criticism of Bo, indicating that Bo would not be purged because he had just made "working mistakes."[134]

Similar developments also occurred at the NCOW, where An Ziwen "became silent and morose" under "the ferocious attack" by Gao and Rao.[135] The situation was so chaotic that the NCOW was suspended on October 12 to hold a leading-group meeting to "solve the problems of unity within the Organizational Department."[136] Liu Shaoqi presided over the meeting and "took full responsibility" for all the errors allegedly made by the Organizational Department,[137] *except* An's "Politburo list," which Liu insisted that he "did not even know."[138] But Rao continued to "denounce An to attack Liu." Again, Mao sent Deng to the conference, and his speech made the turning point: "The Organization Department has made achievements in the past, [it has] carried out the Center's line. ... This is indivisible from Chairman Mao's leadership and especially Comrade Shaoqi's *direct* leadership. Comrade Ziwen has also made achievements.[139]

---

131 Quoted from Bo, *Huigu*, 1:243.   132 Ibid., pp. 243–4.
133 Deng appeared in Beijing on August 9, when he attended the Politburo meeting to discuss Zhou's summary report for the NCFEW.
134 Bo, *Huigu*, 1:245.
135 Chen and Han, *An Ziwen zhuanlue*, p. 103; and Liao, *Xin zhongguo biannian shi*, p. 63.
136 Bo, *Huigu*, 1:318. The leading group consisted of Liu, Zhu De, Rao, Li Fuchun, Xi Zhongxun, Yang Shangkun, Qian Ying, Hu Qiaomu, An, and the directors of the organization departments in six CCP bureaus.
137 Chen and Han, *An Ziwen zhuanlue*, p. 103.
138 Chen, "Questions concerning opposition to the anti-Party conspiratorial activities," p. 168.
139 Quoted from Liao, *Xin zhongguo biannian shi*, p. 63.

Factionalism in Chinese Communist Politics

Meanwhile, Mao asked Yang Shangkun to pass "the six points" in *History of the CPSU (Bolsheviks): Short Course* to the leading group of the NCOW on October 22. Mao asked them "to read, study, and, wherever possible, discuss [these six points], so that when Comrade Liu Shaoqi and the others reach this issue [on the intra-Party struggles] in their speeches in the conference, they can already have some understanding of it."[140] Obviously, Mao used "the six points," which focus on the necessity of intra-Party struggle against "the opportunists," to justify the attack on Liu and his men, only if they were "opportunists within the Party."[141]

Indeed, the change in Mao's attitude did not mean that Mao had forgiven Liu and his men, but it reflected Mao's reluctance to let them sink deeper. In fact, Mao was tough on Bo, as shown in his speech[142] and his revision of Zhou's summary report[143] at the NCFEW. Bo was dismissed from all his posts except the CFEC vice-director on August 17;[144] and An received a "severe warning" and was removed from his post as deputy director of the CC Organizational Department.[145] Although Liu's mountaintop still stood, it was badly damaged.

The Collapse of Gao-Rao

It is unsustainable that Mao did not stop Gao and Rao earlier on because "he had not been informed earlier."[146] In fact, Mao was well aware of Gao's activities – that is why he urged Gao to have "an exchange" with Liu "to straighten things up" after the NCFEW. Mao's encouraging attitude toward Gao made Liu more nervous. After he learned Mao's intention, Liu initiated two conversations with Gao, in which Liu "examined

---

140 Quoted from Teiwes, *Politics at Mao's Court*, p. 218.
141 Ibid., pp. 218–20. Ironically, Liu also drew heavily on the "six points" in his "On the Inter-Party Struggle" to legitimize Mao's attack on the Wang Ming faction during the YR (see Chapter 3).
142 *SWMZD*, 5:103–11.
143 See Bo, *Huigu*, 1:245–6. Notably, Mao added "banking" to Zhou's list of Bo's "mistakes in taxation, commerce, finance." Since banking was Chen Yun's area, this indicates Mao's displeasure with some of Chen's work, especially that Chen failed to report the hidden deficit in the 1953 budget (see note 118).
144 Ibid., 1:249.
145 There are five levels of the CCP discipline punishment: demerit, warning, severe warning, probation within the Party, and expulsion from the Party.
146 Teiwes, *Politics at Mao's Court*, p. 112.

The Transition of the Yan'an Round Table

his shortcomings and mistakes sincerely." But Gao was cocky and "told people that Liu Shaoqi was unwilling to make a self-criticism."[147]

Indeed, the claim that "at the time [of the NCFEW and the NCOW] the Center [i.e., Mao] was not yet fully aware of the entire plot of the Gao-Rao clique"[148] was comprehensible only in the sense that Mao, without knowing exactly the other leaders' stands in this struggle, was uncertain how far Gao and Rao could go and what consequence his intervention could have on the still unclear situation. It was Mao's ambiguous attitude that further induced Gao, who had gained the momentum in the struggle, to go all out to win over support from the other leaders in order to deliver that last punch.

Gao approached *only the mountaintop leaders* with a theory of "the Red area party" or "the army's party" (*jundang*). The aim was to rally the elite members, especially those in the military, who fought their way up during the revolution, in the struggle against Liu and his men, who all rose from the White areas. Gao first focused on the Party leaders who handled political affairs. Among them, Rao had already been Gao's ally; Gao spent little time on Xi because he was confident that Xi would side with him,[149] given the solid comradeship between the two, which dated back to the pre-1935 northern Shaanxi base area (see Chapter 3). Gao's major targets were Chen Yun and Deng Xiaoping. As Deng recalled in 1980:

> After Comrade Mao Zedong proposed *at the end of 1953* that the work of the CC be divided into a "front line" and a "second line," Gao Gang became very active. He first gained the support of Lin Biao. ... So far as Southwest China was concerned, he tried to win me over and had serious talks with me in which he said that Comrade Liu Shaoqi was immature. He was trying to persuade me to join in his effort to topple Comrade Liu Shaoqi. I

---

147 Bo, *Huigu*, 1:312.
148 Deng, "Report on the Gao Gang, Rao Shushi anti-Party Alliance," p. 260.
149 Teiwes, *Politics at Mao's Court*, p. 107, speculates that Gao had little contact with Xi because "the primary effort [of Gao] to win over the Northwest and its associated field army mountaintop was through Peng Dehuai." But He Long could be a better candidate than Peng. Gao was He's commissar in 1942–5, and Xi succeeded Gao after he left for Manchuria. After the KMT force seized Yan'an in March 1947, the bulk of He's army was put under Peng's command (see Chapter 3). Xi would not be Peng's commissar until late 1949 after He's army left for the Southwest.

made my attitude clear, saying that Comrade Liu Shaoqi's position in the Party was the outcome of historical development, that he was a good comrade on the whole, and that it was inappropriate to try to oust him from such a position. Gao Gang also approached Comrade Chen Yun and told him that a few more vice-chairmanships should be instituted, with himself and Chen each holding one of them. At this point, Comrade Chen Yun and I realized the gravity of the matter and *immediately* brought it to Comrade Mao Zedong's attention.[150]

Deng's account is less than entirely credible. First, it is unlikely that Chen and Deng had any coordination in the toppling of Gao. More questionable is the *timing* in Deng's account.[151] If Gao had first gained Lin's support, he must have done so before Lin went to Hangzhou to "recuperate" in mid-August;[152] and Gao must have approached Deng and Chen before he traveled to East and South China in early October.[153] This can be confirmed by Bo's account: "In October 1953 ... [Gao] said to Comrade Chen Yun: if (we) should have vice-chairmanship, there should be a few of them. One for you, one for me."[154] Obviously, Deng mixed up the events between August and December because only then does it make sense that he "immediately reported [to Mao]," which in fact would not happen until the end of 1953 (see my subsequent discussion).

This leads to another question on whether Deng "made [his] attitude clear" when Gao approached him. It is more likely that Deng and Chen maintained an *unclear* attitude when Gao sought their support, not because they "could not be sure of Mao's aim,"[155] but because the two, who had direct access to Mao at the time,[156] knew exactly that Mao was

---

150 *SWDXP*, 1975–82, pp. 278–9 (emphasis added).
151 Cf. Teiwes, *Politics at Mao's Court*, pp. 108–9.
152 Lin left for Hangzhou after Peng Dehuai came back from Korea on August 11.
153 The exact date of Gao's trip cannot be pinned down. The last time Gao appeared in Beijing was on October 2 when he attended a Politburo meeting to discuss the state monopoly for the purchasing and marketing of grain. Gao reappeared in Beijing on November 14 to host King Il Sung. Teiwes (ibid., p. 93) speculates that Gao left Beijing in late September, then came back in early October, only to leave again for East and South China.
154 Bo, *Huigu*, 1:315.
155 Teiwes, *Politics at Mao's Court*, p. 150.
156 A major reason Mao called Chen and Deng back from "the patients club" was to solve the grain crisis in 1953. From early August to October 16, Chen and Deng worked

The Transition of the Yan'an Round Table

unsure how to handle this looming crisis that Gao initiated at Mao's tacit encouragement. Thus, they followed Mao's example – to maintain an ambiguous attitude – when Gao approached them in early October. While this made Gao more desperate in his search for support in order to knock out Liu, it also provided Gao with hopes because Mao, Chen, and Deng at least did *not* oppose his clearly expressed intention. So Gao turned to the military for support, which was a crucial mistake, because Gao sought support from the system to which he did not belong without Mao's consent.

Gao took full advantage of An's "Politburo list," in which the military was obviously underrepresented. Gao had to be careful with Nie Rongzhen, who had a long-term relationship with the North China party. It would be hard for Gao to have Chen Yi's support, although Chen had harbored an antipathy toward Liu Shaoqi because of Liu's patronage of Rao Shushi, who attacked Chen in the YR. Now Rao became Gao's ally. He Long and Xu Xiangqian were not worthy of Gao's effort, for their influence in politics was limited because they came from outside of Mao's Jinggang mountaintop (see Chapter 3). Thus, Gao focused on Defense Minister Peng Dehuai, Lin Biao, and Luo Ronghuan, director of the PLA General Political Department.

There is little evidence that Peng played a substantial role in the Gao-Rao Affair, as he was charged at the 1959 Lushan Conference.[157] Source B recalled that Gao told Peng that "there is a Right-opportunist tendency in the Party" in a private meeting in September; but Gao did not name any names and said little about personnel affairs. According to this source, although Gao got along with Peng, he saw Peng as "a fearless fighter" but "too upright and volatile to play politics."

Gao's major effort was reserved for Lin: Gao's trip to Hangzhou and Guangzhou in October was to win over Lin and his mountaintop. The frequent contacts between the two in Beijing and Hangzhou[158] indicated

---

closely with Mao on the state monopoly for the purchasing and marketing of grains. See Fang, *Jingji dashi ji*, pp. 103–5; and Bo, *Huigu*, 1:261–6.
157 Cf. Roderick MacFarquhar, *The Origins of the Cultural Revolution*, 2: *The Great Leap Forward, 1958–1960*, New York: Columbia University Press, 1983, pp. 231, 234.
158 See Yu Nan, "*Lin Biao jituan xingwang chutan*" (A preliminary research of the rise and fall of the Lin Biao clique), in Tan Zhongji, Zheng Shui, et al., eds., *Shinian hou de pingshuo – Wenhua dageming shilunji* (Appraisal and Critique after Ten Years – Collection of Historical Essays on the CR), Beijing: CCP Historical Materials Press, 1987, p. 61.

that Gao achieved a certain success. It is evident that Lin was more deeply involved than it has been believed, and Lin's support of Gao had a substantial impact on the affair.[159] Indeed, just by allowing Gao to use his name in his lobbying effort, Lin gave Gao what he wanted. Otherwise, Gao's trip to South China would make little sense.[160]

Gao must have talked to Luo more than once, but the most important contact had to be the one after Gao's trip to South China. Gao paid an unexpected visit to Luo after he learned that Mao paid much attention to the upcoming Conference of the High-Ranking Party Cadres in the Military. He persuaded Luo to support the Soviet system of the Council of Ministers, with Lin as its chairman. According to Luo, he "asked [Gao] right away: 'Has the issue been discussed at the CC? Is this Chairman Mao's intention?'" After Gao told him that "the CC has not discussed it yet, neither has Chairman Mao known this," Luo said to Gao: "it is inappropriate for us to discuss such an important issue."[161]

Luo's words are less than wholly credible because they are from Luo's report to the Center *after* the Gao-Rao Affair. But Luo's stratagem is well displayed in his account. First, he did not mention Liu Shaoqi at all. For those who appeared in his account – Mao, Lin, Luo, and Gao – Luo gave Lin an easy out: if the CC had not discussed Lin's prospective assignment, whether Gao and Lin had any deal on this would at best be a case of one's words against another's. Furthermore, Luo ingeniously cleared Mao, and himself, too, from any involvements through Gao's

---

159 Teiwes, *Politics at Mao's Court*, pp. 103–4, believes that Lin's involvement was passive, and his support to Gao constituted little more than lip service. But Wei Li, *1965 nian qian de Lin Biao* (Lin Biao Pirior to 1965), Lhasa: Tibet People's Press, pp. 318–25, shows that Lin was actively involved in the background. Although Wei's account is obviously dramatized, his work reveals a substantial amount of firsthand materials.

160 Tao Zhu, first secretary of the CCP South China Subbureau, was Gao's major target in Guangzhou. Allegedly, Gao promised Tao a position of vice-premier had he succeeded. Unlike Lin, Tao was cautious and his reaction was little more than lip service. See Teiwes, *Politics at Mao's Court*, pp. 224–5. Bo, *Huigu*, 1:241, says that Gao approached Tao during the NCFEW, asking him to attack Bo, but Tao declined.

161 See "*Zai Mao zhuxi guanghui qizhi xia zhandou de guanghui yisheng*" (A brilliant life of battle under Chairman Mao's great banner), compiled by the General Political Department Theory Group, *Lishi yanjiu* (Historical Research), no. 9 (1978), p. 8.

The Transition of the Yan'an Round Table

mouth: Mao was not aware of Gao's idea, so Luo refused to discuss it with Gao. But Luo's account confirmed at least that Gao used Lin's name in his lobby and, like the other elite members, Luo's primary concern was Mao's attitude.

The elite members' attitudes toward Gao, except those from Liu's mountaintop, are different in degree rather than kind. Essentially, all of them wisely followed Mao's example by taking an ambiguous attitude. Yet, their tendencies could be known through their *guanxi* networks through which they exchanged information and coordinated actions. As Gao and Rao geared up their lobby activities in September–November 1953, confusion began to emerge among the elite members. While their tendencies were made known to each other by Gao's "roving talks," Mao, who was preoccupied with two "big" policy issues – the state monopoly for the purchase and marketing of grain and the agricultural cooperativization[162] – maintained an ambiguous attitude. Yet, Mao's criticism of Liu's idea of "sustaining private ownership" and his attack on Bo, coming as late as November,[163] seemed to suggest that he still leaned toward Gao.

Only in early December was Mao alerted by Gao's activities. The Conference of the High-Ranking Party Cadres in the Military was convened on December 7, 1953. Mao paid much attention to this conference, for its agenda was how to transform the PLA from a revolutionary force into a regular army under the Party's command.[164] Yet Gao's theory of "the army's party" became such a hot topic at the conference that, as an attendee recalled, the conference could not focus on its predesigned agenda.

Concerned with such a situation, Mao and Deng had a conversation. It is more likely that it was in this conversation that Deng reported to Mao about his concern for Gao's activities.[165] The same source believes that it was after this conversation that Mao "sent Chen Yun to win over Lin Biao,"[166] although it remains unknown when and how Chen told Mao

---

162 Liao, *Xin zhongguo biannian shi*, pp. 63–5; cf. also *Wengao*, 4:354–66, 379–85.
163 See *SWMZD*, 5:138–9.
164 Cf. Liao, *Xin zhongguo biannian shi*, p. 68; also "*Luo Ronghuan zhuan*," pp. 66–7.
165 Source D holds that Deng was gambling because Mao's attitude still remained unclear.
166 See Yu, "*Lin Biao jituan xingwang chutan*," p. 61.

about Gao's approach to him.[167] In order to secure his control, Mao took a crucial measure in mid-December: he "had a special conversation" with Luo Ruiqing, minister of public security, who was also in charge of the Central Bodyguards. Luo's daughter recalled:

> One day in 1954, the Chairman told father: do you know that there are people going for conspiracies, and organizing an underground headquarters in Beijing? ... The one who is conspiring and organizing an underground headquarters is Gao Gang.... he wants to be a Party vice-chairman. He told •• [i.e., Chen Yun], "you will be a Party vice-chairman and so will I." *You think he supports Lin Biao?* This time there is no Lin Biao here.... He will not only strike down Liu Shaoqi, he will strike down me, and he will strike down Lin Biao. For father, *this was a great shock.* The Chairman finally said: This man *has deceived some cadres and we must win them back.*
>
> After that talk, Chairman Mao went to Hangzhou and father also went with him. Prior to leaving, Chairman Mao convened a meeting. Father attended, so did Gao Gang. The Chairman explained that while he was away from Beijing, Comrade Liu Shaoqi would act on his behalf.[168]

This conversation is obviously misdated,[169] for Mao went to Hangzhou on December 25, 1953. From the context, the change in Mao's attitude toward Gao was dramatic, for Mao's words on Gao were "a great shock" to Luo who, as head of the Central Bodyguards, had daily contact with

---

167 Teiwes, *Politics at Mao's Court*, p. 111, speculates that Chen had told Zhou about Gao's activities before he went to Mao. But it was known among those who worked for Chen that "on matters concerning principles, Chen either talked to Mao directly, or did not talk at all." This, according to a close friend of Chen's family, was "a major reason (that) Mao could never find fault with Chen." If Chen never talked to Liu about Gao because, as Teiwes holds, "the matter was primarily directed against him [Liu]," it seemed unwise for Chen to talk to Zhou, who Teiwes believes was the other target of Gao.
168 Luo Diandian, *Feifan de niandai* (Extraordinary Years), Shanghai: Shanghai Wenhui Press, 1987, p. 149 (emphasis added).
169 Teiwes, *Politics at Mao's Court*, 229, 311n21, believes the Mao-Luo talk was in early December. He asserts that Luo's daughter has conflated at least two Politburo meetings. This seems unlikely. There was only one meeting: the enlarged Politburo meeting held on December 24, 1953.

The Transition of the Yan'an Round Table

Mao. Also noteworthy is that Mao defended Lin who was seen as Gao's ally. This indicated that Chen had fulfilled his mission of "winning over Lin Biao" and informed Mao of Lin's stand.[170]

On December 24, an enlarged Politburo meeting was convened. Mao accused Gao of underground activities and forming a second headquarters in Beijing.[171] Mao's words indicated that Gao had indeed achieved much success: "One can catch sparrows on the doorstep of Junian Hall [where the Politburo held meetings], but there is an incessant stream of horses and carriages at 8 Dong-jiao-min Alley [where Gao resided]."[172]

Mao's criticism threw Gao into panic. According to Luo Ruiqing's daughter, in the evening prior to Mao's leaving for Hangzhou – the evening of December 24, right after the Politburo meeting – Gao "suddenly phoned father, saying he wanted to come over. Father asked him not to come, but father would go to his place if there was anything to talk about. Putting down the phone, father phoned Chairman Mao immediately, telling him of the event. The Chairman said: *Go quickly, see what he has to say*. Father went to Gao Gang's residence. Gao . . . said repeatedly that father must pay attention to [Mao's health] and not be careless. He also said: should the Council of Ministers be set up, I would agree that Lin Biao [be its head]."[173] Indeed, Gao had little to say but to hint at his loyalty by showing his concern for Mao's health and by asserting his support for Lin Biao. Interestingly, Mao was *also eager* to learn Gao's intention. But none of them would, or could, initiate a direct exchange – another case in point that the system was unable provide the leaders with effective channels for communication, especially during the period of crisis.

While Mao was in Hangzhou, Gao wrote to him, asking if he could come to see Mao and "to discuss his [Gao's] self-criticism" at the upcom-

---

170 Yu, "*Lin Biao jituan xingwang chutan*," p. 61, says: "at the end of November Lin Biao handed a letter to Gao Gang's wife and asked her to ensure that the letter was passed to Gao Gang personally. . . . In 1962 . . . Ye Qun (Mme Lin) made up a story regarding this letter to Gao Gang's wife, saying that Lin Biao wrote it to criticize and warn Gao Gang about the danger of Gao's underground activities; as for the secrecy of the letter, it was to exhort Gao to rectify privately his mistakes." Ye might have told the truth, at least part of it, only if Chen Yun had already contacted Lin by the end of November.
171 *SWMZD*, p. 162.   172 Quoted from Bo, *Huigu*, 1:252.
173 Luo, *Feifan de niandai*, p. 150 (emphasis added).

ing Fourth Plenum. Mao did not respond to Gao. Instead, Mao wrote to Liu, instructing him, together with Zhou and Deng, to talk to Gao about his self-criticism.[174] With Mao's support, Liu convened the Fourth Plenum of the Seventh CC to "resolve the problem of the Party's unity" in February 6–10, 1954.[175] Gao was doomed. After an unsuccessful suicide attempt in late February, he killed himself on August 17, 1954.[176]

The Gao-Rao Affair demonstrated some crucial features of the faction-ridden nature of CCP politics. First, a major cause of Gao-Rao's collapse was, ironically, their success in rallying support from various mountaintops, for this success posed a potential threat to Mao's command. The structure of the Yan'an Round Table determined that Mao was the pivot of communications. This enabled Mao to control the flow of information and therefore manipulate the other leaders' behavior in decision making. As such a control became vulnerable, however, so did Mao's command, as Gao's aggressive lobbying activities made the intention of various mountaintop leaders known to each other. The free flow of information among the elite members not only made Mao less authoritative, but also enabled the subleaders to make deals without Mao's knowledge. As a result, two, or even more, "headquarters" would emerge in political affairs. Indeed, Mao felt threatened not so much by whether Gao had gained support as by the way Gao pursued his allies. As Mao emphasized, the problem was not caused by An's "Politburo list" per se but rather by those who spread it.[177]

Moreover, Gao's lobbying activities, especially among the military leaders, not only disturbed entire leadership relations but also threatened Mao's own position. Had Gao been successful in rallying the military leaders, he would have achieved the position only Mao had at the Yan'an Round Table: the control of both the Party and military systems. Thus, Mao had to act resolutely to stop him.

Lastly, once a conflict broke out, any compromise would undermine

---

174 See *Wengao*, 4:440–1.
175 After the plenum, two special forums were convened to expose Gao-Rao's underground activities: Zhou and Luo presided over the one dealing with Gao; Deng, Chen, and Tan Zhenlin presided over the one dealing with Rao.
176 See *Wengao*, 4:451–2; also Quan Yanchi, *Long kun – He Long yu Xue Ming* (The Siege of a Dragon – He Long and Xue Ming), Guangzhou: Guangdong Tourist Press, 1997, p. 492. After his first suicide attempt on February 25, 1954, failed, Gao accumulated sleeping pills by hiding his daily dose under his tongue.
177 Bo, *Huigu*, 1:318; also *SWMZD*, 4:161–2.

The Transition of the Yan'an Round Table

the Party's unity, which was a prerequisite for the CCP political system. Thus, all leaders, including Mao himself, were forced to take a stand whether they had been involved or not; and a participant's rationale was drawn eventually from calculations of his position and his relationship with others, instead of from his views in terms of issues. Only in this sense can the shift of Mao's attitude in the course of the Gao-Rao Affair be comprehensible. Intentionally or not, it was Mao who spurred Gao to take on Liu; as Liu was weakened, however, Mao shifted to an ambiguous neutral position; and finally, when Gao had gathered more strength, Mao stood by Liu and crushed Gao. This shows what really mattered to Mao: not policy issues, but ultimately his command, which could be best secured when a balance of power was maintained among the subleaders. Thus, at the Fourth Plenum where Gao and Rao were denounced, it was Liu and his men who were made to criticize themselves on policy issues, confessing that they had made "Right-opportunist mistakes" on socialist transformation.[178] Indeed, Mao backed up Liu at the last moment not because Mao "retained a substantial trust in Liu,"[179] but because he saw his interests as parallel with Liu's in the toppling of Gao and Rao, thus securing his command and Liu's survival.

Deng Xiaoping tersely summed up the cause of Gao and Rao's doom: "All in all, we had no choice but to expose Gao Gang and Rao Shushi and deal with their case as we did... but so far as Gao Gang's line is concerned, actually, I cannot see that he had one, so it's hard to say whether we should call it (i.e., the Gao-Rao Affair) a struggle between two lines."[180] Indeed, in the Mao period Gao and Rao were the only leaders who were purged without the necessary conviction for "an error of line," for they were on Mao's side as far as the line was concerned.

THE STRUCTURAL CHANGE OF THE YAN'AN ROUND TABLE

Changes in Leadership Relations

The Gao-Rao Affair resulted in significant changes in leadership relations. However, the redistribution of power did not depart from the

---

178 Cf. Bo, *Huigu*, 1:194, 252.   179 Teiwes, *Politics at Mao's Court*, p. 43.
180 *SWDXP*, 1975–82, p. 279.

designed course: to prevent any single mountaintop from obtaining dominance in the policy process in order to secure Mao's command.

Although Liu Shaoqi survived this ordeal, the dominance of his forces at the CC vanished after centralization.[181] As leaders from various mountaintops were moved up to Beijing, they took away substantial power from Liu and his men at the CC apparatus. Besides the "five horses," Ye Jizhuang from the Northeast, Zeng Shan from East China, and Jia Tuofu from the Northwest were all appointed CFEC vice-directors, taking charge of commerce, foreign trade, and light industry;[182] Ma Mingfang from the Northwest was appointed a deputy secretary-general and concurrently a deputy director of the Organizational Department;[183] and Tan Zhenlin from East China was named a deputy secretary-general in charge of agriculture in late 1954.[184] Liu's men who still played a role at the elite level were either in trouble, like Bo and An, or kept a low profile, like Peng Zhen and Liu Lantao. Liu's setback was well demonstrated by the formation of the Politburo at the Eighth PC in September 1956.[185] Among seventeen members and six alternate ones, only Peng Zhen and Bo Yibo were Liu's associates. But Peng's rank dropped beneath Lin Boqu and Dong Biwu, who used to be listed after Peng; and Bo was bottom man among the alternate members.

Deng Xiaoping benefited most from the Gao-Rao Affair, and his rise further restrained Liu's power. Deng was appointed the CC secretary-general and director of the Organizational Department on April 27, 1954.[186] This deprived Liu of the control of two extremely important areas: information flow and organizational affairs. Thus, Deng was recognized among the elite members as Mao's "true successor in the Party." Deng became a member of Mao's "personal clique" after he was purged

---

181 The centralization ended officially at the enlarged Politburo conference on April 27, 1954, which decided to dissolve all of the six regional administrations. See Liao, *Xin zhongguo biannian shi*, p. 71.
182 All three were promoted to Beijing in October–December 1952. Notably, no vice-directorships of the CFEC were given to the Southwest and the Central South, the so-called *chiliang hu* (households that have to be fed) at that time.
183 "*Ma Mingfang zhuan*" (A Biography of Ma Mingfang), *RWZ* (1989), 40:295.
184 "*Tan Zhenlin zhuan*" (A Biography of Tan Zhenlin), *RWZ* (1987), 31:93.
185 See Roderick MacFarquhar, *The Origins of the Cultural Revolution*, 1: *Contradictions among the People, 1958–1960*, New York: Columbia University Press, 1974, p. 165.
186 Yue Zong and Xin Zhi, eds., *Deng Xiaoping shengping yu lilun yanjiu huibian* (Collection of Studies on Deng Xiaoping's Career and Theory), Beijing: CCP History Materials Press, 1988, p. 303.

The Transition of the Yan'an Round Table

by the returned students as a follower of Mao's "rich peasant line" in 1933.[187] After Mao gained dominance in the Party, Deng rose rapidly from a county-level cadre to a major mountaintop leader in three "great leaps upward" under Mao's patronage. The first leap was his appointment as commissar of the 129th Division in early 1938; the second occurred on November 16, 1948, when he was appointed secretary of the CMC Front Committee, commanding the Second and Third Field Armies in the Huaihai Campaign against the KMT forces (see Chapter 3).[188] This appointment indicated that Deng had obtained a higher status than Liu Bocheng and Chen Yi, although both had been Deng's seniors. The CCP's triumph in this campaign, in which over a million troops were involved, boosted Deng's prestige and, moreover, demonstrated his ability to perform above the individual mountaintops.

After Ren Bishi, who was in charge of organizational affairs and information flow at the center, ceased to work in 1949 due to his poor health, it was expected that Mao would move Deng and Chen Zhengren[189] to the Center to take over Ren's duties: Deng would resume his old job, the CC's secretary-general,[190] to handle the information flow, and Chen would be involved in organizational affairs. But Liu and his men picked up most of Ren's work.[191] Deng went to Beijing as the executive vice-premier in July 1952 to strengthen the Party's leadership in the administration. Obviously, Mao wanted Deng to be a watchdog in the GAC. But Deng, who then had not developed a power base in Beijing, could hardly fit in, and there was not much for Deng to do but attend some routine meetings. Frustrated, Deng pleaded illness in early 1953.

It was the Gao-Rao Affair that cleared the way for Deng's third leap into the leadership core. Deng was called back to Beijing in early August to become Mao's troubleshooter. On August 17, he took over the two positions from Bo Yibo: the CFEC's first vice-director and finance min-

---

187 See Deng Maomao, *My Father Deng Xiaoping*, New York: Basic Books, 1995; also Li, *Huiyi yu yanjiu*, 1:336–8.
188 Yue and Xin, *Deng Xiaoping shengping*, p. 301.
189 Chen was also seen as a member of Mao's "personal clique." See MacFarquhar, *The Origins*, 1:142.
190 After the 1935 Zunyi Conference, Deng replaced Deng Yingchao (Mme Zhou) as the CC's secretary-general until August 1937.
191 Gao Gang claimed that Liu was against appointing Chen Zhengren the deputy director of the Organizational Department. See Bo, *Huigu*, 1:313.

ister.¹⁹² From then on, Deng became extremely active in political affairs.¹⁹³ As Source C remembered, "Deng was seen as Mao's messenger and was involved in everything." Indeed, Deng consolidated his position by playing a key role in the Gao-Rao Affair. He was appointed the fourth vice-premier on September 27, and a member of the CMC on September 29, 1954. After the Gao-Rao Affair was concluded at the CCP National Conference in March 1955, Deng entered the Politburo on April 4.¹⁹⁴ Finally, Deng accomplished his third "great leap upward" at the Eighth PC. As MacFarquhar observed: "The most spectacular promotion was that of Teng Hsiao-p'ing from bottom man on the precongress Politburo to sixth place in the postcongress one. He was also accorded a place on the newly created six-man Politburo Standing Committee, from then on the supreme policy-making organ. But perhaps the most significant aspect of Teng's elevation was the change of his title from secretary-general to general secretary."¹⁹⁵

Chen Yun also played a crucial role in the Gao-Rao Affair, partly because, ironically, he had wisely withdrawn into the background with the excuse of illness prior to the redistribution of power, but largely because he had not developed a mountaintop of his own yet.¹⁹⁶ Given his seniority and low profile, Chen was acceptable to all mountaintop leaders. Indeed, Mao called Chen back in August to mediate the Liu-Gao strife because Chen was the only one who could communicate with the three key players in the crisis: Liu, Gao, and, more importantly, Lin. Yet, compared with Deng, and even with Lin who had actually supported Gao, Chen's gain in this affair was less than substantial: his status – ranked fifth in the Politburo – remained unchanged. However, his power – in charge of financial systems – was actually weakened as Li Xiannian would become finance minister. After all, Chen did not rise from Mao's mountaintop.

Zhou Enlai was also a crucial figure in this affair. The CCP official accounts allege, and most analysts have accepted, that Zhou was the

---

192 Ibid., p. 249.
193 Cf. ibid., pp. 243–4, 261–70, 288, 316, 321.
194 Yue and Xin, *Deng Xiaoping shengping*, p. 303.
195 See MacFarquhar, *The Origins*, 1:140.
196 In fact, Gao's power was gained largely at Chen's expense; most areas assigned to Gao had been managed by Chen's CFEC. Cf. Bo, *Huigu*, 1:71–2; also *Jingji guanli dashi ji*, p. 41.

The Transition of the Yan'an Round Table

other target of Gao's conspiracy. But little evidence supports this claim, save for the allegation that Gao wanted to be premier himself. The two accusations Gao raised against Liu, forming a "circle of the White area party" and committing an error of a Right-opportunist line, could not be imposed on Zhou, who deliberately avoided forming a "circle" of his own. Nor could Zhou fit in the category of "White area," although he was periodically in charge of underground work during the revolution. As far as the line is concerned, Zhou was rarely seen as a "line" maker but a policy executor.

The other argument of Zhou's involvement is that Gao saw the dissolution of the GAC's General Party Group led by Zhou on March 10, 1953, as an indication of Zhou's decline, so he attempted to take over Zhou's position as premier.[197] However, as a member of the inner circle, Gao should have known that this dissolution would put the GAC under the Politburo's direct supervision so as to prevent inconsistency in policy making. In fact, when this happened, Gao's "conspiracy to usurp the Party's leadership" had already been under way. Zhou, the coordinator in the policy process who reported to Mao regularly, should have been the one Gao tried to win over. Soon after the affair broke out, Zhou stopped going to Gao's weekend dancing party – though he was always invited – because, as Zhou *later* implied, he could not stand Gao's shameless womanizing in the ballroom.[198] A more logical reason seems to be that, as a seasoned politician, Zhou distanced himself from Gao for his own protection before the situation became clear.

The available evidence suggests that Zhou was *passively* involved in this affair.[199] As Mao's housekeeper (see Chapter 3), Zhou could not keep outside this strife. Although Zhou's criticism of Bo was ferocious,

197 Bo, *Huigu*, 1:310; Liao, *Xinzhongguo biannian shi*, p. 59.
198 A well-informed source told me that Zhou stopped going to Gao's parties because Mme Zhou (Deng Yingchao) was unhappy that Zhou spent weekend nights in Gao's ballroom. But a former chief secretary of Zhou regards this explanation as "total nonsense" (*yipai huyuan*). He said that Zhou attended Gao's parties as a perfunctory response (*yinfu*) to Gao's invitation – Zhou was the only one whom Gao invited regularly. Gao's womanizing just gave Zhou an excuse not to get involved in those "filthy activities" (*wuqi bazao de shi*). But this source's words reveal that Gao at least tried to keep a cozy relationship with Zhou – Gao rarely invited Liu and his men.
199 It is noteworthy that in all Zhou's publications after the affair, Zhou only mentioned Gao *once* when he was criticizing Liu during the CR. Zhou said that Liu made the Right-opportunist mistakes in September 1945, which "gave a handle to Gao Gang [to attack Liu] later." *Materials on Liu Shaoqi*, p. 552.

he was merely following Mao's cue rather than cooperating with Gao. But it was Zhou's job to keep the damage as small as possible when the Gao-Rao Affair was under way; this made Zhou a formidable obstacle to Gao, who struck to blow up Liu's entire mountaintop after he gained the momentum. It was also up to Zhou to clean up the mess when the turmoil was over, which made Zhou an executor of the victimized. Thus, Zhou was most active in two phases of the Gao-Rao Affair: in March–August 1953, when the battle was engaged, and from the Fourth Plenum in 1954 to the CCP National Conference in 1955, when the dust was settling down. But little evidence has shown that Zhou was actively involved in the affair from September 1953 to January 1954, when the struggle was white-hot. The official account exaggerates in claiming that Zhou was Gao's number 2 target in order to justify further the purge of Gao and Rao. If Zhou actually gained anything from this affair, it was that he remained the regime's chief administrator.

Li Fuchun was actively involved in the affair, although little about his participation has been said. Like Deng, Li had been close to Mao since the 1930s (see Chapter 3). It was well known, according to Source B, that Li had developed a close relationship with Gao after he was sent to Manchuria on October 4, 1945. Li was promoted to the Center in June 1952 as the CFEC's vice-director, assisting Chen Yun in economic planning, and concurrently as minister of heavy industry.[200] Allegedly, friction soon occurred between Li and Bo as they jockeyed for position in the policy process. Li also felt bitter about An's "list," in which Bo would be a Politburo member but Li an alternate one. Thus, it was not surprising that Li, a leading member at both the NCFEW and NCOW, was ferocious in the attack on Bo and An after he came back from Moscow on June 9, 1953.[201] It is believed that Li got off the hook mainly because of Mao's protection.[202] After Gao's suicide, Li became the SPC chairman and was appointed the ninth vice-premier on September 25. Li remained the Party's chief planner until December 1964, when he was replaced by Yu Qiuli.[203]

200 See "*Li Fuchun zhuan*," p. 61.   201 Ibid., p. 67.
202 In my interview with Source C, I raised the question on Deng's words in "On Drafts of the Resolution on CCP History," *SWDXP*, 1975–82, p. 279: "In fact, care was taken to protect a number of cadres [involved in the Gao-Rao Affair]." He replied: "For example, Lin Biao and Li Fuchun."
203 See "*Li Fuchun zhuan*," pp. 54, 109.

The Transition of the Yan'an Round Table

Li Xiannian was a major beneficiary of the affair, although he was not involved at all. As a former leader of the Fourth Front Red Army, Li had held various positions in the forces led by Chen Yi, Liu Bocheng and Deng Xiaoping, and Lin Biao before he was appointed the Party secretary of his native province, Hubei, in May 1949.[204] As a major rice growing area, Hubei under Li's leadership played a crucial role in relieving the grain crisis in the early 1950s. This lifted Li to the policy process at the national level.[205] After the Gao-Rao Affair, Deng, the newly promoted secretary-general and director of the Organizational Department, recommended Li to succeed him as finance minister, a crucial position that would send Li into the Politburo (as bottom man) at the Eighth PC. This was quite surprising because Li had little previous financial experience and, moreover, he rose from Zhang Guotao's Fourth Front Red Army, the mountaintop Mao had tried to tear down ever since his clash with Zhang during the Long March (see Chapter 3). But Deng's recommendation showed his extraordinary political foresight. As with Chen Yun's appointment as the CFEC Director in 1949, Li's lack of support from the dominant mountaintops at the Center made him easier for Mao to control and acceptable to those who had eyed this position, especially when a power struggle had just ended.

But Deng had a personal incentive. Since he was appointed commissar of the 129th Division in January 1938, Deng had commanded a headless but potentially strong mountaintop growing out of the Fourth Front Red Army. Although Deng had won certain loyalty from this force during the war, it still had its symbolic leaders: Xu Xiangqian, Wang Shusheng, and Li Xiannian. Yet, Xu and Wang became inactive in politics after 1949. Thus, Li Xiannian was the one those from the Fourth Front Army looked up to. By recommending Li to the position of finance minister, Deng not only made an ally for himself, but he also further incorporated this powerful mountaintop. Undoubtedly, Li's rise to the

---

204 Li Xianian was a major leader of the Fourth Front Red Army. After he was rescued from the disastrous Western Expedition in 1936–7 (see Chapter 3), Li was dispatched to the Hubei-Henan area in January 1939, and he developed a force there. But Li's troop was merged into Chen Yi's army in June 1946 under the attack of the KMT forces. On May 9, 1948, Li was appointed vice-commander in Liu Bocheng and Deng Xiaoping's army. After Wuhan was seized by Lin Biao's Fourth Field Army on May 14, 1949, Li was appointed the Party secretary of Hubei and commissar of the Hubei Military Command.

205 See Bo, *Huigu*, 1:264.

Center was seen as "recognition of the Fourth Front Army,"[206] but, more importantly, it signified that a seemingly impoverished mountaintop had finally tied a knot with a promising leader, Deng Xiaoping. Indeed, some firm Deng supporters in the Deng period, like Hong Xuezhi, Li Jukui, Wang Shoudao, and Qin Jiwei, rose from the Fourth Front Red Army.

The military leaders – Peng Dehuai, Lin Biao, Luo Ronghuan, Chen Yi, Liu Bocheng, and He Long – also gained substantially. It is true that Lin and Peng's support of Gao could have been much less but for their factional ties, but their involvement reflected a shared frustration among the high-ranking officers. The fact that Gao could stir up such an excitement in the military revealed a potential threat to the stability. Indeed, in a society where the notion that "those who fought to win the state power rule the country" (*da tianxia zhe zuo tianxia*) had been a political tradition, it was seen as a great injustice to leave the soldiers outside the palace. Thus, although these military leaders did not have any substantial administrative duties, they were all appointed vice-premiers at the First NPC, held in September 1954 after the Gao-Rao Affair. Lin entered the Politburo at the Fifth Plenum on April 4, 1954, and the others followed at the Eighth PC (Table 4.2).

However, Nie Rongzhen, Xu Xiangqian, and Ye Jianying were the odd men out. The decline of Xu's and Ye's status was not unexpected, for Xu's mountaintop had been incorporated by Deng, and Ye hardly had any mountaintops of his own. Nie's case was strange. Nie, who rose from Mao's Jinggang mountaintop, controlled the military force in North China. A well-informed source attributes this to the sour relationship between Nie and Deng dating back to the 1940s, when the two had personality clashes and jockeyed for positions in the Jin-Cha-Ji base areas.[207] The other explanation is that, given Nie's close relationship with Liu's North China mountaintop, he was left out in the cold in order to restrain Liu's forces at the Center. As Liu's mountaintop began to recover, which was marked by Bo's return to the CC leadership, Nie was finally appointed a vice-premier in June 1956.

---

206 Teiwes, *Politics at Mao's Court*, p. 315n88.
207 A reliable source told me that after the 1989 crisis, Nie Rongzhen and Xu Xiangqan had a private conversation on Deng's handling of the crisis. Nie complained that ever since the 1940s he had known that Deng was stubborn, and that he was rude and reckless (*maocao*) in handling political affairs.

The Transition of the Yan'an Round Table

Table 4.2. *Positions of the Military Leaders after the Gao-Rao Affair*

Name/Mountaintop	Post in Government, 1954	Rank in Politburo, 1956
Lin Biao/4th FA	2nd vice-premier	7
Peng Dehuai/1st FA	3rd vice-premier	14
(Deng Xiaoping)/2nd FA	4th vice-premier	6/standing committee
Luo Ronghuan/4th FA	NPC vice-chairman	11
(Deng Zihui)	5th vice-premier	—
He Long/Northwest FA	6th vice-premier	16
Chen Yi/3rd FA	7th vice-premier	12
Liu Bocheng/2nd FA	NPC Standing Committee	15
Nie Rongzhen/North China FA	Vice-premier (June 1956)	—

Note: FA = Field Army.

The Two-Front Arrangement: A Structural Change of the Yan'an Round Table

A dilemma Mao faced constantly in maintaining his command was that he had to let the subleaders enjoy a substantial independence from each other in the policy process, yet he could not afford to let them make decisions without consulting him beforehand. The solution, as Mao saw it,

> hangs on strengthening the collective leadership and opposing decentralism.... The directive issued by the CC to its bureaus and army commanders on February 2, 1941, stipulates that all circular telegrams, declarations, and inner-Party directives bearing on the country as a whole *must have the Center's prior approval*.... In 1948 the CC issued more directives to the same effect. It issued a directive on setting up *a report system* on January 7 and a supplementary directive in March. The Politburo met in September and adopted *a resolution on rules governing reports to and requests for instructions from the Center.* On September 20, the CC made a decision on strengthening the Party committee system. On March 10, 1953, the CC adopted a

decision on strengthening its leadership over the work of the government in order to *avert the danger of government departments drifting away from its leadership.*[208]

Mao's unusually long-winded recollection was to remind his colleagues of one thing: all decisions had to have his prior approval. Indeed, the "report system" – the subleaders had to report to Mao regularly on their work – was crucial to Mao's command, for it enabled Mao to be better informed in a leadership structure in which deficient institutional arrangements hindered communications among the subleaders (see Chapter 3). Thus, the "collective leadership" in Mao's sense did not mean collective decision making, but it was a way in which Mao persisted in order to keep himself better informed in the policy process. The leader who failed to inform Mao of his activities would be accused of "decentralism."

Mao's words revealed that the effort to fight decentralism was made mainly in two periods. One was in the early 1940s, when the Yan'an Round Table was just formed. The other period started in 1948, when the mountaintops were expanding rapidly as the revolution was heading to a triumphant end. As the policy process became increasingly complicated after the CCP seized the state power, however, it was more difficult for the subleaders to keep Mao informed of everything in their decision making. Thus, as Mao complained, "decentralism has grown since we entered the cities."[209] But the problem was that, even if the leaders would adhere to the report system, it would be too much of a task for Mao to follow every policy issue closely.

Evidently, Mao had noticed this problem. His solution was to create a structure in which the CCP leadership would consist of "two fronts": the first front would be formed by Mao's colleagues who would take care of the daily policy process, while Mao would stay at the second front to concentrate on fundamental issues. This idea and "the related issues were under discussion within the CC leadership from the summer of 1952."[210]

Yet, in 1952–3 this was only a *tentative idea*. No CCP documents have given an exact date when the issue was raised, nor have we seen any pre-1956 official descriptions about "the two fronts." Two essential prob-

208 *SWMZD*, 5:108–9.   209 Ibid., p. 109.   210 Teiwes, *Politics at Mao's Court*, p. 32.

The Transition of the Yan'an Round Table

lems remained unsolved in Mao's two-front idea before the Gao-Rao Affair. How should leadership relations at the first front be structured, and by what means could Mao maintain his control of the first front? Given the faction-ridden structure of leadership relations, deficient understanding of – and, hence, the lack of organizational preparations for – these two problems caused the Gao-Rao Affair in the process of centralization.

The solution of the Gao-Rao Affair led to a structural change in the Yan'an Round Table. This change was officially completed at the Eighth PC in 1956, at which, as MacFarquhar points out, the "two fronts" practically came into being.[211] Compared with the structure formed at the Seventh PC (see Figure 3.4), the basic element of the new structure – Mao's command based on the support from the Party and military systems – remained intact, but there was a fundamental change in leadership relations in policy making: the two-front arrangement (Figure 4.2).

First of all, a Stalin-type party state was created. Mao stayed at the second front, watching over the first-front institutions: the Politburo managed by Liu, the State Council led by Zhou, and the Secretariat headed by Deng. Mao personally chaired the CMC, the supreme organ in the military system. Moreover, the Politburo was dramatically enlarged not just because of the inclusion of military leaders, but because it actually became a council of leaders, including *all* the leaders in charge of various policy areas. The aim was to improve policy coordination while maintaining the "collective leadership" under Mao's command. Thus, the supremacy of the Politburo in policy making was defined by its institutional relations with the organs under its supervision: the State Council and the CC Secretariat.

There was little change, however, in the structure of the military system, except that Mao extended his direct control over the Regional Military Commands (RMCs) – their commanders and commissars could now report to Mao directly. As a result, the grasp of the CMC members over their mountaintops was weakened, although they still maintained direct access to the RMCs, which were built upon their former armies.

Thus, the transition of the Yan'an Round Table was unsymmetrical:

---

211 MacFarquhar, *The Origins*, 1:152–3.

Factionalism in Chinese Communist Politics

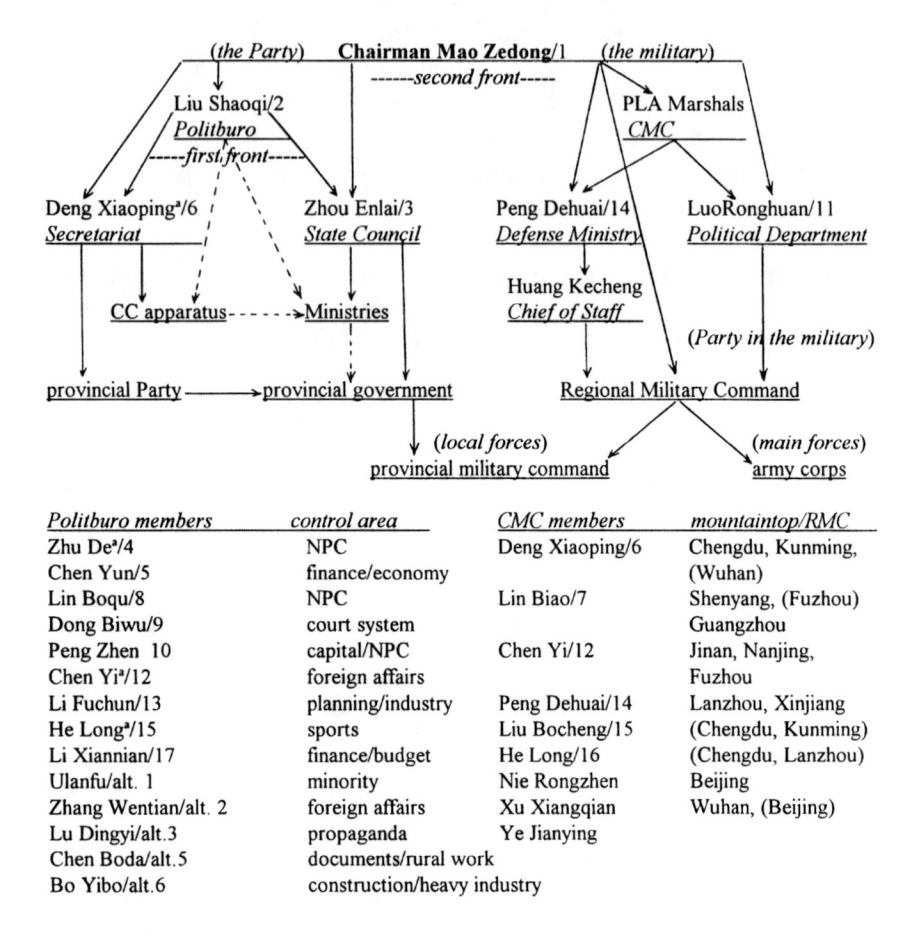

```
                (the Party)    Chairman Mao Zedong/1   (the military)
                                  -----second front-----
                  Liu Shaoqi/2                    PLA Marshals
                  Politburo                       CMC
                  -----first front-----

     Deng Xiaoping*/6        Zhou Enlai/3      Peng Dehuai/14     LuoRonghuan/11
     Secretariat              State Council     Defense Ministry   Political Department

                                                  Huang Kecheng
              CC apparatus------>Ministries       Chief of Staff
                                                                   (Party in the military)

     provincial Party -------->provincial government    Regional Military Command

                                        (local forces)            (main forces)
                                     provincial military command   army corps
```

Politburo members	control area	CMC members	mountaintop/RMC
Zhu De*/4	NPC	Deng Xiaoping/6	Chengdu, Kunming,
Chen Yun/5	finance/economy		(Wuhan)
Lin Boqu/8	NPC	Lin Biao/7	Shenyang, (Fuzhou)
Dong Biwu/9	court system		Guangzhou
Peng Zhen 10	capital/NPC	Chen Yi/12	Jinan, Nanjing,
Chen Yi*/12	foreign affairs		Fuzhou
Li Fuchun/13	planning/industry	Peng Dehuai/14	Lanzhou, Xinjiang
He Long*/15	sports	Liu Bocheng/15	(Chengdu, Kunming)
Li Xiannian/17	finance/budget	He Long/16	(Chengdu, Lanzhou)
Ulanfu/alt. 1	minority	Nie Rongzhen	Beijing
Zhang Wentian/alt. 2	foreign affairs	Xu Xiangqian	Wuhan, (Beijing)
Lu Dingyi/alt.3	propaganda	Ye Jianying	
Chen Boda/alt.5	documents/rural work		
Bo Yibo/alt.6	construction/heavy industry		

/number = rank in the Politburo.
[a] Leaders who have access to the military mountaintops.

Figure 4.2. The transition of the Yan'an Round Table at the Eighth Party Congress, 1956 (solid arrow = direct control; dashed arrow = indirect control)

the structural changes were seen only in the Party system. In the military system leadership relations were based not so much on institutional arrangements as on personal loyalties, and a leader's influence was measured not so much by his institutional position as by the size of his mountaintop and his relationship with Mao. This unsymmetrical change in the leadership structure indicated that the change was made *passively* under

The Transition of the Yan'an Round Table

the pressure of the new situation. The aim was to stabilize leadership relations in the policy process in order to avoid strife like the Gao-Rao Affair and, in the long run, to prevent a succession crisis, as happened in Soviet politics (see Chapter 2).

Obviously, Mao believed that he had eventually worked out an effective solution to the dilemma he faced, namely to maintain his command while freeing himself from the energy-consuming bureaucratic routines. As Figure 4.2 shows, Mao entrusted Deng, a member of Mao's clique since the early 1930s, with the Party's daily affairs; he left administration to Zhou, his housekeeper since the Yan'an period; and let Liu manage the Politburo, the supreme organ in policy making. Thus, a system of checks and balances among the first-front leaders was established. Because Mao maintained direct control over each of them, it seemed that his command was secure.

But it was not to be. Although Mao might have done many things differently, the two-front arrangement was the only one he ever regretted personally. He admitted in October 1966: "For seventeen years, there is one thing that, to my mind, has not been done properly. Originally, for the sake of state security and in view of the lessons from Stalin of the Soviet Union, we created the first front and the second front. I was with the second front while the other comrades were with the first front."[212]

Essentially, the two-front arrangement was a step toward institutionalization. With this arrangement, a leader's duty was not determined by the area that happened to be controlled by his mountaintop. Rather, he was assigned to a policy area according to his status determined by the size of his mountaintop and, more importantly, his personal relationship with Mao. But after he was assigned to this position, more decisive to his personal well-being and influence were the objective policy outcomes in the area under his leadership; and his relations with the other leaders were reshaped by the interests that emerged in the policy process. Thus, in the Party system, common interests began to override personal ties forged during the revolution, and due procedures began to prevail over factional connections in policy making. As a result, the two-front arrangement would undermine, rather than secure, Mao's command, for it helped to promote common interests among the Party bureaucrats at the expense of their personal loyalties to Mao.

---

212 Quoted from ibid., 1:152.

Eventually, as the analysis in the next chapter shows, an unprecedented threat to Mao's command, and ultimately to the integrity of the Yan'an Round Table, would emerge as the Party state went its own way in the policy process; and Mao's desperate effort to stop it led to an overall crisis in leadership relations prior to the Cultural Revolution.

5

Crises in Leadership Relations with the Two-Front Arrangement

Why did Mao Zedong launch the Cultural Revolution? Few would dispute that the answer lies in CCP politics between 1956 and 1966, but explanations vary greatly. The CCP official account explains the CR as a result of the conflict between Mao's "Left-deviationist error" and his colleagues' persistence in the "correct policies."[1] Numerous scholars also attribute the CR to policy differences among the CCP leaders.[2] A few emphasize Mao's deep-seated antibureaucratism,[3] or focus on "the politics of succession" in the leadership,[4] or see the CR "essentially as an aberration," resulting from changes in the political environment that put different constraints on Mao and his colleagues in decision making. The power-struggle analysts see the CR originating in the elite struggles for power, although these struggles were often triggered by policy disputes.[5]

This chapter examines CCP politics in 1956–66 from the perspective of the *structure* of leadership relations. It shows that the CCP leaders' policy choices were essentially *structure-induced* after the two-front arrangement was set up in policy making (see Chapter 4). That is, given his policy preferences and *guanxi* with the other leaders, a leader's ratio-

---

1 See *Jueyi*, pp. 312–13; and Wang Nianyi, *1949–1989 nian de zhongguo: da dongluan de niandai* (China in 1949–1989: The Years of Great Turmoil), Henan: Henan People's Press, 1988, pp. 13–14.
2 See Harry Harding, "Chinese state in crisis," in Roderick MacFarquhar and John K. Fairbank eds., *The Cambridge History of China*, Cambridge: Cambridge University Press, 1991, 15:113 and n2.
3 See Maurice Meisner, *Mao's China and After: A History of the People's Republic*, New York: Free Press, 1988.
4 See Stuart Schram, *Mao Tse-tung: A Political Biography*, New York: Simon and Schuster, 1966.
5 See MacFarquhar's three-volume work, *The Origins of the Cultural Revolution*, New York: Columbia University Press, 1974, 1982, 1997.

nale in decision making was eventually subject to the constraints of the two-front arrangement.

The two-front arrangement was adopted to solve Mao's dilemma in the policy process: Mao had to keep all manner of control flowing to him in order to maintain his command, yet it was too much a task for him to follow every policy issue closely. Staying with the second front, Mao could shake off the burden of, and responsiblity for, the daily routine, while maintaining his command through his direct control over each of the first-front leaders, among whom a system of checks and balances was established.

This arrangement, however, brought about a structural change in leadership relations with profound implications in the shaping of each leader's rationale in decision making. When a problem emerged, the first-front leaders' view would not always be in accord with Mao's vision due to varied perspectives of, and hence different policy preferences in, their evaluations. There was little doubt of the first-front leaders' loyalty to Mao, but their responsibility for the policy process pinned their well-being eventually on the objective policy outcomes, rather than its ideological implications, which usually underlay Mao's policy preferences. When differences emerged between Mao and the first-front leaders, the latter had to stick together in order to achieve their policy goals. As a result, common interests overrode personal loyalty, and the two-front arrangement undermined Mao's command, rather than securing it as he expected.

The analysis in this chapter focuses on two periods: 1956–8 and 1962–5, during which time policy outcomes were the most inconsistent prior to the CR, despite seemingly stable leadership relations. We witnessed the changes from "leap forward" to "retreat" and to the Great Leap Forward (GLF) in 1956–8, and a pragmatic approach in economic development versus the increasingly radical policy in the political arena in 1962–5. My analysis shows:

1 As a formal policy-making process, the two-front arrangement created common interests among the first-front leaders despite their different factional backgrounds. Thus, a formal process could overcome, if not fully suppress, factional tendencies in policy making.
2 The two-front arrangement empowered the Party bureaucrats (PB) but exerted constraints on Mao in policy making. Any policy initiatives from Mao would have to go through this arrangement to be converted into

The Two-Front Arrangement

concrete policies. Thus, Mao felt that "the great power is taken away" [*daquan pangluo*]. This formed the essential source of Mao's frustration against and suspicion of the PB, who managed the policy process at the first front.

3 To maintain the dominance of his vision, and ultimately his power, in policy making, Mao constantly violated the two-front arrangement, usually by initiating a new policy and then taking over the policy-making process at the first front. This was the essential cause of policy inconsistency.

4 In order to minimize the damage caused by policy inconsistency, the first-front leaders would try to integrate Mao's initiatives into the ongoing policy process. Their success, however, would only provoke Mao to make a new initiative in order to maintain his control. This not only created a vicious cycle in policy making but also destabilized leadership relations, which eventually led to an overall crisis of the Yan'an Round Table. The CR resulted.

THE RISE OF THE PARTY BUREAUCRATS

Mao's Setback in 1956

Inspired by the "high tide of socialism" but frustrated by the moderate speed of development, Mao lashed out repeatedly at "Right-conservatism" in late 1955.[6] As a leader in charge of the first front, Liu convened a "big forum" of 122 leading cadres on December 5. Elaborating on Mao's directive, Liu asserted that "our work in various spheres lags behind the development of the situation [because] many of our comrades are following *a conservative line*."[7]

Liu's speech represented the stand of the Party leadership and was transmitted within the Party, which resulted in "an enormous pressure" on all fields of work.[8] Meanwhile, the Twelve-Year (1955–67) Agricultural Program, drafted under Mao's supervision, was dispatched to localities on December 21.[9] In this program all agricultural targets were increased drastically from those set in the previous August

---

6 See Liao Gailong, *1949–1989: Xin zhongguo biannian shi* (1949–1989: A Chronology of the New China), Beijing: People's Press, July 1989, pp. 92, 94–5; and Bo Yibo, *Ruogan zhongda juece yu shijian de huigu* (Review of Several Important Decisions and Events), Beijing: CCP Party School Press, June 1991, 1:394–4, 522–5 (hereafter *Huigu*).
7 Ibid., p. 522 (emphasis added).
8 Ibid., p. 532.
9 See *SWMZD*, 5:277–80; and MacFarquhar, *The Origins*, 2:27–8.

Table 5.1. *Changes in Production Targets for 1967*

Product	1955 Output	1967 Target (Made in 8/1955)	1967 Target (Made in 1/1956)
Grain	184 million ton	300 million ton	500 million ton
Cotton	1.52 million ton	2.8 million ton	6 million ton
Steel	2.85 million ton	18 million ton	24 million ton
Coal	98 million ton	280 million ton	330 million ton
ICC[a]	10.36 billion yuan	11.27 billion yuan	20 billion yuan
GNP	110.4 billion yuan	326.7 billion yuan	467.5 billion yuan

[a] Investment in capital construction.
Sources: Bo Yibo, *Ruogan zhongda juece yu shijian de huigu* (Review of Several Important Decisions and Events), Beijing: CCP Party School Press, 1991, 1:527–8; Fang Weizhong, ed., *Zhonghua renmin gongheguo jingji dashi ji, 1949–1980* (The Economic Chronology of the PRC), Beijing: Chinese Social Science Academy Press, 1984, pp. 160–1, 182.

(Table 5.1). Moreover, Mao made these targets public in his "Prefaces to *Socialist Upsurge in China's Countryside*" without consulting his colleagues.[10]

Spurred by Mao's initiative, the State Planning Commission (SPC) increased all major industrial targets for 1967, the final year of the third five-year-plan (FYP), from those previously set in August 1955.[11] The revised plan, adopted by the SPC on January 14, 1956, marked the beginning of the first "leap forward" with Mao in command.[12]

The "planners,"[13] however, soon realized that these newly pledged high targets were not achievable. For example, the investment in capital construction (ICC) in 1956 would nearly double the amount in 1955 (see Table 5.1), despite a 9.29 percent increase in the 1956 revenue.[14] Thus,

10 Cf. Bo, *Huigu*, 1:525–6.
11 In August 1955, the State Council convened a conference at Beidaihe, at which the second and third FYPs, and a fifteen-year plan (1953–67) were adopted. But Mao complained that these plans were too cautious. Bo, *Huigu*, 1:523.
12 Cf. MacFarquhar, *The Origins*, 1:26–32.
13 The "planners," coined by MacFarquhar (ibid., pp. 59–74), refers to those leaders who were in charge of the economic planning. Zhou, Chen Yun, Li Fuchun, Li Xiannian, and Bo Yibo were then the most notable ones.
14 Bo, *Huigu*, 1:531–2.

The Two-Front Arrangement

Zhou Enlai urged retreat even before the production drive started. Seeing that unrealistically high targets were proposed at the Planning and Financial Conferences in January 1956, Zhou summoned SPC Chairman Li Fuchun and Finance Minister Li Xiannian, who chaired the two conferences respectively, on February 3 and 6. Zhou warned them that "a phenomenon of impetuosity and adventurism" had emerged, and he asked them to "cut down" the targets because they were "all too grandiose."[15] Zhou's effort turned the two conferences into what he called "the conferences of promoting retreat [*cutui*]."[16] Zhou said at the twenty-fourth session of the State Council on February 8: "The numbers in the plans submitted by specific conferences [held] by various departments are very grandiose. *All of us must seek truth from facts.... Those leaders who are hot-headed* [tounau fare] *should be washed with cold water*; [then they] may become a little bit sober."[17]

While Zhou was organizing a retreat,[18] Mao preoccupied himself with an "unexpected" event: thirty-four ministry leaders were sent to report to Mao from February 14 to April 23.[19] All Mao did during this period, as he complained, was to "[sleep] in bed and [listen to reports] on the ground."[20] Thus, the disagreement would not surface until an enlarged Politburo conference, April 25–28.[21] Although Mao sounded sober in his

---

15 "*Zhou Enlai zhuan*" (A Biography of Zhou Enlai), *RWZ* (1991), 106.
16 See Bo, *Huigu*, 1:532–3.
17 *SWZEL*, 2:190–1 (emphasis added).
18 See "*Zhou Enlai zhuan*," pp. 106–8.
19 Bo, *Huigu*, 1:466–7, recalls that, after Mao returned to Beijing from Hangzhou on January 12, Bo went to Mao to report on his work. Bo "*accidentally mentioned*" that Liu was listening to the report from various ministries and committees in order to prepare for "the drafting of the CC's report to the upcoming Eighth PC." To Bo's surprise, Liu's arrangement was unbeknownst to Mao, and Mao "*was unexpectedly* very interested in this matter" and asked Bo to make a similar arrangement for him.

There are two notable points in Bo's description: (1) contrary to some official accounts that Liu had little to do with the drafting of the CC's report to the Eighth PC (see Xue Qingqing and Wang Diming, *Mao Zedong lingdao le bada wenjian de qicao gongzuo* [Mao Zedong led the work drafting the documents of the Eighth PC], *Yaniju* 2, 1990, 2:64–6), Liu was indeed in charge of the drafting (see MacFarquhar, *The Origins*, 1:100–3); and (2) Mao's "unexpected" eagerness to follow Liu's example reflected his fear of being kept out of the policy process.
20 Bo, *Huigu*, 1:469–70.
21 See "*Zhou Enlai zhuan*," pp. 108–9.

speech *On Ten Great Relationships*,[22] his general policy approach in this speech did not reflect his own idea on the speed of economic development. Rather, it was "designed to prevent the abuse of Stalin's Russia – as outlined in the secret speech [at the CPSU's Twentieth Congress] – from being duplicated in China."[23] At the same conference Mao actually demanded a substantial increase in the ICC in 1956–7. Mao's proposal caught the planners by surprise, for a high target had already been set for the ICC and, moreover, Mao made such a proposal without consulting them beforehand. Zhou "objected to it [i.e., Mao's proposal] and expounded upon his reasons."[24] Mao was not convinced, but he was not prepared to confront the planners, nor was he willing to compromise. Thus, the conference failed to achieve its goal: to decide on the economic plans submitted by the State Council.

These plans, however, had to be presented at the annual CC work conference that was to be held in July. Learning that Mao was about to leave for East China, "Zhou called on Mao and [they] had a conversation on May 2, shortly before Mao left Beijing." Little is known about how this conversation went, except that Mao maintained an ambiguous attitude toward Zhou's proposal to cut down production targets.[25]

Mao's hand-off attitude and his absence from Beijing emboldened Zhou to push for a retreat. On May 11, Zhou convened a State Council conference on the 1956 budget report. Zhou made his stand clear in his opening speech: "We have been opposing conservatism for eight or nine months since last August. [We] cannot continue to keep doing so forever."[26] Zhou further pointed out at a plenary session of the State Council on June 5, one day after the 1956 budget report was formally submitted to the CC: "Adventurism [i.e., to pursue unrealistically high targets] appeared after last December. *Now it is not how to prevent, but how to oppose it.*"[27]

The budget report was approved at a Politburo meeting on June 10

---

22 The section on industrial policies in this speech was based on Zhou's notes of the conversations between Mao and ministry leaders in February–April 1956. Ibid., pp. 106–7.
23 MacFarquhar, *The Origins*, 1:48. Also see Bo, *Huigu*, 1:470–2, 486–90.
24 See "*Zhou Enlai zhuan*," p. 108.   25 Ibid., pp. 108–9.
26 Quoted from Shi Wei, *Maojin, fanmaojin, fan fanmaojin* (Adventurism, antiadventurism, and opposing antiadventurism), *Dangde wenxian* (The Party's Historical Documents), 1990, 2:9.
27 Ibid., p. 8.

The Two-Front Arrangement

due to "firm support" from Liu Shaoqi, who chaired the meeting.[28] Liu instructed Hu Qiaomu, deputy director of the CC Propaganda Department, to "put more emphasis on opposing adventurism" in this report before its final version was submitted to the Third Session of the First NPC on June 15. Hu added these "key words" to the report: "While opposing conservatism, we must at the same time oppose the tendency toward impetuosity and adventurism. This tendency has already appeared in many departments and many places in the past few months."[29] On the next day, a *People's Daily* editorial pointed out: "The most noteworthy aspect [of the 1956 budget report] is that it raises the slogan of opposing impetuosity and adventurism."

An overall retreat resulted. At the Beidaihe Conference, cochaired by Zhou and Chen Yun in August 1956 to discuss the economic section of the CC's report to the upcoming Eighth PC, all targets were cut down drastically, and all plans "were readjusted."[30] Thus, the first "leap forward" ended as swiftly as it had emerged.[31]

But how could the CCP leaders stand up to Mao who had unmistakably expressed his preference for fast development? More surprisingly, Liu made a 180-degree turnaround during Mao's absence from Beijing: all of sudden Liu changed from a zealot of "anticonservatism" to an advocate of "antiadventurism." After the State Council conference on May 11, Liu "instructed the Propaganda Department to draft an editorial on opposing the two -isms [i.e., conservatism and adventurism] for the *People's Daily*."[32] This front-page editorial, "One Must Oppose Conservatism and Also a Disposition Toward Impetuosity," published on June 20, points out specifically that "the reason why impetuosity and adventurism have become a serious problem is that they . . . exist in the leading cadres at the top of various systems. In many cases impetuosity and adventurism among the subordinates emerged because of the pressure from the top."[33]

---

28 See "*Zhou Enlai zhuan*," p. 108. Zhou, Zhu De, Chen Yun, Li Fuchun, Li Xiannian, Bo, Li Weihan, and Hu Qiaomu attended this meeting.
29 Bo, *Huigu*, 1:536.   30 Shi, *Maojin, fanmaojin, fan fanmaojin*, 8–9.
31 Cf. MacFarquhar, *The Origins*, 2:86–91.   32 See Bo, *Huigu*, 1:534.
33 The draft of the editorial was revised by Lu Dingyi, Hu Qiaomu, and Liu Shaoqi. See Zhang Qiuyun and Zheng Shulan, *Yipian fanmaojin shelun de youlai* (The Origin of an Editorial of Antiadventurism), *Dangde wenxian* (The Party's Historical Documents), 1990, 2:11–2.

This editorial turned an economic retreat, initiated and organized by the planners, into a political campaign led by the Party. The momentum of the "leap forward" was reversed to antiadventurism, but Mao was humiliated.[34] When the editorial was submitted to him for approval, Mao's comment was: "I am not going to read it" (*wo bu kan le*) because, as Mao lashed out later: "This editorial appears to oppose Rightism as well as 'Leftism.' In fact it is not against Rightism at all. It criticizes 'Leftism' only, and it is diametrically pointed at me."[35]

This brought up another puzzle. Why did Mao, with such a strong feeling against the retreat, fade into the back scene after the leap was launched? Was it because Zhou convinced Mao in their conversation on May 2? Obviously not – otherwise Mao would not have denounced the retreat in early 1958. Had Mao remained active in the policy process, the first leap could have been carried out, or at least would not have ended so swiftly.

A close examination of the choices available to Mao, Liu (head of the PB), and Zhou (head of the planners) after the first leap was launched can shed light on these questions. At the time, each of the three players had three choices in decision making: to carry out the leap, to retreat from the leap, or to withdraw from the policy process into the background.

Mao's first choice was "to carry out the leap," because he saw the leap as the way to turn China into a strong country *rapidly*. However, Mao faced a difficult situation after the planners expressed their objection to the leap. Mao could not carry out the leap without their support, for Mao never had any concrete plans and, moreover, he would be held responsible if the leap turned out to be what Zhou had warned: a disaster. Yet it would be hard for Mao to accept the retreat before his vision of fast development was proved wrong. Moreover, to cave in under the pressure of his colleagues would undermine Mao's authority in decision making. Thus, "withdrawal" appeared as an option for Mao. Withdrawing to the second front, Mao could still claim credit if the leap was successful; if the leap failed, Mao could shake off much of the responsibility.

---

34 See MacFarquhar, *The Origins*, 1:87; also cf. Bo, *Huigu*, 1:537–8.
35 Quoted from Wu Lengxi, *Yi Mao zhuxi* (Memorize Chairman Mao), Beijing: Xinhua Press, 1995, p. 49.

The Two-Front Arrangement

In case the leap was stopped, Mao could at least save his face because he was not in charge of the concrete policy issues; and as the supreme leader, Mao would have the last say should the first-front leaders seek a policy change. Indeed, the rationale of the two-front arrangement was to enable Mao to maintain his command while shaking off the responsibility for daily affairs.

But "to carry out the leap" was Zhou's last choice, for Zhou realized that he would be responsible for carrying out the leap, and therefore for the consequent disaster. Yet, as a first-front leader in overall charge of the economy, Zhou would not be allowed, and could not afford, to choose "withdrawal," for it would be seen as a sign of his breaking up with Mao. Thus, "retreat" was Zhou's first choice. Although insisting on "retreat" would annoy Mao, it could relieve Zhou of an unbearable responsibility. Moreover, Zhou had the planners' support. Given that the leap had been launched, Zhou's priority was not how to maximize the gain, but how to minimize the loss of the state as well as his own.

Liu's first choice, it seems, should also have been "to carry out the leap," given his zealous support to Mao. Yet Liu was thrown into an uncertain situation once the Mao-Zhou dispute surfaced. Had Mao insisted on "carrying out the leap," Liu would have followed Mao for a free ride: Liu could claim the credit had the leap been successful, and he would share little responsibility had the leap failed, because he just followed Mao. However, the free ride no longer existed if Mao chose "withdrawal" and let Liu take charge of the policy process at the first front. If Liu chose "to carry out the leap," he would have to share the responsibility for the leap if Zhou would go along with him; but he would be fully responsible for the leap had Zhou chosen either "retreat" or "withdrawal." As a first-front leader, Liu could not "withdraw" from the policy process for the same reasons that applied to Zhou. Given that Liu's political well-being depended eventually on the objective policy outcomes because he was in overall charge at the first front, it would serve Liu's best interest to cooperate with his partner, namely Zhou, when Mao had withdrawn into the background.

Thus, it is not surprising that, when Mao was in charge of the policy process, Liu would support whatever Mao chose. Yet, after Mao withdrew to the second front, Liu's rational choice was to cooperate with Zhou, despite Mao's clearly expressed intention "to carry out the leap."

Factionalism in Chinese Communist Politics

As a result, a policy inconsistency occurred in June 1956: from anticonservatism to antiadventurism in politics, and from leap to retreat in the economy.

Liu's opportunistic behavior revealed a dilemma in his relationship with Mao in the two-front arrangement. Given the faction-ridden nature of leadership relations, Liu had to be loyal to Mao in order to maintain his position as Mao's successor (see Chapter 2); yet as the leader in charge at the first front, Liu's political well-being depended eventually on the objective policy outcomes. This dilemma determined a two-dimensional conflict in the Mao-Liu relationship. First, as the supreme leader who decided on issues of principle at the second front, Mao would pay more attention to the political consequences of policy making, and therefore he appeared idealistic, and even romantic, in decision making. But as the leader in charge of the first front, Liu had to be realistic in handling daily affairs. Second, given the faction-ridden structure of leadership relations, Mao was intolerant of any tendencies among his followers toward forming a coalition. But Liu had to have the cooperation of the other first-front leaders in order to achieve the desired policy goals. Thus, Liu had to be opportunistic in decision making in order to dodge confrontation with Mao, on the one hand, and to win cooperation from the other leaders, on the other.

More importantly, the episode of "antiadventurism" demonstrated how the two-front arrangement could undermine Mao's command, instead of securing it as Mao expected. This arrangement enabled the first-front leaders – the PB headed by Liu and the planners led by Zhou – to form a de facto coalition when Mao's idea was at odds with their desired policy goals. Thus, common interests overrode personal loyalties which had glued the Yan'an Round Table together (see Chapter 3). Facing a majority of his comrades, Mao had to subject his command to the "collective leadership" in decision making.[36]

As a result, Mao's grandiose idea for development "was firmly rejected" at the Eighth PC.[37] Although Mao was upset and, in fact, expressed his disagreement to Liu three days after the Eighth PC, there

---

36 See Shi Zhongquan, "*Fan maojin yu fan fanmaojin*" (Antiadventurism and opposing antiadventurism), in Jiang Mingwu, ed., *Zhou Enali de licheng* (Zhou Enlai's Career), Beijing: PLA Art Press, 1996, 2:82–102, esp. p. 88.
37 See MacFarquhar, *The Origins*, 1:122–6.

The Two-Front Arrangement

was little he could do but go along with his comrades.[38] At the Second Plenum in November 1956, the plenum Mao saw as "a concentrated exhibition of antiadventurism,"[39] Zhou and Chen's proposal for a further retreat in 1957 was adopted with Liu's "firm support," the Twelve-Year Agricultural Program was shelved,[40] and all economic plans "were adjusted."[41] Again, Mao's dismay was obvious, yet there was nothing he could do but keep quiet in front of the coalition of the PB and planners.[42] According to Party historian Zhang Xingxing, Mao said to a group of provincial leaders in December, with "a mocking taste" (*xixue weidao*): "What you all support is the Eighth PC, but not me!"[43]

The Great Leap Forward under the Party's Command

But Mao would soon intervene in the first front. Citing the 1957 Rectification Campaign and the successive Anti-Rightist Campaign as the evidence,[44] Mao insisted at the Third Plenum of the Eighth CC, held September–October 1957, that "the struggle between the proletariat and bourgeoisie is the major contradiction" in China.[45] Thus, as *Jueyi* points out, Mao "in fact denied the political line of the Eighth PC," that "the major contradiction" in China was between "the increasing socioeconomic demands and the inability of the current economy to meet these demands."[46] Mao also complained that "antiadventurism" had wiped out the spirit of "more, faster, better, and more economically" and the

---

38 See Wang Guangmei, "*Yujun tongzhou, fengyu wuhui*" (No regret for being your company for life), *Xinhua wenzhai* (New China Digest), no. 240 (December 1998), p. 129.
39 Bo, *Huigu*, 1:556.
40 Cf. MacFarquhar, *The Origins*, 2:90–1. Bo, *Huigu*, 1:557–8, recalls that Zhou argued in his report that the *Twelve-Year Program* was "just a draft of suggestions"; it should not be enforced if there were difficulties in its implementation.
41 Liao, *Xin zhongguo biannian shi*, p. 114.
42 Bo, *Huigu*, 1:556–7, recalls when Liu "quoted Chen Yun's words" in his report, saying that "to be a little bit Right is better than to be a little bit Left," Mao was oviously dismayed and questioned the implication of these words. Liu answered bluntly: "to be a little bit Right" meant "to be slow" in the development.
43 Zhang Xingxing, *Zhonggong bada luxian weineng jianchi xiaqu de yuanyin* (The reasons why [the party] failed to adhere to the correct line of the Eighth PC), *Yanjiu 2*, 1988, 5:34.
44 See MacFarquhar, *The Origins*, 1: chaps. 13–15, 18.
45 See *Wansui*, 2:123–4.   46 See *Jueyi*, p. 308.

Twelve-Year Agricultural Program.⁴⁷ The first-front leaders, however, saw Mao's speech at this plenum not so much as a criticism of their policy as a political conclusion of the Anti-Rightist Campaign. They failed to realize that what they were giving up was their "political line" and, hence, the ideological legitimacy for their entire policy approach.

Mao's effort to "put politics in command" was echoed by Khrushchev, who declared that it was "a political phenomenon" to overtake the United States in economic matters. Khrushchev's grandiose plan further spurred Mao when he visited Moscow in November 1957.⁴⁸ While still in Moscow, Mao revised and approved a *People's Daily* editorial, which would be published on December 12.⁴⁹ As Mao was stepping into the first front, Liu, who was notably inactive at the CC's Third Plenum (presumably because he was unsure of Mao's intention), quickly switched to Mao's side. Before the editorial revised by Mao in Moscow was published, Liu and his men rushed to publish a *People's Daily* editorial on November 13.⁵⁰ This editorial readvocated the Twelve-Year Agricultural Program and implied that "antiadventurism" had disheartened the peasants in socialist construction. As the National Planning Conference opened on November 28, a week after Mao returned from Moscow, Bo Yibo, a Liu confidant who headed the State Economic Commission, announced an increase in the ICC for 1958 from 11.713 to 13.059 billion yuan.⁵¹ Four days later, at the Eighth Congress of the All-China Federation of Trade Unions, Liu declared on behalf of the CC the goal Mao made on his own while in Moscow: "(China will) catch up with and

---

47 See Liao, *Xin zhongguo biannian shi*, p. 132.
48 See MacFarquhar, *The Origins*, 2:15–17.
49 See Wu, *Yi Mao zhuxi*, pp. 47–8.
50 Wu's claim (ibid., p. 47) that this editorial "was written by the editorial department of the *People's Daily* itself" is not accurate. According to a reliable source, this *People's Daily* editorial was drafted under the supervision of Lu Dingyi, a Liu confidant who headed the CC Propaganda Department, and approved by Liu himself.
51 Cf. Fang Weizhong, ed., *Zhonghua renmin gongheguo jingji dashi ji, 1949–1980* (The Economic Chronology of the PRC, 1949–1980), Beijing: Chinese Social Science Academy Press, 1984, p. 201. But Bo, *Huigu*, 2:635–43, does not even mention this speech in his account of opposing antiadventurism. Rather, Bo implies that he was a major "victim" of the event. According to a source close to Li Xiannian, Li complained about Bo's description of antiadventurism. Li said: "Bo is very slippery [*huatou*].... At the [National] Planning Conference at the end of 1957, he unexpectedly increased the ICC. This put Premier Zhou in a difficult situation." Obviously, Bo would not dare to increase the ICC without the approval of Liu, or maybe Mao himself.

The Two-Front Arrangement

surpass the United Kingdom in the output of iron, steel, and other major industrial products."[52] On December 12, the *People's Daily* published the editorial Mao revised in Moscow. It criticized antiadventurism as "a Right-conservative tendency" against the principle of "more, faster, better, and more economically."

Open criticism of "antiadventurism" appeared first at the CCP congresses of Zhejiang and Shanghai in early December 1957 when Mao was at Hangzhou, the capital of Zhejiang Province. The attack on antiadventurism soon spread to all the provincial CCP congresses, held variously from late 1957 to early 1958 to prepare for the upcoming Second Session of the Eighth PC.[53] With support from the local leaders, most notably Ke Qingshi (East China), Li Jingquan (Southwest), and Tao Zhu (South), Mao convened two CC conferences *outside* Beijing – the Nanning and Chengdu Conferences – in early 1958, where he fiercely attacked the planners.[54] Mao argued at the Nanning Conference in January that "antiadventurism" was not just about policy differences but involved "a political issue," because the planners blocked the information from him and enforced their choice on him.[55] Under Mao's "furious attack," Zhou, who arrived in Nanning on the evening of January 13,[56] caved in. He said in a self-criticism the next day: "[Antiadventurism] is a vacillation and error in terms of *fangzhen* [fundamental policy]. It is of the Right-conservatist thinking.... This is a *fangzhen* that promotes retreat, as opposed to the Chairman's *fangzhen*, which promotes progress.... I must take the major responsibility."[57]

Triumphantly, Mao warned at an enlarged Politburo meeting in mid-February: "From now on, [we] can only oppose Right-conservatism, but cannot oppose adventurism."[58] Chen Yun, who did not attend the Nanning Conference, made a self-criticism at this meeting.[59] Moreover,

---

52 See MacFarquhar, *The Origins*, 2:17; also Liao, *Xin zhongguo biannian shi*, pp. 132–3.
53 Ibid., p. 133.
54 Besides most of the Politburo members, a dozen provincial leaders attended the Nanning Conference; and leaders from the Northeast, Northwest, and Southeast attended the Chengdu Conference. Wu, *Yi Mao zhuxi*, p. 47, provides a list of participants of the Nanning Conference.
55 See *Wansui*, 2:145–53.
56 See *"Zhou Enlai zhuan,"* p. 110.
57 Quoted from Shi, *"Maojin, fanmaojin, fan fanmaojin,"* p. 9.
58 Quoted from *"Zhou Enlai zhuan,"* p. 110.
59 Shi, *"Maojin, fanmaojin, fan fanmaojin,"* p. 9.

Mao declared at the Chengdu Conference in March that "adventurism is Marxism, antiadventurism is anti-Marxism."[60] Thus, Mao denounced the retreat in 1957 in terms of ideology. Under Mao's pressure, Zhou and the planners made self-criticisms at the conference and, later, at the Second Session of the Eighth PC, held May 5–23, 1958.[61]

How could the planners cave in without any resistance? While Mao's success in rallying support from local leaders was a factor, a key reason was that Liu and the PB, as the preceding analysis shows, switched to Mao's side after Mao stepped into the first front. Liu even chided those at the Chengdu Conference as if he had always been on Mao's side: "[We] must pay more attention to correcting 'the disease of slowness' [*manxing bing*]. The danger of Right-deviationism is still the principal one at present."[62] Moreover, in his report at the Second Session of the Eighth PC, Liu attacked the retreat as "an expression of Right-deviationism in our Party" without a sheer reflection on his active role in this episode. He claimed that the situation from 1956 to 1958 had undergone a U-shaped development from good (early 1956), to bad (1956–7), and to good again (1958), corresponding with "a leap forward, a conservative retreat, and a big leap forward."[63] This was a distortion of reality, for 1957 was the best year regarding economic development in the entire Mao period.[64] It was Liu's report that sounded the bugle call for the GLF, although it would not be fully launched until the Enlarged Politburo Conference at Beidaihe in August.[65] As MacFarquhar points out, Liu was the organizer of the GLF.[66]

60 Quoted from "*Zhou Enlai zhuan*," p. 111.
61 Zhou made an 8,000-word self-criticism at the Second Session of the Eighth PC. The other planners like Chen Yun and Li Xiannian also made self-criticisms at the meeting. Zhou was so depressed that he was often lost in reflection. See "*Zhou Enlai zhuan*," pp. 111–12.
62 Quoted from "*Liu Shaoqi zhuan*" (A Biography of Liu Shaoqi), *RWZ* (1991), 49:103. A Party historian who specializes on Zhou believes that opposing antiadventurism and the GLF in 1957-8 could have been prevented had Liu sided with Zhou. His opinion represents the mainstream among the Party historians on this issue. This was the second time that Zhou suffered from Liu's attack – the first happened during the YR (see Chapter 3). This may be part of the reason why Zhou Enlai rarely protected, but rather helped to attack, Liu and those from Liu's mountaintop during the CR – Bo Yibo, for example.
63 See Liu's Shaoqi, *Communist China*, Cambridge, MA: Harvard University Press, 1962, p. 427.
64 Cf. Fang, *Jingji dashi ji*, pp. 203–5.
65 See Liao, *Xin zhongguo biannian shi*, pp. 138–9, 144–9.
66 See MacFarquhar, *The Origins*, 2:51–4.

The Two-Front Arrangement

Major personnel adjustments were made at the Fifth Plenum, held immediately after the Second Session of the Eighth PC. Lin Biao entered the PSC and was named a vice-chairman of the CCP. The regional leaders who had supported Mao – Tan Zhenlin, Ke Qingshi, and Li Jingquan – entered the Politburo. More important, however, was that this plenum marked the beginning of the dominance of the PB, led by Liu and Deng Xiaoping, in policy making. Li Fuchun and Li Xiannian, the two planners who were the Politburo members, joined in the CC Secretariat led by Deng,[67] an indication of the increase in Deng's power at Zhou's cost. This plenum also decided that Liu would succeed Mao as the PRC chairman at the Second NPC, which would open on April 18, 1959. This arrangement increased Liu's power, again at Zhou's cost, because it legitimized Liu's supervision over the State Council. Thus, the system of checks and balances at the first front was broken. Policies were no longer produced through the Politburo–State Council axis. Instead, the CC Secretariat, which had been mainly in charge of daily Party affairs, replaced the State Council as the key organ in policy making. Notably, in this new PSC-Secretariat axis, the newly expanded Politburo as a whole played a lesser role in the policy process. The Secretariat could step over the Politburo and report directly to the PSC, because all its key members were concurrently Politburo members.[68] As a result, the first front, which had been comanaged by Liu (in general charge), Zhou (administration and economy), Chen Yun (finance), and Deng (daily Party affairs), was now dominated by the PB led by Liu, Deng, and Liu's long-term associate Peng Zhen (the number 2 figure in the Secretariat).

Crestfallen and virtually powerless, Zhou submitted his resignation on

---

67 Ibid., 2:60–1.
68 Noticeably, Deng Xiaoping inherited the same mechanism in the post-Mao period when the State Council was not in his control. After Deng established his dominance in the Party, he restored the CC Secretariat, led by his man Hu Yaobang, at the Fifth Plenum of the Eleventh CC in February 1980 in order to diminish the role of the State Council, then still a domain of the "whateverists," in policy making. When Deng dominated both the Party and government in the mid-1980s, the Secretariat became an auxiliary organ in policy making. The influence of the Secretariat increased again after the Thirteenth PC in October 1987, at which the hardliners gained control of the State Council. Again, the Secretariat rose as the key organ in policy making at the Fourteenth PC in 1989, while the power of the enlarged Politburo declined (see Chapter 7).

June 9.[69] Although it was turned down at an elite meeting,[70] Zhou's voice would rarely be heard thereafter until the late 1960s, and the State Council would function merely as auxiliary organ to the Politburo-Secretariat axis in the policy process.[71]

Noticeably, only after the momentum of antiadventurism was halted by the joint forces of Mao and the local leaders was the GLF launched through the Party machine. As Mao admitted later, there would not have been the GLF without the Nanning Conference.[72] This phenomenon was significant. It demonstrates not only the difficulty Mao faced in reversing a policy adopted by the first-front leaders, but also the incompleteness of the transition of the Yan'an Round Table. Although the two-front arrangement put constraints on Mao's power, his ability to intervene in the policy process from the bottom up revealed that the faction-ridden nature in the distribution of power remained intact: a leader's command was based on his personal access to the subordinate levels of authority. Indeed, as my examination shows repeatedly, the vulnerability of relations between the central and local elite members was exploited frequently by Mao, and later by Deng, in order to maintain his dominance.

Launching the GLF through the Party machine also revealed the other crucial feature of leadership relations: political loyalty prevailed over policy preferences based on the objective evaluation of issues in decision making. But only after Mao violated the two-front arrangement, a formal policy-making process, could this feature play a full role in decision making. During the launching of the GLF, decision making was

69 Zhou believed that Mao intended to replace him with Ke Qingshi, the Shanghai Party secretary who played a leading role in opposing antiadventurism. See Wen Ze, "1958 nian Nanning huiyi shang de yichang jilie douzheng" (A fierce struggle at the 1958 Naning Conference), in Jiang, *Zhou Enlai de licheng*, 2:122.
70 Those who attended this meeting include Mao, Liu, Zhu De, Chen Yun, Lin Biao, Deng, Peng Zhen, Peng Dehuai, He Long, Luo Ronghuan, Chen Yi, Li Xiannian, Chen Boda, Ye Jianying, and Huang Kecheng. (Noticeably, among fifteen attendees, eight – Zhu, Lin, Peng Dehuai, He Luo, Chen Yi, Ye, and Huang – were military leaders.) See "*Zhou Enlai zhuan*," p. 112.
71 After the Second Session of the Eighth PC, major policies were made through the SPC-Secretariat-Politburo axis. All the important meetings and documents were held and issued in the name of the CC, instead of the State Council. Although Zhou would become active again in CCP politics after the GLF, he would not reobtain the position as a major policy maker until after the Party collapsed during the CR.
72 See Liao, *Xin zhongguo biannian shi*, p. 136.

The Two-Front Arrangement

based not so much on calculations of costs and gains as on the media "reports" of wildly exaggerated achievements, which were competitively cooked up by subordinate leaders.[73] While decisions of the leadership reflected its "anxiety to enhance China's capacity rapidly,"[74] production targets pledged by cadres at each level of authority were loyalty-oriented, in response to their leaders' desire on the one hand and in emulation of their peers on the other hand. The economic consequence was overlooked by the ambitious leaders and ignored by their subordinate cadres in their vying of pledge making.

Moreover, as the Party rallied behind Mao in the launching of the GLF, not only was Mao put in a position of accountability, but the Party's fate was also linked with the outcome of the GLF. Thus, the GLF was transformed from an economic policy into *a political line* that supported the legitimacy of the Party's rule as well as Mao's leadership. This change enabled Mao to resume his *absolute* authority in policy making, a position Mao once obtained at the Seventh PC in 1945 (see Chapter 3) but virtually lost at the Eighth PC in 1956.[75]

Thus, although a series of CC meetings was held from November 1958 to April 1959 to find a remedy for the looming problem caused by the GLF,[76] and a retreat was arranged at Chen Yun's suggestion,[77] little evidence has suggested that the CC leadership would give up the GLF when the Lushan Conference opened on July 2, 1959. Mao insisted in his opening speech that the GLF was fundamentally correct and that the problems were caused by the Party's inexperience in

---

73 Cf. *Jueyi*, p. 311.
74 Cf. Bo, *Huigu*, 1:485, 522, 528–9.
75 See MacFarquhar, *The Origins*, 1:99–109. 76 Ibid., 1:119–80.
77 As problems in the GLF emerged, a Central Financial and Economic Group was created in late 1958, and Chen was named its head. On May 11 and 15, 1959, Chen suggested to Mao in writing to cut the production targets. According to his suggestions, the SPC drafted a report in early June, in which all major targets were cut down. On June 13, Mao approved this report and issued an "Emergency Directive," a directive that virtually halted the GLF (see *Cankao*, 23:100–3). However, Chen's suggestions were concerned not so much with the GLF itself as with concrete problems during the GLF. According to Ding Shu, *Ren huo, "da yuejin" yu da jihuang* (Human Calamity, the "Great Leap Forward," and the Great Famine), Hong Kong: Nineties Monthly, 1991, p. 109, Chen told Xue Moqiao, then a top economic advisor to the CC, in early 1959 that the GLF was disastrous. Xue urged Chen to talk to Mao, but Chen said: "I cannot speak out. I still want to keep the Party membership I have had for over thirty years."

economic affairs on the one hand and insufficient regulations on the other hand.[78]

When Peng Dehuai criticized the GLF in a *private* letter to Mao on July 14, what he eventually challenged was the Party's line, rather than Mao's leadership as conventionally explained. It must be noticed that before his counterattack against Peng, Mao suggested on July 16 to rotate "the [leading] comrades from Beijing" in their participation in the submeetings of the regional groups – moving those who had been with the East China group to the South China group and so on.[79] Obviously, this was to break any possible coalitions between the central and local leaders. Then, without consulting the other leaders, Mao distributed Peng's letter with an added title: "Comrade Peng Dehuai's Letter of Opinion,"[80] although Peng had specifically marked on his letter: "To be opened by the Chairman himself."[81] Mao's message was clear: this was a letter to the Party – after all, it was the Party that had launched and organized the GLF – rather than Mao himself. In his speech on July 23, Mao warned explicitly: had the GLF been nothing but "errors," the Party "would surely be overthrown," so he "would go to the countryside ... and look for the Red Army."[82]

Peng was doomed, for although Mao could have been wrong, the Party had to be forever right. Indeed, Peng's official crime was not so much his attack on the GLF as his alleged "anti-Party activities."[83] Thus, it is not surprising that the Party leaders were more involved in the attack on Peng.[84] At the Enlarged CMC Conference, held from

---

78 See *Wansui*, 1:63–6; 2:278, 288, 294.
79 See *Wengao*, 8:355. It has been a routine that participants of a central conference are grouped, according to the areas (*diqu*) or systems (*xitong*) where they come from, for discussions. A central leader would usually participate in the group of a region or system where he originated. For example, Chen Yun was usually with the group of East China, and Deng Xiaoping, Southwest China.
80 Mao summoned Liu and Zhou to his residence at noon on July 16, showing them Peng's letter which he had already distributed. See Ma Lu, Pei Pu, and Ma Qinquan. *Peng Dehuai lushan qi huo* (The Fall of Peng Dehuai at Lushang), Hong Kong: Yalin Press, 1990, pp. 52–3.
81 Peng Dehuai, *Peng Dehuai zishu* (Autobiography of Peng Dehaui), Beijing: People's Press, 1981, p. 269, emphasized that he hoped to settle the difference with Mao privately.
82 *Wansui*, 2:300.   83 See *Cankao*, 23:119–21.
84 Cf MacFarquhar, *The Origins*, 2:229–33, 250.

The Two-Front Arrangement

Table 5.2. *High-Ranking Officers Implicated in Peng's Case*

Name	Rank/Position	Fate
Huang Kecheng[a]	Senior general/Chief of Staff	Purged
Teng Daiyuan[a]	General/Commander of the PLA Railway Corps	Demoted
Deng Hua[a]	General/Commander of Shenyang RMC	Demoted
Zhou Huan[a]	General/Commissar of Shenyang RMC	Demoted
Zhong Wei[a]	Lieutenant general/Chief of Staff, Beijing RMC	Purged
Hong Xuezhi[b]	General/Director of PLA General Logistic Department	Demoted
Fang Qiang[a]	Vice-admiral/Vice-commander, PLA Navy	Demoted
Wan Yi[b]	Lieutenant general/Director of PLA Equipment Department	Purged

Note: PLA = People's Liberation Army; RMC = Regional Military Command.
[a] Rising from Peng's mountaintop – the Third Red Army Group.
[b] Relationship developed during the Yan'an Period.

August 18 to September 12, 1959, to "eliminate Peng's influence in the army," Liu's attack on Peng was the most ferocious and, indeed, groundless.[85]

Not surprisingly, as I have explained in Chapter 2, Peng's fall was followed by a nationwide purge, especially in the military. Those high-ranking officers who affiliated with Peng were either purged or demoted (Table 5.2). Yet, more urgent for the Party leadership was to prove the correctness of the GLF so as to prove the Party's correctness. Thus,

---

85 See Ding, *Ren huo*, pp. 143–4; also Liao, *Xin zhongguo biannian shi*, pp. 161–2, 204. In his speech, Liu not only accused Peng of "having the foreign [i.e., Soviet] connections," but he also claimed that "for several decades Peng had sneakingly bad-mouthed the Chairman and the other CC leaders on the sly, behind the back of Chairman Mao and of the CC. He scheme to build up his personality cult." The other key speakers were Zhou Enlai, Lin Biao, and Zhu De. Zhou's speech, though biased (but not groundless), focused on "Peng's historical problems" – mainly differences between Mao and Peng during the revolution. Zhu's speech was in fact a self-criticism. And Lin's speech, though ferocious indeed, was well thought out, being not so much an attack on Peng as a praise of Mao. According to Ma, Pei, and Ma, *Peng Dehuai lushan qi huo*, pp. 114–15, Liu's speech "hurt Peng most."

"the leap was resumed, the problems were compounded, and disaster was the result."[86] As Deng admitted twenty-two years later, "Comrade Mao Zedong was carried away when we launched the GLF, but didn't the rest of us go along with him? Neither Comrade Liu Shaoqi nor Comrade Zhou Enlai nor I for that matter objected to it, and Comrade Chen Yun didn't say anything either ... it is the collective rather than a particular individual that bears the responsibility."[87] Deng told only half the truth. Mao and his comrades might have been carried away during the launching of the GLF. Resuming the leap after Peng's fall, however, was the choice they made in an effort to save the Party, although they might not have fully realized how costly it would be.

The Rise of the Party Bureaucrats

Mao veered "Right" at an enlarged Politburo conference, held in Shanghai in June 1960, as the famine began to spread across China.[88] Admitting that "there was an enormous blindness" in economic policy making, Mao demanded that the production targets be adjusted so as to "draw a lesson from the GLF and the People's Commune movement."[89] As a result, "retrenchment, not expansion, was in the air"[90] at the annual CC work conference at Beidaihe in July. On September 30, the CC dispatched the SPC's *Report on Adjusting the Targets in the 1961 Economic Plan*, in which the Eight-Character Principle – adjustment, consolidation, filling out, and improvement – was put forward as the new guideline for economic affairs. On November 3, the CC issued a 12-article *Urgent Directive* on the problems in the People's Commune movement.[91] These two documents virtually halted the GLF.

However, the retreat was not so much a self-conscious effort to redress the erroneous GLF as a hasty response to the looming disaster. That was why, at the Ninth Plenum in January 1961, the Party leadership still insisted that the GLF was correct but that problems were caused mainly by the lopsided development in which agriculture was over-

---

86 MacFarquhar, *The Origins*, 2:251.   87 *SWDXP*, 1975–82, p. 281.
88 See Fang, *Jingji dashi ji*, pp. 272–3.   89 Liao, *Xin zhongguo biannian shi*, pp. 173–4.
90 MacFarquhar, *The Origins*, 2:323.   91 See *Cankao*, 24:373–81.

The Two-Front Arrangement

looked. The new *fangzhen* (fundamental policy) adopted at this plenum was "taking agriculture as the foundation and going in for agriculture in a big way."[92]

Mao also insisted in his self-criticism at a CC work conference, held from May 21 to June 12, that insufficiency in "concrete working policies" had caused the loss of control during the GLF, because localities acted on their own according to their interests.[93] Thus, after the Ninth Plenum, the PB worked out numerous regulations and rules for various fields of work,[94] making 1961 the most productive year in regard to the working policies in CCP history.

Yet, the local cadres had difficulties adapting to this abrupt policy reversal. They also resisted to various degrees the new regulations and rules, which explicitly prohibited them from abusing their power as they used to do during the GLF.[95] Under such circumstances, a huge conference was convened from January 11 to February 7, 1962. Over seven thousand cadres at and above the county level attended this conference.

The 7,000-Cadre Conference was a victory for the Mao-Liu leadership in the sense that not only did it achieve a consensus on "carrying out resolutely the *fangzhen* of adjusting the national economy,"[96] but the Party elites also successfully convinced their followers that, as Liu emphasized in his marathon report, "*Our domestic situation is good. Work in every aspect of economic construction is advancing forward gradually and healthily along the correct track.... We should say that our experience in building socialism becomes richer instead of poorer through the work during the last four years [1958–61]. We are stronger instead of weaker.... The mistakes we made are not ones concerned with line. They are the problems in the implementation of the General Line.*[97]

---

92 Liao, *Xin zhongguo biannian shi*, p. 183.
93 See *SWLSQ*, 2:367n164.
94 The major working policies made in 1961 include *Sixty Articles on Agriculture, Seventy Articles on Industry, Forty Articles on Commerce, Thirty-five Articles on Handicraft Industry, Fourteen Articles on Science and Technology, Nine Articles on Nonagricultural Population and Rationing, Eighteen Articles on Forestry, Eight Articles on Literature and Art,* and *Sixty Articles on Higher Education.*
95 Sha Qing's "*Yixi dadiwan*" (The vague horizon), *Shiyue* (October), 5, 1988, pp. 17–44, provides a detailed account of the abuse of power by local cadres.
96 Liao, *Xin zhongguo biannian shi*, p. 193.
97 *SWLSQ*, 2:361, 422. Emphasis added.

Liu's report was in full accord with Mao's views.[98] Mao reemphasized Liu's major points, including these words just cited, in his own speech at the conference.[99] Seeing that the conference had unified the thinking of high-ranking cadres, Mao again withdrew to the second front, letting Liu take charge of the policy process at the first front.

But this conference also sowed the seeds of a rift among the CCP leaders. "Differences within the core of the CC leadership on the appraisal of the situation, the understanding of major causes of difficulties, and the evaluation of achievements and errors in the work were not addressed, and [these differences] developed even further."[100] This was clearly shown by Liu's report. Although Liu put forward a tentative Ten-Year Plan, a plan in which the targets for 1967 and even for 1972 were set, there was not even a word for any concrete plans for 1962, except the "ten tasks," which were nothing but empty slogans.[101]

Only after they began to work out concrete plans did the first-front leaders find out that the situation was worse than they expected. They were especially "shocked" by "an unexpectedly huge deficit of several billion yuan in the 1962 budget."[102] Liu convened a three-day Politburo conference on February 21. In his speech Chen Yun argued that the situation was so bad that it would take five years for the economy to recover to the level of 1957. Chen suggested dividing the next ten years into two five-year periods: the first would be solely for recovery, and only in the second period would further development be the goal.[103] Although Chen's negative but realistic appraisal of the situation was a far cry from the one Liu made two weeks earlier at the 7,000-Cadre Conference, Liu "firmly supported Chen." He authorized the dispatch of Chen's speech within the Party. After "consulting with the other CC leaders," Liu decided to restore the Central Financial and Economic Group (CFEG) with Chen as its head. Seeing that Chen was reluctant to head the CFEG,

---

98 See Tang Qun, Wu Xuesheng, and Yang Maorong, "*Tongyi sixiang renshi, zongjie jingyan jiaoxun – qi qian ren dahui wenxian zongshu*" (Unify the thinking, summarize the experience – a general description of the 7,000-Cadre Conference), *Dang de wenxian* (The Party's Historical Documents), 1991, 2:27–36.
99 *Wansui*, 2:410.
100 Liao, *Xin zhongguo biannian shi*, p. 194.
101 See *SWLSQ*, 2:369–72.
102 Huang Zeng, "*Liu Shaoqi yu lishi niandai chu de guomin jingji tiaozheng*" (Liu Shaoqi and the readjustment of the national economy in the early 1960s), *Yanjiu 1*, 1986, 1:4.
103 See *SWCY*, pp. 182–97.

The Two-Front Arrangement

an organ that would coordinate the policy process during the economic adjustment, Liu promised Chen: "I shall support you with all my strength and support you through to the end."[104]

Consequently, the entire policy approach was reversed abruptly from "continuous development through adjustment" to "a resolute retreat." Based on the consensus that "the recovery" was the goal for the next five years, the first-front leaders led by Liu made radical policy changes in February and March 1962:

1 Resolute centralization, especially in the financial system, in order to tame wild inflation and prevent "unauthorized" spending by localities.
2 Agricultural supremacy over all other economic goals in plan making.
3 Drastic cutting of industrial targets, especially the ICC and heavy industry.
4 Resolute reduction of the state-owned economy and downsizing of administration in order to further reduce nonagricultural population. (Over 18,000 state enterprises were shut down in 1962, reducing the total number of state-run enterprises to 53,000, less than half of the amount in 1958 [119,000].)
5 A sharp increase in the prices of all the consumer goods, except for daily necessities supplied through a rigid rationing system, to promote a rapid withdrawal of currency from circulation.[105]

However, a negative appraisal of the situation and the radical policy changes were made without consulting Mao. So Liu, Zhou, and Deng went to Wuhan, where Mao stayed, on March 14. The trio went there not just to "keep Mao informed."[106] The aim of this unprecedented trip was to demonstrate to Mao a united front formed by the first-front leaders on the policy they had adopted during Mao's absence and, moreover, against his ideas. As Liu admitted later in his self-criticism on October 23, 1966: "A more serious mistake [I made] was that I presided at a Politburo meeting from February 21 to 23, 1962, to discuss the 1962 budget.... Chairman Mao was not in Beijing at the time. So the other

---

104 Huang, "*Liu Shaoqi yu liushi niandai chu de guomin jingji tiaozheng*," p. 4. The former Central Finance and Economic Group headed by Chen Yun (see note 77) was dissolved after the 1959 Lushan Conference (see Liao, *Xin zhongguo biannian shi*, p. 195).
105 See Fang, *Jingji dashi ji*, pp. 313, 321, 327, 336, 338–41, for details of these policies.
106 Avery Goldstein, *From Bandwagon to Balance-of-Power Politics: Structural Constraints and Politics in China, 1949–1978*, Stanford: Stanford University Press, 1991, p. 149.

CC leaders and I went to him to report on some issues that had been discussed in Beijing.... *I knew afterward that Chairman fundamentally disagreed with our appraisal of the situation and some of our doings at that time.*"[107]

The word "afterward" is less than credible, for Liu knew exactly what was in Mao's mind at that time. First, Chen's negative evaluation of the situation virtually denounced the GLF – if it needed five years to recover the economy to the level of 1957, the GLF was nothing but a disaster. No wonder that Chen's speech, as Liu admitted in his self-criticism, "encouraged the appearance of various evil winds and noxious influences all over the country. Some people fundamentally denied the Three Red Banners. As a result, many of those who had been active in socialist construction during the preceding years [1958–61] felt crestfallen."[108] But Mao was the one who felt the most crestfallen.

Second, not only did the Mao-Liu leadership assert at the 7,000-Cadre Conference that the economy was "advancing forward gradually and healthily along the correct track," but they also held that "the broad masses can carry out socialist construction more effectively" once the Party worked out concrete policies.[109] Now Liu insisted that "the economy was severely damaged and dislocated in every aspect,"[110] and a radical policy change was made: from "continuous development through adjustment" to "resolute retreat," and from mass movement to strict centralization.[111] All this was done before the trio went to see Mao in Wuhan.

Moreover, the decision to restore the CFEG with Chen as its head was made without consulting Mao, though it was pending Mao's approval. This was the first time since the formation of the Yan'an Round Table that a decision concerning the distribution of power was made behind Mao's back. It is worth noticing that though Chen's speech on February 21 was dispatched on March 18, three days after the trio returned from Wuhan, the CFEG would not be formally restored until

---

107 *A Special Collection of Materials on Liu Shaoqi*, compiled by the Institute for the Study of Chinese Communist Problems, Taibei, 1970, p. 623 (hereafter *Materials on Liu Shaoqi*).
108 Ibid., p. 623. The Three Red Banners refer to the General Line of Building Socialism, the GLF, and the People's Commune Movement.
109 See *Wansui*, 2:416; *SWLSQ*, 2:361, 367–8.
110 Fang, *Jingji dashi ji*, p. 335.   111 See *SWCY*, pp. 182–97.

The Two-Front Arrangement

April 19.[112] Ironically, by then Chen had already quit again on the excuse of "illness," presumably because he sensed the risk of the job.[113]

The trio's awareness of Mao's unhappiness was best shown by their evident failure to inform Mao of Chen's talk on March 7 at the first meeting of the CFEG, an organ that had not yet been approved by Mao at that time. In this talk, Chen denounced the steel campaign, a drive in steel production Mao advocated as late as 1961.[114] Chen also advocated deep cuts in industry, which would "injure tendons and bones" (*shangjin ddonggu*).[115] Moreover, Chen's warning at the end of his talk sounded similar to what Peng Dehuai said at Lushan in 1959: "Comrades, it took several decades for us to succeed in our revolution. Under no circumstances can we allow the revolutionary achievement to be lost in our hands.... The key is to arrange the life of 600 million people well and to work earnestly for the people's interests."[116] Yet Mao would not hear these words until April 16, when Liu wrote to Mao:

> I asked Deng Liqun to collect Comrade Chen Yun's recent suggestions and talks on the economic work. Deng worked out an abstract [of Chen's talks]. *I have only read the abstract.* Now I submit it to Chairman. *Comrade Chen Yun also made some very important suggestions at a CFEG meeting on March 7.* They are worth reading. I have asked the General Office to distribute all these documents *among the members of the PSC, the Secretariat, and the CFEG.* Should these documents also be distributed to any other comrades? Please consider it after Chairman reads them. Then [I will] ask Comrade Chen Yun for his opinion.[117]

This note shows Liu's political skill as well as his awareness of differences between Mao and himself. Liu claimed that he had "only read the abstract" of Chen's talks that he submitted to Mao. Thus, in case Mao found something offensive in Chen's talks – Liu knew Mao would – Liu could clear himself on the excuse that he had only read the abstract made by Deng Liqun, Liu's secretary at the time. However, Liu told Mao that Chen's talks, including the one on March 7, had already been distributed

---

112 See Huang, "*Liu Shaoqi yu liushi niandai chu de jingji tiaozheng,*" p. 4.
113 See Liao, *Xin zhongguo biannian shi*, p. 197.
114 Ibid., p. 181.   115 *SWCY*, p. 198.   116 Ibid., p. 201.
117 Huang, "*Liu Shaoqi yu liushi niandai chu de jingji tiaozheng,*" p. 4.

235

among the first-front leaders, implying that a consensus on Chen's suggestions had been achieved among them. Thus, Mao, who was the last one to read these documents, had either to go along with or to oppose his comrades in Beijing.

Liu's opportunistic behavior in the policy process was not unexpected in a game played in the two-front arrangement. What seems surprising was that Liu acted first and reported to Mao afterward. Why did not Liu consult Mao on the problems, as Zhou did in April–May 1956, before he abruptly led the first-front leaders in turning right? Didn't Liu realize that this could cause severe damage to his relationship with Mao? As Mao recalled on February 3, 1967, referring to the eventual Mao-Liu split: "For many years the struggle in our Party has not been known to the public. We convened the 7,000-Cadre Conference in January 1962.... [I] saw the problem at that time."[118]

Liu's behavior seemed odd, but not irrational, given the situation he was facing in early 1962. Unlike the 1956–7 retreat, during which the planners and the PB comanaged the policy process, now the PB led by Liu were in charge of the policy process. Facing enormous difficulties in carrying out the policies adopted previously according to Mao's vision, Liu had to change the entire policy approach in order to fulfill his mission, namely, to rescue the CCP regime from collapse. Liu had only two choices to get Mao's approval: to consult Mao first on the necessity of such a policy change; or to make the change first and report to Mao afterward. Obviously, Mao would be reluctant to accept any policy changes against his vision. Moreover, a radical policy change based on a negative appraisal of the situation, even if with a low-profile, amounted to a denunciation of the GLF, and therefore of Mao's leadership during the GLF. Such a change was even harder for Mao to swallow given the 1959 Lushan Conference and its aftermath. But, still, Mao could choose to support the policy change, or oppose it, or show no opinion and keep his attitude ambiguous.

The game models in Appendix 5.1 explain why Liu acted first and reported to Mao afterward in the policy change in early 1962. Moreover, as the models show, it was necessary for Liu not just to act first and report afterward but, more importantly, to keep Mao *uninformed* of the policy change until it was completed. Had Mao known that the first-

118 *Wansui*, 2:663–4.

The Two-Front Arrangement

front leaders would make a policy change against his vision, to oppose it openly beforehand would serve his best interests. That was why Mao felt so bitter about what Liu did in early 1962, because Liu, with the first-front leaders' support, enforced a fait accompli on Mao against his own will.

Yet, how was it that none among the first-front leaders informed Mao of the happenings in Beijing before the trio's Wuhan trip on March 14? Undoubtedly, this was a factor Liu had to take into account prior to any policy changes behind Mao's back. Although any first-front leaders could have reported to Mao, Deng Xiaoping should be held accountable, not just because of his close personal ties with Mao (see Chapter 3), but because, as the general secretary, Deng's principal task was to keep Mao informed (see Chapter 4). If Liu chose to consult Mao before the policy change, whether Deng reported to Mao or not would make little difference; but when Liu chose to make the change first and report to Mao afterward, Deng's choice between reporting to Mao and keeping quiet would be a factor in the shaping of Mao and Liu's preferences. (See Appendix 5.2.)

Adding the Deng factor to the game played between Mao and Liu, however, has little effect on the outcome. Liu's rational choice was still to make the change first and report to Mao afterward; and Mao's, still to keep his attitude ambiguous, if and *only if* Liu moved first. The result of the game also explains why to go along with Liu, rather than report to Mao, served Deng's best interests. Deng's behavior during the policy change in early 1962 was a typical example of how common interests overrode personal loyalty in decision making in the two-front arrangement. No wonder Mao felt betrayed. His talk at a Politburo meeting in October 1966 revealed his bitterness toward Deng in this case: "Deng Xiaoping is deaf [to my words]. He sits far from me whenever [we] have a meeting. *He has never reported to me on his work in the past six years since 1959....* [The way] Deng treated me is to stay at a respectful distance."[119]

Bitter though he was, Mao could not afford to stand up to the first-front leaders when the economy was at the verge of collapse. As the games in the appendixes predict, Mao maintained an ambiguous attitude when the trio "made a special trip to Wuhan to report to him"; he neither

---

119 Ibid., 2:661–2 (emphasis added).

clearly supported their decisions nor "expressed any disagreement."[120] Seeing that Mao's attitude was unclear, Liu convened a CC conference from May 7 to 11. In his speech, Liu stressed that "the situation was no good at all." He pointed out specifically: "At present, the principal danger is to underestimate the difficulties.... One who denies the obvious difficulties... [or] underestimates the difficulties in order to console himself is not a Marxist at all."[121] If these words soured Mao, a more devastating result for Mao was that after the first-front leaders' approach – "to adjust the national economy by a big margin" – was formally adopted,[122] Mao lost his dominance in decision making. As *Jueyi* points out, although "Mao's Left-leaning ideas [and its influence] in the political and cultural spheres were in fact further escalated," his vision "failed to dominate the overall situation" during the 1962–5 period.[123]

MAO VERSUS THE PARTY STATE

The Tenth Plenum, a Compromise between Mao and the Party Bureaucrats

After Mao again withdrew to the second front in early 1962, the PB led by Liu and Deng dominated the policy process. When differences emerged between Mao and the PB, the latter had to stick together to fulfill their mission of rescuing the regime from collapse. Their success not only increased their power but also strengthened their de facto coalition. Moreover, while the radical policy change was carried out, regulations and rules made in 1961 to strengthen the central authority were also implemented. All this not only greatly increased the CC's control[124] but also *bureaucratized* the Party's center authority. A Party state emerged, from which Mao was procedurally an outsider.

The extent to which Mao was kept out of the policy process was best shown by his own complaint on August 9, 1962:

120 Liao, *Xin zhongguo biannian shi*, p. 195.
121 See *SWLSQ*, 2:444–6, 447–8.   122 See Liao, *Xin zhongguo biannian shi*, pp. 202–3.
123 *Jueyi*, pp. 312–3; also see Deng Linqun, "*Xuexi 'guanyu jianguo yilai dang de ruogan lishi wenti de jueyi' de wenti he huida*" (Questions and answers for the study of *The Resolution on Several Questions of Our Party's History since the Establishment of the PRC*), *Zhuanji*, 2:143–4.
124 Cf. Liao, *Xin zhongguo biannian shi*, p. 189.

The Two-Front Arrangement

The financial and economic ministries and commissions never report [to me]. They do not ask for [my] instructions beforehand, nor do they report to [me] afterward. [They are] independent kingdoms.... We know the happenings in foreign countries, [we] even know what Kennedy wants to do. But who knows what various ministries in Beijing are doing? I have no idea what is going on in the major economic departments. If I don't know, how can I make decisions? This problem also exists in various provinces.[125]

In order to seize the initiative in policy making, Mao stepped into the first front again in August 1962 after he was sure that the situation had turned for the better due to a good wheat harvest.[126] Mao appeared extraordinarily active at the annual CC work conference, held at Beidaihe from July 23 to September 23, 1962. Mao took the floor six times and interrupted the other leaders repeatedly.[127] He totally ignored the predetermined agenda: the economy, economic plans, and agriculture. All his talks focused on politics, and specifically on classes, class struggle, and contradictions.[128] Insisting that "the class struggle is still the major contradiction" in China, Mao further advanced a new theory: differences in the Party were the expression of class struggle in the society.[129] This theory was expressed pithily in the *Communique of the Tenth Plenum of the Eighth CC*, held in September 1962: "Class struggle is bound to find its expression in our Party.... At the time when we wage struggles against class enemies at home and abroad, we must be promptly vigilant of and firmly opposed to various ideological tendencies of opportunism in our Party."[130]

---

125 *Wansui*, 2:429.
126 Ibid., p. 599, recalled on December 28, 1964: "During April and May [1962], none of the civilian comrades said that the situation was good.... In June, when I went to Jinan, several comrades told me that the situation was very good. Why was there such a change within just a month? The wheat was not harvested in May, but it was harvested in June." Also cf. Fang, *Jingji dashi ji*, p. 344.
127 Wei Weijun, *Dangde bajie shizhong quanhui* (The Tenth Plenum of the Eighth PC), *Zhonggong dangshi zhuanti jiangyi* (Teaching Materials on Specific Issues in the CCP History), Beijing: CC Party School Press, 1988, pp. 148–9; see also Liao, *Xin zhongguo biannian shi*, p. 205.
128 See *Wansui*, 2:423–9.   129 Ibid., pp. 430–4.
130 *People's Daily*, September 29, 1962.

Although this theory would eventually be elaborated to legitimate the all-out assault to the Party state during the CR, its immediate purpose at the time was to justify Mao's attack on the PB's pessimistic appraisal of the situation. Mao blamed such an appraisal for the emergence of *heian feng* (trend of darkness) which, as Mao insisted, denied the Party's achievements and echoed "the anti-China chorus" sung by the class enemies at home and abroad.[131] Mao implied that the first-front leaders' negative appraisal of the situation benefited the enemy or, so much the worse, even expressed the enemy's interests within the Party. Mao leveled his attack on two specific policies adopted by the PB:

1 *Baochan daohu*, to divide the land to each household with the fixed output quotas.
2 *Zhenbie pingfan*, to reexamine the [mishandled] cases and rehabilitate [those who were wrongly purged].

The first policy was initially adopted by the Anhui Party authorities on March 6, 1961. In his letter to Mao on March 20, Anhui Party Secretary Zeng Xisheng explained that this policy would not undermine the People's Commune, but would instead give the peasants incentives to increase production: the more they produced, the more surplus they could keep. "In July, Zeng reported to Mao directly on the results of the policy implementation, and received Mao's approval."[132] This policy was again advocated by Deng Zihui, director of the Rural Work Department, in early 1962.[133] The other leaders, including Liu, Deng, and Chen Yun, also endorsed the policy.[134] Liu told a group of cadres on July 18 that *baochan daohu* was "fully practicable."[135] Moreover, Mao himself also seemed supportive of the policy as late as July. Tao Zhu, first secretary of the CCP South China Bureau, convened a forum

---

131 See Wei, *Dangde bajie shizhong quanhui*, pp. 150–1.
132 See Liao, *Xin zhongguo biannian shi*, pp. 184–5. But Mao changed his mind in October and Zeng was criticized for this matter at the 7,000-Cadre Conference.
133 Deng advocated *baochan daohu* at the February Politburo Conference and at the May work conference. He submitted a report on *baochan daohu* on May 24. In his debate with Ke Qingshi, who was against this policy, Deng Zihui quoted a Anhui peasant's words: "No matter if it is a white cat or a yellow cat, the one that catches the mouse is a good cat." See *"Deng Zihui zhuan"* (A Biography of Deng Zihui), RWZ (1982), 7:370–4.
134 See Wei, *Dangde bajie shizhong quanhui*, pp. 151–2; also *Materials on Liu Shaoqi*, p. 623.
135 *SWLSQ*, 2:463.

The Two-Front Arrangement

on the rural economy in July. Mao was so delighted by the report of the forum that he recommended it to the whole Party on July 22. Mao stated that "all suggestions and analysis made by this forum were in full accord with Marxism" – *baochan daohu* was a key policy this forum suggested.[136]

The second policy of *zhenbie pingfan* was also within Mao's knowledge. The decision to reexamine the cases in the 1959 Anti-Right-Deviationist Campaign was made as early as May 1961 at a CC work conference, held at Beijing from May to June 1961. Deng Xiaoping, who was in charge of the work, elaborated on this policy at the 7,000-Cadre Conference. On April 27, the CC issued *The Circular on Speeding-up Reexamination of the Cases of Party Members and Cadres*. Deng made a report on this policy at the CC Work Conference in May. By the time of the Tenth Plenum, over 3.65 million wrongly purged cadres had been rehabilitated.[137]

Thus, it was evident that both policies were made and implemented with Mao's agreement, at least his tacit consent. Yet Mao turned against these two policies in August,[138] blaming them for having provoked *dangan feng* (the tendency to return to individual farming) and *fan'an feng* (the trend of reversing verdicts), which would "lead to the capitalist restoration." As my analysis shows, this was the strategy Mao used often to turn the situation around – to use the policy issues as means to legitimate his attack on his perceived opponents.

The PB caved in. The two policies of *baochan daohu* and *zhenbie pingfan* were revoked. Deng Zihui became a scapegoat for the policy of *baochan daohu*. His Rural Work Department was dissolved on November 9, and he was dismissed from all the posts he had held.[139] Peng Dehuai was picked out as the symbol of *fan'an feng* largely because of an 8,000-word letter he wrote to the CC on June 16.[140] Vice-Premier Xi Zhongxun, Jia Tuofu, a deputy director of the State Economic Commission, and "over three hundred cadres and officers" who rose from the

---

136 See Fang, *Jingji dashi ji*, pp. 342–3.
137 See Liao, *Xin zhongguo biannian shi*, pp. 201–2.
138 Ibid., p. 206, see also *Wansui*, 2:423–8, 435.   139 See "*Deng zihui zhuan*," pp. 379–80.
140 Peng wrote this letter to refute Liu's groundless attack. In his report at the 7,000-Cadre Conference Liu said: "For a long time, Peng Dehuai had a small faction within the Party. He was a key member of the Gao-Rao anti-Party clique. They all had international [the Soviet] background . . . and engaged in anti-Party activities behind the CC's back." See Liao, *Xin zhongguo Biannian shi*, pp. 204–5.

Northern Shaanxi base area were purged because of their alleged attempt to "reverse the Gao Gang verdict."[141]

The abrupt policy changes at the Tenth Plenum and the consequent purges were inconsistent with the overall policy orientation: a cautious economic retreat aimed at the recovery and a moderate political profile in order to create a harmonious atmosphere.[142] The CCP official accounts attribute this policy inconsistency to the further development of Mao's "Left-deviationist errors" on the one hand, and the first-front leaders' persistence in "the correct *fangzhen* [the fundamental policy] of adjusting the economy" on the other.[143] Some scholars also hold that this policy inconsistency reflected policy differences among the CCP leaders.[144]

The "policy-difference" interpretation is subject to argument. As I have examined earlier, Mao had at least tacitly agreed to the policies he condemned in August. Moreover, Mao did not challenge the PB on their general policy approach, although he was unhappy with their entire economic policy. His criticism focused on political issues, and his attack on *baochan daohu* and *zhenbie pingfan* was about their potential political impact – the alleged *dangan feng* and *fan'an feng* – instead of their objective outcomes: the increase of grain production under *baochan*

141 Xi Zhongxun, *Xiaoshuo* "'*Liu Zhidan*' *yuanan*" (The unjust verdict on the novel *Liu Zhidan*), *Zhongguo qingnian* (Chinese Youth), 4 (April 1979), pp. 6–8. This purge originated in the Novel *Liu Zhidan*, written by Liu's sister-in-law Li Jiantong in 1959. The novel described how Liu and his comrades developed the northern Shaanxi base area in the early 1930s. Xi, Jia, and other senior cadres who participated in this struggle made positive comments in this novel. Though Gao Gang, a major leader of the northern Shaanxi base area, was not mentioned in this novel, his shadow could be seen in the activities of Jia Yan, a fictional hero in the story. Yan Hongyan, then the Yunnan Party secretary who had a faction opposed to the dominant faction led by Liu, Gao, and Xi in the northern Shaanxi base area, tipped Kang Sheng that Jia Yan incarnated Gao. Kang therefore charged that the novel's intent was to "reverse the Gao Gang verdict." Mao, who never read the novel, used Kang's accusation as an example of "class struggle in the Party." As a result, all those who rose from Liu and Gao's "donkey faction" (see Chapter 3) were purged. Also see Zhong, *Kang sheng pingzhuan* (A Critical Biography of Kang Sheng), Beijing: Red Flag Press, 1982, pp. 155–61.
142 See Liu Qingwen, *Liushi niandai chu zhengzhi guanxi tiaozheng shuxi* (Description and analysis of the adjustment of political relations in the early 1960s), *Dang de wenxian* (The Party's Historical Documents), 1995, 1:43–8.
143 *Jueyi*, pp. 312–13.
144 See Harding, "Chinese state in crisis," p. 113 and n2.

The Two-Front Arrangement

daohu, and the rehabilitation of millions of cadres through *zhenbie pingfan*.

A close examination of the choices available to Mao and the PB in their interactions can shed light on our understanding of this policy inconsistency. Either because Mao disliked the policies the PB adopted at the first front, or because he was afraid that his dominance in policy making was eroding, Mao had three choices in dealing with the PB:

1 *An overall attack.* Mao could repeat what he did against the planners in early 1958, that is, denounce the PB's policy approach and revoke the policies they had adopted.
2 *A limited attack.* Instead of denouncing the PB's policy approach. Mao could attack them in a specific area where he held an advantageous position. The aim was not so much to reject the PB's policies as to seize the initiative, and therefore resume his dominance, in policy making.
3 *Staying put at the second front.*

Correspondingly, the PB who managed the policy process at the first front also had three choices:

1 *Persistence.* The PB could persist in their policy choices despite Mao's unhappiness and even attack.
2 *Retreat.* In order to assure Mao of their loyalty, the PB could try to execute Mao's policy initiatives. Yet they would not surrender the control of the policy process; nor would they give up their general policy approach.
3 *Surrender.* The PB could abandon their policies and take a new approach in full accord with whatever Mao envisioned.

Obviously, an overall attack would have been Mao's first choice in order to seize back his dominance in policy making, given Mao's unhappiness with the policies the PB adopted and, moreover, his increasing suspicion that his command was being taken away. But this could lead to an overall confrontation with the PB, who might have to persist in their policy approach in order to rescue the regime from collapse – after all, they had adopted this approach with full knowledge of Mao's unhappiness. Moreover, unlike the case of antiadventurism in early 1958 in which Mao rallied the PB in his attack on the planners, this time it would be hard for Mao to find any substantial support among the first-front leaders. Not only had the PB dominated the first front since the planners, who used to be a balancing force against the PB, were disintegrated in 1958, but the mission to rescue the regime had also created among them strong common interests, which overrode their different factional backgrounds, and even their loyalty to Mao – Deng, for example. Lastly, even if Mao could have prevailed in an overall attack, he was neither qualified nor prepared to run the economy.

Thus, the rational choice for Mao was to initiate a limited attack on the PB. Unlike his attack on the planners in early 1958, what Mao actually did from August to September 1962 was to initiate an offensive against the PB in the political area where, as I have explained in previous chapters, Mao always held an advantageous position due to the ideological legitimacy of his command and his direct control of the military. In fact, Mao himself stressed at the Tenth Plenum that "class struggles must not interfere with the [economic] work."[145] This indicated that his aim was not to reject the PB's general policy but to regain his dominance in policy making.

Indeed, it would be unimaginable for the PB to confront Mao in the political area, not necessarily because of their loyalty to Mao, but because of the lack of legitimacy – Mao's command was guaranteed essentially by the Party's adoption of MZT as its guiding principle (see Chapter 3). Seeing that Mao did not intend to roll back their general policy approach, the PB made a retreat in the political area in order to dodge a confrontation with Mao. They stopped talking about the "bad situation" (the good-situation propaganda reappeared in a *People's Daily* editorial on the National Day, October 1), Mao's theory on the internal danger of revisionism was written in *Communique of the Tenth Plenum*, and the two policies of *baochan daohu* and *zhenbie pingfan* were revoked. In return, the PB maintained their control of the routine policy process at the first front, and "the overall work was still carried out according to their preadopted plans."[146]

Thus, what appeared to be a policy dispute among the CCP leaders around the Tenth Plenum of the Eighth CC was actually underlain by Mao's effort to seize back his lost dominance in policy making. The consequent policy inconsistency reflected not so much policy differences in the CCP leadership as a compromise between Mao and the PB in a struggle for power. This formed a sharp contrast with the

---

145 *Wansui*, 2:435.
146 Liao, *Xin zhongguo biannian shi*, p. 206.

The Two-Front Arrangement

ordeal the planners suffered in early 1958: Mao not only rejected their entire policy approach but also deprived them of power in policy making.

This compromise was well demonstrated in the personnel changes made at the Tenth Plenum. Kang Sheng and Luo Ruiqing, the PLA's new chief of staff, replaced Huang Kecheng and Tan Zheng in the Secretariat.[147] The entrance of Kang and Luo into the Secretariat seemed to have increased Mao's influence in decision making. But Kang was assigned to the ideological area, where his influence was limited because Lu Dingyi, a Liu confidant who directed the Propaganda Department, also entered the Secretariat. Luo Ruiqing was in charge of defense affairs, which would bring him into a conflict with Lin Biao (see Chapter 6). Tan Zhenlin, a firm GLF supporter, was appointed director of the Office of Agriculture and Forestry.[148] But daily agricultural affairs were handled by his deputy director Liao Luyan, who rose from Liu's mountaintop.

Thus, the victory Mao scored at the Tenth Plenum brought little change to leadership relations in decision making. With respect to the structure of policy making, the two-front arrangement remained intact, and the PB still managed the policy process at the first front. Mao's newly advanced theory – "the danger of revisionism exists in the Party" – had little effect on the policy process. It was in fact downplayed by the first-front leaders, whose attitude toward Mao's new theory was best reflected by Liu's words at the Plenum: "It is enough to use a few people to cope with the antirevisionism struggle within the Party. But the whole Party must not be involved in and disturbed by this struggle so much that [it will] hinder our work."[149] Liu further emphasized in his speech at the Fourth Enlarged Conference of the Chinese Social Science Academy in January 1963: "At present, the principal task for our theoretical workers was to criticize revisionism abroad. So long as we carry on the struggle

---

147 Huang Kecheng was purged together with Peng Dehuai. Tan Zheng, director of the PLA Political Department, would not dance to Lin Biao's baton after Lin became the defense minister in 1959. With Mao's consent, Lin launched an attack on Tan at the enlarged CMC conference in September 1960. Tan was demoted to deputy director of the department (see Chapter 6). See Huang Yao, Li Zhijing, and Yang Guoqing, *Luo shuai de zuihou shiwu nian* (The Last Fifteen Years of Marshal Luo Ronghuan), Beijing: People's Press, 1987, pp. 104–6.
148 Liao, *Xin zhongguo biannian shi*, p. 208.
149 *"Liu Shaoqi zhuan,"* p. 115.

against the modern revisionism [abroad] through to the end, . . . it would be difficult for revisionism to appear in China.[150]

More importantly, the compromise at the Tenth Plenum set up a pattern of interactions between Mao and the PB during the 1962–6 period: Mao had to keep a high political profile in order to keep his initiative in policy making, while the PB would try to cope with Mao and integrate whatever he initiated into the policy process. The stability of leadership relations was maintained through constant compromises, yet the essential dilemma of the two-front arrangement remained unsolved and would develop further. The PB, who were responsible for the policy outcomes at the first front, had to maintain a stable policy environment, either in the execution of Mao's injunctions or in the implementation of the policies they adopted. However, the more effectively they ran the policy process, the more influential they appeared in policy making, and therefore the more frequent was Mao's intervention in the policy process in order to secure his dominance, and, in return, the greater the effort of the PB to keep the situation under control. As my examination will show, this vicious circle eventually brought an overall crisis to the Yan'an Round Table.

Socialist Education Campaign: Mao's Struggle to Maintain His Command

Mao toured eleven provinces in early 1963 to gather materials to show the existence of a revisionist tendency in the Party.[151] The aim was, as it was prior to the attack on antiadventurism in 1957, to rally support from the localities for his new initiatives. Immediately after the tour, Mao recommended two reports from the Party committees in Hunan and Hebei at a CC work conference in February 11–28, 1963. Both reports asserted that there was a "dark counterrevolutionary trend" in China, especially in the rural areas. They argued that the corruptions among the CCP cadres were "vivid examples of the expression of class struggle in the

---

150 *Materials on Liu Shaoqi*, p. 542.
151 See Wei Weijun, "*Shehui zhuyi jiaoyu yundong*" (On the Socialist Education Campaign), *Zhonggong dangshi zhuanti jiangyi* (Teaching Materials on Special Topics in CCP History), Beijing: CCP Party School Press, 1988, p. 160; also *Wansui*, 2:441.

The Two-Front Arrangement

Party."[152] Based on these two reports, Mao urged the Party to wage a socialist education *movement* in the rural areas and a new Five Anti *movement* – antigraft and antiembezzlement, antiextravagance and antiwaste, antispeculation and antiprofiteering, antidecentralization, and antibureaucracy – in the cities in order to "uproot revisionism" in China.[153]

Again, the PB dutifully executed Mao's injunction. On March 1, the CC issued a directive on the launching of a Five Anti Campaign to "prevent the corrosive influence of capitalism and revisionism." However, the directive pointed out explicitly that the ultimate goal was "to ensure the full accomplishment of the national economic plan," so the campaign had to "be carried out step by step under the Party's leadership."[154] Thus, the campaign was not launched as a nationwide movement, as Mao wanted. Rather, while the Five Anti Campaign "was carried out gradually in a few cities," some local Party authorities began to "train cadres on how to conduct the Socialist Education Campaign (SEC) experimentally at selected places."[155]

But a Party-controlled campaign, which would strengthen the PB's dominance, was not what Mao had in mind. Mao wanted a *mass movement* in which the leader's vision could be transmitted directly to the broad masses. Taking advantage of Liu's absence from Beijing between April 12 and May 16,[156] Mao "summoned some Politburo members and secretaries of the six CCP bureaus to Hangzhou, and convened a *small-scale meeting*" during May 2–12.[157] Mao emphasized: "This *revolutionary movement* [i.e., the SEC] is the biggest struggle since the [1951] land reform. There has not been such a large-scale class struggle inside or

---

152 See *Zhongguo gongchan dang lishi dashi ji* (Chronology of the CCP History), compiled by CCP Party History Research Center, Beijing: People's Press, 1991, p. 259.
153 Liao, *Xin zhongguo biannian shi*, p. 221.
154 *Cankao*, 24:189–96.
155 See Wei, *Shehui zhuyi jiaoyu yundong*, pp. 159–60.
156 Liu was visiting Indonesia, Burma, Cambodia, and Vietnam.
157 Liao, *Xin zhongguo biannian shi*, p. 214 (emphasis added). According to Zheng Qian and Han Gang, *Mao Zedong zhilu: wannian suiyue* (Mao Zedong's Road: The Later Years), 7th ed., Beijing: Chinese Youth Press, 1996, p. 246, Peng Zhen, Ke Qingshi, Tao Zhu, Li Jingquan, Jiang Hua, and some provincial party leaders attended the meeting. Song Rengqiong, Li Xuefeng, Liu Lantao, Hu Yaobang, and Chen Boda attended the meeting "a few days later." Zhou Enlai and Deng Xiaoping came to the meeting in its final days.

outside our Party in the past ten years. This [struggle] should be [carried out] *from within the Party to outside the Party, from the top to the bottom, and from cadres to masses.*"[158]

This meeting produced a ten-article *Resolution* on the SEC, known as the *Former Ten Articles*. It asserted that a large-scale "class struggle appeared in Chinese society," the class enemy had "tried by all means to usurp the leadership," and the power in some places had "already been in their hands." The problems were so serious that it was "necessary to launch a large-scale mass movement," in which "revolutionary masses would be reorganized" in order to "beat back the class enemy's savage onslaught." Otherwise, the document warned, "a nationwide capitalist restoration will inevitably appear, our Marxist-Leninist Party will become a revisionist and fascist party, and all China will change color."[159]

Although the *Former Ten Articles* was produced at an informal "small-scale meeting," the Party state responded to it promptly. On May 20, four days after Liu returned to Beijing, the CC dispatched the *Former Ten Articles*, praising it as a "programmatic document" for the SEC. Simultaneously, the CC also issued a circular emphasizing unmistakably that the SEC was "a campaign led and organized by the Party." This circular required all local Party authorities to "work out plans, conduct experiments, and exercise leadership in carrying out [the SEC] step by step, place after place at different times."[160]

In order to ensure the Party's control, the PB drew up a ten-article *Stipulation for Some Concrete Policies of the SEC*, known as the *Latter Ten Articles*, at the annual CC work conference in September 5–27. Although it affirmed the theme of the *Former Ten Articles* that the campaign involved "essentially a class struggle," the *Latter Ten Articles* pointed out that most problems in the SEC belonged to the category of "contradictions among the people." Thus, "the campaign must rely on the [Party] organizations and cadres at the grass-root levels ... and be integrated in the economic production."[161] The *Latter Ten Articles*, dispatched on November 14, replaced the *Former Ten Articles* as the policy for the SEC.

Not surprisingly, the PB's effort to rein in the SEC intensified Mao's suspicion that his command was being nibbled away. This further con-

---
158 *Wansui*, 2:437 (emphasis added).
159 *Cankao*, 24:212.   160 Ibid., pp. 203–4.   161 Ibid., pp. 241–2.

The Two-Front Arrangement

vinced him that there were "revisionists" in the Party. Mao expressed his concern repeatedly during his meetings with the delegations of Communist Party members from Albania, Japan, and Indonesia in February and April 1964. Mao even asserted that these "revisionists" in the CCP included "some CC members, CC secretaries, and vice-premiers." He accused them of carrying out "revisionist programs ... at home and abroad" in order to "sabotage our socialist system." Mao even asked the foreign communists to "help Chinese Marxists oppose Chinese revisionists" in case "a Khrushchev appears in China."[162] This was the first time that Mao alleged the existence of "Khrushchev-type revisionists" in the Party leadership.

Seeing that his words drew little attention from the PB,[163] Mao brought his concern to the CC work conference, which was held in May 15–June 17. More significant was that Mao raised the issue of successor at this conference: Mao urged the leaders at all levels to "pay special attention to the training of revolutionary successors" in order "to prevent the leadership from falling into the revisionists' hands."[164] Mao's words sent a clear warning to Liu, who had long been seen as Mao's successor. Mao even asked Liu provocatively: "What should be done if a Khrushchev appears in China?" Liu replied: "A province can claim its independence, it can rebel."[165]

Alarmed and probably panicky, Liu tried his best to please Mao. Liu became unusually radical at this conference. He asserted that "one-third of authorities at the primary level were no longer in our hands" and suggested that the SEC should "focus on the struggle to seize back power."[166]

---

162 See Liao, *Xin zhongguo biannian shi*, pp. 226–7.
163 According to the normal procedure, Mao's talk to the foreign communists would be passed to Zhou Enlai via the Foreign Ministry, and to Kang Sheng via the CCP Central Foreign Relations Department. But it was unclear whether the two relayed the words to the Politburo and the Secretariat. I asked Liao Gailong how the Party leaders responded to the words of Mao that he quotes in his book. He sent me to a source familiar with the issue. This source told me that "someone" did ask Zhou whether Mao's talks with "the foreign comrades" should be passed to the other Party leaders. Zhou replied that this should be decided by the Chairman himself. It is unclear whether Kang Sheng relayed the words to the others. But it would be surprising if Zhou and Kang would not pay serious attention to Mao's allegation that there were "revisionists" in the Politburo and the Secretariat.
164 See *Wansui*, 2:501–3.
165 Quoted from Liao, *Xin zhongguo biannian shi*, p. 229.
166 See Wei, *Shehui zhuyi jiaoyu yundong*, p. 164.

Liu's effort turned a virtual anticorruption campaign into a large-scale purge of local cadres who were accused of being representatives of the class enemy. Liu's radical attitude was to assure Mao of his loyalty, although such an attitude was sharply inconsistent with his cautious approach in the economic sphere. But Liu could do so as long as his Party state had control of the policy process.

Indeed, as the radical policy adopted at the May conference began to provoke nationwide chaos in the SEC, Mao had no choice but to "recommend Liu as the commander [of the SEC], with Deng and Peng to assist Liu," in early August.[167] Liu convened a CC conference in late August to revise the *Latter Ten Articles* in the light of the *Taoyuan Experiences*, a report on how Mme Liu (Wang Guangmei) had conducted the SEC at Taoyuan Village in Hebei from November 1963 to May 1964.[168] Based on Mme Liu's report, it was required in the *Revised Latter Ten Articles* that work teams be sent to the rural areas to lead the SEC on behalf of the Party, under the assumption that local cadres were too corrupt to be trustworthy. Thousands of work teams went to the rural areas to "lead the struggle to seize power" after the *Revised Latter Ten Articles* was dispatched on September 18.[169] A CC circular, issued on November 13, bestowed so much power on a work team that it could not only purge any cadres at the county level or below, but also arrest, detain, and sentence anyone who was perceived as a class enemy.[170] The *Revised Latter Ten Articles* brought the SEC to its extremes, involving a nationwide purge in which "many cadres at the grass-roots levels suffered unfair treatment."[171] Yet, as thousands of work teams took over the local authorities, the control of the Party state was strengthened.

But Liu's extraordinary effort to fulfill Mao's intention failed to please Mao. Instead, it made Mao more vigilant of Liu's increasing power.

---

167 Liao, *Xin zhongguo biannian shi*, p. 234.
168 See *Cankao*, 24:472–84; also Jia "*siqing,*" *zhen fubi* (False "Four Clean-ups," True Restoration), *PsD*, September 5, 1967. It is known that Liu authorized the dispatch of *Taoyuan Experiences* in the CC's name on September 1, 1964. Yet Liao, *Xin zhongguo biannian shi*, p. 234, says: "Mao approved Liu's report that Chen Boda suggested [to dispatch *Taoyuan Experiences*] on August 27." This seems odd because Chen had direct access to Mao.
169 See *Cankao*, 24:508–9.   170 See ibid., 24:509–10.
171 *Jueyi*, p. 313. These words in *Jueyi*, according to Deng Liqun, *Xuexi "Jueyi" de wenti he huida*, pp. 83–4, embodied a criticism of Liu, who was more radical than Mao in the SEC and caused more damage to the Party.

The Two-Front Arrangement

Seeing that the SEC was carried out all over the country soon after the *Revised Latter Ten Articles* was issued, Mao said: "I have talked [about the SEC] for two years, [but] no one ever listened to [me]. Yet, once Comrade [Liu] Shaoqi paid special attention, the whole country is moving."[172] Mao's words sounded not so much a praise to Liu as a complaint. Evidently, it was by then that Mao's attitude toward the PB underwent a fundamental change. This change was well seen in his comment on December 12 on Chen Zhengren's report about the SEC at the Luoyang Tractor Factory: "The class of bureaucrats is a class sharply opposed to the working class and poor and lower-middle peasants.... *These leaders who take the capitalist road* have become, or are becoming, the capitalists who suck workers' blood. How can they sufficiently understand the necessity of socialist revolution? They are the targets of our struggle and targets of revolution. The SEC can never depend on them."[173]

This was the first time that Mao referred to the bureaucrats as *a class*, a class that took the capitalist road and was therefore opposed to the working class. Mao made similar comments on the other two documents on the same day.[174] But this was a class that grew out of the CCP administration, which was supposed to represent the proletariat.

Obviously uneasy with Mao's inference, Liu convened a CC work conference on December 15 to discuss the problems in the SEC. Mao insisted that the SEC involved the struggle between the two classes, so the contradictions in the campaign were "between the enemy and ourselves."[175] But Liu confronted Mao in no time. He interrupted Mao and said: "Various contradictions interweave with one another. There are contradictions between the four cleanups and four not-cleanups, and interactions of contradictions within and outside the Party. It is proper [for us] to solve these contradictions as they are."[176] This is not surpris-

---

172 Ibid., p. 84.
173 *Wansui*, 3:31 (emphasis added). Chen Zhengren was then a deputy minister of Agricultural Machinery.
174 See Zheng and Han, *Mao Zedong zhilu: wannian suiyue*, pp. 264–5.
175 Liao, *Xin zhongguo biannian shi*, p. 238.
176 Quoted from Jin Chunming, *"Wenhua da geming" shigao* (A Draft of History of the "Cultural Revolution"), Chengdu: Sichuan People's Press, 1995, p. 254. But Jin says that the event happened at a CC working conference in January 1965, which is obviously inaccurate. The conference was held in December 15–28, 1964. See *Zhongguo gongchan dang lishi dashi ji*, p. 269. Unless specifically noted, my analysis of the information between Mao and Liu at this conference and in its aftermath is based on my interviews with a few well-informed sources.

ing because, as the leader in charge of daily affairs at the first front, Liu had to deal with various "contradictions as they are" instead of treating them all as the ones "between the enemy and ourselves." Liu's words reflected his stance that different problems in the SEC should be dealt with according to different policies.[177] That was why, as Liu insisted, the SEC should be called the Campaign of Four Cleanups (political, economic, organizational, and ideological).[178]

What is surprising, and unprecedented indeed, was that instead of exchanging their differences privately, Liu confronted Mao at a formal conference. At the time when Mao knew better than anyone else that he had fumbled badly on the GLF – the purge of Peng Dehuai made it even worse – and that he had played little part in the remarkable recovery after the GLF, Liu's interruption, not to endorse but to "*correct*" (*jiuzheng*) what Mao had just said, was read by Mao as a subtle but significant challenge. To make it worse, Deng Xiaoping visited Mao after the meeting. Given that Mao was not feeling well, Deng suggested to Mao that he should not attend the next day's meeting because, as Deng explained, what would be discussed were routine affairs for the ongoing First Session of the Third NPC. It would be overstretching to assume that this was a coordinated move by Liu and Deng. But this seems to be exactly what Mao believed at the time. The next day, Mao appeared at the meeting with the PRC Constitution and the CCP Constitution. Throwing the two pamphlets at the table, Mao announced that, as a citizen and Party member, he was entitled by these two constitutions to participate in and to talk at the meeting. He then lashed out: "one [i.e., Deng] tries to block me from attending the meeting, the other [i.e., Liu] would not allow me to talk."[179]

Seeing that Mao was upset, Xie Fuzhi and Luo Ruiqing suggested

---

177 Deng Liqun, *Xuexi "Jueyi" de wenti he huida*, p. 85.
178 *Siqing* was originally raised by the Party authority of Baoding in Hebei in its report to the CC (see note 152). It refers to "cleaning up [*qing*] accounts, warehouse stocks, work points, and properties," so as to expose the corruption of cadres at the grassroots level. Wang Guangmei gave *siqing* new interpretations in her *Taoyuan Experiences*, because she believed that "the SEC involved the interactions of all contradictions in the fields of politics, economy, organization, and ideology." See *Cankao*, 24:484.
179 Jin, *"Wenhua da geming" shigao*, p. 254. Li Zhishui, *The Private Life of Chairman Mao*, New York: Random House, 1994, pp. 416–17, also described the event. But like Jin, he misremembers the time of the meeting as in January 1965.

The Two-Front Arrangement

after the meeting to hold a birthday party for Mao on his coming birthday, December 26. Mao accepted their suggestion, which was unprecedented because Mao was opposed to birthday celebrations. Mao set up three dinner tables at his residence and invited three groups of people to the party: the top leaders like Liu, Zhou, Deng, and Peng Zhen sat at one table; the ministry-level leaders like Tao Zhu, Xie Fuzhi, Luo Ruiqing, Li Fuchun, and Chen Boda sat at another table; and the "model workers" like Qian Xuesen, Xing Yanzi, Chen Yonggui, and Dong Jiageng sat at a third. Mao chose, as a political statement, to sit with the model workers. Jiang Qing served as the hostess. When all the guests had barely arrived, Mao started his oblique accusations. Mao claimed that "some big-time leaders [*da guan*] forgot their origins [*wangben*]" and "they think 'investigation' [*diaocha*] is out of date." Mao warned explicitly: "Don't consider that only your own opinion is right because you are in authority. Consider yourself as always correct. But there is no one who considers himself wrong. Why do we hold meetings? It is [because] we have different opinions. Why should we have meetings if [we all hold] the same opinion?"

While the model workers were confused,[180] the others knew who was Mao's target: Liu Shaoqi, not only because Liu had confronted Mao at the previous meeting, but also because Liu, in praise of his wife Wang Guangmei's experience of *dundian* (stay in) at Taoyuan, said at the August Conference that "investigation [*diaocha*] is out-of-date. Now [one] has to stay in the place [*dundian*] [to learn first-hand information]."

As Li Fuchun entered the room, Mao raised his voice: "There is also an independent kingdom in Beijing. That is the SPC [led by Li Fuchun]. They never reported to me." Although the CC leaders were confused this time because Li belonged to Mao's personal clique (see Chapters 3 and 4), they soon recognized Mao's real target: Deng Xiaoping and his Secretariat, since Mao was looking at Deng while saying the above words. But Liu and Deng remained quiet the whole evening.

Mao repeated most of what he said at the meeting next day. When Chen Boda argued in Mao's favor that "there are factions within our Party," Mao said: "There are at least two factions in our Party. One is the

---

180 Chen Yonggui, for example, told Ji Dengkui that only years later did he realize that "the Chairman was criticizing Liu Shaoqi," although he could see Mao's unhappiness at the time.

Factionalism in Chinese Communist Politics

socialist faction, the other is the capitalist faction."[181] Mao made his stand clear on December 28, the last day of the conference. He emphasized: "The name of the campaign is the SEC. It is not a Four Cleanups campaign, nor an educational campaign of the so-called interactions of [various] contradictions."[182]

However, Liu still made things go his way in the seventeen-article *Summary of Discussion* of the conference. In this summary the SEC was named the Four Cleanups Campaign, arguing that "the nature of the SEC involved interactions of various contradictions in all fields of work."[183] Mao was furious when he saw this summary, which was distributed on December 30, the last working day of 1964. On January 3, the first working day of 1965, Mao convened a CC meeting. At this meeting Mao "criticized Liu Shaoqi. He [i.e., Mao] criticized the formulations [*tifa*] that the nature of the campaign involved the interactions of contradictions ... within and outside the Party, between the enemy and ourselves, and among the people.... He also claimed that there were the two 'independent kingdoms' in Beijing [referring to the Secretariat led by Deng, and the SPC led by Li Fuchun]." Under Mao's supervision, important revisions were made on the *Summary of Discussion*, and more articles were added. On January 14, the final draft came out as the *Twenty-three Articles*.[184]

The *Twenty-three Articles* redressed the Leftist policy of the *Latter Ten Articles*, denounced the practice of work teams, especially their treatment of local cadres. More significantly, it announced that "the focus of the SEC is to punish those in power who take the capitalist road," and stressed that "the broad revolutionary cadres and masses," rather than the work teams, were "the main forces in the SEC."[185] Thus, the grassroot cadres were no longer the targets of the SEC, but "the spearhead of struggle was directed at the leading bodies and the leaders at various levels of authority, including the CC."[186]

About this time Mao made up his mind to get rid of Liu, although Liu made a self-criticism at a Politburo meeting after Zhou Enlai and He Long talked to him about his "unrespectable interruption of the

181 *Wansui*, 2:598. 182 Ibid., p. 599. 183 See *Cankao*, 25:267–8.
184 Liao, *Xin zhongguo biannian shi*, p. 239.
185 See *Cankao*, 24:559–60, 561.
186 See Wei, *Shehui zhuyi jiaoyu yundong*, p. 167.

The Two-Front Arrangement

Chairman." Mao "saw Liu Shaoqi's problem not as one about whether [Liu] showed respect to him, but as a major problem of principle."[187] Mao admitted on October 25, 1966, at a CC work conference: "I put too much trust upon the other people [i.e., Liu, Deng, and Peng]. It was at the time when the *Twenty-three Articles* was made that this problem [i.e., Liu being against Mao] raised my vigilance."[188] Zhou Enlai also revealed on August 9, 1967, that "The most serious [criticism Mao made against Liu] was the one during the drafting of the *Twenty-three Articles*.... By that time, Mao was totally disappointed in Liu."[189] On December 18, 1970, Edgar Snow asked Mao when he decided to topple Liu, Mao replied: "In January 1965, the *Twenty-three Articles* was issued. Among the twenty-three articles, there is one that says that the target of the Four Cleanups was to punish the people in authority in our Party who were taking the capitalist road. Liu Shaoqi opposed it right on the spot."[190]

It is surprising, however, that Mao's severe criticisms of Liu drew little response in the Party. As a result, Mao complained to some provincial leaders on January 13, 1965: "Since last October, I have talked about what you local [leaders] would do if Beijing goes in for revisionism.... I always feel that there will be problems. After I said that, I have heard little response when I traveled through many areas from Tianjin to Nanjing."[191] This was unimaginable indeed when compared with the Gao-Rao Affair in 1954, the attack on "antiadventurism" in 1958, and Peng Dehuai's fall in 1959. In these cases, Gao Gang, Zhou Enlai, and Peng became the targets of attack as soon as Mao made his stand clear.

That Mao's attack on Liu failed to draw attention in the Party showed the extent of control exerted by the Party state. What mattered ultimately in the policy process was not so much Mao's ideas but whether

---

187 Jin, *"Wenhua da geming" shigao*, p. 254. But Jin does not give the names of "a few senior comrades who approached Liu Shaoqi after the meeting; [they] criticized him that he should not have interrupted [Mao] and did not show enough respect to the Chairman." Although the sources I interviewed disagree on the exact time when "a few senior comrades" talked to Liu – late December 1964 or early January 1965 – all of them said that Zhou Enlai and He Long approached Liu. While Zhou's involvement is not surprising, He's presence in the "private talk with Liu" was revealing. As the one who was then in charge of daily military affairs, He's involvement must have reminded Liu of the military support for Mao.
188 *Wansui*, 2:658.   189 *Materials on Liu Shaoqi*, p. 553.
190 Liao, *Xin zhongguo biannian shi*, p. 239.   191 Ibid., p. 247.

255

the PB would execute them. Although Mao initiated the SEC and struggled to maintain his initiative during the campaign, the SEC failed to strengthen Mao's position in decision making because he was unable to seize back the control of the policy process. An essential source of Mao's increasing frustration and suspicion of the PB led by Liu was the fact that the PB would take over whatever policies Mao initiated and then make things go their way through manipulation of the policy process, with Mao barely able to do anything about it.

CONCLUSION: THE OVERALL CRISIS OF THE YAN'AN ROUND TABLE

The Yan'an Round Table was in an overall crisis in 1965. First of all, Mao felt that his command was threatened, and this was clearly shown by Mao's reluctance to convene the Ninth PC, which, according to the CCP Constitution, should have been convened in 1961. As the economy recovered to prosperity in 1964–5, there was an increasing pressure to convene the Ninth PC.[192] But this was not what Mao wanted at the time when the PB dominated in the policy process,[193] for the major tasks of a PC were to produce a new leadership and adopt new policies. Kang Sheng explained on January 21, 1968, why the Ninth PC could not be held before the CR: "Think about it, comrades. Had we held the Ninth PC [before the CR], those cuckolds and sons of bitches, such as Liu Shaoqi, Peng [Zhen], Luo [Ruiqing], Lu [Dingyi], and Yang [Shangkun], would all have been promoted.... It would have been a disaster had we held the Ninth PC [before the CR]."[194] Zhang Chunqiao explained more explicitly on January 15, 1969: "Like the Liu Shaoqi problem, how terrible it was! Had the Ninth PC been held before the movement [i.e., the CR], it is very likely that *Liu would have been the chairman, Chairman Mao would have been the honorary chairman....* According to the former Party Constitution, the Ninth PC should have been held a long

---

192 After the Third NPC in December 1964, the expectation for the opening of the Ninth PC was so high that, according to Source C, some local Party authorities were preparing the lists of delegates.
193 A former secretary of Mao told me in June 1993: "everyone expected the Ninth PC be held in 1964–5. But none dared to bring it to Mao because he was obviously reluctant even to mention this topic."
194 Quoted from Ding, *Ren Huo*, p. 272.

The Two-Front Arrangement

time ago, and Liu Shaoqi would have been the chairman, Deng Xiaoping and Luo Ruiqing would all have been promoted. It was a trump card for the counterrevolutionary revisionists."[195] Indeed, the *CCP Constitution* adopted at the Eighth PC, had a specific article that stipulated that the CCP could have "an honorary chairman" if necessary.[196] Mao explained on September 22, 1961, that this article was added to the CCP Constitution on the expectation that he would be the "honorary chairman" when Liu succeeded during Mao's lifetime.[197] This could have happened at the Ninth PC had it been convened in 1965 when the PB led by Liu not only dominated the policy process but were also credited for the remarkable economic recovery. No wonder Mao was reluctant to convene even a CC plenum, which had not been held since 1962, for it could have been proposed and passed at the plenum to convene the Ninth PC.

The threat Mao felt was unprecedented indeed: it was not caused just by the increase in power of any individual leaders. Rather, it was rooted in a well-organized Party state, which was nibbling away Mao's dominance. True, Mao's repeated interventions in the policy process on the one hand and the opportunistic behavior of the PB on the other resulted in constant policy inconsistency during the 1962–5 period: a pragmatic economic approach versus increasingly radical political policies. But the trade-off was that the PB dodged confrontations with Mao. Meanwhile, they stonewalled Mao's effort to seize back his dominance in the policy process. The control of the Party state was so formidable that although Mao had kept the initiative on the political front since August 1962, the PB was capable of taking over Mao's initiatives and making their way by manipulating the policy process. Thus, Mao felt he was being manipulated rather than manipulating, not necessarily because his comrades were opposed to him – in fact, they tried their best to please him – but because all manner of control, including reports, information, directives, and the like, had to be filtered through the Party state before flowing to and from Mao.

Further, the growth of the Party state was destroying the very foundation of the Yan'an Round Table – namely, *personal loyalty*, on which

---

195 Ibid., pp. 271–2 (emphasis added).
196 *The Documents of the 8th National Congress of the CCP*, compiled by the CC General Office, Beijing: People's Press, 1957, p. 834.
197 Ding, *Ren Huo*, pp. 273–4.

Mao's command had been established and the stability of relationships among its members had been maintained. It would be groundless indeed to argue that any members of the Yan'an Round Table ever betrayed Mao. On the contrary, they tried their best to maintain their loyalty to Mao – that was why Zhou could swallow the pain and humiliation of being deprived of power in 1958, Peng could endure such an enormous injustice in 1959, and Liu could subject his policy choices repeatedly to Mao's ideas during the 1962–5 period. The *foundation* of the Yan'an Round Table was endangered essentially because the personal loyalty forged during the revolution was overridden by common interests in policy making, and particularly when these interests were not in harmony with Mao's vision, given varied responsibilities, hence varied goals and preferences, among the CCP leaders in the policy process. It was common interests that made Liu cooperate with Zhou in 1956, although the two had a sour relationship during the revolution (see Chapter 3). It was also common interests that alienated Deng from his long-term patron, Mao, during the rise of the Party state. These common interests emerged through, and were consolidated by, the *structure* of the policy-making process: the two-front arrangement.

Finally, as policy making was increasingly institutionalized under the control of the Party state, Mao's intervention caused more instability and inconsistency in the policy process. Unable to prevent Mao's intervention, the PB had to extend their control to every aspect of the policy process so as to increase their ability to absorb Mao's interventions. As a result, not only the domain of the Party state kept expanding, but the power of the PB also increased and, more significantly, became *institutionalized*. But the institutionalization of political power was incompatible with Mao's command, which had personalized Mao's authority in decision making.

Policy differences could hardly change Mao from a "charismatic and benign leader" into a Machiavellian ruler. What made Mao increasingly suspicious of, and alienated from, the PB was the fear that he was losing his command because of his inability to fuse his leadership within the Party state, on the one hand, and the PB's difficulty in maintaining their absolute loyalty to Mao at the expense of their interests, on the other hand. As a result, the Yan'an Round Table was no longer a cohesive entity. As the Party state kept looming large, Mao tried desperately to prevent it from becoming an "independent kingdom."

The Two-Front Arrangement

Yet, the Party state Mao faced was like a huge ball filled with air: the harder Mao hit it, the faster and higher it bounced back, and the more threatening it appeared to Mao. Unable to subdue it, Mao had to blow it up in his effort to maintain his command. But the cost would be beyond Mao's imagination.

Appendix 5.1

The Game between Mao and Liu in Early 1962

After the 7,000-Cadre Conference, the first-front leaders led by Liu had to make a radical policy change in order to fulfill their mission – to rescue the CCP regime from collapse. Liu had only two choices to get Mao's approval: l1, to consult Mao first on the necessity of policy change; or l2, to make the change first and report to Mao afterward. Meanwhile, Mao could choose m1, to support the policy change; m2, to oppose the policy change; or m3, to keep his attitude ambiguous. There could be the following outcomes O and corresponding payoffs for Liu and Mao, u(L, M), depending on their choices, s(L, M) (see Table 5.A1).

Liu has a *dominant strategy* l1 in this noncooperative game (see Figure 5.A1) because:

$$u.l1(2, -2, 2) \geq u.l2(2, -3, 2).$$

Yet, the domination of l1 is very weak because l1 slightly dominates l2 only in case Liu loses:

$$u.l1(-2) > u.l2(-3).$$

Otherwise, l1 is indifferent as l2 for Liu because

$$\text{if } u.l1(2, 2) = u.l2(2, 2), l1 \: I \: l2.$$

Mao first choice m2 is also his *best-response strategy* if and *only if* Liu chooses l1 because

$$u.m2(2) > u.m3(0) > u.m1(-2).$$

Thus, Liu is the loser, but Mao is the winner because the payoffs for Liu and Mao in the vector of strategies s(l1, m2) are:

$$u(-2, 2).$$

The Two-Front Arrangement

Table 5.A1. *Outcome, Strategy, and Payoffs in the Mao-Liu Game*

O1 s(l1, m1) u(2, −2)	Liu is the winner. Mao is the loser. By agreeing to Liu's idea of change, Mao in fact accepts the responsibility for the failure of old policies adopted according to his vision.
O2 s(l1, m2) u(−2, 2)	Mao objects to Liu's idea of change, and his dominance continues. Liu is the loser. He is trapped in a deadly dilemma after Mao's objection: if he insists on the policy change, he has to challenge Mao and could end up being purged; if he caves in, he can hardly fulfill his mission.
O3 s(l1, m3) u(2, 0)	Liu is the winner. But Mao neither gains nor loses by keeping an ambiguous attitude when Liu consults him. As the supreme leader, Mao has the last say on the final policy outcomes: he can claim credit if the new policy is successful; if it fails, Mao will be in a better position to counterattack.
O4 s(l2, m1) u(2, −1)	Liu is the winner. Although Liu makes the policy change without consulting Mao, Mao still supports Liu, which means that Mao virtually accepts the responsibility for the failure of the old policy made according to his vision. Yet Mao can be partly compensated by the success of the new policy.
O5 s(l2, m2) u(−3, −2)	Both Mao and Liu suffer, but Liu suffers more. Mao rejects the policy change Liu has already made. Although the dominance of his vision continues, Mao is now solely responsible for the "continuous leap forward" which is bound to fail. Moreover, his objection to the new policy destabilizes leadership relations as well as policy making. Liu can hardly prevail in a head-to-head confrontation with Mao, given the legitimacy of Mao's command. Liu will be purged.
O6 s(l2, m3) u(2, 0)	Liu is the winner: he changes the policy without consulting Mao beforehand. Mao neither gains nor loses by keeping his attitude ambiguous. As the supreme leader, Mao has the last say on the final policy outcomes: he can claim credit if the new policy is successful; if it fails, Mao will be in a better position to counterattack.

Factionalism in Chinese Communist Politics

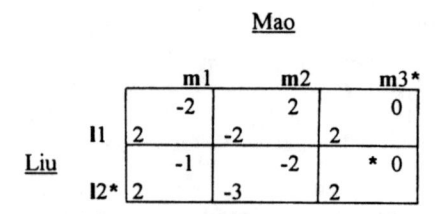

```
              Mao
         m1      m2      m3*
       ┌─────┬─────┬─────┐
       │ -2  │  2  │  0  │
    l1 │  2  │ -2  │  2  │
Liu    ├─────┼─────┼─────┤
       │ -1  │ -2  │ * 0 │
    l2*│  2  │ -3  │  2  │
       └─────┴─────┴─────┘
```

Figure 5.A1. Normal form of the game between Mao and Liu

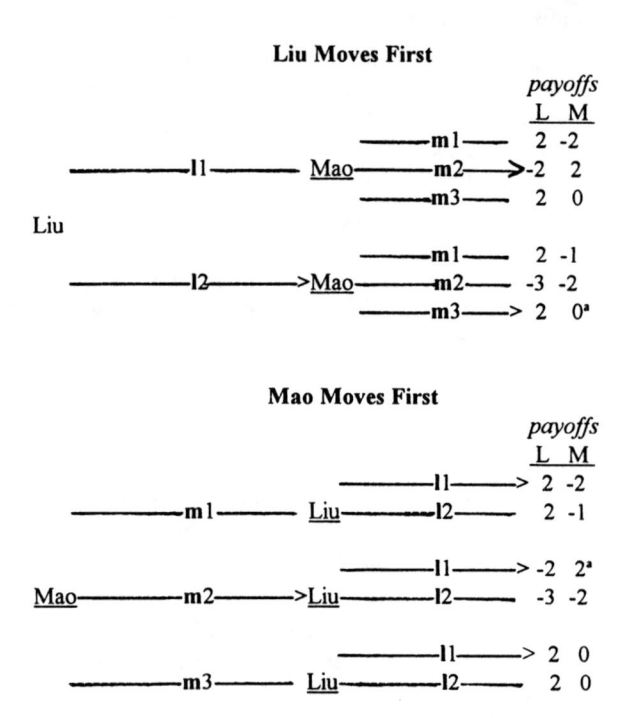

Liu Moves First

```
                                              payoffs
                                               L   M
                           ────m1────       2  -2
       ────l1──── Mao ────m2────►-2  2
                           ────m3────       2   0
Liu
                           ────m1────       2  -1
       ────l2────►Mao ────m2────      -3  -2
                           ────m3────► 2   0ᵃ
```

Mao Moves First

```
                                              payoffs
                                               L   M
                           ────l1────► 2  -2
       ────m1──── Liu ────l2────       2  -1

                           ────l1────►-2   2ᵃ
Mao────m2────►Liu ────l2────      -3  -2

                           ────l1────► 2   0
       ────m3──── Liu ────l2────       2   0
```

ᵃ Pure-strategy (Nash) equilibrium.

Figure 5.A2. Extensive form of the game between Mao and Liu (solid arrow = best-response strategy)

The Two-Front Arrangement

However, Mao's *best-response strategy* is **m3*** if and *only if* Liu chooses **l2***, because

$$\mathbf{u.m3^*}(0) > \mathbf{u.m1}(-1) > \mathbf{u.m2}(-2).$$

Therefore, it is rational for Liu to abandon **l1** but choose his *best-response strategy* **l2***. In this case, Mao is forced to choose his *best-response strategy* **m3***. As a result, the vector* of strategies s(**l2***, **m3***) is the *pure-strategy equilibrium* of the game, where the payoffs for Liu and Mao are: **u**(2, 0). Liu is the winner because he achieves his desired goal – to make the policy change without heading into a direct confrontation with Mao. Virtually, what Liu did was to enforce a fait accompli on Mao, for **m3*** was Mao's rational choice if and only if Liu chose **l2***.

However, the above result can be yielded *only if Liu moves first* (Figure 5.A2). Otherwise, if *Mao moves first*, **m2** is the *best-response strategy* for Mao. Given that **l1** dominates **l2** if and *only if* Mao chooses **m2** because **u.l1**(−2) > **u.l2**(−3), the vector of strategies s(**l1**, **m2**) is the *pure-strategy (Nash) equilibrium* of the game, and **u**(−2, 2) are the payoffs for Liu and Mao. Thus, Mao is the winner and Liu, the loser. Indeed, if Mao moves first and chooses his *best-response strategy* **m2** – to oppose the policy change – Liu will be the loser no matter what choice he makes because **u**(−2, −3) are all the possible payoffs for Liu.

The different outcomes between Liu-moves-first and Mao-moves-first reveal the importance of the sequence of players' moves in a *noncooperative game of perfect information*.[198] This explains the necessity for Liu not just to act first and report afterward but, more importantly, to keep Mao *uninformed* of the policy change until it was completed.

---

198 See Peter Ordeshook, *Game Theory and Political Theory*, Cambridge: Cambridge University Press, 1986, pp. 108–9, 120–1.

Appendix 5.2

The Game with the Deng Factor in Early 1962

During the policy change in early 1962, whether Deng reported to Mao or not would have made little difference had Liu consulted Mao before the policy change. But when Liu chose l2, that is, to make the change first and report to Mao afterward, Deng's choice between **d1**, to report to Mao, and **d2**, to go along with Liu in policy change, was a factor in the shaping of Mao's and Liu's preferences. Adding the Deng factor to the game in Appendix 5.1, there could be the following outcomes, **O**, and corresponding payoffs for Liu, Mao, and Deng **u**(L, D, M), depending on their choices **s**(L, D, M) (Table 5.A2).

The result of the game, yielded by either its normal or its extensive forms (Figure 5.A3), shows that d2# is Deng's *dominant strategy* because

$$\mathbf{u}.d2\#(1, -1, 1) > \mathbf{u}.d1(-2, -2, -2).$$

The Two-Front Arrangement

Table 5.A2. *Outcome, Strategy, and Payoffs with the Deng Factor*

O1 s(l2, d1, m1) u(2, −2, −2)	Liu is the winner. The policy change is made even though Deng has reported to Mao on Liu. Both Deng and Mao are losers. Deng sells himself cheaply. Mao is blamed for the failure of the old policy made according to his vision.
O2 s(l2, d1, m2) u(−2, −1, 2)	Liu is the loser. Mao rejects the policy change after Deng's report. Thus, Liu was trapped: if he insists on the change, he has to challenge Mao and can end up being purged; yet if he caves in, he can hardly fulfill his mission. Deng loses more than he gains. Liu and the first-front leaders will shun him and, moreover, he will be more responsible for the "continuous leap forward." Mao is the winner. The dominance of his vision continues in policy making.
O3 s(l2, d1, m3) u(2, −2, 0)	The same as O1 except that Mao keeps an ambiguous attitude toward the policy change. As the supreme leader, he has the last say on final policy outcomes.
O4 s(l2, d2, m1) u(2, 1, −1)	Liu is the winner, Deng also gains by sharing the credit, and Mao suffers. By supporting the policy change, Mao virtually accepts the responsibility for the failure of the old policy. But Mao is compensated by the success of the new policy.
O5 s(l2, d2, m2) u(−3, −1, −2)	All three suffer. Mao rejects Liu's policy change. Not only does this abrupt objection destabilize leadership relations and the policy process, but it also makes Mao solely responsible for the continuous leap, which is bound to fail. Deng loses Mao's trust because he fails to report to Mao. Liu can hardly prevail in a direct confrontation with Mao. He will be purged.
O6 s(l2, d3, m3) u(2, 1, 0)	Same as O4 except that Mao maintains an ambiguous attitude toward the policy change. As the supreme leader, he has the last say on the final policy outcomes.

Factionalism in Chinese Communist Politics

Normal Form of the Game

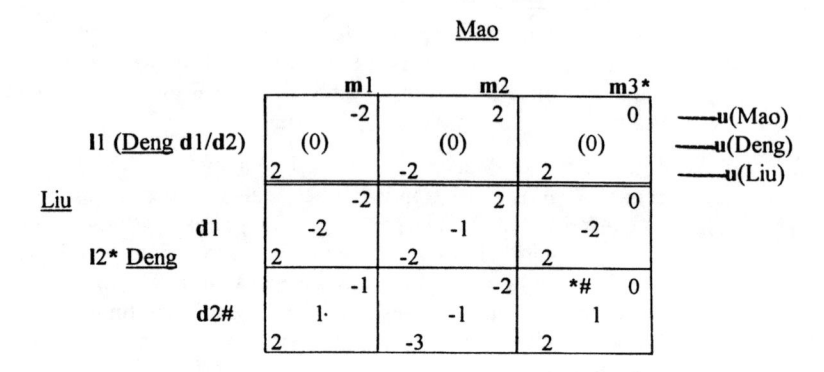

Mao

		m1	m2	m3*	
l1 (Deng d1/d2)		-2 (0) 2	2 (0) -2	0 (0) 2	——u(Mao) ——u(Deng) ——u(Liu)
l2* Deng	d1	-2 -2 2	2 -1 -2	0 -2 2	
	d2#	-1 1· 2	-2 -1 -3	*# 1 2	

(Liu labels rows at left; "0" in m3* row marked with * and #)

Extensive Form of the Game

```
                                                        payoffs
                                                        L, D, M
         ——l1—— (The Deng factor is non-existent.)
                              ——m1——  2 -2 -2
            ——d1—— Mao ——m2——> -2 -1  2
                              ——m3——  2 -2  0
Liu——l2——>Deng
                              ——m1——  2  1 -1
            ══d2══>Mao ——m2—— -3 -1 -2
                              ——m3—> 2  1  0ᵃ
```

ᵃ Pure-strategy (Nash) equilibrium.

Figure 5.A3. The game between Mao and Liu with the Deng factor (solid arrow = best-response strategy; double arrow = Deng's dominant strategy)

6

The Collapse of the Yan'an Round Table and the Unleashing of Factionalism

How could Mao do away with the Party state? Why did Mao initiate his assault in the cultural field? Most Western analysis and the CCP official accounts blame Mao's absolute power and his personality cult, and see as random its initial unfolding in the cultural field.[1] Yet my examination in Chapter 5 shows that Mao's authority was at its lowest ebb in 1965. By then, the Party bureaucrats (PB) had controlled the policy process, and the remarkable recovery from the GLF under their management had increased their reputation and influence. Their control was so extensive that Mao was virtually incapable of doing anything in Beijing without their cooperation.[2]

Mao had to find the *legitimacy* – that is, an ideological justification – and a *force* to break the Party state. He obtained the legitimacy by provoking a confrontation with the PB in the cultural field, which is why the Cultural Revolution preluded an all-out assault on the Party establishment; and he organized his forces outside the Party state, which is why his personality cult was created in order to impel and control a broad but poorly organized mass movement.[3] Thus, Mao's personality cult and his absolute power were not so much the cause as the result of the CR.

---

1 See *Jueyi*, pp. 314–18; Wang Ruoshui, "*Mao Zedong yu wehua da geming*" (Mao Zedong and the Great Cultural Revolution), *Tan-so* (Quest), no. 111 (March 1993), pp. 10–14, and no. 112 (April 1993), pp. 60–6; Lee Hong Yung, *The Politics of the Chinese Cultural Revolution*, Berkeley: University of California Press, 1978; and Jin Chunming, "*Wenhua da geming" shigao* (A Draft of History of the "Cultural Revolution"), Chengdu: Sichuan People's Press, 1995, pp. 130–4.
2 See *Wansui*, 2:641, 658, 674.
3 Mao implied that he encouraged the creating of his personality cult at the eve of the CR in order to "stimulate the masses to dismantle the anti-Mao Party bureaucrats." See Edgar Snow, *The Long Revolution*, New York: Random House, 1972, p. 169.

Factionalism in Chinese Communist Politics

Vicious factional struggles broke out immediately after the first wave of purges, not just because such massive purges created a huge power vacuum, but essentially because the collapse of the Party state removed the *organizational* shackle of factionalism embedded in the CCP political system (see Chapter 2). Mao's effort to stabilize the situation resulted in a prisoners' dilemma between Mao and his successor, Lin Biao. Although Lin was victimized, his fall cut off Mao's access to the military system. Mao's command was thus in great jeopardy because the two systems that his leadership was based on, the Party and military, had been either paralyzed or disconnected. Desperately, Mao brought back Deng Xiaoping, who had access to the mountaintops in both the Party and military. Yet Deng's effective work led to "reversing the verdict [*fanan*] of the CR." Furthermore, the struggle with the Gang of Four forced Deng into Zhou Enlai's arms. Deng was bound to fall again because the Zhou-Deng alliance posted an unprecedented threat to Mao's dominance. Deng's second fall marked the final collapse of the Yan'an Round Table, the very base of Mao's command. Thus, Mao was increasingly Machiavellian, and his cult reached the climax in his final days; only through his cult could he maintain his power, which appeared so absolute yet so fragile that it could not tolerate the slightest differences in policy making.

The most significant impact of the CR, however, was the loss of the Party's coherence and the comradeship among the CCP leaders. As a result, personal relations overruled the due procedures in decision making, and factional interests prevailed over principle in political affairs. Factionalism in CCP politics was thus fully unleashed.

THE DESTRUCTION OF THE PARTY SYSTEM

The Hai Rui Affair: A Trap

Mao's siege of the Party state began with the criticism of *The Dismissal of Hai Rui*, a Beijing opera written by Wu Han, a deputy Beijing mayor and a historian of the Ming Dynasty, on how Hai Rui (A.D. 1515–87), a ranking Ming Dynasty official, was dismissed from his office after he criticized the emperor.[4] Although Jiang Qing wanted to criticize the

---

4 Liao Gailong, *1949–1989: Xin zhongguo biannian shi* (1949–1989: A Chronology of the New China), Beijing: People's Press, July 1989, p. 248. After Mao advocated "the Hai Rui

The Collapse of the Yan'an Round Table

opera as early as July 1962, and Kang Sheng reminded Mao in 1964 that Hai Rui's dismissal paralleled Peng Dehuai's fall,[5] Mao turned a deaf ear to them, for he then saw that "at least in its origins the Hai Rui 'affair' was perfectly innocent."[6]

The Hai Rui Affair was rooted in the struggle between Mao and the PB in the ideological field, a field one had to control in order to prevail in CCP politics (see Chapter 2). As early as September 28, 1963, one day after the *Latter Ten Articles* was worked out (see Chapter 5), Mao instructed that "special attention must be paid to the ideological field."[7] Although a cultural rectification campaign was launched immediately in Shanghai, little attention was paid to Mao's injunctions in Beijing. Frustrated, Mao lashed out at Peng Zhen and his lieutenant Liu Ren on December 12: "Many communists are enthusiastic for advocating the arts of feudalism and capitalism, but shy away from advocating the arts of socialism. Isn't it monstrously absurd?!"[8]

In response to Mao's criticism, the CC Secretariat decided to follow Shanghai's example and launched an ideological rectification in March 1964. Three months later, Lin Muohan, a deputy cultural minister, drafted a summary report on the campaign to the Center. But Zhou Yang, a deputy director of the CC Propaganda Department in charge of the campaign, withheld the report because he thought it was not good enough. Mme Mao obtained a copy and sent it to Mao *before* the report was submitted to the Secretariat.[9] Mao was upset by the report, especially by its conclusion that the problems exposed in the campaign were "mainly concerned with the misunderstanding of the

---

spirit" in April 1959, Hu Qiaomu, an alternate CC secretary, conveyed Mao's injunctions to Wu Han and urged him "to write a play with Hai Rui as the hero." See also Jin, *"Wenhua dageming" shigao*, p. 141.

5 Zhong Kan, *Kang Sheng pingzhuan* (A Critical Biography of Kang Sheng), Beijing: Red Flag Press, 1982, pp. 174–6.

6 Roderick MacFarquhar, *The Origins of the Cultural Revolution, 2: The Great Leap Forward 1958–1960*, New York: Columbia University Press, 1983, p. 212.

7 Liao, *Xin zhongguo bianian shi*, p. 222.

8 *Wansui*, 3:25. These words are part of the comment Mao wrote on a report, submitted by Shanghai Party Secretary Ke Qingshi, on the cultural rectification campaign in Shanghai. Also see Liu Zhijian, "*Budui wenyi gongzhuo zhuotanhuai jiyao chansheng qianhou*" (The making of *The Summary of the Forum on the Work in Literature and Art in the Armed Forces*), *Zhonggong dangshi ziliao* (Source Materials of the CCP History) (1989), 30:3.

9 See Zheng Qian and Han Gang, *Mao Zedong zhilu: wannian suiyue* (Mao Zedong's Road: The Later Years), Beijing: Chinese Youth Press, 1996 pp. 241–2.

Party's policy."[10] Mao felt that the PB once again tried to stall him. He commented harshly on the report on June 27:

> For the past fifteen years, these [literary] associations and most of the periodicals under their control *have basically failed to carry out the Party's policy*. They have ... failed to reflect socialist revolution and socialist construction. In recent years, they have even fallen to the verge of revisionism. If they do not remold themselves earnestly, someday in the future they will inevitably become the organizations like *The Petofi Circle* in Hungary.[11]

Not surprisingly, the PB responded promptly as Mao became ferocious. A five-man Cultural Revolution Group (CRG) headed by Peng Zhen was created in early July, with Lu Dingyi, Kang Sheng, Zhou Yang, and Wu Lengxi (director of the *People's Daily*) as its members. A nationwide Cultural Rectification was launched. Although Mao's injunctions were executed – almost the entire literary administration was toppled and thousands of scholars, writers, and artists were purged[12] – Mao's control of the ideological field was undermined rather than strengthened. In the five-man CRG that was in overall charge of ideological affairs, Peng, Lu, Zhou, and Wu all rose from Liu's mountaintop (see Chapter 4). Kang, the only one Mao could trust, was just an ordinary member, although he had been specifically assigned to take charge of ideological affairs at the CC's Tenth Plenum in 1962 (see Chapter 5).

This was intolerable to Mao, who had felt that the Party state was nibbling away his command. It was no coincidence that when the Secretariat was about to conclude the Cultural Rectification in March 1965,[13] Mao, who by then had already made up his mind to topple Liu (see Chapter 5), began to deploy the criticism of *The Dismissal of Hai Rui*. Liao Gailong, former director of the CCP Party History Research Center, says:

> In early 1965, as his discontent with and suspicion of the first front Party leaders intensified, Mao agreed with Jiang Qing's suggestion to criticize *The Dismissal of Hai Rui*.... The drafting

---

10 Liu, "*Budui wenyi gongzhuo zhuotanhuai jiyao*," p. 4.
11 Ibid., p. 26 (emphasis added).
12 Except Zhou Yang, five deputy cultural ministers, and most leaders of the National Federation of Arts and Culture and its subordinate associations were purged.
13 See Liao, *Xin zhongguo biannian shi*, p. 242.

The Collapse of the Yan'an Round Table

[of the article] started in March. . . . The criticism of *The Dismissal of Hai Rui* was launched as a matter of overall importance. [It] took the field of literature and art as a breakthrough point . . . and [the attack] was directed against the Beijing Party Committee and the first front CC leaders.[14]

The PB's control was so tight, however, that Mao had to deploy the engagement outside Beijing with such secrecy that, "except for Mao, none of the PSC members was aware of it."[15] With Shanghai Party Secretary Ke Qingshi's support, Mme Mao assigned Yao Wenyuan, an editor of the *Liberation*, a monthly published by the CCP Shanghai Municipal Committee, to draft an article criticizing *The Dismissal of Hai Rui*. Zhang Chunqiao, a Shanghai Party secretary in charge of propaganda, supervised Yao's work and liaisoned with Mme Mao, who would pass each draft to Mao and convey Mao's injunctions to Zhang and Yao.[16]

Meanwhile, the situation was developing in a direction unfavorable to Mao. As the third Five-Year Plan was approved in October at a CC work conference, it was widely expected that the Ninth PC, or at least a CC plenum, would be held soon.[17] But a congress was not what Mao wanted at the time when the PB had not only dominated the policy process, but was also credited with the remarkable recovery from the disastrous GLF (see Chapter 5). Eager to engage the PB, Mao approved the publication of Yao Wenyuan's *On the New Historical Opera "The Dismissal of Hai Rui"* in Shanghai on November 10. On the same day Yang Shangkun, director of the CC General Office, was replaced by Wang Dongxing, who had been in charge of Mao's security since the Yan'an period.[18] Yao's article charged that *The Dismissal of Hai Rui* was

14 Ibid., pp. 248–9 (emphasis added).   15 Ibid., p. 248.
16 Jin, *"Wenhua da geming" shigao*, p. 140.
17 Cf. Fang Weizhong, ed., *Zhonghua renmin gongheguo jingji dashi ji, 1949–1980* (The Economic Chronology of the PRC, 1949–1980), Beijing: Chinese Social Science Academy Press, 1984, pp. 395, 397–400 (hereafter *Jingji dashi ji*); Liao, *Xin zhongguo biannian shi*, pp. 244–5.
18 Huang Yao, *"Luo Ruiqing zhuanlue"* (A brief biography of Luo Ruiqing), pt. 2 in *Zhongong dangshi ziliao* (Source materials of the CCP History) (1991), 37:180. Yang got in trouble when a tapping device was found in Mao's bedroom in the summer of 1965 (see *Ziliao*, 1:25). Seeing that Mao was upset, Wang Dongxing, the deputy director of the General Office who was in charge of Mao's security, accused Yang of espionage against Mao. Though the investigation turned out to be inconclusive,

"antiproletarian and antisocialist" and its author Wu Han was "an anti-Party revisionist."

Peng Zhen and Lu Dingyi put up a strong resistance. Peng ordered all newspapers in Beijing to block Yao's article. Although the blockade failed due to the intervention by Zhou Enlai and Luo Ruiqing at Mao's behest,[19] Peng organized a vigorous defense of Wu Han. A series of articles written by Peng's associates appeared in the *Beijing Daily* and *People's Daily* in December.[20] All of them argued that the criticism of *The Dismissal of Hai Rui* involved an "academic debate" in which "everyone is equal before truth" – a tune set by Peng himself in the editorial note of the *Beijing Daily* on November 29.

"the CC suddenly issued a telegram in early November, saying that ... Yang was removed from the CC General Office." See Liao, *Xin zhongguo biannian shi*, p. 267.

19 Ibid., p. 249. After Mao arrived in Shanghai on November 19, he "called Zhou, requiring him to reprint Yao's article in various newspapers." (Mao left Beijing on November 13.) Wu Lengxi, director of the *People's Daily*, was also in Shanghai at the time to celebrate the eightieth birthday of Ana Louise Strong. Before he left for Shanghai, Wu asked Peng Zhen how to deal with Yao's article. Peng replied: "the matter needs to be discussed [*shangliang*]." So when Wu saw Mao in Shanghai, he did not mention the issue. See Wu Lengxi, *Yi Mao zhuxi* (Memorizing Chairman Mao), Beijing: New China Press, 1995, p. 150. Wu's account reveals at least that the PB tried to keep the issue under their control.

Huang Yao, *Sanci danan busi de Luo Ruiqing da jiang* (Senior General Luo Ruiqing's Three Escapes from Death), Beijing: CCP History Press, 1994, pp. 278–80, reveals that when Luo Ruiqing and Zhou Enlai arrived in Shanghai on November 25, Shanghai Party Secretary Chen Peixian told Luo Ruiqing that Mao was mad at Peng and that Mao ordered that Yao's article by published as a pamphlet. The next day, Luo met with Jiang Qing, who informed him of more details about the event. Luo "immediately" ordered the *Liberation Army News* to reprint Yao's article with a supportive editorial (see also Liu, "Budui wenyi gongzhuo zhuotanhuai jiyao," p. 6). On November 27, Luo Ruiqing told Zhou what he had learned and done. But Zhou, who had already learned the whole thing from Mao, pretended that he did not know it and asked Luo to give him a copy of Yao's article, so that he could read it on the airplane back to Beijing. According to a well-informed source, Zhou had "a serious talk with" Peng on November 28 after he returned to Beijing. Peng compromised on the conditions that the major newspapers in Beijing should reprint Yao's article and include editorial notes to downplay Yao's attack. Yao's article was reprinted in the *Beijing Daily* on the 29th, and in the *People's Daily* on the 30th. Yet, their editorial notes differed: the one in the *Beijing Daily*, dictated by Peng, emphasized that the Hai Rui Affair involved an *academic* debate, implying that Yao's accusation was fallacious. The one in the *People's Daily*, also dictated by Peng but revised by Zhou, endorsed Yao's article, but it also emphasized that the policy of "letting a hundred flowers blossom" had to be followed in the criticism.

20 See "*Deng Tuo zhuan*" (Biography of Deng Tuo), *RWZ* (1993), 50:294–5.

The Collapse of the Yan'an Round Table

Peng's defiance seemed irrational indeed, compared with the behavior pattern of the PB in dealing with Mao – executing his injunctions, but keeping effective control through maneuvering the policy process. There was no doubt Peng Zhen was enraged, for Yao's attack on Wu without the Center's approval not only grossly violated the Party's rules, but also flagrantly challenged Peng's authority – as head of the five-man CRG, the number 2 figure in the CC Secretariat, and the Beijing Party secretary, Peng should have been consulted beforehand. Yet it was unimaginable that Peng could have failed to see Mao's role in this affair. Peng might have "failed to realize Mao's true intention" when Mao asked him provocatively in September whether Wu Han could be criticized,[21] but he could clearly see Mao's involvement and resolve when Luo Ruiqing called him from Shanghai on November 26, telling him that the publication of Yao's article as a pamphlet was Mao's idea. Luo also hinted broadly that Mao was upset about what he had done to Yao's article.[22] Still, Peng ordered the bookstores in Beijing not to distribute the pamphlet. Moreover, after Mao made the home thrust on December 21, charging that Wu Han intended to parallel Hai Rui's dismissal with Peng Dehuai's fall in 1959, Peng Zhen told Mao that there was "no organizational relation between Wu Han and Peng Dehuai." After that, Peng and Lu Dingyi continued to "suppress" Yao's article and those which were supportive to Yao's.[23] How could Peng dare to defy Mao?

The reason is that Mao's surprise attack trapped Peng Zhen.[24] Had Peng caved in and admitted that he had "protected bad people" like Wu,[25] his fate would have been left at Mao's mercy, for it was Peng's mission to expose "the anti-Party revisionists like Wu Han" during the Cultural Rectification. Although Wu was seen as a literati cadre rather than a ranking Party official, he "was Peng Zhen's man."[26] That was why

---

21 Yan Jiaqi, *"Wenhua da gemig" shinian shi 1966–1976* (The Ten-Year History of the "Great Cultural Revolution," 1966–1976), Tianjin: Tianjin People's Press, 1986, pp. 7–8 (hereafter *Wenge shinian shi*).
22 See Huang, *Sanci danan busi de Luo Ruiqing da jiang*, p. 280.
23 See *Zilaio*, 1:6–8.
24 See Roderick MacFarquhar, *The Origins of the Cultural Revolution*, 3: *The Coming of the Cataclysm*, New York: Columbia University Press, 1997, pp. 439–60.
25 *Wansui*, 2:641.
26 Source C explains: "Wu Han was a confidant of Deng Tuo, and Deng [a Beijing Party secretary in charge of cultural affairs] was Peng's confidant."

while other literati cadres like Deputy Cultural Minister Xia Yan were purged during the Cultural Rectification, Wu was well protected, even though *The Dismissal of Hai Rui* was distributed as a sample of "the works with bourgeois influence."[27] No wonder that Mme Mao saw Wu Han's case as "a super bomb"; as she said: "once a Wu Han is dug out, a whole bunch will follow!"[28]

Peng had to defend Wu in order to prevent the Maoists from framing him. Although his choice would lead to a confrontation with Mao, Peng at least could have a chance to defend himself if, according to the Party's rules, Mao would have to resolve the conflict through the due procedure – through discussions at a CC conference, or at least at the Politburo. If so, Peng could count on his patron Liu Shaoqi and other PB to come to his rescue.

But Mao would follow the rules no more. He did not bring the issue to the Politburo, nor did he consult Liu or Deng, who were supposed to handle such a problem. Instead, Mao *privately* contacted two leaders. One was Zhou Enlai, a unique go-between among the CCP elite members due to his seniority, nonfactional background, and extraordinary personality (see Chapter 2). As previously discussed, Zhou's intervention brought down Peng's blockade of Yao's article and hence sank Peng and his associates deeper: it was now their responsibility to prove that Wu and *The Dismissal of Hai Rui* were not "anti-Mao, anti-Party, and antisocialist."

The other was Defense Minister Lin Biao. After Peng confronted Mao on Wu Han's case, Mao complained to Lin: "Haven't you seen it? Except the army's newspaper which has clearly pointed out the political nature of *The Dismissal of Hai Rui*, the rest [of the newspapers] have just gone through the motions. In Beijing, my words have no effect already. . . . they [the PB] feign obedience to me in the public but oppose me covertly." Mao also asked Lin to pay close attention to the armed forces to make sure that they would be under control.[29] Lin replied: "This is intolerable! We shall resolutely do away with those who dare to reverse Peng Dehuai's verdict, just like what we did to Peng Dehuai in that year [1959]."[30]

27 Yan, *Wenge shinian shi*, p. 6.   28 Zhong, *Kang Sheng pingzhuan*, p. 175.
29 Quan Yanchi, *Long kun – He Long yu Xue Ming* (The Siege of a Dragon – He Long and Xue Ming), Guangzhou: Guangdong Tourist Press, 1997, pp. 95–6.
30 Quoted from Liao, *Xin zhongguo biannian shi*, p. 249.

The Collapse of the Yan'an Round Table

"The Struggle Between Two Lines"

But Peng Zhen was no Peng Dehuai. Unlike Peng Dehuai whose *official* crime was opposing the Party's *line* (see Chapter 5), Peng Zhen could hardly be faulted in principle. Moreover, with the PB's cooperation, Peng Zhen was trying to keep the situation under control.

On January 23, 1966, Liu Shaoqi and Deng Xiaoping coauthorized the dispatch of *The Outline Report Concerning Several Problems in Our Current Cultural Work* as the "guiding policy" in an attempt to "cool down" the fire ignited by Yao's article.[31] On February 4, the five-man CRG worked out an *Outline Report Concerning the Current Academic Discussion* – known as the *February Outline* – specifically on the Hai Rui affair. Not surprisingly, the two outlines echoed one another in content, for both were drafted under Peng's supervision. Although both outlines acknowledged that there were "problems of the bourgeois tendency in the literary world," they proposed that these problems be solved "prudently under the Party's leadership" and through an "academic debate" under the principle of "seeking truth from facts."[32] The *February Outline* even warned some "Leftists" – obviously pointing at Yao and those like him – who acted like "scholar-tyrants" and tried to purge, instead of helping, "people like Wu Han" who had "made mistakes in their work."

The *February Outline* was promptly approved at an enlarged PSC meeting, chaired by Liu on February 5. On February 8 Peng and Lu flew to Wuhan, where Mao stayed, to report to Mao. (Kang also went with them to report to Mao on "something else.") Although Mao was obviously unhappy with the outline, Peng claimed that Mao "did not express any disagreement." So, while still in Wuhan, Peng dictated a comment to endorse the *February Outline* in CC's name and cabled it to Beijing on February 12. The same day, the CC dispatched the outline, together with the CC's – actually Peng's – comments.[33]

Peng's inept maneuvering of the policy process was a brazen replay of

---

31 See Yan, *Wenge shinian shi*, pp. 11–12.
32 See "Outline Report Concerning the Current Academic Discussion of the Group of Five in Charge of the Cultural Revolution," in *CCP Documents of the Great Proletarian Cultural Revolution, 1966–67*, Hong Kong: Union Research Institute, 1968, pp. 7–12.
33 See *Ziliao*, 1:8–9.

what Liu Shaoqi did to Mao in March 1962 – enforcing on Mao the policy he disliked in the name of "collective leadership" (see Chapter 5). But this time Mao would not give up because he was well prepared. While the PB were working on their two outlines, Mao and his followers were framing up a legitimate charge against Peng and his associates.

On January 21 Mme Mao went to Lin Biao's winter residence at Hangzhou to, in her words, "borrow Commander Lin's power" against the PB. Lin gave her what she needed: on January 31 Mme Lin, Ye Qun, called Liu Zhijian, a deputy director of the PLA Political Department, and conveyed Lin's injunctions: "Comrade Jiang Qing is very competent in politics. She is also an expert in literature and art. She has many valuable ideas. You must take [her ideas] seriously and execute Comrade Jiang Qing's suggestions earnestly."[34]

Lin's support gave Jiang the legitimacy to convene a Forum on the Work in Literature and Art in the Armed Forces, February 2–22, in Shanghai. She announced to the attendees: "This [forum] is a top secret. [You] must not divulge it to the outside, especially not to Beijing."[35] The *Summary* of this forum, virtually drafted by Chen Boda under Mao's supervision and revised by Mao himself,[36] had a decisive impact on CCP politics for the years to come. First and foremost, as Mao pointed out, "this *Summary* unmistakably raised *the question of line*, i.e., *the question of two lines*."[37] Thus, the *Summary* provided Mao with the *legitimacy* to topple Peng and Lu Dingyi because the struggle against them was no longer on concrete policy issues but on the Party's line. Declaring that the literary world was "under the dictatorship of a sinister anti-Party and antisocialist line,"[38] the *Summary* implied what Peng defended was not just a Wu Han but "a sinister line opposed to Chairman Mao's revolutionary line," and that the conflict on the Hai Rui Affair involved not just different opinions but a *"struggle between two lines"* – the legitimacy of the entire CR was thus produced.

Moreover, it "forged the political alliance between" the Maoist radicals and Lin Biao,[39] who headed the largest military mountaintop. Mao

34 Quoted from Liu, "*Budui wenyi gongzhuo zhuotanhuai jiyao*," p. 9.
35 Ibid., p. 10.   36 Ibid., pp. 17–30.   37 *Wansui*, 2:674 (emphasis added).
38 See *Hong Qi* (Red Flag), 9 (1967), pp. 11–21.
39 Cf. Harry Harding, "Chinese state in crisis," in Roderick MacFarquhar and John. K. Fairbank, eds., *The Cambridge History of China*, Cambridge: Cambridge University Press, 1989, 15:130.

The Collapse of the Yan'an Round Table

saw this alliance as the essential *force* for him to destroy the Party state. That was why the very first change Mao made to the draft was to add, *with Which Comrade Lin Biao Entrusted Comrade Jiang Qing*, to its original title: *Summary of the Forum on the Work in Literature and Art in the Armed Forces*.[40] This title legitimated not only Jiang's involvement in military affairs, which were otherwise none of her business, but also Lin's intervention in civilian affairs, which were otherwise not under his authority.

Lastly, the procedure through which the *Summary* was issued showed further that Mao was to rely on the military in the struggle against the PB. On March 17, Mao released the final draft of the *Summary* to Jiang with this instruction: "I have read the document twice, and it is good. I suggest to distribute it among some CC leading comrades for their opinions *in the name of the CMC*.... Surely, we should *first of all* seek opinions from the comrades at the CMC."[41] It must be noticed, however, that Mao *deliberately* kept the *Summary* from the Party leaders before he was sure that the military leaders would rally behind him. That was why, though most Central Military Commission (CMC) leaders attended an enlarged PSC meeting at Hangzhou from March 17 to 20, the draft of the *Summary*, which Lin received on the 19th, would not be passed to He Long, who was in charge of the CMC during Lin's absence, until the 22nd, two days after the meeting was over. True, Mao attacked Wu Han at the meeting, but he did not mention anything about "the two-line struggle," nor did he criticize Peng Zhen,[42] who was in fact still in charge of Luo Ruiqing's case.[43] As Jiang Qing warned Liu Zhijian and his colleagues who were involved in the drafting of the *Summary* on March 19: "You ... must not divulge [the *Summary*] to the outside before it is formally issued. This is discipline!"[44]

The *Summary* was "approved" by He Long, Nie Rongzhen, Chen Yi, Xu Xiangqian, and Ye Jianying before it was "submitted" to the CC

---

40 Liu, "*Budui wenyi gongzhuo zhuotanhuai jiyao*," p. 25.
41 Quoted from ibid., p. 30 (emphasis added).
42 Peng actually appeared very active at the meeting, interrupting Mao at least seven times during Mao's talk on March 20. Cf. *Wansui*, 2:634–40.
43 See Li Xuefeng, "*Wo suo zhidao de 'wen ge' fadong neiqing*" (The inside stories that I know about the launching of the "Cultural Revolution"), *Bainian chao* (Hundred Year Tide), no. 4 (1998), p. 16.
44 Liu, "*Budui wenyi gongzhuo zhuotanhuai jiyao*," p. 31.

Secretariat in the name of the CMC on March 30.[45] Such a procedure was unprecedented indeed: never before had a civilian policy been adopted by the military leaders first and then enforced on the Party ever since the establishment of the Yan'an Round Table! It violated the basic principle that "the Party commands the gun" (see Chapter 3), not necessarily because of Mao's distrust of the PB but because Mao would have been unable to dominate the policy-making process had the normal procedure been followed.

On March 28, two days after Liu Shaoqi left Beijing for Pakistan and Afghanistan, Mao had three conversations with Kang Sheng, Jiang Qing, and Zhang Chunqiao. Alleging that the *February Outline* was to "suppress the Leftists and protect the Rightists," Mao attacked Peng by name for the first time: "If Peng Zhen, the [CCP] Beijing Committee, and the Propaganda Department (headed by Lu Dingyi) continue to protect the bad people, the Propaganda Department has to be dissolved, the [CCP] Beijing Committee has to be dissolved, and the five-man CRG has to be dissolved!"[46]

On March 31, Kang conveyed Mao's words to Zhou Enlai and Peng.[47] Meanwhile, the CMC also sent twenty copies of the *Summary* to Peng, who distributed it among the CC leaders on April 1.[48] Mao's attack on Peng and the sharp contrast between the *Summary* and the *February Outline* showed clearly "a two-line struggle" between Mao and Peng; and the CMC's approval of the *Summary* suggested unmistakably that Mao had the military's support. Peng and Lu became the targets of criticism at a Secretariat meeting, April 9–12, chaired by Deng Xiaoping.[49] A crucial decision made at this meeting was to set up a CC Document Drafting Group led by Chen Boda; the control of document-drafting would enable the Maoists to interpret leadership decisions in their terms.

There exists an interesting correspondence between Liu Shaoqi's

45 Ibid., p. 32; also see *Ziliao*, 1:10.
46 *Wansui*, 2:641. Cf. Liao, *Xin zhongguo biannian shi*, pp. 257–8.
47 See Jin, *"Wenhua da geming" shigao*, p. 149.
48 Liu, *"Budui wenyi gongzhuo zhuotanhuai jiyao,"* p. 34. The *summary* was sent to Peng because Deng Xiaoping was not in Beijing at the time.
49 *Ziliao*, 1:11–12; also see Jin, *"Wenhua da geming" shigao*, pp. 149–50. A document I saw at Source A's place shows that a focus of the criticism of Peng is on his "dishonesty" (*bu laoshi*) in the making of *February Outline*. In fact, even in the post-Mao period there was little sympathy for Peng regarding Wu Han's case. Some senior leaders still hold that Peng's behavior in this case was "at least inappropriate." This may be why *Jueyi* does not mention the Hai Rui Affair at all in its discussion of the CR.

The Collapse of the Yan'an Round Table

Table 6.1. *Liu's Whereabouts and the Happenings in Beijing, March 26–April 19*

Date	Liu's Whereabouts	Happenings in Beijing
March		
26	Liu left Beijing for Pakistan.	
28		Mao attacked Peng and Lu.
30		Mao's attack on Peng and the *Summary* were sent
31	Liu returned to Xinjiang.	to the CC Secretariat.
April		
4	Liu left Xinjiang for Afghanistan.	
8	Liu returned to Xinjiang again.	
9–12	Liu stayed in Xinjiang.	Peng-Lu was criticized at a Secretariat meeting.
10		The *Summary* was dispatched to the whole Party.
15	Liu left Xinjiang for the ex-Eastern Pakistan via Kunming, Yunnan Province.	
16		Mao convened an enlarged PSC meeting at which Peng and Lu were toppled and the five-man CRG was dissolved.
17	Liu left Dacca for Rangoon.	
18		
19	Liu returned to Beijing.	

Sources: *People's Daily*, *Xinjiang Daily*, and *Yunan Daily*.

whereabouts and the happenings in Beijing from March 30 to April 19, 1966 (Table 6.1). Liu Shaoqi left for Pakistan on March 26, but he returned to Xinjiang on March 31, a day after Mao's attack on Peng was convened to the Secretariat. Liu left Xinjiang for Afghanistan on April 4, but he came back again on the 8th, a day before the decisive Secretariat meeting was conveyed. Liu stayed in Xinjiang until April 15, when he flew to the former Eastern Pakistan. The next day, Mao convened a four-day enlarged PSC meeting in Hangzhou, at which the five-man

CRG was dissolved and Peng and Lu were purged.⁵⁰ Liu returned to Beijing on April 19, only to see his two most important men fall. Why were Peng and Lu toppled during Liu's absence? Why did Liu twice interrupt his visit to Pakistan and Afghanistan? Why did Liu, during his twenty-three-day absence from Beijing, stay in Xinjiang for thirteen days at a time when Peng and Lu's fate was being decided? It is hard to imagine that these were sheer coincidences. But Liu's absence from Beijing surely contributed to Peng's dramatic fall, a fall that triggered the collapse of the entire Party state.

"Bombarding the Headquarters" with the Military Support

A CC circular, drafted by Kang Sheng and Chen Boda under "Mao's personal supervision," was approved on May 16 at an enlarged Politburo meeting, held May 4–26, without "changing a word."⁵¹ The significance of this *May 16 Circular* was that it legitimated an all-out assault on the PB, who, as the words Mao added to its conclusion read, "are representatives of the bourgeoisie . . . in our Party." Thus, the aim of the CR was to "eliminate these people [who] are reactionary revisionists . . . of the Khrushchev brand."⁵²

More important was a series of structural changes in leadership relations that enabled Mao to launch the CR. First of all, "Mao personally chaired the entire preparation of the meeting."⁵³ All the agenda and documents were prepared by the Maoists and approved at the enlarged PSC meeting chaired by Mao in April *during Liu's absence*. Notably, the Secretariat was excluded from the process for the first time since its establishment. This was not a mere violation of the two-front arrangement by Mao, but it indicated that Mao had discarded this arrangement and "replaced the CC's collective leadership with his personal leadership."⁵⁴

50 Liao, *Xin zhongguo biannian shi*, p. 262. But Li Xuefeng, "*Wuo suo zhidao de 'wen ge' fadong neiqing*," pp. 16–17, recalls that this conference formally started on April 19, the day Liu returned from the former Eastern Pakistan, and ended on April 24. Liu arrived in Hangzhou on April 21 to cochair this conference with Zhou Enlai. But Zhou actually presided over the conference because Liu "had no clue about the situation" during his absence from Beijing.
51 "*Liu Shaoqi zhuan*" (A Biography of Liu Shaoqi), *RWZ* (1991), 49:122.
52 Quoted from Liao, *Xin zhongguo biannian shi*, p. 265.   53 Ibid., p. 262.
54 *Jueyi*, p. 318.

The Collapse of the Yan'an Round Table

Consequently, a new CRG, with Chen Boda as the head, Kang Sheng as the adviser, and Mme Mao and Zhang Chunqiao as vice-heads,[55] replaced the five-man CRG. The new CRG stood out not only for its radical approach, but also for "the enormous power" Mao entrusted to it in decision making.[56] Notably, Chen and Kang received significant promotions at this meeting: from alternate Politburo members to membership in the PSC. This was a crucial change: it enabled the new CRG to report "directly to the SCP [i.e., to Mao] rather than to the CC Secretariat [i.e., to Deng Xiaoping and Liu Shaoqi] as its predecessor."[57] More importantly, it indicated that Mao was setting up a *new CRG-PSC policymaking axis* to replace the old Secretariat-PSC axis that had been established since the CC's Fifth Plenum in 1958 (see Chapter 5). As a result, the Secretariat, the de facto headquarters of the Party state, was deprived of its power.

Last but not least was the purge of Luo Ruiqing, the PLA's chief of staff. The change in leadership relations underlying this event was so fundamental that it reshaped the structure of the Yan'an Round Table, initiating the process that led to its final collapse. It was argued that Luo's fall was caused by a conflict between Luo and Lin Biao, which "reached its climax in early September [1965] when the two men published articles... that contained very different implications for Chinese defense policy": Luo stressed military professionalization while Lin preached "people's war."[58] However, the two articles were symbolic rather than substantial. While Luo's article was drafted by the PLA Political Department, Luo himself personally revised *Long Live the Victory of People's War*, which was published under Lin's name.[59] Essentially, Luo's fall resulted from the struggle over the control of the military, which emerged during the changes in Party-military relations after the tenth Plenum in 1962.

Traditionally, the principle that "the Party commands the gun" was executed through the PLA's Political Department led by Luo Ronghuan, a Politburo member who was the *only* marshal rising as a commissar. But

---

55 Liao, *Xin zhongguo biannian shi*, p. 269.   56 *Jueyi*, p. 318.
57 Harding, "Chinese state in crisis," p. 133.   58 Ibid., p. 126.
59 Huang, "*Luo Ruiqing zhuanlue*," pt. 2, p. 180. Both Lin's article (*BR*, September 3, 1965, pp. 9–30) and Luo's, "The people defeated Japanese fascism and they can certainly defeat US imperialism, too" (*CB*, September 14, 1965, pp. 1–12), were published in the *People's Daily*.

after Lin Biao was named the defense minister in 1959, the tension between Luo Ronghuan and Lin emerged, resulting in the "criticism" of Tan Zheng, Luo's protégé, in September 1960.[60] Luo Ruiqing kept neutral in this strife despite Lin's pursuit.[61] Luo Ruiqing's refusal to take sides soured his relationship with Lin. As Lin told Mao on December 2, 1965: "Luo Ruiqing's cooperation with me was good in 1960. He has estranged himself from me and isolated me since 1961. He is openly against me in 1965."[62]

However, just like Lin himself could not make his candidate, Luo Ruiqing, the PLA's chief of staff in 1959,[63] Lin alone could not topple Luo all by himself, either. He needed Mao's support and, furthermore, the other CMC leaders' cooperation, or at least their consent. In essence, what "alienated" Luo from the CMC leaders was not his "disrespect" for them,[64] but his unremitting effort to "professionalize" the PLA, of which a top priority was to institutionalize its commanding systems. This effort

60 From January 22 to February 27, 1960, the CMC convened an enlarged meeting in Guangzhou, at which both Lin and Luo Ronghuan made reports. While Lin advocated that the PLA should "carry forward the Yan'an tradition" and focus on studying Mao's works, Luo emphasized the Party command over the gun. But Tan Zheng only relayed Luo's report at the PLA Political Conference held in March–April. With Mao's approval, Lin convened an enlarged CMC meeting in September 13–October 20, at which Tan was accused of opposing "putting politics in command" and, more seriously, forming an "anti-Party faction." Tan was thereafter demoted to deputy director of the PLA Political Department. Yet, all this was done without consulting Luo Ronghuan who was in charge of the PLA's political work. Mao, after consulting Luo Ruiqing and Xiao Hua, renamed Luo Ronghuan the director of the PLA Political Department, but the appointment was never formalized because of Lin's opposition. The influence of the Political Department dropped dramatically since then. For the clash between Lin and Luo Ronghuan, see *"Luo Ronghuan zhuan"* (A Biography of Luo Ronghuan), *RWZ* (1987), 32:104–5; Huang Yao, Li Zhijing, and Yang Guoli, *Luo shuai zuihou shiwu nian* (The Last Fifteen Years of Marshal Luo [Ronghuan]), Beijing: People's Press, 1987, pp. 103–8, 127–35; and Wei Li, *1965 nian qian de Lin Biao* (Lin Biao Prior to 1965), Lhasa: Tibet People's Press, 1996, pp. 358–63.
61 See Wei, *1965 nian qian de Lin Biao*, p. 364. Lin charged that Luo Ronghuan was anti-Party and asked for Luo Ruiqing's support in a private conversation with Luo Ruiqing in June 1961. But Luo Ruiqing refused to take sides. Also see Huang, *Sanci danan busi de Luo Ruiqing da jiang*, pp. 203–5.
62 Liao, *Xin zhongguo biannian shi*, pp. 168, 182.
63 Huang, *"Luo Ruiqing zhuanlue,"* pt. 2, p. 165.
64 Luo admitted in his self-criticism at a CMC meeting on March 12, 1966, "a major mistake" he had made: "I have alienated myself from senior marshals [*lao shuai*] because of my disrespect to them in my work." Cf. Huang, *"Luo Ronghuan zhuanlue,"* pt. 2, p. 184.

The Collapse of the Yan'an Round Table

undermined the miliary leaders' control of their mountaintops through their *guanxi* networks forged during the revolution (see Chapter 3). Moreover, after Luo entered the CC Secretariat in 1962, his efforts paralleled the PB's drive to formalize the policy process, a drive that had threatened Mao's command based on personal loyalties. No wonder that Liu openly promised that Luo was "the successor of the defense minister."[65]

A compelling explanation of Luo's fall is that Mao had to sacrifice Luo, and later He Long, in order to secure Lin Biao's support.[66] In other words, "the fall of Luo Ruiqing was a political deal between Lin Biao and Mao Zedong."[67] The significance of this explanation, which has been accepted by most Party historians in China,[68] is that it demonstrates that Mao's authority was far from absolute as conventionally believed at the eve of the CR; the military support was so vital in Mao's struggle against the PB that he would rather sacrifice one of his most loyal followers, Luo Ruiqing, to please Lin Biao.

A more profound reason for Luo's fall, however, was that he had functioned as the *organizational link* between the Party and military since he entered the CC Secretariat in 1962. His increasingly prominent role in military affairs tended to overshadow Lin, not necessarily because of Mao's long-term trust in Luo Ruiqing or Lin's "chronic illness,"[69] but because, as the only military man in the CC Secretariat, Luo had the blessing of the Party state in military affairs. As Mao was preparing an all-out assault on the Party state, this link had to be eliminated. That was why Mao eventually agreed to put Luo away, even though he admitted that Luo had always been loyal to him.[70] Mao instructed on December 2, 1965: "[We] must watch out for those who oppose putting politics in

---

65 Yan, *Wenge shinian shi*, p. 195.   66 See Quan, *Long kun*, pp. 90–8.
67 Jin, *"Wehua da genming" shigao*, p. 155.
68 All but one Party historian I have interviewed agree with this explanation. The one who disagrees argues that Luo's fall was not so much caused by Mao's decision as by the fact that Luo's no-nonsense style had offended many high-ranking officers.
69 Yan, *Wenge shinian shi*, pp. 192–4; and Harding, "Chinese state in crisis," pp. 124–5.
70 Huang, "*Luo Ruiqing zhuanlue*," pt. 2, pp. 159, 181–2. Lin wrote to Mao on "Luo's problems" on November 18. On the 29th Ye Qun went to Hangzhou, where Mao stayed, with eleven pieces of evidence against Luo – mainly reports from Lin's followers. Mao never really believed in the allegation that Luo was "anti-Mao and anti-Party," despite Ye's six-hour report to Mao on Luo's problems. Mao said to Lin on December 2, the day he approved the toppling of Luo: "He [i.e., Luo] opposes you, but hasn't opposed me yet.

command... but spread a kind of eclecticism [i.e., opportunism] of their own."[71] The key word is "eclecticism," implying that Luo had failed not so much to follow Mao as to break up with the PB. Luo, who had been "urgently" summoned back from the Sino-Vietnam border on December 11, was dismissed from his military posts at an enlarged PSC meeting chaired by Mao in Shanghai, December 8–15. Notably, at the meeting and during the "face-to-face" struggle against Luo in March 1966, none among the military leaders defended Luo, but the Party leaders – Liu, Deng, Peng, and Lu Dingyi – expressed serious doubts about the charges against Luo.[72] Luo's case was officially handled by the three-man group formed by Zhou Enlai, Deng Xiaoping, and Peng Zhen. But their attitude toward Luo was at least lenient, if not overtly defensive.[73] It was the inquisitorial group led by Marshal Ye Jianying, Xiao Hua (director of the PLA Political Department), and Yang Chengwu (first deputy chief of staff) that decided Luo's verdict: "Luo Ruiqing opposed the MZT, opposed 'putting politics in command,' and schemed to usurp power [from Lin Biao]."[74]

Indeed, Luo's fall was a *necessary* step for Mao to separate the military from the Party state. Thereafter, the PLA was turned from "the Party's army" to what Lin claimed was "an army Chairman Mao *personally* created and has since *directly* commanded" in his infamous "May 18 Speech."[75] No wonder that Mao, who had never dressed in uniform since 1949, appeared in PLA uniform at almost all the public occasions in the initial years of the CR, for Mao no longer led the army as the CCP chairman, but as "the PLA's supreme commander."

The most important victory Mao achieved at the May Politburo

71 Quoted from Liao, *Xin zhongguo biannian shi*, p. 251.
72 See Huang, "*Luo Ronghuan zhuanlue*," pt. 2, pp. 182–4.
73 Ironically, even after Lin Biao's fall, Deng Xiaoping still criticized himself in his letter to Mao on August 3, 1972, for his "unforgivable mistake on the handling of Luo's [Ruiqing] problem," namely, Deng's attempt to defend Luo. (See "Comrade Deng Xiaoping's Letter [to Mao]," August 3, 1972, located at the John K. Fairbank Center Library, Harvard University, Cambridge, MA, pp. 2–3.) This indicates further that the purge of Luo Ruiqing was ultimately Mao's decision. This may be why Mao declined Luo's repeated requests to see him after he was told that Mao made a "self-criticism" on his case on December 21, 1973. See Huang Yao and Zhang Mingzhe, eds., *Luo Ruiqing zhuan* (A Biography of Luo Ruiqing), Beijing: Contemporary China Press, 1996, p. 586.
74 Ye was the leader of the group, but the actual job was done by Xiao and Yang.
75 Lin, "Address to Politburo," *CLG*, 2, no. 4 (Winter 1969–70), pp. 53–4 (emphasis added).

The Collapse of the Yan'an Round Table

meeting was the total isolation of the Party state. The purge of Peng, Luo, Lu, and Yang "was by no means a coincidence."[76] As Roderick MacFarquhar points out, by purging the four, Mao cut off the PB from all the crucial areas in CCP politics: the capital (Peng), the army (Luo), the propaganda apparatus (Lu), and the information flow (Yang).[77] Thus, the "political and organizational preparations for the overall launching of the CR" were completed.[78] Although the PB struggled to have the situation under control, similar to what they did during the 1963–5 SEC (see Chapter 5) – they sent work teams to the campuses in an attempt to put down the rebellious students – their effort only made it evident that they were suppressing "a great revolution" initiated by Mao.[79]

The Eleventh Plenum of the Eighth CC was held from August 1 to 12, 1966. Obviously, Mao would not have convened this plenum had he not regained the dominance at the Center – this plenum had been long overdue since the Tenth Plenum in 1962. The new CRG had made all the preparations for the plenum. Moreover, Mao made his stand clear to the local leaders who were to attend the plenum. Mao said to the secretaries of six CCP bureaus and some provincial Party leaders on July 24: "The work teams have obstructed the mass movement. Obstructing the revolution will surely help counterrevolutionaries and help the sinister gangs."[80]

In contrast, the PB were so poorly prepared for the plenum that Liu did not even complete a draft of the report he was to make on the CC's behalf.[81] The controversy over the work teams made the PB the targets of attack from the very beginning of the plenum. Mao openly attacked Liu, claiming that Liu's decision to send work teams to campuses was to "suppress the students and exercise terror."[82] Mao dropped his super bomb: "bombarding the headquarters," on August 5. In this *dazibao* (big-character poster) Mao exposed succinctly all the major "crimes" committed by the PB led by Liu since 1962: "the Right-deviationism in 1962 ... the erroneous tendency of 'Left' in form but Right in essence in 1964,

---

76 Wu, *Yi Mao zhuxi*, p. 153.
77 Roderick MacFarquhar, lectures on *The Cultural Revolution* at Harvard University, 1991.
78 Liao, *Xin zhongguo biannian shi*, p. 263.
79 See ibid., pp. 270–3; Yan, *Wenge shinian shi*, pp. 18–38; Harding, "Chinese state in crisis," pp. 134–7.
80 "*Liu Shaoqi zhuan*," p. 126.   81 Liao, *Xin zhongguo biannian shi*, p. 276.
82 *Wansui*, 2:650; also see "*Liu Shaoqi zhuan*," pp. 127–8.

... [and] exercising a bourgeois dictatorship for the past 50 days." Thus, Mao's *dazibao* "indicated the main direction of attack for the CR" – the PB led by Liu Shaoqi.[83]

Although there was no mention of reorganizing the CC leadership in the original agenda, Mao suggested a new list of the Politburo members at the plenum.[84] Noticeably, except for Peng Dehuai (purged) and Luo Ronghuan (died), all the PLA marshals entered the leadership core for the first time, with Lin Biao and Zhu De as PSC members, and Chen Yi, Liu Bocheng, He Long, Xu Xiangqian, Nie Rongzhen, and Ye Jianying as Politburo members. (Lin was announced as the CCP vice-chairman *after* the plenum.) It must be noted, however, that the sixteen-article *Decision on the Great Proletarian Cultural Revolution* stipulated specifically that the PLA "must not be involved in the CR" and the CR policies "must not be implied to the armed forces."[85] In other words, the army was ordered to stand by as the Party establishment was under siege "in this great two-line struggle."[86] By the time the mass organizations led by Wang Hongwen overthrew the Shanghai Party authority in January 1967, all the Party authorities across China had virtually collapsed in the storm of "seizing-power."[87]

Although it is still subject to argument whether Mao had envisioned that his "bombarding the headquarters" would lead to the collapse of the entire Party establishment, what Mao failed to foresee was that such an outcome would result in the loss of the *organizational control* of the society that had been effectively organized and governed by the Party state. As a result, while Mao's command relied solely on the military support, his grasp of the society at large had to be achieved by the preaching of the myth of his constant correctness – the very source of Mao's personality cult. As Lin Biao pointed out on August 9, 1967, "Two conditions are indispensable for us to launch the CR: one is Chairman Mao's high prestige, the other is reliance on the PLA's strength.[88]

83 Liao, *Xin zhongguo biannian shi*, p. 278.
84 See "*Tao Zhu zhuan*" (A Biography of Tao Zhu), *RWZ* (1989), 43:58; also see MacFarquhar and Fairbank, *Cambridge History of China*, 15: table 33, p. 884.
85 The stipulation was suggested by Ye Jianying and endorsed by Lin Biao and the other CMC leaders. See "*Tao Zhu zhuan*," p. 60.
86 *Hong Qi* (Red Flag), 13 (October 1966), p. 1.
87 Liao, *Xin zhongguo biannian shi*, pp. 289–91.
88 Quoted from Wang, "*Mao Zedong yu wenhua da geming*," pt. 2, p. 62.

The Collapse of the Yan'an Round Table

Yet, the Mao cult did not yield any definitions for Liu Shaoqi's "bourgeois reactionary line," or for his own "revolutionary line."[89] Although everyone claimed that he was loyal to Mao, people were judged not so much by their political attitudes as by their *personal backgrounds* and their *personal relations* with those who were in power, or with those who were purged.[90] As the collapse of the Party created a power vacuum at every level of authority, the "two-line struggle" soon evolved into unprincipled factional struggles throughout the system, with rival factions attacking each other as "the followers of the sinister line." Indeed, the most devastating impact of the collapse of the Party state was that it removed the *organizational* shackles of factionalism embedded in the CCP political system (see Chapter 2).

LIN BIAO'S RISE AND FALL: DISCONNECTION OF
THE MILITARY FROM THE YAN'AN ROUND TABLE

The Relationship of Mutual Dependence between Mao and Lin

Although Lin was posted next to Mao at the Eleventh Plenum, his power base in Beijing was not as solid as it appeared. Many key positions at the PLA Headquarters were held by the officers rising from the other mountaintops (see Figure 6.1). But Mao's patronage enabled Lin to expand rapidly at the other leaders' cost. Marshal He Long was the first victim of Lin's expansion.

As the commander of the 1927 Nanchang Uprising, which gave birth to the PLA, He Long enjoyed seniority next to Zhu De among the ten PLA marshals. Although he stood firmly by Mao in the struggles against Zhang Guotao, He Long's mountaintop had been constantly contained because it was not part of Mao's First Front Red Army. In 1947 Peng Dehuai took over the bulk of He's forces, which later grew into the First Field Army (see Chapter 3). He entered the Politburo after the transition of the Yan'an Round Table in 1953–4 (see Chapter 4), yet he was assigned to a humble position: director of the National Sports

---

89 Zhou Enlai once asked the Maoists for a definition of "the bourgeois reactionary line," coined by Lin Biao in his speech on October 1, 1966. Zhou's request was ignored. Cf. Liao, *Xin zhongguo biannian shi*, pp. 281–2.
90 See Lee, *The Chinese Cultural Revolution*, pp. 64–139, 204–43.

Factionalism in Chinese Communist Politics

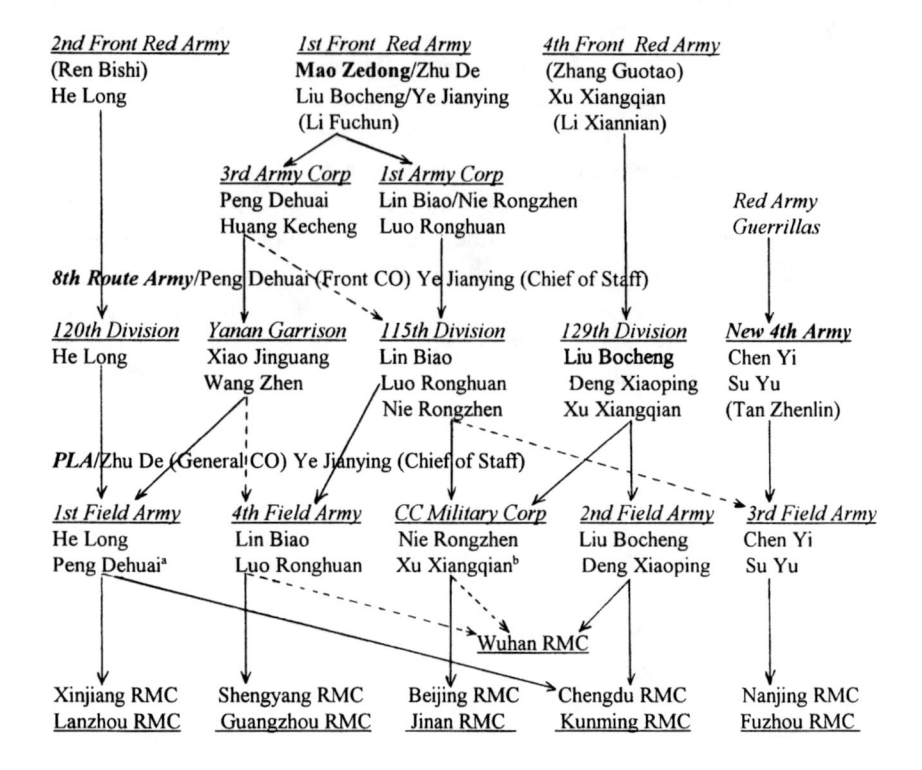

```
2nd Front Red Army        1st Front Red Army        4th Front Red Army
(Ren Bishi)               Mao Zedong/Zhu De         (Zhang Guotao)
He Long                   Liu Bocheng/Ye Jianying   Xu Xiangqian
                          (Li Fuchun)               (Li Xiannian)

                    3rd Army Corp    1st Army Corp
                    Peng Dehuai      Lin Biao/Nie Rongzhen            Red Army
                    Huang Kecheng    Luo Ronghuan                     Guerrillas

8th Route Army/Peng Dehuai (Front CO) Ye Jianying (Chief of Staff)

120th Division     Yanan Garrison    115th Division    129th Division    New 4th Army
He Long            Xiao Jinguang     Lin Biao          Liu Bocheng       Chen Yi
                   Wang Zhen         Luo Ronghuan      Deng Xiaoping     Su Yu
                                     Nie Rongzhen      Xu Xiangqian      (Tan Zhenlin)

PLA/Zhu De (General CO) Ye Jianying (Chief of Staff)

1st Field Army     4th Field Army    CC Military Corp  2nd Field Army    3rd Field Army
He Long            Lin Biao          Nie Rongzhen      Liu Bocheng       Chen Yi
Peng Dehuaiª       Luo Ronghuan      Xu Xiangqianᵇ     Deng Xiaoping     Su Yu

                                     Wuhan RMC

Xinjiang RMC       Shengyang RMC     Beijing RMC       Chengdu RMC       Nanjing RMC
Lanzhou RMC        Guangzhou RMC     Jinan RMC         Kunming RMC       Fuzhou RMC
```

[a] In March 1947, Peng Dehuai took over the command of He Long's Northwestern Field Army, which later grew into the 1st Field Army (see Chapter 3).

[b] Xu Xiangqian's troop merged into Nie Rongzhen's force in May 1948 (see Chapter 3).

Figure 6.1. Ties between PLA leaders and their mountaintops (solid arrow = direct/strong ties; dashed arrow = indirect/weak ties).
Source: Zhang Guoqi and Li Guoxiang, *Zhongguo renmin jiefangjun fazhan yange, 1927–1949* (The Organizational Development of the PLA, 1927–1949), Beijing: PLA Press, 1984

The Collapse of the Yan'an Round Table

Commission, and his role in the military was symbolic rather than substantial.[91]

Peng Dehuai's fall in 1959, however, brought He back into military affairs, presumably because he was the only PLA marshal available at the time.[92] Although Mao shared Luo Ronghuan's concern that the "defense minister cannot always be from the First Front [Red] Army [i.e., Mao's grand mountaintop]" – Luo therefore recommended He to succeed Peng in order to balance the power among various military mountaintops[93] – the job was eventually given to Mao's man, Lin Biao. He Long was named the second vice-chairman of the CMC, assigned to "take charge of the work at the CMC when Lin is not available."[94] Given Lin's chronic illness, He was in actual charge of daily CMC affairs.

Lin soon became suspicious of He's increasing influence, especially his close relationship with Luo Ruiqing.[95] Lin felt that he was treated as a figurehead because He and Luo often bypassed him and "reported to Mao directly." Lin wrote in the summer of 1965 after he learned that He and Luo had flown to Lanzhou to see Mao without consulting him beforehand: "Let them go. Let them do things to the extreme. In the end they will be another Peng (Dehuai) and Huang (Kecheng)!"[96]

---

91 He Long was named director of the National Sports Commission when he was visiting North Korea in December 1953. It is believed that a factor in He's appointment was his tense relationship with Peng Dehuai. Allegedly, He was very disappointed about this appointment, as a widely circulated poem He then wrote reads: "A sheer order from the Grand Commander deprives me of the command of my army" (*dashuai yisheng ling, duo le wo bingquan.*).

92 Zhu De was an inept administrator. Chen Yi was the full-time foreign minister. Liu Bocheng had been deactivated since he was criticized for "military doctrinism" in 1958. See Xiao Ke, *"Yi 1958 nian jundui fan 'jiaotiao zhuyi' douzheng"* (The 1958 struggle against "doctrinism" in the military), *Bainian chao* (Hundred Year Tide), no. 2 (1997), pp. 4–10. Nie Rongzhen was preoccupied with the defense industry. Xu Xiangqian, the former commander of Zhang Guotao's Fourth Front Red Army, had never been fully trusted – previously Xu had always been a vice-commander. Ye Jianying did not really have a mountaintop (see Chapter 3) and his relationship with Lin Biao had been tense since the early 1950s (see Zhao Wei, *Zhao Ziyang zhuan* [A Biography of Zhao Ziyang], Beijing: China News Press, 1989, pp. 63–6).

93 See *"Luo Ronghuan zhuan"* (A Biography of Luo Ronghuan), *RWZ*, 1987, 32:103–4.

94 See Quan, *Long kun*, pp. 26–8.

95 Ibid., pp. 48–68. In fact, it was Mao's instruction that Luo should "often ask for He Long's instructions" on military affairs, not because Mao trusted He more than Luo, but because Mao did not want the Party to get involved in military affairs, given Luo's dual prominent positions in the Party and the military.

96 Huang, *"Luo Ruiqing zhuanlue,"* pt. 2, p. 175.

Indeed, He was the first obstacle Lin had to remove in order to achieve dominance at the CMC. Although Lin had initiated a few oblique attacks on He before the CR, accusing He's men of "using military training to push aside politics,"[97] his effort was barely fruitful because of Lin's limited influence in decision making when the PB dominated in the policy process. But soon after the Eleventh Plenum was over, letters against He from Lin's followers, including Wu Faxian and Li Zuopeng, began to flood to Mao.[98] All these letters accused He of being Luo Ruiqing's backstage boss and claimed the two "schemed to usurp the supreme command of the army."[99] Evidently, Mao never believed these allegations. Mao summoned He to his residence on September 5, reaffirming his trust to He. Mao even promised that he would stand in He's defense.[100] Yet, Mao's promise was nothing but a way to free himself from the guilt in the purge of He.

Indeed, Lin's ferocious attack on He put Mao in a difficult situation: Mao has to choose between Lin and He. Lin's attack on He was reckless but well calculated: once the Lin-He strife broke out, Mao's rational choice had to be Lin, not just because Lin rose from Mao's First Front Red Army, but because Lin controlled the strongest mountaintop in the military and Mao became dependent on the military support to maintain his command after the Party collapsed. Although Mao did try to bring peace between the two marshals, his effort was fruitless because Lin refused to compromise.[101]

Unknown to He, however, was that Mao had just approved Lin's request to conduct an investigation of He.[102] Obviously, Mao gave up on He and left him to the prey of Lin and his men. Desperately, He sought Zhou Enlai's help – he moved into Zhou's residence on January 11, 1967.

---

97 See Quan, *Long kun*, pp. 48–68.   98 Ibid., pp. 245–57.
99 See Xue Ming, "*Xiang dang he renmin de baogao*" (A report to the party and people), in Zhou Ming, ed., *Lishi zai zheli chensi – 1966–1976 nian jishi* (Deep Reflections on This Period of History – True Stories in 1966–1976), Beijing: Huaxia Press, 1986, 1:131.
100 See Quan, *Long kun*, pp. 258–63.
101 Mao's secretary Xu Yefu called He on September 9, telling He that Mao had "talked with Lin and the other senior comrades, [and your] problems have been solved. But you should pay a visit [to Lin] and solicit the opinion of the involved comrades." See Li Lie, *He Long nian pu* (Chronology of He Long), Beijing: People's Press, 1996, pp. 780–2. Although He did pay a humble visit to Lin the next day, the conversation went nowhere because Lin was determined to get rid of He. See Quan, *Long kun*, pp. 268–72.
102 See ibid., p. 264. Also cf. Li, *He Long nian pu*, p. 781.

The Collapse of the Yan'an Round Table

Zhou made a well-calculated arrangement: he invited Mme Mao, who was Lin's ally and had direct access to Mao, and Li Fuchun, who had close relationships with both Mao and Lin (see Chapter 3), to have a conversation with He on January 19. But Li had few words to say; and Jiang did not show up.[103] Although Zhou promised that He's problem would be solved soon, he sent He and his wife to a military camp in the western suburb of Beijing, where He was under house arrest till his death on June 9, 1969.

He would never have believed what actually transpired. As the pressure from Lin and the Maoist radicals increased, He's nephew, a general who was the Beijing RMC commissar, wrote an "exposing letter" to the CC, accusing He of having a covert relationship with the KMT in late 1933.[104] Moreover, Zhou Enlai, who should have known He's innocence because he was in charge of military operations in the early 1930s, drafted a one-and-half-page report on September 8, 1967, requiring a special investigation of "He Long's historical problems." Mao wrote on the report the word "agree," on January 13; but Lin just encircled his name, which meant that he had read the report and did not have any disagreements.[105] A Special Investigation Group on He Long's Case was set up the same day. He was doomed. Notably, this special group was also in charge of the "investigation" of twenty-three high-ranking officers rising from He's Second Front Red Army.[106]

---

103 According to a well-informed source, Quan Yanchi's description of this meeting, *Long kun*, pp. 368–79, "is incredibly accurate."
104 In later 1933 the KMT sent Xiong Gongqing, an acquaintance of He Long, to He's army to lobby He to surrender to the KMT. Not only did He refuse, but he also executed Xiong on January 23, 1934, after reporting to the CC. See *He Long zhuan* (A Biography of He Long), compiled by the He Long zhuan Writing Group at PLA Headquarters, Beijing: Contemporary China Press, 1993, p. 157.
105 According to a most reliable source, a former Politburo member, who was in charge of all special cases involving the central leaders after Lin Biao's fall, was so shocked when he saw Zhou's handwritten report on He Long that his entire view of the CR changed. The same source also told me that among all the "exposing letters" against He Long, two of them hurt He most. One was written by one of He's closest followers, an RMC commander; the other by He's nephew. He also confirmed that Lin Biao did not leave "a single word in writing" in He's case, although it was known that Lin was the driving force in the purge of He Long. This is yet another example in CCP history when "such a thing happened absolutely, but no solid evidence can be found" (*que you qi shi, cha wu shi ju*).
106 See Li, *He Long nian pu*, pp. 791–2, 795.

Factionalism in Chinese Communist Politics

The He-Lin strife was just a prelude to the outbreak of factional struggles. Furthermore, it revealed Mao's reluctance to stop Lin's expansion at the other leaders' cost. This reluctance is seen in the CCP official account as "a gross mistake in Mao's later years."[107] Yet, as my examination shows, it was not that Mao was unwilling but that he was *unable* to check the ongoing factional struggles, given that the collapse of the Party had not only broken the organizational shackles on factionalism that were embedded in CCP politics, but also resulted in an extremely unbalanced distribution of power among the three elite groups: the Maoists at the CRG, the planners at the State Council, and the military leaders at the CMC.

The prominence of the Maoists, led by Jiang Qing, Kang Sheng, and Chen Boda, was rooted in their direct access to Mao and close affiliation with mass organizations. But their social forces would soon disintegrate as these organizations turned on each other in power struggles after the Party collapsed. Thus, although they appeared influential in policy making due to their control of propaganda and document drafting, they barely had any solid power bases. That is why they had to remain *unconditionally* loyal to Mao on the one hand, and maintain an alliance with Lin on the other hand. While Mao's protection was vital for their survival, Lin's cooperation was necessary for them to achieve their political goals.

Noticeably, except for Bo Yibo, who rose from Liu Shaoqi's mountaintop, all planners – Zhou, Chen Yun, the two Lis, Tan Zhenlin, Yu Qiuli, and Gu Mu – survived the first wave of purges. This indicated further that the initial aim of the CR was just to topple the PB, not "all the authorities," as the CCP official account claims. True, few planners had ever won Mao's full trust, but Mao had to depend on them for housekeeping because of their expertise in economy and administration. More importantly, as the housekeepers rather than organizers, they had posed little threat to Mao's command since antiadventurism in 1956 (see Chapter 5). There were policy disputes between the planners and the Maoists: the former preferred stability, but the latter advocated "continuous revolution."[108] Beneath these disputes was a power struggle between the two elite groups. "Continuous revolution" would enable the

---

107 See *Jueyi*, pp. 314–16.   108 See Harding, "Chinese state in crisis," pp. 167–8.

The Collapse of the Yan'an Round Table

Maoists to grasp more power, but the planners could have more say in policy making should the stability be restored.

The military leaders formed the most powerful force in the leadership. It was essentially their support that enabled Mao to launch the CR. Moreover, the military was the only organized force left after the Party collapsed. Yet, unlike the Party system, which had been institutionalized since 1956, a military leader's power was still measured by the size of his mountaintop. Although the field armies were divided into eleven RMCs, the ties between the military leaders and their former mountaintops remained intact (Figure 6.1).

The planners also had access to the military. But unlike the Maoists, who allied only with Lin Biao's force, the planners had forged their ties with various military mountaintops during the revolution: Li Fuchun rose from the First Front Red Army; Li Xiannian rose from the Fourth Front Red Army; Tan Zhenlin had close ties with both the First Front Red Army and the New Fourth Army, Yu Qiuli and Gu Mu had been soldiers themselves before being transferred to the oil industry. Notably, although there is little evidence that Lin had taken on the planners – Lin, in fact, sincerely cared about Zhou's health[109] – relations between Lin and the planners deteriorated rapidly, not only because Lin stood with the Maoists, but also because Lin's expansion was made at the expense of the mountaintops with which the planners affiliated.

Undoubtedly, all military leaders were loyal to Mao. But they saw each other as rivals in political affairs. Stability in their relationships had been maintained essentially because they had largely been kept out of the policy process and, more importantly, their decision making had been subject to the Party's command. Once the Party collapsed, factional struggles broke out among them immediately. While the Maoists eagerly participated in these struggles for more gains, the planners were also involved due to their ties with various military mountaintops.

Without the organizational shackles by the Party, there were few

---

109 Zhang Zuoliang, Zhou's personal doctor from 1965 to 1976, recalled that, after Zhou's first heart attack in early 1966, "Lin Biao let Ye Qun call Big Sister (Zhou's wife Deng Yingchao), saying: Vice-commander Lin cared greatly about Premier's health. He instructed: 'The doctor, nurses and oxygen must not be away [from Zhou], they must be with [Zhou] wherever he goes.'" Chen Hua, *Zhou Enlai he ta de mishu men* (Zhou Enlai and His Secretaries), Beijing: China Media and Television Press, 1992, p. 526.

Factionalism in Chinese Communist Politics

means available to Mao to suppress factional strife among his followers. The unbalanced distribution of power and, more importantly, Mao's reliance on the military made the situation more difficult to control. As my examination shows, the aim of Mao's manipulation was not so much to stabilize leadership relations as to maintain his own command. Only in this sense can we comprehend Mao's letter to Jiang Qing on July 8, 1966, in which Mao expressed his concern and distaste for Lin's activities, yet admitted that he had to go along with Lin in order to "do away with the Rightists."[110] This letter indicated that Mao "had long been aware of Lin Biao's wild ambition."[111] Yet "it underlined rather than explained away Mao's failure to prevent this dangerous man from emerging as his officially anointed successor."[112] What this letter really demonstrates is Mao's *helplessness* and *inability* to prevent his relationship with Lin, which had been based on trust and loyalty, from evolving into one of mutual dependence. Mao wrote: "I am forced to go to Liang Mountain. I see that their [i.e., Lin Biao and his followers'] real intention is to draw support from Zhong Kui in order to attack [their] devils. I therefore become the CCP's Zhong Kui in the sixties of the twentieth century."

But Mao only told half the truth by likening himself to Zhong Kui, a legendary figure who had the power to subdue devils. True, without Mao's patronage, Lin could hardly excel in CCP politics at other leaders' costs, but Lin's support was also necessary for Mao to topple the PB and, furthermore, to maintain his command thereafter. Thus, Mao and Lin served as each other's Zhong Kui. Mao obviously realized the risk of this relationship of mutual dependence. That is why Mao showed this private letter to Zhou Enlai and Wang Renzhong,[113] not necessarily because he intended to inform them of his true opinion of Lin, but as a *precaution* to prevent the forces the two represented – the planners and local leaders – from merging into Lin's mountaintop. This is also why Mao approved Zhou's suggestion to pass Mao's intention to Lin. It served as a *warning*

110 "Mao Zedong's Private Letter to Jiang Qing (July 8, 1966)," *Chinese Law and Government*, 6, no. 2 (Summer 1973), pp. 96–100.
111 See Yao Wenyuan, *On the Social Basis of the Lin Biao Anti-Party Clique*, Beijing: Foreign Language Press, 1975. Also cf. Hao and Duan, *Liushi nian*, 2:625–6; Liao, *Xin zhongguo biannian shi*, pp. 273–5.
112 Roderick MacFarquhar, "The succession to Mao and the end of Maoism," in MacFarquhar and Fairbank, *The Cambridge History of China*, 15:335–6.
113 See Wang, *Da dongluan de niandai*, p. 7.

The Collapse of the Yan'an Round Table

to Lin: the Zhong Kui (i.e., Mao) Lin used to get rid of his "devils" (i.e., Luo Ruiqing and He Long) was nobody's fool.[114]

Mao was never able to free himself from this mutually dependent relationship with Lin, though he managed to contain Lin within his power base – Lin's rise was based on the expansion of his mountaintop rather than the merging of other forces. Because of this mutually dependent relationship, Mao had to connive at Lin's expansion at the other leaders' cost and then had to withstand a destructive blow resulting from Lin's fall in 1971.

Lin Biao's Expansion Amid Factional Struggles

Despite the policy adopted at the Eleventh Plenum that the PLA "must not be involved in the CR," the army was soon involved because a large number of cadres came from the army through *zhuanye* (transferring the officers to civilian positions) and therefore had *guanxi* with various armed forces (see Chapter 3). As the assault on the cadres escalated, local military leaders began to give refuge to their former comrades-in-arms who were under attack. This brought about conflicts between the army and the mass organizations,[115] not because the generals stood by the Party establishment, but essentially because they felt threatened as more and more ex-officers from their mountaintops were purged, resulting in a sharp decline of their influence.

Obviously, had this situation continued, the army, which had been separated from the Party, could again come to the Party's defense. Seeing the danger, Mao reversed the "noninvolvement" policy in a series of injunctions to Lin and the CMC in January 1967: "The PLA should support the broad masses of Leftists... The so-called 'noninvolvement' is untrue. It has long been involved. The problem is not whether [the PLA] should be involved, *it is on which side it should stand.*"[116] On January 23, the CC, State Council, CMC, and CRG issued a joint

---

114 Although Lin felt uneasy and pleaded illness after he learned Mao's intention (see Quan, *Long kun*, p. 31), his behavior later shows that he did not really hear Mao.

115 Jurgen Domes, "The role of the military in the formation of revolutionary committees," 1967–8, *CQ*, 44, pp. 112–45, shows that twenty-four out of twenty-nine military district commanders were to various degrees in conflict with the local mass organizations. Wang, *Da dongluan de niandai*, p. 286, says that "almost all the RMCs sided with the so-called 'conservative organizations.'"

116 *Wansui*, 3:12–13 (emphasis added).

directive, ordering the PLA to "give resolute support to the broad masses of revolutionary Leftists" and stop serving as "air-raid shelters for a handful of capitalist-roaders in the Party."

But there were neither clearly defined criteria nor unified organizations for "the Leftists." Thus, the military commanders chose to support the mass organizations whose interests fit theirs, and attack those who were at odds with them. This led to more chaos and, moreover, brought about more violence in the movement. Indeed, it was *after* the military involvement in the CR that the conflicts between the mass organizations escalated from *wendou* (verbal argument) to *wudou* (violent fight) across China.

More devastating was that military intervention brought out the covert rifts among the military mountaintops. Table 6.2 shows that in the CCP's former base areas where the armed forces often shared the same roots, such as Beijing and Shenyang (cf. Figure 6.1), there were few conflicts in the armed forces. Consequently, the situation in these areas was soon under control after military involvement. Yet we witnessed fierce conflicts among the armed forces in the "liberated areas" that the PLA seized from the KMT during the war. In these areas, such as the Wuhan, Nanjing, Chengdu, Kunming, and Lanzhou RMCs, the armed forces often grew out of different mountaintops (cf. Figure 6.1). It was not surprising that the armed forces in these RMCs supported the opposing mass organizations in the struggles, resulting in prolonged chaos and fierce *wudou* in the society.

The emerging conflicts within the PLA worried the CMC leaders. They feared that such a situation would lead to disorder in the army. The danger was fully demonstrated by the episode on January 19, 1967, at a joint meeting of the CMC and CRG. The official account later describes this event as a struggle between the Maoists and the CMC leaders.[117] But what really happened was a struggle involving four parties: the Maoists, Lin Biao, Xu Xiangqian (the newly appointed head of the military CRG),[118] and Ye Jianying and Nie Rongzhen. The event was triggered

---

117 See Jin, *"Wenhua da geming" shigao*, pp. 230–1.
118 Xu Xiangqian, *Lishi de huigu* (History in Retrospect), Beijing, PLA Press, 1987, 2:821–2, says that it was Jiang Qing who nominated him for the job. But the idea was originally from Lin, who saw Xu as the most manipulable among the existing marshals, not only because he had been virtually cut off from his mountaintop, but also because he had lived under the shadow of history – Xu's past included his

Table 6.2. *Factional Conflicts in the PLA Regional Military Commands (1967–8)*

RMCs	Dominant Forces/Factional Tie	Opposition Forces/Factional Tie
Shenyang	Main and local forces/Lin Biao	None
Beijing	Main and local forces/Nie Rongzhen	None
Jinan	Main forces/Nie Rongzhen	Local forces and navy/Chen Yi
Xinjiang	Main and local forces/He Long and Peng Dehuai	None
Lanzhou	Main forces/Peng Dehuai and He Long,	Air force/Lin Biao
Wuhan	Main and local forces/Xu Xiangqian (Deng Xiaoping)	Air force and navy/Lin Biao
Nanjing	Main forces/Chen Yi and Xu Xiangqian Navy/Chen Yi (pre-July 1967)[a]	Air force and navy/Lin Biao
Fuzhou	Main forces/Lin Biao and Chen Yi	Local forces/Chen Yi
Guangzhou	Main forces/Lin Biao	Local forces (Guangdong)/local party
	Local forces (Guangxi)/Deng Xiaoping	
Chengdu	Main forces/Deng Xiaoping	Air force/Lin Biao, local forces/local party
Kunming	Main forces/Deng Xiaoping	Air force/Lin Biao, local forces/local party

Notes: The results are from a survey I conducted in 1983.

[a] The Eastern Sea Fleet originated from Chen Yi's Third Field Army. However, Lin Biao's forces prevailed in the fleet after the mysterious "suicide" of the Fleet Commander Tao Yong, who was found drowned in a three-foot-deep well in early morning of January 21, 1967. See Li Yong, ed., *"Wenhua da geming" zhong de mingren zhi si* (Death of the Celebrities in the CR), Beijing: Central Nationality College Press, 1993, pp. 63–9.

Factionalism in Chinese Communist Politics

by Ye Qun's attack on Xiao Hua, director of the PLA Political Department. Ye Qun accused Xiao of opposing Lin Biao and sabotaging the CR.[119] Ye's attack was part of the compromise between Lin and Jiang Qing,[120] but an essential reason for Lin to turn on Xiao, whose relationship with Lin could be traced back to the late 1920s, was that Xiao had alienated himself from Lin after the CR was launched.[121] Xu Xiangqian was also unhappy with Xiao, who, as the deputy director of the military CRG, often bypassed Xu and reported to Ye Jianying and Nie Rongzhen because of his close relationship with the two. A more profound factor in the Xu-Xiao tension was the friction between Xiao and Yang Yong, commander of the Beijing RMC who rose from Xu's Fourth Front Red Army.[122] Not surprisingly, Ye Jianying defended Xiao vigorously. As Xiao's "backstage boss," Ye knew that Xiao's fall could drag him down. Ye took on Xu Xiangqian, rather than the Maoists as the official account claimed, because he thought that Xu should have protected Xiao instead of letting him hang out to dry in front of the Maoists. The quarrel

relationship with Zhang Guotao and the total defeat of his army in 1936 in the Northwest (see Chapter 3). Mao endorsed Lin's nomination of Xu essentially because, as the only marshal who had been kept out of the Party leadership, Xu had few ties with the Party establishment.

119 See ibid., p. 824.
120 Cf. Wen Feng, *Shentan xia de Lin Biao* (Lin Biao Out of the Shrine), Beijing: Huaqiao Press, 1993, pp. 68–9.
121 Xiao was sandwiched between Lin Biao and Luo Ronghuan when their relationship went sour in the early 1960s. After Lin managed to topple Luo's protégé Tan Zheng in 1960, Xiao and Luo Ruiqing suggested to Mao that Luo Ronghuan resume the directorship of the PLA Political Department. This annoyed Lin to such an extent that he blocked the publication of Luo's appointment (see note 60). After the CR was launched, Xiao was put at in even more difficult position. As the deputy director of the military CRG, Xiao appeared to be supportive of the mass organizations in the PLA headquarters, which in turn brought him into conflict with Lin's trio: Wu Faxian, Li Zuopeng, and Qiu Huizuo, who tried to keep the situation at the PLA headquarters under control. What further annoyed Lin was that, although Xiao knew clearly that Lin was trying to isolate He Long in order to create an impression that He would be gone soon, he still arranged for He, together with Chen Yi, Nie Rongzhen, and Xu Xiangqian, to speak at a mass rally on behalf of the CMC on November 13, 1966. Thus, Lin decided to "throw Xiao Hua out," which in turn soured Lin's relations with Nie Rongzhen and Ye Jianying, who tried to protect Xiao.
122 The tension between Yang Yong and Xiao Hua started on the evaluation of "the great contest of military training [*da biwu*]" in 1964. Following Lin's cue, Xiao criticized *da biwu* as showman activities that "squeezed out" more important political work in the military. As a major organizer of *da biwu*, Yang counterattacked that Xiao was "ill-minded" (*bie you yongxin*). Cf. Quan, *Long kun*, pp. 52–3.

The Collapse of the Yan'an Round Table

between the two marshals was so fierce that Ye broke his palm when smiting the table. Although Xiao was saved temporarily due to Mao's last-minute intervention (he would be purged a few months later), Yang's premature announcement of Xiao's fall – Yang convened a conference at the Beijing RMC to announce Xiao's fall before Mao's words arrived in the late afternoon of January 19 – turned him into an anti-Maoist right on the spot.

The episode exposed the factional cleavages in the military. It also revealed differences between the Maoists and the military leaders on how the CR should be carried out in the armed forces. The Maoists insisted that the mass movement was necessary in the military because it would give the CRG, the headquarters of mass organizations, more leverage in decsion making. The military leaders, however, were unanimously opposed to this proposition. This is not surprising because the mass movement could provoke an outbreak of factional conflicts among the armed forces, which would jeopardize the status quo of power distribution in the commanding system. Thus, on January 24, 1967, one day after the joint directive on military involvement in the CR was issued, Xu Xiangqian visited Lin. The two marshals shared the same concern: the expanding conflicts in the armed forces had to be stopped. While Xu might be genuinely anxious to restore stability, Lin's worry was that increasing chaos in the military could undermine his own power base as his men were also under the indiscriminating attack from those CR zealots. Lin dictated a nine-article order and then summoned Ye, Nie, and Yang Chengwu to his residence to obtain their consent. After that, Xu called up Chen Yi. Then the four marshals – Chen, Nie, Xu, and Ye, with Lin's support – went to the Maoists to inform them of their decision.[123] This order put strict limits over the military involvement in the CR, ordering that all the servicemen "must stand fast at their posts" and "must not leave their units without permission." It stipulated specifically that "the movement must be contained within each unit," and "assaults on the military's leading bodies must be strictly prohibited."[124] Although all this was in sharp contrast to the Maoists' policy preferences, they did

---

123 See Hu Changshui, "*Lin Biao yu zhongyang junwei 'batiao mingling'*" (Lin Biao and the *Eight-Article Order* of the CMC), in Jiang Bo and Li Qing, eds., *Lin Biao, 1959 nian yihou* (Lin Biao after 1959), Chengdu: Sichuan People's Press, 1993, pp. 171–87; also Xu, *Lishi de huigu*, 2:828.
124 See *Ziliao*, 1:262.

not put up much resistance when faced with the solidarity of the CMC leaders. The only change was that the nine articles were slightly revised into seven. Later, one more article was added concerning the discipline of children of the high-ranking officers.[125]

On January 28 Lin and Xu brought the *Eight-Article Order* to Mao for his approval. When Mao endorsed the *Order*, Lin could not help chanting "long live, and long long live [Mao]."[126] Lin appeared so grateful not necessarily because Mao approved the *Eight-Article Order*, but because Mao did not find fault with Lin for initiating this policy without consulting Mao beforehand. Furthermore, this policy virtually reversed the joint *Directive* by the CMC and CRG, which was issued just five days earlier, ordering the PLA to "actively participate in the CR." The *Eight-Article Order* was dispatched in no time, together with a new *CMC Directive*, which suspended the CR movement in the Jinan, Nanjing, Fuzhou, Guangzhou, Kunmimg, Xijinag, and Wuhan RMCs[127] – all were then involved in fierce factional struggles (cf. Table 6.2).

Such an abrupt reversal of policy on military involvement in the CR demonstrated further the relationship of mutual dependence between Mao and Lin. More importantly, the obvious policy inconsistency exposed a dilemma Mao faced after the collapse of the Party: he could not keep the military out of the CR as planned because the army was the only organized force left to keep the situation under control, yet military involvement would inevitably provoke conflicts in the armed forces, not necessarily because of the "structural cleavages between the local and main forces,"[128] but because military intervention in "seizing power" would unleash the factionalism embedded in the military. Essentially, it was Mao and the CMC leaders' *inability* to solve this dilemma, rather than Lin's and the Maoists' "rebuff and sabotage," as the official account claims,[129] that caused the escalating conflicts in

---

125 These children used to be the most zealous participants of the CR because they saw it as their exclusive privilege to carry on their fathers' revolutionary cause. Yet they became increasingly frustrated as the CR went on, partly because their fathers began to have troubles, but largely because they felt that their "privileges" were eroding as more and more ordinary people, or even those with "bad" family backgrounds, began to play the major role in the CR. Frustration and confusion turned them from leading Red Guards into troublemakers for the Maoists.
126 See Quan, *Long kun*, p. 395.   127 *Ziliao*, 1:263.
128 Harding, "Chinese state in crisis," p. 170.
129 Liao, *Xin zhongguo biannian shi*, p. 293.

The Collapse of the Yan'an Round Table

the armed forces, which in turn provoked more chaos and violence in the society.

The *Eight-Article Order* was a victory for the CMC leaders indeed. The planners also benefited from it given their preference of stability. By coincidence, Mao learned on February 20 that Tao Zhu, a newly promoted leader who then ranked fourth behind Mao, Lin, and Zhou in the PSC, was purged because of a plot by Jiang Qing and Chen Boda, instead of "simultaneous action by the revolutionary masses," as Mao had been informed.[130] Outraged, Mao lashed out at Chen and Jiang so harshly that Chen intended to commit suicide.[131] This further emboldened the CMC leaders and the planners to take on the Maoists. The result was the so-called February Adverse Current – an open confrontation at two "joint CC meetings" chaired by Zhou Enlai on February 11 and 16, 1967.[132]

The clash was triggered by Ye Jianying's attack on the Maoists at the meeting on February 11. Xu Xiangqian soon followed suit. Both men blamed the Maoists for their "attempt to stir up chaos in the army." But the onslaught to the Maoists took place at the meeting on February 16, partly because their defensive posture at the previous meeting further encouraged the CMC leaders and planners, partly because more details about Mao's anger at Jiang and Chen were known among the elite members. Tan Zhenlin, a senior leader whose relationship with Mao

---

130 Tao had been the secretary of the CCP South China Bureau before he was promoted to the executive CC secretary at the 1966 May Politburo Conference. He was further promoted into PSC at the Eleventh Plenum. But he soon found himself in a clash with the Maoists, partly due to his reluctance to purge the PB, especially Deng Xiaoping, but largely because of his disgust with Jiang Qing and her followers. A head-to-head confrontation between Jiang and Tao took place at a CRG meeting. When Jiang asked Tao to entitle a "rebellious leader" from the Social Science Academy as a "revolutionary leftist," not only did Tao refuse, but his counterattack on Jiang was so harsh that she burst into tears. On January 4, 1967, Jiang and Chen Boda, without consulting Mao or any other Politburo members, launched a "surprise attack" on Tao, denouncing him as "a follower of the reactionary bourgeois line" in front of a group of Red Guards. Their denouncement of Tao spread throughout the country overnight, and Tao was toppled. But Jiang reported to Mao that Tao was knocked down by "simultaneous action of the revolutionary masses" and forced Mao to accept it as a fait accompli. See Quan Yanchi, *Tao Zhu zai "wenhua da geming" zhong* (Tao Zhu in the "CR"), Beijing: CCP Central Party School Press, 1991, pp. 158–63. Also cf. Jin, "*Wenhua da geming*" *shigao*, pp. 225–6.
131 Cf. Quan, *Long kun*, pp. 403–4.
132 Unless noted specifically, my analysis of this event is based on Quan, *Long kun*, pp. 402–14, and my interviews with several reliable sources.

started in the late 1920s, took the lead in the attack. He interrogated Zhang Chunqiao on the whereabouts of Chen Peixian, the Shanghai Party secretary who rose from Chen Yi and Tan's mountaintop. Tan soon escalated his attack on all the Maoists, particularly Jiang Qing, accusing them of scheming to purge all the senior cadres. The other CMC leaders and planners joined in: first Chen Yi, then Ye Jiangying, Yu Qiuli, Li Xiannian, and Nie Rongzhen.[133] All of them accused the Maoists of attempting to destroy the Party's leadership through massive purges. When Zhang Chunqiao jeered that "the Party has been useless" in the mass movement, Tan lashed out: "What does 'the masses' mean? [You] always [talk about] the masses, but there must be the Party's leadership! [You] abandon the Party's leadership, but preach day and night about self-liberation, self-education, and self-revolution of the masses. What is this nonsense? It is nothing but metaphysics!"[134]

Tan's condemnation reflected the frustration of the CMC leaders and planners who saw their power drop rapidly since the launching of the CR. Although the joint meetings of the CMC, State Council, and CRG were held regularly after the Eleventh Plenum, the CRG had manipulated policy making to such an extent that more often than not the CMC leaders and planners had to obtain the information through their informal personal ties.[135] In fact, what upset the CMC leaders and planners was not so much the assault on the Party as the chaos caused by the collapse of the Party; what made them feel threatened was not so much the purge of senior cadres as the paralysis of their factional networks resulting from the massive purge; and what underlay their emphasis on the Party's leadership was a strong demand for power, which was legitimate indeed, given that they were all Politburo members. By contrast, except for Chen Boda and Kang Sheng who had just been promoted into the PSC, most of the CRG members were not even the CC members at the time! Their onslaught reached its climax when Chen Yi took the floor:

133 Although Xu Xiangqian and Li Fuchun were also presented at the meeting on February 16, the minutes of the meeting shows that they said few words.
134 Quoted from Liao, *Xin zhongguo biannian shi*, p. 295.
135 For example, Liu Zhijian and Wang Renzhong, both deputy directors of the CRG, were purged in December 1966 because of their alleged "underground contacts and leaking of the CC's secrets." Yet the people Liu and Wang contacted were Chen Yi, Nie Rongzhen, Ye Jianying, and Li Xiannian. The two had been the main sources of the CMC leaders and planners for the information about decisions made by Mao and the CRG.

The Collapse of the Yan'an Round Table

These scoundrels [i.e., the Maoists] have climbed onto the stage. It is them who are engaging in revisionism. *At Yan'an, Liu Shaoqi, Peng Zhen, and people like Bo Yibo, Liu Lantao, and An Ziwen, they also supported MZT zealously.* They [claimed that they] were never against Chairman Mao. But they had never seen Chairman Mao! It was people like us who were criticized for opposing Chairman Mao. Wasn't Premier [Zhou] also a target of criticism? Hasn't history proved who really opposed Chairman Mao? [We] will have to see later, for [history] will prove again. *Stalin relayed the leadership to Khrushchev.* Didn't Khrushchev carry on revisionism?[136]

Chen drew two parallels in his words. The first parallel was between Liu Shaoqi and the Maoists. Liu and his men had supported Mao zealously in the Yan'an Rectification (YR; see Chapter 3), as did the Maoists in the CR. Thus, like Liu and his men who became the "anti-Maoists" in the CR, the Maoists could also become anti-Maoists in the future. The second parallel was between Lin Biao and Khrushchev. Both were chosen as successors, and, just as Khrushchev denounced Stalin, Lin could denounce Mao after his death.

But Chen overplayed his hand, which turned out to be disastrous for the CMC leaders and planners. First and foremost, Chen's comparison between Liu in the YR and the Maoists in the CR unnerved Mao himself. It is true that Liu and his men were zealous Mao supporters, and their attacks on Wang Ming and the "empiricists" like Zhou Enlai and Chen Yi were ferocious during the YR. But it was Mao who was behind Liu and his men then, and now it was Mao again who was behind the Maoists in the CR. Thus, what Chen truly exposed was Mao himself as a cunning and untrustworthy leader who used people to do dirty jobs and then dumped them when they became useless. Moreover, Chen's comparison revealed the true nature of the CR and the YR: they were not "the two-line struggles" but power struggles for Mao to establish and maintain his command.

The second parallel between Lin and Khrushchev was also a vital mistake because it virtually pushed Lin to the other side. True, Lin gave decisive support to Mao in the launching of the CR, as did all the other CMC leaders; also true is that Lin had allied with the Maoists in order

---

136 Quoted from Jin, *"Wenhua da geming" shigao*, p. 236 (emphasis added).

to get rid of He Long. But there were common interests between Lin and the CMC leaders, namely, to maintain stability in the army; that is why Lin, together with the other CMC leaders, worked out the *Eight-Article Order* despite a potential confrontation with Mao. Although Lin still needed the Maoists' cooperation in his expansion, he would have thought twice about it if he knew the price would be total alienation from all the CMC leaders. By likening Lin to Khrushchev, however, Chen not only excluded Lin from their camp, but also left Lin with little room but to support Mao because any hesitations on Lin's part could raise Mao's suspicion that Lin could be a Khrushchev indeed.

Not surprisingly, Mao burst into anger as soon as Zhang Chunqiao and Yao Wenyuan, who were reporting to him at midnight of February 16, told him about Chen's words. Mao rebuked: "What? Does that mean the YR was wrong? [Should we] reverse the verdict [of the YR]? [Should we] invite Wang Ming back?" After Zhou Enlai's "objective report" later confirmed what Mao had learned from the Maoists, Mao summoned the CMC leaders, the planners, and the Maoists to his residence at midnight of February 18. Mao appeared so upset that he virtually "shouted" to these senior leaders:

> [I] have read the minutes of the meeting at Huairen Hall [on February 16] and have a few words to say. The CRG has implemented the principles of the Eleventh Plenum. [Their] mistake is 1, 2, or 3 percent, but 97 percent [of what they have done] is correct. I will resolutely oppose those who are against the CRG! You want to denounce the CR. No way! You said that Jiang Qing and Chen Boda are no good. Fine, let you, Chen Yi, be the head of the CRG. Arrest Jiang Qing and Chen Boda and shoot them! Let Kang Sheng be exiled! I will also step down! You can invite Wang Ming back to be the chairman! You, Chen Yi, want to reverse the verdict of the YR. The whole Party will not allow you [to do so]! You, Tan Zhenlin, are counted as a senior Party member. How could you speak on behalf of the bourgeois line?

Mao's anger was real. But Mao knew that it would be difficult for him to resolve this crisis without Lin's support, given that all the CMC leaders and planners were involved. That is why he turned to Ye Qun, who was also present, and said provocatively: "Comrade Ye Qun, go and tell Lin

The Collapse of the Yan'an Round Table

Biao [that] his status is also shaky. Someone wants to seize his power. Let him be prepared. If the CR would fail this time, *he and I* would have to withdraw from Beijing and go to Jinggang Mountain again to wage a guerrilla war." But Lin did not need to be reminded that Mao had threatened to go back to Jinggang Mountain once before – at the 1959 Lushan Conference when he was challenged by Peng Dehuai (see Chapter 5). Noticeably, however, Mao was not as confident as in 1959, although his personality cult peaked. Instead of doing it himself, this time Mao wanted Lin to be his company, which again indicated their mutually dependent relationship.

To make sure that Lin would be on his side, Mao sent Jiang Qing to "report to Vice-Chairman Lin" the next day, although Ye Qun had already dutifully told Lin what had happened. Not surprisingly, the CMC leaders and planners also tried to win Lin's support. When Jiang arrived in Lin's residence, Lin had already received a letter from Tan Zhenlin on behalf of the CMC leaders and planners. Tan reported to Lin that they had been "driven beyond forbearance . . . and determined to fight to the end."[137] Lin's preference of stability and his risk-taking decision on the *Eight-Article Order* made Tan and his colleagues believe that Lin was persuadable despite Chen Yi's misfiring at the meeting. Given Tan's close relationship with Chen, Tan's letter itself implied that Chen's attack on Lin reflected only his own opinion.

But this time the context was quite different from that which prevailed when the *Eight-Article Order* was issued. Then it was Lin, together with all CMC leaders, who initiated the *Order* and presented it to Mao as a fait accompli. But now an open clash between the senior leaders and the Maoists had already taken place, and the stakes were so high that the outcome would affect not just policy but also the very legitimacy of the CR. Lin was not directly involved in this clash; he could not afford to go along with his colleagues, given what Chen Yi had said at the meeting and, moreover, having learned Mao's attitude via his wife. Jiang's visit on Mao's behalf further indicated to Lin that Mao was counting on his support. As "Mao's best pupil," Lin chose to support Mao. Lin asked Jiang to pass Tan's letter to Mao with the following comment: "Chairman: Indeed, the tree prefers calm, but the wind will not subside.

---

137 For the whole text of Tan's letter, see See Li Yong, ed., *"Wenhua da geming" zhong de mingren zhi yu* (The Purge of the Celebrities in the CR), Beijing: Central Nationality College Press, 1993, pp. 110–11.

It is totally unexpected that recently Tan Zhenlin's thinking has become so muddled and degenerated to such a low level."

Zhou Enlai also played a crucial role, although the official account deliberately avoids any discussions about Zhou's role in the solution of this crisis. As the head planner, Zhou did lean toward the planners at the meeting on February 11 – he warned that the CR should not undermine the economy. Even at the meeting on February 16, Zhou's neutral attitude helped the senior leaders. Otherwise, as the one who chaired the meeting, he could at least have suspended the meeting so as to relieve the Maoists from the relentless attack. But few could see Mao's intention clearer than Zhou. In fact, when Chen Yi misfired at the meeting, two people saw the problem immediately: Ye Jianying and Zhou Enlai. But unlike Ye, who interrupted Chen and changed the topic back to the protection of senior cadres, Zhou distanced himself from Chen right away. When Chen reminded Zhou that he was "also the target of criticism" in the YR, Zhou corrected Chen immediately: "the criticism to me was fully correct." Moreover, as the one who chaired the meeting and was responsible for reporting to Mao, Zhou let Jiang Qing make arrangements for Zhang and Yao to report to Mao first at midnight of February 16, but Zhou astutely waited until the 18th to give his report to Mao.

Leaderless – neither Lin nor Zhou sided with them – the CMC leaders and the planners had no choice but to cave in. At Zhou's "patient persuasion," Ye made his self-criticism first; the others soon followed suit. In the end Mao decided Chen, Xu, and Tan had to "be on leave to make self-criticisms";[138] the two Lis and Yu Qiuli had to make self-criticisms but, at Zhou's request, were allowed to assist Zhou at the State Council; and Ye would take care of daily affairs at the CMC due to his "good attitude and profound self-criticism."

The crisis was over. Although the basic structure of leadership relations – the three elite groups under Mao's command – still remained, there was a drastic change in the distribution of power. The joint meeting of the CMC, State Council, and CRG was suspended, and except for Lin and Zhou, the CMC leaders and planners ceased to play any substantial roles in policy making. The Maoist radicals came out as winners, as Mao decided to let the CRG assume the functions of the

---

138 Liao, *Xin zhongguo biannian shi*, p. 296.

The Collapse of the Yan'an Round Table

Politburo.[139] Their victory, however, was symbolic rather than substantial. From then on, the CR became the very source of the legitimacy for Maoists' power. The "class struggle" and "continuous revolution" were no longer just policy choices for them, but the *necessity* for their survival. As a result, they could not help going to the extreme Left in policy making, which would alienate them from all the social forces and, more devastatingly, make it suicidal for anyone to form coalitions with them. Thus, their glorious victory in February 1967 sowed the seeds for their inevitable doom.

Zhou actually benefited from the event. His biggest reward was that he had been transformed from the head planner into an *indispensable mediator* in political affairs. For Mao, Zhou was a reliable messenger and housekeeper, not necessarily because Zhou had Mao's trust, but because he had access to all the three elite groups and, more importantly, did not pose any substantial threat to Mao, because Zhou cautiously avoided any impression that he would develop his own mountaintop. For the CMC leaders and planners, Zhou provided not only protection when things went sour, but also a source of information and access to Mao, so that they could maintain a meaningful influence in the policy process from which they had been virtually excluded. Although the Maoists never liked Zhou, his expertise in administration and, moreover, his access to various factional networks were indispensable for the Maoists to have their policy implemented. Essentially, playing the role of mediator enabled Zhou to maneuver in the stormy political weather in 1967–73. As my examination shows, once the structure of leadership relations among the three elite groups changed due to Lin's fall and Deng's return, Zhou's role as the mediator vanished, and so did his "good luck" in political affairs.

The biggest beneficiary, however, was Lin Biao. All Lin's potential rivals – those CMC leaders who had their own mountaintops: Chen, Xu, and Nie – were either knocked out or badly mauled. More importantly, as the senior leaders faded out, Lin was the only one left in the leadership who maintained a substantial mountaintop, a position that essentially secured Lin's undisputed number two status. Lin wasted no time to consolidate his newly achieved position: he convened a month-long conference of high-ranking officers from February 26 to March 25. The aim was

---

139 See Jin, *"Wenhua da geming" shigao*, pp. 242–3.

to make sure that the PLA would "unite firmly under the new CMC leadership."[140] Lin made his most notorious comment in his summary speech at the conference: "the achievement of the CR is the biggest; the loss is the smallest" – a true statement from Lin's perspective.

But Lin would pay dearly for this "biggest achievement": he was thereafter perceived as a perpetual partner of the Maoists, even though they would soon become rivals. More devastatingly, Lin had antagonized virtually all the CMC leaders and planners, who thereafter saw him as a traitor. One of the involved leaders later explained why they could not forgive Lin: "Lin Biao could have at least followed Premier Zhou's example – pretend that he was deaf and mute and not show his attitude [*zhuanlong zuoya bu biaotai*]. But he not only supported the Gang of Four but also sold out all of us [by turning in Tan's letter]."[141] But betrayal of his colleagues was what Lin had to do, given his ambition, Chen Yi's words, and, most of all, Mao's mounting pressure. Tragically, the rejection of the senior leaders made Lin feel friendless and hence more insecure despite the substantial consolidation of his position. As a result, Lin was more aggressive in his expansion, which in turn not only created more enemies but also made Mao feel threatened.

The ultimate price, however, was to be paid by Mao himself. First, Mao had to survive a virtually unbearable burden – to stand with the Maoists. Although Mao would soon realize their increasing unpopularity – he did try to distance himself from them in his later years, declaring in July 1974 that "Jiang Qing represented only herself" – he had to back them up whenever they were in real danger because their existence symbolized the legitimacy of the CR, which had become part of the Mao legacy. As the Maoists went to the extreme Left, Mao was transformed from a charismatic chairman, who could always "unite the majority" in decision making, into a Machiavellian tyrant who was alienated but feared by everyone around him. Moreover, as the CMC became defunct, Mao became more dependent on Lin, for now it was through Lin's factional networks that Mao's command could penetrate into the system. This enabled Lin to expand more aggressively, which would lead to a deadly prisoners' dilemma between Mao and Lin.

140 See Liao, *Xin zhongguo biannian shi*, pp. 298–9.
141 This former leader said these words in September 1995 when I asked him why he would "resolutely oppose" any efforts to reverse Lin's verdict, even though he did acknowledge that Lin had made "a substantial contribution to the revolution."

The Collapse of the Yan'an Round Table

An immediate consequence of the event, however, was the disconnection between the Center and the military mountaintops other than Lin's, resulting in a substantial decrease in the Center's control of the military. This was vividly shown by the Wuhan Incident of July 20.[142]

The situation in Wuhan provided an example of how the CR provoked factional struggles in the armed forces. Most civilian and military leaders in Wuhan, like Provincial Party Secretary Wang Renzhong, RMC Commander Chen Zaidao, and Commissar Zhong Hanhua, rose from the Fourth Front Red Army, which originated in this area, but the armed forces garrisoned there came from various mountaintops.[143] The factional cleavages were exposed in the CR. When the Workers' Headquarters, a coalition of mass organizations, began to "seize power" in February, the PLA air force in Wuhan, which was controlled by Lin's mountaintop, declared its endorsement. Yet the Wuhan RMC, dominated by those rising from the Fourth Front Red Army, issued a statement on March 18. This statement, approved by the military CRG led by Xu Xiangqian, former commander of the Fourth Front Red Army, declared that the armed forces that supported the Workers' Headquarters did "not represent the PLA." Moreover, the Wuhan RMC disbanded the Workers' Headquarters and arrested its leaders in March, accusing them of "attacking the military commanding system" – the act that was prohibited by the *Eight-Article Order*.

The Maoists saw this episode as a typical example of collusion between the local Party leaders and generals to suppress the Leftists. A *People's Daily* editorial on April 2 implied that the Wuhan RMC had "cracked down on the Leftists." On April 16 Jiang Qing declared that it was justified to "attack the Wuhan RMC where serious problems existed." Meanwhile, Chen Zaidao and Zhong Hanhua were summoned

---

142 Unless noted specifically, my analysis of this event is based on Chen Zaidao, "*Wuhan '7-20 shijian' shimo*" (The beginning and the end of the "July 20 Incident in Wuhan"), in *Zhongguo laonian* (Chinese Seniors), 1 (1983) to 1 (1984); Liao, *Xin zhongguo biannian shi*, pp. 302–4; and Gao Zhenpu, "*7.20 shijian qianhou*" (The period around the July 20 Incident), in Wang Mingwu, ed., *Zhou Enlai de licheng* (Zhou Enlai's Career), Beijing: PLA Art Press, 1996, 2:358–67.

143 Wuhan was seized by Lin's Fourth Field Army in May 1949, but the countryside around it had been occupied by Deng Xiaoping and Liu Bocheng's Second Field Army, which grew out of the Fourth Front Red Army. After Lin, Deng and Liu's armies marched southward, the vacancy was filled by Xu Xiangqian's troop in the Central Military Corps.

to Beijing to report to the CRG instead of the CMC. The meeting, chaired by Zhou Enlai on April 19, was fruitless because Chen and Zhong refused to cave in. The situation in Wuhan deteriorated after Chen and Zhong returned to Wuhan on April 29. With support from the Wuhan RMC, a new "mass organization," the Million Heroes, was set up in opposition to the Workers' Headquarters backed by the air force. The struggle between the two mass organizations soon escalated into massive violence, paralyzing the economy of Central China.

Mao went to Wuhan himself on July 14.[144] After a two-day meeting, followed by a two-day "persuasion" by Zhou, a compromise was achieved on July 18: the Wuhan RMC would endorse the Workers' Headquarters, and Mao personally promised Chen and Zhong that they would not be toppled despite their "error of line." It was also agreed that the change would be made gradually in order to avoid more chaos. Yet two CRG members, Wang Li and Xie Fuzhi, leaked the deal to the Workers' Headquarters. The next day, while the radicals celebrated their victory, members of the Million Heroes surrounded the Donghu Hotel where Wang and Xie stayed, unaware that Mao also stayed there. Trailing Chen Zaidao who "went to talk to Wang and Xie" in the early morning of July 20, the soldiers from the local garrison dashed into the room and detained Wang Li in Chen's presence. A civil war broke out in Wuhan immediately.

When the news arrived in Beijing, Zhou, who had just left Wuhan, rushed back to Wuhan – the situation was so bad that Zhou had to sneak into the city in the night. Also arriving with Zhou was Lin Biao's confidant Qiu Huizuo, director of the PLA Logistic Department. Qiu brought to Mao a joint letter from Lin and Jiang Qing, urging Mao to "leave Wuhan immediately." In the night, while Mao boarded a warship in the Yangtze River for Shanghai, Wang was released at Zhou's "stern order" (*zeling*). Wang and Xie flew to Beijing on July 22. As soon as they arrived, Lin Biao convened a meeting attended by Ye Jianying; Yang Chengwu; all the CRG members; and Lin's confidants Wu Faxian, the air force commander, and Li Zuopeng, the navy commissar, both of whom had just returned from Wuhan. They decided to mobilize the airborne forces and the Eastern Sea Fleet to take over Wuhan and to summon

---

144 According to Gao Zenpu (Zhou's body guard), "*7.20 shijian qianhou*," p. 358, Mao went to Wuhan because he "wanted to swim in the Yangtze River," and Zhou went there ahead of Mao to ensure Mao's security.

The Collapse of the Yan'an Round Table

Chen and Zhong to Beijing. Chen and Zhong arrived in Beijing at 3:30 A.M. on July 24 and were immediately detained. On July 26, Lin chaired an enlarged PSC meeting, at which Chen and Zhong were purged, and, not surprisingly, Xu Xiangqian was criticized as their backstage boss.

This episode exposed the extent to which Beijing had lost control of the RMCs – the commander (CO) at Wuhan RMC would not cave in even with Mao's personal intervention, for these COs' power rested not so much in their offices as in their mountaintops. Humiliation through public criticism at mass rallies, dismissals, and purges – the methods that could effectively eliminate a civilian leader's influence – had little effect on the RMC COs but could provoke violent reactions from their forces. Thus, Chen and Zhong were treated leniently, although they were accused of staging a "counterrevolutionary coup d'etat."[145] In August, Mao resolutely stopped a radical surge against military leaders consequent to the Wuhan Incident. Wang Li and Guan Feng, the two most radical CRG members, became the scapegoats and were thrown out.[146]

More importantly, the event fully exposed Mao's dependence on Lin during the crisis. Lin virtually made all the decisions and his men played crucial roles in suppressing the insurgency. Not surprisingly, Lin, as he said at a mass rally on July 25, "made [the Wuhan Incident] a big issue [*dazuo wenzhang*] concerning the whole country." The aim, as Kuai Dafu, a Red Guard leader explained, was to "knock down those rising from the Fourth Front Red Army ... in order to clear the obstacles for Lin to be [Mao's] successor."[147] Thus, while Xu Xiangqian was attacked as the backstage boss, a large number of high-ranking officers rising from the Fourth Front Red Army were toppled after the Wuhan Incident. As a result, for the first time since the establishment of the Yan'an Round Table, the officers rising from Mao's grand Jinggang Mountaintop achieved full control of the PLA Headquarters: besides Lin and his men, other leaders were Nie Rongzhen, who remained in charge of the defense industry and China's strategic forces, and Nie's associates, Yang Chengwu, acting chief of staff, and Fu Congbi, commander of the Beijing

---

145 Chen Zaidao, "*Nanwang de huiyi*" (Unforgettable memory), in Ke, *Mao Zedong de licheng*, 2:329, claimed that Mao saved his life by adding "comrade" in front of his name in the document, which denounced their "error of line."
146 See Harding, "The Chinese state in crisis," p. 183.
147 Yan, *Wenge shinian shi*, p. 267.

Garrison. Mao's command over the military seemed stronger than ever before.

But it was not to be. The tension between Mao's two most trusted marshals, Lin and Nie, soon surfaced. Although both of them rose to power from Mao's Jinggangshan base area and cocommanded the First Red Army Corp, and later the 115th Division (see Chapter 3), the relationship between the two was not so much a partnership as a rivalry. After the two departed in October 1938, Lin led the main force of the 115th Division going south, and eventually settled in Shandong. Nie was left in the Jin-cha-yi area with merely 3,000 people.[148] But Nie later developed a big mountaintop which was predominant in North China. Thus, not only did Nie have a substantial influence in the Beijing RMC, but his men were also a major force at the PLA Headquarters. Yet, when the CMC Caretaker Group was set up on August 17 to handle daily affairs on behalf of the CMC, it was headed by Wu Faxian, with Ye Qun and Lin's other two confidants, Qiu Huizuo and the navy's vice-commissar Zhang Xiuchuan, as members.[149] Yang Chengwu, acting chief of staff who was with Mao touring the East and South China, was an odd man out,

---

148 See Wei Wei and Zhou Junlun, eds., *Nie Rongzhen zhuan* (A Biography of Nie Rongzhen), Beijing: Contemporary China Press, 1994, pp. 179–81; also see Nie Rongzhen, *Nie Rongzhen huiyi lu* (Nie Rongzhen's Memoir), Beijing: PLA Press, 1984, 2:363–5. Even in these official accounts, one can sense the tension between Lin and Nie. A source who had worked with Nie since the 1930s pointed out: "The relationship between Lin and Nie was not as good as it appeared. It had always been tense. But neither intended to break it open." When asked if Mao knew the tension between the two, he replied: "Of course. Nothing could escape the Chairman's eyes. But I think he liked Lin better than Nie. Lin could read Mao's mind, but Nie just followed orders."

149 After criticizing Xu Xianqian, the CMC was virtually defunct, given that Ye had pleaded illness after being criticized (see Quan, *Long kun*, pp. 415–16). So Zhou Enlai suggested to Lin to set up a temporary organ – the CMC Caretaker Group – to handle daily affairs on behalf of the CMC. But when the order was issued, Xu Shiyou, a general who was the Nanjing RMC commander, complained to Mao, who was then in Shanghai: "How could they let Wu Faxian be in charge? He is just a lieutenant general!" Obviously, Xu resented that Wu was put in the position to command people like himself and Yang Chengwu, who were both senior generals. Although it seemed unlikely that Lin and Zhou could make the decision without consulting Mao beforehand, Mao mentioned the issue to Zhou when he returned to Beijing. So Zhou had to go between Mao and Lin again to put Yang as the head of the group. The name of the office was also changed to the CMC Administrative Group. Lin was obviously unhappy with all this, and he later blamed Yang, accusing him of "asking the Party for power" (*xiang dang yao quan*).

The Collapse of the Yan'an Round Table

although he also started his career under Lin's command during the Red Army period. Only after Mao returned to Beijing on September 23 was Yang appointed the head of the group, which was renamed the CMC Administrative Group, *at Zhou Enlai's suggestion*, and Wu Faxian was demoted to its vice-head.[150]

What alienated Yang even further from Lin was that he declined Lin's request on what Mao had said to the regional commanders during his tour in East and South China. Although Lin had learned that Mao had some negative words on him in these conversations, he did not know exactly to whom and in what context Mao made these comments. As the one who accompanied Mao throughout the tour, Yang obviously had the full information. Lin summoned Yang to his residence and asked Yang personally about Mao's conversations. But Yang declined, saying that he was not clear himself. Furthermore, as Yang and Wu jockeyed for positions, strife emerged between Lin's trio, Wu Faxian, Li Zuopeng, and Qiu Huizuo, and Nie's trio, Yang Chengwu, Yu Lijin (the air force commissar), and Fu Congbi, over the control of the PLA Headquarters.[151]

However, like Xu Xiangqian's men in the Wuhan Incident, Nie's trio had to face the joint forces of Lin and the Maoists because the close ties between Nie's mountaintop and the local authorities in North China disposed them to oppose the mass organizations backed by the CRG.[152] Two minor but dramatic events in March 1968 triggered the purge of Yang, Yu, and Fu. First, Wu Faxian's people detained Yu Lijin's secretary on March 5, accusing him of "leaking military secrets." But the actual reason was that Ye Qun and Wu Faxian wanted to embarrass Yang Chengwu, because Yu's secretary, who was a married man, was having an affair with Yang's unmarried daughter. Enraged, Yang forced Wu to release Yu's secretary immediately and to apologize to Yu.

Second, Fu Congbi, with Yang's approval, led a group of soldiers to the CRG on March 8, searching for the lost manuscripts of Lu Xun, a most influential left-wing writer before 1949. The action enraged Jiang

---

150 Liao, *Xin zhongguo biannian shi*, p. 305.
151 Unless noted specifically, my analysis on the Yang-Yu-Fu Incident is based on my interviews with several reliable sources and on Dong Chunbao, *Zai lishi de xuanwo zhong – yu Mao Zedong you guan de wangshi* (In the Whirlpool of History – the Happenings Related to Mao Zedong), Beijing: Zhongwai wenhua chuban gongsi (Publishing Company of China-Foreign Culture), 1990, pp. 3–136.
152 See Harding, "The Chinese state in crisis," p. 186.

not only because she was not notified beforehand, but also because she was embarrassed when the manuscripts were recovered in her safe.[153] Jointly, Lin and Jiang brought the cases to Mao. After what Lin called "four CC meetings at Mao's place," *all* the officers at the regiment level and above in the Beijing area – over 10,000 of them – were summoned to the People's Hall at midnight on March 24. Lin announced the dismissal of Yang, Yu, and Fu for the alleged crime of "anti-Party factionalism."[154] The aim of this unprecedented grand meeting and the blitz tactics was to prevent any resistance from Nie's people, given that the Beijing RMC had been their domain. Zhou Enlai warned repeatedly in his speech that officers who dared to stand with Yang, Yu, and Fu would "be sternly punished." Mao appeared at the end of the conference to show his support for Lin.[155] On the same day, Huang Yongsheng and Wen Yucheng – both were Lin's men – were appointed the PLA's chief of staff and commander of the Beijing Garrison. Given that the CMC was virtually defunct, Mao agreed to suspend the CMC meetings. Thereafter, all military affairs were handled by the CMC Administrative Group, which was virtually Lin's personal office formed by Huang, Wu, Ye, Li Zuopeng, Qiu Huizuo, and Zhang Xiuchuan. Lin's dominance at the PLA Headquarters was established.

Mao versus Lin: A Prisoners' Dilemma

"The CCP's Ninth Congress in April 1969 was a triumph for Lin Biao individually and for the PLA institutionally."[156] More significant was that this triumph resulted in a *structural* change of the Yan'an Round Table (Figure 6.2). Compared with the pre-CR Yan'an Round Table (cf. Figure 3.4 and Figure 4.2), a most visible change was the vanishing of the Party system. The effort to reconstruct the Party since late 1967 was barely fruitful.[157] The civilian affairs were managed by two elite groups: the Maoists and the planners. The former were flying high and controlled propaganda, document drafting, information flow, and public security; the latter, though severely mauled in the February Adverse Current, still

---

153 See Yan, *Wenge shinian shi*, pp. 272–5, 332.
154 Liao, *Xin zhongguo biannian shi*, pp. 308–9.   155 Yan, *Wenge shinian shi*, p. 271.
156 MacFarquhar, "The Succession to Mao," p. 306.   157 See ibid., pp. 312–13.

The Collapse of the Yan'an Round Table

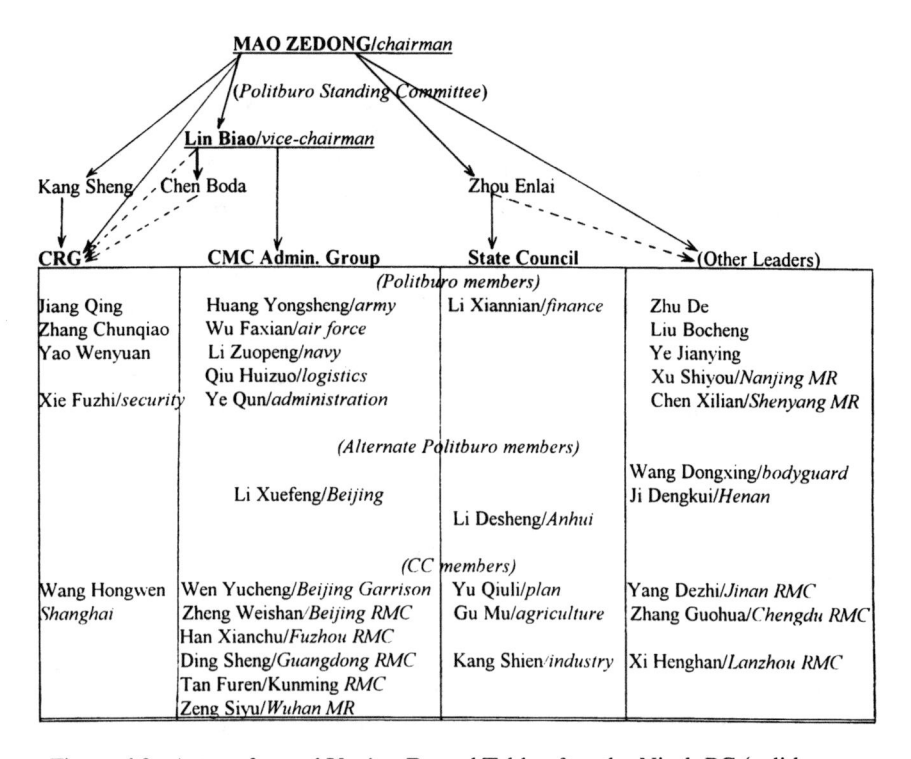

	MAO ZEDONG/*chairman*		
	(Politburo Standing Committee)		
	Lin Biao/*vice-chairman*		
Kang Sheng	Chen Boda	Zhou Enlai	
CRG	CMC Admin. Group	State Council	(Other Leaders)
	(Politburo members)		
Jiang Qing	Huang Yongsheng/*army*	Li Xiannian/*finance*	Zhu De
Zhang Chunqiao	Wu Faxian/*air force*		Liu Bocheng
Yao Wenyuan	Li Zuopeng/*navy*		Ye Jianying
	Qiu Huizuo/*logistics*		Xu Shiyou/*Nanjing MR*
Xie Fuzhi/*security*	Ye Qun/*administration*		Chen Xilian/*Shenyang MR*
	(Alternate Politburo members)		
			Wang Dongxing/*bodyguard*
	Li Xuefeng/*Beijing*		Ji Dengkui/*Henan*
		Li Desheng/*Anhui*	
	(CC members)		
Wang Hongwen	Wen Yucheng/*Beijing Garrison*	Yu Qiuli/*plan*	Yang Dezhi/*Jinan RMC*
Shanghai	Zheng Weishan/*Beijing RMC*	Gu Mu/*agriculture*	Zhang Guohua/*Chengdu RMC*
	Han Xianchu/*Fuzhou RMC*		
	Ding Sheng/*Guangdong RMC*	Kang Shien/*industry*	Xi Henghan/*Lanzhou RMC*
	Tan Furen/*Kunming RMC*		
	Zeng Siyu/*Wuhan MR*		

Figure 6.2. A transformed Yan'an Round Table after the Ninth PC (solid arrow = direct/full control; dashed arrow = indirect control)

managed economic affairs. Yet neither group had penetrating factional networks, except "the petroleum faction" – Yu Qiuli, Kang Shien, and Gu Mu – who had cultivated the oil industry as their power base,[158] and the Maoists who had a firm grasp of Shanghai.

The lack of penetrating factional networks handicapped the civilian leaders' capability in the policy process. Moreover, it furthered Mao's dependence on military support. This resulted in a remarkable increase in the military representation in the leadership. However, the military by now was virtually fragmented. Unlike the pre-CR Yan'an Round Table

---

158 All three rose from the petroleum industry in 1960s. See Lieberthal and Oksenberg, *Policy Making in China*.

at which military affairs were comanaged by the leaders from various mountaintops under Mao's command, now Lin's dominance was absolute: all the officers listed in the second column of Figure 6.2 were his men. Evidently, Mao tried to balance Lin's power. Three marshals, Zhu, Liu, and Ye, remained in the Politburo, and two RMC commanders, Xu Shiyou and Chen Xilian, who rose from the Fourth Front Red Army, were promoted into the Politburo. Yet, the officers in the fourth column either did not have their own mountaintops, like Zhu and Ye, or appeared lonely in the new environment, like Xu and Chen. The other RMC COs in this column had little influence in decision making because the bosses of their mountaintops had been toppled – Yang Dezhi rose from the Central Military Corps; Zhang Guohua, the Second Field Army; and Xi Henghan, the First Field Army.

The most significant change, however, was that Lin's dominance was institutionalized through the CMC Administrative Group, the only organ in the leadership that commanded a penetrating mountaintop. Indeed, the most substantial consequence of changes in leadership structure at the Ninth PC was that the entire leadership was largely based on support from Lin's mountaintop. No wonder that Mao felt threatened, because the godfather-like position he had maintained through his firm grasp of *all* the mountaintops appeared all of sudden like a figurehead position resting solely on Lin's mountaintop.

Mao had two choices in this situation: to continue his patronage of Lin or to contain Lin in order to secure his command. Lin also had two choices: to stop his expansion or to continue his expansion in order to strengthen his position. A prisoners' dilemma resulted between the two (see Introduction and Chapter 2). Obviously, Mao realized the danger. Even before the Ninth PC Mao hinted broadly his suspicion of Lin in front of some regional commanders and acting chief of staff Yang Chengwu in his tour of East and South China in August–September 1968. Mao ridiculed the "four greats" (great teacher, leader, commander, and helmsman) innovated by Lin, and he also expressed his dismay at the formulation that "the PLA was created by Chairman Mao and commanded by Vice-Commander Lin." Mao complained: "Why cannot I command myself if I could create it?"

To contain Lin, Mao had to seek support from the other military mountaintops, although they had been substantially damaged by Lin's attack. That was why Mao began to cultivate their leaders – Chen Yi, Nie

The Collapse of the Yan'an Round Table

Rongzhen, and Xu Xiangqian – soon after the Ninth PC.[159] Mao let Ye Jianying convene the three, who had no official positions at the time, to work on a "strategic plan" for China's foreign relations, especially the relationships with the United States and the Soviet Union. The meetings of the four marshals, which were held regularly for over four months, were such a top secret that even the four marshals' secretaries were not informed. All the arrangements, including the meetings, transportation, security, minute keeping, and report drafting, were handled by Xiong Xianghui, a top CCP secret agent who had close ties to Zhou Enlai.[160] The four marshals concluded that China's major threat was from the Soviet Union, while the United States, which was deeply involved in the Vietnamese War, posed no immediate danger to China. They suggested a focus on economic development at home and reconciliation with the United States abroad. However, Lin and his people, who had no idea about the four marshals' work, were working on the same topic at the time. At Lin's order, the CMC Administrative Group convened a month-long forum on "strategic policies" in June. Contrary to the four marshals' evaluation, Lin's people held that there was a great danger of war due to the tension between the two superpowers and, furthermore, their hostility to China. Thus, this forum produced a plan claiming that "the preparation for war is our overriding task."[161]

Although Mao, with Zhou's assistance, began to maneuver China's foreign relations covertly according to the four marshals' suggestions,[162] it was Lin's plan that prevailed in policy making, resulting in a substantial increase in the defense budget – 34 percent in 1969, 15 percent in 1970, and 16 percent in 1971 – and a massive migration of defense industries to the "strategic third front," the mountainous Southwest. This

---

159 Unless noted specifically, my analysis of the four marshals' work on international relations is based on Xiong Xianghui, "*Dakai zhongmei guanxi de qiancou*" (The prelude to the opening of the Sino-American relations), *Zhonggong dangshi ziliao* (Source Materials of the CCP History) (1992), 42:56–96.

160 Xiong, a secret CCP member, joined the KMT forces in 1933 at Zhou Enlai's instruction. He soon won the trust of Hu Zongnan, commander of the KMT forces in the Northwest. Xiong had since been the major source of intelligence for the CCP on the KMT in 1930s and 1940s. In 1948 the KMT regime sent him to the United States to be trained as a next-generation leader. After Xiong finished his study at the University of Minnesota, however, he appeared in Beijing in 1949 as a high-ranking CCP diplomat, and he has since worked on "diplomatic affairs" for the PRC.

161 Fang, *Jingji dashi ji*, p. 455; Liao, *Xin zhongguo biannian shi*, p. 324.

162 See "*Mao Zedong zhuan*," p. 185.

Factionalism in Chinese Communist Politics

policy cost China dearly and "severely hindered the development of the national economy."[163] Yet Mao achieved what he desired: while avoiding a premature confrontation with Lin, who never knew that there was another plan recommended by his rivals, Mao reconciled with Marshals Chen, Xu, and Nie by entrusting them with China's "strategic policy" behind Lin's back. Moreover, Mao also sent a clear message to Zhou Enlai and Ye, the two go-betweens in this affair. Thus, Mao had covertly prepared the siege of Lin, who was then at the peak of his power.

A crisis broke out in 1970 on whether the state chairmanship, which Mao abdicated in favor of Liu Shaoqi in 1959, should be abolished. Despite Mao's repeated rejections, Lin persisted that Mao should reassume this position.[164] Because Mao declared that he would not take the job, Lin's people hinted that Lin should be the candidate. The tension between Mao and Lin surfaced after the central work conference from March 17 to 20. At Mao's injunctions, it was decided at this conference to start two projects in order to reconstruct the state structure: revision of the state Constitution, and the preparation of the Fourth NPC to determine personnel arrangements for the state structure. Kang Sheng, Zhang Chunqiao, Wu Faxian, Li Zuopeng, and Ji Dengkui took charge of the first project; Zhou Enlai, Zhang Chunqiao, Huang Yongsheng, Xie Fuzhi, and Wang Dongxing were in charge of the second one. Notably, Zhang Chunqiao's influence increased; he was the only one who was involved in both groups. By contrast, Chen Boda was the odd man out. Most distinctive, however, was that Vice-Chairman Lin was virtually excluded from the reconstruction of state, for both groups reported to Mao directly!

This arrangement was read by Lin and his men as a sign of Mao's distrust, or at least that Mao had shifted his trust from Lin to the Maoists, especially Zhang Chunqiao. More agonizing was the expectation that, as a military leader, Lin would have little legitimacy to intervene in, let

---

163 Ibid., p. 186.
164 Unless noted specifically, my analysis of this episode is based on Jin Chongji, "*Lushan huiyi yu Lin Biao shijian*" (Lushan conference and the Lin Biao Incident), *Bainian chao* (Hundred Year Tide), no. 5 (1997), pp. 9–22; Wang, *1949–1989 nian de zhongguo*, pp. 382–434; "*Mao Zedong zhuan*," pp. 181–2; Wang Dongxing, "*Jiujie erzhong quanhui fengbo*" (The storm at the Second Plenum of the Ninth CC), in Ke, *Mao Zedong de licheng*, 2:335–57; Liao, *Xin zhongguo biannian shi*, pp. 328–9, 332–3; and my interviews with a few reliable sources.

The Collapse of the Yan'an Round Table

alone to lead, the policy process once the state structure was reestablished. As a result, Lin's position as Mao's successor would become vulnerable. Contrary to the CCP official account that Lin's pushing Mao to assume the state chairmanship was prompted by "his own wild ambition" to be the head of state, Lin's effort appeared genuine, for what really mattered to Lin was not so much whether he could be the head of state as whether his status as Mao's successor would be legitimized in the reconstruction of the state. Had Mao assumed the state chairmanship, Lin, Mao's successor, would naturally assume the vice-chairmanship and therefore obtain legitimacy in the state leadership. Lin's intention was clearly revealed by Ye Qun's complaint to Wu Faxian in July: "If there is no state chairmanship, what will Lin Biao do? Where will [Lin] be located?"

However, viewed from the perspective of the structure of Yan'an Round Table, in which the separation of the Party and military systems was vital for Mao's command (see Chapter 3), it was a rational choice for Mao to prevent Lin from expanding into the civilian system, especially when Lin had achieved predominance in the military. Given that the reconstruction of the state essentially embodied Mao's effort to restore the two-system structure of the Yan'an Round Table, it was not surprising that Mao was determined to deny Lin any access to the new state structure – that was why Mao not only refused to assume the state chairmanship but also insisted that the entire institution of state chairmanship be abolished.

The crisis in the Mao-Lin relationship became more explosive as Chen Boda jumped into Lin's boat because of his rivalry with Zhang Chunqiao, which started during the drafting of the political report for the Ninth PC. Originally, Chen was assigned to take overall charge of the drafting, in which Zhang and Yao Wenyuan also participated. But Zhang and Yao would submit their draft directly to Mao via Jiang Qing, instead of Chen Boda. Chen was very upset and decided to do the same, to submit his own draft to Mao. As a result, two drafting groups emerged, and Mao later decided to use Zhang and Yao's draft, but with major revisions. Chen's depression at feeling forsaken by Mao and his bitterness at Zhang and his patron, Jiang, drove him to Lin's camp.

Soon, Lin and his men were also offended by Zhang in the drafting of the new state constitution before the Second Plenum. Zhang suggested cutting off the words that Mao "brilliantly and constructively developed Marxism and Leninism." But this was seen by Lin's men as a gross insult to Lin rather than Mao because these words were Lin's innovation. Moreover, when Wu Faxian and Li Zuopeng managed to insert a clause on the head of state in the draft,[165] Zhang picked out their insertion, saying that it was "against the Chairman's instruction." All this was seen as unacceptably rude to Lin: how dare Zhang, a newly promoted pen handler, turn down Vice-Chairman Lin's idea with such an arrogance! More significant was that Zhang's comment highlighted differences between Mao and Lin on this issue, turning a low-profile disagreement into a high-profile policy dispute. No wonder that Zhang became the target of oblique attacks by Lin's associates at the Second Plenum, and he was also the only person besides Mao on the assassin list of Lin's son Lin Liguo.

The showdown occurred at the Second Plenum of the Ninth CC, held from August 23 to September 6 at Lushan, where Peng Dehuai had fallen eleven years earlier. But Lin had learned Peng's lesson well. He carefully avoided all the missteps Peng had made. First of all, instead of exchanging *privately* with Mao as Peng did, Lin raised the issue of the head of state at the PSC meeting at the eve of the plenum. Although Mao again expressed his objection, Lin, as if he had already had Mao's approval, raised the issue again and urged Mao to assume the state chairmanship in his speech at the opening session of the plenum the next morning. Lin's speech was so long that Zhou had to cancel his prescheduled speech on economy. Lin's aim was obvious: to make the state chairmanship a *legitimate* issue before Mao could make his stand clear at the plenum, so that Mao would have to go along with it once the momentum was created.

Second, instead of challenging Mao as Peng did, Lin praised Mao as the greatest genius whose "position as the great leader, head of state, and supreme commander" had to be written in the Constitution. Thus, Lin attempted to use Mao's prestige against Mao, and he was "threatening that the opponents of retaining the state chairmanship could be accused of being anti-Mao."[166]

Third, instead of losing the momentum by waiting for Mao's response as Peng did, Lin had his followers promote his idea immediately after

165 Cf. Hao and Duan, *Liushi nian*, p. 613.
166 MacFarquhar "The Succession to Mao," p. 317.

The Collapse of the Yan'an Round Table

Lin's speech. Lin's tactics appeared successful. Although Mao refused to assume the state chairmanship at the PSC meeting, he could no longer insist that the position had to be abolished. In fact, Mao did not even mention the state chairmanship at all at the plenum after Lin's speech.

But never would Mao give up. As a master strategist, Mao counterattacked the weakest part of Lin's camp while dodging a direct confrontation. Zhang Chunqiao took the floor on the morning of August 24. *Unexpectedly*, Zhang challenged the genius theory Lin had preached: "Marxism holds that a great leader is produced in the revolutionary struggle of broad masses, not by self-claimed genius." Zhang's speech drew attack from Lin's camp immediately, not just because Zhang again dared to stick his neck out against Lin, but, more importantly, because Zhang's criticism of the genius theory hit right on the ideological base of Lin's proposal of the state chairmanship. Not surprisingly, Chen Boda took the lead in attacking Zhang at the North China group, clamoring: "those who attempt to deny Chairman Mao as the greatest genius ... must be thoroughly denounced and cut into thousands of pieces [*doudao pichou, qiandao wangua*]!"[167] Chen praised Lin's speech, claiming that it "represented the desire of the entire Party, entire army, and entire people," who all "strongly requested that [Mao] assume the state chairmanship and [Lin], the vice-chairmanship." Meanwhile, Lin's people, Ye, Wu, Li, and Qiu, promoted the same ideas at the Central-South, Southwest, and Northwest regional groups. (Huang Yongsheng was in Beijing.) The attack on Zhang was so overwhelming that even Wang Dongxing jumped onto the bandwagon, and Wang Hongwen, Zhang's protégé, also prepared a speech, vowing to defend "the Greatest Genius Leader Chairman Mao."

However, the fierce attack on Zhang *transformed* the issue from whether the state chairmanship should be retained to whether Mao should be seen as "the greatest genius," which further extended to whether Mao's leadership was based on his genius or on his revolutionary practice. Thus, Mao had his opponents trapped – the aim of preaching Mao's genius is to deny Mao's revolutionary practice! On August 25 Mao convened an enlarged PSC meeting, at which Mao attacked Chen's speech as "anti-Marxism" and ordered Chen to make a self-criticism.

---

167 See Liao, *Xin zhongguo biannian shi*, p. 333.

Thus, "Mao set the tone for a counterattack by circulating, on August 31, *A Few of My Opinions*."[168]

Mao's attack was *strategic* because it focused on Chen rather than Lin, and on the genius theory rather than the issue of state chairmanship; it was *legitimate* because the genius theory was against the tenets of Marxism; it was *lethal* to Lin's effort on the state chairmanship because it tore apart its ideological basis; and hence it was *overwhelming* because it smashed Lin's momentum by taking away its ideological legitimacy.

True, Chen's fall seemed to have caused little substantial damage to Lin's force, for Chen did not really have his own power base – that was presumably why Lin gave up on him so easily.[169] It was also true that Lin encouraged his people after the plenum: "[We] are not good at playing theories, but good at playing the guns." But this was self-consoling, for Lin had long realized that, in his words, one "could not succeed without two barrels: the barrel of a gun and the barrel of a pen." Like Peng Zhen's fall, which gave Mao the ideological legitimacy to purge the PB, Chen's fall secured Mao's ideological superiority in the struggle against Lin. Without the ideological high ground, Lin had to take defensive stance, while Mao was gradually wearing down Lin's mountaintop.

Yet Mao did not have a *force* that could overwhelm Lin's mountaintop. That was why, instead of a frontal assault as he did against the PB, Mao adopted a guerilla strategy – "throwing stones, mixing in sand, and digging up the cornerstones" – to force Lin to chicken out.[170] The CC Organization and Propaganda Group was set up on November 16, with Kang Sheng as head, Jiang, Zhang, Yao, Ji Dengkui, and Li Desheng as members; the inclusion of Ji and Li marked the entrance of local mountaintop leaders into the core of decision making. The group reported to Mao directly. Thus, Lin and his men were deprived of their say in propaganda and organizational affairs, the two most important areas in CCP politics. On the same day, Mao threw out his first "stone": the CC dispatched an instruction on Chen's "anti-Party crimes."[171] In order to

---

168 MacFarquhar, "The Succession to Mao," p. 319.
169 Ye Qun and Wu Faxian actually attacked Chen after the plenum. They complained to Jiang Qing that Chen "had fooled" them.
170 Cf. MacFarquhar, "The Succession to Mao," pp. 323–34.
171 See Liao, *Xin zhongguo biannian shi*, p. 334.

The Collapse of the Yan'an Round Table

"expose Chen's crime," two conferences were convened in December: the CMC forum on the 9th, which was chaired by Ye Jianying and attended by 143 high-ranking officers, and the North China conference on the 22nd, which was chaired by Xie Fuzhi and attended by 449 leading cadres and officers in North China. Yet, the attempt to abuse Lin and his men by criticizing Chen was stonewalled at both conferences. As Mao complained, "the CMC forum had been held for over a month, but Chen was not criticized at all. . . . During the first part of the North China conference, the criticism of Chen Boda was also superficial and perfunctory."[172] The inability of the Maoists and the newly promoted local leaders to shake up Lin exposed their vital weakness: they did not have access to the factional networks. Moreover, it also indicated that the massive purge and replacement of military leaders during the heyday of Lin's expansion had not only damaged these military mountaintops but also cut off their ties with the Center.

Zhou Enlai, the political mediator, was the only one who had maintained his access to various mountaintops and, more importantly, he was *trusted* by their leaders because Zhou had at least tried to provide certain protections to them. Although Mao had apparently been reluctant to have Zhou involved in the struggle against Lin, he had no choice but to let Zhou take charge after he realized that the joint force of the Maoists and the newly promoted local leaders was unable to shake up Lin's mountaintop. Thus, Zhou, who was then preoccupied with the National Planning Conference (held from December 16, 1970, to February 29, 1971),[173] was called up to take over the operation. This was the first time that Zhou had been entrusted with the top command position in an intra-Party struggle since the establishment of the Yan'an Round Table.

Zhou lived up to Mao's expectation. With the newly entrusted authority over military affairs, Zhou merged the CMC forum into the North China conference on January 9. He announced that North China had been "a major disaster zone [*zhong zaiqu*] of Chen Boda's sinister influence." Zhou instructed that the criticism of Chen had to be focused on the questions Mao raised on December 16 on a report from the Thirty-eighth Army Corps: "Why was Chen Boda allowed to fool around and spread gossip [in North China]? He had no position in the Beijing RMC,

---

172 Ibid., 339.   173 See Fang, *Jinji dashi ji*, pp. 470–1.

nor did the Center entrust him with any military or civilian problems in the Beijing RMC. For what reasons could Chen become the backstage boss of the Beijing RMC and the North China region?"[174]

Zhou's criticism of Chen was essentially a covert attack on Lin because it was Lin who authorized Chen to intervene in affairs of the Beijing RMC and therefore in civilian affairs in North China. In his summary speech on January 24, Zhou shocked the attendees by announcing a reorganization of the Beijing RMC: Commissar Li Xuefeng and Commander Zheng Weishan would be replaced by Xie Fuzhi and Li Desheng. Lin's "cornerstone" was thus dug up, although the conference failed to achieve Mao's desired goal: to force Lin's men – Huang, Wu, Ye, Li, and Qiu – to make self-criticisms in order to shake up Lin's mountaintop.

After he had the Beijing RMC under control, Zhou convened another conference in April 15–29 to criticize Chen. This time Huang, Wu, Ye, Li, and Qiu were all forced to make self-criticisms in front of 449 leading cadres. Zhou declared in his summary speech: "Politically, they [i.e., Huang, Wu, Ye, Li, and Qiu] have committed the *error of line*; and organizationally, they have committed the *error of factionalism*."[175] This was virtually a death sentence in CCP politics – no wonder that Lin's son Lin Liguo and his associates decided to "speed up" the preparation for an armed uprising after this conference. Yet, without ideological legitimacy and being cut off, Lin had little chance. After the desperate plan to assassinate Mao aborted, Lin, his wife, and son flew to the Soviet Union on September 13, 1971. They were all killed as their plane crashed.[176]

Lin's fall dealt a devastating blow not only to Mao personally – "How could Mao have been so wrong for so long?" – but also to the legitimacy of the CR – "Was [the treachery and intrigue worthy of the palace politics] the purified politics the CR should have produced?"[177] A more substantial damage was the disconnection between the Yan'an Round Table

---

174 Quoted from Liao, *Xin zhongguo biannian shi*, p. 336.
175 Ibid., pp. 339–40 (emphasis added).
176 Frederick Teiwes and Warren Sun, *The Tragedy of Lin Biao: Riding the Tiger during the Cultural Revolution, 1966–1971*, London: C. Hurst, 1996, offer a new perspective of Lin's case. They try to prove that Lin was virtually innocent but he was manipulated by his wife, son, and the men around him.
177 Liao, *Xin zhongguo biannian shi*, pp. 335–6.

The Collapse of the Yan'an Round Table

and factional networks, for none among those who remained at the Center had any penetrating mountaintops. As a result, Mao's command, which had been based on his firm grasp of various mountaintops, appeared more vulnerable than ever before. On October 3, a new CMC General Office was set up to handle military affairs, with Ye Jianying as its head, and Xie Fuzhi, Zhang Chunqiao, Li Xiannian, Li Desheng, Ji Dengkui, Wang Dongxing, Chen Shiqu, Zhang Caiqian, and Liu Xianquan as members. It was striking that the representation of the major military mountaintops, particularly Mao's First Front Red Army, was barely existent in this new supreme military organ: Ye Jianying and his long-term secretary Liu Xianquan barely had any mountaintops; Xie Fuzhi and Li Xiannian had been kept out of military affairs since 1949; Zhang Caiqian rose from the local forces in Hubei; Li Desheng, Ji Dengkui, and Wang Dongxing had yet to develop their influence in the armed forces. Thus, Chen Shiqu, who had been the chief of staff of the Third Field Army, was the only one who had certain influence in a major military mountaintop. Zhang Chunqiao, who had no military experience at all, entered the military high command, for there were few left in the military whom Mao could fully trust.

DENG XIAOPING'S RETURN AND FALL: THE COLLAPSE OF THE YAN'AN ROUND TABLE

Containing Zhou Enlai

Zhou benefited most from Lin's fall. True, Zhou's significant role in the opening to the United States attracted worldwide attention,[178] but his increasing prominence during the Lin Biao affair and its aftermath was rooted essentially in his access to various mountaintops. The prime commandership in the struggle against Lin also enabled Zhou to cash in on his political investment – he had protected the senior cadres and officers (except those from Liu Shaoqi's mountaintop) from Lin's prey.[179] As the new number two figure in the leadership, Zhou was actu-

---

178 Cf. Nathan Pollack, "The opening to America," in MacFarquahar and Fairbank, *The Cambridge History of China*, 15:419–26.
179 During the Lin Biao Incident, Zhou had such an authority that he kept all elite members, including Mao himself, in the People's Hall until after the Chinese Embassy

ally more influential than his predecessors, Liu Shaoqi and Lin Biao, as his authority extended to both the civilian and military systems during the Lin Biao Affair. This development was what Mao had tried to prevent since the establishment of the Yan'an Round Table and it posted a bigger threat to Mao's command.

Thus, it was not surprising to see Zhou's power being contained soon after the Lin Biao Affair. His authority in maneuvering the military, which had been entrusted to him during the struggle against Lin, was taken away immediately after Lin's fall. Ye Jianying was entrusted with all military affairs. Meanwhile, Zhang Chunqiao, whom Mao had considered to be a "good candidate" for successor,[180] took over the PLA Political Department. Zhang used the position quite effectively to check Zhou's influence after Lin's fall. In February 1972 and February 1973, Zhang twice vetoed the *Outline on National Economic Plans* drafted under Zhou's supervision, claiming rightfully that they were "anti-CR."[181] By October 1972, the Maoists, who had been in disarray since Lin's fall, regrouped and reversed Zhou's antileftist offensive with Mao's support. Contrary to Zhou's claim that "the Lin Biao anti-Party clique was ultraleft," Mao decreed on December 17 that Lin "was an ultrarightist," which the Maoists had advocated.[182]

The effort to contain Zhou's power was best shown in the new leadership formed at the Tenth PC in August 1973 (Table 6.3). Personnel arrangements in the Politburo were obviously aimed at checking Zhou's power, although Zhou's bladder cancer, which was diagnosed on May 18, 1972,[183] had been wearing him down. Not only did Zhou's prominence diminish among the unprecedented number of vice-chairmen – five of

in Mongolia confirmed Lin's death on September 16. During those days, only Li Xiannian and Li Desheng were allowed to leave the People's Hall. See Cheng, *Zhou Enlai he tade mishumen*, pp. 448–9.
180 Wang, *Da dongluan de niandai*, pp. 397–8, says that Mao once mentioned to Lin that "Xiao [little] Zhang is a good candidate" for Lin's successor. But a well-informed source doubts the credibility of the story. One thing, he pointed out, is that Mao never referred to Zhang Chunqiao as "Xiao Zhang," but always "Chunqiao." Jiang Qing was the one who often used "Xiao Zhang" to reminded him of his inferior status in front of her.
181 Fang, *Jingji dashi ji*, pp. 487–8, 508–9.
182 See Wang Ruoshui, "*Cong pi 'zuo' daoxiang fanyou de yici geren jingli*" (My individual experience in the reversal from criticizing "leftism" to opposing rightism), *China Daily News*, New York, March 12–21, 1989.
183 See Cheng, *Zhou Enlai he ta de mishumen*, pp. 527–8.

The Collapse of the Yan'an Round Table

Table 6.3. *The Leadership Formed at the Tenth PC (August 24–28, 1973), Mao Zedong/Chairman*

Radicals	Beneficiaries	Mao Followers	Moderates
Politburo Standing Committee			
Wang Hongwen/ vice-chair	Li Desheng/ vice-chair	Zhu De/ vice-chair	Zhou Enlai/ vice-chair
Kang Sheng/ vice-chair		Ye Jianying/ vice-chair	
Zhang Chunqiao		Dong Biwu	
Politburo			
Jiang Qing (Mme Mao)	Ji Dengkui	Liu Bocheng	Li Xiannian
Yao Wenyuan	Wang Dongxing	Xu Shiyou	
	Wei Guoqing	Chen Xilian	
	Hua Guofeng	Chen Yonggui	
	Wu De		

them – but he was also in an absolute minority at the Politburo: only Ye, Xu, and Chen, who were politically the Mao followers but moderates in policy preferences, were his potential supporters. The Maoists outnumbered the moderates. The majority in the Politburo, the beneficiaries,[184] maintained an ambiguous attitude in the conflict between the Maoists and the moderates unless Mao's stand was clear. Thus, with his firm control of the Maoists, the beneficiaries, and his own followers, Mao seemed to have once again consolidated his command at the Tenth PC.

However, Mao's command was baseless because the entire leadership was disconnected from the major mountaintops after Lin's fall. Moreover, Zhou and his associates still had considerable influence in the policy process because of their access to the local factional networks. Thus, although the Maoists repeatedly blocked Zhou's policy initiatives, Zhou's ideas were still put into practice to various degrees across China.[185] But access to factional networks was not enough to have the

---

184 For the definition of "beneficiaries," see MacFarquhar, "The succession to Mao," p. 338.
185 See Fang, *Jingji dashi ji*, p. 609; and Hao and Tuan, *Liushi nian*, p. 626.

Factionalism in Chinese Communist Politics

situation under full control, and Zhou's influence was belittled further as he lacked the majority support at the Center. The inability of either side to dominate on the one hand and the leadership's impotence to subdue factional networks on the other hand not only resulted in an ebb of economic growth in 1972–4,[186] but also provoked the resurgence of chaos in some key areas like Zhengzhou in Central China, Shijiazhuang in North China, and Zhijiang in East China.

Deng Xiaoping's Return and the Decline of Zhou's Power

Apparently, Mao saw the danger of losing control of factional networks, and he also realized that the leaders who remained at the Center could neither subdue the existing mountaintops nor develop their own in a short period of time. To stabilize the situation, he had to bring back someone who had certain control over the factional networks.

Deng Xiaoping was the only one available at that time who had access to mountaintops in *both* the civilian and military systems. As I have discussed in Chapter 3, Deng was one of the few CCP leaders who had power bases in both systems. Deng's forces – the 129th Division, which later grew into the Second Field Army (see Figure 6.1) – were always assigned to the most difficult tasks during the revolution: the opening of the Jin-Yi-Lu-Yu base area in the late 1930s; the frontal resistance of the KMT forces in North China in 1946–7; the march into Central China in 1947; the Huaihai Campaign in 1948; and the march into the Southwest in 1949.[187] Moreover, whenever there was a chance, Mao would shift Deng's troops into other forces: two detachments to Shandong in 1938; an entire army to Central China in 1940; seven regiments to Henan in 1944; and a force with a framework for twenty-five regiments to Manchuria in 1945.[188] All these were aimed at wearing down

---

186 Percentage rates of yearly economic growth in China from 1966 to 1975, expressed by growth of GNP, with corresponding industrial and agricultural growth in parentheses, are as follows: 13.4% (15.8%, 9.2%); –9.6 (–13.8, 1.6); –4.2 (–5, –2.5); 23.8 (34.3, 1.1); 25.7 (—, —); 12.2 (14.9, 3.1); 4.5 (6.6, –0.2); 9.2 (9.5, 8.4); 1.4 (0.3, 4.2); and 11.9 (15.1, 4.6). Fang, *Jingji dashi ji*.
187 Deng Maomao, *My Father Deng Xiaoping*.
188 See Zhang Guoqi and Li Guoxiang, *Zhongguo renmin jiefangjun fazhan yange yange, 1927–1949* (The Organizational Development of the PLA, 1927–1949), Beijing: PLA Press, 1984, pp. 167–9; also cf. Deng, *My Father Deng Xiaoping*, p. 367.

The Collapse of the Yan'an Round Table

the forces growing out of Zhang Guotao's Fourth Front Red Army (see Chapter 3). These deployments, however, helped Deng extend his influence throughout the armed forces and all over the country because Deng had fostered contacts between these forces and his own mountaintop after he was appointed commissar of the 129th Division in January 1938. Thus, "Commissar Deng" became the earmark title addressed *only* by those who rose from the 129th Division and later the Second Field Army.

More importantly, Deng still had Mao's trust. Although Deng had been purged as the number two "capitalist roader" next to Liu, their cases were fundamentally different. Liu's rise to power resulted from his political marriage with Mao in the struggle against the Wang Ming faction (see Chapter 3). This marriage ended as soon as Mao could no longer benefit from it. Liu was Mao's *personal victim* in the sense that Mao was determined to destroy Liu in order to secure his command. But Deng's "three great-leaps" in his rise to power – commissar of the 129th Division in 1938, secretary of the CMC Front Committee of the Huaihai Campaign in 1948, and general secretary of the CC Secretariat in 1956 – were all achieved with Mao's patronage (see Chapters 3 and 4). After the Eighth PC it was well known in the elite circle that Lin was Mao's "best student" in the military, and Deng was Mao's most-favored Party leader. The Mao-Deng relationship began to sour in the early 1960s largely because as a major first-front leader, Deng's choice in policy making was subject to the structural constraints of the two-front arrangement, where Deng's well-being depended not so much on his loyalty to Mao as on policy outcomes (see Chapter 5). Thus, Deng was an *institutional victim* of the CR in the sense that he fell with the Party state, which Mao was determined to destroy. That was why Mao kept Deng in the Party while Liu was "expelled from the Party forever" at the Twelfth Plenum of the Eighth CC.[189]

This special bond with Mao emboldened Deng to write to Mao as soon as he learned of Lin's fall on November 15, 1971. He asked Mao for "a chance to correct [his] mistakes in practice."[190] Obviously, Deng's

---

189 See Ke, *Mao Zedong de licheng*, 2:333–4.
190 Yue Zong and Xin Zhi, eds., *Deng Xiaoping shengping yu lilun yanjiu huibian* (Collection of Studies on Deng Xiaoping's Career and Theory), Beijing: CCP Historical Materials Press, 1988, p. 308.

letter drew Mao's attention. He told Mme Chen at Marshal Chen Yi's memorial ceremony on January 6, 1972, that Deng's case belonged to the "contradictions among the people." Mao's words were soon passed to Deng, who had been in Jiangxi since 1969.[191]

However, despite Mao's words, which had been spread among the elite members, Deng was left out in the first wave of rehabilitation started in April 1972 under Zhou's leadership.[192] It was not surprising that no one from Liu's mountaintop was rehabilitated; they would not return until the Deng period. But Deng was disappointed as well as spurred by seeing the rehabilitated leaders appear at the celebration of the Army Day on August 1. He wrote to Mao again on August 3. Compared with his first letter, Deng was more anxious to return, and therefore his words were more flattering and self-abased. Deng vowed that should he be allowed to work, he would "never reverse the verdict" of the CR.[193] Mao was obviously touched. He urged the Politburo to rehabilitate Deng on August 14. Mao's comment on Deng's letter reads:

> The mistake *Comrade* Deng Xiaoping made is serious. But he must be distinguished from Liu Shaoqi: (1) He was the target of attack in the Central Soviet Area.... [He] was *the head of the so-called Mao faction*. Zhang Wentian was the one who purged him. (2) He has no historical problems, i.e., he never surrendered to the enemy. (3) He ... had merits during the War. In addition, ... *he did not yield to the Soviet revisionists*. I have talked about these things *many times* in the past. Now [I] repeat them once more.[194]

But Deng would not return until March 1973. Given Mao's absolute power, it was incredible that it took so long to rehabilitate Deng despite Mao's repeated intervention since early 1972. Who tried to block Deng? Why?

Not surprisingly, the CCP official account lays the blame conveniently

---

191 Liu Jintian, ed., *Deng Xiaoping de licheng – yige weiren he ta de yige shiji* (Deng Xiaoping's Career – a Great Man and His Century), Beijing: PLA Art Press, 1994, 2:155.
192 Liao, *Xin zhongguo biannian shi*, p. 348.
193 See *Deng Xiaoping gei Mao zhuxi de xin*, August 3, 1972 (located in the John K. Fairbank Center Library, Harvard University).
194 Quoted from Ke, *Mao Zedong de licheng*, 2:384 (emphasis added).

The Collapse of the Yan'an Round Table

on the Gang of Four, although little evidence has been produced to support the assertion. A reliable source told me that Deng's return was delayed simply because "no one mentioned his name when the issue [of rehabilitation] was discussed at the Politburo." Given that this source was close to a Politburo member who was among the beneficiaries, it seems that resistance to Deng's return came mainly from this silent majority at the Politburo. It is not hard to see why they were reluctant. Naturally, they felt nervous about the return of Deng and other veteran leaders, because they rose essentially at the veteran leaders' expense. Moreover, they realized that the veteran leaders' return would undermine their positions in the leadership, given their newly promoted status, lack of connections, and inexperience.

Reluctant though they were, the beneficiaries were not powerful enough to block Deng's return; otherwise, leaders like Chen Yun, Tan Zhenlin, and Wang Zhen could not have come back so quickly.[195] But they had a willing collaborator in Zhou Enlai, who was in charge of the rehabilitation. Indeed, there is little evidence to substantiate the CCP official account that Zhou played a major role in bringing Deng back.[196] The fact that the two would become allies or, more precisely, be pushed together in the fight against the Maoists, does not prove that Zhou played a crucial role in Deng's return. The only piece of evidence for the official argument is a note Zhou dropped to Ji Dengkui, who was then in charge of organizational affairs, and Wang Dongxing, head of the Central Body Guards, on December 12, 1972, four months after Mao's comment on Deng's second letter. Zhou wrote: "Deng Xiaoping and his family once asked to have a little work to do. Please consider it. The Chairman has also mentioned it several times."[197] Judging from the context, it is hard to see that Zhou was urging Ji and Wang to solve Deng's problem. Rather, it appeared more like a reluctant and, indeed, very much belated relay of Mao's instructions on Deng's return.[198]

---

195 According to Liao, *Xin zhongguo biannian shi*, pp. 347–8, Zhou played a crucial role in bringing back these senior leaders.

196 In July 1996 I confronted a former leader of the CC Department for Research on Party Literature (*zhongyang wenxian yanjiu shi*). Although he defended Zhou zealously, he had little evidence to substantiate his assertion that Zhou played a major role in bringing Deng back.

197 Quoted from Jiang, *Zhou Enlai de licheng*, 2:466.

198 A reliable source told me that Ji Dengkui, who was then in charge of organization affairs, was very much confused by Zhou's reluctance on solving Deng's case despite

Factionalism in Chinese Communist Politics

Objectively, Zhou had little to gain from Deng's return. First, the relationship between the two was not as close as the official account claims. True, both of them were active among the radical students in France in the 1920s, but Zhou, a major leader of the CCP European Branch, was too prominent to notice Deng, a teenager then, who was not even a CCP member when Zhou left France in 1924.[199] Deng, a major front-line commissar, did not have significant contact with Zhou. The two began to work together after Deng was appointed a vice-premier in 1952, apparently a watchdog for Mao at the State Council. But the job was obviously not so enjoyable for Deng, who virtually quit and joined the "patient club" with Lin Biao, Chen Yun, and Kang Sheng. Deng became active at the Center only after the 1954 Gao-Rao Affair (see Chapter 4).

Moreover, the power that was likely to be entrusted to Deng would come mostly at Zhou's cost. Deng would certainly not be entrusted with propaganda and ideology – the Maoists' domain – because as a major victim of the CR, it was unlikely that Deng could carry on the ideological approach that had legitimated the CR. Neither would Deng be entrusted with organizational affairs, for that would confuse and even panic all the beneficiaries who rose to power virtually at the cost of Deng and his like. Thus, the areas that Deng was expected to take over would be the areas in administration, foreign relations, the military, and the economy – all were under Zhou's control or influence. In general, Mao's aim to bring Deng back was to resume control of the factional networks, but a practical reason for Mao to call Deng back was to contain Zhou's power – that was why the Maoists actually helped Deng's comeback rather than opposing it. Notably, the official account falls short in pro-

---

Mao's repeated instructions. But he explains this as the way Zhou dealt with Mao when he was not sure of Mao's true intention: "Mao could have used Deng's case to test Zhou's true attitude on the CR. Zhou would have had trouble had he been too enthusiastic on bringing Deng back." But after hearing my explanation that Zhou did not really want Deng back, this source responded: "It is possible, given Deng's personality and his well-known stubbornness. But Zhou was reluctant to let Deng come back indeed. The official propaganda has [its own] purpose."

199 Cf. Deng, *My Father Deng Xiaoping*. Notably, she used a lot of space describing her father's friendship with Chen Yi, Li Fuchun, and Nie Rongzhen, which started during their stay in France. Most Party historians would agree that Deng Maomao at least exaggerates her father's "close relationship" with Zhou in France.

The Collapse of the Yan'an Round Table

viding evidence to support its claim that Zhou helped bring Deng back; neither does it substantiate its blame that the Maoists tried to block Deng's return. During the 1980 trial of the Gang of Four, which was broadcast live, Jiang Qing challenged the court: "it was me who nominated and proposed [*timing jianyi*] to the Politburo to let Deng Xiaoping resume his work [at the Center]."[200] None, including Deng himself, ever denied Jiang's claim.

Indeed, only *after* Zhou's antileftist offensive was halted in October 1972 was substantial progress made in Deng's return. Notably, a trip to the former Jiangxi Soviet area was arranged for Deng before he returned to Beijing.[201] This trip would surely remind Deng that is was Mao who had brought him up after his first fall in 1933 (see Chapter 3). Furthermore, it would also remind Deng who purged him then: it was Zhang Wentian, as Mao pointed out specifically in his comment on Deng's letter. Needless to say, Zhou was then a major leader beside Zhang.

Moreover, although Deng was named a vice-premier immediately after his rehabilitation, he had little to show for almost an entire year after his return, which suggested that his treatment at the State Council was no better than the one he experienced in 1952 – he had little to do except attend routine meetings (see Chapter 4). Seeing that Deng got the cold shoulder in the administration, Mao let Deng start in the military. But before that, Deng made a special trip to Shaoshan, Mao's hometown, on October 19.[202] Again, the visit was more than a show of respect; it was a ritual demonstrating Deng's loyalty to Mao. On December 12, Mao convened a Politburo conference at his residence and announced that he had appointed Deng a Politburo member, a CMC member, and the PLA's chief of staff. Mao specifically pointed out that Deng was "the former superior" of most Politburo members, indicating that Deng resumed the status of general secretary, although Deng declined the title. Mao also announced at this conference his plan to rotate eight major RMC commanders.[203] The plan was put into action in ten days.

---

200 Also cf. Ban Ying and Zuo Xiaowei, "*Heimao baimao – ping Han Shanbi 'Deng Xiaoping zhuan'*" (Black cat or white cat – a critique to Han Shanbi's *A Biography of Deng Xiaoping*), *Tansuo* (Quest), no. 3 (1992), p. 71.
201 Yue and Xin, *Deng Xiaoping shengping yu lilun*, pp. 308–9.
202 See Liu, *Deng Xiaoping de licheng*, 2:147–52.
203 Ke, *Mao Zedong de licheng*, 2:386–7.

Factionalism in Chinese Communist Politics

Evidently, Deng's return had little to do with Zhou, nor did it strengthen Zhou's position as the official account implies. On the contrary, Deng's return undermined Zhou's position. It was by no means accidental that Deng's comeback coincided with a decline of Zhou's power (Table 6.4). The parallel was underlain by an intriguing power struggle between Zhou and the Maoists, and ultimately Mao himself. Of course, Zhou would never dare to challenge Mao, not necessarily because of his unfading loyalty to Mao, but because, like Liu and Lin, he never had the ideological legitimacy to do so. However, during the Lin Biao Affair and its aftermath, Zhou's short but effective control of the PLA, his seizure of the ideological high ground in the antileftist offensive, and his access to various mountaintops had posted an unprecedented threat to Mao's command. Although Mao was able to deprive Zhou of his *official* role in military affairs and help the Maoists recapture the ideological high ground, he could hardly go any further after that. Unlike Mao's previous struggles against his perceived opponents – Peng Dehuai, Liu Shaoqi, and Lin Biao – Mao could hardly diminish Zhou's power because no one in Mao's camp had the ability to block Zhou's access to various mountaintops. Mao was eager to call Deng back because only Deng could help him resume control of these mountaintops; and the Maoists had to help Deng come back – an odd but rational choice for them – because only Deng could help them cut off Zhou from the mountaintops and therefore root out his influence. No wonder that as soon as Deng had the military under control in December, the Campaign of *pi Lin pi Kong* (criticizing Lin and Confucius) was launched in January 1974. The aim "was to undermine Zhou Enlai, as had been clear from the first salvo the previous August."[204]

Deng's Dilemma and His Second Fall

With reliable access to the mountaintops, Deng soon accomplished what the previous CMC leaders could not achieve: the rotation of major RMC commanders. Chen Xilian of Shenyang changed places with Li Desheng of Beijing; Yang Dezhi of Jinan, with Zeng Siyu of Wuhan; Xu Shiyou of Nanjing, with Ding Sheng of Guangzhou; and Pi Dingjun of Lanzhou,

---

[204] See MacFarquhar, "The succession to Mao," p. 346.

The Collapse of the Yan'an Round Table

with Han Xianchu of Fuzhou.[205] As these RMC commanders were pulled out of their power bases and entrusted with the forces from different mountaintops, their dependence on the central authority increased, while their factional networks, which were now headless, were vulnerable to reorganization. Moreover, except Chen Xilian and Li Desheng, all exchanges were made between the non–Lin Biao followers and those rising from Lin's forces. As these commanders were cut off from their forces, Lin's mountaintop was finally torn apart.

Indeed, that Lin's men like Zeng Siyu, Ding Sheng, and Han Xianchu could remain in their powerful RMC CO positions for over two years after Lin's fall indicated not only difficulties in eliminating the influence of a fallen mountaintop leader but also the ineffectiveness of a leadership that was not connected with the mountaintops. Deng's comeback changed all of this. Like Lin, Deng was a leader with a substantial mountaintop, but Deng was actually more influential than Lin because his *guanxi* penetrated both the Party and military systems.

Notably, Beijing RMC Commander Li Desheng, who had been Zhou's major aid during the Lin Biao affair,[206] was replaced by Shenyang RMC Commander Chen Xilian, who rose from Deng's mountaintop. It must also be noticed that the commanders of the Chengdu, Kunming, and Xinjiang RMCs remained untouched in this unprecedented reshuffle, for the Chengdu and Kunming RMCs had been controlled by Deng's forces (see Chapter 4), and the Xinjiang RMC had been the turf of Wang Zhen, who would be a key supporter of Deng in the years to come. Thus, this reshuffle not only consolidated Deng's position in the leadership, but it also paved the way for his overall *zhengdun* (rectification and reorganization) in the coming year.

---

205 Liao, *Xin zhongguo biannian shi*, p. 363, says that the rotation of the RMC commanders was initiated by Mao himself. But the idea came originally from Ye Jianying, who was in charge of the CMC after Lin's fall. (See Ke, *Mao Zedong de licheng*, 2:386.) Although Mao endorsed the plan, the CMC was unable to do the job due to resistance from these powerful commanders. In fact, at that time people like Ji Dengkui, who was in charge of organizational affairs, did not even know how to draft the order on behalf of the CMC, let alone put the idea in practice (see ibid., pp. 382–3). One of these rotated commanders told me in September 1995: "Marshal Ye is a nice guy. It is easy to talk with him [*hao jianghua*]. But Deng is tough [*lihai*], and he knew all of our backgrounds [*zhigen zhidi*]."

206 See Cheng, *Zhou Enlai he tade mishumen*, pp. 449, 480.

Factionalism in Chinese Communist Politics

Table 6.4. *Deng Xiaoping's Return and the Decline of Zhou Enlai's Power (1971–3)*

Time	Progress of Deng's Return to Power	Changes in Zhou's Capacity
1971		
9/13	The Lin Biao Incident occurred.	Zhou took overall charge during the Lin Biao affair.
11/15	Deng wrote his first letter to Mao.	
1972		
1/6	Mao said at Chen's memorial ceremony that Deng's case belonged to "the contradictions among the people."	Zhou made the memorial speech at Chen Yi's memorial ceremony.
2	Mao's words were passed to Deng.	Zhang Chunqiao vetoed the documents that substantiated Zhou's economic policy.
4		The senior cadres started at Zhou's leadership were rehabilitated.
8/3	Deng wrote to Mao again, vowing that he would "never reverse the verdict."	Chen Yun, Wang Zhen, Teng Daiyuan, and others appeared in public on August 1.
8/14	Mao made a positive comment on Deng's letter, urging to rehabilitate him.	
10	Jiang Qing raised the issue of Deng's rehabilitation at the Politburo sometime in October.	Zhou's antileftist offensive was resisted by the Maoists.
12/17		Mao reversed Zhou's antileftist offensive, saying that Lin was ultraright. The Maoists recaptured the ideological high ground.
12/18	Deng was told that his case would be solved soon, and a trip was arranged for Deng to visit the former Jiangxi Soviet Area before returning to Beijing.	Zhou sent a note to Ji Dengkui and Wang Dongxing, reminding them that Mao had mentioned Deng's return several times.

The Collapse of the Yan'an Round Table

Table 6.4. (*cont.*)

Time	Progress of Deng's Return to Power	Changes in Zhou's Capacity
1973		
2/20	Deng returned to Beijing.	Zhang again vetoed the document of Zhou's economic policy.
3/10	Deng was named a vice-premier.	
5		Mao proposed to criticize Confucius.
7/4		Mao criticized the Foreign Ministry led by Zhou for its "revisionist tendency." Mao linked Lin Biao with Confucius.
8/24	Deng entered the CC at the Tenth PC.	Zhou was contained at the Tenth PC.
9		Jiang Qing went to Qinghua to brew the Campaign of Criticizing Lin and Confucius.
10/19	Deng visited Mao's hometown.	
12/12	Mao announced that Deng would enter the Politburo and CMC.	
12/22	Deng took charge of the CMC and had a seat at the Politburo.	
1974		
1/24		The Campaign of Criticizing Lin Biao and Confucius began.

Deng's second coming could not be more promising: Mao trusted and, as a matter of fact, increasingly relied on him; the survivors were overwhelmed; and the beneficiaries were not even up to his caliber. As Zhou's cancer continued to take its toll, Mao entrusted more power to Deng. Yet Deng faced a looming dilemma. Undoubtedly, Deng knew why he was called back and realized that he was empowered so rapidly because

Mao, and to certain extent the Maoists, expected him to counterbalance Zhou's power. But as an astute politician, Deng also saw the disastrous consequence of being perceived as the Maoists' ally, not only because it would alienate Deng from all those who had suffered during the CR – the last thing Deng would want was to be perceived as Lin Biao II – but also because their policy approach of "continuous revolution" was at odds with Deng's mission, namely, to stabilize the situation and to subdue various mountaintops. Although Deng tried to maintain neutrality between Zhou and the Maoists, his increasing power and ambiguous attitude only encouraged both sides to woo him, wishing to win him as an ally, or at least not to make him an enemy. When Deng led the Chinese delegation to the United Nations on April 6, 1974, for example, Zhou, who was very ill at the time, struggled to go to the airport, but Jiang Qing and Zhang Chunqiao were also there to see him off.

This subtle but complicated situation – the Maoists mounted their attack on Zhou with Deng being sandwiched in between, trying to do his job – was the essential reason for "Mao's periodic dissociation from Jiang Qing and her Shanghai followers, while they remained so important to the promotion and preservation of his CR goals."[207] A careful examination of the progress of Deng's work and the timing of Mao's criticism of the Maoists shows that the aim of Mao's periodic whipping at the barking Maoists was to hold them in the right direction, so that they would not bite a wrong person: Deng, who was accomplishing his mission. But Mao rarely attempted to stop the radicals' innuendo against Zhou. Indeed, as Deng's power increased, the relations among Mao, Deng, Zhou, and the Maoists underwent a gradual change, which I examine in *three phases* (Table 6.5).

Phase I. From January to October 1974, Deng could remain neutral in the strife between Zhou and the Maoists, for his power just began to expand from the military into the administration, largely due to Zhou's declining health. Mao's expectation was that, while the Maoists carried out *pi Lin pi Kong*, a campaign that was aimed at wearing Zhou down, Deng would not only restore the Center's control of the military but also gain ground in civilian affairs at Zhou's cost. Thus, Mao would not allow the Maoists to undermine Deng. That was why

---

207 MacFarquhar, "The succession to Mao," p. 348.

The Collapse of the Yan'an Round Table

Mao aborted their attack on *zou houmen* (obtaining personal favors through the back door), which, as Ye Jianying's letter to Mao on February 15 complained, had threatened stability in the military, because most of those who got special treatment were the children of high-ranking officers.[208] But Mao's major concern was that, as he pointed out in his comment on Ye's letter, "the attack on *zou houmen* could weaken the effect of *pi Lin pi Kong*."[209] For the same reason, Mao criticized Jiang Qing on March 20 and stopped the Maoists' attempt to promote a mass movement of *pi Lin pi Kong* in the military.[210]

When Deng took overall charge after Zhou was hospitalized on June 1, 1974,[211] he faced a falling economy caused largely by factional struggles provoked by *pi Lin pi Kong*.[212] On July 1 the Politburo issued a circular, which stressed that *pi Lin pi Kong* should neither interrupt the production nor undermine stability. Not surprisingly, the Maoists did not like this circular, arguing that "production must not be used to suppress revolution." Seeing that Deng had a hard time pushing through the Maoists's resistance, Mao whipped the Maoists on June 17. Mao pointed out at a Politburo meeting that Jiang Qing represented "only herself but not me," and warned the Maoists for the first time "not to form a gang of four."[213] Yet, given the context of the event, this whip was less severe than the official account implies.[214] Mao's warning was essentially to urge

---

208 The attack on *zou houmen* was sparked by a *People's Daily* article on January 18, 1974. In this article a high-ranking officer's son, who had joined the army and then entered an elite college through the "back door," declared that he would give up all his privileges and start a life of his own. The Maoists took advantage of the social unrest caused by this article and targeted their criticism at the senior leaders. The aim was to boost their popularity and to undermine Zhou, given that most senior cadres and officers looked to Zhou for protection.
209 Fan Shuo and Gao Yi, "*Gandan xiangzhao, gong jie guonan – Ye Jianying he Deng Xiaoping zai dang he guojia weinan de shi ke*" (Cooperation with utter devotion to each other to solve the national crisis – Ye Jianying and Deng Xiaoping in the crisis periods of the party and nation), in *Dang de wenxian* (The Party's Historical Documents), 1995, 1:79–80.
210 Liao, *Xin zhongguo biannain shi*, p. 369.
211 *Zhou zongli shengping dashi ji* (Major Events in Premier Zhou's Life), Chengdu: Sichuan People's Press, 1986, p. 504.
212 For the first time since 1967, the industrial production fell 6% in April, 3% in May, and 12% in June. Fang, *Jingji dashi ji*, pp. 528–9.
213 Liao, *Xin zhongguo biannain shi*, p. 372.
214 Unless cited specifically, my analysis of Mao's criticisms of the Maoists from July 1974 to January 1975 is based on my interviews with two sources: one was close to Ji Dengkui, the other was Source C, whom I have quoted previously.

339

Factionalism in Chinese Communist Politics

Table 6.5. *Deng's Progress and Mao's Criticism of the Gang of Four (1974–6)*

Time	Deng's Progress	Mao's Whip at the Maoists and Their Activities
Phase I, 1974		
2/15	The Maoists attack *zou houmen* (getting special treatment through back doors) for the children of senior officers and cadres.	Mao criticizes Jiang, pointing out that the attack on *zou houmen* could "undermine Criticizing Lin and Criticizing Confucius."
2/20		
3	The Maoists incite their followers in the PLA to attack their leaders.	Mao criticizes Jiang again, forcing her and the Maoists to make self-criticisms.
4/6	Deng leads the Chinese delegation to the UN's sixth Special Session.	
6/1	Zhou is hospitalized.	
7/1	The Politburo issues a circular drafted with Deng's supervision. It calls to restore order and increase industrial production.	On July 17 Mao criticizes Jiang and warns the Maoists for the first time "not to form a Gang of Four."
Phase II, 1974		
10/14		Mao suggests letting Deng be the first vice-premier.
10/17	Deng has his first clash with the Maoists at the Politburo on *Fengqing* freighter.	
10/18	Zhou summons Wang Hairong and Tang Wensheng to coach them how to report to Mao on Deng's clash with the Maoists.	Mao criticizes Wang Hongwen, who flies to Changsha to tell Mao about Zhou and Deng's "abnormal activities." Mao warns him not to become Jiang's cat's paw.
10/20	Wang Hairong and Tang Wensheng arrive in Changsha and report Zhou's version of the story to Mao.	Mao decides to let Deng be the first vice-premier and PLA chief of staff.
11/6	Zhou writes to Mao, "firmly supporting" Mao on Deng's appointment.	
12	Mao encourages Deng to "shoulder the load of government and military works."	Mao criticizes Jiang, warning her not to be "the backstage boss."
12/23	Zhou flies to Changsha to report to Mao on the preparation of the Fourth NPC.	

340

The Collapse of the Yan'an Round Table

Table 6.5. (cont.)

Time	Deng's Progress	Mao's Whip at the Maoists and Their Activities
12/24	Mao approves Zhou's suggestion that Deng take overall charge of the administration.	Mao urges the Maoists not to "form a Gang of Four" but to "unite" with Deng.
Phase III, 1975		
1/5	Deng is appointed the CMC vice-chairman and the PLA's Chief of Staff.	Zhang Chunqiao is appointed the director of the PLA Political Department.
1/8	Deng is appointed the CCP vice-chairman.	
1/13	After the Fourth NPC, Deng takes overall charge of daily affairs at the Center.	
1/25	Deng's *zhengdun* is started in the military.	
2/25	*Zhengdun* starts in the transportation system.	
3/1	The Maoists take the "antiempiricism" offensive against the senior cadres.	
4/23		Mao criticizes the Maoists and halts their "antiempiricism" offensive.
5/3		Mao emphasizes the unity again, asking Deng and the Maoists to straighten out the problems between them.
6/4	*Zhengdun* starts in the heavy industry and soon spreads to the other fields.	
6/24	Deng intensifies *zhengdun* in the military, focusing the attack on "factionalism."	
9/15	Deng stresses the importance of an overall *zhengdun* at the National Learn-from-Dazhai Conference. Jiang also makes a speech that is at odds with Deng's.	Mao criticizes Jiang's speech as "nonsense!" and orders that she not dispatch her speech.
10/20	Deng and his associates work out the *General Program* in order to legitimize his *zhengdun*, which is essentially to "reverse the verdicts of the CR."	Mao is alerted to Deng's "true intention" by his nephew Mao Yuanxin.
	Deng refuses to work on "a resolution on the CR" with an excuse that he knows little about it because he was purged.	Mao instructs the Politburo to work on "a resolution on the CR."
11/3		Mao decides to topple Deng again.

the Maoists to cooperate with Deng, who was now in charge of daily affairs.

Phase II. The controversy about the *Fengqing* freighter in October 1974 started the second phase, which continued until the Fourth NPC in early 1975. The freighter was made in Shanghai in early 1974. Skeptical about its quality, the Transportation Ministry, presumably with Zhou's support, was reluctant to let it join in China's oceangoing fleet formed almost entirely by imported ships. Under the Maoists' pressure, *Fengqing* was allowed to sail across the ocean in May 1974 and returned on September 30. The successful voyage gave the Maoists leverage to accuse the Transportation Ministry, and ultimately Zhou, of "worshiping the foreigners." When they tried to force their view on the Politburo at a meeting on October 17, Deng, who was now in overall charge, disagreed, not necessarily because he wanted to defend Zhou, but because, had the Maoists prevailed, a witch-hunt would have started in the entire administration, making it difficult for Deng to fulfill his mission. A clash occurred between Deng and the Maoists,[215] who had just been soured by the rumor that Mao would let Deng be the first vice-premier, a position that would lead to the premiership, given Zhou's deteriorating health.[216] The next day, the Maoists sent Wang Hongwen to Changsha, where Mao stayed, to report on Zhou and Deng's "abnormal activities." Meanwhile, Jiang summoned Wang Hairong and Tang Wensheng, Mao's translators who were going to see Mao with foreign guests on October 20. Jiang asked them to tell Mao that "Deng had jumped in Zhou's boat" and was therefore no longer trustworthy.

Yet Wang Hongwen received a cold shoulder in Changsha: Mao told him that it was not proper for him to come to Changsha "behind the back of the other Politburo comrades" – Mao was too seasoned to get involved before he knew the whole story. Meanwhile, Jiang was double-crossed: Ms. Wang and Tang went to see Zhou on October 19, asking for

---

215 See Liu, *Deng Xiaping de licheng*, 2:163–4; also Jiang, *Zhou Enlai de licheng*, 2:478–9.
216 The source of rumor was Mao's concubine Zhang Yufeng. She passed to Wang Hongwen a log note of Mao's phone call on October 4. It reads: "Who will be the first vice-premier? (Deng)." (Based on this note, the official account suggests that Mao made the decision to let Deng take the position on October 4. Cf. Liao, *Xin zhongguo biannian shi*, p. 372.) But "(Deng)" was not in the original but added later.

The Collapse of the Yan'an Round Table

his advice on Jiang's story. Zhou astutely told them that the Maoists' real target was not him but Deng because of their jealousy of Deng's achievement. Thus, Zhou shrewdly distorted the Maoists' intention from "attacking Deng because he switched to Zhou's side" to "attacking Deng because of his achievement." Wang and Tang retold Zhou's version to Mao after they arrived in Changsha the next day. Convinced by their story, Mao was upset that the Maoists picked on Deng on "this tiny issue [of *Fengqing*]." Since Wang Hongwen had just left Changsha in the morning, Mao asked his two translators to pass his words to Zhou and Wang Hongwen: Deng would be the first vice-premier and the PLA's chief of staff.

Zhou wrote to Mao on November 6, "firmly supporting the Chairman's decision."[217] On November 12, Mao told Deng, who also went to Changsha with a foreign delegation, that he "was unhappy" with what the Maoists had done to Deng. Mao also encouraged Deng to "shoulder the load" of both the civilian and military works.[218] On December 23, Zhou and Wang flew to Changsha to report to Mao on the preparation for the Fourth NPC, which would open in the coming January. In their two-hour meeting on December 24, Mao decided that in addition to being the first vice-premier and the PLA's chief of staff, Deng would also be the vice-chairman of the CCP and the CMC. Meanwhile, it was also decided to appoint Zhang Chunqiao the second vice-premier and the director of the PLA Political Department. After the meeting Mao, who had been unable to talk clearly, told Wang in writing: "Don't form a gang of four. *Unite!* It does no good for you four to stick together!"[219]

Mao's intention was obvious: Jiang, Zhang, Wang, and Yao should stop indulging in their myopic factional activities. Instead, they should cooperate with Deng, to whom Mao intended to pass the baton of leadership. Mao had entrusted so much power to Deng, essentially at Zhou's cost, not necessarily because he trusted Deng more than the Maoists, but because Mao knew that Deng, with his access to the mountaintops in both the Party and the military, was the only one who could replace Zhou and get the job done. Mao wished that the Maoists would "unite" with Deng because he realized that the Gang of Four would have no future unless they would join with Deng. Zhang's simultaneous appointments

217 Quoted from Yan, *Wenge shinian shi*, p. 532.
218 See Ke, *Mao Zedong de licheng*, 2:434–5.
219 Quoted from Liao, *Xin zhongguo biannian shi*, pp. 373–4 (emphasis added).

as the second vice-premier and director of the PLA Political Department were not so much to balance Deng's power as the official account claims. It is more comprehensible to see it as Mao's effort to bring the Maoists and Deng together. Otherwise, why should Mao entrust Deng with so much power in the first place? Mao's criticisms of the Maoists in this phase reflected his frustration with the Maoists' myopic behavior, rather than an effort to diminish their influence.

But a unity between Deng and the Maoists was a wishful thinking, given their conflicting interests and goals. And their competition for the first vice-premiership accelerated the breakup. No wonder that Zhou, who was known for his extraordinary self-restraint, could not help celebrating after the meeting on December 24, 1974, in Changsha. Zhou's bodyguard, Gao Zhenpu, recalled that Zhou was "unusually relaxed and happy" after the meeting. On December 26, Zhou held a private party to "celebrate" Mao's birthday – the first time Zhou ever did so. Zhou specially invited Ms. Wang and Tang, who, consciously or not, had given Zhou decisive assistance in this affair.[220] Zhou was so happy not just because the Maoists had lost their bet for the first vice-premiership but because Zhou knew that he had won or, more precisely, been given a powerful ally.

Phase III. Deng also realized that the breakup was inevitable. But he also knew that as long as he could maintain a facade of peace with the Maoists, Mao would support him, given Mao's goal to restore control of the mountaintops, a goal that Mao could hardly achieve without Deng's help. Thus, interactions among the elite members in the third phase, from the Fourth NPC to November 1975, were the most complicated and intriguing. Zhou still had substantial influence through planners like Li Xiannian, Yu Qiuli, and Gu Mu, although he was too ill to perform an active role.[221] Deng carried out a relentless *zhengdun* (rectification and reorganization), while dodging direct confrontations with the Maoists.

---

220 Cheng, *Zhou Enlai he tade mishumen*, pp. 458–9. Notably, only after making sure that Wang Hongwen, who was still at Changsha at the time, was not invited did Wang and Tang come to the party.
221 Deng replaced Li Desheng, who had been close to Zhou after Lin's fall, as a CCP vice-chairman and PSC member at the Second Plenum in January. Li's ousting, though in a low-profile manner, was a further step to cut off Zhou's military linkages.

The Collapse of the Yan'an Round Table

The beneficiaries were overwhelmed despite their reluctance to support Deng's *zhengdun*, which undermined their still-growing factional networks. The Maoists kept barking (which was all they could do, indeed), but they could not get a good bite on Zhou, who cleverly hid behind Deng, nor could they stop Deng's *zhengdun*, which had the support of the senior cadres and, more importantly, Mao's blessing. Indeed, Mao remained supportive of Deng's work and intervened whenever the Maoists hindered Deng's mission, which was to bring mountaintops back under Mao's command.

Deng, now a CCP vice-chairman, a PSC member, first vice-premier and PLA's chief of staff, wasted no time in launching an overall *zhengdun*, which started in the military at a meeting of high-ranking officers on January 25, 1975. Deng made it clear that the aim of *zhengdun* was to "eliminate factionalism."[222] *Zhengdun* in the civilian system started at the National Conference of the Party Secretaries in Charge of Industry, held from February 25 to March 8. Deng pointed out again in his speech at the conference that the major task was to "combat factionalism," which had "seriously jeopardized our overall interests."[223] Deng emphasized that the struggle against factionalism had to be focused on "the leading bodies" at each level of authority. The aim, as Deng pointed out repeatedly, was to "build up a strong, fearless, and able leading body.... Find and recruit [into the leadership] those who dare to adhere to the principles, are not afraid of being knocked down, dare to take responsibility, and dare to struggle."[224] Needless to say, Deng was targeting the factions that did not belong to him. Indeed, once Deng had the mountaintops under his control and his men entered the leadership at each level of authority, it would be impossible to eliminate his influence.

The Maoists sensed Deng's real intention. They felt specifically uncomfortable with the massive return of senior cadres during *zhengdun*. So they initiated an antiempiricism campaign in March.[225] While the offensive was part of the innuendo against Zhou, who was criticized as "the representative of empiricism" during the 1943–5 YR (see Chapter 3), the other objective was to warn the returning senior cadres not to

---

222 See *SWDXP*, 1975–82, pp. 11–13.   223 Ibid., p. 16.
224 Quoted from Yan, *Wenge shinian shi*, pp. 544–5.
225 See Liao, *Xin zhongguo biannian shi*, pp. 380–1.

embark on the same road for which they had been toppled during the CR. Yet again, Deng won Mao's support through his "secret weapon": Ms. Wang and Tang, who were sent to see Mao and convinced him that the Maoists' antiempiricism undermined stability.[226] Mao was apparently unhappy with the Maoists, for the situation appeared to be developing in the direction Mao had designed: Zhou was fading out; Deng was subduing the mountaintops; and the economy was beginning to improve.[227] Seeing the Maoists' behavior as harmful to his goals, Mao whipped them again and halted their antiempiricism propaganda on April 23.[228] Jiang Qing was forced to make a self-criticism at the Politburo on April 27. On May 3, Mao summoned the Politburo to his residence, "emphasizing repeatedly the [importance of] stability and unity." Mao ordered the Maoists to "make self-criticisms" and again urged them to *unite* with over 200 hundred members of the CC."[229] Deng seized the momentum and convened two Politburo meetings on May 27 and June 3 to criticize Jiang and her gang, who all made self-criticisms.[230]

Deng's *zhengdun* won great success in both the military and civilian systems.[231] Yet it further exposed Deng's dilemma: his mission was essentially at odds with the ultimate goal of the CR. A crucial part of Deng's mission was to subdue factionalism in order to restore stability. So he had to bring back the senior cadres and officers, for they had access to various mountaintops. By doing so, however, Deng had to get rid of those who rose to power during the CR, not just because the senior cadres resented greatly those former Red Guards, but because their positions in the authority blocked the returned cadres' links to each other and to their mountaintops. Yet these former Red Guards represented not just the forces supportive to the Maoists but ultimately the legitimacy of the CR. As Deng's overall *zhengdun* penetrated into the entire system, Deng had no choice but to "do away with the leftist views and ideas" in order

---

226 Several sources confirmed that, after the fall of the Gang of Four, the Foreign Ministry wanted to criticize Wang and Tang for their "close ties with Jiang Qing." But Deng stopped it, saying that "the two ladies must not be criticized! They had big merit in the struggle against the Gang of Four!"
227 Fang, *Jingji dashi ji*, pp. 548–9.   228 Liao, *Xin zhongguo biannian shi*, p. 381.
229 For a detailed and objective record of this meeting, see Jia Sinan, "*Sanyao san buyao*" (Three do's and three don'ts), in Ke, *Mao Zedong de licheng*, 2:450–8.
230 See Fan and Gao, "*Gandan xiangzhao, gong jie guonan*," pp. 80–1.
231 See Zhang Mingjun, "*1975 nian quanmian zhengdun de lishi kaocha*" (A historical review of the overall rectification in 1975), in *Dang de wenxian*, 1995, 1:74–5.

The Collapse of the Yan'an Round Table

to provide his *zhengdun* with a "theoretical base" or, in other words, ideological legitimacy.[232]

Thus, Deng pieced together the words Mao said at various occasions – "to study [Marxist] theory, to maintain stability and unity, and to increase the national economy" – claiming that these "three important instructions" of Mao were the "guiding principle" in all fields of work. Deng argued that the essential tenet of Marxism and the ultimate goal of revolution were to "increase social production," and for this purpose "the stability and unity" had to be maintained because it was necessary for economic growth. Deng's idea was fully expressed in *On the General Program of Work for the Whole Party and Nation*, drafted by Deng Liqun.

Not surprisingly, Mao was upset when he saw the draft on October 20, 1975, because the "three important instructions" were a shameless distortion of Mao's words out of their context. Mao's call to study Marxist theory in December 1974 was to highlight the importance of class struggle and the danger of commodity exchange, which could undermine the socialist economy.[233] Mao's emphasis on unity and stability was to urge the Maoists to cooperate with Deng, who Mao believed was doing the right thing; but Mao denied flatly that the phrase "increasing the national economy" was his.[234] Mao finally realized what the Maoists had tried to tell him: he had been duped, for what Deng had been doing was not to preserve the achievements of the CR but to "reverse the verdict of the CR"; not to promote "continuous revolution" but to undermine its legitimacy; and not to consolidate Mao's command but to cultivate his own mountaintop.

But Mao would not knock down his longtime protégé again without giving him a last chance to redeem himself. Mao claimed that he had done "two important things" in his life: the Chinese revolution and the CR.[235] Since *The Resolution on Several Historical Problems* adopted at the Seventh PC in 1945 had documented Mao's role in the Chinese revolution (see Chapter 3), Mao instructed the Politburo to make a similar resolution on the CR. But Deng, who was in charge of the Politburo, turned down the job flatly with an excuse that he knew little about the CR because he was purged.[236] Mao was enraged, and humiliated, because

---

232 Liao, *Xin zhongguo biannian shi*, p. 388.
233 See ibid., pp. 378–9; also MacFarquhar "Succession to Mao," p. 354.
234 See Fang, *Jingji dashi ji*, p. 561.   235 See Jin, *"Wenhua da geming" shigao*, p. 398.
236 See Fan and Gao, *"Gandan xiangzhao, gong jie guonan,"* pp. 82–3.

Deng's refusal was virtually an open announcement of rebellion, for it was Mao's CR that brought Deng down. Indeed, Deng, whom Mao described as "a needle wrapped with cotton,"[237] stung Mao badly in his final days. Mao, who just whipped Jiang Qing as late as September 20 for Deng's sake,[238] lashed out on November 2 and 3: Deng "is not happy with the CR. He wants to settle accounts, to settle accounts of the CR. . . . [This is] not an isolated problem. It reflects the struggle between the two lines at present. . . . The spearhead is pointing at me."[239]

At Mao's injunction, the Politburo held several meetings, at which Deng was criticized and deprived of all power except "taking care of foreign affairs." On November 23, a CC meeting was convened to notify the high-ranking cadres and officers that Deng's problem involved "a struggle between the two classes, two roads, and two lines." Deng's leadership was ended promptly, and so was his *zhengdun*.

Deng's second fall marked the final collapse of the Yan'an Round Table, the essential base of Mao's command. After Deng's fall, Mao could not find, and in fact there was not, anyone who had reliable access to the mountaintops. Knowing that one's leadership could not be sustained without solid control of the factional networks, Mao at the end relayed the baton to Hua Guofeng, the head of beneficiaries, instead of the Maoists, for although the beneficiaries did not have solid ties to major mountaintops, they at least had their own bases in various localities or systems. The Maoists had nothing except Mao's favor.

Deng was toppled again, but he gained tremendously in his year in charge. Through his *zhengdun*, Deng had not only consolidated and expanded his force, but his toughness in the fight against those who rose to power during the CR had also convinced the veteran cadres and officers that he was their man. All this was Deng's vital asset that he would not trade for anything, even Mao's blessing. Thus, it was not that Deng

---

237 Mao said the words when he announced to bring Deng back to the leadership of the CMC on December 12, 1973. See Liu, *Deng Xiaoping de licheng*, 2:147–52.
238 Jiang rebutted Deng repeatedly during Deng's speech at the National Learn-from-Dazhai Conference on September 15. When Mao learned about it, he said: Jiang's words were "nonsense [*fangpi*]! . . . The draft of her speech must not be dispatched; the tape must not be heard; and her speech must not be printed." See Liao, *Xin zhongguo biannian shi*, p. 387.
239 Ibid., pp. 389–90.

The Collapse of the Yan'an Round Table

failed Mao's last test, as Wang Dongxing claimed.[240] Had Deng made a positive resolution on the CR as Mao wanted, he would have become Lin Biao II and alienated himself from the mountaintops he had worked so hard to bring under his control. In fact, Deng was so confident after he was toppled again that he told his supporters: "Don't' be afraid of criticizing Deng Xiaoping. Criticize me as hard as you can. The harder you attack me, the safer you are, and the more hope [there would be]."[241] Deng knew that he would again make a comeback, because no one among the remaining elite members – the survivors led by Ye Jianying, the beneficiaries headed by Hua Goufeng, and the Maoists – had any reliable access to the mountaintops.

---

240 Wang said on several occasions: "Deng Xiaoping was far less capable than Chairman Hua [Guofeng]. In fact, Chairman [Mao] had already relayed all the power to him. All the Chairman wanted from him was a resolution [on the CR]. But he would not do it. So the Chairman dumped him."
241 These words are confirmed by several well-informed sources.

7

Deng Xiaoping's Dominance: Factionalism Prevails over the Party Spirit

THE ESTABLISHMENT OF DENG XIAOPING'S DOMINANCE

Deng Xiaoping's Comeback

The coalition of beneficiaries and survivors, led by Hua Guofeng and Ye Jianying, "smashed" the Gang of Four, which had little support from mountaintops except Shanghai, four weeks after Mao's death on September 9, 1976.[1] The new leadership was haunted immediately by Deng's case.[2] Little evidence shows that the survivors abandoned Hua for Deng, as the official account implies.[3] But their continuous support of Hua was half-minded, not only because they realized that Deng's return was inevitable, given his control of mountaintops in both the Party and military systems, but also because their own power rested essentially on the support from the veteran cadres and officers rather than those who rose to power during the CR. Allegedly, Ye Jianying sent his children for Deng "immediately" after the Gang of Four was arrested on October 6. Ye told Deng not only of the Gang's arrest but also the details about the Politburo conference on the aftermath.[4] Li Xiannian also said to Hua privately a few days after the Gang's arrest that the verdict on the

---

1 See Roderick MacFarquhar, "The succession to Mao and the end of Maoism," in Roderick MacFarquhar and John K. Fairbank, eds., *Cambridge History of China*, Cambridge: Cambridge University Press, 1989, 15:366–70.
2 See Ma Licheng and Lin Zhijun, *Jiao feng: dangdai zhongguo san ci sixiang jiefang shilu* (Crossing Swords: True Record of the Three Emancipations of Mind in Contemporary China), Beijing: Jinri Zhongguo Press, 1998, pp. 17–18.
3 Ibid., pp. 19–20, 27–8. See also Jin Chunming, *"Wenhua da geming" shigao* (A Draft of the History of the "Cultural Revolution"), Chengdu: Sichuan People's Press, 1995, pp. 470–87.
4 Fan Shuo and Gao Yi, "*Gandan xiangzhao, gongjie guonan – Ye Jianying he Deng Xiaoping zai dang he guojia de weinan shike*" (Cooperation with utmost devotion in the

350

Deng Xiaoping's Dominance

Tiananmen Incident in April 1976 "appeared shaky" (*kao buzhu*), hinting that Deng's verdict should be reconsidered because Deng was officially brought down by the allegation that he was behind the "anti-Party and anti-Mao" Tiananmen Incident.[5]

Despite all this pressure, Hua instructed Li Xin, Kang Sheng's former secretary who was now a deputy director of the CC General Office, on October 26 to "concentrate on criticizing the Gang of Four and relate it to the criticism of Deng. The Gang of Four's line is an extreme rightist line. *Don't criticize whatever Chairman Mao had said or agreed to.* Head off any discussion about the Tiananmen Incident."[6]

Hua's words resulted in the formulation of "two whatevers," expressed by a *People's Daily* editorial on February 7, 1977, as: "We shall resolutely defend *whatever* policy Chairman Mao decided upon; steadfastly abide by *whatever* decisions Chairman Mao made."[7] The official account claims that the "two whatevers" was put forward to "prevent Deng Xiaoping from returning to work and to hinder the reversal of the verdict of Tiananmen Incident."[8] Yet a more important aim was to create political legitimacy for Hua's leadership, which was virtually baseless except for Mao's blessing. Thus, Hua further highlighted the "two whatevers" in his speech at the CC work conference, held March 10–22, 1977. Although Chen Yun and Wang Zhen requested that the conference reconsider Deng's case and the verdict of the Tiananmen Incident, Hua and the other beneficiaries rejected their demand flatly, arguing that the verdicts of the Tiananmen Incident and Deng were made by Mao and

---

solution of the national crises – Ye Jianying and Deng Xiaoping in the periods of crises for the party and the nation), in *Dang de wenxian* (The Party's Historical Documents), 1995, 1:86.

5 A reliable source recalls that the conversation happened soon after "the meeting of notification" (*da zhaohu*), October 7–14, 1976. Hua replied to Li: "Let's see. It will be difficult because it was the Chairman who decided on the verdict." For the Tiananmen Incident and its implications on Deng's second fall, see MacFarquhar, "The succession to Mao," pp. 361–5.

6 Quoted from Liao Gailong, ed., *1949–1989: Xin zhongguo biannian shi* (1949–1989: Chronology of the New China), Beijing: People's Press, July 1989, p. 406 (emphasis added).

7 A reliable source told me that it was Gong Yuzhi, later a deputy director of the CCP Propaganda Department in charge of the drafting of political documents for Jiang Zemin, who put the formulation of "two whatevers" in writing.

8 Liao, *Xin zhongguo biannian shi*, p. 407.

the reversal of these verdicts would therefore damage "our great banner of Chairman Mao."[9]

But Deng wasted no time in mobilizing his forces to mount pressure on the whatever faction. Xu Shiyou and Wei Guoqing, commander and commissar of the Guangzhou RMC, wrote to Hua in early April. They reminded Hua that, although Mao had let Hua "take charge at the Center," Hua's chairmanship still had to be decided by a CC plenum according to the Party Constitution.[10] It was not surprising that the letter came from the two generals, for both of them rose from Deng's mountaintop and, more importantly, Deng stayed with them in Guangzhou for a while after his second fall.[11] The letter, which was circulated among the high-ranking officers via private channels, sent a clear message: if Hua insisted on blocking Deng's return, his chairmanship would be challenged at least by the powerful military leaders. Meanwhile, Deng wrote to the CC and Hua on April 10. While Deng asked humbly for "a chance to work for the Party and people," he made a subtle but significant statement: "we must ... understand Mao Zedong Thought [MZT] accurately as an integral whole [*zhunque wanzheng*]," not simply as "two whatevers."[12]

The CC dispatched Deng's letter on May 3 – a signal of Deng's return. Yet Deng knew that he had to restore his control of the military before he could make any substantial progress. Although Deng had strong support from the RMC leaders, the relationship between Deng and those at the PLA Headquarters had been soured by the latter's "thorough criticism" of Deng during the campaign of Criticizing Deng Xiaoping in 1976. True, Deng encouraged people to criticize him for their own protection, but he did not expect that Yang Chengwu, then the acting chief of staff, would expose Deng's "ten private talks with the leading comrades at the PLA Headquarters" during his *zhengdun* campaign in 1975

---

9 See Ma and Lin, *Jiao feng*, pp. 28–9; also Fan and Gao, "*Gandan xiangzhao, gongjie guonan*," p. 85.
10 Jurgen Domes, *The Government and Politics of the PRC: A Time of Transition*, Boulder, CO: Westview Press, 1985, p. 146, seems to put the time of this letter *before* the CC work conference, March 10–22. But I saw a copy of the letter circulating in Sichuan in April 1977.
11 Liu Jintian, ed., *Deng Xiaoping de licheng – yige weiren he ta de yige shiji* (Deng Xiaoping's Career – a Great Man and His Century), Beijing: PLA Art Press, 1994, p. 190.
12 See Ma and Lin, *Jiao feng*, p. 30.

Deng Xiaoping's Dominance

(see Chapter 6). These "ten private talks" were all about Deng's ideas on the personnel arrangements of high-ranking officers in the ongoing *zhengdun* in order to strengthen Deng's control of the military. Yang's disclosure hurt Deng most, for these "ten talks" provided not only solid evidence of Deng's "vicious ambition to usurp the supreme command of the army," but also a name list of those who had participated in Deng's "anti-Party factional activities."[13] Given Yang's close relations with Ye Jianying and Nie Rongzhen, it would be surprising that he would have dared to do so without the consent of the two marshals.[14]

But Deng would not settle the account with Yang Chengwu at this time, for Deng still needed the support, or at least the cooperation, from Yang and his patrons in his effort to resume his dominance. On May 14, 1977, Ye Jianying held a private party to celebrate his eightieth birthday. Ye invited most of the military leaders in Beijing, including Nie Rongzhen, Xu Xiangqian, Su Yu, Yang Chengwu, Su Zhenhua, Yu Qiuli, and Wang Zhen. But Deng was not invited. As the party started, however, Deng walked in. Deng sat next to Ye and made himself the center of attention by assuming the role of master of ceremonies.[15] Deng's behavior was somewhat unexpected to Ye and the others at the party, but his appearance and his self-assertiveness impressed the people from the outside of the circle that Deng and Ye were in the same boat, and it would be silly, and self-destructive indeed, for Ye and his men to declare otherwise.

Soon, the effect was shown. Wang Dongxing and Li Xin visited Deng on May 24. They notified Deng on behalf of the CC that Deng would assume all his former positions – CCP vice-chairman, CMC vice-chairman, PSC member, vice-premier, and the PLA's chief of staff – on the condition that Deng would not challenge Hua's leadership at the coming Third Plenum of the Tenth CC. Although Deng criticized the "two whatevers" in his conversation with Wang Zhen and Deng Liqun

---

13 Not surprisingly, Yang was later severely criticized for what he did in 1976. His "gross error" was summarized as "ten (disclosure of Deng's ten private talks), hundred (selection of a hundred anti-Party and anti-Mao quotations from Deng's speeches), thousand (a rally of over a thousand high-ranking officers to criticize Deng), and ten thousand (a rally of ten thousand officers to criticize Deng)."
14 Yang never admitted that he had consulted Ye or Nie for what he did in 1976.
15 I interviewed several sources on this event. Except one who is not sure, all confirmed that Deng was not invited to the party. Also cf. Fan and Gao, "*Gandan xiangzhao, gongjie guonan,*" pp. 85–6.

three days later (May 27),[16] he kept his promise at the Third Plenum, held July 16–21, 1977. In his speech at the plenum on July 21, Deng went along with the formulation of "two whatevers" and called the Party "to unite around our wise leader Chairman Hua."[17] Deng did emphasize that "MZT must be understood accurately as an integral whole," but most attendees failed to see the difference, because "MZT understood accurately as an integral whole" should naturally include whatever Mao said.[18] The new leadership produced at the Eleventh PC, held August 12–18, "was weighted in favor of survivors and beneficiaries of the CR." Among the five PSC members – Hua, Ye, Deng, Wang Dongxing, and Li Xiannian – Deng "was the only one who would later emerge as a strong critic of Hua and the whatever faction."[19]

"Practice Is the Sole Criterion of the Truth": The Fight for Legitimacy

Although Deng's control of mountaintops enabled him to made a quick comeback after Mao's death, Mao's condemnation of Deng in his final

---

16 Deng told Wang and Deng: "The two whatevers cannot hold water. According to the two whatevers, you cannot answer the question on the reversal of my verdict, nor can you answer the question why [we] affirm that the mass's activities in Tiananmen Square were 'reasonable.'" See *"Deng Xiaoping jiejian Deng Liqun shi de jianghua"* (Deng Xiaoping's talk during the meeting with Deng Liqun), May 27, 1977, located in the library of the John K. Fairbank Center for East Asian Studies, Harvard University, Cambridge, MA.
   But the two meetings are mixed up in the published official account. (Ma and Lin, *Jiao feng*, p. 31, for example, claim that Deng met Wang Zhen and Deng Liqun on May 24, implying that Deng met Wang Dongxing and Li Xin "a few days ago.") This is a mistake. Or it could be an attempt to cover up the compromise Deng made with Hua's people on May 24. Notably, the gist of Deng's conversation with Wang and Li on May 24 is selected in *SWDXP*, 1975–82, pp. 53–4. But there is no mention of "genuine MZT taken as an integral whole" at all, nor the criticism of the "two whatevers." Had Deng criticized the "two whatevers" in his meeting with Wang Dongxing and Li Xin, as he later claimed, it makes no sense that he should be denied the credit, given that *SWDXP* was printed after Deng gained his dominance.
17 This part is not seen in Deng's speech printed in *SWDXP*, 1975–82, pp. 55–60.
18 See Wang Hongmo, *"Shiyijie sanzhong quanhui zai dangshi shang de diwei he gongxian"* (The status and impact of the Third Plenum of the Tenth CC in our Party's history), in *Quanguo dangxiao xitong zhonggong dangshi xueshu taolunhui zhuanti baogao he fayan huibian* (Collected speeches and papers on special topics at the National Academic Conference of Party Schools on the CCP History), 1980, 2:82.
19 MacFarquhar, "The succession to Mao," p. 376.

Deng Xiaoping's Dominance

days – Deng "knew little about Marxism-Leninism" and he was too "highly problematic" to be entrusted with "a leading position."[20] – was an inescapable curse on Deng as long as MZT was taken as the Party's guiding principle. By contrast, Hua was chosen by Mao and his leadership had Mao's blessing: "with you in charge, I am at ease."[21]

Deng had to deprive Hua's leadership of its legitimacy in order to establish his dominance. Yet Deng would not try until he was well prepared. Not surprisingly, the first step Deng took was to restore his control of the military. After the Eleventh CC a dispute emerged between Deng and Ye Jianying over the nomination of the PLA's chief of staff.[22] Deng wanted Yang Yong, who had been commander of the Xinjiang RMC since May 1973, to succeed him as the PLA's chief of staff. This was not surprising given that Yang rose to power from Deng's mountaintop (see Chapter 6). But Ye Jianying, with support from Nie Rongzhen, insisted that the job be given to their man Yang Chengwu, acting chief of staff after Deng's second fall. Eventually, both sides settled on Li Xiannian's nominee: Yang Dezhi. Although this Yang rose to power from Nie's mountaintop, he was a close friend of Yang Yong,[23] and he had also been under Deng's command during the resistance war. Moreover, Yang Yong was named the executive deputy chief of staff. By contrast, Yang Chengwu was virtually demoted to a deputy chief of staff, and he was soon kicked out of Beijing by a concurrent appointment as commander of the Fuzhou RMC, the smallest one among the eleven RMCs. Only by then did Yang Chengwu fully realize the price he had to pay for his "thorough criticism of Deng Xiaoping."

In order to secure his control, Deng also nominated Luo Ruiqing as

---

20 See Michael Schoenhals, "The 1978 truth criterion controversy," *CQ* (June 1991), pp. 249–50.
21 These words, according to Deng Liqun, "*Xuexi 'Guanyu jianguo yilai dang de ruogan lishi wennti de jueyi' de wenti he huida*" (Questions and answers for the study of *The Resolution on Several Questions of Our Party's History since the Establishment of the PRC*), *Zhuanji*, 2:86–7, were written down by Mao in June 1976 after Hua reported to Mao "about the work in several provinces." Mao, who could hardly speak at the time, meant to approve Hua's work, not his succession.
22 Unless noted specifically, the analysis of this episode is based on my interviews with several reliable sources.
23 After Yang Yong was purged and hunted by the Red Guards, Yang Dezhi, then commander of the Jinan RMC, invited Yang Yong to Jinan and provided him with much needed protection. See Jiang Feng, Ma Xiaochu, and Dou Yishan, *Yang Yong jiangjun zhuan* (A Biography of General Yang Yong), Beijing: PLA Press, 1991, pp. 446–7.

the CMC's secretary-general in charge of daily military affairs. Within the next few months, Deng managed to put his men in all the key positions at the PLA Headquarters: Wei Guoqing was named director of the Political Department, Hong Xuezhi, director of the Logistic Department, and Zhang Zhen was in charge of the training of high-ranking officers.[24] As a result, Ye Jianying, who was still officially in charge of the CMC, was virtually a figurehead.

Once he had the headquarters under control, Deng resumed his *zhengdun* in the military in late 1977. The aim, as Deng pointed out in his speech at a CMC conference on December 28, was to "solve the problems of . . . *leading bodies*" at each level of the commanding system. Deng requested that every officer be evaluated by his behavior during the CR. Deng emphasized specifically to eliminate "the mountaintop mentality" (*shantou zhuyi*) – that is, factionalism, which was shown through "exercising favoritism in the appointment of officers."[25] Yet, the officers whom Deng accused of "engaging in factional activities" and who therefore had to be expelled from the military were those who did not belong to his mountaintop. With the effective management of Luo Ruiqing, Yang Yong, and Wei Guoqing, all the positions of commanders and commissars at the army level and above had been rearranged by April 1978. In some key RMCs like Beijing, Jinan, Wuhan, and Nanjing, the rearrangements were made down to the division level. Once his control of the military was consolidated, Vice-Chairman Deng wasted no time in challenging Chairman Hua's authority.

On April 12 Hua instructed the navy that after his scheduled visit to North Korea in May, he would go to Dalian, the home base of the PLA North Sea Fleet, to inspect the navy.[26] Hua's intention was obvious: at the time when Deng's influence was rising, Hua wanted to make a show

---

24 Cf. Ma and Lin, *Jiao feng*, p. 41. Unlike Wei and Hong, who rose from Deng's mountaintop, Zhang Zhen rose from the New Fourth Army, which later grew into the Third Field Army. But he developed a close relationship with Deng after the 1948 Huaihai Campaign, during which he was chief of staff of the campaign's Front Committee, of which Deng was general secretary.
25 *SWDXP*, 1975–82, pp. 90–1.
26 The analysis of this episode is based on Huang Yao and Zhang Mingzhe, *Luo Ruiqing zhuan* (A Biography of Luo Ruiqing), Beijing: Contemporary China Press, 1996, pp. 607–8; *Zhongong dangshi ziliao* (Source Materials of the CCP History) (1991), 37:198–9, and my interviews with two former navy officers whose fathers were both former top commanders of the PLA navy.

that he, the CMC chairman, was in charge of the military. "A major naval leader," undoubtedly Navy Commissar Su Zhenhua who was also a Politburo member, agreed after he "consulted a CMC leader," obviously Ye Jianying. Su then ordered all the naval forces to go to Dalian to prepare for Hua's inspection. But Commander Xiao Jinguang and Chief of Staff Yang Yanguo cautioned that such a massive maneuver had to be *formally* reported to the CMC. When the report reached the CMC on April 17, Luo Ruiqing ordered the suspension of all activities before he reported to "Vice-Chairman Deng." Luo called Deng immediately. While still *on the phone*, Deng ordered cancellation of the inspection. Obviously, Deng did not consult either Chairman Hua or Vice-Chairman Ye, although both were officially ranked above Deng at the CMC and the Politburo. Hua was so upset that he "refused to answer the phone" when Luo called to inform him that the inspection had been canceled. This incident demonstrated that Deng already had the military under his control. And Deng's camp wasted no time in putting up a bigger challenge to Hua, only this time it was to the legitimacy of his leadership.

On May 4 Deng went to see Hua off when he left for Pyongyang, and he met Hua at the train station when he came back on the 11th.[27] But it was during this week that the final revision of the article, "Practice is the sole criterion of the truth," was accomplished – it was revised ten times – under the supervision of Hu Yaobang, Deng's hit man who had been director of the CCP Organizational Department since December 10, 1977. On May 11, the day of Hua's return from Pyongyang, *Guangming Daily*, which then covered mainly intellectual and educational affairs, published the article.[28] The article argued that all the truth, including Marxism and MZT, had to be tested and enriched through practice. Otherwise, they would ossify into the "lifeless dogma." The *People's Daily* reprinted this article the next day. This article struck at the roots of the "two whatevers." Its implication was obvious: even if Hua's

---

27 See *PD*, May 4 and 11, 1978.
28 For the details on how this article was produced, see Shen Baoxiang, "*Zhenli biaozhun wenti taolun jishi*" (Chronology of the truth criterion debate), in Zhang Shujun and Gao Xinmin, eds., *Zhonggong shiyi jie sanzhong quanhui lishi dangan* (Historical Archives of the CCP Third Plenum of the Eleventh CC), Beijing: China Economy Press, 1998, 2:185–206; see also Chai Hongxia, Shi Bibo, and Gao Qing, *Hu Yaobang moulue* (Hu Yaobang's Resources and Astuteness), Beijing: Red Flag Press, 1997, pp. 5–8.

leadership did have Mao's blessing, its correctness had to be tested by practice. No wonder that the whatever faction was furious about it. Wang Dongxing pointed out correctly that the "spearhead [of this article] is virtually directed at the Chairman's thought as well as the present central Party leadership."[29] But all Hua and his men could do to suppress it was to order that the official media "not be involved" in the debate triggered by this high-profile article.

Deng seized the opportunity and turned the fray to his own advantage. One week after the article was published, on May 19, Deng said bluntly to a group of leaders from the Cultural Ministry: "This article is in full accord with Marxism. It cannot be pulled down [*ban budao*]!"[30] Deng did not hesitate to seek support from the military. He called up Luo Ruiqing, who was presiding over the All-Army Conference on Political Work, held from April 27 to June 6. Deng told Luo that he "had to make a speech" at the conference to roll back an erroneous "ideological trend."[31] In his speech on June 2 Deng emphasized that the essence of MZT was "seeking truth from fact." Notably, in his speech Deng did not mention the debate on the truth criterion at all, nor did he attack the "two whatevers" as the official account implies. Instead, Deng debated with the whatever faction on a seemingly generic issue. Contrary to Hua's rhetorical slogan, "carry out the policies previously made by Chairman Mao in *the new historical era*," Deng argued that "seeking truth from facts" was more important than ever before because the Party was facing "*new historical conditions*." Astutely, Deng added a subtle but significant footnote to the thesis of the truth criterion. That is, if "seeking truth from fact is a fundamental principle of MZT," which was itself the product of "integration of Marxist theory with practice," then for the same reason, as Deng implied, whether Mao's teachings in the past could still hold water "in today's situation" had to be tested through practice because of *the changes in historical conditions!*[32] No wonder that the words "new historical

---

29 Liao, *Xin zhongguo biannian shi*, p. 425.
30 See Ma and Lin, *Jiao feng*, pp. 60–1.
31 See Shen Baoxiang, "*Deng Xiaoping zhichi zhenli biaozhun wenti taolun jingguo*" (The course of Deng Xiaoping's support to the debate on the problem of truth criterion), *Bainian chao* (Hundred Year Tide), CCP Research Center of Party History, no. 3 (1997), pp. 4–5.
32 See *SWDXP*, 1975–82, pp. 130–4.

conditions" drew attacks immediately from the whatever faction at the conference.[33]

Although both *People's Daily* and *Liberation Army News* printed Deng's speech on their front pages the next day, Deng's point was too oblique to put down the vigorous resistance by the whatever faction. According to Hua's injunction that the media should "ignore" and "not be involved" in the debate, the CC Propaganda Department ordered all the major newspapers across China not to print any articles about the truth criterion. But the block was soon broken once the military was involved. Yang Yong, Deng's man in the military, who also happened to be Hu Yaobang's cousin, ordered Chi Haotian, then a deputy chief of staff who was concurrently director of the political department of the PLA Headquarters, to organize a thorough study of the article on the truth criterion. When Chi told Yang that he had not heard any instructions from the General Political Department, Yang said bluntly: "go ahead and do it. I will take the full responsibility." Chi did a good job: he organized the officers at the division level and above to "study the article" in order to "unify their thinking" on the truth criterion.[34] It was not surprising that Chi rose rapidly to the office of defense minister thereafter.

Meanwhile, Deng's forces launched an even more lethal attack. The *Liberation Army News* published "A most basic principle of Marxism" on June 24 as a result of Luo Ruiqing's direct intervention. This article, which forcefully reiterated the thesis of practice criterion, was drafted by the same group of ghostwriters as the article on truth criterion. But it was "personally revised three times by Luo Ruiqing."[35] Deng's influence was undeniable this time, although "no evidence" has shown that he had anything to do with the first article.[36] The second article dealt a lethal

---

33 See Zha Ruqiang, "*Guanyu quandang gongzuo zhongxin de zhuanbian he shijian biaozhun*" (The change of the focus of the entire Party's work and the practice criterion), *Xueshu yanjiu dongtai* (Development of academic research), 7 (July 1997), pp. 9–10.
34 Jiang, Ma, and Dou, *Yang Yong jiangjun zhuan*, pp. 486–9.
35 Huang, "*Luo Ruiqing zhuanlue*," p. 201.
36 Cf. Schoenhals, "The 1978 truth criterion controversy," pp. 263–4. But Chai, Shi, and Gao, *Hu Yaobang moulue*, p. 7, imply that the article of the truth criterion was read by Deng Xiaoping and Li Xiannian before publication. A reliable source, who had a conversation with Hu Yaobang a few days before his death, told me in June 1993 that he had asked Hu about how the article could be published and reprinted quickly by the

blow to Hua's camp. Only then did Deng come into the ring from the back scene to deliver the final punch. Deng summoned Zhang Pinghua, a Hua supporter who was director of the CC Propaganda Department, on July 21, ordering him to stop repressing the debate on the truth criterion.[37] The next day, Deng pointed out explicitly in his talk with Hu Yaobang that "The debate [on the truth criterion] is inevitable. It is good. The root [of the debate] is 'two whatevers.'"[38] When Deng openly attacked the "two whatevers" on September 16 in Jilin on his way back from Pyongyang,[39] the whatever faction was under siege. By early November all the RMCs and the provincial Party authorities, except Hunan, "had thrown their weight on Deng's side."[40]

The debate about the truth criterion had a tremendous impact on CCP politics. Were it not for this debate, "the fundamental change, not only in the balance of forces within the leadership, but also in the Party's line and in the whole intellectual climate prevailing in China, would not have been possible."[41] The immediate and most important result, however, was the collapse of the *ideological legitimacy* of Hua's leadership. Mao's blessing on Hua had since lost its ideological significance because it had to be retested through practice under "new historical conditions." Thus, the last obstacle to Deng's achieving his dominance was removed.

The Establishment of Deng's Dominance

As soon as his force prevailed in the debate on the truth criterion, Deng proposed to convene a CC conference in early September.[42] Yet the conference would not be held until November. The reason, according to a former leader at the CC Organizational Department, was that "the department [led by Hu Yaobang] had to fight [with the whatever faction]

People's Daily and *Liberation Army News*. Hu replied: "It is unnecessary to get the bottom out [*shuiluo shichu*]. What is important is its result." Thus, "no evidence" could be the best evidence of Deng's involvement in this affair.
37 See ibid., p. 12; and Ma and Lin, *Jiao feng*, p. 62.
38 Quoted from Shen, "*Deng Xiaoping zhichi zhenli biaozhun wenti taolun jingguo*," p. 5.
39 See *SWDXP*, 1975–82, pp. 141–4.
40 MacFarquhar, "The succession to Mao," p. 379; see also Liao, *Xin zhongguo biannian shi*, p. 426.
41 Schram, "Economics in command?" p. 419.
42 Hao Mengbi and Duan Haoran, *Zhongguo gongchandang liushi nian* (The Sixty Years of the CCP), Beijing: PLA Press, 1984, 2:682–3.

Deng Xiaoping's Dominance

for almost every name on the attendee list." While Hua wanted all the members of the Eleventh CC, among whom a majority rose to power during the CR, to attend the conference, Deng insisted that the attendees should also include the leaders from various central apparatuses, the RMCs, and provinces – most of them were Deng supporters. Again, Deng prevailed. Among 219 attendees of this CC work conference, held from November 10 to December 18, 1978, only 42 percent were the members or alternate members of the Eleventh CC, and 137 attendees were Deng supporters or leaned toward Deng.[43]

Deng's forces were well prepared for this conference. The breakthrough issue they chose was the prohibition of the veteran cadres who had been wrongly purged. This was a two-birds-with-one-stone strategy indeed, for the massive comeback of the veteran cadres would not only further undermine the whatever faction, but also strengthen Deng's forces. After painstaking preparation and investigation, the materials for the reversal of the verdict of "61 traitors" headed by Bo Yibo, An Ziwen, and Liu Lantao (see Chapter 3) were ready to be delivered when the CC work conference opened.[44] These materials, in the words of the source just cited, became "the bombshell" immediately after they were submitted to the conference on November 20.

Although the whatever faction was prepared for the challenge on the verdict on the Tiananmen Incident – four days after the conference opened, it was announced that the event was "fully revolutionary"[45] – they were caught by surprise at the onslaught led by Chen Yun, who raised "six issues" on the Party's history, including the wrong verdicts on Bo Yibo, Tao Zhu, Wang Heshou, and Peng Dehuai, the Tiananmen Inci-

---

43 See Yu Guangyuan, "*Gaibian zhongguo jincheng de sanshi liu tian – shiyi jie sanzhong quanhui qian de zhongyang gongzhuo huiyi zhuiji*: 1" (The thirty-six days that changed China's historical process – recall of the CC Work Conference prior to the Third Plenum of the Eleventh CC), *Bainian chao* (Hundred Year Tide), no. 5 (1998), pp. 7–8.
44 See Dai Huang, *Hu Yaobang yu pingfan yuan jia cuo an* (Hu Yaobang and the Rehabilitation of the Wrong, False, and Mistaken Verdicts), Beijing: New China Press, 1998, pp. 93–119.
45 Liao, *Xin zhongguo biannian shi*, p. 432. The reversal of the verdict on the Tiananmen Incident, however, seems conspiratorial. It was not a decision made by the CC leadership at this CC work conference; rather, it was virtually enforced on Hua Guofeng as a fait accompli by Deng's forces during this conference. See Yu Guangyuan, "*Gaibian zhongguo jincheng de sanshi liu tian:* 2," *Bainian chao* (Hundred Year Tide), no. 6 (1998), pp. 6–8.

dent in 1976, and Kang Sheng's grave errors.[46] Because all these cases were either decided or approved by Mao, the reversal of their verdicts essentially denounced the "two whatevers."

Indeed, the most significant achievement scored by Deng and his allies at this conference was the discarding of the "two whatevers." Those who had defended the "two whatevers" in the debate of truth criterion, like Wang Dongxing and Xiong Fu, chief editor of *Hongqi* (Red Flag), the Party's theoretical monthly, were fiercely criticized. Thus, the Deng forces achieved their designed goal of the debate of truth criterion, that is, to deprive Hua Guofeng's leadership of its ideological legitimacy.[47]

Deng and his allies wasted no time in holding the Third Plenum of the Eleventh CC (December 18–22), a plenum that the official account claims "has started a new era of the overall reform." However, a close examination of the policies adopted at this plenum reveals they resembled those made by the Party bureaucrats in 1962–5 (see Chapter 5). The general approach returned to the line adopted at the Eighth PC in 1956, declaring that "the massive class struggle" was over and the focus of the Party's work "must be shifted on the economic construction." Consequently, the agricultural policies returned to those in the early 1960s, emphasizing the three-level *collective* ownership by the people's commune, production brigades, and production teams, with the team as the basic accounting unit. Although the practice of "household responsibility" was *secretly* adopted by the peasants in Anhui, it would not become a formal policy until September 1980. The industrial policies were also Chen Yun's old remedy in 1962 – that is, to retreat from Hua's "great leap forward" in 1977–8 but to concentrate on "readjustment, reorganization, consolidation, and improvement." The decentralization, especially expanding the authority of enterprises, would not be tested until July 1979, and be adopted as a formal policy in July 1980. The policy of openness to the outside world would not be tried out cautiously in Guangdong and Fujian until July 1979, and it would not be adopted as a formal policy until early 1982.[48]

---

46 See ibid., pp. 4–5; Ma and Lin, *Jiao feng*, pp. 73–5. Also cf. *Chen Yun wenxuan 1956–1985* (Selected works of Chen Yun, 1956–1985), Beijing: People's Press, 1986, pp. 208–10.
47 See Yu, "*Gaibian zhongguo jincheng de sanshi liu tian: 2,*" *Bainian chao* (Hundred Year Tide), pp. 10–11.
48 See *Xuandu*, 1:4–8; Liao, *Xin zhongguo biannian shi*, pp. 434–5, 441–2, 447, 450, 461, 465–6, 492–3, 495–6; and Fang, *Jingji dashi ji*, pp. 661–2, 615–16, 629–30, 664–5.

Deng Xiaoping's Dominance

What really marked this plenum as the "starting point of a new era" were the fundamental changes in leadership relations. Deng's ally Chen Yun resumed the CCP vice-chairmanship. Their supporters, Hu Yaobang and Wang Zhen, entered the Politburo. Deng Yingchao, Zhou Enlai's widow, also joined the Politburo so that the new leadership could cash in on her late husband's popularity. The Discipline Inspection Commission was created, with Chen Yun as the first secretary, Deng Yingchao, the second secretary, Hu Yaobang, the third secretary, and Huang Kecheng, the secretary. But daily affairs were handled by Vice-Secretary Wang Heshou, who was a Chen Yun follower. The commission was set up to purify the Party ranks and strengthen the Party's discipline, which justified its real task: to keep a close watch on the whatever faction and its followers, most of whom were leftists who had risen to power during the CR.

However, substantial changes in personnel arrangements in favor of the Deng-Chen alliance were made *after* the plenum at a Politburo conference on December 25. The reason was obvious: if these arrangements had been made at the plenum as required by the Party Constitution, it would have been very difficult for them to be passed because a majority of the CC members were still whateverists or their sympathizers. But at this virtually enlarged Politburo conference, the Deng-Chen forces were superior (Table 7.1).

At this conference, the Deng-Chen alliance obtained nearly all the substantial power at the Center. Notably, the changes already embodied an embryo of the CC Secretariat, led by Hu Yaobang, Hu Qiaomu, and Yao Yilin. As the front office of the Deng-Chen alliance, it not only made Chairman Hua a mere figurehead, but also turned the Politburo into a de facto rubber stamp in the policy process. "Wang [Dongxing] and other members of the whatever faction maintained their positions on the Politburo, but the writing was on the wall for them."[49]

More importantly, these arrangements virtually structured new leadership relations in the years to come: the power in decision making was shared by Deng and Chen, with Li Xiannian, and later Peng Zhen, as the balancing weights. But Deng's dominance was indisputable, not just because his followers outnumbered those of Chen, but because, like

---

49 MacFarquhar, "The succession to Mao," p. 381.

Table 7.1. *Personnel Arrangements at the Politburo Meeting (December 25, 1978)*

Name	Position/Duties	Affiliation
Politburo members		
Chen Yun	Vice-chairman/*discipline, security, law, civil administration*	
Hu Yaobang	CC secretary-general, director of Propaganda Department/*daily party affairs, propaganda, media*	Deng
Wang Zhen	Defense industry	Deng
Deng Yingchao	Mass organizations	
CC members		
Hu Qiaomu	Vice-secretary-general/*editing and publication of Mao's works*	Deng
Yao Yilin	Vice-secretary-general/*economic affairs*	Chen
Song Renqiong	Director of Organizational Department/*personnel affairs*	Deng
Wang Renzhong	Vice-premier, director of Agricultural Commission/*agriculture*	Li Xiannian
Feng Wenbin	Vice-president of Central Party School, first deputy director of CC General Office/*party history, file keeping*	Hu
Ma Wenrui	Party secretary of Shaanxi Province	Hu
Yang Dezhong	Commander of central bodyguard	Deng
Jin Ming	Commercial minister	Chen
Chen Guodong	Head of financial and trade group/*credit, commerce*	Chen
Whatever faction		
Wang Dongxing	Dismissed from all substantial posts	
Zhang Pinghua	Demoted from director of Propaganda Department to vice-president of the Central Party School	
Li Xin	Dismissed from the post of deputy director of the CC General Office	

Deng Xiaoping's Dominance

Mao, Deng was the *only* one in the leadership who had control of the mountaintops in both the Party and military systems.

FACTIONALISM OVER THE PARTY SPIRIT

Deng's Dominance without Its Own Ideological Legitimacy

It must be noticed that although the Third Plenum denounced the "two whatevers," its evaluation on "practice as the sole criterion of truth" was made with carefully selected words: the *Plenum Manifesto* says, "the plenum sets a high value [*gaodu pingjia*] on the discussion of the issue that practice is the sole criterion of truth."[50] The implication is obvious: the debate on the truth criterion was appreciated for its breaking down of the legitimacy of Hua's leadership, that is, the "two whatevers." But neither Deng nor Chen had vigorously insisted on "practice as the sole criterion of truth," not necessarily because people from their own camp like Wu Lengxi and Hu Qiaomu also rightfully accused it of aiming at "cutting down the banner" of MZT,[51] but because it was a double-edged sword that could also be used against the Deng-Chen dominance – whether their leadership was correct could be tested through practice, too. What Deng always insisted upon was "seeking truth from fact." Although there is only one truth, one can always explain it from his own perspective.

Deng's equivocal attitude on the truth criterion revealed a dilemma he faced in establishing his dominance. On the one hand, Deng had to denounce the "two whatevers" in order to break down the legitimacy of Hua's leadership; on the other hand, he could not afford to undermine MZT, which had provided the *ideological legitimacy* for the CCP's rule. This dilemma formed a virtually insuperable barrier for Deng in converting his dominance into the absolute command Mao had enjoyed, for in a totalitarian system in which "an elite bureaucracy sanctioned simply by its commitment to and mastery of a totalist ideology that claimed to

---

50 *Xuandu*, 1:12. So far, this author has not seen any CCP documents that violate this formula (*tifa*) except, ironically, Ye Jianying's speech at the PRC's thirtieth anniversary. Ye said: "The Third Plenum . . . clearly *affirms* this unshakable tenet of Marxist epistemology that practice is the sole criterion of truth." Ibid., p. 84.
51 See Michael Schoenhals, "The 1978 truth criterion controversy," pp. 260–2, 265.

explain the world and man's place in it,"[52] the ideological legitimacy was indispensable for absolute authority. Mao achieved the ideological legitimacy for his command during the YR (see Chapter 3). But could Deng do it? Obviously, Deng tried.

Soon after Deng achieved his dominance, the Forum on the Principles for the Party's Theoretical Work, attended mostly by the Party's theoreticians, was convened from January 18 to April 3, 1979.[53] The aim, as Hu Yaobang pointed out in his opening speech, was to work out some ideological principles to justify the new policy approach adopted at the Third Plenum. Hu emphasized that the fundamental task for "the Party's theoretical workers was to study and solve the new problems; try our best to advance our ideological work ahead of our practice; and *enrich and develop* Marxism and MZT continuously."[54] Spurred by Deng's call of "emancipating the mind, seeking truth from fact," and still excited by the debate on truth criterion, "all of us," said a participant whom I interviewed in March 1990,

> saw Hu Yaobang's speech as a go-ahead encouragement [for us] to reevaluate MZT. The aim was to see whether it was still suitable to "the new historical conditions." If not, a new theory had to be developed. No matter what, we all knew that *Deng Xiaoping needed an ideological base for his reform*. (Emphasis added.)

Yet, the participants soon split into two groups. The liberals like Yu Guangyuan, Hu Jiwei, Li Honglin, and Su Shaozhi – many of them would later become dissidents – held that Mao's gross error during the CR was rooted in his "class struggle" theory developed after 1958. So at least this part of MZT had to be abandoned or, better, denounced in order to justify the declaration at the Third Plenum that "the massive class struggle is over." Some of them even questioned whether the socialist economy was really good for China. They argued that China would have been better-off had "the new-democratic system" in the early 1950s been sustained (see Chapter 4), for it was more

---

52 MacFarquhar, "Succession to Mao," p. 399.
53 Unless noticed specifically, my analysis of this forum is mainly based on my interviews with Professor Su Shaozhi, a former leader at the CC Organizational Department, and two other sources, who all attended this conference.
54 Quoted from Liao, *Xin zhongguo biannian shi*, p. 442 (emphasis added).

suitable to the small-scale peasant economy that had been predominant in China.

The hardliners led by Hu Qiaomu and Deng Liqun, however, insisted that MZT had to be firmly upheld, although they acknowledged Mao's mistakes and agreed that the "class struggle" theory was wrong. Resenting any doubts about socialism, they argued that China's problem was that "socialism had never been truly practiced." They cited the 1962–5 period as an example during which, as Yao Yilin, a long-term associate of Chen Yun, claimed, "the true central-planned economy brought about a miracle." They attacked the proposal of returning to "the new democratic system" as "a reactionary retrogression."

The differences were so fundamental and the relationship between the two groups was so tense that by mid-February the forum could hardly continue. Hu Yaobang, who oversaw the forum, knew all about it, and so should Deng. Yet, Hu asked both sides to put their differences on the table, and to "emancipate the mind and *bravely explore* in the theoretical field." Hu's words were taken as an indirect encouragement to the liberals. Given their superiority in both theory and number and, more importantly, the momentum of "emancipating the mind," the liberals began to gain the upper hand at the forum.

Coincidently, a naive but enthusiastic demand for "democracy" also began to arise in the society, especially in big cities like Beijing where some young people posted their opinions and discussions on "a wide range of political and social problems" on the Democracy Wall, a stretch of wall along Changan Avenue west of the Tiananmen Square.[55] Among them, the most controversial were the demand to "criticize Mao" for his role during the CR and the call for a democratic system. Notably, the reaction of Deng and his followers to the Democracy Wall corresponded with their attitude toward the liberals' unorthodox views at the theoretical forum. Little evidence shows that Deng really understood, let alone believed in, a democratic system. Yet, at the beginning he saw this liberal momentum as positive, not only because it could generate the wide social support necessary for a radical departure from Mao's legacy in policy making, but also, and more importantly, because the more Mao's legacy was undermined, the less difficult it would be for Deng to establish *ideological legitimacy* for his own leadership. Thus, when Wang Zhen asked

---

55 See MacFarquhar, "The succession to Mao," pp. 382–4.

Deng to crack down on the Democracy Wall in early March, accusing it of provoking an "anti-Party and antisocialist" tendency, Deng said: "Of course, [we] must suppress the counterrevolutionaries and restrict their sabotage. But to walk back down the old road of suppressing differing opinion and not listening to criticism will cost us the trust and support of the broad masses."[56]

The Mao bashing, however, soon turned out to be counterproductive for Deng's camp. In late March, a leaflet signed by "The Society for the Study of Marxism-Leninism and MZT" appeared in Beijing. This leaflet charged that Deng Xiaoping and Hu Yaobang "are deeply engaged in revisionism. They oppose Chairman Mao, oppose the line of the Eleventh PC, oppose our Party's policy and constitution.... With Deng Xiaoping's support, Hu Yaobang has openly opposed Chairman Mao, and he cannot deny it."[57] It was not difficult to see that this leaflet was the product of the leftists. Yet it represented a looming trend which forced the elite members to take a stand on this issue. Ironically, while a telling silence remained in the whatever faction, the survivors and the returned leaders formed a hardline coalition at a Politburo meeting in March 21–23. While Ye Jianying expressed his deep concern about the Mao bashing, Wang Zhen vowed to risk his life to defend the late chairman. But Chen Yun, who would later be seen as the leader of the hardliners, scored again, arguing that Mao bashing would eventually undermine the Party's cause. Allegedly, Chen said at the meeting that "There is a dangerous trend recently. Some people attempt to make an issue on the Chairman [*zai zhuxi shenshang zuo wenzhang*]. We must not allow this to distract us from the focus of our Party's work on economic construction. If we fail in economic construction [this time], there would be nothing to justify our Party's cause."[58]

Indeed, "widespread political debate could get out of hand and undermine the stability and unity."[59] More dangerous was that the Mao bashing and skepticism about socialism could eventually undermine the Party's

---

56 Quoted from ibid., 385. According to a reliable source, after the CMC decided to withdraw all the troops from Vietnam on March 5, 1979, Wang said to Deng: "now the problem abroad has been solved. Now we should turn around to teach those cocky young fellows [*buzhi tiangao dihou de xiaozi*] a good lesson."
57 Quoted from *Zhengming* (Contend), August 1980, p. 63.
58 Several sources confirmed Chen's words. They said that Hu Qiaomu used these words as "a big stick" to suppress different views at the theoretical forum.
59 MacFarquhar, "The succession to Mao," p. 384.

barely existent legitimacy, although it had indeed helped Deng to mobilize the social support for his leadership. Indeed, any doubt, let alone denouncement, of MZT would be self-destructive because, were it not for MZT, the entire cause of the CCP could hardly be justified by the orthodox communist ideology in the first place (see Chapter 3). True, all the returned cadres rallied behind Deng in attacking the whatever faction, but their aim was not to denounce MZT but essentially for the convenience of proving that Mao's decision on their cases was wrong. Ironically, their zeal and eagerness in breaking down the "two whatevers" showed exactly their *ideological dependence* on Mao: they had to acknowledge Mao's mistakes so that they could legitimately reverse their verdicts during the CR without substantially undermining "MZT as an integral whole."

Deng changed his attitude all of sudden after the March Politburo meeting. He rushed to the theoretical forum on March 30 and declared the Four Cardinal Principles (FCP):

1 Uphold the socialist road.
2 Uphold the dictatorship of the proletariat.
3 Uphold the leadership of the CCP.
4 Uphold Marxism-Leninism and Mao Zedong Thought.

Deng's speech refroze the thaw that had been started by his own drive to "emancipate the mind." It yielded an unexpected victory for the hardliners, who would later use the FCP as the most effective weapon in their constant struggle against Deng's reform forces. But Deng had to cave in. Otherwise, the hardliners and the whatever faction might be pushed into an alliance, which was the last thing Deng wanted to see.

But the FCP were essentially opposed to the newly adopted policy approach centered on reform. The first two principles were practically phony. "The socialist road" would disappear completely in agriculture within a few years because of the "household responsibility" system,[60] and the market economy Deng was to introduce massively into China's economy is fundamentally at odds with the planned economy on which socialism is established. Deng's description of "the dictatorship of the

---

60 Ironically, the Heilongjiang Party authority, which first officially endorsed that "the practice is the sole criterion of truth" in August 1978 (see Shen, "*Zhenli biao zhun wenti*," p. 206), was the last one to abandon the people's commune system and accept the "household responsibility" system in 1983.

proletariat" was evidently self-contradictory. Deng insisted in his speech that "We do not believe that there is a bourgeoisie within the Party, nor do we believe that under the socialist system a bourgeoisie or any other exploiting class will reemerge after exploiting classes and the conditions of exploitation have really been eliminated."[61] It is not difficult to see why Deng firmly denied the existence of classes in the Party and in the socialist system, for this denial was essential for denouncing Mao's "class struggle" theory, which had created the legitimacy of the CR (see Chapter 6). However, if the bourgeoisie no longer existed, how could a proletariat, let alone its dictatorship, still exist?

Deng's desire to "uphold the leadership of the CCP" was sincere. As Deng later stressed repeatedly, this principle was "the essence of the FCP."[62] The Party's leadership was necessary not only because Deng could not tolerate a democracy, no matter how emancipated his mind could be, but also because the Party's leadership was an indispensable check for Deng on factionalism embedded in the CCP organizations (see Chapter 2). That was why Deng wrote "opposing factionalism, enhancing the Party spirit" on his banner during his 1975 *zhengdun* (see Chapter 6), and he had since used it as a weapon against his opponents. Essentially, it was Deng's need for the Party's leadership in order to maintain his dominance over the mountaintops that forced him to "uphold MZT," which provided the CCP's rule with the ideological legitimacy.

In essence, the FCP were incompatible with the principle of "seeking truth from fact," for this principle would be virtually meaningless if the FCP were the inviolable truth. In this sense, the FCP that Deng established in a hurry in order to appease his conservative opponents were a stunning setback for Deng because, as my examination shows, they exerted an ideological constraint on Deng's reform and sowed the seeds for all the troubles Deng's reform forces were to endure in the years to come. Their impact was shown immediately.

First of all, it halted the momentum of a departure from Mao's legacy in policy making. Not only would the whatever faction hang on in the leadership for nearly another two years, but the Fourth Plenum from September 25 to 28 also failed to achieve the expected policy breakthrough. All it did was to pass Ye Jianying's speech at the thirtieth

---

61 *SWDXP*, 1975–82, p. 176. 62 Ibid., p. 369. Also see *Xuandu*, 1:68.

anniversary of the PRC. The economic policy, as expressed in Ye's speech, was virtually a mixture of the leftovers of Hua's rhetorical "four modernizations" and the remedy of retreat prescribed by Chen Yun in 1978. Politically, Ye's speech was a tedious repeat of the line adopted at the Third Plenum.[63] Although Zhao Ziyang, a key Deng supporter, entered the Politburo, so did Peng Zhen, who would more often than not be a headache to Deng. Eight senior leaders reentered the CC: Yang Shangkun, Hong Xuezhi, Bo Yibo, Wang Heshou, Liu Lantao, Liu Lanbo, An Ziwen, and Jiang Nanxiang. Except for Yang and Hong, who were Deng's men, all the others rose to power from Liu Shaoqi's mountaintop (see Chapter 4). It was true that this force would be far less effective than it used to be due to the heavy damage it endured during the CR and, moreover, the rivalry between Peng Zhen and Bo Yibo. It was also true that Deng and Chen Yun had to join forces to block Peng Zhen's entrance into the PSC, partly due to Peng's no-nonsense, and indeed bullish, style, but essentially because of his soured relationship with Chen Yun.[64] But the conservative attitude of these returned leaders and their sustaining influence in North China turned them more often than not into a formidable obstacle to reform. For example, the resistance to the reform policy from Hebei Province, where Liu's mountaintop originated (see Chapter 3), was so strong that it would not implement the "household responsibility" system until 1983, three years after the policy was adopted; and it did so only after Hu Yaobang dispatched a special work team to Hebei and "thoroughly reorganized the provincial leading bodies."[65]

A more substantial compromise on which Deng had to yield was the virtual takeover of the entire economic front by the conservatives. An Economic and Financial Commission in overall charge of the economy

63 Ye Jianying, "*Yanzhe sige xiandaihua de hongwei mubiao qianjin*" (March forward towards the magnificent goal of four modernizations), *PD*, October 1, 1979.
64 It is well known among the elite members that Chen despised Peng, seeing Peng as a dishonest and treacherous person. Allegedly, the tension between the two started in the Yan'an period (1937–45) when Chen Yun was in charge of organizational affairs and Peng Zhen was entrusted with the training of the high-ranking cadres and officers at Yan'an. Peng obviously did not show much respect to Chen at the time. The relationship between the two was further soured in 1945–47 in Northeast China (see Chapter 3).
65 See Chai, Shi, and Gao, *Hu Yaobang moulue*, pp. 109–11. The authors blamed the "sinister impact of the CR" for Hebei's resistance to reform, although they acknowledge these problems were rooted in "Leftism and factionalism."

was established at the March Politburo conference, at which Deng was obliquely blamed for Mao bashing. When it was formally set up on July 1, 1979, Chen Yun was its director and Li Xiannian, deputy director, with Yao Yilin as the secretary-general. Its members included Yu Qiuli, Wang Zhen, Fang Yi, Gu Mu, Bo Yibo, Wang Renzhong, Chen Guodong, Kang Shien, Zhang Jinfu, and Jin Ming.[66] All the members at this newly created supreme economic organ were known for their conservative approach in policy making. So it is not surprising that none would turn out to be a reformer; and, except for Wang Zhen, none of them was Deng's man!

However, the most profound and far-reaching loss Deng suffered in the establishment of the FCP was his inability, once and forever, to establish ideological legitimacy for his leadership. As a result, although his exclusive accesses to the mountaintops in both the Party and military systems secured his dominance, Deng's choices in policy making would forever be subject to the ideological justification of MZT, as were those of the other leaders. Compared with Mao, whose own thought, MZT, had provided his command with ideological legitimacy, it was much harder for Deng to prevail in a policy dispute because his opponents could always find and use some of Mao's words to justify their own choices. Even if he did prevail, Deng would be very vulnerable if things went wrong. Mao would have few problems justifying whatever decision he made in the policy process, given that MZT was established as the ideological guidance for the Party. So if his choice turned out to be correct, Mao could claim the credit; but if it was wrong – like the GLF and even the CR – the whole Party had to be responsible for it. But Deng, like his colleagues, had to depend on MZT for ideological justification for his policy choices. If his choice turned out to be wrong, not only would he be held responsible, but his opponents could also easily accuse him of violating MZT. No wonder that "wading through the river by groping for the stepping-stones" had been Deng's guiding principle since he achieved prominence in policy making.

However, it was virtually impossible to avoid missteps because the

---

66 Li Yongchun, Shi Yuanqin, and Guo Xiuzhi, eds., *Shiyijie sanzhong quanhui yilai zhengzhi tizhi gaige dashi ji* (Major events in the reform of political institutions since the Third Plenum of the Eleventh CC), Beijing: Chunqiu Press, 1987, p. 48; and Liao, *Xin zhongguo biannian shi*, pp. 450–1.

Deng Xiaoping's Dominance

river Deng had to ford was so big and turbulent. Thus, Deng had to put someone in front of him to take the lead in the groping, so that Deng could always step on a solid stone; and, needless to say, this leading person had to be absolutely loyal to Deng, so that the march would head toward the direction Deng wanted. This was essentially why, although his dominance was undisputed, Deng was reluctant to take the top position in the Party. Deng wanted to make the call in decision making without taking the direct hit if things went sour. But Deng was equally reluctant to give up the CMC chairmanship, so that he could maintain his dominance with the military support.

"Wading through the River by Groping for the Stepping-Stones": The Making of Reform Policies

Deng recovered quickly from his setback in 1979. But his recovery resulted largely from the successes of the reform practices innovated by his followers at various localities. Although Deng achieved dominance at the Third Plenum, his influence was hardly seen in the making of economic policies after the plenum. The policies adopted in 1979 were based on Chen Yun's prescription of readjustment and reorganization, namely, to retreat from Hua Guofeng's "great leap" in 1977–8. But Chen's remedy turned out to be ineffective,[67] partly because of the resistance from the whatever faction, and particularly the petroleum faction, which had been the driving force in Hua's "great leap,"[68] and partly because of Chen's forces' lack of penetrating factional networks within the administrative system.

From late 1978 on, Deng's followers began to practice the reform measures *on their own* in the areas under their control. Local leaders

---

[67] The economic situation in 1979 turned out to be worse than expected. The most serious problems were a deficit of 17.7 billion yuan in the government budget and a trade deficit of 2.1 billion yuan – both were the largest since 1949. See Fang, *Jingji dashi ji*, p. 641; and Liao, *Xin zhongguo biannian shi*, pp. 457–8.

[68] Although Chen, Bo, and Yao were appointed the vice-premiers at the Second Session of the Fifth NPC, daily affairs at the State Council were still in large part handled by Ji Dengkui, Yu Qiuli, Gu Mu, and Kang Shien. Their resistance to the retreat policy was blamed for the ineffectiveness of "readjustment" at the Third Session of the Fifth PCN in September 1980, though Chen Yun and Li Xiannian had been in overall charge of the economy since March 1979.

like Wan Li, the Anhui Party secretary, Zhao Ziyang, the Sichuan Party secretary, Liu Jie, the Henan Party secretary, and Song Ping, the Gansu Party secretary endorsed the "household responsibility" system in their provinces: the land was divided up among individual households, which would turn over certain quotas of grain to the state each year and retain the rest of their products.[69] Zhao also experimented with the management autonomy in state-owned enterprises and reformed the financial relationship between the state and enterprises: the profit turnover system was divided into two levels, the state and the locality.[70] The aim was to enable the enterprises to retain more profit so that they could depend less on the state in expanding their production. Leaders like Yang Shangkun and Xi Zhongxun in Guangdong and Xiang Nan in Fujian opened their areas to the world market and promoted the market economy in their provinces' development.[71]

All these practices were obviously inconsistent with the socialist economy and therefore were opposed by the central elites to various degrees. The most controversial policy was the "household responsibility" system. Except for Deng and his men, nearly all the central leaders were opposed to this "antisocialist policy." Moreover, most provincial Party authorities were also against the household responsibility system, for dividing up the land among individual households was virtually a return to individual farming, which the CCP cadres had been trying to eliminate in China's rural economy ever since the CCP seized the state power in 1949.[72] As a matter of fact, up to October 1981 when reform had already gained momentum in policy making, only about 45 percent of the production teams across China had adopted the household responsibility system, and most of these teams were in the provinces like Anhui, Fujian, Gansu, Guangdong, Guangxi, Guizhou, Henan, and Inner Mongolia where Deng's forces dominated, or in the

---

69 *Xin zhongguo jishi 1949–89* (Major Events of New China, 1949–1984), compiled by the Association of Party History of Jilin Province, Changchun: Northeastern Teacher's University Press, 1986, p. 567. For a detailed description of how the Household Responsibility System was developed, see Ma and Lin, *Jiao feng*, pp. 125–42.
70 See *Sichuan Daily*, February 15, 1979; and Liao, *Xin zhongguo biannian shi*, p. 452.
71 Ibid., 450. Also cf. Liu Jintian, *Deng Xiaoping de licheng*, pp. 278–9.
72 See Zhang Guangyou and Han Gang, "*Wan Li tan longcun gaige shi zenme gao qilai de*" (Wan Li on how the reform was initiated in the rural areas), *Bainian chao* (Hundred Year Tide), 3 (May–June 1998), pp. 4–7.

remote areas like Ningxia and Yunnan.[73] However, while Deng maintained "a neutral position" in this policy dispute between the central and local leaders, Hu Yaobang and Song Renqiong, who took charge of propaganda and personnel affairs respectively (see Table 7.1), held their fronts firmly so that the central authority could neither discipline nor wage a propaganda attack on the reform-minded local leaders. Luo Xiaopeng, former director of the Research Office of Rural Development of the State Council, points out:

> Deng's attitude [of keeping neutral in the policy dispute on the household responsibility system] was *extremely unusual* in CCP history. He virtually let these two policies [of household responsibility system and collectivization], which were essentially opposed to each other, coexist. With Deng's silent encouragement, the household responsibility [system] was applied first at the poorest areas.... Yet, *once the ideological taboo was broken through, it was difficult to prevent [this policy] from spreading on its own.*... As a result, this three-year long and unprecedented policy competition ended with the overall victory of the household responsibility [system].[74]

More significantly, the triumph of the household responsibility system, which the reformers likened to the strategy of "surrounding the city from the countryside," set a successful precedent for Deng to prevail in policy making, namely, Deng would overcome the weakness of his leadership – the lack of its own ideological legitimacy – with the strength of his mountaintop. Unable to get his way at the Center, Deng would rely on his followers to "conduct policy experiments" in localities under their control, while Deng would prevent these experiments, which were usually at odds with the general policy approach adopted by the Center, from being suppressed from above. Once the experiments turned out to be successful, Deng would force his colleagues to adopt this policy, using the justification of "seeking truth from facts."

---

73 See Huang Daoxia, "*Quxiao renmin gongshe de qiangian houhou*" (A whole story of the abolition of the People's Commune), *Xinhua wenzhai* (New China Digest), 1998, 2:75.
74 Luo Xiaopeng, "*Gaige yu zhongguo dalu de dengji chanquan*" (Reform and China's hierarchic ownership system), *Modern China Studies*, 41 (April 1994), Princeton: Center for Modern China, p. 41 (emphasis added).

In retrospect, all Deng's major reform policies – the household responsibility system, extending the autonomy of enterprises, and the opening to world markets – originated not so much from a top-down effort as from a bottom-up resistance to the policies adopted at the Center. Such a resistance could be successful essentially because of Deng's protection at the top on the one hand and the control of his factional networks at the localities on the other hand. In return, the success achieved by Deng's followers at the localities not only justified his policy preferences, but also boosted his strength at the Center. Thus, "reform and openness" became the legacy of Deng's leadership, although his reform policies were a far cry from "the socialist road" he had vowed to uphold. However, Deng's strategy of empowering his followers at the cost of the collective authority of central elites further promoted factionalism in policy making. Ironically, the FCP now evolved into a double-edged sword: while the conservatives used them as a taming whip whenever they saw Deng's reform go too far down the road of "bourgeois liberalization," Deng used them as an effective constraint on factional activities against his mountaintop.

The troubled national economy, on the one hand, and the success of Deng's followers in promoting local economies, on the other, enabled Deng's forces to take the offensive again on the economic front. Seeing that the "readjustment" policy failed to solve the problem of overinvestment in capital construction and that an unprecedented deficit was predicted in October 1979, Deng lashed out at the forum of first provincial Party secretaries, held October 4–10: "The economic work, the economic problems are *the biggest political problem* [at present]. To be precise, it is a political problem that overrides everything else."[75] Hu Yaobang, who was not assigned to any economic duties, also made a speech at this forum, lecturing that the economic problems should be thoroughly studied in order to "learn the basic lessons."[76] Notably, this forum required all the provinces, except Guangdong and Fujian where the experiment of "openness" had been conducted, to prepare for financial reform "according to the measures adopted in Sichuan."[77] Zhao Ziyang, who would soon take over Chen Yun's job, said in a speech on November 6 at the conference of county Party secretaries in Sichuan:

75 Quoted from Liao, *Xin zhongguo biannian shi*, p. 451 (emphasis added).
76 See *The Economic Daily*, December 10, 1979.
77 Fang, *Jingji dashi ji*, p. 635.

Deng Xiaoping's Dominance

> At present, the economic work is the most important politics. . . . In order to concentrate on doing a good job in the economy, we must further *emancipate our mind*. . . . Sure, we have to uphold the socialist road in economic construction. *But what is socialism?* We have had many muddled ideas in the past, attached many things [to socialism] that do not belong to socialism at all, taken them as inviolable holy principles, kowtowed to them, and failed to emancipate our mind. As a matter of fact, Marx, Engels . . . just set up some socialist principles like public ownership and distribution according to work. But they did not, and could not, make any *concrete executive plans* for socialist construction beforehand.[78]

Zhao's words virtually challenged the orthodox concept and practice of socialism and prepared for the theory of "the initial stage of socialism with Chinese characteristics," which Zhao would elaborate eight years later at the Thirteenth PC. Given that the FCP were reemphasized at the Fourth Plenum just a month ago, and the household responsibility system Zhao had applied in Sichuan was labeled "antisocialist," Zhao's speech was bold and unprecedented indeed. Were it not for Deng's support, Zhao would not have dared to do so.

Deng appeared to sit in the driver's seat again in economic affairs at the National Planning Conference, held from November 20 to December 21, 1979. It was decided at this conference that except for Beijing, Shanghai, Tianjin, and the minority areas, all the provinces would follow the "Sichuan model" in financial reform, which would increase the power of local authorities in financial affairs. The decentralization of the financial system, though still in its initial stage, would undermine not only the centrally planned economy, which was the essence of socialism, but also the conservative forces led by Chen Yun, whose strength had been rooted largely in his control of central finance since the financial centralization in the early 1950s (see Chapter 4).

Deng had a good year in 1980. The whatever faction was finally put away at the Fifth Plenum, held from February 23 to 29. With Wang Dongxing, Ji Dengkui, Chen Xilian,[79] and Wu De resigning from their

---

78 *Sichuan Daily*, November 11, 1979 (emphasis added).
79 As an army corp commander in Deng's Second Field Army, Chen Xilian had been close to Deng and, moreover, had been of substantial help to Deng during the 1975 *zheng-*

offices, the days of Hua Guofeng were numbered. Meanwhile, Deng's lieutenants, Hu Yaobang and Zhao Ziyang, entered the PSC. Hu had been a close associate of Deng since the early 1950s.[80] But it was during the 1975 *zhengdun* that Hu became a firm Deng supporter; and he had been Deng's political hit man ever since Deng came back again in 1977. At the Fifth Plenum, Hu was named the General Secretary of the newly restored CC Secretariat, with Wan Li, Wang Renzhong, Fang Yi, Gu Mu, Song Renqiong, Yu Qiuli, Yang Dezhi, Hu Qiaomu, Yao Yilin, and Peng Chong as secretaries. The Secretariat was virtually Deng's front office. Besides Hu Yaobang, a majority of its members – Wan, Fang, Song, Yang, Hu, and Peng – were Deng supporters. (Hu Qiaomu would later lean toward Chen Yun as Deng's reform departed further from "the socialist road.")

Zhao rose to power from Deng's mountaintop. His relationship with Deng could be traced back as early as 1939 when Zhao was a twenty-year-old cadre. But he won Deng's attention in early 1940s with his organizational skill and down-to-earth working-style. During Deng's 1975 *zhengdun*, Zhao was appointed the first Party secretary of Sichuan, China's biggest province and Deng's hometown. He lived up to Deng's expectation and turned Sichuan into a reform model.[81] Soon after the Fifth Plenum, Zhao was appointed the head of the Financial and Economic Leading Group, which was created on March 17 to replace the Economic and Financial Commission led by Chen Yun. Not surprisingly, Deng's men were predominant in this newly created supreme organ in economic policy making. Its members included Yu Qiuli, Fang Yi, Wan Li, Yao Yilin, and Gu Mu. Zhao virtually took over the State Council after he was appointed a vice-premier at the fourteenth session of the Standing Committee of the Fifth NPC, held April 8–16, 1980.[82]

---

dun. However, Chen was deeply involved in some affairs during the CR because of his close relationship with Mao Yuanxin, Mao's nephew who had been Chen's commissar at the Shenyang RMC during the CR. Deng had to let Chen go partly because Chen was involved in the whatever faction, partly because Chen had to shoulder some of Mao Yuanxin's "crimes," and partly because Deng had to appease those returned officers like Luo Ruiqing and Yang Yong.

80 Deng and Hu were acquainted with each other in late 1930s. But their close relationship started after the Eighteenth Army Corp led by Zhou Shidi and Hu Yaobang joined in Deng's Second Field Army in its march to the Southwest in December 1949.

81 See Zhao Wei, *Zhao Ziyang zhuan* (A Biography of Zhao Ziyang), Beijing: China News Press, 1989.   82 Ibid., p. 233.

Deng Xiaoping's Dominance

By now Deng had obtained firm control of the situation, with Hu Yaobang as his political executive and Zhao Ziyang, his economic executive. All Deng needed was a CCP National Congress to formalize such a structure of power distribution. Thus, it was announced at the Fifth Plenum that "the Twelfth PC will be convened *ahead* of the schedule"[83] (which meant it should have been held before 1981, four years after the Eleventh PC in August 1977). Yet Deng had to clear the field for his team so that his policy approach could be fully implemented. This turned out to be more difficult and hence took longer than expected due to strong resistance from the other mountaintops – that was essentially why the Twelfth PC would not be held until September 1982, which was not before, but *after*, the original schedule.

First of all, Deng needed to prevent the conservative senior leaders like Chen Yun and Peng Zhen from intervening in the work of his front offices, namely the CC Secretariat led by Hu and the State Council led by Zhao. On April 23 Deng made the Politburo pass a resolution that stipulated: "the senior comrades who are too old and have lost the ability to work ... shall neither be the representatives of the Twelfth PC nor candidates for the CC."[84] The aim was to undermine the conservative forces that concentrated among the senior leaders. Yet, this resolution met with strong resistance. Most of the senior leaders refused to leave their offices, insisting that they would follow the example of the old-generation revolutionary leaders, like Deng himself, who were "still working for the Party and people." Thus, all Deng could do was to take Chen, Li, Wang Zhen, Xu Xiangqian, and himself off the list of vice-premiers at the Third Session of the Fifth NPC, held from August 30 to September 10, 1980. Except Liu Bocheng, all the senior leaders would be on the Politburo at the Twelfth PC.

Second, Deng had to make sure that his reform policies would be fully adopted at the Twelfth PC. Yet these policies could hardly be justified by MZT, so they had to prove correct through practice. Again, Deng encountered strong resistance from the conservative forces. Although the household responsibility system proved successful in Anhui and Sichuan, it failed to be adopted as a formal policy at the forum of the first provincial Party secretaries, held from September 14 to 22, 1980. The summary of the forum recognized the household responsibility system

---

83 *Xuandu*, 1:186.   84 Li, Shi, and Guo, *Shiyijie sanzhong quanhui yilai*, p. 77.

only as a "necessary measure" suitable to "the remote mountainous districts and the poor and backward areas," but it emphasized that "collective economy is the unshakable base" for agricultural development.[85] The implementation of reform policies in industry also turned out to be more difficult. The State Council dispatched a report on September 2, 1980, asking to "extend decision-making powers of the enterprises." Yet by the end of 1980 the management autonomy had been applied to only about eighty state-owned enterprises despite the fact that experiments had already been conducted in over six thousand industrial units.[86] An essential reason, as a former aid to Zhao observed, was that the financial system "was reluctant to cooperate." This was not surprising because, as I have discussed before, financial decentralization would undermine the conservative forces led by Chen Yun, whose power was rooted in their control of finance. Thus, although Deng eventually ousted Hua and made Hu Yaobang the CCP chairman at a series of enlarged Politburo meetings in November–December 1980, and the arrangements were formalized at the Sixth Plenum in June 27–29, 1981, the Twelfth PC had to be postponed for nearly two years so that the reform policies could be fully accepted in practice.

The conflict between Deng's force and the conservative forces was fully shown at a CC work conference held from December 16 to 25, 1981. Chen warned in his speech on December 16 that though the opening to the outside world had brought about certain benefits, "our cadres must remain sober-minded" in dealing with the foreign investors who "after all are still capitalists." Complaining that financial decentralization had increased the power of local authorities at the cost of the Center, Chen suggested "freezing all the surplus money at localities so that the money can be used by the Center." Chen's stand was clearly expressed:

> Ours is a country with *the central-planning economy as the mainstream*. Therefore, the state intervention is necessary in many respects within a certain period. . . . In a country like ours *it won't do without [financial] centralization*. Otherwise, everything will be in the muddle, which is no good for the reform, either. . . .
>
> We must reform, but our steps must be steady. We must not be

85 See Liao, *Xin zhongguo biannian shi*, p. 466.
86 Fang, *Jingji dashi ji*, pp. 663–4.

Deng Xiaoping's Dominance

rash because the problems in our reform are complicated.... So the initial steps must be small. Go slowly. This is by no means to abandon the reform, but *to make the reform serve readjustment*, and for the success of the reform itself, too.

Now [we] must rehabilitate the good reputation of the financial system. Those which have quick accesses to the information and can respond promptly are the financial, banking, and commercial departments. We learn the general situation from these departments.[87]

Obviously, Chen saw "reform" as a means to, rather than the end of, his "readjustment," so it should strengthen financial centralization, not vice versa. This understanding was fundamentally different from the reform Deng had in mind. It was not surprising that Chen did not like financial decentralization at all, because it substantially undermined the central-planning economy, and Chen's power base as well. No wonder that Chen defended the financial system, the uncooperativeness of which had been widely resented among the local leaders.

Although Zhao also said in his speech at the conference that it was necessary to make "a big readjustment" in order to avoid "an economic crisis," he emphasized that this was not to "slip back into the old rut" but to "open a new route in our economic development" – that was why the reform was needed. Zhao implicitly refused Chen's suggestion to return to centralization, that is, "the old rut." He argued that the most important task in the near future was to "bring the capacity of the [state-owned] enterprises into full play and enhance their efficiency." Needless to say, these were exactly what management autonomy and profit retention aimed at.[88]

Deng claimed at the beginning of his speech on December 25 that he "fully agreed to" Chen's speech as well as Zhao's. Yet Deng's stand was also clearly expressed:

The responsibility system in agricultural production has produced good effects and should continue to be implemented in earnest. ... This year the number of industrial enterprises experimenting

---

87 *Xuandu*, 1:235–8 (emphasis added).
88 See *Dangde shiyijie sanzhong quanhui yilai dashi ji* (Major events since the Third Plenum of the Eleventh CC), compiled by the Research Office of the CC Secretariat, Beijing: Red Flag Press, 1987, p. 124.

with extended decision-making power has risen to more than 6,000.... We have begun to find better ways of integrating the interests of the state, the enterprises, the production, and office workers, stimulating the initiative of all....

It is absolutely necessary to have a high degree of centralism and unification during the readjustment. *But we should continue to enforce those reform measures that have proved effective and should not backtrack.* We should continue to stimulate the economy and to *mobilize the initiative of the localities and enterprises*.[89]

From these words, it is hard to see how Deng could "fully agree to" Chen's speech.

The discord resulted in an obscure policy approach that combined the preferences of both sides. The CC issued a circular on January 5, 1981, requiring all the local authorities to adhere to the principle of reform and openness. Meanwhile, it also stipulated that all the localities should "unconditionally keep step with the CC" in the policy process – a CCP jargon refering to centralization. However, Chen and his associates had to give up. Although they continued to resist the reform policies, their approach – an overall retreat under strict central control, which had been mainstream policies – proved ineffective again in 1980. Besides a huge budget deficit of 12.75 billion yuan and a trade deficit of $1.28 billion, inflation had reached over 6 percent, and the food prices had increased 13.8 percent – both were the highest since 1951. Thus, the reform policy began to prevail throughout the country after the summer of 1981.

By the time the national agricultural work conference was convened in October, the household responsibility system had been practiced across China. On January 1, 1982, the CC issued the famous 1982 Number 1 Document, in which the household responsibility system was formally adopted as "a long-term policy" because it had proved "tremendously successful" – by then the "policy" had already been practiced by over 90 percent of production teams. The next day, the CC and the State Council issued a resolution jointly on "overall reorganization of the state-owned enterprises," which would also center on the production responsibility system, namely, to grant the enterprises management autonomy on the condition that they would be responsible for their production activities

[89] *SWDXP*, 1975–82, p. 343 (emphasis added).

Deng Xiaoping's Dominance

and for turning over a certain amount of profit in the form of taxes. Thus, after over three years of struggle, Deng eventually overcame the ideological barrier; overwhelmed his opponents; and ensured that the reform policy, which departed radically from the orthodox doctrine expressed as the FCP, was formally adopted at the Twelfth PC in September 1982.

Leadership Relations under Deng's Dominance

The most substantial victory Deng achieved at the Twelfth PC was the establishment of a new leadership structure under his dominance. Despite the "new historical conditions," however, this structure inherited all the basic features of the Yan'an Round Table before the CR (see Chapters 3 and 4) because the *independent variable*, factionalism, in CCP politics remained unchanged. It was still a two-system structure, in which the Party and military systems were virtually independent of each other and leaders were linked to each other by personal ties rather than institutional arrangements. The two-front arrangement also existed in the Party and administrative system, with Hu and Zhao managing the policy process at the first front, and Deng staying at the second front with *the other senior leaders* to wrestle with "the principal issues." Like Mao's command, Deng's dominance was essentially based on his exclusive accesses to *both* the Party and military systems (Figure 7.1).

However, this structure was not exactly a copy of the Yan'an Round Table under Mao's command. A significant difference was that the nature of the two-front arrangement was fundamentally different from the one at Mao's Yan'an Round Table in that there was not an absolute supreme commander, although Deng's dominance was unquestionable. Mao's aim in setting up a two-front arrangement was to relieve himself of the burden of daily affairs and responsibility without undermining his command (see Chapter 4), but Deng needed this arrangement partly to head off attack in case things went sour under his leadership and in large part to make up the lack of ideological legitimacy of his dominance.

Second, Deng, who stayed at the second front with Chen Yun and Ye Jianying, was officially inferior to his follower Hu Yaobang, who was general secretary of the CCP in charge of the first front. The aim for such an arrangement was obvious: as a Deng follower, Hu would execute the

Factionalism in Chinese Communist Politics

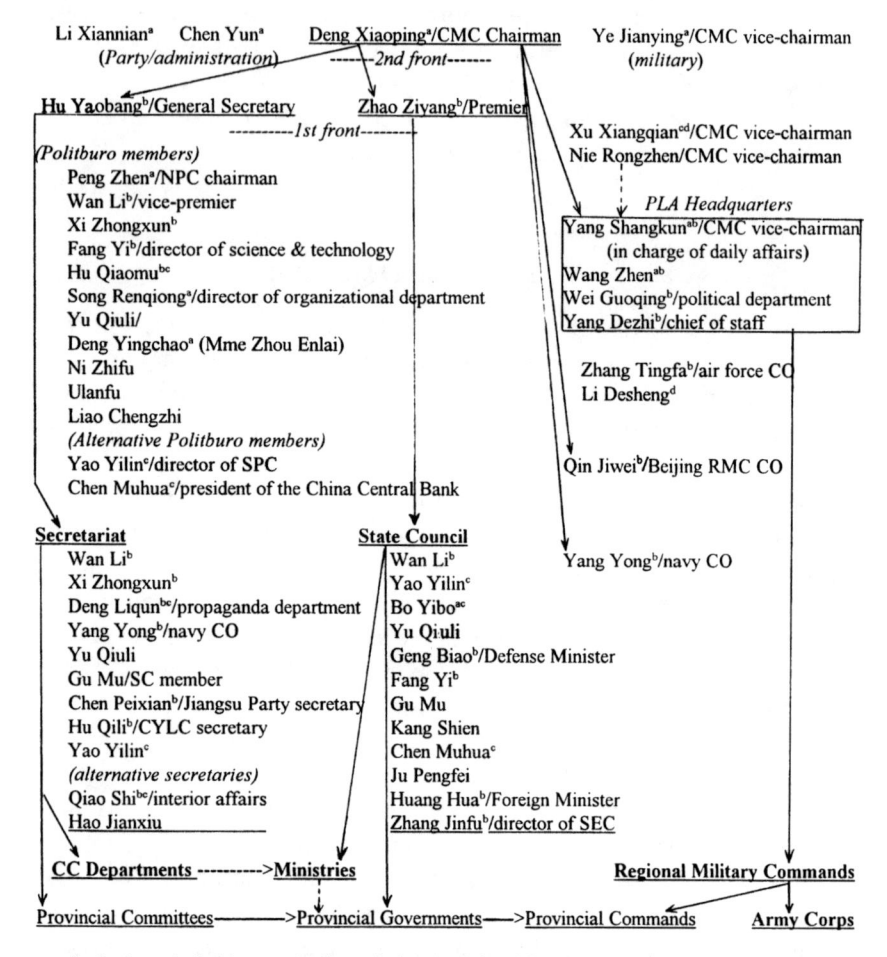

Li Xiannian[a]   Chen Yun[a]   Deng Xiaoping[a]/CMC Chairman   Ye Jianying[a]/CMC vice-chairman
(*Party/administration*)   ------2nd front-------   (*military*)

Hu Yaobang[b]/General Secretary   Zhao Ziyang[b]/Premier
----------1st front--------   Xu Xiangqian[cd]/CMC vice-chairman
(*Politburo members*)   Nie Rongzhen/CMC vice-chairman
Peng Zhen[a]/NPC chairman
Wan Li[b]/vice-premier   PLA Headquarters
Xi Zhongxun[b]   Yang Shangkun[ab]/CMC vice-chairman
Fang Yi[b]/director of science & technology   (in charge of daily affairs)
Hu Qiaomu[bc]   Wang Zhen[ab]
Song Renqiong[a]/director of organizational department   Wei Guoqing[b]/political department
Yu Qiuli/   Yang Dezhi[b]/chief of staff
Deng Yingchao[a] (Mme Zhou Enlai)
Ni Zhifu   Zhang Tingfa[b]/air force CO
Ulanfu   Li Desheng[d]
Liao Chengzhi
(*Alternative Politburo members*)
Yao Yilin[e]/director of SPC   Qin Jiwei[b]/Beijing RMC CO
Chen Muhua[e]/president of the China Central Bank

Secretariat   State Council
Wan Li[b]   Wan Li[b]   Yang Yong[b]/navy CO
Xi Zhongxun[b]   Yao Yilin[e]
Deng Liqun[bc]/propaganda department   Bo Yibo[ac]
Yang Yong[b]/navy CO   Yu Qiuli
Yu Qiuli   Geng Biao[b]/Defense Minister
Gu Mu/SC member   Fang Yi[b]
Chen Peixian[b]/Jiangsu Party secretary   Gu Mu
Hu Qili[b]/CYLC secretary   Kang Shien
Yao Yilin[e]   Chen Muhua[e]
(*alternative secretaries*)   Ju Pengfei
Qiao Shi[be]/interior affairs   Huang Hua[b]/Foreign Minister
Hao Jianxiu   Zhang Jinfu[b]/director of SEC

CC Departments ---------->Ministries   Regional Military Commands

Provincial Committees--------->Provincial Governments---->Provincial Commands   Army Corps

[a] senior leaders who had been at the Center before the Cultural Revolution.
[b] affiliated with Deng Xiaoping.
[c] affiliated with Chen Yun.
[d] affiliated with Li Xiannian.

Figure 7.1. Leadership relations under Deng Xiaoping's dominance, 1982 (solid arrow = direct control; dashed arrow = indirect control)

decisions made by Deng; but as the top leader of the Party, Hu, and the Party as well, had to shoulder the responsibility if policies failed. It has to be noticed, however, the CCP chairmanship Hu had enjoyed for fifteen months was abolished. The ultimate power that Hu had as the CC

Deng Xiaoping's Dominance

general secretary, according to the new Party Constitution, was to convene (*zhaoji*) a Politburo meeting. But even this was not an exclusive privilege – the other senior leaders, namely Deng and Chen, could also convene a Politburo meeting on their own initiatives.

Third, unlike Mao, who was increasingly aloof after the arrangement had been made, Deng was still very much involved in the policy process, even though he would vow repeatedly to quit. To Mao, the first front was essentially *an institution* under his command. He could always replace any individual leaders there without substantially undermining his command. Yet, when Mao realized that it was the institution that had been undermining his command, he felt compelled to get rid of it, even though that meant the whole Party state had to go (see Chapter 6). But to Deng, the first front was like his *personal offices*. Anything wrong there would have negative implications for Deng's own position, although an original aim of this arrangement was to make someone there a scapegoat when necessary.

Last, although Mao rose to power by "the barrel of a gun," he put the gun under the Party's command because the legitimacy of his leadership, as well as the Party's cause, came from the same source: MZT. Mao relied on the army again and cut off the Party from the gun only *after* he was determined to do away with the Party bureaucrats (see Chapter 6). But Deng was never able to convert his control of the gun into the kind of command Mao had enjoyed. As a result, he had to hold the CMC chairmanship while letting his follower head the Party. In order to justify his CMC chairmanship, Deng even managed to add a new clause to the 1982 Party Constitution: the CMC chairmanship must be assumed by a PSC member, instead of *the* Party leader as required by all the previous Party constitutions.[90] Thus, at the Yan'an Round Table it was the Party that commanded the gun, which was why Mao advocated that "rebellion is justified" when this relationship was reversed during the CR. But in the Deng period, it was the military's support that enabled Deng to dominate, which was why Deng's opponents applauded the FCP, and particularly "the leadership of the CCP," for these symbolic principles would at least make it illegitimate for Deng to take over the Party by the barrel of gun.

The most *fundamental* change, however, occurred in the nature of

---

90 See 1982 CCP Constitution, Article 21, in *Xuandu*, 1:541.

personal relations which fostered factional activities. Personal loyalties of course still played an essential role in leadership relations, especially among the senior leaders (those who had been at the Center before the Cultural Revolution) who survived the collapse of the Yan'an Round Table. This is best demonstrated by the relationship between Deng and Wang Zhen. Although the two had totally different attitudes toward policy making – Deng wanted to reform and Wang was a diehard hardliner – Wang's loyalty to Deng kept him on Deng's side whenever he was really needed. The relationship between Chen Yun and Peng Zhen provides an opposite example. Both were conservatives who resented any departure from "the socialist road," but a personality clash kept them apart. According to at least two reliable sources, including one of Chen's former political secretaries, it was Chen who resolutely blocked Peng from entering the PSC at the Fifth and Sixth Plenums, and then again at the Twelfth PC.[91]

Among the younger leaders, however, similar policy preferences played a more important role in their political alignments. True, their loyalties toward those who had promoted them, namely the mountaintop bosses, were unquestionable, but they themselves knew little about each other until they were promoted into the Center. Even after they were acquainted, the kind of personal loyalties commonly seen among the senior leaders barely existed among the young generation, partly because few of them had endured the hardships *together* as the senior leaders did during the revolution, but essentially because the intrigue, treachery, betrayal, and inhuman struggles during the CR had virtually destroyed that kind of trust and comradeship within the Party, especially among the local leading cadres who had suffered most because of the overall assault on the Party bureaucrats, on the one hand, and fierce factional struggles during the 1967–8 "Red Storm of Seizing the Power," on the other (see Chapter 6). Indeed, from the very beginning, similar views had brought them together. They were not very fond of the "Party spirit" because they had hardly ever benefited from it; they were more faction-

---

91 Chen's strategy was a typical character assassination. Citing Peng's behavior in the making of the *February Outline* as an example, Chen questioned Peng's honesty as a Party leader. Allegedly, Chen even held that Peng's dishonesty in this case had "implicated the Party" (*tuolei le dang*), because it yielded an excuse to Mao to launch the CR. It has to be noticed that the verdict on the *February Outline* has not been officially reversed.

Deng Xiaoping's Dominance

oriented because it was their patrons who had brought them into the leadership, and it was in factional interactions that they acquired most of their political skills.

Thus, leadership relations under Deng's dominance were more faction-ridden because of the decline in the "Party spirit"; more vulnerable to crisis during a policy dispute because of *different understandings* of the ideological principles these leaders had committed themselves to; and more unpredictable because of the weaker personal loyalties on the one hand, and the even weaker incentive to abide by the rules in the game on the other.

DENG'S STRUGGLE TO MAINTAIN HIS DOMINANCE

"Two Principal Points" versus "Two Civilizations"

Although Deng scored an overall victory at the Twelfth PC, he still faced strong opposition from the conservatives in policy making. His followers were doubtless a dominant force at the Center, but they could not form a majority if the other leaders stood together in a policy dispute. At the Politburo, fourteen out of twenty-eight members were Deng followers, but Hu Qiaomu had already began to lean toward the other side, and Wang Zhen – Deng's "big gun" – was a diehard hardliner. Deng could have followed Mao's strategy in decision making, that is, to surpass the Politburo by using the CC Secretariat-PSC line (see Chapter 5), given that six out of eleven CC secretaries were his followers. Yet he could hardly prevail at the six-man PSC if the other three senior leaders – Chen, Ye, and Li – stood together against him. The situation was more difficult for Deng among the ten senior leaders – Deng, Chen, Ye Jianying, Li, Peng, Nie Rongzhen, Xu Xiangqian, Yang Shangkun, Wang Zhen, and Deng Yingchao – who all carried substantial weight in decision making. It was true that Nie, Xu, Yang, and Wang, all military leaders, tended to stand by Deng, but all of them had a conservative political attitude.

The senior military leaders' attitude – supportive of Deng's economic reforms (but with varied limits) and opposed to political changes – revealed a dilemma shared by most of the CCP cadres. Like Deng, whose reform policy resulted not so much from a self-conscious effort as from his pragmatic approach, these cadres supported the reform largely because they had learned from the repeated economic failures since the 1950s that the orthodox, centrally planned economy did not work. More substantially, they were thrilled by the increase in their economic and political powers brought about by the decentralization in the reform. When the reform provoked political challenges to their authorities, however, they tended to be reactionary and therefore support the hardliners in political affairs. Indeed, few of the CCP cadres foresaw or were prepared for political changes brought about by the reform, which they wished would just create economic prosperity.

As the reform policy prevailed, a thaw also set in, resulting in a surge of "scar literature" that implicitly criticized the CCP's rule by exposing the social "scars" caused by the political campaigns from the 1957 antirightist movement through the CR.[92] What was more devastating to the Party was that the reform had created so many opportunities and temptations that corruption soon became a widespread phenomenon. All this had created an excellent excuse for the conservatives, who were losing on the economic front, to take on Deng in the ideological field where his dominance was always liable to challenge due to his lack of ideological legitimacy. According to a former leader of the CC Propaganda Department, as soon as the Sixth Plenum (June 27–29, 1981) was over, Deng Liqun and Hu Qiaomu submitted a report, together with some materials, to the CC with Chen's support. They claimed that the "scar literature in the literary world" and corruptions among the cadres in "the economic spheres" reflected "a trend of bourgeois liberalization," which was undermining the Party and its "socialist cause."[93]

The report drew Deng's attention, not necessarily because the blame was laid virtually at his doorstep, given that the literary world was Hu Yaobang's domain and Zhao Ziyang had just taken over the economy from Chen Yun, but essentially because Deng also shared the fear that "bourgeois liberalization" could bring about challenges to the CCP's rule. He summoned all the leading cadres in charge of ideology and propaganda on July 17, and he attacked the liberal tendency in the literary world: "The essence of the FCP is to uphold the Communist Party's lead-

---

92 See Cyril Birch, "Literature under communism," in Roderick MacFarquhar and John Fairbank, eds., *Cambridge History of China*, Cambridge: Cambridge University Press, 1991, 15:799–806.
93 Also cf. Ran Ming, *Deng Xiaoping diguo* (The Deng Xiaoping Empire), Taipei: Shipao Press, 1992, pp. 128–9.

ership. Without the Party's leadership there definitely will be nationwide disorder and China will fall apart.... *The keystone of bourgeois liberalization is opposition to the Party's leadership.*"[94] However, this did not mean that Deng would yield to the hardliners. Rather, his reaction revealed the dilemma he shared with most of the CCP cadres, namely, that they needed the reform for economic prosperity, which was becoming the only source of legitimacy for the CCP's rule, but they were unwilling, and could not afford, to tolerate any trends that would lead to the challenges to the CCP's rule. Deng's solution to this dilemma, as Zhao Ziyang summed up later, was the "two principal points":

> [The Party's] line since the Third Plenum [of the Eleventh CC] is to proceed from China's reality and build socialism with Chinese characteristics. This line embodies two principal points. One is to *uphold the FCP*; and the other is to adhere to the *fundamental policy* of reform and openness. The two points are interrelated and neither can be dispensed with. Should we fail to uphold the FCP, reform and openness would lose their direction and would not have any guarantees. Should we fail to carry out reform and openness, we could not rapidly develop our productive capacity, let alone build socialism with Chinese characteristics.[95]

Deng himself expressed these two principal points as "grasping things with two hands" (*liangshou zhua*), with one hand grasping the reform, the other hand political stability and unity. He wished that this strategy would enable him to carry out the reform that would promote a fast economic growth with little change in the political system. But this was wishful thinking. First of all, Deng failed, or was unwilling indeed, to see that the hardliners were exploiting his commitment to the FCP to roll back the gains he obtained through his reform in the economic sphere. As a result, Deng's "grasping things with two hands" evolved into grasping the reform with one hand, but letting the other hand endure the pounding from the hardliners.

Furthermore, the strategy of "grasping things with two hands" virtually split Deng's forces in the economic and political spheres and therefore weakened the strength of his forces on both fronts. Not surprisingly,

---

94 *SWDXP*, 1975–82, p. 369 (emphasis added).
95 *Xuanbian*, 3:1261 (emphasis added).

while Zhao Ziyang, Deng's economic executive in charge of the "economic basis," was increasingly prominent due to the offensive Deng took on the economic front, Hu Yaobang, Deng's political executive who was assigned to defend the political front, was losing ground to the hardliners. Moreover, the separation made Deng's followers, and particularly Zhao, turf-oriented in the policy process, which gave the conservatives more leverage in the struggle against Deng.

Yet, the vital flaw of the "two principal points" was that they were essentially self-contradictory in theory as well as in practice. Deng's reform policy was a departure from "the socialist road." What is more, as the economy grew rapidly, so did people's socioeconomic expectations, which in turn provoked their interests and demands for political participation. The so-called bourgeois liberalization was essentially a reflection of these increasing demands. As my examination shows, this innate self-contradiction in Deng's "two principal points" enabled the hardliners to maintain their ideological superiority in the struggle against Deng, although they had little social support and their strength was no match to that of Deng's forces; that was why Deng could repeatedly roll back their attack. Ironically, the more success Deng achieved in his reform, the further he had to depart from "the socialist road," and therefore the more ideological advantage the hardliners could take in their struggle against Deng's forces.

In 1983 the household responsibility system was implemented in all the provinces after the CC issued another Number 1 CC Document on January 2, 1983. Meanwhile, the reformers began to take on the conservatives in their traditional domain: the financial system. The National Conference on the Work of Converting Profits into Taxes (*li gai shui*) was held March 17–29 in order to work out a system in which the state-owned enterprises would no longer turn over their profits to the state; rather, they would pay taxes according to their productive capacity.[96] This change would undermine the centrally planned economy because it would transform the previous *administrative* relationship between the state and enterprises into one in which *economic interests* would be an essential factor. The substantial gain for Deng's forces in this change was obvious for the profit turnover system, which had been an important part of the economic planning led by Yao Yilin, Chen Yun's protégé, but the

---

96 See Liao, *Xin zhongguo biannian shi*, pp. 514–15.

tax system would be managed by a new vice-premier, Tian Jiyun, who was Zhao's confidant.[97] At the Sixth NPC, held June 6–21, not only were the reformers' budget and economic plans adopted, but Deng's forces also gained more ground at the State Council: besides Premier Zhao, Vice-Premiers Wan Li and Tian Jiyun were in charge of agriculture and finance respectively, while Chen's associates, Yao Yilin and Li Peng, were assigned to take charge of planning and to "assist" Zhao in industrial affairs.

Not surprisingly, the reform momentum also encouraged the liberal Party theoreticians. At the initiative of Zhou Yang, a vice-chairman of the All-China Writers Association, Wang Ruoshui, deputy general editor of the *People's Daily*, and Su Shaozhi, director of the Marxism-Leninism Institute, a discussion on the Marxist alienation theory emerged in the ideological field in the first half of 1983. Some participants implied that a socialist system could also become "alienated into an oppressive system," and "public servants could evolve into lords over the people."[98] This not only provided the hardliners with an excuse to attack Hu Yaobang, who was in charge of the theoretical field, but it also agitated Deng, who was also "concerned about the emergence of ideological trends that, if unchecked, might ultimately challenge political stability."[99] Thus, Deng criticized the alienation theory, and the discussions about it as well, at the Second Plenum of the Twelfth CC on October 12, accusing it of "spreading spiritual pollution on the ideological front."[100]

However, when a jubilant Deng Liqun was drumming up "an overall struggle against spiritual pollution in all fields of the work," Deng Xiaoping resolutely stopped such an attempt. At the suggestions of Zhao Ziyang, Wan Li, and Fang Yi, the CC issued a circular on November 9,[101] stipulating that the campaign against spiritual pollution should be carried out "only on the ideological front" and should not intervene in the work of the other fields. Thus, this campaign against the

---

97 Tian had been the financial boss of Sichuan. Zhao promoted him to Beijing soon after he was appointed vice-premier.
98 See Zhou Yang, "*Guanyu Makesi zhuyi de ji ge lilun wenti*" (Explorations of a few theoretical questions of Marxism), *PD*, March 16, 1983.
99 Harry Harding, *China's Second Revolution*, Washington, DC: Brookings Institution, 1987, p. 189.
100 See *Xuandu*, 2:721–4. Deng's speech was drafted by Deng Liqun.
101 See *PD*, November 10, 1983.

spiritual pollution was aborted twenty-eight days after it was officially launched.

The year of 1984 was Deng's year. It started with his tour of the "special economic zones" of Shenzhen and Zhuhai in Guangdong and Xiamen in Fujian, from January 24 to February 10. Deng's tour generated the momentum for the reform to move up to the second stage – openness to the world economy and a massive introduction of the market economy, a stage that was further away from "the socialist road." It was decided at a forum of leaders of the coastal provinces, convened by the CC Secretariat and the State Council from March 26 to April 6, that another fourteen costal cities would be opened to the world market, which meant that the bulk of China's industry would be fully exposed to the capitalist market economy.[102] On May 10, the State Council issued *The Regulations on Further Extending the Management Autonomy of the State-Owned Enterprises*. The document increased the managers' power remarkably: they were now allowed to alter the state plans according to the market, which was a radical departure from the centrally planned socialist economy.[103] In his report to the Second Session of the Sixth NPC, held May 15–31, Zhao suggested that reforming the *economic system* and opening China to the outside world were the "two major tasks" in the future. Zhao further emphasized that antispiritual pollution should be confined to the ideological field and should not intervene in the economic work, nor should it be used against "the people's normal demands to improve their spiritual and material lives."[104]

On October 20, the CC held its Third Plenum at which two documents were approved: "The Resolution on the Reform of the Economic System," and "Ten Policies for Further Stimulating the Rural Economy." This resolution defined China's economy as "a *planned market economy* based on public ownership." This new jargon was practically meaningless indeed – how can a market economy be planned? But it marked the *ideological breakthrough* the reformers had long wanted. From now on, the market economy no longer just belonged to capitalism, but it was also part of "the socialist road."[105] The "Ten Policies" declared that the state would no longer monopolize the purchasing and marketing of

---

102 *Xuandu*, 2:735–46. 103 Ibid., pp. 747–54. 104 See *PD*, June 1, 1984.
105 See "*Zhonggong zhongyang guanyu jingji tizhi gaige de jueding*" (The CC's resolution on the reform of the economic system), *Xuandu*, 2:775–8.

Deng Xiaoping's Dominance

major agricultural products like grain and cotton – a policy that was initiated by Chen Yun in 1953 and had ever since been strictly enforced (see Chapter 4).[106] Thus, after the household responsibility system had destroyed the people's commune, the abandoning of the state monopoly of the market of major agricultural products finally eliminated "the socialist road" in the rural economy.

This reform momentum, which pushed Deng's reform and his reputation to the climax, continued until the Third Session of the Sixth NPC in April 1985. In his report to the NPC, Zhao put forward the idea of "reforming the price system" in accord with the market economy.[107] This was another major step away from "the socialist road" because price controls were essential to a socialist economy. Politically, the price reform would undermine Chen Yun's force because it would be managed by the State Economic Commission and the Commerce Ministry, which were led by Tian Jiyun, but the price system had been managed by the State Planning Commission, which was Yao Yilin's domain.

Yet an inevitable consequence of the transition toward a market economy in a system of single-party rule was the rampant corruption among the Party cadres. Increasing corruption provided the hardliners with an opportunity to substantiate their attack on the reformers. In late June the CC Discipline Inspection Commission, which had been controlled by the hardliners ever since its establishment, convened a national conference on rectifying the Party's work-style. Chen Yun made a written speech at the conference on June 29. He emphasized:

> We must let the whole Party understand that *our cause is the socialist cause*. Its ultimate goal is to realize communism. This is a very important point. Economic construction that is under way in our country is *socialist* economic construction under the central leadership [of the CCP]. The reform of the economic system is a *socialist reform* of the economic system. . . .
> If we fail to build *socialist spiritual civilization* while building *socialist material civilization*, the construction of material civilization will drift off the correct course. . . . Our comrades of the

---

106 "*Zhonggong zhongyang, guowu yuan guanyu jinyibu huoyue nongcun jingji de shiyang zhengce*" (Ten policies of the CC and the State Council on further stimulating the rural economy), *Xuandu*, 2:805–6.
107 Zhao, "*Guanyu jingji tizhi gaige*," *Xuandu*, 2:866–72.

whole Party must always pay special attention to the building of spiritual civilization while developing material civilization.[108]

Chen's speech fully exposed the ideological contradiction of Deng's "two principal points." Chen *reminded* Deng of his commitment to the FCP – Deng's first "principal point" – pointing out explicitly that "*our cause is the socialist cause*," an ideological principle that Deng never dared to deny. Implicitly but forcefully, Chen challenged the departure from "the socialist road," which was the essential nature of Deng's reform policy – Deng's second "principal point." Thus, the innate contradiction in Deng's "two principal points" enabled Chen Yun to capture the ideological high ground for his forces. With ideological superiority, Chen put forward the "two civilizations": socialist *spiritual* civilization and socialist *material* civilization. Emphasizing the necessity to "build the two civilizations simultaneously," Chen implicitly criticized Deng's emphasis on the economic development, warning Deng that his reform aimed at economic growth could "drift off the correct course" if he failed to build "socialist spiritual civilization" simultaneously. Compared with Deng's "two principal points," Chen's "two civilizations" was ideologically consistent and hence stronger, not just rhetorically but politically as well. No wonder that it has since been taken by the conservatives as a political line opposed to Deng's "two principal points" and used effectively in their attack on Deng's forces.

With Chen's support, the Discipline Inspection Commission exposed two "big cases" in July. One involved the massive production of "fake medicines" in Jinjiang of Fujian. Some local leading cadres, who had been bribed, either turned a blind eye to or participated in the illegal activity.[109] The other case involved the massive smuggling of foreign-made cars via Hainan, then a region of Guangdong Province. Liang Xiang, a local leader who was a close associate of Zhao Ziyang, was involved in this case.[110] The hardliners fully capitalized on these two cases: they publicized the two cases to make a high-profile political issue; demoted or even sentenced the involved cadres; and removed Xiang Nan, the Party secretary of Fujian Province, and Ren Zhongyi, the Party secretary of Guangdong from the two provinces that were at the forefront of the reform – not surprisingly, both were Deng's men. More

---

108 Chen, "*Liangge wenming yao yiqi zhua*," *Xuandu*, 2:897–8 (emphasis in original).
109 See *PD*, July 13, 14, 22, 1985.   110 See *PD*, August 1, 1985.

Deng Xiaoping's Dominance

importantly, they forced Deng to accept their political agenda. Although the seventh five-year plan made under Zhao's supervision and the reformers' agenda – an overall reform of the economic system – were approved at the CCP National Conference held from September 18 to 23, Deng had to endorse Chen's proposal of "building the two civilizations simultaneously" in his speech on September 23.[111] Chen wanted more in his speech on the same day:

> [Ours is] a *socialist economy*, [it] still needs the plans and [must be developed] in proportion. Our Party is the Communist Party. *The Communist Party must carry out socialism*. The *socialist reform* of the economic system that is now under way is the self-perfection and development of the socialist system. . . .
>
> When viewed from the work of the whole country, *the planned economy plays the principal role and the market adjustment a subsidiary role*. These words are not outdated. . . .
>
> [We must] strengthen the ideological and political work, vindicate the authority of the departments in charge of ideological and political work.

Chen ended his speech with an explicit warning, obviously intended for Deng's ears:

> Persist in democratic centralization. This is the principle stipulated by our Party Constitution. . . . *Decisions on important issues must be fully discussed by the collective leadership* in order to reduce mistakes.[112]

A campaign against "spiritual pollution" was launched immediately after the conference. This time the hardliners were better prepared than in the first round. Under the banner of Chen's "building the two civilizations simultaneously," they took full ideological advantage over the innate contradiction between Deng's "two principal points" – to carry out a reform that was departing from "the socialist road" while insisting on the leadership of the CCP, which had to "carry out socialism." In practice, they made full use of their control of the Central Discipline Inspection Commission to find fault with the reform-minded cadres. As a result, the reform momentum was halted by the end of 1985, and Hu

---

111 See *Xuandu*, 2:969–71.   112 Ibid., pp. 977–8 (emphasis added).

Yaobang was assigned to take charge of a campaign to rectify the Party in 1986, a job that would lead to his fall.

"Separating the Party from the Government" and the Fall of Hu Yaobang

Deng realized that unless he could find a way to contain the conservative forces, especially their effective use of their ideological superiority and their control of the Discipline Inspection Commission to check out and deter the reform-minded cadres, his reform could hardly continue smoothly. Deng's solution was to *institutionally* separate the political front from the economic front in the policy process, namely, to "separate the party from government." This was the essential aim of the political reform Deng *reinitiated* in 1986.

True, Deng made a speech "On the Reform of the System of the Party and State Leadership" at an enlarged Politburo meeting on March 18, 1980. Yet, Deng's main concern at that time was to prevent power from "overconcentrating in the hands of individual leaders" like Mao,[113] which Deng believed was *the* cause of the CR. Except for pointing out the problems he had observed within the leadership, Deng's ideas about political reform were vague and inconsistent. In fact, this speech was shelved soon after Deng's dominance was established at the Sixth Plenum of the Eleventh PC in June 1981. Obviously, had Deng's proposal of checking the power of individual leaders been put into practice at the time, it was his increasing power that would have been checked first.

In retrospect, the idea of "separating the party from the government" was substantiated in the struggle against the conservative forces in 1985–6.[114] Seeing that the conservative forces had used their control of the Discipline Inspection Commission to deter the reform-minded

---

113 *SWDXP* 1975–82, pp. 303, 311–13.
114 Cf. Shiping Zheng, *Party vs. State in Post–1949 China: The Institutional Dilemma*, Cambridge: Cambridge University Press, 1997, pp. 197–8. Zheng's analysis shows that "separating the Party from the government" was Zhou Ziyang's top priority in political reform because Zhao realized that "the Party" had increasingly become an obstacle for the reform. Yet his implication that the policy was adopted *after* Hu Yaobang was toppled at the end of 1986 is arguable. In fact, the policy had been proposed before Hu's fall, which made it more urgent for the reform-minded leaders to carry out the policy in an attempt to fend off the attack from the conservative forces, which, not surprisingly, concentrated in the Party organizations.

Deng Xiaoping's Dominance

cadres and to sabotage reform in the name of anticorruption, Deng adopted Hu's suggestion to launch a nationwide anticorruption campaign within the Party. The aim, as a provincial CYLC secretary in South China, who was a close associate of Hu, pointed out in an interview in May 1986, was "to rehabilitate the reputation of reform [cadres], on the one hand, and to take over the initiative from the antireform factions, on the other." Thus, the CC Secretariat convened a grand conference from January 6 to 8, 1986, with eight thousand cadres and officers in Beijing in attendance. Hu Yaobang, Tian Jiyun, Wang Zhaoguo, and Yang Shangkun – all Deng's men – made speeches at the conference. Hu pointed out repeatedly in his summary speech that the coming rectification campaign was not to slow down, let alone stop, the reform. Rather, its aim was to consolidate "the achievements of the reform in the first five years of the 1980s" so as to promote the reform in the future. Hu called the cadres at the Center "to make an example" in keeping the fine work-style of the Party, and to "unite around the CC leadership" in the reform.[115]

However, although the launching of an anticorruption campaign enabled Deng's forces to resume the political initiative and might have helped them to get even with the conservative factions on the ideological front, it could not effectively stop the purge of the reform-minded cadres by the Discipline Inspection Commission, which had become so powerful during the rectification that it could not only discipline the cadres but also force the judicial offices to indict and even sentence them to jail in the name of the Party's leadership. During his inspection in Fujian, where the reform cadres endured the hardest hit, Hu Qili, Hu Yaobang's confidant who was newly promoted to the CC Secretariat, complained about the old-style purge of cadres. He said on May 24:

> In order to steadfastly and relentlessly push the overall reform forward, we have to protect the enthusiasm of cadres. . . . The aim of rectification of the Party is to educate and prevent our cadres from sinking into the hole of corruption, not to find fault with them and then knock them dead with one blow [*yi gunzi dasi*]. Now we are facing many new problems, but [these problems]

---

115 Hu Yaobang, "*Zhongyang jiguan yaozuo quanguo de biaoshuai*" (The CC apparatus must make an example for the whole country), *Xuandu*, 2:990–3.

have to be solved through further reform. It is hopeless to follow the beaten track.¹¹⁶

Indeed, Deng had to contain the power of the CC Discipline Inspection Commission and stop its onslaught on the reform forces. In his speech at a PSC meeting on June 28, Deng said:

> Some comrades have raised the question of how to distinguish between the work of rectifying the Party's work-style and that of checking unhealthy [social] tendencies. In fact, the main question is not how to distinguish these two things, but the problem in *the relationship between the Party and the government. It is inappropriate to let the Party interfere in some problems, of which* [the solutions] *belong to the scope of law.* Too much interference by the Party will hinder the establishment of the concept of the rule of law among the people. *The Party should mind the problems concerning the Party's discipline.* The problems within the scope of law have to be taken care of by the state and government. . . . *All in all, to include some criminal problems in the scope of rectifying the Party's work-style and let* [them] *be handled by the system of the CC Discipline Inspection Commission are not helpful to the establishment of the concept of the rule of law among the people.*¹¹⁷

Two points must be highlighted in Deng's words. First, it was for the first time in CCP history that the issue of distinguishing between the law and the Party's discipline was raised in a CCP leader's speech. But Deng warned the Party not to interfere in the law not necessarily because he really wanted the rule of law, but because he had to contain the hardliners who, using their control of the Discipline Inspection Commission, had been undermining the reform forces in the name of anticorruption. Ironically, it was factionalism that helped Deng to prevail on this issue. Despite his conservative attitude, Peng Zhen zealously supported Deng's idea of distinguishing the law from the Party's discipline. As the leader in charge of law, strengthening the legal institutions at the expense of the CC Discipline Inspection Commission could not only increase Peng's power but also enable him to get back at Chen Yun, Peng's rival since

---

116 Quoted from *Fujian Daily*, May 26, 1986. Also see *Shiyijie sanzhong quanhui yilai*, p. 246.   117 *Xuandu*, 2:1077–8 (emphasis added).

the 1940s. No wonder that Peng suddenly changed his uncooperative attitude and became a zealous advocate of reform in the summer of 1986. Peng said during his tour of Shanxi and Henan on June 2:

> All those in production relations and in the superstructure who are not suitable to the development of productive forces must be adjusted and reformed. *Reform is in accord with the tenets of Marxism.* At present, our central task is construction, reform, and stimulation of the productive forces. No matter how many contradictions, twists, and difficulties we will encounter during the process of reform, our direction and the fundamental policy of reform of the [economic] system will not be altered. . . .
> We must maintain a political situation of stability and unity. To maintain the political situation of stability and unity, we must rely on correct leadership and line; *we must all unite and work as one*; and we must also have the guarantee provided by developing the socialist democracy and *strengthening the socialist rule of law*.[118]

In his meeting with a Polish delegation on June 9, Peng again sounded like Deng's copycat, but he did not fail to point out what he really wanted:

> *Reform is necessary* in historical development. China needs reform, so does Poland. The aim of reform is to develop the productive capacity of our society. . . . This is a tenet of Marxism. According to our historical experience since the establishment of our country, special attention must be paid to *strengthening and perfecting the socialist rule of law* during socialist construction toward modernization.[119]

Peng's switch to Deng's side broke the conservative coalition and reversed their momentum, so it prompts little wonder that Chen allegedly lost his temper when he learned of Peng's comments.[120]

---

118 Quoted from ibid., 247 (emphasis added).
119 Quoted from *PD*, June 10, 1986 (emphasis added).
120 According to a source who had been Chen's secretary, Chen lashed out when he was told about Peng's open support for the reform: "What an old slick bustard [*lao huatou*]! I've always known he [i.e., Peng] is unreliable."

On July 10, the CC issued a circular that stipulated that "the whole Party must steadfastly abide by the socialist rule of law." It pointed out that some Party leaders and Party organs

> flagrantly interfere in the normal work of the judicial offices; force the judicial offices to act according to their intentions; ... remove at will the judicial cadres who have handled the cases impartially. ... Some of them even used the judicial cadres and police as the instruments for their coercion and pursuit for self interests. These phenomena ... have exerted infamous influence, severely damaged the party's prestige and the seriousness of the socialist rule of law. This must draw full attention from the Party.

Not surprisingly, the circular used Deng's line of "grasping things with two hands," requiring that, "under the new historical conditions, [we] must earnestly put in effect the thought of 'grasping construction with one hand and the rule of law with the other hand.'"[121] But now Deng had to let Peng Zhen's hands "grasp the rule of law," so that his hands could keep "grasping construction."

The second point Deng made in his speech on June 28 is "the relationship between the Party and the government." Obviously, Deng realized that although he could effectively contain the influence of his opponents within the Party, it was very hard to prevent them from interfering in the reform as long as the Party had the last say in the policy process. So Deng readvocated the idea of "the reform of political *institutions*" (*zhengzhi tizhi gaige*) in the summer of 1986 in order to roll back the attack from the conservative forces.[122] Given that Deng's primary goal was to prevent the conservatives, who had formed a formidable force within the Party leadership, from undermining the reform in the name of "strengthening the Party's leadership," the political reform was

---

121 "*Zhonggong zhongyang guanyu quandang bixu jianjue weihu shihui zhuyi fazhi de tongzhi*" (The CC's circular on that the whole Party must steadfastly abide by the socialist rule by law), *Xuandu*, 2:1080–2.

122 The formula "the reform of political institution [*tizhi*]" – not system (*zhidu*) – first appeared in Peng Zhen's report to the NPC Standing Committee on April 22, 1982. Hu Yaobang used it in his political report at the Twelfth PC in 1982. Deng also mentioned it in his speech at the Second Plenum of the Twelfth CC on October 2, 1983. It disappeared thereafter in China's political language until May 20, 1986, when Deng met Australian Prime Minister Hawke. Deng told Hawke that "the reform of political institutions was "aimed at eliminating overstaffing and bureaucracy."

soon substantiated by another so-called fundamental policy of the reform: "separating the party from government."

On September 4, the CC Secretariat issued a circular, requiring all the cadres at the Center to study "On the Reform of the System of the Party and State Leadership," a speech Deng had given six years before.[123] The circular asked specifically that "special attention" be paid to Deng's "discussion on the relationship between the Party and government," though Deng only mentioned this issue once at the beginning of the speech: "It is time for us to distinguish between the Party's responsibilities and those of the government and to stop substituting the former for the latter."[124] On September 13 Deng expressed his ideas on the content of the political reform at the CC Financial and Economic Leading Groups led by Zhao Ziyang: "What should be the contents of the reform of political institutions? It is necessary to discuss it. In my view, ... these contents are: first, *the Party has to be separated from government* in order to solve the problem of how the Party should provide a leadership, and be good at providing the leadership. This is the key."[125]

Deng's aim of "separating the Party from government," however, was not to "democratize the policy process," as Deng and his followers claimed. It was to confine the conservative forces within the Party so that they could not interfere directly in the economic spheres controlled by Deng's forces in the government, and their ideological strength would also be limited *truly* to the ideological front. Thus, an objective consequence of "separating the Party from government" was that Hu was virtually left alone to fight the stronger and better organized conservative forces in the Party organization. This was best shown by the fact that a "Political Reform Office" was set up under the State Council led by Zhao Ziyang. Its job was to work on concrete policies and procedures for the reform of political institutions, especially on a mechanism to "limit the Party's intervention in government affairs."[126] There are various explanations and speculations on why Deng gave this job, which should

---

123 See *Shiyijie sanzhong quanhui yilai*, p. 258.
124 *SWDXP* 1975–82, pp. 303.
125 *Deng Xiaoping tongzhi lun gaige kaifang* (Comrade Deng Xiaoping on the Reform and Openness), Beijing: People's Press, 1991, p. 108 (emphasis added).
126 See Wu Guoguang, *Zhao Ziyang yu zhongguo zhengzhi gaige* (Political Reform under Zhao Ziyang), Hong Kong: Pacific Century Institute, 1997, chaps. 1, 2, 3, 5.

have been Hu Yaobang's, to Zhao.[127] From the perspective of factionalism, however, this was because Deng had predetermined to let Hu concentrate on coping with the conservative forces, so that Zhao could expand his force, and eventually Deng's, to the largest extent in the government.

But the hardliners immediately saw what Deng was really up to. A commentator's article, drafted by Deng Liqun, was printed in *Guangming Daily* on September 18, only two days after Deng's talk to Zhao was transmitted in the Party. The article emphasized that there were "two dividing lines that must be drawn clearly in the reform of political institutions."

> First, like the reform of the economic system, the reform of political institutions is for *the self-perfection and self-development of the socialist system*.... Second, the reform of political institutions must be helpful to improving and strengthening the Party's leadership. It is by no means to make a fundamental change in our socialist system. The viewpoint that the implementation of the reform of political institutions will weaken and abolish the Party's leadership and change the essential nature of the socialist system is incorrect.[128]

In retrospect, "separating the Party from the government" was barely put into practice because of the resistance from the conservative forces. As a matter of fact, this policy soon evolved into symbolic jargon after Zhao Ziyang replaced Hu Yaobang as the CCP General Secretary in early 1987. Its effects on the reform, if there were any, were negative, rather than positive as Deng had expected. It was true that Deng's intention was that, by separating the Party from government in the policy process, he could confine the effect of hardliners' exploitation of his ideological weakness within the Party. But Deng miscalculated. Although the policy of separating the Party from government might give Zhao Ziyang and his associates in the government more freedom to push for the reform, it fully exposed Hu Yaobang, who had already been weakened largely because he had, in fact, single-handedly held the conservative forces at bay. In practice, "separating the Party from government" unloaded two virtually impossible tasks Deng had faced

127 Ibid., pp. 23–5. 128 *Guangming Daily*, September 18, 1986 (emphasis added).

Deng Xiaoping's Dominance

onto Hu Yaobang's back, and these two tasks would eventually break Hu's back.

First of all, Hu had to continue the campaign of rectifying the Party, a campaign that was entering a dead end. In his written speech to the Sixth Session of the CC Discipline Inspection Commission on September 24, 1985, Chen Yun emphasized that a focus in the rectification of the Party's work-style was "the rampant corruption among the children of the high-ranking cadres and officers." Chen argued that unless they were punished, "the Party's work-style and social tendencies could not be fundamentally improved."[129] By the time Hu Yaobang took over the campaign in January 1986, the Discipline Inspection Commission had already started the investigations of a number of the privileged children, including Hu Qiaomu's son Hu Shiying and Wang Zhen's son Wang Jun. The commission dumped all these cases in Hu's offices, implicitly daring him to solve them. Hu was trapped. Had he continued the investigations impartially, he would have to take the same approach to the "bigger fishes" – there were widespread rumors that Ye Jianying's grandson and Zhao Ziyang's sons were guilty of serious wrongdoings. By doing so, however, Hu would become the most wanted man in the elite circle, for corruption did not discriminate against either the hardliners' or the reformers' children.

Second, as I have discussed already, Deng had yielded to the conservative forces repeatedly on the ideological front, not only because of his weakness on this front, but also because he shared the same fear with them – namely, the "spiritual pollution" would provoke challenges to the CCP's rule if unchecked. Thus, Deng and his conservative colleagues had common interests in the campaign of rectifying the Party's work-style and clearing up the spiritual pollution – differences between Deng and the conservatives were in degree rather than in kind. In other words, Deng also wanted Hu to purge those liberal Party cadres like Su Shaozhi, Wang Ruoshui, Yu Guangyuan, Li Honglin, and the like. Again, Hu was trapped in a situation similar to what Peng Zhen faced ten years ago in the Wu Han affair (see Chapter 6). He was in a no-win situation. Even if Hu had done what Deng and the hardliners wanted him to do – that

---

[129] Chen Yun, "*Bixu zhongshi hushi jingshen wenming jianshe*" (We must pay attention to the phenomenon of overlooking the building of the spiritual civilization), *Xuandu*, 2:984–5.

is, to purge those liberals in the Party – he could hardly have been better-off; he would have been blamed anyway for having encouraged and supported them in the first place. A former leader of the CC Organizational Department, who was close to Hu, said in his discussion of this issue with the author in the summer of 1993:

> Yes, [Hu] Yaobang was facing a very difficult situation. You see, Yaobang not only agreed with them [i.e., the so-called bourgeois liberals in the Party] on many issues, but also had good personal relations with them. As a matter of fact, they represented the social forces that supported Yaobang. But Deng wanted Yaobang to expel most of them from the Party. Yaobang could not make up his mind [to do so] because he knew he would be blamed no matter whether he went ahead to do it, or stood there doing nothing. Yaobang chose the latter, presumably because he did not expect that Deng would have been so heartless [*jueqing*]. Hu miscalculated [*shisuan*].

Indeed, the purge of the liberal cadres would inevitably undermine Hu's power base, given the faction-ridden structure of leadership relations. But Hu's reluctance to attack the liberal forces was seen by his patron Deng Xiaoping as a sign of political prematurity and, moreover, disobedience. Deng was further dismayed as Hu emphasized repeatedly in 1986 the importance of promoting the younger cadres to the leading posts. Given that the other senior leaders like Chen Yun, Li Xiannian, and Peng Zhen had hinted broadly that they would follow Deng's example on the issue of retirement – that they would not retire unless Deng set up an example – Hu's genuine effort further raised Deng's suspicion that Hu, who had been recognized as Deng's successor, attempted to be the real boss instead of a front-stage puppet. Deng's suspicion seemed to be proved by Hu's interview with Katharine Graham, president of the *Washington Post*, on September 23, 1986. When Graham doubted whether the succession problem had been solved, given that Deng still remained in his office, Hu replied:

> He [Deng] is a figure who has played the central role.... So the Chinese people hope that he will remain in the leading positions of the Party and state. This is natural and understandable. From this point of view, *it makes certain sense to say that the succession*

problem of our Party and state leaders has not been fully solved yet. . . . I believe that *at the 13th National Congress of our Party next year, there will be a more complete solution to the succession problem of our Party and state leaders.*[130]

Hu's words not only drew international attention, but also "aroused tremendous response" in the Party after being transmitted.[131] People read Hu's words as an indication that Deng would retire at the Thirteenth PC. No wonder that, according to a reliable source who had been close to Hu, these words from Hu would later become key evidence of Hu's gross error. As the hardliners claimed at a series of Politburo meetings after Hu's fall, Hu not only "leaked a top Party secret to the foreign media," but his "extremely irresponsible remarks on such an important issue [of leadership succession] caused unnecessary chaos in the thinking of the broad Party members and cadres." Thus, as Deng became increasingly suspicious of Hu, a *prisoners' dilemma* emerged between the two, given the faction-ridden structure of leadership relations (see Chapter 2). Hu, however, did not expect that Deng would join forces with the hardliners to unseat him from his post, although this would eventually undermine Deng's own position. But as I have explained in Chapter 2, Deng had to make such a compromise with the hardliners and victimize Hu in order to maintain his dominance.

Hu's "resignation" was triggered by the prodemocratic student movement in late 1986.[132] Seeing that the movement was beginning to spread all over the country, Deng summoned most of the central leaders like Hu, Zhao, Peng Zhen, Yang Shangkun, Wang Zhen, Bo Yibo, Wan Li, Hu Qili, and Li Peng to his residence on December 30 to discuss how to put down the student movement.[133] Deng lashed out at Hu, accusing him of protecting the bourgeois liberalists, being soft on the ideological front, and failing to transmit Deng's words against bourgeois liberalization at

---

130 Quoted from Chai, Shi, and Gao, *Hu Yaobang moulue*, pp. 208–9 (emphasis added).
131 Ibid., p. 209.
132 On December 5, 1986, the students at the National University of Science and Technology at Hefei, Anhui Province, rallied to oppose the "officially named representatives" to the NPC. They demanded the right to hold a democratic election for their "true representatives." The demonstration soon spread to other major cities and ignited the first nationwide prodemocratic student movement.
133 Cf. Wu, *Zhao Ziyang yu zhingguo zhengzhi gaige*, pp. 240–1. Notably, Chen Yun, who was at Suzhou, and Li Xiannian, who was in Shanghai, did not attend this informal meeting, at which Hu's fall was virtually decided.

the Sixth Plenum in September. Hu's "resignation" was virtually decided at this *informal* meeting. The decision was formalized at another meeting at Deng's residence, which was attended by the same group of leaders, except for Hu himself, on January 4, 1987. Thus, the CCP general secretary was toppled by a group of senior leaders without the approval of the CC, a gross violation of the CCP constitution.

Hu Yaobang's Fall: Factionalism Prevails over the Party Spirit

Deng could be blamed as politically myopic and strategically inept in handling Hu's case. Yet beneath Deng's seemingly irrational choice was a dilemma Deng was never able to solve because the CCP political system he had to defend prevented him from providing his dominance with ideological legitimacy. On the one hand, Deng was dependent on the FCP not only to legitimize his dominance but also to provide the ideological constraint on factional activities, which had been rampant essentially because the organizational shackles on factionalism had never really been restored after the CR. On the other hand, Deng had to carry out the reform that departed radically from "the socialist road," because Deng needed the economic success to make up for his ideological weakness and, ultimately, to maintain the existence of the regime. In retrospect, it was Deng's inability to solve this innate dilemma in his policy approach – best shown by his stubborn insistence on the FCP while groping for the next stepping-stone in his reform – that resulted in a vicious cycle during the ten-year reform from 1978 to 1987. That is, the more successful his reform was, the more vulnerable Deng appeared on the ideological front because the departure from "the socialist road," for the economic prosperity would inevitably bring about more challenges to the socialist system. The more difficulties Deng endured in politics, however, the more vigorous he would have to be in pushing for reform, so as to make up the ground he had yielded to the hardliners and the diminishing social support due to his repression of the demands for political participation.

Ironically, this vicious cycle was best summed up by Deng Liqun from his conservative point of view. As a diehard opponent of the reform, Deng Liqun took the lead in the criticism of Hu Yaobang at a series of enlarged Politburo meetings, held January 10–15, 1987. According to Ruan Ming, Deng Liqun divided the ten years of reform (1978–87) into

Deng Xiaoping's Dominance

five pairs, and he argued that "bourgeois liberalization" was rampant in every even year, and a struggle against it would follow in every odd year[134] (Table 7.2).

Deng Liqun's timetable virtually reflects the cycle of power struggles between Deng's men and the conservative forces I have discussed in this chapter. That is, whenever Deng's forces held the upper hand and their reform policy became successful, the conservative forces would try to roll back the reform and, not surprisingly, they always initiated their offensive on the ideological front. Hu Yaobang's "resignation" in early 1987 fully exposed this division within the CCP leadership. More significantly, it marked the final prevalence of factionalism over the Party spirit, not necessarily because Hu fell victim to factional strife – numerous leaders had fallen victim to factional struggles – but because those who toppled Hu were never able to justify their action with a "political line." This was essentially why Hu was allowed to keep his seat in the Politburo, although thereafter he would be virtually nonexistent in policy making. In retrospect, although intra-Party struggles had always existed, the CCP leadership had at least been able to maintain a facade of unity with a predominant "political line." This line provided not only the guidance for their decision making, but also the ideological justification for the purges of those who had failed in these intra-Party struggles. The toppling of Hu Yaobang, however, could hardly be justified by any lines because there had never been one since Deng achieved his dominance. Rather, Hu's case revealed that the reform policy was not, and would not be, glorified as the CCP's political line, but it was always a *pragmatic policy*, through which the CCP leaders, including Deng himself, hoped to reenergize the falling "socialist system." This was essentially why the more successful the reform policy was, the more vulnerable the reform leaders appeared, because a successful reform would inevitably provoke challenges to the CCP's political system, the system on which not just the reform leaders stood but on which the entire CCP's rule was based. Thus, the tragedy of Hu, and later Zhao Ziyang, was essentially the same as Gorbachev's. The difference is that Hu was victimized as a scapegoat, but Gorbachev had no scapegoat but himself to be victimized.

Indeed, what Hu's case really revealed was the inability of Deng and his colleagues to work out an overriding political line for the Party. This

---

134 See Ruan, *Deng Xiaoping diguo*, pp. 168–71.

Table 7.2. *Power Struggles between Deng and the Hardliners (1978–87)*

The Achievement of the Reform Forces	The Rollback by the Conservative Forces
1978. Deng broke down the "two whatevers." Ideas of reform began to brew and he experimented with the household responsibility system. Demands for democracy appeared within the Party and were echoed by the Democracy Wall.	*1979.* The conservative leaders blamed Deng for Mao bashing at the March Politburo meeting. Deng had to make the commitment to the FCP. Chen Yun and his men took over the economy.
1980. The reform measures practiced by Deng's men in various localities turned out to be successful, while Chen's retreat remedy failed to yield the desired outcome. Hu Yaobang was named general secretary of the Secretariat and entered the PSC at the Fifth Plenum in February. Zhao took over economic policy in March.	*1981.* The hardliners put up a strong resistance at the CC work conference in December 1980. Deng later joined with them in July and launched the first antibourgeois liberalization campaign.
1982. The reform policies were implemented across China. Deng's dominance, with Hu and Zhao managing the Party and government respectively, was formally established at the Twelfth PC in September.	*1983.* The hardliners initiated a campaign against "spiritual pollution." Deng endorsed the campaign at the Second Plenum in October, saying that "spiritual pollution will not be allowed on the ideological front."
1984. Deng resolutely stopped the hardliners' attempt to extend the campaign against spiritual pollution into the economic field. The Third Plenum of the Twelfth CC adopted "The CC's Resolution on the Reform of the Economic System" in October.	*1985.* The Central Discipline Inspection Commission exposed two "big corruption cases" in Fujian and Guangdong, Xiang Nan and Ren Zhongyi, the reform-minded Party secretaries of the two provinces, were forced out. The anticorruption campaign evolved into a witch-hunt aimed at the reform-minded cadres.
1986. Deng substantiated the idea of political reform: to *separate the Party from government* in policy making. The aim was to confine the hardliners in the political sphere to prevent them from undermining the economic reform which had become the legacy of Deng's leadership.	*1987.* Deng suffered his second major setback since 1979. Hu Yaobang was toppled as a compromise with the hardliners who, seizing the opportunity of the nationwide prodemocracy student movement, had formed a coalition with the military leaders.

Deng Xiaoping's Dominance

not only prevented the CCP leadership from fully repairing the damage to the Party caused by the CR, but also made it unable to contain the factionalism embedded in the CCP political system. Thus, although Deng, like Mao, had exclusive access to the mountaintops in both the Party and military systems, he had never been able to subdue the other factions like Mao did. As a result, instead of engaging in a "life-and-death struggle of line" like Mao, Deng had to make constant compromises with his opponents, which in turn not only undermined his reform policy, but also his own mountaintop. Although Deng managed to keep the top Party office under his control after Hu's "resignation" – Zhao Ziyang was immediately named the acting general secretary of the CCP and was made general secretary at the Thirteenth PC in October – Deng's political vulnerability was further exposed, for Hu's fall not only weakened his forces, especially on the political front, but also alienated Deng further from the social forces that had provided broad support for his reform.

More devastatingly, Hu's fall virtually bankrupted Deng's grand strategy of "grasping things with two hands (separately)," the strategy that had just been substantiated by the policy of "separating the Party from government." With Zhao moved to the top Party office, the hardliners turned this policy against Deng himself. They not only forced Zhao to give up his premiership to Li Peng, a diehard hardliner,[135] but also blocked all the effort of Deng's forces to reform the banking and financial systems thereafter. Thus, when Zhao was forced to "break a bottleneck" (*chuangguan*) – the price system – of the economic reform that had been centered on developing a "socialist market economy," his effort was virtually suicidal without the cooperation of the banking and financial systems.[136] The soaring inflation and the rampant corruption essentially caused by the "two-price systems" – one set by the state, the other by the market – eventually brought about the May 1989 crisis, which was a combination of radical demands by the students and liberal-minded intellectuals, the outbreak of the social disgust against widespread corruption, and the inability of the leadership to provide any effective

---

135 Zhao's reluctance to give up the premiership was obvious. Even at the news conference after the Thirteenth PC, which marked the highest point in Zhao's career, Zhao openly admitted that he was "more suitable to be the premier." See *PD*, November 3, 1987.
136 Cf. Wu, *Zhao Ziyang yu zhingguo zhengzhi gaige*, pp. 524–39.

solutions because of the internal split between Zhao and his conservative opponents. Zhao's luck was no better than Hu Yaobang's: Zhao was also victimized. Although Deng managed to put down the crisis with a violent military intervention, Deng lost another round to the hardliners. The damage to Deng's forces would be so severe that he would not regain the momentum in policy making until 1992.

8

Conclusion

FACTIONALISM AND POLITICAL OUTCOMES IN CHINA

Factionalism, an Essential Dynamic in CCP Politics

The system of single-party dictatorship imposes a double dilemma on the CCP leaders. In order to maintain the image of the Party's unity, which is the prerequisite for its rule, they have to deny any differences among themselves in public, but differences are inevitable in the policy process; and they need support in a policy dispute, but they cannot generate support through an open debate because that would undermine the image of unity. This double dilemma has forced the CCP leaders to engage in factional activities: when a policy dispute emerges, they pass information and seek support through informal channels provided by *guanxi* (personal ties). Moreover, it has also brutalized CCP politics: the weaker ones must be victimized once the dispute breaks open, even though their policy preferences might be correct, because any compromises would expose the division within the leadership and hence undermine the image of unity. Thus, we have observed fierce factional activities whenever a policy dispute emerged among the CCP leaders, and those who had control of the strongest factional networks would prevail. Indeed, the extent of a CCP leader's power is measured essentially by his ability to manipulate factional activities in political affairs. Mao and Deng were, in this sense, the supreme leaders of their times, and Mao was a stronger leader than Deng in this respect.

But it is hard to distinguish among the CCP factions in terms of ideology, for they all exist under the same ideological principles in a system of single-party dictatorship. Ironically, only *after* a faction was defeated would it be recognized due to the ideological denunciation befalling its members in order to justify the purge. Nor can we define and see a CCP faction as a political organization. Although a CCP faction assumes some key functions – the exclusive channels of communications among political associates, the outlets of their particular interests, and the commanding system of their forces (see Introduction and Chapter 2) – of a political organization in political affairs, it lacks the key elements necessary for the existence of a formal organization: well-defined ideology, independent leadership, formal organizational arrangements, and stable financial sources. Indeed, the very nature of the CCP system would not tolerate the existence of any such organizations except the CCP itself. Thus, although factionalism is a well-observed phenomenon in CCP politics, none of the CCP leaders has ever admitted that he has a faction, and they have always vowed to eliminate factionalism, which they see as "a formidable enemy [*dadi*] of the Party's cause." Again, only *after* a purge befalls one or more elite members would his or their faction be identified and denounced.

With shared ideological and organizational identity, factions in CCP politics are formed and operated for only one ultimate purpose: power. Although a faction, or factional coalition, can be trademarked by its preferred policy approach (such as conservatism or reform), whether its policy preference can prevail depends essentially on the strength of its networks, rather than the extent to which its advocated policy can solve the existing problems. More often than not we have witnessed a bad policy prevail in CCP politics simply because its advocates were more powerful. Endless factional struggles for power have not only turned power into an overriding goal – rather than the means to make one's policy choice prevail – in CCP politics but have also made the system sensitive to even a slight change in the distribution of power at the top. Figure 8.1 demonstrates how factionalism has become an essential dynamic in CCP politics.

When an emerging problem broke the established consensus and set off a policy-making process, factional activities would be activated immediately, because this process creates an opportunity for the redistribution of power. Consequently, any changes in the distribution of power at the top, usually caused by the rise and/or fall of elite members, would lead to a top-down *zhengdun* (rectification) in the whole system. The aim is to consolidate the forces of the dominant leaders, and to eliminate those of the fallen ones (see Chapter 2 and Figure 2.1). Centering around *factional activities*, Figure 8.1 is composed of three circles:

Conclusion

```
                    AN EMERGING PROBLEM
                            │
                            ▼
                 BREAKDOWN OF CONSENSUS
                     AND STATUS QUO
                ╱        │        ▲
POWER STRUGGLE  circle 1  │        │
      ▲                   ▼        │           ┌─────────────────────┐
      │         FACTIONAL ACTIVITIES ◄──────── │ Figure 2.1 (Chap. 2)│
      │               ▲                        │ ZHENGDUN, or        │
      │               │                        │ RECTIFICATION       │
REDISTRIBUTION         │         circle 3      ├─────────────────────┤
  OF POWER     circle 2│                       │ Figure 8.2          │
      ▲                │                       │ FACTIONALISM &      │
      └────────SOLUTION/NEW CONSENSUS          │ POLICY OUTCOME      │
               RISE/FALL OF ELITE MEMBERS      └─────────────────────┘
```

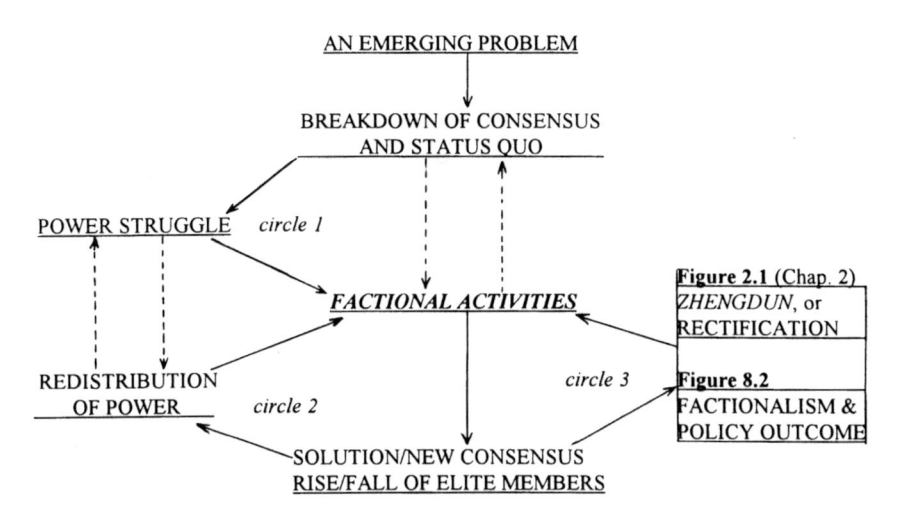

Figure 8.1. Factionalism and power struggle in CCP politics (solid arrow = direction of the causal relation; dashed arrow = correlation)

1 From the breakdown of consensus and status quo, to power struggle, to *factional activities*.
2 From *factional activities* (among the leaders), to solution and new consensus, resulting in the rise and fall of the elite members, to redistribution of power at the top, to *factional activities* (realignments and reorganization in the whole organization).
3 From the rise and fall of the elite members, to *zhengdun* (rectification) campaign (see Figure 2.1) and policy changes (see Figure 8.2), to a new round of *factional activities* that are activated in the political process.

Factionalism and Policy Outcomes

Factional struggles for power impose a primary dilemma on the CCP policy makers: as leaders, they have to comply with the adopted policy, which is based essentially on the dominant leader's vision; yet their rationale in decision making is ultimately drawn from the calculations of the consequence of this policy upon the strength of their factional networks and their positions in the distribution of power. Thus, while a leader has to commit himself to the adopted policy, he will try to distort this policy in its implementation according to his best interests in the area or the system controlled by his mountaintop.

The two-level policy-making process in China has provided leaders with opportunities and convenience to cash in their interests. A policy-making process usually involves decision making at two levels: (1) the buildup of *fangzhen* (the political line or guiding principle like the reform and openness), which embodies the political consensus reached among the top leaders; and (2) the making of *zhengce* (concrete policies that deal with specific problems in a given policy area) under the guidance of the adopted *fangzhen*. Usually, the Politburo determines *fangzhen*, which reflects the vision of the dominant leader(s). But *zhengce* is usually produced by governmental agencies, or even the provincial authorities, to deal with specific policy issues. The making and implementation of *zhengce* constitute routine affairs of the Chinese bureaucracy.

The consensus on *fangzhen*, however, cannot embody everyone's priority; nor can it provide a solution for every concrete problem. Thus, various *zhengce*, or concrete policies, are needed under the guidance of *fangzhen*. The making and implementation of *zhengce* provide factions with opportunities to manipulate the policy process on their turfs according to their particular interests. The faction-ridden structure of the distribution of power, the cellularly structured administrative system, and the dependence on personalized authorities in the operation of the system all provide the factions with great leverage to skew the outcomes of *zhengce* to their own advantage. As a result, although the nature of the single-party dictatorship requires the unconditional implementation of the adopted *fangzhen*, the whole system is swamped by the so-called *tu zhengce* (ad hoc policies made by various government agencies and local authorities), which are inconsistent and even contradictory with one another. Thus, policy making becomes ideologically symbolic and practically meaningless in terms of principle, and collectively irrational and separately inconsistent and even contradictory in terms of issues.

Figure 8.2 demonstrates how factionalism has affected the policy process. In order to justify its manipulation of *zhengce* in the areas or systems controlled by its networks, a faction will try to interpret the adopted *fangzhen* in terms of its interests. Not surprisingly, its leader(s) at the Center will tacitly consent to, or even encourage, such a manipu-

Conclusion

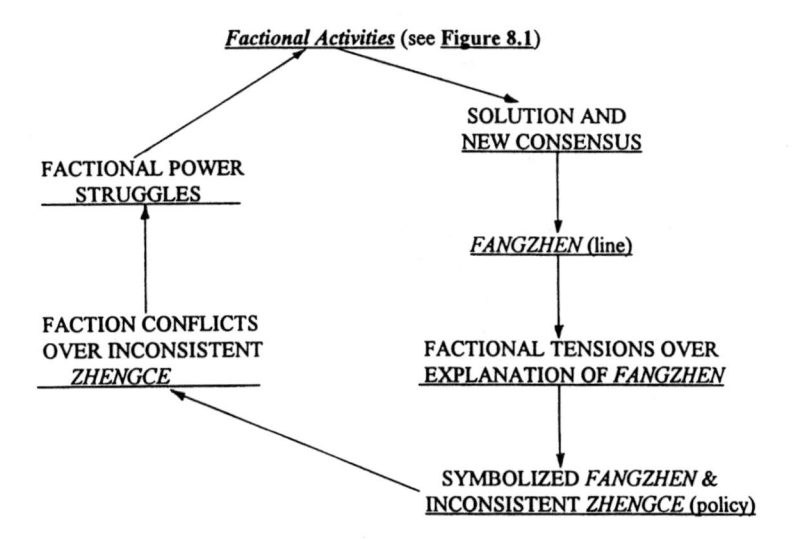

Figure 8.2. Factionalism and policy outcomes in CCP politics (solid arrow = direction of the causal relation)

lation in their struggle for power. It is over these *zhengce* that endless factional conflicts take place. Not only does a faction make and implement *zhengce* according to its interpretation of the adopted *fangzhen*, but its leaders also use the particular *zhengce* to represent their positions at the Center. As a result, the adopted *fangzhen* will be increasingly symbolic and drained of its substance in the endless squabbling among the factions, while inconsistent and even contradictory *zhengce* made by the sublevel authorities flood the policy process.

The abuse of inconsistent *zhengce* under the symbolized *fangzhen* is perhaps best shown by the policy issues on "separating the Party from the government." The aim of this *fangzhen* is to restructure the distribution of power, so as to check intervention by the conservative forces in the policy process (see Chapter 7). Not surprisingly, Deng's idea (of separating the Party from the government) "immediately provoked speculations and chaos in political circles,"[1] even before the policy process was

---

1 Wu Guoguang, *Zhao Ziyang yu zhongguo zhengzhi gaige* (Political Reform under Zhao Ziyang), Hong Kong: Pacific Century Institute, 1997, p. 122.

started. Despite disputes among the elite members on how to convert this *fangzhen* into applicable *zhengce*,[2] a number of *zhengce* were devised and put into practice, especially in the economic sphere where more power was given to managers at the expense of the Party secretaries. However, given fierce factional struggles involved in the process, not only were these policies mostly ad hoc and inconsistent, but their implementations also varied greatly. In some places the administrators assumed more power in the name of "separating the Party from the government"; in the other places the Party secretaries expanded their influence, emphasizing the necessity of strengthening the Party's leadership.[3] What really counted was to whom the power was to be entrusted. In places where the administrators controlled the local factional networks, they were glad to expel the Party. If the factional networks were led by the Party secretaries, then the Party's leadership was of course the most important. As a result, while there were the wants of consistent policies under the adopted *fangzhen*, inconsistent and even contradictory working policies became rampant in the practice of "separating the Party from the government." After 1987, however, "separating the Party from the government" became rhetoric and eventually disappeared from the CCP political vocabulary. This is not surprising because the leadership of Zhao Ziyang, and later Jiang Zemin, was based on his position in the Party after he replaced Hu Yaobang as the CC general secretary in 1987.

True, the symbolic *fangzhen* does play an important role in the maintenance of stability. But such stability is vulnerable, given the increasing tension between the factions caused by the endless frictions over *zhengce*. Sooner or later, an emerging problem serious enough to break the consensus will spark an explosion of factional activities. The solution will lead to a major change in the policy approach in accord with the redistribution of power among the triumphant leaders. A new round of the same games begins.

Thus, it is not surprising that "reform and openness," the *fangzhen* that brought about tremendous changes in China, became increasingly symbolic during the Deng period. It could actually be used by both the reform-minded leaders and the hardliners (quite oddly but logically),

---

2 Ibid., pp. 124–42.
3 Also see Shiping Zheng, *Party versus State in Post-1949 China: The Institutional Dilemma*, Cambridge: Cambridge University Press, 1997, pp. 195–7.

Conclusion

including Chen Yun, Peng Zhen, Bo Yibo, and even Li Peng, to justify their positions in the policy process. Yet the fierce struggles on how to reform and what was to be reformed never ceased. The prodemocracy student movement in May 1989 eventually triggered a disastrous explosion of factional strife, which resulted in severe damage to the reform.

THE IMPACT OF FACTIONALISM ON CHINESE POLITICS

Importance of Ideological Consensus

Factionalism in CCP politics cannot be eliminated because it is innate to the system. The excessive factional struggles for power, however, can lead to an explosion that will undermine not only stability but also the supreme leader's position, given that his dominance is essentially based on his control of various mountaintops. Thus, it is in his best interest to keep factional activities under control.

Inevitably, consistent with the supreme leader's dominance is the necessity of political consensus based on his vision. "All who participate in elite affairs must acknowledge as imperative the maintenance of consensus," not necessarily because "[t]he requirement that everyone must appear to be in agreement with everyone else has the consequence of erecting a wall around Chinese politics,"[4] but because such a consensus provides an *ideological mandate* for leadership relations. Those who violate this mandate must be purged because their behavior endangers the status quo – the stability of leadership relations under the supreme leader's command. In this sense, Gao and Rao's failure in 1954 was rooted in their attempt to distinguish between the "red area" and "white area" leaders, which stirred up the factional strife and therefore jeopardized stability under Mao's command (see Chapter 4). Peng Dehuai's tragedy in 1959 was rooted in the fact that he "implicitly but unmistakably laid the blame [of the Great Leap Forward]...at the door of the Chairman,"[5] violating the code of "shared responsibility" that had been tacitly accepted in the previous CC meetings on the

---

4 Lucian Pye, *The Dynamics of Chinese Politics*, Cambridge, MA: Oelgeschlager, Gunn & Hain, 1981, esp. p. 3.
5 Roderick MacFarquhar, *The Origins of the Cultural Revolution, 2: The Great Leap Forward 1958–1960*, New York: Columbia University Press, 1983, p. 216.

GLF.[6] The fall of Liu Shaoqi and of Lin Biao had different causes, but they did share an essential one: their increasing power constituted an objective threat to Mao's command, the inviolable code in the Mao era. And Deng's second fall in 1976 was caused by his violation of the consensus that "the verdict of the CR must never be reversed" – the commitment Deng himself had vowed to keep in his two letters to Mao in November 1971 and August 1972 (see Chapter 6).

Factional activities in the post-Mao period appear to be less brutal with respect to the fate of the toppled leaders. But such "gentleness" is due to the fact that none of the leaders, including Deng, was powerful enough to knock out his rival(s). Since all the conditions for factionalism continued, but the political consensus was much weaker than in the Mao period, factional activities during this period became more visible and more difficult for the supreme leader to control. Any changes in leadership relations would provoke an explosion of factional activities because of the absence of absolute dominance. Thus, ironically but logically, it is more vital for the leaders to maintain a political consensus when none among them is able to obtain absolute dominance. As an embodiment of the code of agreement among the dominant leaders, the consensus exerted an ideological constraint over factional activities. That is why the maintenance of the adopted consensus, the Four Cardinal Principles (FCP), has been imperative and increasingly coercive, although the elite members' preferences are so different from each other that they have rarely reached a substantial agreement on any particular issue.

The vital importance of consensus in the Deng period was best shown by the CCP leadership's insistence on the FCP, which was obviously inconsistent with the reform policy (see Chapter 7). In fact, the FCP, put forward by Deng in a rush at the end of March 1979, was not based on careful consideration of long-term interests, particularly Deng's own. But at the time when the whatever faction had just been pushed aside, Deng's dominance had barely been established upon a loose factional alliance, the hardliners were alienated by Deng's radical reform, the mountaintops were still to be overhauled, and the "punishment of Vietnam" had not yet achieved the desired result, it could not be more dangerous for

---

6 The CC held a series of meetings from November 1958 to May 1959, discussing how to retreat from the GLF. For details of these conferences, see MacFarquhar, ibid., pp. 119–80.

Conclusion

Deng to allow the luxury of "discussing theoretical principles" when a political consensus was barely existent within the CCP leadership. Not surprisingly, the debate on the truth criterion that Deng had used to tear down the ideological legitimacy of Hua Guofeng's leadership was brought to an abrupt end; the Democracy Wall, which had played a role in mobilizing social support to Deng, was repressed; and Deng took a sudden left turn and changed from the enthusiastic advocate of "emancipating the mind" to the headstrong guard of the FCP.

True, Deng's dominance was based on his exclusive access to the mountaintops in both the party and military systems. But he had to depend on the FCP for the ideological legitimacy of his leadership. Moreover, the FCP has since become an indispensable ideological constraint for Deng, and now Jiang Zemin, to hold factional activities in check. Whenever a clash between the competing factions broke out, Deng would paint himself as the standard-bearer of the FCP, rather than a reformer with an "emancipated mind."

Thus, the supreme leader has to keep a tight grasp on ideology in order to maintain his dominance. Granted, ideology is crucial to any totalistic system. But, in CCP politics, the occupation of the ideological high ground is necessary for the dominant leader to justify his attacks on his opponents and to legitimate his leadership. In CCP politics a fight in the ideological field was always a prelude to the outbreak of a power struggle among the elite members; the winner always claimed ideological correctness; and the losers were always denounced ideologically. The emphasis on the ideological legitimacy has not only further brutalized the political conflicts, but also led to deliberate ignorance of the substantial issues in the policy process, although the conflict might have indeed originated from a genuine policy dispute on these issues.

The importance of ideology in CCP politics has been displayed vividly by two significant phenomena. First, the control of propaganda, including the information flow, is so crucial that in this area we have observed the most frequent and intense conflicts in CCP politics. In fact, this area has been a barometer of the political weather in China: the faction that dominates the propaganda must be in the driver's seat. For example, "emancipating the mind" was put forward by Deng himself during the debate on the truth criterion in 1978 (see Chapter 7). It was soon adopted as an ideological *fangzhen* at the Third Plenum of the Eleventh CC in order to justify the attack upon the whatever faction. But after Deng established his dominance in 1980, Deng's forces used this *fangzhen* to justify their struggles against the conservative factions. Thus, we saw this *fangzhen* being downplayed and even criticized obliquely during the 1983 Anti–Spiritual Pollution Campaign and the 1987 Anti–Bourgeois Liberalization Campaign when the hardliners were on the offensive; but it was reemphasized in 1984–5 and 1987–8 as the reformers got the upper hand. Beneath the surface of whether to adhere to or drop this *fangzhen* were the fierce power struggles in which the propaganda area has been the battlefront. Thus, the hardliners such as Deng Liqun, Hu Qiaomu, and Wang Renzhi were extraordinarily active and riding high in 1983, early 1987, and after the May 1989 crisis when this *fangzhen* was downplayed; but Deng's men, leaders like Hu Yaobang, Hu Qili, and Zhu Houze, controlled the propaganda in the late 1970s and early 1980s, 1984–6, and 1987–8 when this *fangzhen* was emphasized.

The second phenomenon is that the factions are so sensitive to any slight change on the ideological front that even a subtle difference in their *tifa* (the way of description) was usually underlain by a fierce power struggle,[7] especially during the periods of political transition. For example, both Ye Jianying and Deng Xiaoping made speeches at the All-Army Conference on Political Work (April 27 to June 6, 1978). Ye insisted on "maintaining [*baochi*] the glorious tradition" of the PLA; but Deng emphasized "restoring" (*huifu*) the PLA's fine tradition.[8] It is not difficult to see the difference: Ye wanted to keep the status quo, but Deng asked to restore the old order *before* the CR. Six months later at the memorial meeting for Peng Dehuai and Tao Zhu in December 1978, Deng changed his *tifa*, talking about "*maintaining and restoring*" the PLA's fine tradition.[9] This contradictory *tifa* (how can one maintain and restore something simultaneously?) indicated that Deng and Ye had reached a deal so that the Deng-Chen alliance could launch a lethal attack on the whatever faction at the Third Plenum (December 18–22,

---

7 *Tifa* is jargon in the CCP political language. It refers to "the way of description" of a principle, which includes both the selection of words and the arrangement of the selected words in a certain order, so that one can express his intentions precisely, although the characters one selects or the order one arranges – but never both – may appear similar to those used by his opponents. Michael Schoenhals translates *tifa* as "formulation" in his *Doing Things with Words in Chinese Politics*, Berkeley: University of California Press, 1992.
8 See *SWDXP*, 1975–82, pp. 137–8.
9 Deng, "The Memorial Speech to Peng Dehuai," *PD*, December 24, 1978.

Conclusion

1978). In the Deng period, we have observed repeatedly the switch of *tifa* between "promoting" (*tuidong*) and "deepening" (*shenhua*) the reform. When reform needed to be "promoted," Deng was undoubtedly in the driver's seat; but when it had to be "deepened," his rivals must have gotten the upper hand. Zhao Ziyang called on the Party to "construct" (*jianshe*) socialism with Chinese characteristics at the Thirteenth PC in 1987, but the CCP leadership since the May 1989 crisis has been stressing "insisting on [*jianchi*] socialism with Chinese characteristics" – one can "construct" something new, but he has to "insist on" the old rut.

Continuity and Changes in Factionalism in CCP Politics

The continuity of factionalism from the Mao period to the Deng period is obvious. This is shown not only by the similar structure of leadership relations but also by the design of the policy-making process. Thus, although there were enormous differences between Mao and Deng in personality, experience, knowledge, vision, and policy orientation, their behaviors in political affairs were strikingly similar to each other. A strong case emerging from this study is that factionalism in CCP politics is essentially *system-created*, and so is a leader's political behavior.

However, there were substantial changes between the Mao and Deng periods. Mao's command was based not only on his firm control of political factions but also on the ideological legitimacy provided by his own Mao Zedong Thought. Mao could manipulate factional interactions at will because he was virtually free from the ideological constraint that was imposed on his colleagues.

But Deng never quite achieved the ideological legitimacy for his dominance. As a result, his choices were also subject to the ideological constraints applied to his colleagues, and the theoretical justification he worked out for his attack on his opponents could also backfire. Undoubtedly, the insistence on the Four Cardinal Principles (FCP) helped Deng maintain stability as well as his dominance. Yet the FCP also exerted constraints on his reform. The hardliners never hesitated to use the FCP as a taming whip whenever they saw Deng's forces going too far down the road toward "bourgeois liberalization" (see Chapter 7).

Moreover, the lack of ideological legitimacy has prevented Deng from achieving the absolute command Mao had enjoyed. Deng was at best seen as a "big brother" among the elite members. He could maintain his dominance, though just barely, because he was the only leader who had access to the factional networks in both the military and civilian systems. Compared with Mao, Deng's dominance was displayed by his ability to initiate an agenda that could bring about an outcome favorable to him during the crisis periods. In fact, Deng never failed to form a coalition with the other leaders at crucial moments. His shrewdness as a politician and toughness as a fighter were shown by his tactical behavior, or pragmatism, in pursuing his goals. Yet he always depended on allies in political affairs, though he was the strongest in the coalition. The final outcome of an elite conflict during the Mao period was often determined by which side Mao was on; during the Deng period, however, it depended on who sided with Deng.

Different structures of power distribution determine different manifestations of factionalism in leadership relations. Mao's supreme position enabled him to function as an outside arbiter, rather than a participant, of elite conflicts. As the godfather in CCP politics, he could pose as being neutral in power struggles between competing leaders who tried to win his favor. In fact, Mao's command was secured by his ability to manage a balance of power between his competing followers. He virtually kept an equal distance from all the factions in the normal conditions but tended to lean toward the weak ones during crisis periods.[10]

It was in such a situation that Zhou Enlai became an indispensable middleman between Mao and his competing followers. Besides his extraordinary intelligence and energy, modest attitude, adept communications skill, and rich experience, Zhou's most remarkable ability was to attach himself to power. Yet Zhou, an able bureaucrat rather then a revolutionary throughout his career, never developed his own faction and therefore could not pose a real threat to Mao. Thus, Zhou was seen as Mao's most reliable messenger, and his eminence was in a large part based on his close relation with and special access to Mao. Zhou was also

---

10 This phenomenon is the centerpiece of Avery Goldstein's balance-of-power argument (see Avery Goldstein, *From Bandwagon to Balance-of-Power Politics: Structural Constraints and Politics in China, 1949–1978*, Stanford: Stanford University Press, 1991, esp. pp. 36–42, 185–202). His interpretation, however, shortchanges the factionalism analysis as he attributes this phenomenon to the alleged "anarchic structure." He has overlooked its essential causes and its particular manifestations. In fact, the balance-of-power game generally exists in all domestic politics. What differs, and indeed matters, are its causes and the way it is played.

Conclusion

the most acceptable mediator between the competing factions because his senior yet factionless status enabled him to maintain real neutrality in factional conflicts. This may best account for Zhou's "mystery": as a very senior leader, he was in the center of almost every intra-Party conflict in CCP history, but he always maintained a stable number three position in the leadership. Zhou's incredible luck came to an end – and he knew this better than anyone else – when he formed an alliance with a leader who had strong factional networks, namely Deng Xiaoping, in the struggle against the Gang of Four in 1974. Thereafter Mao spurred the Gang of Four to attack Zhou. His death in January 1976 saved his career but victimized Deng's in the Mao period.

In the post-Mao period, however, the dramatic increase of social demands due to rapid development has created a bigger arena in which factions compete for dominance. A double irony has resulted. While the elite members, both hardliners and reformers, have become more strategic in the policy process, the political consensus is increasingly important for holding factional strife in check. While their collective authority has decreased to its lowest ebb due to the absence of an absolute authority, their individual influence has increased, resulting from the dependence on personalized authorities. In this situation, it is unnecessary and dangerous indeed for leaders, who are competing for dominance at an equal level, to have a go-between like Zhou Enlai, because no one will be able to control him. This further impedes communications among the elite members, who are more strategic in the situation where the rules and procedures are uncertain and the actors change their positions constantly in a noninstitutional environment. As a result, the outcomes seem more unpredictable and more explosive; and it is therefore more difficult to recover from the resulting damage.

Yet a more fundamental change has taken place in the orientation of factional alignment in CCP politics. During the Mao period, factional networks were bound by personal loyalties forged during the revolution. Such alignments are virtually *policy-blind* – members of a faction are bound by their mutual loyalty rather than their policy preferences. Essentially, this very nature caused the *incompatibility* between Mao's command, which was based on personal *loyalties*, and the institutionalization of the Party organization, a process in which leadership relations were defined by the *interests* that emerged in the policy process. The inability of the CCP leaders, including Mao, to overcome this incompatibility brought about constant policy inconsistency, and also continuously destabilized leadership relations, which eventually led to the CR, in which Mao destroyed the entire Party establishment in order to maintain his command. As a result, correspondent to the rise of Mao's cult, the loyalty-oriented factionalism went to its extreme – loyalty toward Mao became essential in the shaping of leadership relations and leadership decision making during the CR (see Chapter 6).

Personal loyalties, however, have become less important in the shaping of leadership relations since China moved into the post-Mao period, especially among the younger-generation leaders, partly because few of them have endured any hardships *together* as the senior leaders did – they barely knew each other before being promoted to the Center – but essentially because the inhuman struggles during the CR destroyed the kind of comradeship that existed among the older generations. As a result, although loyalty still played a substantial role in factional alignments, factions tended to be earmarked by certain policies and factional members identified or labeled by their policy preferences. A significant impact of this fundamental change is that policy outcomes are more sensitive to changes in leadership relations. Since policy-oriented factional alignments have substantially related the factional interests with the policy outcomes, even a slight change in the distribution of power among the elite members can result in a radical switch in the policy orientation. This has been best shown by the constant shift of the CCP leadership between the "two principal points" in the 1980s and the early 1990s (see Chapter 7). As a result, power becomes even more important to the well-being of a political faction, and beneath the constant policy disputes are fierce power struggles among the elite members.

Moreover, policy-oriented factional alignments have forced the CCP elite members, especially among the reform-minded leaders, to pay more attention to the *objective outcomes* of the policy process rather than the *ideological justification* for their policy proposals. This change has enabled Deng and his followers, and now an even more pragmatic Jiang Zemin, to push continuously for the reform with the principle of "seeking truth from fact," even though their policy approach was obviously inconsistent with the Party's ideological obligation, namely the FCP. A substantial consequence of China's overall political development is the gradual but irreversible weakening of the socialist practice – the centrally

Conclusion

planned economy – in the economic base and the fading away of communist ideology in the superstructure.

Factionalism and Political Development in China

The conventional wisdom believes that factionalism hinders political development because factional politics tends to be temporary, unstable, and potentially chaotic. This also implies that hegemony by a dominant faction is necessary not just because it is an inevitable outcome of factional politics, but because it is the normal and stable state of affairs we can expect of CCP politics.[11] The findings in this study, however, demonstrate that political stability became vulnerable after a mountaintop had achieved the hegemony in CCP politics and its predominance was then faced by a credible challenge when a policy dispute emerged. In this situation, the dominant leader(s) were reluctant to make any compromises not just because this would undermine his power, but essentially because a compromise would exert a negative impact on the Party's image of unity under his leadership. As a result, a genuine policy dispute usually evolved into a showdown of power in which the weak would be purged, but the problems would remain unsolved. We have witnessed fierce power struggles among the elite members in the early 1950s when Liu Shaoqi's mountaintop seemed to have achieved dominance in the policy process at the Center (see Chapter 4), but the most turbulent political situation emerged during the CR after Mao had achieved the absolute authority in decision making (see Chapter 6). During the post-Mao period, explosive political events took place after Deng's forces had achieved nearly complete dominance in decision making in 1984–5, and again after Deng had nearly fully restored his dominance in 1987–8, after Hu Yaobang's "resignation" in early 1987 (see Chapter 7). The most stable political situation and consistent policy making, however, occurred in 1962–5 when Mao's authority was virtually balanced by the Party bureaucrats' control of the policy process at the first front (see Chapter 5). In Deng's period, it is surprising but significant that political stability was maintained with economic prosperity after the 1989 crisis. When viewed from the perspective of this study, an essential reason for these

---

11 See Tang Tsou, *The Cultural Revolution and Post-Mao Reform: A Historical Perspective*, Chicago: University of Chicago Press, 1986, pp. 105–10.

Factionalism in Chinese Communist Politics

periods of stability and policy consistency is that the absence of absolute dominance forced the CCP leaders, including Mao and Deng, to seek compromises in the policy process instead of engaging in "life-and-death struggles" that could end in brutal purges. In this sense, the slow but steady improvement of the political situation in China since the 1989 crisis – with delicate stability being maintained – is not necessarily because the reform-minded leaders gained the upper hand in political struggles. On the contrary, it is the inability of any single faction to dominate in CCP politics that has compelled the elite members to be more compromising and tolerant in handling political affairs.

What factionalism, an essential source of the intra-Party strife, has constantly undermined is not so much China's overall development as the coherence and unity of the CCP. This has been increasingly obvious in the past two decades, during which the departures of the veteran leaders have caused two profound changes in factional politics. First, factionalism-induced power struggles have become more visible since the mid 1980s. Unlike those among the veteran leaders, factional activities among the younger-generation leaders are motivated not so much by personal loyalty as by *common interests* emerging from the policy process. Although its consequence has yet to be fully appreciated, this change is significant because it has undermined a vital principle of the CCP's rule – *an absolute ideological consensus* – which is indispensable for the maintenance of the Party's unity. As my analysis in Chapter 7 shows, the prevalence of factionalism in CCP politics since the mid 1980s is in large part due to the failure of the CCP leaders to establish a political line consistent with their pragmatic reform policies. As a result, unprincipled power struggles have become routine in political affairs.

Second, factionalism tends to become localized. Unlike the veteran leaders, whose factional connections originated in their mountaintops developed in the revolution, the younger-generation leaders rose to the Center from various localities, where their factional alignments are rooted.[12] The uneven developments across China, which have given rise

---

12 In fact, even the vocabulary in CCP politics can reflect this change (though superficially). The terms referring to one's factional ties, such as Shanghai *bang* (faction), Guangdong *bang*, Shandong *bang*, and the like, have replaced the old ones such as the mountaintop of the First Front Army, the mountaintop of the Fourth Front Army, and the like.

Conclusion

to diverse interests and demands from various localities, have reinforced this tendency of localization of factionalism.[13] The increasing influence of the leaders from some localities such as Shanghai, Sichuan, and Shandong at the Center and frequent changes in personnel arrangements at the provincial level in the past decade reflect not only the Center's effort to check the rising localism[14] but also Jiang Zemin's attempt to maintain a balance in the distribution of power among various factions.

Evidently, factionalism will remain an essential dynamic in CCP politics in the post-Deng period, for all the conditions for the development of factionalism (see Chapter 2) still exist in CCP politics. Factional struggles, however, will no longer be confined to the Party as before, but they will become more compromising in nature and, more importantly, involve participation of social forces outside the CCP. As rapid but extremely *uneven* economic growth across China has greatly diversified the Chinese society, the social classes formed by the workers, the peasants, the soldiers, the cadres, and so on, which were traditionally dominant in China, have been evolving into many small social groups with their specific economic and political interests and demands. As a result, differences among the CCP factions have been dramatically enlarged, given that various socioeconomic interests, in Mao's words, "will eventually find expression in the Party." This makes it more and more difficult for any single faction to retain dominance in policy making because it is impossible for one faction to represent many social groups with different interests simultaneously.

Constant power struggles among the factions and the increasingly diversified agenda they present in policy making have made it virtually impossible to maintain the facade of Party unity. Yet the fear of instability on the one hand and the increasingly balanced distribution of power among factions on the other make it politically more affordable for the CCP leaders to seek compromises rather than to plot a purge, as they used to do in solving differences among them. As a result, the *uncompromising nature* of the single-party dictatorship has gradually

---

13 See Jing Huang, "*Buduan zengda de diqu chaju dui wuoguo zhengzhi wending de weihai*" (Continuous increase in regional differences and its negative impact on political stability in our country), *Gaige* (The Reform), no. 5 (August 1996), pp. 34–9.

14 See Wu Guaguang, "*Gaige guocheng zhong zhongyang yu difang guanxi de bianhua*" (Changes in central-local relations during the reform,), paper for the International Forum on Economic Reform and Political Change: Reflections on Twenty Years of Reform, Hong Kong, December 11–12, 1998.

changed. More significant is that, unable to dominate within the Party, each faction has to seek as much support as possible from the society in order to make the best deal in making compromises. As a result, a greater range of social interests can be expressed and more social forces can participate in the political process. For example, whenever Deng Xiaoping encountered strong resistance in the policy-making process, he would tour East and Southeast China to seek support directly from the society for his policy choice. The last time he made such a tour was in 1992 in his effort to regenerate the momentum of reform. This is not surprising because his reform forces enjoyed strong support in these areas. But contrary to Deng's repeated tours along the coastal areas, the hardliners were reluctant to go to these places, and in fact, few of them have stepped on the soil that was "polluted by the dirty bourgeois influence." Chen Yun, for example, did not go to any special economic zones before his death. Rather, the hardliners have tended to seek support from the hinterland, which lags behind in the development. Moreover, whereas the intellectuals, self-made entrepreneurs, and farmers tend to support the reform-minded leaders, the Party cadres and workers at the state-owned enterprises usually maintained a skeptical and conservative attitude toward the reform policies.

This tendency of the CCP leaders to seek support from different localities and social groups is encouraging indeed, for in their search for support from *outside* of the CCP organization, the CCP factions have began to integrate their interests with those of specific areas or social groups in the political process. Given that communist ideology and practice have been fading away, the findings in this study tend to predict that factionalism in CCP politics may actually play a positive role in the political development of China – a kind of development we have witnessed in Japan, Korea, and Taiwan – in which the process toward political pluralism can be set off not by multiparty competitions but through interactions among various factions within the ruling party.

Selected Bibliography

Ahn, Byung-joon. *Chinese Politics and the Cultural Revolution*, Seattle: University of Washington Press, 1976.
Arrow, Kenneth. *Social Choice and Individual Values*, 2nd ed., New Haven, CT: Yale University Press, 1963.
Bachman, David. *Bureaucracy, Economy, and Leadership in China: The Institutional Origins of the Great Leap Forward*, Cambridge: Cambridge University Press, 1991.
  Chen Yun and the Chinese Political System, China Research Monograph, no. 29, Berkeley: University of California, 1985.
Ban Ying and Zuo Xiaowei. "*Heimao baimao – ping Han Shanbi 'Deng Xiaoping zhuan'*" (Black cat or white cat – a critique to Han Shanbi's *A Biography of Deng Xiaoping*), *Tansuo* (Quest), no. 1 (1992), pp. 51–5; no. 2 (1992), pp. 60–3; and no. 3 (1992), pp. 69–74.
Barnett, Doak A. *Cadres, Bureaucracy and Political Power in Communist China*, New York: Columbia University Press, 1967.
  Uncertain Passage, Washington, DC: Brookings Institution, 1974.
Baum, Richard, ed. *Reform and Reaction in Post-Mao China: The Road to Tiananmen*, New York: Routledge, Chapman and Hall, 1991.
Bo Yibo. *Ruogan zhongda juece yu shijian de huigu* (Review of Several Important Decisions and Events), 2 vols., Beijing: CCP Party School Press, 1991, 1995.
Brandt, Conrad, Benjamin Schwartz, and John K. Fairbank, eds. *A Documentary History of Chinese Communism*, New York: Atheneum, 1967.
Bridgham, Philip. "Mao's Cultural Revolution, 1: Origin and development," *CQ*, 29 (January 1967), pp. 1–35.
  "Mao's Cultural Revolution, 2: The struggle to seize power," *CQ*, 34 (April 1968), pp. 6–37.
  "Mao's Cultural Revolution, 3: The struggle to consolidate power," *CQ*, 41 (January 1970), pp. 1–25.
Brzezinski, Zbigniew K., and Carl J. Friedrich. *Totalitarian Dictatorship and Autocracy*, New York: Praeger, 1961.
Chai Hongxia, Shi Bibo, and Gao Qing. *Hu Yaobang moulue* (Hu Yaobang's Resources and Astuteness), Beijing: Red Flag Press, 1997.

Selected Bibliography

Chang, Parris H. *Power and Policy in China*, 2nd ed., University Park: Pennsylvania State University Press, 1978.

Chen Hua. *Zhou Enlai he ta de mishu men* (Zhou Enlai and His Secretaries), Beijing: China Media and Television Press, 1992.

Chen Wei. "*Jiben wancheng shehui zhuyi gaizao de qinian*" (Seven years of basical completion of socialist transformation), *Zhuanji*, 1:97–116.

Chen Yeping and Han Jingcao. *An Ziwen zhuanlue* (A Brief Biography of An Ziwen), Taiyuan: Shanxi People's Press, 1985.

Chen Yun. "*Bixu zhongshi hushi jingshen wenming jianshe de xianxiang*" (We must pay attention to the phenomenon of overlooking the building of spiritual civilization), *Xuandu*, 2:983–6.

Chen Yun wenxuan 1956–1985 (Selected Works of Chen Yun, 1956–1985), Beijing: People's Press, 1986.

"*Liangge wenming yao yiqi zhua*" (The two civilizations must be developed simultaneously), *Xuandu*, 2:897–8.

Selected Works of Chen Yun, Beijing: Foreign Languages Press, 1984.

Chen, Zaidao. "*Wuhan '7-20 shijian' shimo*" (The beginning and the end of the July 20 Incident in Wuhan), *Zhongguo laonian* (Chinese Seniors), 1 (1983) to 1 (1984).

Cheng Tiejun. "The Household Registration (Hukou) System in China," Ph.D. dissertation, Binghamton: State University of New York, 1992.

Clapham, Christopher S., ed. *Private Patronage and Public Power: Political Clientalism in the Modern State*, New York: St. Martin's Press, 1982.

The Collection of Laws and Orders of the People's Central Government, Beijing: Law Press, 1958.

Dai, Huang. *Hu Yaobang yu pingfan yuan jia cuo an* (Hu Yaobang and the Rehabilitation of the Wrong, False, and Mistaken Verdicts), Beijing: New China Press, 1998.

Dangde shiyijie sanzhong quanhui yilai dashi ji (Major Events since the Third Plenum of the Eleventh CC), compiled by the Research Office of the CC Secretariat, Beijing: Hongqi Press, 1987.

Dangshi huiyi baogao ji (Collection of Speeches at the Party History Conference), compiled by the Secretariat of the National Working Conference on Collecting Materials of CCP History, Beijing: Central Party School Press, 1982.

Daniels, Robert. "Soviet politics since Khrushchev," in John W. Strong, ed., *The Soviet Union under Brezhnev and Kosyqin*, New York: Van Nostrand-Reinhold, 1971.

Deng Liqun. "*Xuexi 'guanyu jianguo yilai dang de ruogan lishi wenti de jueyi' de wenti he huida*" (Questions and answers for the study of *The Resolution on Several Questions of Our Party's History since the Establishment of the PRC*), *Zhuanji*, vol. 2.

Deng, Maomao. *My Father Deng Xiaoping*, New York: Basic Books, 1995.

Deng Xiaoping. "Report on the Revision of the CCP Constitution at the 8th PC,"

Selected Bibliography

Documents of the 8th National Congress of the CCP, Beijing: People's Press, 1957, pp. 73–110.

Selected Works of Deng Xiaoping, 1975–1982, Beijing: Foreign Languages Press, 1984.

Deng Xiaoping tongzhi lun gaige kaifang (Comrade Deng Xiaoping on the Reform and Openness), Beijing: People's Press, 1991.

"*Deng Zihui zhuan*" (A Biography of Deng Zihui), *RWZ* (1982), 7:366–84.

Ding Shu. *Ren huo, "da yuejin" yu da jihuang* (Human Calamity, the "Great Leap Forward," and the Great Famine), Hong Kong: Nineties Monthly, 1991.

Dittmer, Lowell. *China's Continuous Revolution*, Berkeley: University of California Press, 1987.

——. *Liu Shao-ch'i and the Chinese Cultural Revolution: The Politics of Mass Criticism*, Berkeley: University of California Press, 1974.

The Documents of the Eighth National Congress of the CCP, compiled by the CC General Office, Beijing: People's Press, 1957.

Domes, Jurgen. "The Gang of Four and Hua Kuo Kuao-feng: Analysis of political events in 1975–76," *CQ*, 71 (September 1977), pp. 473–97.

——. *The Government and Politics of the PRC: A Time of Transition*, Boulder, CO: Westview Press, 1985.

Dong Chunbao. *Zai lishi de xuanwo zhong – yu Mao Zedong you guan de wangshi* (In the Whirlpool of History – the Happenings That Related to Mao Zedong), Beijing: *Zhongwai wenhua chuban gongci* (Publishing Company of China-Foreign Culture), 1990.

Falkenheim, Victor, ed. *Citizens and Groups in Contemporary China*, Michigan Monographs in Chinese Studies, no. 56, Ann Arbor: University of Michigan, Center for Chinese Studies, 1987.

Fan Shuo and Gao Yi. "*Gandan xiangzhao, gongjie guonan – Ye Jianying he Deng Xiaoping zai dang he guojia de weinan shike*" (Cooperation with utmost devotion in the solution of the national crises – Ye Jianying and Deng Xiaoping in the periods of crises for the party and the nation), *Dang de wenxian* (The Party's Historical Documents), 1995, 1:78–88.

Fang, Weizhong, ed. *Zhonghua renmin gongheguo jingji dashi ji, 1949–1980* (The Economic Chronology of the PRC, 1949–1980), Beijing: Chinese Social Science Academy Press, 1984.

Farquharson, Robin. *Theory of Voting*, New Haven, CT: Yale University Press, 1969.

Goldstein, Avery. *From Bandwagon to Balance-of-Power Politics: Structural Constraints and Politics in China, 1949–1978*, Stanford: Stanford University Press, 1991.

Goodman, David, ed. *Groups and Politics in the People's Republic of China*, New York: M. E. Sharpe, 1984.

"*Guanyu fanmaojin de wenxian sipian*" (Four documents about antiadventurism), *Dang de wenxian* (The Party's Historical Documents), 1990, 2:4–7.

Guanyu jianguo yilai dang de ruoganlishi wenti de jueyi (The Resolution on

Selected Bibliography

Several Questions of Our Party's History since the Establishment of the PRC), Beijng: CCP Central Committee, 1981.

Han, Xianchu. "*Siping baoweizhan*" (The battle of defending Siping), *Dangshi yanjiu ziliao* (Research Materials of CCP History), 1986, 1:1–5, 2:1–6.

Hao Mengbi and Duan Haoran. *Zhongguo gongchandang liushi nian* (The Sixty Years of the CCP), Beijing: PLA Press, 1984.

Harding, Harry. *China's Second Revolution*, Washington, DC: Brookings Institution, 1987.

Organizing China, Stanford: Stanford University Press, 1981.

He Long zhuan (A Biography of He Long), compiled by the *He Long zhuan* Writing Group at PLA Headquarters, Beijing: Contemporary China Press, 1993.

Hough, Jerry. *Soviet Union and Social Science Theory*, Cambridge, MA: Harvard University Press, 1977.

Hough, Jerry, and Merle Fainsod. *How the Soviet Union Is Governed*, Cambridge, MA: Harvard University Press, 1979.

Hu Qiaomu. *Hu Qiaomu huiyi Mao Zedong* (Hu Qiaomu's Memory of Mao Zedong), Beijing: People's Press, 1994.

Hu Yaobang. "*Zhongyang jiguan yaozuo quanguo de biaoshuai*" (The CC apparatus must make an example for the whole country), *Xuandu*, 2: 990–7.

Hua Shijun and Hu Yumin. *Yanan zhengfeng shimo* (The Whole Story of Yan'an Rectification), Shanghai: Shanghai People's Press, 1985.

Huang Yao. "*Luo Ruiqing zhuanlue*" (A brief biography of Luo Ruiqing), part 2 of *Zhongong dangshi ziliao* (Source Materials of the CCP History), 37 (1991), pp. 155–204.

Sanci danan busi de Luo Ruiqing da jiang (Senior General Luo Ruiqing's Three Escapes from Death), Beijing: CCP History Press, 1994.

Huang Yao, Li Zhijing, and Yang Guoqing. *Luo shuai de zuihou shiwu nian* (The Last Fifteen Years of Marshal Luo Ronghuan), Beijing: People's Press, 1987.

Huang Yao and Zhang Mingzhe, eds. *Luo Ruiqing zhuan* (A Biography of Luo Ruiqing), Beijing: Contemporary China Press, 1996.

Huang Zeng. "*Liu Shaoqi yu liushi niandai chu de guomin jingji tiaozheng*" (Liu Shaoqi and the readjustment of the national economy in the early 1960s), *Yanjiu 1*, 1986, 1:1–7.

Huiyi Wang Jiaxiang (Memory of Wang Jiaxiang), compiled by the Editing Group of *Selected Works of Wang Jiaxiang*, Beijing: People's Press, 1985.

Ji Xichen. "*Eryue niliu shimo ji*" (The beginning and the end of the February Adverse Current), *Shidai de baogao* (Reports of an Era), Beijing, 1 (January 1980).

Jiang Bo and Li Qing, eds. *Lin Biao, 1959 nian yihou* (Lin Biao after 1959), Chengdu: Sichuan People's Press, 1993.

Jiang Mingwu, ed. *Zhou Enlai de licheng* (Zhou Enlai's Career), Beijing: PLA Art Press, 1996.

Selected Bibliography

Jin Chongji, ed. *Zhou Enlai zhuan* (A Biography of Zhou Enlai), Beijing: People's Press, 1988.

ed. *Mao Zedong zhuan, 1983–1949* (A Biography of Mao Zedong, 1983–1949), Beijing: Central Document Press, 1996.

Jin Chunming. "*Wenhua da geming*" *shigao* (A Draft of History of the "Cultural Revolution"), Chengdu: Sichuan People's Press, 1995.

Jin, Daying. "*9.13 shijian shimuo ji*" (The whole story of the September 13 Incident), *Shidai de baogao* (Reports of an Era), Beijing, 4 (December 1980), pp. 1–47.

Joffe, Ellis. *Chinese Military after Mao*, Cambridge, MA: Harvard University Press, 1987.

Party and Army: Professionalism and Political Control in the Chinese Officer Corps, Cambridge, MA: Harvard University, East Asian Research Center, 1965.

Ke Yan, ed. *Mao Zedong de lichenn – yige weiren he ta de huihuang shidai* (Mao Zedong's Career – a Great Man and His Splendid Era), 2 vols., Beijing: PLA Art Press, 1996.

Lampton, David, ed. *Policy Implementation in the People's Republic of China*, Berkeley: University of California Press, 1987.

Lewis, John W. *Leadership in Communist China*, Ithaca: Cornell University Press, 1963.

"*Li Fuchun zhuan*" (A Biography of Li Fuchun), *RWZ* (1990), 44:1–112.

Li Lie. *He Long nian pu* (Chronology of He Long), Beijing: People's Press, 1996.

Li Rui. "*Chongdu Zhang Wentian tongzhi de 'Lushan fayan'*" (Reread Comrade Zhang Wentian's "Lushan Speech"), in *Huiyi Zhang Wentian* (Memory of Zhang Wentian), Changsha: Hunan People's Press, 1985, pp. 13–47.

Li Ruqing. *Bixue huangsha* (Red Blood and Yellow Sand), *Kunlun*, no. 2, Beijing: PLA Literature Press, 1988.

Wannan shibian (The Wannan Incident), Shanghai: Shanghai Literature and Art Press, 1987.

Li Weihan. *Huiyi yu yanjiu* (Memory and Study), 2 vols., Beijing: CCP Historical Materials Press, 1986.

Li Yongchun, Shi Yuanqin, and Guo Xiuzhi eds. *Shiyijie sanzhong quanhui yilai zhengzhi tizhi gaige dashi ji* (Major Events in the Reform of Political Institutions since the Third Plenum of the Eleventh CC), Beijing: Chunqiu Press, 1987.

Liao, Gailong, ed. *1949–1989: Xin zhongguo biannian shi* (1949–1989: A Chronology of the New China), Beijing: People's Press, July 1989.

Liao Kuang-sheng. "Linkage politics in China: Internal mobilization and articulated external hostility in the Cultural Revolution," *World Politics*, 28, no. 4 (July 1976), pp. 590–610.

Lieberthal, Kenneth. *A Research Guide to Central Party and Government Meetings in China, 1949–75*, Armonk, NY: M. E. Sharp, 1976.

Selected Bibliography

Lieberthal, Kenneth, and Michael Oksenberg. *Policy Making in China: Leaders, Structure, and Processes*, Princeton: Princeton University Press, 1988.

Lin Biao. "Address to Politburo" (May 18, 1966), *CLG*, 2, no. 4 (Winter 1969–70), pp. 42–62.

Lin Boqu zhuan (Biography of Lin Boqu), Beijing: Red Flag Press, 1987.

Lindbeck, John M. H. *China: Management of a Revolutionary Society*, Seattle: University of Washington Press, 1971.

Liu Jintian, ed. *Deng Xiaoping de licheng – yige weiren he ta de yige shiji* (Deng Xiaoping's Career – a Great Man and His Century), Beijing: PLA Art Press, 1994.

Liu Shaoqi. "On inner-party struggle," *SWLSQ*, 1:180–216.

Selected Works of Liu Shaoqi, Beijing: Foreign Languages Press, 1984.

Liu Shaoqi lun Dang de jian she (Liu Shaoqi on the Construction of the Party), compiled by the Department for Research on Party Literature, Beijing: CCP Central Document Press, 1991.

Liu Shaoqi zai wandong (Liu Shaoqi in East Anhui), Beijing: CCP History Press, 1990.

"*Liu Shaoqi zhuan*" (A Biography of Liu Shaoqi), *RWZ* (1991), 49:1–130.

Liu Zhijian. "*Budui wenyi gongzhuo zhuotanhuai jiyao chansheng qianhou*" (Around the making of *The Summary of the Forum on the Work in Literature and Art in the Armed Forces*), *Zhonggong dangshi ziliao* (Source Materials of the CCP History), 30 (1989), pp. 1–44.

Liuda yilai – dangnei mimi wenjian (Since the sixth PC – the Party's Secret Documents), Beijing: People's Press, 1980.

Luo Diandian. *Feifan de niandai* (Extraordinary Years), Shanghai: Shanghai Wenhui Press, 1987.

"*Luo Ronghuan zhuan*" (A Biography of Luo Ronghuan), *RWZ* (1987), 32:1–119.

Ma Licheng and Lin Zhijun. *Jiao feng: dangdai zhongguo san ci sixiang jiefang shilu* (Crossing Swords: True Record of the Three Emancipations of Mind in Contemporary China), Beijing: Contemporary China Press, 1998.

Ma Lu, Pei Pu, and Ma Qinquan. *Peng Dehuai lushan qi huo* (The Fall of Peng Dehuai at Lushan), Hong Kong: Yalin Press, 1990.

MacFarquhar, Roderick, ed. *China under Mao*, Cambridge, MA: MIT Press, 1966.

The Origins of the Cultural Revolution, 1: *Contradictions among the People, 1956–1957*, New York: Columbia University Press, 1974.

The Origins of the Cultural Revolution, 2: *The Great Leap Forward, 1958–1960*, New York: Columbia University Press, 1983.

The Origins of the Cultural Revolution, 3: *The Coming of the Cataclysm*, New York: Columbia University Press, 1997.

ed. *The Politics of China: 1949–1989*, New York: Cambridge University Press, 1993.

MacFarquhar, Roderick, and John K. Fairbank, ed. *Cambridge History of China*, vol. 15, Cambridge: Cambridge University Press, 1991.

Selected Bibliography

Mao Zedong. *Jianguo yilai Mao Zedong wengao* (The Manuscripts of Mao Zedong since 1949), 13 vols., Beijing: CCP Central Archives Press, 1987–98.

Mao Zedong sixiang wansui (Long Live Mao Zedong Thought), 3 vols., n.p., 1967, 1969.

Mao Zedong xinwen gongzuo wenxuan (Selected Works of Mao Zedong on Journalism), Beijing: Xinhua Press, 1983.

Selected Works of Mao Zedong, Beijing: Foreign Languages Press, 1981.

"*Mao Zedong zhuan*" (A Biography of Mao Zedong), *RWZ*, 1991, 50:1–196.

"Mao Zedong's private letter to Jiang Qing (July 8, 1966)," *CLG*, 6, no. 2 (Summer 1973), pp. 96–100.

Mei Jian, ed. *Yan'an mishi* (The Untold Stories of Yan'an), 2 vols., Beijing: Red Flag Press, 1996.

Meisner, Maurice. *Mao's China and After: A History of the People's Republic*, New York: Free Press, 1986.

Moody, Peter R., Jr. *Chinese Politics after Mao: Development and Liberalization, 1976 to 1983*, New York: Praeger, 1983.

Nathan, Andrew. *China's Crises, Dilemmas of Reform and Prospects for Democracy*, New York: Columbia University Press, 1990.

"A factionalism model for CCP politics," *CQ*, 53 (January 1973), pp. 34–66.

Nie Rongzhen. "*Guanyu Lin Biao de jige wenti*" (Several questions about Lin Biao), *Xinhua yuebao* (New China Monthly), 18–19 (October 1984).

Nie Rongzhen huiyi lu (Nie Rongzhen's Memoirs), Beijing: PLA Press, 1984.

Oi, Jean C. *State and Peasant in Contemporary China*, Berkeley: University of California Press, 1989.

Oksenberg, Michael. "Policy making under Mao," in John M. H. Lindbeck, ed., *China: Management of a Revolutionary Society*, Seattle: University of Washington Press, 1971, pp. 75–115.

"Politics takes command: An essay on the study of post-1949 China," in Roderick Macfarquhar and John. K. Fairbank, eds., *Cambridge History of China*, vol. 14, Cambridge: Cambridge University Press, 1987.

Ordeshook, Peter C. *Game Theory and Political Theory: An Introduction*, Cambridge: Cambridge University Press, 1986.

Parrish, William L. "Factions in Chinese military politics," *CQ*, 56 (October 1973), pp. 667–99.

Peng Dehuai. *Peng Dehuai zishu* (Autobiography of Peng Dehaui), Beijing: People's Press, 1981.

Pillsbury Barbara. "Factionalism observed: Behind the face of harmony in a Chinese community," *CQ*, 74 (January 1978).

Pye, Lucian. *The Dynamics of Chinese Politics*, Cambridge, MA: Oelgeschlager, Gunn & Hain, 1981.

Quan Yanchi. *Long kun – He Long yu Xue Ming* (The Siege of a Dragon – He Long and Xue Ming), Guangzhou: Guangdong Tourist Press, 1997.

Selected Bibliography

Ran Ming. *Deng Xiaoping diguo* (The Deng Xiaoping Empire), Taipei: Shipao Press, 1992.
Reynolds, Bruce, ed. *Chinese Economic Policy*, New York: Paragon House, 1989.
Rice, Edward E. "The second rise and fall of Teng Hsiao-p'ing," *CQ*, 67 (September 1976).
Rostow, Walt W. *The Prospects of Communist China*, New York: John Wiley and Sons, 1954.
Saich, Tony, and Hams van de Ven, eds. *New Perspective of Chinese Communist Revolution*, New York: M. E. Sharp, 1995.
Schmidt, Steffan W., Laura Guasti, Carl H. Lande, and James C. Scott, eds. *Friends, Fellows, and Factions: A Reader in Political Clientalism*, Berkeley: University of California Press, 1977.
Schoenhals, Michael. *Doing Things with Words in Chinese Politics*, Berkeley: University of California Press, 1992.
Schram, Stuart. "China after the 13th congress," *CQ*, 114 (June 1988), pp. 177-97.
"'Economics in command?' Ideology and policy since the Third Plenum, 1978-1984," *CQ*, 99 (September 1984), pp. 417-61.
Mao's Road to Power, vols. 1–, New York: M. E. Sharp, 1992–.
Mao Tse-tung: A Political Biography, New York: Simon and Schuster, 1966.
Schwartz, Benjamin. *Chinese Communism and the Rise of Mao*, Cambridge, MA: Harvard University Press, 1961.
Schwartz, Thomas. *The Logic of Collective Choice*, New York: Columbia University Press, 1986.
Sha, Qing. "*Yixi dadiwan*" (The vague horizon), *Shiyue* (October), 5 (1988), pp. 24-87.
Shanxi geming huiyi lu (Reminiscence of Revolution in Shanxi), compiled by the Shanxi Social Science Academy, Taiyuan: Shanxi People's Press, 1983.
Shepsle, Kenneth A., and Barry Weingast. "Structure-induced equilibrium and legislative choice," *Public Choice*, 37 (1981), pp. 503-19.
"Uncovered sets and sophisticated voting outcomes with implications for agenda institutions," *AJPS*, 28 (1984), pp. 49-74.
Shi Wei. *Maojin, fanmaojin, fan fanmaojin* (Adventurism, Antiadventurism, and Opposing Antiadventurism), *Dang de wenxian* (The Party's Historical Documents), 1990, 2:7-10.
Shirk, Susan. *The Political Logic of Economic Reform*, Berkeley: University of California Press, 1993.
Snow, Edgar. *The Long Revolution*, New York: Random House, 1972.
Solinger, Dorothy. *Chinese Business under Socialism*, Berkeley: University of California Press, 1984.
Solomon, Richard. *Mao's Revolution and Chinese Political Culture*, Berkeley: University of California Press, 1971.
A Special Collection of Materials on Liu Shaoqi, compiled by the Institute for the Study of Chinese Communist Problems, Taipei, 1970.
"Summary of the Forum on the Work in Literature and Art in the Armed Forces

Selected Bibliography

with which Comrade Lin Biao entrusted Comrade Jiang Qing," *Peking Review*, 10, no. 23 (June 2, 1967), pp. 10–16.

"*Tan Zhenlin zhuan*" (A Biography of Tan Zhenlin), *RWZ* (1987), 31:25–104.

Tang Peiji. "*Jianguo yiqian ershiba nian lishi de huigu*" (Review of Twenty-eight years of history before the establishment of the PRC), *Zhuanji*, 1:51–96.

"*Tao Zhu zhuan*" (A Biography of Tao Zhu), *RWZ*, 43.

Teiwes, Frederick C. *Leadership, Legitimacy, and Conflict in China*, New York: M. E. Sharpe, 1984.

Politics and Purges in China, Rectification and the Decline of Party Norms, 1950–1965, New York: M. E. Sharpe, 1979.

Politics at Mao's Court: Gao Gang and Party Factionalism in the Early 1950s, New York: M. E. Sharpe, 1990.

Tsou, Tang. *The Cultural Revolution and Post-Mao Reform: A Historical Perspective*, Chicago: University of Chicago Press, 1986.

Vogel, Ezra. *Canton under Communism*, Cambridge, MA: Harvard University Press, 1969.

Walder, Andrew. *Communist Neo-Traditionalism: Work and Authority in Chinese Industry*, Berkeley: University of California Press, 1986.

Waltz, Kenneth. *Theory of International Politics*, Reading, MA: Addison-Wesley, 1979.

Wan Li. "*Lun juece de kexuehua yu zhidu hua*" (On the scientification and institutionalization of policy making), *PD*, 1987.

Wang Jianying. *Zhongguo gongchandang zuzhi shiliao huibian* (Collection of Materials of CCP's Organizational History), Beijing: Red Flag Press, 1983.

Wang Ming yanlun xuanji (Selected Speeches and Articles of Wang Ming), *Neibu* ed., Beijing: People's Press, 1982.

Wang Mingwu, ed. *Zhou Enlai de licheng* (Zhou Enlai's Career), 2 vols., Beijing: PLA Art Press, 1996.

Wang Nianyi. *1949–1989 nian de zhongguo: da dongluan de niandai* (China in 1949–1989: The Years of Great Turmoil), Henan: Henan People's Press, 1988.

Wang Ruoshui. "*Cong pi 'zuo' daoxiang fanyou de yici geren jingli*" (My individual experience in the reversal from criticizing "leftism" to opposing rightism), *China Daily News (Huaqiao Ribao)*, New York, March 12–21, 1989.

"*Mao Zedong yu wenhua da geming*" (Mao Zedong and the Great Cultural Revolution), *Tan-so* (Quest), no. 111 (March 1993), pp. 10–14; no. 112 (April 1993), pp. 60–66.

Wei Wei and Zhou Junlun, eds. *Nie Rongzhen zhuan* (A Biography of Nie Rongzhen), Beijing: Contemporary China Press, 1994.

White, Lynn. *Policies of Chaos: The Organizational Causes of Violence in China's Cultural Revolution*, Princeton: Princeton University Press, 1989.

Whitson, William. *The Chinese High Command*, New York: Praeger, 1978.

Witke, Roxan. *Comrade Chiang Ch'ing*, Boston: Little, Brown, 1977.

Wu Guoguang. *Zhao Ziyang yu zhongguo zhengzhi gaige* (Political Reform under Zhao Ziyang), Hong Kong: Pacific Century Institute, 1997.

Selected Bibliography

Wu Lengxi. *Yi Mao zhuxi* (Memorizing Chairman Mao), Beijing: Xinhua Press, 1995.

Xiang Qing. *Gongchan guoji he zhongguo geming guanxi lunwenji* (Collection of Papers on the Relationship between the Comintern and China's Revolution), Shanghai: Shanghai People's Press, 1985.

Xiao Chaoran and Sha Jiansun, eds. *Zhongguo geming shigao* (History of the Chinese Revolution), Beijing: Beijing University Press, 1984.

Xiao Jinguang. *Xiao Jinguang huiyi lu* (Xiao Jinguang's Memoir), Beijing: PLA Press, 1987.

Xiao Yang. "*Yi Lushan huiyi qianhou de Zhang Wentian tongzhi*" (Memory of Comrade Zhang Wentian at the Lushan Conference), in *Huiyi Zhang Wentian* (Memory of Zhang Wentian), Changsha: Hunan People's Press, 1985, pp. 87–96.

Xin zhongguo jishi 1949–1984 (Major events of New China, 1949–1984), compiled by the Association of Party History of Jilin Province, Changchun: Northeastern Teacher's University Press, 1986.

Xiong Xianghui. "*Dakai zhongmei guanxi de qiancou*" (The prelude to the opening of the Sino-American relations), *Zhonggong dangshi ziliao* (Source Materials of the CCP History), 42 (1992), pp. 56–96.

Xu Xiangqian. *Lishi de huigu* (History in Retrospect), Beijing: PLA Press, 1987.

Xue Muqiao. *Zhongguo shehui zhuyi jingji wenti yanjiu* (The Study of the Problem in China's Socialist Economy), Beijing: Social Science Academy Press, 1981.

Xue Qingqing and Wang Diming. "*Mao Zedong lingdao le bada wenjian de qicao gongzuo*" (Mao Zedong led the work drafting the documents of the Eighth PC), *Yanjiu 2*, 1990, 2:64–6.

Yan Huai. "Understanding the political system of contemporary China," *Papers from the Center for Modern China*, 10 (August 1991).

Yan Jiaqi. "*Wenhua da geming shinian shi 1966–1976*" (The Ten-Year History of the "Great Cultural Revolution," 1966–1976), Tianjin: Tianjin People's Press, 1986.

Yang Benjamin. *From Revolution to Politics: Chinese Communists on the Long March*, Boulder, CO: Westview Press, 1990.

Yang Shangkun. "*Huainian Shaoqi tongzhi*" (Memorize Comrade Shaoqi), in *Mianhui Liu Shaoqi* (Cherish the Memory of Liu Shaoqi), Beijing: CC Document Press, 1988, pp. 2–14.

Yang Zhongmei. *Hu Yaobang: A Chinese Biography*, trans. William A. Wycoff, New York: An East Gate Book, 1988.

Yao Wenyuan. *On the Social Base of Lin Biao Anti-Party Clique*, Beijing: Foreign Language Press, 1975.

Yu Jundao. *Zhongguo geming zhong de gongchan guoji renwu* (People from the Comintern in China's Revolution), Chenqdu: Sichuan People's Press, 1986.

Yu Nan. "*Lin Biao jituan xingwang chutan*" (A preliminary research of the rise

Selected Bibliography

and fall of the Lin Biao clique), in Tan Zhongji and Zheng Shui, eds., *Shinian hou de pingshuo – Wenhua dageming shilunji* (Appraisal and Critique after Ten Years – Collection of Historical Essays on the CR), Beijing: CCP Historical Materials Press, 1987.

Yue Zong and Xin Zhi, eds. *Deng Xiaoping shengping yu lilun yanjiu huibian* (Collection of Studies on Deng Xiaoping's Career and Theory), Beijing: CCP Historical Materials Press, 1988.

"*Zai Mao zhuxi weida qizhi xia zhandou de guanghui yisheng*" (A brilliant life of battle under Chairman Mao's great banner), compiled by the General Political Department Theory Group, *Lishi yanjiu* (Historical Research), no. 9 (1978).

Zhang Guoqi and Li Guoxiang. *Zhongguo renmin jiefangjun fazhan yange, 1927–1949* (The Organizational Development of the PLA, 1927–1949), Beijing: PLA Press, 1984.

Zhang Guotao. *Wode huiyi* (My Memoirs), 3 vols., Hong Kong: Mingpao Monthly Press, 1973.

Zhang Qiuyun and Zheng Shulan. *Yipian fanmaojin shelun de youlai* (The Origin of an Editorial of Antiadventurism), *Dangde wenxian* (The Party's Historical Documents), 1990.

Zhang Shujun and Gao Xinmin, eds. *Zhonggong shiyi jie sanzhong quanhui lishi dangan* (Historical Archives of the CCP Third Plenum of the Eleventh CC), 2 vols., Beijing: China Economy Press, 1998.

Zhang Xingxing. *Zhonggong bada luxian weineng jianchi xiaqu de yuanyin* (The reasons why [the party] failed to adhere to the correct line of the Eighth PC), *Yanjiu 2*, 1988, 5:33–6.

Zhang Zhenglong. *Xuebai xuehong* (Red Blood on White Snow), Beijing: PLA Press, 1991.

Zhao Wei. *Zhao Ziyang zhuan* (A Biography of Zhao Ziyang), Beijing: China News Press, 1989.

Zhao, Ziyang. "*Guanyu jingji tizhi gaige*" (On the reform of the economic system), *Xuandu*, 2:861–72.

"The Political Report to the 13th PC," *PD*, November 4, 1987.

Zheng Qian and Han Gang. *Mao Zedong zhilu: wannian suiyue* (Mao Zedong's Road: The Later Years), Beijing: Chinese Youth Press, 1996.

Zhong Kan. *Kang Sheng pingzhuan* (A Critical Biography of Kang Sheng), Beijing: Red Flag Press, 1982.

Zhonggong dangshi zhuanti jiangyi (Teaching Materials on Specific Issues in the CCP History), Beijing: CC Party School Press, 1988.

"*Zhonggong zhongyang guanyu jingji tizhi gaige de jueding*" (The CC resolution of the reform of the economic system), *Xuandu*, 2:776–95.

"*Zhonggong zhongyang guanyu quandang bixu jianjue weihu shihui zhuyi fazhi de tongzhi*" (The CC's circular on that the whole party must steadfastly abide by the socialist rule by law), *Xuandu*, 2:1080–85.

"*Zhonggong zhongyang, guaowu yuan guanyu jinyibu huoyue nongcun jingji de*

Selected Bibliography

shiyang zhengce" (Ten policies of the CC and the State Council on further stimulating the rural economy)," *Xuandu*, II, pp. 804–13.

Zhonggong zhongyang wenjian xuanji (A Selected Collection of Documents of the CCP Central Committee), vol. 11 (1936–8), compiled by the CCP Central Archives, Beijing: CC Party School Press, 1991.

Zhongguo gongchan dang lishi (The CCP History), compiled by *zhonggong zhongyang dangshi yanjou shi* (CCP Party History Research Center), Beijing: People's Press, 1991.

Zhongguo gongchan dang lishi dashi ji (Chronology of the CCP History), compiled by CCP Party History Research Center, Beijing: People's Press, 1991.

Zhongguo gongchan dang lishi jiangyi (Teaching Materials of CCP History), compiled by the Drafting Group of CCP History, Shanghai: Shanghai People's Press, 1984.

Zhongguo renmin jiefangjun zhanshi jianbian (A Concise History of the PLA), compiled by the Editing Group of PLA's Concise History in the Chinese Military Academy, Beijing: PLA Press, 1989.

Zhonghua renmin gongheguo jingji guanli dashiji (Chronology of the PRC Economic Management), compiled by the "Contemporary China's Economic Management" Editorial Board, Beijing: China's Economy Press, 1986.

Zhou Enlai. "*Quanguo caijing huiyi shang suozhuo de jielun*" (Conclusion of the National Conference on Financial and Economic Work, *Cankao*, 20:132–43.

"*Zai guanyu Gao Gang wenti de zuotanhui shang de fayan tigang*" (Speech outline at the forum on the Gao Gang question, *Cankao*, 20:267–9.

"*Zhou Enlai zhuan*" (A Biography of Zhou Enlai), *RWZ* (1991).

Zhou Guoquan, Guo Dehong, and Li Mingsan. *Wang Ming pingzhuan* (A Critical Biography of Wang Ming), Hefei: Anhui People's Press, 1989.

Zhou Ming, ed. *Lishi zai zheli chensi – 1966–1976 nian jishi* (Deep Reflections on This Period of History – True Stories in 1966–1976), vols. 1–3, Beijing: Huaxia Press, 1986; vols. 4–6, Taiyuan, Shanxi: Baiyue Art Press, 1989.

Zhou Yang. "*Guanyu Makesi zhuyi de ji ge lilun wenti de tantao*" (An exploration of a few theoretical questions of Marxism), *PD*, March 16, 1983.

Zhou zongli shengping dashi ji (Major Events in Premier Zhou's Life), Chengdu: Sichuan People's Press, 1986.

Zhu De nianpu (A Chronicle of Zhu De's Life), compiled by the CC Documentary Study Office, Beijing: People's Press, 1986.

Zhu Zhongli (Mme Wang Jiaxiang). *Liming yu wanxia* (Dawn and Sunset), Beijing: PLA Press, 1986.

Zweig, David. "Dilemmas of partial reform," in Bruce Reynolds, ed., *Chinese Economic Policy*, New York: Paragon House, 1989, pp. 13–40.

Index

adventurism, 52, 222, 226, 246, 255, 292; and first leap forward, 216, 217, 218, 220, 221; left-, 2, 128n89, 130; Mao on, 221, 223, 224, 243
agriculture: collectivization of, 169–70, 171n53, 185–6, 193, 362; and economic reform, 240–5, 369, 380, 393; and GLF, 227, 230–1, 233; production targets for, 213–14, 227; in socialist transition, 169–71. *See also* household responsibility system
Ai Siqi, 123n64
Albanian Communist Party, 249
alienation theory, 391
All-China Federation of Trade Unions, 222
An Pingsheng, 87
An Ziwen, 152, 183, 187n136, 303, 361, 371; and Gao Gang, 173, 185–8, 198; and Liu Shaoqi, 68n29, 86, 150; and Mao, 184n114, 188; Politburo list of, 177–80, 181, 187, 191, 196, 202; and rural capitalism, 164, 165, 166
antiadventurism. *See* adventurism
anti-bourgeois liberalization campaigns, 405, 408, 420; and CCP rule, 388–9; and Deng's reforms, 376, 407, 421
antiempiricism, 341, 345–6
Anti-Japanese War, 77, 115, 129
Anti-Rightist Campaign (1959–61), 83, 221, 241, 388; Mao's role in, 52n82, 222
August 1 Declaration (1935), 112

balance-of-power theory, 49–54
bandwagon theory, 49–54
baochan daohu (dividing land by household), 240–3, 244. *See also* household responsibility system
Barnett, Doak, 29, 30
Beidaihe Conference (1956), 217

Bo Gu, 111n13, 112, 113n21, 115, 116n35, 123n64
Bo Yibo, 12, 80n, 303, 361, 417; and CR, 224n62, 292; and Deng, 199, 384; and economic policy, 151, 156, 170, 181, 182, 183, 184n117, 214n13, 372; and first leap forward, 215n19, 217n28; and Gao Gang, 185–8; and Gao-Rao Affair, 159n3, 173, 190, 198; and GLF, 222; and Hu Yaobang, 405; and Li Fuchun, 202; and Liu Shaoqi, 129, 130n96, 131n101, 140, 204; and Liu's Tianjin talks, 161nn10,11, 162, 163, 165n27; and Mao, 188; positions of, 118, 137, 142, 150, 152, 178, 179, 208, 371, 373n68; tax reform of, 37n39, 173–6; and Zhou Enlai, 201
"bombarding the headquarters" (Mao), 285–6
bourgeois liberalization. *See* anti-bourgeois liberalization campaigns
bureaucracy: of CCP, 238; institutionalization of, 13, 158; literary, 270–1; and Mao, 15, 17–18, 211; Soviet, 66; in structure model, 32, 33
bureaucratic politics, theory of, 3, 31
bureaucrats, Party (PB), 212, 213–38, 284, 290, 301n130; and CR, 280, 286, 292, 386; and GLF, 224, 225, 236, 267; and Hai Rui Affair, 269–78; and Mao, 230–46, 251, 256, 267–8, 285, 294, 322, 385, 425; and policy making, 257–9, 283, 362; and SEC, 247, 248, 255–6; and two-front arrangement, 220–1

cadres: CR attacks on, 295; literati, 273–4; local, 231, 250, 254; rehabilitation of, 361; rural, 74n43; transfers of, 76–7, 85–6. *See also* leaders
Cai Chang, 124n66
Cai Hesen, 124n66

441

Index

Cao Yiou, 122
capitalism, 168, 392; Liu Shaoqi on, 161–6; rural, 164, 165, 166; and SEC, 247, 248, 254
capitalist roaders, 83, 251, 254, 255, 296, 329
CCP. *See* Chinese Communist Party
Central China Bureau (CCB), 132, 143
Central Committee (CC), 79, 302, 400; leaders of, 107, 111, 124, 126, 127, 128, 130, 146n135, 165n27; and Liu's Tianjin talks, 162; Number 1 Documents of (1982–3), 382, 390; Party School of, 128, 129n92, 132; power of, 226n71, 238, 406; pre-1949, 107–8, 113, 114, 115, 116, 124, 126, 127, 130; Propaganda Department of, 121, 128; revenue sources of, 151, 155; and SEC, 248; and two-front arrangement, 205, 208; Work Conference of (1978), 360–1
Sixth, 128n89
Seventh: First Plenum, 128; Second Plenum, 156, 162, 169, 176; Third Plenum (1950), 168; Fourth Plenum (1954), 196, 197, 202; Fifth Plenum (April 1954), 204
Eighth: Second Plenum (1956), 58; Third Plenum (1957), 59, 221, 222; Fifth Plenum (1958), 281; Tenth Plenum (1962), 132n104, 238, 239, 241, 242, 244, 245, 246, 270, 281, 285; Eleventh Plenum (1966), 285, 287, 290, 295; Twelfth Plenum, 329
Ninth: Second Plenum, 319–20
Tenth: Third Plenum (1977), 353–4
Eleventh, 355, 361, 368; Third Plenum (1978), 362–3, 365, 366, 371, 373, 389, 419, 420; Fourth Plenum (1979), 370; Fifth Plenum (1980), 225n68, 377, 378, 379, 386, 408; Sixth Plenum (1981), 380, 386, 388
Twelfth: Second Plenum (1983), 391, 408; Third Plenum (1984), 392, 408; Sixth Plenum (1986), 406
Central Financial and Economic Committee (CFEC), 156, 157, 182, 185, 188, 199; and new tax law, 173, 175
Central Financial and Economic Group (CFEG), 232–3, 234, 235
Central High-Ranking Cadre Study Group, 127–8
Central Military Commission (CMC), 122, 133, 292, 307, 310, 325; Administrative Group of, 312–13, 314, 315, 316, 317; Caretaker Group for, 312; and CR, 295, 300; and Deng, 333, 337, 341, 343, 356, 357, 373, 385; *Directives* of, 300; and *Eight-Article Order*, 300–1; Forum of (1970–1), 323; and Hai Rui Affair, 277–8; and He Long, 289, 290; and Lin Biao, 282, 304, 305, 308; and Mao, 108, 128, 207, 314; and Maoists, 301, 302, 303, 304, 306; and PLA, 295, 296
Central Plain Bureau (CPB), 117, 132
centralization, 198, 207; after GLF, 233, 234; and economic reform, 382, 395; of financial system, 380–1, 382; of leadership, 10, 57–58, 125, 159–60
CFEC. *See* Central Financial and Economic Committee
Chen Boda, 78, 171n53, 226n70; and beginnings of CR, 280, 281; criticism of, 79n51, 304, 323; and Hai Rui Affair, 276, 278; and Mao, 139, 292, 321; and Mao-Lin conflict, 319, 322, 323–4; positions of, 137, 208, 302, 315, 318; and rectification campaigns, 83, 122; and SEC, 247n157, 250n168, 253; and Tao Zhu, 301; in YR, 122, 123
Chen Changhao, 108n5
Chen Duxiu, 107, 133
Chen Geng, 137, 154
Chen Guodong, 364, 372
Chen Muhua, 88, 384
Chen Peixian, 272n19, 302, 384
Chen Shiqu, 325
Chen Xilian, 78, 315, 316, 327, 334, 335, 377
Chen Yi, 226n70, 277, 298n121, 330; and Deng, 199, 332n199; and Gao-Rao Affair, 191, 204, 205; and Li Xiannian, 203; and Lin Biao, 305, 307, 308; and Liu Shaoqi, 58n4, 131n101, 143; and Maoists, 302–3, 304, 306; and military, 57n2, 109, 117, 120n48, 142, 144n129, 146, 147, 149, 297, 299; mountaintop of, 288, 302; and policy making, 155, 316–17, 318; positions of, 58, 109, 118, 137, 153, 208, 286, 289n92
Chen Yonggui, 253, 327
Chen Yun, 44, 121, 226n70, 292, 405n133; allies of, 87n, 367, 428; and Deng, 5, 102, 351, 361–2, 365, 383, 384, 385, 387, 420; and Deng's retirement, 404; and economic policy, 184, 184n117, 202, 214n13, 362, 371, 372; and economic reform, 240, 373, 376–80, 388, 390, 393–5, 408; and financial system, 139, 151, 156,

442

Index

157, 182, 380–1, 382; and first leap forward, 217, 221; and Gao-Rao Affair, 189–91, 193–5, 196n175, 200; and GLF, 52, 223, 224n61, 225, 227, 230, 234; and GLF's reversal, 232–3, 235, 236; illnesses of, 200, 235, 332; and Liu Shaoqi, 143, 187; and Manchurian strategy, 144, 145, 146, 147; and Mao, 31, 58, 111, 157, 188n143, 368; and military, 8, 73, 136; and new tax law, 174, 175, 176; and Peng Zhen, 4, 37, 144, 147, 371, 386, 398, 399; positions of, 112, 115, 116n35, 118, 137, 153, 177, 178, 208, 363, 364; and rectification campaigns, 84, 122, 123, 125n69, 403; and reform policies, 37n40, 388, 417; rehabilitation of, 331, 336; and urban administration, 160n6, 161
Chen Zaidao, 86; and Wuhan Incident, 309–10, 311
Chen Zhengren, 122, 123, 199, 251
Cheng Zihua, 143
Chengdu Conference (1958), 223, 224
Chi Haotian, 359
Chiang Kai-shek, 113n21, 131, 143
Chinese Communist Party (CCP): and class stuggle, 239; and Comintern, 110, 115, 116, 120, 125; Constitution of, 68n29, 256, 257, 352, 363, 385, 395, 406; corruption in, 400; and CR, 16, 287, 293, 409; and Deng, 68n29, 80, 97, 105, 111, 329, 335, 341, 343, 350, 365, 372, 383–5, 409, 419, 422; dictatorship of, 61–4; dismantling of, 238, 268–87; and economy, 368, 395; and executions, 133; and factionalism, 20, 24, 43–4, 45, 107–8, 120, 292, 293, 406–10, 428; and Gao-Rao Affair, 160; and GLF, 221–30, 236; informal channels within, 62–3; institutionalization of, 258, 293, 423; and KMT, 112, 113, 115–16, 117, 130, 317n160; leadership of, 22, 107, 119, 302, 369, 370; legitimacy of, 9, 10, 135, 227, 368–9; Mao's control of, 9–10, 11, 35, 59–60, 107–11, 135–6, 207, 268, 365; and military, 72, 135–6, 138, 281, 289n95, 290, 295, 309, 319, 385; purges in, 45, 230; rectification campaigns in, 403–4; and reform, 388–9, 395, 396n114, 403, 407; and revolutionary base areas, 56–7, 145; in rural areas, 74n43; and SEC, 246–7, 249; separation from government of, 398–402; system of, 6–7, 96, 208, 268–87; in totalitarian model, 26; unity of, 1–2, 5, 7, 48, 51, 62–4, 140, 159, 197, 411, 425–7;

and Zhou Enlai, 326. *See also* Party Congresses; Party state
class struggle, 307, 370; criticism of, 366, 367, 370; Mao on, 132n104, 239, 244, 347; and SEC, 246, 247, 248
clientalism, 1, 46. *See also* patron-client relationships
CMC. *See* Central Military Commission
Colton, Timothy J., 66n23
Comintern: antifascist front of, 112, 115, 130; and CCP, 110, 120, 125; and Mao, 116, 119; and Wang Ming, 111, 114
Communique of the Tenth Plenum of the Eighth CC, 239, 244
Communist Youth League of China (CYLC), 86
Conference of the High-Ranking Party Cadres in the Military (1953), 192, 193
conflict models, 26–42
Confucius, Campaign to Criticize Lin and, 334, 337, 338, 339, 340
Constitution, state, 318, 319, 320
"continuous revolution," 292, 307, 338, 347
contradictions, 251–6, 330
corruption, 388, 393, 394, 396–8, 403, 408, 409
Counterattacking the Right-Deviationist Restoration Campaign (1976), 83
CRG. *See* Cultural Revolution Group
Cultural Revolution (CR): beginnings of, 69, 280–2, 285; beneficiaries of, 84, 327, 331, 332, 337, 345, 348, 349, 350–4; causes of, 31, 211, 213; and CCP, 16, 287, 293, 409; and CMC, 295, 300, 302; compared to YR, 303; criticism of, 37, 304–5, 366, 367, 369; and Deng, 37, 281, 329, 330, 332, 336, 338, 346, 348, 371; and economy, 306, 326; and factionalism, 16, 18, 24, 35, 267–349, 298; Gang of Four during, 4, 42; and *guanxi*, 53n88, 287, 302; ideological consensus on, 418; leaders from, 361, 363, 378n79; and leadership relations, 4, 47, 210, 268, 280, 281, 306, 386, 424; legitimacy of, 16, 276, 280, 305, 307, 308, 324, 332, 346, 347, 370; and Lin Biao, 4, 19, 96, 308; and Liu Shaoqi, 90, 131n101; and Mao, 13, 15, 35, 69, 132n104, 211, 267, 280–7, 372, 386n, 396, 425; military in, 16, 17, 73, 280–7, 293, 295–6, 299, 300, 308, 309, 356, 385; and Party state, 240, 281, 287; and PB, 256, 280, 286, 292, 386; purges during, 64, 87; reversal of verdicts of, 80, 341, 347; and "scar literature," 388; survivors of,

443

Index

Cultural Revolution (CR) (*cont.*)
139, 349; theories on, 28, 50–4; and Zhou Enlai, 224n62, 332n198
Cultural Revolution Group (CRG), 292, 306, 313, 315; and CMC, 296, 302; creation of, 270; dissolution of, 279–80; and Hai Rui Affair, 273, 275, 278; and military, 295, 299, 300; new, 281, 285; in Wuhan Incident, 309, 310, 311

Daniels, Robert, 65
danwei (unit) system, 46, 62
decentralization, 81n, 206, 377, 388. *See also* centralization
Decision on the Great Proletarian Cultural Revolution, 286
Democracy Wall, 367–8, 408, 419
Deng Fa, 112
Deng Hua, 229
Deng Liqun, 42, 87n, 235, 367, 388, 420; and Deng, 88, 353, 384; and reform, 402, 406–7; in YR, 122, 123
Deng Tuo, 273n26
Deng Xiaoping: and CCP, 68n29, 80, 97, 105, 111, 329, 335, 341, 343, 350, 365, 372, 383–5, 409, 419, 422; and centralization of leadership, 58, 159; comebacks of, 16–17, 45, 79, 83, 84, 139, 307, 328–34, 350–4; compromises of, 22–4, 426; and CR, 37, 281, 329, 330, 332, 336, 338, 346, 348, 371; criticism of, 352, 368; dominance of, 5, 7, 24, 29, 32, 39, 54, 60, 75–7, 360–5, 387–410, 425; dual civilian-military control of, 105, 328, 335, 343, 350, 365, 372, 383, 409, 419, 422; economic reforms of, 37n40, 240, 332, 346, 347, 373–83, 406, 408; and factionalism, 20–5, 44, 78, 341, 346, 383, 386–7, 398, 411, 421–2; followers of, 86, 87–8; and Gao-Rao Affair, 185, 189, 191, 193, 196, 197, 198–200, 205, 332; and GLF, 225, 230, 233, 237; and Hai Rui Affair, 274, 275, 278; and Hu Yaobang, 406–10; and ideology, 391, 418–22, 420; illnesses of, 199, 332; and leadership relations, 20–1, 158, 226, 383–7; legitimacy of, 21–2, 347, 354–60, 365–73, 375, 388, 421–2; and Lin Biao, 268; and Liu Shaoqi, 164, 187, 199, 330; and Luo Ruiqing, 284; and Mao, 30, 52, 87, 88, 111, 138, 198–200, 244, 258, 334–49, 354–55, 365, 372; and Maoists, 331, 332, 333, 338–49; and military, 20, 22, 72, 73, 79, 80, 97, 105, 106, 140–50, 297,
309n143, 328–38, 350–5, 365, 372, 373, 383–7, 409, 419, 422; and mountaintops, 203–4, 288, 342–9; and MZT, 21, 366–70; and new tax law, 174, 175; policy making under, 182, 183, 238, 329, 363, 372–3, 385–7, 390; political reform of, 37n40, 69, 396–406, 415; positions of, 109, 111, 142, 154, 241, 257; purges of, 11, 16, 45, 64, 105, 111, 138, 334–49, 418; and rectification campaigns, 79, 82, 83–4, 124, 335, 341, 344–8, 352–3, 356, 370, 378; and reorganization of Politburo, 178, 179; and SEC, 247n157, 250, 252, 253, 254, 255; successors to, 2, 19–20, 21, 42, 90, 96–104, 404–5; support for, 301n130, 386, 428; and "ten private talks," 352–3; and two-front arrangement, 13, 14, 21, 106, 207–9, 329, 383; in Yan'an Round Table, 20, 118, 137, 383; and Zhou Enlai, 225, 226n70, 268, 423
Deng Yingchao, 199n190, 201n198, 293n, 363, 364, 384, 387
Deng Zihui, 58, 159, 178, 185, 205, 240, 241; policy areas of, 182, 183
Ding Sheng, 315, 334, 335
Discipline Inspection Commission (CC), 363, 393–4, 395, 396–8, 403, 408
The Dismissal of Hai Rui (Wu Han), 268–74, 270, 271, 272, 274
Dittmer, Lowell, 21n37
dogmatism, 119, 120
Dong Biwu, 113n21, 156, 182, 198, 208, 327; in Politburo, 151, 177, 178
Dong Jiageng, 253
"donkey faction," 126, 127, 140, 242n141

East China Bureau (ECB), 143, 148n143, 181
East-Central China, 142, 143, 146
economic reform, 22, 387–9, 390, 401, 416; and Deng, 37n40, 240, 332, 346, 347, 373–83, 406, 408; and legitimacy, 389, 406; opposition to, 30–1, 392–6, 408
economy: and CCP, 368, 395; conservative control of, 250, 371–2; and CR, 306, 326; decline of, 234, 237, 382; and factionalism, 328; and first leap forward, 213–21; growth of, 24, 224, 346, 425, 427; market, 3, 22, 31, 369, 374, 392, 409; and military budget, 318; planned, 3, 26, 30–1, 169, 171–2, 173, 367, 377, 380–1, 388, 390, 395, 424–5; planned market, 392; planners' management of, 184–5,

444

Index

243, 245, 314–15; policies on, 15, 69, 212, 230–8, 326, 362, 371; and political campaigns, 247, 248, 339; and price controls, 233, 393, 409; recovery of, 27, 52, 176, 242, 256, 257; rural, 164–6, 241; socialist, 347, 366–7, 392, 424–5; socialist market, 409; socialist transformation of, 161–6; urban, 161, 166; world, 317, 374, 376, 380, 392; and Wuhan Incident, 310. *See also* Great Leap Forward
Eight-Article Order, and Lin Biao, 299–301, 304, 305, 309
Eighth Route Army, 108, 111, 114, 119, 129n94
"emancipation of the mind," 2, 33, 367, 369, 377, 419–20

factional networks, 78, 315, 335, 345; and Deng, 332, 348; and *guanxi*, 44, 74–7; of Yan'an Round Table, 324–5; of Zhou Enlai, 327, 328
factionalism: conditions for, 6–8; and conflict models, 34–42; continuity of, 421–5; criticism of, 120, 121, 345; defined, 1; as dependent variable, 4, 42; as essential dynamic, 411–13; as independent variable, 5, 6, 55, 104, 383; at lower levels, 35, 45n; and pluralism, 25, 46, 61, 81, 428; and stability, 2, 10, 16, 17, 24, 44, 158; Western analysis of, 3–5
Fang Qiang, 229
Fang Yi, 372, 378, 384, 391
fangzhen (political line), 223, 231, 242, 407, 414–16, 419–20
February Adverse Current, 301, 314
February Outline, 275, 278, 386n
Feng Wenbin, 364
Fengqing freighter controversy, 342–3
A Few of My Opinions (Mao), 322
Field Armies, 1, 34, 76n46, 293; First, 179, 287, 288, 316; Second, 142, 288, 309n143, 316, 328, 329; Third, 145n129, 146, 288, 325, 356n24; Fourth, 143, 160–1, 288, 309n143
financial system, 175, 181, 185–8, 202, 378; decentralization of, 380; and factionalism, 151, 155–8; reform of, 380–1, 382, 390–1, 409; unification of, 151–8. *See also* Central Financial and Economic Committee; Central Financial and Economic Group
First Front Red Army, 293; and Lin Biao, 288, 290; and Mao, 124, 287, 288, 325
first leap forward, 213–21

Five Anti Campaign (1963), 171, 172, 173, 181, 247
Five Year Plans, 184–5, 214, 271, 395
foreign relations, 317, 332, 348, 362; economic, 374, 376, 380, 392
formal political process, 42, 53, 62–3, 121; constraints of, 23–4, 33–4; and factionalism, 36–7, 412; and institutionalization, 66, 67; and leadership relations, 17, 39, 70; and Mao's authority, 12–14; violations of, 37, 39, 59
Former Ten Articles, 248
Forum on the Principles for the Party's Theoretical Work (1979), 366–7
Forum on the Work in Literature and Art in the Armed Forces, 276; *Summary* of, 277, 278, 279
Four Cardinal Principles (FCP), 22, 33, 369–70, 377, 394; and Deng, 372, 385, 388–9, 406, 408, 421; as ideological consensus, 418–19; and reform, 376, 383, 424
Four Cleanups Campaign, 251, 252, 254
"four modernizations," 371
Fourth Front Red Army, 56n, 108, 109, 288, 311; and Deng, 203–4, 329; leaders from, 110, 147, 289n92, 293, 298, 309, 316
France, 332
Fu Congbi, 78, 311, 313–14
Fu Qiutao, 109

Gang of Four, 42, 44, 83, 139; and beneficiaries, 84, 351; and Deng, 268, 331; fall of, 346n226, 350; and Lin Biao, 4, 308; Mao on, 339, 340, 341, 343; and Zhou Enlai, 79, 423. *See also* Maoists
Gao Gang, 11–12, 36n37, 37n39, 116n36; and centralization of leadership, 57–8, 159; factionalism of, 44, 127, 140; and financial system, 155, 156; and Lin Biao, 189, 190, 191; and Liu Shaoqi, 160–7, 169, 171–3, 176–7, 185–8, 202; and Manchuria, 145, 147, 149; and Mao, 118, 125, 126, 128, 144, 172–3, 255; and military, 77, 122; policy areas of, 182, 183; and Politburo, 128, 176–80; positions of, 127, 132, 140, 146, 152, 184–5; purge of, 138; relations with leaders of, 86, 177, 200, 201; in Yan'an Round Table, 118, 137; in YR, 122, 123
Gao Jingting, 109
Gao Zhenpu, 310n, 344

445

Index

Gao-Rao Affair (1954), 36n37, 37n39, 68, 104, 173–205, 417; aftermath of, 197–205; and Chen Yun, 189–91, 193–5, 196n175, 200; and Deng, 191, 193, 196, 197, 198–200, 205, 332; end of, 188–97; and factionalism, 1, 45, 51; *guanxi* in, 64n, 193; and leadership relations, 10–12, 58, 160, 196, 197–205; and Mao, 160, 161n11, 188–97; and military, 160, 189, 191, 196, 204–5; and Peng Dehuai, 190n152, 191, 204, 205, 241n140; and political campaigns, 83, 255; reversal of verdict on, 242; and two-front arrangement, 160, 189; and Yan'an Round Table, 11, 159, 196; and Zhou Enlai, 161n11, 194n167, 196, 200–2
Geng Biao, 384
genius theory, 321–2
Goldstein, Avery, 49–51, 53, 54, 59, 64n
Gong Yuzhi, 351n7
Gorbachev, Mikhail, 407
Government Administration Council (GAC), 156, 157, 182, 184, 199; General Party Group (GPG) of, 181, 183, 201
Graham, Katherine, 404
Great Leap Forward (GLF), 15, 29, 53, 221–38, 245; criticism of, 59, 228–30; and ideology, 224, 417–18; and Liu Shaoqi, 222, 224, 225, 230, 231–8, 240; and Mao, 59, 252, 372; recovery from, 267, 271; reversal of, 230–8; revival of, 31, 33; and two-front arrangement, 212, 226, 236; and Zhou Enlai, 52, 223, 224, 230, 233, 236
Green, Barbara B., 66n23
Gu Mu, 292, 293, 315, 344, 384; and economic policy, 372, 373n68, 378
Guan Feng, 311
Guan Xiangying, 109, 116n35, 118, 122, 123, 137
guanxi (personal ties), 7–8, 36, 58n4, 226, 424; *vs.* common interests, 44, 426; and CR, 53n88, 287, 302; and Deng, 335, 383, 386–7; and factional networks, 74–7; and factionalism, 41, 42, 44, 49, 411; in Gao-Rao Affair, 64n, 193; and institutionalization, 64–5, 67, 70, 71–2, 423; in military, 57, 73, 149, 283, 295; of new-generation leaders, 80; and patron-client relationships, 46–9; and personal entrustment of power, 55, 56, 61; in policy making, 43, 63–4, 426; from revolutionary period, 6, 423; in Soviet system, 66; in structure model, 4–5, 40;

and two-front arrangement, 208, 209, 211–12, 220

Hai Rui Affair, 268–74
Han Jingcao, 181n108
Han Xianchu, 315, 335
Hao Jianxiu, 384
Harding, Harry, 3, 30
He Bingyan, 154
He Long, 123, 131n101, 254, 255n187, 283, 298n121; and Gao-Rao Affair, 189n149, 191, 204, 205; and Hai Rui Affair, 277; and Lin Biao, 287–92, 295, 303–4; and military, 108, 109, 122, 141, 145n129, 147, 289, 290, 297; positions of, 58, 116n36, 118, 125, 137, 154, 159, 208, 286; and Zhou Enlai, 226n70, 290–1
Hebei province, 129, 149, 246, 250
History of the CPSU (Bolsheviks): Short Course, 188
Hong Xuezhi, 204, 229, 356, 371
household responsibility system, 362, 369, 376, 377, 408; implementation of, 381, 382, 390, 393; and local leaders, 374–5; opposition to, 371, 379–80
Hu Jintao, 86
Hu Jiwei, 366
Hu Qiaomu, 68n29, 217, 269n4, 365, 388, 403, 420; and Deng, 88, 384, 387; and Mao, 124, 125n69, 367; positions of, 187n136, 363, 364, 378; in YR, 122, 123
Hu Qili, 87, 384, 397, 405, 420
Hu Shiying, 403
Hu Yaobang: criticism of, 368, 391; and Deng, 19, 20, 21, 87, 90, 357, 383, 384, 406–10, 425; and economic reform, 371, 375, 376, 379, 380; and factionalism, 44, 360; fall of, 2, 45, 69, 396–410; and *guanxi* networks, 75, 76; and hardliners, 390, 410, 420; and ideology, 366, 367; and political campaigns, 83, 84n58, 86, 247n157; and political reform, 400n122, 401–2; positions of, 113n20, 154, 225n68, 363, 364, 378, 383, 408; and scar literature, 388; in succession struggles, 96, 97, 103, 104, 105; support for, 80n, 86; and truth criterion, 42, 359, 360; and Zhao Ziyang, 4, 38, 416
Hu Zongnan, 317n160
Hua Guofeng, 78, 80, 83, 84, 327; and Deng, 350–4, 361–5; economic policy of, 371, 373, 380; fall of, 2, 37, 378; legitimacy of, 351, 354–60, 362, 365, 419; in succession struggle, 105, 106, 348, 349

446

Index

Huaihai Campaign, 356n24
Huang Hua, 384
Huang Jing, 162n14
Huang Kecheng, 161n8, 162n14, 226n70, 229, 245, 288, 289; and military, 142, 160; positions of, 137, 152, 208, 363
Huang Yongsheng, 78n49, 86, 314, 321, 324; positions of, 153, 315, 318
Hungary, 270
ideology: in conflict models, 27, 28, 29; consensus on, 417-21, 426; and control, 118, 123; decline of, 425, 428; and Deng, 80, 332, 365-73, 388, 391, 407, 418-42; and economic reform, 392, 394, 395; in factional conflicts, 269, 322, 387, 390, 411-12, 414; and GLF, 224, 417-18; and legitimacy, 21-2, 59, 119, 123, 135, 140, 222, 334, 365-73, 375, 388, 406, 419, 421; and Mao, 59, 123-4, 136, 244, 324, 365, 369, 372; and policy, 366, 419, 424; and political campaigns, 270, 347, 397; and reform, 396, 401, 402, 403. *See also* Mao Zedong Thought

"independent kingdoms," 57, 86, 239, 253, 254, 258
Indonesian Communist Party, 249
industry, 362, 391; autonomy in, 374, 376, 380, 381, 382-3, 392; and GLF, 227, 233, 235; production targets for, 213-14, 222, 227
information, 38, 53, 62, 70-1, 307, 419; asymmetry of, 94, 95, 98, 102, 103; complete, 91; control of, 39, 198, 199; in Gao-Rao Affair, 193, 196; incomplete, 95, 99, 101, 102
institutionalization of political process: and bureaucracy, 13, 158; and CCP, 258, 293, 423; and Deng, 60, 383; and factionalism, 64-72; and *guanxi*, 64-5, 67, 70, 71-2, 423; and leadership relations, 95, 139, 160, 167, 181-2; at lower political levels, 35; and military, 72-3, 106, 282-3; in multiparty systems, 43; and policy making, 7, 38, 41, 58, 64-5, 67, 70-1, 283; and redistribution of power, 179, 184; and two-front arrangement, 206, 208, 209

Japan, 141, 428; united front against, 110, 112, 114, 115, 119, 130, 131; war against, 77, 115, 129
Japanese Communist Party, 249
Ji Dengkui, 78, 253n, 322, 339n214, 373n68;

and Deng, 331, 336; positions of, 315, 318, 325, 327, 335n205; resignation of, 377
Jia Tuofu, 155, 176n86, 182, 198, 241, 242n141
Jiang Chunyun, 80n
Jiang Hua, 247n157
Jiang Nanxiang, 371
Jiang Qing, 78, 162n14, 296n118, 306, 326n180; and CR, 17, 281; criticism of, 302, 304, 339, 340, 341; and Deng, 333, 336, 338, 342, 343, 346, 348; and Hai Rui Affair, 268-71, 272n19, 274, 276, 277, 278; and Lin Biao, 291, 294, 298, 305; and Mao, 292, 308, 339, 340, 341; and Mao-Lin conflict, 322; and political campaigns, 253, 337; positions of, 315, 319, 327; and Tao Zhu, 301; and Wuhan Incident, 309, 310; and Yang-Yu-Fu Incident, 313-14
Jiang Zemin, 80n, 351n7, 416, 419, 424, 427; and Deng, 2, 87; survival of, 105, 106
Jiefang ribao (Liberation Daily), 123, 132
Jin Ming, 364, 372
Jinggang Mountain, 56n, 108, 146-7, 305, 311
Ju Pengfei, 384

Kai Feng, 112, 115, 122, 123
Kang Sheng, 77-8, 242n141, 249n163, 304, 351, 362; and CR, 270, 280, 281; and Hai Rui Affair, 269, 275, 278; illnesses of, 175, 332; and Mao, 111, 125-6, 139, 292, 322; positions of, 112, 115, 116n35, 121, 122, 177, 178, 245, 256, 302, 315, 318, 327; and Wang Ming, 121, 125; in Yan'an Round Table, 118, 137; and YR, 122, 123-4
Kang Shien, 315, 372, 373n68, 384
Ke Qingshi, 86, 122, 226n69, 240n133, 247n157; and GLF, 223, 225; and Hai Rui Affair, 269n8, 271
Khrushchev, Nikita, 66n23, 67, 222, 249, 280; and Lin Biao, 303, 304
Kim Il Sung, 190n152
Korea, 428
Korean War, 27, 151, 168, 169
Kuai Dafu, 311
Kuomintang (KMT), 10, 124n66, 166, 291, 296, 328; and CCP, 112, 113, 117, 130, 317n160; defeat of, 115-16, 129, 147-8, 150; Provisional National Congress of, 114; in southern Manchuria, 144, 146; *vs.*

447

Index

Kuomintang (KMT) (*cont.*)
  Red Army, 110, 141, 143; Wang Ming and, 114

land reform, 12, 165, 166, 168–9, 172, 247
Latter Ten Articles, 248, 269; *Revised*, 250, 251
leaders: of CCP, 22, 107, 119, 302, 369, 370; centralization of, 10, 57–8, 125, 159–60; collective leadership of, 206, 207, 220, 276, 280; communications between, 90, 91, 95, 139, 160, 167, 179, 195, 196, 206, 412, 423; and CR, 16, 280, 285, 361, 363, 378n79, 386; and economic reform, 373–5, 376, 381, 382; and military, 96, 204–5, 293; mountaintops of, 112n18, 116, 141–51, 157, 288, 293, 334–5; new-generation, 80; personal entrustment of power to, 6, 55–61, 70, 71, 72, 73, 74–5, 184; purges of, 64, 78, 82, 83, 87, 107–8, 124, 268; redistribution of power among, 181–4, 412–13; retirement of, 379, 404; in revolutionary base areas, 56–7; senior, 371, 379, 383, 386, 387, 404, 406, 424, 426; systems-based, 80. *See also* Yan'an Round Table
leaders, local: and concrete policies, 414; and Deng, 226, 374–5, 428; and economic reform, 231, 374–5, 428; and factional networks, 80–1, 323; and GLF, 223, 224, 225; and Mao, 86, 87, 138; relations with center of, 80n, 86–7, 226, 228; and SEC, 250, 254. *See also* Regional Military Commands
leadership decision making, 2, 3–5; in Deng period, 21, 158; and factionalism, 42, 55, 413–17; formal process for, 6, 39; *guanxi* in, 7–8, 42, 226, 237; institutionalization of, 7, 71, 158; Mao's dominance of, 124, 238; and new CRG 281; and two-front arrangement, 12–18, 211–12, 220; and Zunyi Conference, 113n20, 121. *See also* policy making
leadership relations: changes in, 81–8, 307, 363–4; compromise in, 22–4, 246, 425, 426, 428; in conflict models, 26, 33; and CR, 4, 47, 210, 268, 280, 281, 306, 386, 424; under Deng, 20–1, 158, 226, 383–7; factionalism in, 42, 55, 77–81, 142, 157, 404, 405; and formal process, 17, 39, 70; and Gao-Rao Affair, 10–12, 58, 160, 196, 197–205; and ideological consensus, 417–21; institutionalization of, 95, 139, 160, 167, 181–2; local-elite, 86–7, 226,

228; and Mao, 77–8; Mao's control of, 8–12, 59, 139–40, 158, 338–49; and military, 73, 293, 294; personal loyalty in, 257–8; and policy making, 41, 158, 167, 423–4; in post-Mao period, 421–5; and prisoners' dilemma, 180; and redistribution of power, 58, 177, 182, 184, 422; stability of, 2, 10, 16, 17, 158; and succession struggles, 18–20, 96, 104, 105; trust in, 19–20, 91–2; and two-front arrangement, 12–18, 106, 207–66, 220, 245; Western analysis of, 3–5. *See also* *guanxi*; Yan'an Round Table
Left-deviationism, 127, 162, 166–7, 211, 242
Left-opportunism, 121, 125, 128
legal system, 182, 183, 398–9, 400
legitimacy: of CCP, 9, 10, 135, 227, 368–9; of CR, 16, 276, 280, 305, 307, 308, 324, 332, 346, 347, 370; of Deng, 21–2, 347, 354–60, 365–73, 372, 375, 388, 421–2; and economic reform, 389, 406; and GLF, 222; in Hai Rui Affair, 276; of Hua Guofeng, 351, 354–60, 362, 365, 419; and ideology, 21–2, 59, 119, 123, 135, 140, 222, 334, 365–73, 375, 388, 406, 419, 421; of Lin Biao, 318–19; of Mao, 10, 51, 118–19, 128, 135, 267, 322, 324, 365–6, 385, 421; of Maoists, 307; Marxism-Leninism as source of, 119, 120, 134, 135, 322; and MZT, 10, 21, 119, 140, 244, 369, 385, 421; of Zhou Enlai, 334
Lenin, V. I., 27, 131, 135
Leninism, 2, 320
Li Desheng, 78, 87, 326n179, 344n221, 384; and Mao-Lin conflict, 322, 324; positions of, 315, 325, 327, 334, 335
Li Fuchun, 202, 225, 291, 292, 332n199; and economic policy, 176n86, 182, 184n117, 214n13, 215, 217n28; and Mao, 124, 144; and Maoists, 302n133, 306; mountaintop of, 288, 293; positions of, 116n35, 177, 178, 179, 187n136, 208; and SEC, 253, 254; in Yan'an Round Table, 118, 137; and YR, 122, 123, 124
Li Honglin, 366, 403
Li Jiantong, 242n141
Li Jingquan, 154, 223, 225, 247n157
Li Jukui, 204
Li Lanqing, 80n
Li Lisan, 64, 107, 133
Li Peng, 80n, 86, 87n, 405; and Deng, 88, 96; and reform, 391, 409, 417
Li Rui, 19n34
Li Ruihuan, 80n, 87n

448

Index

Li Weihan, 116n35, 122, 123, 128n89, 217n28
Li Xiannian, 200, 222n51, 292, 326n179, 359n36, 405n133; and Deng, 350–1, 354, 355, 384, 387; and economic policy, 214n13, 215, 217n28, 372; and Gao-Rao Affair, 203–4; and GLF, 224n61, 225; and Maoists, 302, 306; mountaintop of, 288, 293; positions of, 137, 155, 208, 315, 325, 327, 363; and reform, 37n40, 373n68, 379; and retirement, 404; and Zhou Enlai, 226n70, 344
Li Ximing, 88
Li Xin, 351, 353, 354n16, 364
Li Xuefeng, 68n29, 247n157, 315, 324
Li Yunchang, 142n123
Li Zhusheng, 111n13
Li Zuopeng, 78n49, 290, 298n121, 310, 313; and Mao-Lin conflict, 320, 321, 324; positions of, 314, 315, 318
Liang Xiang, 86, 394
Liao Chengzhi, 384
Liao Gailong, 249n163, 270
Liao Hansheng, 154
Liao Luyan, 150, 152, 245
Lieberthal, Kenneth, 2, 3, 31, 38, 40, 42
Lin Biao, 110, 129n94, 287–325; Campaign to Criticize Confucius and, 334, 337, 338, 339, 340; and centralization of leadership, 58, 159; and CMC, 282, 304, 305, 308; and CR, 4, 17, 19, 96, 281, 286, 299, 300, 308; criticism of, 303, 304; fall of, 2, 11, 33, 45, 64, 78–9, 131n101, 138, 147, 268, 307; followers of, 86, 139, 203, 335; and Gang of Four, 4, 44, 308; and Gao-Rao Affair, 189, 190, 191–5, 200, 202n202, 204, 205; and Hai Rui Affair, 274, 276, 277; and He Long, 287–92, 295, 303–4; illnesses of, 175, 283, 289, 295n114, 332; and Jiang Qing, 291, 294, 298, 305; and Liu Shaoqi, 145n134; in Manchuria, 144, 145, 146, 147, 149; and Mao, 4, 16, 19, 20, 31, 52, 79, 87, 90, 143–7, 151, 229n, 283, 287–95, 300, 304–5, 311, 314–25, 329, 418; and Maoists, 293, 296, 304–5, 307–8; and military, 57n2, 78n49, 108, 149, 160, 268, 282, 287, 297, 304, 314, 316, 329; mountaintop of, 288; opponents of, 245, 282, 289n92, 298, 312; positions of, 109, 153, 155, 177n94, 178, 179, 208, 225, 286, 301, 315; rise of, 295–314; in succession struggles, 92, 93, 95, 96, 104; and Wuhan Incident, 310, 311; in Yan'an Round Table, 118, 137; and Yang-Yu-Fu Incident, 313, 314; and Zhou Enlai, 17, 226n70, 293, 294, 326, 334
Lin Biao Incident (1971), 75, 83, 324, 336; and Zhou Enlai, 96, 325–6, 334, 335
Lin Boqu, 112, 198; positions of, 113n21, 177, 178, 208; and Wang Ming, 115, 121; and YR, 122, 123
Lin Feng, 143, 144, 152
Lin Liguo, 79, 320, 324
Lin Muohan, 269
Lin Yuying (Zhang Hao), 110–11, 116n35
Liu Bocheng, 199, 203, 204, 205, 309n143, 379; and military, 108, 109, 110, 142, 144n129, 147, 150; mountaintop of, 288; positions of, 155, 208, 286, 289n92, 315, 316, 327; in Yan'an Round Table, 118, 137
Liu Jie, 374
Liu Lanbo, 371
Liu Lantao, 170, 198, 247n157, 303, 361, 371; positions of, 68n29, 142, 150, 152, 178, 179
Liu Ren, 269
Liu Shaoqi: and CC, 128, 130, 165n27; and centralization of leadership, 57n3, 58, 182–3, 198; and CR, 37, 270, 281, 286, 287; criticism of, 256, 257, 285, 303; and Deng, 164, 187, 199, 330; dominance of, 10, 24, 151, 425; in factional conflicts, 24, 44, 78, 130, 145, 147, 156, 245–6, 283, 284, 318; fall of, 2, 15, 64; and first leap forward, 213, 215n19, 217–21; followers of, 86, 122n62, 142n122, 245, 325, 371; and Gao Gang, 36n37, 37n39, 160–7, 185–8, 201, 202; and Gao-Rao Affair, 51, 173–81, 188–97, 198, 200, 204; and GLF, 222, 224, 225, 230, 231–8, 240; and Hai Rui Affair, 274, 275, 278–80; and Mao, 4, 19, 20, 30, 31, 52, 67n29, 87, 90, 112, 115, 118, 125, 130–5, 140, 143, 146, 163, 183–8, 257, 276, 418; and military, 8, 73, 77, 117, 118, 120n48, 136, 138; mountaintop of, 149–50; opponents of, 58n4; and Peng Dehuai, 228n80, 229, 241n140; and Peng Zhen, 145, 146; and policy making, 12, 151, 175, 238; and Politburo, 112, 115, 128, 177, 178, 179, 180; positions of, 116n35, 117, 129, 152, 176n91, 187n136; and Rao Shushi, 180–1; rise of, 128–33, 149–50, 156; and SEC, 247–56; in succession struggles, 92, 93, 95, 96, 104, 257; Tianjin talks of, 161–6, 170n50; in two-front arrangement, 13–14, 207, 208,

449

Index

Liu Shaoqi: and CC (*cont.*)
  209; in Yan'an Round Table, 118, 137, 258; and YR, 131–3; and Zhou Enlai, 224n62, 226n70, 326, 334
Liu Xianquan, 325
Liu Yalou, 153
Liu Zhidan, 126n75, 127n80, 242n141
Liu Zhijian, 276, 277, 302n135
Long March, 107, 108, 125, 126
Lu Dingyi, 123, 150, 217n33, 222n50, 284, 285; and Hai Rui Affair, 272, 273, 276, 278, 279, 280; positions of, 152, 183, 208, 245, 256, 270
Lu Xun, 313
Lu Zhengcao, 142n123
Luo Ronghuan, 129n94, 144, 226n70, 281–6, 289, 298n121; and CR, 281–2; and Gao-Rao Affair, 191, 192–3, 196n175, 204, 205; and Lin Biao, 282–3; and military, 142, 151; mountaintop of, 288; positions of, 109, 116n36, 146, 154, 155, 208; in Yan'an Round Table, 118, 137
Luo Ruiqing, 37n40, 182, 281–4, 298n121, 359, 378n79; and Deng, 355–6, 357, 358; and Gao-Rao Affair, 194–5; and Hai Rui Affair, 272, 273, 277; and He Long, 289, 290; and Lin Biao, 282, 295; positions of, 116n36, 142, 151, 153, 245, 256, 257; purge of, 16; and SEC, 252, 253
Luo Xiaopeng, 375
Luochuan Politburo Conference, 108, 112n16
Lushan Conference (1959), 37, 52, 191, 305; and GLF, 31, 33, 59, 227, 235, 236

Ma Bufang, 109n5
Ma Mingfang, 68n29, 198
Ma Wenrui, 364
MacFarquhar, Roderick, 9n19, 135, 207, 214n13, 224, 285; on conflict models, 27, 28, 29–30, 31; on Eighth PC, 68n29, 200
Manchuria, 129n92, 141–7, 149
Mao Hong, 153
Mao Yuanxin, 341, 378n79
Mao Zedong: birthday party for, 253; and CC, 128, 165n27; and CCP, 9–10, 11, 35, 59–60, 107–19, 135–6, 149, 207, 268, 365; checks on power of, 58, 113; and Chiang Kai-shek, 143; on class struggle, 132n104, 239, 244, 347, 370; and CMC, 128, 207; and Comintern policy, 112, 116, 119; compromises of, 426; in conflict models, 28; and CR, 13, 15, 24, 35, 69, 132n104, 211, 267, 280–7, 298n118, 300, 372, 386n, 396, 425; criticism of, 366, 367, 368, 372, 408; and Deng, 30, 52, 87, 88, 111, 138, 198–200, 244, 258, 32849, 354–5, 365, 372; dominance of, 8–12, 29, 32, 106, 124, 139, 158, 238, 383, 385, 417–18, 425; dual civilian-military control of, 11, 135–6, 141, 160, 196, 207, 268, 319, 365, 409; and economic reform, 156, 240–1; and factionalism, 411, 421–2; and first leap forward, 213–21; and Gao Gang, 118, 147, 197; and Gao-Rao Affair, 160, 161n11, 188–97; and GLF, 59, 230–8, 252, 372; and Hai Rui Affair, 268–74; as honorary chairman, 256, 257; and Hua Guofeng, 358; and ideology, 59, 123–4, 136, 244, 324, 365, 369, 372; and leadership relations, 8–12, 59, 77–8, 139–40, 158, 226, 338–49; legitimacy of, 10, 51, 118–19, 128, 135, 267, 322, 324, 365–6, 385, 421; and Lin Biao, 4, 16, 19, 20, 31, 79, 87, 90, 143–7, 151, 229n, 283, 287–95, 300–25, 329, 418; and Liu Shaoqi, 4, 19, 20, 30, 31, 52, 67n29, 87, 90, 112, 115, 118, 125, 130–5, 140, 143, 146, 163, 183–8, 257, 276, 418; and local leaders, 86, 87, 138; loss of dominance of, 67, 75, 238; and Maoists, 308, 318, 323, 338–49; and military, 9–10, 11, 57n2, 72, 73, 108–11, 136, 138, 144n129, 207, 244, 268, 290, 294, 300, 312, 315, 316–17; mountaintop of, 288; and new tax law, 174–5, 176; and Party bureaucrats, 230–46, 251; and Party state, 238–59, 267–8, 285, 286, 385; and personal loyalty, 139, 151, 158; personality cult of, 15, 18, 28, 78, 267–8, 286–7, 305, 424; and policy making, 139–40, 182; privileges of, 7, 39; and reorganization of Politburo, 177, 178, 179, 180; and SEC, 246–56; on socialist transition, 167–73; on Soviet model, 68n30; and Stalin, 142n123; and successors, 2, 12, 19–20, 90, 92–7, 104, 249, 257, 294, 303, 311, 319, 326; and "two whatevers," 351, 352, 362; and two-front arrangement, 12–18, 205–10, 219–20, 232; and Wang Ming, 77, 111–17, 119–25, 130; and Wuhan Incident, 310; and YR, 122–5; and Zhang Guotao, 108, 109n5, 110; and Zhou Enlai, 147, 183, 202, 226n70, 325–8
Mao Zedong Thought (MZT), 284, 303; in CCP Constitution, 67, 68n29; and Deng, 21, 352, 354, 355, 366–70, 372, 379; in ideology model, 27; and legitimacy, 10, 21, 119, 140, 244, 369, 385, 421; and Mao's power, 9, 59, 134, 141, 244; and

450

Index

Marxism, 134, 366; and truth criterion, 357, 358, 365, 366
Mao Zhiyong, 85, 86, 87
Mao-in-command model, 28, 33
Maoism. *See* Mao Zedong Thought
Maoists, 301–9, 337–49; and Deng, 331, 332, 333, 337–49; and Lin Biao, 293, 296, 304–5, 307–8, 313; and Mao, 308, 318, 323, 327, 338–49; and military, 298, 299, 301, 306, 339, 340; and Ninth Congress, 314–15; and planners, 292–3, 302–4, 306; of Shanghai, 315; and Zhou Enlai, 304, 306, 307, 334, 336
Marx, Karl, 131
Marxism, 120, 241, 322, 391; and Deng, 347, 399; and Mao, 224, 320; and MZT, 366; and truth criterion, 357, 358, 359, 365n50
Marxism-Leninism, 26, 131, 355, 369; as source of legitimacy, 119, 120, 134, 135
Marxism-Leninism-Mao Zedong Thought, 22. *See also* Four Cardinal Principles
mass organizations, 298n121, 302, 313; and military, 295, 296, 299; in Wuhan Incident, 309, 310
May 16 Circular, 280
McKelvey, Richard D., 71
military: and CCP, 193, 281, 283, 289n95, 290, 309, 385; in civilian posts, 57, 72, 148–9, 151, 295; commanders in, 138, 148n143; corruption in, 339; in CR, 16, 17, 73, 280–7, 293, 295–6, 299, 300, 308, 309, 356, 385; and Deng, 20, 22, 72, 73, 79, 80, 97, 105, 106, 140–50, 297, 309n143, 328–38, 343, 350–5, 365, 372, 373, 383–7, 385, 408, 409, 419, 422; and economic reform, 387–8; factionalism in, 34, 78, 299, 309; and Gao-Rao Affair, 160, 180, 189, 191, 196, 204–5; and Hai Rui Affair, 272n19, 274, 276, 277; and Lin Biao, 268, 289, 316, 329; and Mao, 9–10, 11, 57n2, 72, 73, 108–11, 136, 138, 144n129, 207, 244, 268, 290, 294, 300, 312, 315, 316–17; and Maoists, 298, 299, 301, 306, 339, 340; mountaintops in, 288, 293, 296; and Party state, 284; and policy making, 72–3, 80; political role of, 6, 8; purges in, 229; rectification campaigns in, 345, 356; reorganization of, 108–11, 325; revolutionary base areas of, 6, 55–7, 141–2; and SEC, 255n187; in succession struggles, 96, 106; in Tiananmen crisis, 73, 410; and truth criterion, 358, 359; in two-front arrangement, 13, 14, 207–8; in Yan'an Round Table, 287–325, 319; and Zhou Enlai, 323, 326, 334, 344n221. *See also* Eighth Route Army; First Front Red Army; Fourth Front Red Army; New Fourth Army; People's Liberation Army; Red Army; Second Front Red Army
Military and Administrative Committee (MAC), 148n143
Million Heroes (mass organization), 310
mountaintop mentality (*shantou zhuyi*), 8, 107, 108, 111, 136, 356

Nanchang Uprising (1927), 287
Nanning Conference (1958), 223, 226
Nathan, Andrew, 1, 16n30, 35, 41, 44, 45n
national bourgeoisie, 12, 161–6, 168, 171, 176
National Conference of the Party Secretaries in Charge of Industry (1975), 345
National Conference on Financial and Economic Work (NCFEW; 1953), 185–8, 202
National Conference on Organization Work (NCOW; 1953), 185, 187, 188, 202
National Learn-from-Dazhai Conference, 341, 348n238
National Peoples' Congresses (NPC): *First*, 204, 217; *Second*, 225; *Third*, 252, 256n192; *Fourth*, 318, 340, 341, 342, 343, 344; *Fifth*, 373n68, 378, 379; *Sixth*, 391, 392, 393
Navy, Chinese, 297, 356–7
NCFEC. *See* North China Financial and Economic Committee
neo-institutional analysis, 66n24
new democratic system, 166, 167–9, 171, 366–7
New Fourth Army, 108, 112n18, 113; commanders of, 117–18, 120n48, 142, 147; leaders from, 114, 117, 132, 138, 293, 356n24
Ni Zhifu, 384
Nie Rongzhen, 145n129, 184n117, 277, 311, 314; and CR, 296, 299, 302; and Deng, 332n199, 353, 355, 384, 387; and foreign relations policy, 316–17, 318; and Gao-Rao Affair, 191, 204, 205; and Lin Biao, 307, 312; and military, 109, 129n94, 142, 147, 150, 297, 299, 313; mountaintop of, 288; positions of, 116n36, 151, 153, 208, 286, 289n92; and Xiao Hua, 298, 298n121; in Yan'an Round Table, 118, 137
North China, 141–3, 144, 150, 165–6

451

Index

North China Bureau (NCB), 150, 169–70, 180–1
North China conference (1970–1), 79, 323
North China Financial and Economic Committee (NCFEC), 151, 155, 175, 181, 187
Northeast Bureau (NEB), 143, 144, 146, 160–2, 164–6, 172
Northeast China, 166, 167, 171–2
Northern Bureau (NB), 128–9, 130n96, 142
Northwestern Bureau (NWB), 127, 132, 140, 177
northwestern faction. *See* "donkey faction"
Northwestern High-Ranking Cadre Conference (NWHCC), 127–8, 133

Oi, Jean, 47
Oksenberg, Michael, 2, 3, 9n20, 28, 40, 42; on models, 26, 31, 38
On the General Program of Work for the Whole Party and Nation (Deng), 347
On the New Historical Opera "The Dismissal of Hai Rui" (Yao Wenyuan), 271–2
"On the Reform of the System of the Party and State Leadership" (Deng), 396, 401
Outline Report Concerning the Current Academic Discussion. See *February Outline*

Party Congresses (PC)
  Sixth, 78n48; Fourth Plenum, 56n, 107, 121; Sixth Plenum (1938), 114, 115–19, 120, 125, 131; Seventh Plenum, 124
  Seventh, 68n29, 116n33, 134, 135, 136n117, 141, 207, 227
  Eighth, 208, 215n19, 217, 257, 329, 362; Second Plenum, 221, 223, 224, 225; Fifth Plenum (1958), 225; Ninth Plenum, 230, 231; institutionalization at, 67, 69; MacFarquhar on, 68n29, 200; and Mao, 220–1, 227; and Politburo, 198, 203, 204; and two-front arrangement, 12, 207
  Ninth, 104, 256–7, 271, 314, 315, 316, 319
  Tenth, 64n, 326, 327, 337
  Eleventh, 84, 354, 379, 396
  Twelfth, 379, 380, 383, 386, 387, 400n122, 408
  Thirteenth, 45, 105, 225n68, 377, 405, 409, 421
  Fourteenth, 225n68

Party state, 27, 283, 284, 329; and CR, 240, 281, 287; and Hai Rui Affair, 277, 280; and Mao, 238–59, 267–8, 285, 286, 385; and SEC, 248, 250, 255; Stalin-type, 207; and Yan'an Round Table, 210, 256–9
patron-client relationships, 27, 35, 46–9, 76
Peng Chong, 378
Peng Dehuai, 37, 235, 241, 245n147, 286, 320, 420; and Gao-Rao Affair, 189n149, 190n152, 191, 204, 205, 241n140; and GLF, 31, 59, 228–30; and Hai Rui Affair, 269, 273, 274, 275; and He Long, 141n121, 287, 289; and Mao, 252, 255, 305, 417; and military, 108, 109, 110n9, 141n121, 147, 149, 151, 297; mountaintop of, 288; positions of, 58, 116n35, 152, 159, 178, 208; purge of, 11, 64, 83, 138, 228–30; rehabilitation of, 361; and Wang Ming, 112–13, 115, 119; in Yan'an Round Table, 118, 137; and Zhou Enlai, 226n70, 334
Peng Zhen, 80n, 226n70, 256, 400, 403, 404; and Chen Yun, 4, 37, 147, 371, 386; and CRG, 270; and Deng, 371, 379, 384, 398–9, 405; and factions, 44, 78, 147; and Gao-Rao Affair, 198; and GLF, 225; and Hai Rui Affair, 269, 272–80; and Liu Shaoqi, 86, 129, 130n96, 131n101, 140, 145n134, 150; and Luo Ruiqing, 284; and Manchurian strategy, 145, 146; and Mao, 52n82, 322; and NEB, 143, 144, 145, 146; and policy making, 182, 363, 417; positions of, 116n36, 150, 152, 178, 179, 208; purge of, 16, 285; and SEC, 247n157, 250, 253, 255; in Yan'an Round Table, 118, 136, 137, 258; and YR, 122, 123
People's Communes, 74n43, 230, 240, 393
People's Daily, 217, 222, 223, 244, 339n208, 351; and CRG, 270; and Hai Rui Affair, 272; and truth criterion, 357, 359; on Wuhan Incident, 309
people's democratic dictatorship, 22, 369–70. *See also* Four Cardinal Principles
People's Liberation Army (PLA): and CCP, 26, 193; and civilian posts, 57, 148–9; in CR, 281, 286, 295, 296, 308, 312–14; and Deng, 333, 340, 343, 352, 355, 356; factionalism in, 34, 420; institutionalization within, 282–3; and Lin Biao, 78n49, 282, 287, 312–14; Maoists in, 340; Mao's control of, 284, 311, 316; and mountaintops, 288; Political Department of, 326, 343, 344; in two-front arrangement, 208; and Zhou Enlai, 334

452

Index

The Petofi Circle, 270
"petroleum faction," 3, 39, 40n49, 315, 373
Pi Dingjun, 334
pi Lin pi Kong (criticize Lin and Confucius) Campaign, 334, 337, 338, 339, 340
planners, 292, 293, 301; and Lin Biao, 305, 308; management of economy by, 184–5, 243, 245, 314–15; and Maoists, 292–3, 302–4, 306; and Zhou Enlai, 307, 344
pluralistic systems, 31, 64, 66; and factionalism, 25, 46, 61, 81, 428
policy making: areas of, 182, 209; common interests in, 44, 72, 76, 426; compromise in, 22–4, 32, 425–8; in conflict models, 29, 30, 38, 39; and CR, 211; and CRG, 292, 302; under Deng, 96, 182, 183, 238, 329, 363, 372–3, 385–7, 390, 406–7, 410; diverse interests in, 6, 12, 24–5, 65, 67; economic, 69, 218–20, 371–8; factionalism in, 2, 37, 44, 74, 81, 376, 407, 411–13, 421, 423–8; and FCP, 370–1; and foreign relations, 317–18; formal process for, 8, 14, 36, 158; game theory on, 260–6; and *guanxi*, 43, 63–4; and Hai Rui Affair, 273, 275–6, 278; and ideology, 366, 419, 424; inconsistencies in, 13, 16, 201, 242, 243, 257–8, 300, 424; institutionalization of, 7, 38, 41, 58, 64–5, 67, 70–1, 283; and Liu-Gao conflict, 165, 166, 167; and Mao, 198, 213, 227, 238–46, 243, 244, 246, 256, 268, 276; and Maoists, 307; military involvement in, 72–3, 80, 293, 306, 315, 318–19; outcomes of, 44, 45, 71, 105, 184, 212, 413–17, 424; and Party bureaucrats, 238–46, 257–9; and planners, 292–3; and political reform, 400, 401, 402; and PSC, 200, 225–6; and reversal of GLF, 233, 236; in Soviet Union, 66; supreme leader's dominance of, 34, 140; and two-front arrangement, 12–18, 205–10, 212, 213; two-level, 414; and Zhou Enlai, 327
policy-choice model, 3, 30, 32, 33, 36, 38–9, 93
Politburo: An Ziwen's list of members of, 177–80, 181, 187, 191, 196, 202; changes in, 198, 316, 326–7, 363, 364; and CR, 302, 306–7, 341; and Deng, 331, 333, 336, 337, 340, 342, 347, 348, 350, 385, 387; and Hai Rui Affair, 274; members of, 128, 204, 287, 289, 379, 407; military in, 286; policy role of, 225–6, 414; and political campaigns, 339; reorganization of, 176–81; in two-front arrangement, 13, 14, 207, 208, 209; in Yan'an, 115
Politburo Meetings, 108, 112–14, 120, 128, 130–1, 133, 151; Enlarged, 69, 194n169, 195, 198n181, 215, 224, 230
Politburo Standing Committee (PSC), 4, 38, 128, 225; changes in, 311, 327, 354; and CR, 281, 302; and Deng, 200, 387; and Hai Rui Affair, 271, 275; members of, 301, 371, 386; military in, 286, 385; and state chairmanship, 320, 321
political culture, 1, 45, 48–9, 125
The Political Resolution, 117
power: balance of, 292, 294, 422, 427; distribution of, 97, 234, 292, 294, 299, 306, 379, 412–16, 422, 424; and factionalism, 5, 77–81, 114, 411, 412, 424; and *guanxi*, 41, 64, 71–2; in international politics, 50; in multiparty systems, 43; personal entrustment of, 6, 55–61, 71, 72, 73, 184; redistribution of, 73, 74, 78, 80–1, 137–8, 159, 160, 181–4, 197–205, 286; in succession struggles, 93, 95
power-struggle model, 3–4, 5, 30, 31, 33, 41, 211
"Practice is the sole criterion of truth," 357–60
"Prefaces to *Socialist Upsurge in China's Countryside*" (Mao), 214
prisoners' dilemma, 18–20, 88–92, 180; Deng-Hu Yaobang, 405; Deng-Mao, 79–80; Mao-Lin, 17, 268, 308, 314–25; in succession struggles, 94, 95, 98, 105
Pye, Lucian, 1, 4, 27, 41, 43–4, 46, 49; on CCP leadership, 60, 62–3

Qi Guang, 114
Qian Xuesen, 253
Qian Ying, 187n136
Qiao Shi, 80n, 384
Qin Jiwei, 86, 87, 204, 384
Qiu Huizuo, 78n49, 298n121, 310, 315, 321, 324; and military, 312, 313, 314
Qu Qiubai, 107, 128n89, 133

Rao Shushi (Xiao Yao): and Gao Gang, 177, 185, 188, 189; and Kang Sheng, 78; and Liu Shaoqi, 58n4, 129, 130n96, 132, 140, 143, 180–1, 186, 187; and military, 142, 146n138, 147, 149; policy areas of, 182, 183; positions of, 58, 137, 146, 148n143, 154, 155, 156, 159, 178, 179, 187n136. *See also* Gao-Rao Affair
rational-choice theory, 8, 29, 39

453

Index

rectification (*zhengdun*) campaigns, 81–8, 104, 403–4, 412–13; of 1957, 52, 221; against corruption, 396–8; cultural, 269–70, 273–4; of Deng, 79, 83, 335, 341, 344–8, 352–3, 356, 370, 378. *See also* Yan'an Rectification

Red Army, 110, 129n90; Western Route (WRA), 108n5. *See also* First Front Red Army; Fourth Front Red Army; Second Front Red Army

Red Guards, 52, 131n101, 157, 300n125, 301n130, 346, 355n23

reform: consensus on, 37; and Deng, 21–2, 80, 104, 370, 373–83, 396–408, 418–19; and factionalism, 416–17, 423, 426; and FCP, 421; financial, 374, 377, 380–1, 382, 390–1, 409; "incomplete," 21; institutional, 69, 396, 400, 402; of legal system, 398–9; local support for, 428; opposition to, 371; political, 74n43, 409; and succession struggles, 96, 104; and Tiananmen crisis, 23. *See also* economic reform

Regional Military Commands (RMC), 207, 208, 288, 293, 296, 297, 316, 360; Beijing, 79, 86, 324; in CR, 295n115, 300; and Deng, 352, 356, 361, 384; rotation of, 333, 334–5; Wuhan, 309, 310, 311

Ren Bishi, 108, 109, 125, 127, 199; and CC, 121, 128, 156; mountaintop of, 288; and Politburo, 112, 115; in Yan'an Round Table, 118, 137; and YR, 122, 123, 124n69

Ren Zhongyi, 394, 408

The Resolution on Several Historical Problems, 124, 125

"Resolution on the Reform of the Economic System," 392, 408

revisionism, 54n, 245–6, 257, 303, 368; and Hai Rui Affair, 270, 273; Mao on, 244, 245; and SEC, 246–56; of Zhou Enlai, 337

revolutionary period, 77, 184, 206; *guanxi* from, 60, 106, 258, 283, 423, 426; military base areas in, 6, 55–7, 145; reorganization of leadership during, 107–11

Right-conservatism, 2, 213, 223

Right-deviationism, 83, 224, 241, 285

Right-opportunism, 176, 186, 191, 197, 201

Right-opportunists, 111, 117, 120, 126n76, 127n80

Ruan Ming, 97n, 406

rural areas, 47, 74n43, 246, 250

"scar literature," 388

Schram, Stuart, 21n36

Schurmann, Franz, 27

SEC. *See* Socialist Education Campaign

Second Front Red Army, 288, 291

Secretariat (CC), 56n, 176, 177, 283, 378, 401; and CR, 280, 281; and Deng, 14, 225, 329, 363, 387; and economic reform, 379, 392; and Hai Rui Affair, 269, 273, 277, 279; policy role of, 225–6; and political campaigns, 253, 254, 270, 397; in two-front arrangement, 207, 208

Selected Works of Mao Zedong, 120

"Separating the Party from the Government," 396–406, 408, 409, 415–16

7,000-Cadre Conference (1962), 52, 231–2, 234, 240n132, 241, 260

Shaanxi province, 108, 147, 149

Shandong province, 141, 142, 149, 180–1

Shanghai, 269, 271, 273, 286, 315, 350

Shanxi province, 129, 149; Party Committee of, 169–70, 184n114

single-party rule, 6, 65, 427–8; and factionalism, 42–3, 61–4, 81, 411, 414

Snow, Edgar, 15, 255

socialism, 366–9, 424–5; agrarian, 169–70, 369; with Chinese characteristics, 377, 389, 421; and economic reform, 377, 393, 395

Socialist Education Campaign (SEC), 246–56, 285

socialist road, 22, 369, 386; and economic reform, 376, 377, 390, 392, 393, 394, 395, 406. *See also* Four Cardinal Principles

socialist spiritual civilization, 2, 387, 393–5

socialist transition, 167–73, 197

Solomon, Richard, 46n65

Song Ping, 86, 374

Song Renqiong, 68n29, 247n157, 375, 384; positions of, 154, 364, 378

Southeastern Bureau (SEB), 117, 129n92

Southern Bureau (SB), 117, 132, 148

Soviet Union, 138, 184n117, 209, 216, 241n140, 317, 324; and CCP, 9, 116; institutionalization in, 7n, 65–7; as model, 3, 68, 172, 177, 192; single-party rule in, 61; and Wang Ming, 77, 116

SPC. *See* State Planning Commission

special economic zones, 392, 428

spiritual pollution, campaign against, 83, 391–2, 395, 403, 408, 420

Stalin, Joseph, 7n, 157, 171, 209, 216, 303; and Mao, 135, 142n123

state chairmanship, 318–22

454

Index

State Council, 292, 306, 378, 401; and CR, 295, 302; and Deng, 332, 333, 391; and economic reform, 373n68, 379, 380, 382, 392; and first leap forward, 215, 216; policy role of, 225–6; in two-front arrangement, 207, 208; and Zhou Enlai, 14, 315
State Planning Commission (SPC), 182, 185, 214, 230; and Gao Gang, 172–3, 184; and SEC, 253, 254
Strong, Anna Louise, 272n19
structural theory of international politics, 50, 51
structure model, 3, 4–5, 31–2, 33, 39–40
students: Moscow-trained, 107, 117, 119, 120, 126, 127, 130, 131; prodemocratic, 405, 408. *See also* Tiananmen crisis; Tiananmen Incident
Su Shaozhi, 366, 391, 403
Su Yu, 288, 353; and military, 109, 142, 144n129, 147; positions of, 118, 137, 146, 153
Su Zhenhua, 353, 357
succession struggles, 2, 12, 18–20, 68, 88–104, 209, 249; and CR, 211; Deng's solution to, 96–104; Mao's solution to, 92–6; new players in, 92–8; and prisoners' dilemma, 88–92, 404–5
Sun, Warren, 9n20
Sun Xiushan, 153

Taiwan, 428
Tan Furen, 86, 315
Tan Zheng, 154, 245, 282, 298n121
Tan Zhenlin, 68n29, 196n175, 225, 292, 302; and Lin Biao, 305, 308; and Maoists, 301–2, 304, 306; and military, 109, 142; mountaintop of, 288, 293; positions of, 137, 143, 154, 198, 245; rehabilitation of, 331
Tang Tsou, 23n, 35–6, 67
Tang Wensheng, 340, 342, 343, 344, 346
Tao Yong, 297n
Tao Zhu, 86, 153, 192n160, 223, 240–1, 420; purge of, 301; rehabilitation of, 361; and SEC, 247n157, 253
Taoyuan Experiences (Wang Guangmei), 250, 252n178
taxes, 12, 156; and economic reform, 383, 390–1; new law on, 37n39, 173–6, 181, 184n114
technocrats, 66n23, 80
Teiwes, Frederick, 1, 9n20, 36n37, 37n39, 52, 157, 159, 163n18

"Ten Policies for Further Stimulating the Rural Economy," 392
Teng Daiyuan, 229, 336
Ten-Year Plan, 232
Three Anti Campaign, 171n55, 172
Three Red Banners, 234
"three-category people," 83, 84
Tian Jiyun, 87, 391, 393, 397
Tiananmen crisis (May 1989), 33, 45, 417, 420; and Deng's power, 409–10; military intervention in, 73, 410; stability since, 24, 425, 426; and Zhao Ziyang, 23, 75, 409–10, 421
Tiananmen Incident (April 1976), 350–1, 354n16, 361–2
Tianjin, 128–9, 160–1
totalitarian model, 26, 27
truth criterion debate, 357–60, 362, 370, 375, 419, 424; and MZT, 357, 358, 365, 366
Twelve-Year Agricultural Program, 213, 221, 222
Twenty-three Articles, 254, 255
"two civilizations," 387, 393–5, 395
"two principal points," 387, 389–90, 394, 395, 424
"two whatevers," 351, 353–4, 365, 369, 408; and truth criterion, 357, 358, 360, 362
two-front arrangement, 67, 237, 238, 258, 280; and Deng, 13, 14, 21, 106, 207–9, 329, 383; and Gao-Rao Affair, 160, 189; and GLF, 212, 226, 236; and leadership relations, 211–66; and Liu Shaoqi, 13–14, 207, 208, 209; and Mao, 12–18, 205–10, 219–20, 232; and succession struggles, 96–7, 98, 102; and Tenth Plenum, 245, 246; and Yan'an Round Table, 205–10
two-line struggle, 275–80, 286, 287, 303, 324, 348
"two-price system," 409

Ulanfu, 208, 384
ultrarightism, 33, 326
Uncertain Passage (Barnett), 29, 30
united front, anti-Japanese, 110, 112, 114, 115, 119, 130, 131
United Kingdom, 223
United Nations, 340
United States, 27, 222, 317, 325
unity model, 26–7, 28

Vietnam, 418
Vietnamese War, 317

455

Index

Walder, Andrew, 46, 47
Waltz, Kenneth, 50, 51
Wan Li, 80n, 97, 405; and Deng, 69, 86, 87, 384; and economic reform, 374, 378, 391
Wan Yi, 142n123, 229
Wang Diming, 67n29
Wang Dongxing: and Deng, 331, 336, 349, 353, 354; and Mao, 271, 321, 358; positions of, 315, 318, 325, 327, 363, 364; resignation of, 377; and truth criterion, 358, 362
Wang Guangmei, 130, 163n18, 250, 252n178, 253
Wang Hairong, 340, 342, 343, 344, 346
Wang Hanbin, 88
Wang Heshou, 361, 363, 371
Wang Hongwen, 286, 315, 321, 327, 340, 344n220; and Deng, 342, 343
Wang Jiaxiang, 112, 115, 116, 122, 123
Wang Jun, 403
Wang Li, 310, 311
Wang Ming, 107, 113nn21,22, 116n35, 130, 304, 329; attacks on, 121, 128, 188n141, 303; and Comintern, 111, 115, 116, 119; and KMT, 114–15; and Liu Shaoqi, 131, 133, 186; and Mao, 9, 77, 111–17, 119–25, 130, 188n141; purge of, 64; and Zunyi Conference, 121, 124
Wang Ming faction, 77, 107, 124, 127n80, 132; and YR, 119, 120, 121, 123, 126
Wang Renzhi, 420
Wang Renzhong, 86, 294, 302n135, 309, 364, 372, 378
Wang Ruofei, 122
Wang Ruoshui, 391, 403
Wang Shoudao, 122, 204
Wang Shusheng, 155, 203
Wang Zhaoguo, 397
Wang Zhen, 122, 363, 364, 372, 379, 403, 405; and Democracy Wall, 367–8; and Deng, 335, 351, 353, 384, 386, 387; mountaintop of, 288; rehabilitation of, 331, 336
Wannan Incident (1941), 120, 132
Wei Guoqing, 78, 327, 352, 356, 384
Wen Yucheng, 78n49, 314, 315
Western Expedition, 108, 109n5
"whatever faction," 24, 44, 225n68, 351–4, 363, 373; attacks on, 369, 419; defeat of, 37, 69, 377; and Deng, 360–1, 418, 419; and ideology, 368, 370–1, 420; and rectification campaigns, 84, 85; and truth criterion, 358, 359
White, Lynn, 47

Whitson, William, 1, 34
Workers' Headquarters, 309, 310
Wu De, 327, 377
Wu Faxian, 78n49, 290, 298n121, 310, 322n169; and Lin Biao, 319, 324; positions of, 312, 313, 314, 315, 318; and state chairmanship, 320, 321
Wu Han, 268–77, 403
Wu Lengxi, 270, 272n19, 365
Wu Xiuquan, 143
Wuhan Incident (1967), 309–11

Xi Henghan, 315, 316
Xi Zhongxun, 126, 182, 183, 242n141, 374, 384; and Gao Gang, 185, 189; positions of, 58, 149, 155, 159, 177, 178, 187n136; purge of, 241
Xia Yan, 274
Xiang Ming, 155, 181
Xiang Nan, 374, 394, 408
Xiang Ying, 109, 117, 120; positions of, 113n21, 116n35, 118, 129n92; and Wang Ming, 112, 114, 115, 130
Xiang Zhongfa, 113n20
Xiao Hua, 144, 282n60, 284, 298, 299
Xiao Jinguang, 109, 143–4, 152, 288, 357; in Yan'an Round Table, 118, 137; in YR, 122, 123
Xiao Yao. See Rao Shushi
Xie Fuzhi, 310, 315, 318, 325; and Mao-Lin conflict, 323, 324; and SEC, 252, 253
Xie Hua, 86
Xie Juezai, 122, 123
Xing Yanzi, 253
Xiong Fu, 362
Xiong Gongqing, 291n104
Xiong Xianghui, 317
Xu Guangda, 152
Xu Jiatun, 86
Xu Shiyou, 85, 312n149, 315, 316, 327, 334; and Deng, 87, 352; and Mao, 86, 110n6
Xu Teli, 123
Xu Xiangqian, 191, 204, 277, 296, 379; and CMC, 108, 122, 312n149; and Deng, 353, 384, 387; and foreign relations policy, 316–17, 318; and Lin Biao, 299, 307; and Maoists, 301, 302n133, 306; and military, 108n5, 109, 110, 147, 150, 203, 297, 299, 300; mountaintop of, 288; positions of, 145, 155, 208, 286, 289n92; and Wuhan Incident, 309, 311, 313; and Xiao Hua, 298, 298n121; in Yan'an Round Table, 118, 137

456

Index

Xu Yefu, 290n101
Xue Moqiao, 227n77

Yan Hongyan, 242n141
Yan'an, 77, 132, 141n121, 146n135
Yan'an Rectification (YR), 56n, 78n48, 120, 133, 191; beginning of, 121–2, 127, 132; compared to CR, 303–4; and Liu Shaoqi, 131–3; and Mao, 123, 366; and Wang Ming faction, 119–25, 126; Zhou Enlai in, 224n62, 306, 345
Yan'an Round Table, 9–10, 107–58, 184, 311; collapse of, 17, 18, 158, 267–349, 386; and CR, 16, 281; crisis in, 213, 256–9; and Deng, 20, 348, 383; factions in, 135–41, 147, 151, 157, 324–5; and Gao-Rao Affair, 11, 159, 196; and GLF, 226, 234; and military, 136, 287–325, 385; and Party state, 210, 256–9; structural changes in, 197–210, 314–15; and two-front arrangement, 220, 246
Yang Chengwu, 284, 299, 316; and Deng, 352–3, 355; and Lin Biao, 78, 312–14; positions of, 137, 153; and Wuhan Incident, 310, 311
Yang Dezhi, 315, 316, 334, 355, 378, 384
Yang Dezhong, 364
Yang Lisan, 156n156
Yang Rudai, 86
Yang Shangkun, 68n29, 175, 188, 271, 374, 397, 405; under Deng, 384, 387; and Liu Shaoqi, 163, 183–4; positions of, 116n35, 118, 130n96, 131n99, 187n136, 256, 371; purge of, 105, 285
Yang Xianzhen, 150, 152
Yang Yanguo, 357
Yang Yong, 298, 359, 378n79; and Deng, 355, 356, 384
Yangtze Bureau (YB), 111–15, 113, 114, 117
Yang-Yu-Fu Affair (1968), 78, 313–14
Yao Wenyuan, 304, 306, 322, 343; and Hai Rui Affair, 271, 272, 273, 274, 275; positions of, 315, 319, 327, 373n68
Yao Yilin, 80n; and Chen Yun, 367, 390, 391; and Deng, 88, 384; and economic reform, 176, 372, 378, 390, 391, 393; positions of, 153, 363, 364, 378
Ye Jianying, 113n21, 204, 277, 284, 288, 310, 321, 365n50; and CMC, 108, 312n149, 314, 325; and corruption, 339, 403; and CR, 296, 299; and Deng, 350, 353–7, 383, 384, 387; on economy, 370–1; and foreign relations policy, 317, 318; as leader of survivors, 349; and Mao, 139, 323, 368; and Maoists, 301, 302, 306; and military, 109, 299, 326, 335n205, 420; positions of, 118, 137, 159, 208, 286, 289n92, 315, 316, 327; and Xu Xiangqian, 298, 299; and Zhou Enlai, 226n70
Ye Jizhuang, 153, 176n86, 182, 198
Ye Qun, 195n170, 276, 283n70, 293n, 313, 319, 322n169; and Lin Biao, 298, 324; and Maoists, 304–5; positions of, 312, 315
Ye Ting, 109, 113n21
Ye Xuanping, 80n, 85, 86, 87
Yu Guangyuan, 366, 403
Yu Lijin, 78, 313–14
Yu Qiuli, 292, 293, 344; and Deng, 353, 384; and economic policy, 372, 373n68, 378; and Maoists, 302, 306; positions of, 202, 315, 378
Yuan Guoping, 120n48

Zeng Shan, 176n86, 182, 198
Zeng Siyu, 315, 334, 335
Zeng Xisheng, 240
Zhang Caiqian, 325
Zhang Chunqiao, 78, 302, 304, 306, 319; and CR, 17, 281; and Deng, 338, 343; and Hai Rui Affair, 271, 278; and Lin Biao, 320, 321, 322; positions of, 256, 315, 318, 325, 327, 341, 343–4; and Zhou Enlai, 326, 336, 337
Zhang Dingcheng, 109
Zhang Guohua, 315, 316
Zhang Guotao, 112, 115, 133, 203, 289n92, 298n118, 329; and Mao, 9, 108, 109, 110, 287; mountaintop of, 288
Zhang Hao (Lin Yuying), 110–11, 116n35
Zhang Jinfu, 372, 384
Zhang Kai, 163n18
Zhang Mingyuan, 153
Zhang Pinghua, 360, 364
Zhang Tingfa, 384
Zhang Wentian, 111n13, 123n, 162n15, 330; and Liu Shaoqi, 130, 131n99, 144; and Mao, 115, 121, 124n69, 166n33, 333; and Politburo, 112, 113, 115, 129n90, 177, 178; positions of, 116n35, 127, 176n86, 208
Zhang Xingxing, 221
Zhang Xiuchuan, 312, 314
Zhang Yufeng, 342n216
Zhang Yunyi, 109, 154
Zhang Zhen, 87, 356

457

Index

Zhang Zuoliang, 293n
Zhao Ziyang, 23, 44, 80n, 87, 410, 416, 421; and corruption, 394, 403; and Deng, 19, 20, 21, 42, 90; and economic reform, 374, 376, 377, 379, 380, 381, 388–93, 395, 408; and *guanxi* networks, 75, 76; and Hu Yaobang, 4, 38, 405; and political campaigns, 83, 86, 391; and political reform, 396n114, 401, 402, 407, 409; positions of, 371, 378, 383; purge of, 2, 64; in succession struggles, 96, 97, 103, 104, 105
zhenbie pingfan (reexamine and rehabilitate), 240–3, 244
Zheng Weishan, 315, 324
zhengce (concrete policies), 414–16
zhengdun campaigns. *See* rectification (*zhengdun*) campaigns
Zhong Hanhua, 309–10, 311
Zhong Kui (legendary figure), 294, 295
Zhong Wei, 229
Zhou Enlai, 83, 287n89, 310, 314, 317; and Bo Yibo, 186, 187; and CC, 156nn156,159, 165n27; and CMC, 108, 312n149, 313; containment of, 11, 104–5, 138, 325–8; and CR, 37, 280, 292, 308; criticism of, 255, 303, 345; decline of, 225–6, 326; and Deng, 225, 268, 328–34, 335, 336–49, 341, 342–9; dual civilian-military control of, 326; and economic policy, 174, 175, 184n117, 188, 214n13; and first leap forward, 215, 216, 217–19, 220, 221; and Gang of Four, 79; and Gao-Rao Affair, 161n11, 194n167, 196, 200–2; and GLF, 52, 223, 224, 230, 233, 236; and Hai Rui Affair, 272, 274, 278; and He Long, 226n70, 290–1; illness of, 326, 340; and Lin Biao, 17, 226n70, 293, 294, 326, 334; and Liu Shaoqi, 130, 131nn99,101, 164, 224n62; and Luo Ruiqing, 284; and Mao, 30, 31, 58, 87, 139, 147, 151, 183, 255, 320, 338–49; and Maoists, 304, 306, 307, 334, 336; and Mao-Lin conflict, 318, 323–4; as mediator, 307, 422–3; and Peng Dehuai, 228n80, 229n; and policy making, 182, 183; positions of, 116n35, 117, 132, 176n91, 177, 178, 301, 315, 318; and SEC, 247n157, 249n163, 253, 254, 255; in succession struggles, 92, 93, 96, 104–5; in two-front arrangement, 13, 14, 207, 208, 209; and Wang Ming, 112–13, 115; wife of, 363, 364; in Yan'an Round Table, 118, 137, 258
Zhou Huan, 229
Zhou Shidi, 154, 378n80
Zhou Yang, 269, 270, 391
Zhu De, 121, 165n27, 217n28, 226n70, 229n; and military, 57n2, 108, 109, 287, 288; positions of, 116n35, 177, 178, 187n136, 208, 286, 289n92, 315, 316, 327; in Yan'an Round Table, 118, 136, 137, 139
Zhu Houze, 86, 420
Zhu Rongji, 80n
zhuanye system (transfer of officers to civilian posts), 57, 72, 148–9, 295
zou houmen (special treatment through the back door), 338, 339, 340
Zunyi Conference, 56n, 108, 111, 113n20, 121, 124, 135

458

Printed in the United States
65178LVS00003B/25-42